THE
OFFICIAL
SCRABBLE BRAND
WORD-FINDER

THE
OFFICIAL
SCRABBLE® BRAND
WORD-FINDER

□□□

ROBERT W. SCHACHNER

COLLIER BOOKS
Macmillan Publishing Company
New York

Word lists given in this book have been compiled from the vocabulary of *The Official Scrabble® Players Dictionary,* used by permission of the publishers, Merriam-Webster, Inc., of Springfield, Massachusetts. *The Official Scrabble® Players Dictionary* is the dictionary of first reference for all official Scrabble® Players Crossword game tournaments.

Collier Books
Macmillan Publishing Company
866 Third Avenue, New York, NY 10022
Collier Macmillan Canada, Inc.

Library of Congress Cataloging-in-Publication Data
Schachner, Robert W.
  The official Scrabble® word-finder.
  On t.p. the trademark symbol "R" is superscript following "Scrabble" in the title.
  1. Scrabble® (Game)—Glossaries, vocabularies, etc.
I. Title.
GV1507.S3S3 1988   793.73   87-35453
ISBN 0-02-029802-1

10 9 8 7 6 5 4 3 2

Printed in the United States of America

To Beth, who inspired the concept;
to Marvin, who conspired the pre-text;
and to Alex and Victoria, with love

Acknowledgment is gratefully extended to:

John Whited, who has probably read the dictionary from cover to cover more than any other scholar in history. His help has made this book a better work.

Ellie Gorinstein, who has caressed the word processor with loving care, given of herself with intense dedication, and smiled in the face of adversity—me.

Jerry Houle II, a new friend, who has worked so hard to make this project possible.

Mr. John Williams, president of the Scrabble® Association of America, for his advice and support.

McGladrey, Hendrickson and Pullen, and especially Kathy Zukowski, for their help, their expertise, and their computer program.

The Broward Community College Central Campus library for their patience, and

Victor Scudiery, who kept the faith.

—RWS

CONTENTS

□□□

THE
OFFICIAL
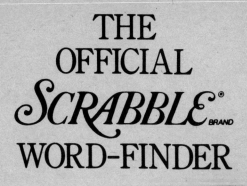
SCRABBLE® BRAND
WORD-FINDER

INTRODUCTION

□□□

*Respect for the word—to employ it with scrupulous
care and heartfelt love of truth—is essential. . . .*

—Dag Hammarskjöld
Markings

This book is the product of a loser—me—a frustrated Scrabble®
player, who has been beaten game after game by a person with
whom I dearly love to play. She always seems to beat the clock and
find the unusual word and the highest-scoring combination of letters,
leading to my almost certain defeat. This has been going on for years,
and I suspect I'm not alone. Scrabble® has been the most popular
word game since its invention by Alfred Butts, at the time an out-of-
work architect, during the Great Depression. Mr. Butts counted the
letters used on the front page of *The New York Times* and produced
what was eventually released commercially as Criss-Crosswords. It
became Scrabble® in 1948 and has since then sold more than 90
million copies worldwide.

Scrabble®'s fun to play, win or lose, but who wants to lose? Who
enjoys watching the score mount against him as round by round the
reservoir of unused letters is depleted? Who enjoys scrambling
through a dictionary, trying to memorize esoteric words? No one
except a masochist. So, if you want to be a winner, this book is for
you.

I began by considering ways of rearranging the dictionary of acceptable Scrabble® words to suit my number one need as a player:
constructing the highest-scoring word in the shortest possible time.
The word lists in this book are the result of that effort.

Word-Finder (Chapter 1) is a powerful new tool providing quick

access to thousands of high-scoring words. For each letter of the alphabet (except vowels) there are three lists:

1. Words beginning with that letter
2. Words ending with that letter
3. Words having that letter in approximately the middle of the word

In Chapter 2 you'll find a listing of all "legal" two-letter words (based on standard Scrabble® rules) for those tough situations that arise during play.

In Chapter 3, we provide an alphabetical listing of two-letter words that can be made into a new word with the addition of one letter. For quick recognition, the letter to be added stands apart from the original two-letter word.

Prefixes, suffixes, and plurals can be a boon to the Scrabble® player and in Chapter 4 we provide a review of the rules for their use. Again, for easy reference, the base word shown is detached from the new addition.

Everyone who has played Scrabble® has experienced an opponent who uses a word drawn from his or her special knowledge. Little-known legal, medical, military, and other specialized words are, if contested, time consuming to check, and, if not challenged, can be very successful for the player using them. In Chapter 5 we present a new kind of word list, a Quick-Check Usage Guide covering these various categories.

Now that you know how the *Official Scrabble® Word-Finder* works, you should be aware of some other aspects of the game and the word usage that affects it.

Players of Scrabble® must, in the interests of their continued friendship and the nonviolent settlement of arguments, have a mutually agreeable dictionary at hand. Since dictionaries vary enormously from publisher to publisher and editor to editor, the agreement on the "standard" or dictionary of play must be made at the outset of any game. The *Word-Finder* is not such a dictionary and does not cover every "legal" word nor provide definitions of the words included, although it does contain approximately 60,000 words culled from the complete *Official Scrabble® Players Dictionary*.

There are also many acceptable variations of play. Only those

actually playing the game can decide by which set of rules they wish to test their vocabulary strength against their opponents. There are also interpretations of rules, both official and those agreed upon by the players. One of the most controversial areas in interpretation of the rules is "designated foreign words." For instance, *oui* (yes) is not found in the Oxford dictionaries, and the word *si* is shown as a musical note in the full *Oxford*. However, in *Funk & Wagnalls, si* is shown as meaning "yes" in Portuguese, Italian, and Spanish, as well as an alternate for *ti* (musical note), and *oui* (yes in French) is permissible for "yes." You can see that with that degree of variation some discussion before the start of play is necessary to agree upon the interpretation of the rules. The *Word-Finder* does not provide a set of rules nor does it attempt to interpret the rules.

Another factor determining the acceptability of words is the particular set of rules chosen by the participants before play begins. The official rules may be used or the rules for any of the many games, such as "theme" Scrabble®, solitaire, clock-racing or timed play, foreign, or even "sex" Scrabble®. The game you choose to play will, of course, affect the "legality" or acceptability of words used in play. (The *Word-Finder* may not always prove useful in these more unconventional games.)

Now go forth, *Official Scrabble® Word-Finder* in hand, and with a new sense of confidence. I'm sure these word lists will prove as useful for you as they have been for me.

—RWS

P.S.

While compiling this book I became fascinated with certain interesting facts and statistics about our language and its cataloging. For instance, there are eighty-two two-letter words in our general use language and seven hundred seventy-nine three-letter words. There are twenty-four kinds of antelope, twenty-eight words for types of carriages, one hundred thirty-seven listings of foreign, domestic, and ancient coins in the dictionary, and fourteen words meaning prostitute, including some that you would probably have never heard of regardless of your sexual proclivities. Whole dictionaries exist on the

subject of underground language like *A Dictionary of Historical Slang* and *A Dictionary of the Underworld.* Words from the American West and words used in obsolete English are cataloged by the thousands in volumes of their own. There are dictionaries of usage, of style, of diplomacy, of dates—even of narcotics. And just in case you are feeling smug because you have a so-called "unabridged," remember that *The Oxford English Dictionary,* in eleven volumes weighing one hundred thirty-two pounds, has 500,000 entries.

Increasing your word power will not just make you a better Scrabble® player, it will enrich your knowledge and understanding of the world in which we live. One method of vocabulary building is to play Scrabble® using *The Official Scrabble® Word-Finder* in combination with *The Official Scrabble® Players Dictionary.* The *Word-Finder* will guide your play and help you obtain the highest possible score, while the dictionary will teach you the meaning of a word that may be new to your vocabulary. Learning the idea behind unfamiliar words will facilitate adding those words to your vocabulary—permanently.

THE
WORD LISTS

□□□

CHAPTER 1

□□□

Word-Finder

Words listed in this section are arranged alphabetically and according to the number of the letters they contain. High-scoring words are shown in boldface type (10–14 points), extra-high-scoring words (15 points or more) are shown with an asterisk in addition to the boldface type. Words with the value of 3 points or less are not shown at all. The vowels have been omitted in Word-Finder as separate categories because most words contain them; their inclusion would make the book cumbersome and difficult to use. Also, having been assigned the most numerous allotment of letters in the game, vowels have the lowest point value (based on face value of the letter). Using your highest point value letters and Word-Finder to maximize your score, the vowels you are holding will most certainly be used.

Based on the standard Scrabble® rules, the following words will also not be contained in Word-Finder since their use is not "legal" in normal play:

Capitalized words
Hyphenated words
Prefixes and suffixes (standing alone)
Abbreviations
Words requiring an apostrophe

The maximum length of words shown in Word-Finder is eight letters (the maximum letters held at any one time, plus one letter

on the board). The skilled vocabularist and experienced player will, at times, construct longer words out of existing words already on the board, but the Scrabble® Word-Finder is designed to be a *quick* reference to locate as high a scoring word as possible in the shortest possible time.

Here's the most effective way to use the Word-Finder. First, turn to the list based on the letter you plan to build onto. You'll notice that the list has three sections: words beginning with that letter, words ending with that letter, and words containing that letter in the middle. Thus, you have a variety of word suggestions built around your key letter. All that is left is for you to choose the highest-scoring word that fits the other letters on your rack.

B

BAAL	BATT	BILE	**BOGY**	BRAW
BABA	BAUD	**BILK**	BOIL	BRAY
BABE	**BAWD**	BILL	BOLA	BRED
BABU	BAWL	BIMA	BOLD	BREE
BABY	BEAD	BIND	BOLE	BREW
BACH	**BEAK**	BINE	BOLL	BRIE
BACK	BEAM	BINT	BOLO	BRIG
BADE	BEAN	BIRD	BOLT	BRIM
BAFF	BEAR	**BIRK**	**BOMB**	BRIN
BAHT	BEAT	BIRL	BOND	BRIO
BAIL	BEAU	BIRR	BONE	BRIT
BAIT	**BECK**	BISE	BONG	BROO
BAKE	BEEF	**BISK**	BONY	BROW
BALD	BEEN	BITE	BOOB	BRUT
BALE	BEEP	BITT	**BOOK**	BUBO
BALK	BEER	*BIZE	BOOM	**BUCK**
BALL	BEET	BLAB	BOON	**BUFF**
BALM	BELL	BLAE	BOOR	BUHL
BAND	BELT	BLAH	BOOT	BUHR
BANE	BEMA	BLAT	BORA	BULB
BANG	BEND	BLAW	BORE	**BULK**
BANI	BENE	BLEB	BORN	BULL
BANK	BENT	BLET	BORT	**BUMF**
BARB	BERG	BLIN	**BOSK**	**BUMP**
BARD	BERM	BLIP	BOSS	BUND
BARE	BEST	BLOB	BOTH	BUNG
BARF	BETA	BLOC	BOTT	**BUNK**
BARK	BETH	BLOT	BOUT	BUNN
BARM	**BEVY**	BLOW	BOWL	BUNT
BARN	BHUT	BLUE	*BOXY	BUOY
BASE	BIAS	BLUR	BOYO	BURA
BASH	**BIBB**	BOAR	*BOZO	BURD
BASK	BICE	BOAT	BRAD	BURG
BASS	BIDE	**BOCK**	BRAE	BURL
BAST	BIER	BODE	BRAG	BURN
BATE	**BIFF**	BODY	BRAN	BURP
BATH	**BIKE**	**BOFF**	BRAT	BURR

BURY	**BATCH**	BETON	**BLESS**	*BOOZE
BUSH	**BATHE**	BETTA	**BLEST**	*BOOZY
BUSK	**BATIK**	BEVEL	**BLIMP**	**BORAX**
BUSS	BATON	**BEVOR**	**BLIMY**	BORED
BUST	BATTU	**BEWIG**	BLIND	BORER
BUSY	**BATTY**	*BEZEL	**BLINI**	BORIC
BUTT	BAULK	*BEZIL	**BLINK**	BORNE
*BUZZ	**BAWDY**	**BHANG**	BLISS	BORON
BYRE	**BAWDY**	**BHOOT**	BLITE	*BORTZ
BYRL	**BAWTY**	**BIALY**	*BLITZ	**BOSKY**
BYTE	**BAYOU**	BIBLE	BLOAT	BOSOM
BABEL	*BAZAR	**BIDDY**	**BLOCK**	BOSON
BABKA	**BEACH**	BIDER	**BLOKE**	**BOSSY**
BABOO	**BEADY**	BIDET	BLOND	BOSUN
BABUL	**BEAKY**	BIELD	BLOOD	**BOTCH**
BACCA	**BEAMY**	*BIFFY	BLOOM	BOTEL
BACON	BEANO	**BIFID**	BLOOP	BOUGH
BADDY	BEARD	**BIGHT**	**BLOWN**	BOULE
BADGE	BEAST	**BIGLY**	**BLOWY**	BOUND
BADLY	BEAUT	BIGOT	BLUED	BOURG
*BAFFY	BEAUX	**BIJOU**	BLUER	BOURN
BAGEL	BEBOP	**BIKER**	BLUET	BOUSE
BAGGY	**BECAP**	BILBO	**BLUEY**	**BOUSY**
BAIRN	BEDEL	BILGE	**BLUFF**	**BOVID**
BAITH	BEDEW	BILGY	BLUME	BOWEL
*BAIZA	**BEDIM**	**BILLY**	BLUNT	**BOWER**
*BAIZE	**BEECH**	**BIMAH**	BLURB	**BOWSE**
BAKER	**BEEFY**	BINAL	BLURT	**BOXER**
BALAS	**BEERY**	BINGE	**BLUSH**	**BOYAR**
BALER	**BEFIT**	BINGO	**BLYPE**	**BOYLA**
BALKY	**BEFOG**	BINIT	BOARD	BRACE
BALLY	BEGAN	**BIOME**	BOART	**BRACH**
BALMY	BEGET	BIONT	BOAST	**BRACT**
BALSA	BEGIN	BIOTA	**BOBBY**	BRAID
BANAL	BEGOT	**BIPED**	**BOCCE**	BRAIL
BANCO	**BEGUM**	**BIPOD**	**BOCCI**	**BRAIN**
BANDY	BEGUN	**BIRCH**	**BOCHE**	**BRAKE**
BANJO	BEIGE	BIRLE	**BOFFO**	**BRAKY**
BANNS	**BEIGY**	BIRSE	BOGAN	BRAND
BARBE	**BEING**	**BIRTH**	**BOGEY**	**BRANK**
BARDE	**BELAY**	BISON	**BOGGY**	BRANT
BARER	**BELCH**	**BITCH**	BOGIE	**BRASH**
BARGE	BELGA	BITER	BOGLE	BRASS
BARIC	BELIE	**BITSY**	BOGUS	**BRAVA**
BARKY	BELLE	**BITTY**	**BOHEA**	**BRAVE**
BARMY	BELLY	**BLACK**	BOITE	**BRAVO**
BARNY	**BELOW**	BLADE	BOLAR	**BRAWL**
BARON	*BEMIX	BLAIN	BOLAS	**BRAWN**
BARRE	**BENCH**	BLAME	BOLUS	**BRAWS**
BARYE	**BENDY**	BLAND	**BOMBE**	*BRAXY
BASAL	BENNE	**BLANK**	BONER	*BRAZA
BASED	BENNI	BLARE	**BONEY**	*BRAZE
BASER	**BENNY**	BLASE	BONGO	BREAD
BASES	BERET	BLAST	BONNE	**BREAK**
BASIC	BERME	BLATE	**BONNY**	BREAM
BASIL	**BERRY**	*BLAZE	BONUS	BREDE
BASIN	**BERTH**	**BLEAK**	*BONZE	BREED
BASIS	**BERYL**	BLEAR	**BOOBY**	BRENT
BASSI	BESET	BLEAT	**BOOMY**	**BREVE**
BASSO	BESOM	BLEED	BOOST	BRIAR
BASSY	BESOT	BLEND	**BOOTH**	BRIBE
BASTE	BETEL	BLENT	**BOOTY**	**BRICK**

BRIDE	BURRY	BANGLE	BATING	BEGGED
BRIEF	BURSA	BANIAN	BATMAN	BEGIRD
BRIER	BURSE	BANING	BATTED	BEGLAD
BRILL	BURST	BANISH	BATTEN	BEGONE
BRINE	BUSBY	BANKER	BATTER	BEGRIM
BRING	BUSHY	BANNED	BATTIK	BEGULF
BRINK	BUSTY	BANNER	BATTLE	BEHALF
BRINY	BUTCH	BANNET	BATTUE	BEHAVE
BRISK	BUTEO	BANTAM	BAUBEE	BEHEAD
BRITT	BUTTE	BANTER	BAUBLE	BEHELD
BROAD	BUTTY	BANYAN	*BAULKY	BEHEST
BROCK	BUTUT	*BANZAI	BAWBEE	BEHIND
BROIL	BUTYL	BAOBAB	*BAWDRY	BEHOLD
BROKE	*BUXOM	BARBAL	BAWLER	BEHOOF
BROME	BUYER	BARBEL	BAWTIE	BEHOVE
BROMO	BWANA	BARBER	BAYAMO	BEHOWL
BRONC	BYLAW	BARBET	BAYARD	BEKISS
BROOD	*BYWAY	BARBUT	*BAZAAR	BEKNOT
BROOK	BABBLE	BARDIC	*BEACHY	BELADY
BROOM	BABIED	BAREGE	BEACON	BELAUD
BROSE	BABIES	BARELY	BEADLE	BELDAM
BROSY	BABOOL	BAREST	BEAGLE	BELEAP
BROTH	BABOON	BARFLY	BEAKER	BELFRY
BROWN	BACKER	BARHOP	BEANIE	BELIEF
BRUGH	*BACKUP	BARING	BEARER	BELIER
BRUIN	BADDIE	BARITE	BEATER	BELIKE
BRUIT	BADGER	BARIUM	BEAUTY	BELIVE
BRUME	BADMAN	BARKER	BEAVER	BELLOW
BRUNT	BAFFLE	BARLEY	BECALM	BELONG
BRUSH	BAGASS	BARLOW	BECAME	BELUGA
BRUSK	BAGFUL	BARMAN	BECKET	BEMEAN
BRUTE	BAGGED	BARMIE	BECKON	BEMIRE
BUBAL	BAGGIE	BARONG	BECLOG	BEMIST
BUBBY	BAGMAN	BARONY	BECOME	BEMOAN
BUCKO	BAGNIO	*BARQUE	BEDAMN	*BEMOCK
BUDDY	BAGUET	BARRED	BEDAUB	BEMUSE
BUDGE	BAGWIG	BARREL	BEDBUG	BENAME
BUFFO	BAILEE	BARREN	BEDDED	BENDAY
*BUFFY	BAILER	BARRET	BEDDER	BENDEE
BUGGY	BAILEY	BARRIO	*BEDECK	BENDER
BUGLE	BAILIE	BARROW	BEDELL	BENIGN
BUILD	BAILOR	BARTER	BEDLAM	BENNET
BUILT	BAITER	BARYON	BEDPAN	BENUMB
BULGE	*BAKERY	BARYTA	BEDRID	*BENZAL
BULGY	BAKING	BARYTE	BEDRUG	*BENZIN
BULKY	BALATA	BASALT	BEDUIN	*BENZOL
BULLA	BALBOA	BASELY	BEDUMB	*BENZYL
BULLY	BALDLY	BASEST	BEEBEE	BERAKE
BUMPY	BALEEN	BASHAW	*BEECHY	BERATE
BUNCH	BALING	BASHER	BEEPER	BERIME
BUNCO	BALKER	BASIFY	BEETLE	BERLIN
BUNKO	BALLAD	BASING	BEEVES	BERTHA
BUNNY	BALLER	BASION	BEFALL	BESEEM
BUNYA	BALLET	BASKET	BEFLAG	BESIDE
BURAN	BALLON	*BASQUE	BEFLEA	BESMUT
BURET	BALLOT	BASSET	BEFOOL	BESNOW
BURGH	BALSAM	BASSLY	BEFORE	BESTIR
BURIN	BANANA	BASTER	BEFOUL	BESTOW
BURKE	BANDER	BATBOY	BEFRET	BESTUD
BURLY	BANDIT	BATEAU	BEGALL	BETAKE
BURNT	BANDOG	BATHER	*BEGAZE	BETHEL
BURRO	BANGER	BATHOS	BEGGAR	BETIDE

BETIME	BIRDER	**BODICE**	**BOTANY**	**BREWIS**
BETISE	BIRDIE	**BODIED**	*BOTCHY	BRIARD
BETONY	**BIREME**	BODIES	**BOTFLY**	**BRIBER**
BETOOK	**BIRKIE**	**BODILY**	**BOTHER**	*BRICKY
BETRAY	**BIRLER**	**BODING**	BOTTLE	**BRIDAL**
BETTED	**BISECT**	**BODKIN**	**BOTTOM**	**BRIDGE**
BETTER	**BISHOP**	**BOFFIN**	**BOUCLE**	BRIDLE
BETTOR	*BISQUE	**BOGGED**	**BOUFFE**	**BRIGHT**
BEVIES	BISTER	**BOGGLE**	**BOUGHT**	BRINER
BEWAIL	BISTRE	BOGIES	BOUGIE	**BRIONY**
BEWARE	BISTRO	*BOHUNK	**BOULLE**	**BROACH**
BEWEEP	*BITCHY	BOILER	**BOUNCE**	**BROCHE**
BEWORM	BITING	BOLERO	**BOUNCY**	BROGAN
BEWRAP	BITTED	BOLETE	**BOUNTY**	**BROGUE**
BEWRAY	BITTEN	BOLIDE	**BOURNE**	**BROKEN**
BEYLIC	BITTER	*BOLLIX	**BOURSE**	**BROKER**
*BEYLIK	*BIZONE	*BOLLOX	**BOVINE**	**BROLLY**
BEYOND	*BLABBY	BOLSON	**BOWERY**	**BROMAL**
*BEZANT	BLAMER	BOLTER	**BOWFIN**	**BROMIC**
*BEZOAR	BLANCH	**BOMBER**	**BOWING**	**BROMID**
*BHAKTA	BLASTY	*BOMBYX	**BOWLEG**	**BROMIN**
*BHAKTI	*BLAZER	BONACI	**BOWLER**	**BRONCO**
*BIAXAL	*BLAZON	**BONBON**	**BOWMAN**	*BRONZE
BIBBED	BLEACH	BONDER	**BOWPOT**	*BRONZY
BIBBER	BLEARY	**BONDUC**	*BOWWOW	**BROOCH**
BICARB	BLENCH	BONIER	**BOWYER**	**BROODY**
BICEPS	BLENDE	BONING	*BOXCAR	**BROOMY**
BICKER	BLENNY	BONITA	*BOXFUL	**BROTHY**
BICORN	BLIMEY	BONITO	*BOXIER	**BROWNY**
BICRON	BLINIS	BONNET	*BOXING	**BROWSE**
BIDDEN	*BLINTZ	BONNIE	BOYARD	BRUCIN
BIDDER	**BLITHE**	BONSAI	BOYISH	BRUISE
BIDING	*BLOCKY	*BONZER	**BRACER**	BRULOT
BIFFIN	BLONDE	**BOOBOO**	**BRAGGY**	**BRUMAL**
*BIFLEX	**BLOODY**	BOODLE	**BRAHMA**	*BRUMBY
BIFOLD	**BLOOMY**	BOOGER	**BRAINY**	**BRUNCH**
BIFORM	BLOTCH	BOOGIE	BRAISE	BRUNET
BIGAMY	BLOTTO	**BOOHOO**	*BRAIZE	**BRUSHY**
BIGEYE	BLOTTY	**BOOKER**	**BRANCH**	BRUTAL
BIGGER	**BLOUSE**	**BOOKIE**	**BRANDY**	**BRYONY**
BIGGIE	BLOUSY	**BOOMER**	**BRANNY**	**BUBALE**
BIGGIN	*BLOWBY	BOOTEE	**BRASHY**	**BUBBLE**
BIGWIG	**BLOWER**	BOOTIE	BRASIL	*BUBBLY
BIKING	BLOWSY	*BOOZER	**BRASSY**	**BUCCAL**
BIKINI	**BLOWUP**	BOPPER	**BRATTY**	**BUCKER**
BILBOA	*BLOWZY	BORAGE	**BRAVER**	**BUCKET**
BILKER	**BLUELY**	BORANE	**BRAWLY**	**BUCKLE**
BILLER	BLUEST	BORATE	**BRAWNY**	**BUCKRA**
BILLET	**BLUESY**	BORDEL	**BRAYER**	**BUDDER**
BILLIE	BLUING	BORDER	*BRAZEN	**BUDDLE**
BILLON	**BLUISH**	BOREAL	*BRAZER	**BUDGER**
BILLOW	BLUNGE	BORIDE	*BRAZIL	**BUDGET**
BINARY	**BLURRY**	BORING	**BREACH**	**BUDGIE**
BINATE	BOATEL	**BORROW**	BREAST	**BUFFER**
BINDER	BOATER	BORSCH	**BREATH**	**BUFFET**
BINDLE	**BOBBER**	**BORSHT**	**BREECH**	**BUGEYE**
BINNED	**BOBBIN**	*BORZOI	**BREEKS**	**BUGGED**
BIOGEN	**BOBBLE**	BOSKER	*BREEZE	**BUGGER**
BIOPSY	**BOBCAT**	BOSKET	*BREEZY	BUGLER
BIOTIC	**BOCCIA**	BOSOMY	**BREGMA**	**BUGSHA**
BIOTIN	**BOCCIE**	*BOSQUE	**BREVET**	**BULBEL**
*BIPACK	**BODEGA**	BOSTON	**BREWER**	**BULBIL**

BULBUL	BUTTER	BALONEY	*BATHYAL	BEDLIKE
BULGER	BUTTON	BAMBINO	BATISTE	BEDMATE
BULGUR	*BUZZER	BANDAGE	BATLIKE	BEDOUIN
BULLET	BYELAW	BANDANA	BATSMAN	BEDPOST
BUMBLE	BYGONE	*BANDBOX	BATTEAU	BEDRAIL
BUMKIN	BYLINE	BANDEAU	BATTERY	BEDRAPE
BUMMED	BYNAME	BANDIED	BATTIER	*BEDROCK
BUMMER	BYPASS	BANDIES	BATTING	BEDROLL
BUMPER	BYPAST	BANDORA	BATTLER	BEDROOM
*BUNCHY	*BYPATH	BANDORE	BATWING	BEDSIDE
BUNDLE	*BYPLAY	BANEFUL	BAUSOND	BEDSORE
BUNGLE	BYRNIE	*BANGKOK	*BAUXITE	*BEDTICK
BUNION	BYROAD	BANKING	*BAWCOCK	BEDTIME
BUNKER	BYSSUS	BANKSIA	BAWDIER	BEDUNCE
BUNKUM	*BYTALK	BANNING	BAWDIES	BEDWARD
BUNTER	*BYWORD	*BANNOCK	*BAWDILY	*BEDWARF
*BUQSHA	*BYWORK	*BANQUET	*BAWDRIC	BEEFIER
BURBLE	*BYZANT	BANSHEE	BAWSUNT	*BEEFILY
BURBLY	BAALISM	BANSHIE	BAYONET	*BEEHIVE
BURBOT	BABASSU	BAPTISE	*BAYWOOD	BEELIKE
BURDEN	BABBITT	BAPTISM	*BAZOOKA	BEELINE
BURDIE	BABBLER	BAPTIST	BEADIER	*BEESWAX
BUREAU	BABBOOL	*BAPTIZE	BEADILY	*BEFLECK
BURGEE	BABESIA	BARBATE	BEADING	BEGGARY
BURGER	*BABICHE	BARBELL	BEADMAN	BEGGING
BURGLE	*BABYISH	BARBULE	BEAMIER	BEGLOOM
BURGOO	BACCARA	BAREFIT	BEAMILY	BEGONIA
BURIAL	BACCATE	BARGAIN	BEAMISH	BEGORAH
BURIED	*BACCHIC	BARGING	BEANBAG	BEGORRA
BURIER	*BACKHOE	BARILLA	BEANERY	BEGRIME
BURIES	*BACKING	*BARKEEP	BEARCAT	BEGROAN
BURKER	*BACKLIT	BARLESS	BEARING	BEGUILE
BURLAP	*BACKLOG	BARMAID	BEARISH	BEGUINE
BURLER	*BACKOUT	BARONET	BEASTIE	*BEHAVER
BURLEY	*BACKSAW	BARONNE	BEASTLY	*BEHOOVE
BURNER	*BACKSET	*BAROQUE	*BEATIFY	*BEJEWEL
BURNET	BADGING	*BARRACK	BEATING	BELABOR
BURNIE	BADLAND	BARRAGE	BEATNIK	BELACED
BURRED	BADNESS	BARRIER	BEBEERU	BELATED
BURRER	*BAFFIES	BARRING	BEBLOOD	BELCHER
BURROW	*BAFFLER	BARROOM	BECAUSE	BELDAME
BURSAR	BAGASSE	BARTEND	*BECHALK	BELIEVE
BURTON	BAGGAGE	BARWARE	*BECHARM	BELLBOY
BUSBOY	BAGGING	BASCULE	BECLASP	BELLEEK
BUSHEL	BAGPIPE	BASEMAN	*BECLOAK	BELLHOP
BUSHER	BAGSFUL	*BASENJI	BECLOUD	BELLIED
BUSIED	*BAGWORM	*BASHFUL	BECLOWN	BELLIES
BUSIER	BAHADUR	*BASHLYK	BECRAWL	BELLMAN
BUSIES	*BAILIFF	BASILAR	BECRIME	BELOVED
BUSILY	BAILOUT	BASILIC	*BECROWD	BELTING
BUSING	BAIRNLY	BASINET	BECRUST	*BELTWAY
BUSKER	*BAKLAVA	BASSIST	BECURSE	BELYING
BUSKIN	*BAKLAWA	BASSOON	BEDDING	BEMADAM
BUSMAN	BALANCE	BASTARD	BEDEMAN	BENCHER
BUSSED	BALCONY	BASTILE	BEDEVIL	BENEATH
BUSSES	BALDISH	BASTING	BEDFAST	BENEFIC
BUSTER	BALDRIC	BASTION	BEDGOWN	BENEFIT
BUSTIC	BALEFUL	BATCHER	BEDIGHT	BENEMPT
BUSTLE	BALLADE	*BATFISH	BEDIRTY	BENISON
BUTANE	BALLAST	*BATFOWL	*BEDIZEN	BENTHAL
BUTENE	BALLOON	BATHING	BEDLAMP	BENTHIC
BUTLER	BALNEAL	BATHTUB	BEDLESS	BENTHOS

*BENZENE	*BICYCLE	*BIVALVE	BLUNDER	BORDURE
*BENZINE	BIDARKA	*BIVINYL	BLUNGER	BOREDOM
*BENZOIN	BIDDING	BIVOUAC	BLURTER	BORNEOL
*BENZOLE	BIFILAR	*BIZARRE	BLUSHER	BORNITE
*BENZOYL	BIFOCAL	*BIZNAGA	BLUSTER	BOROUGH
BEPAINT	BIGGEST	BLABBER	BOARDER	BORSCHT
*BEQUEST	BIGGETY	*BLACKEN	BOARISH	BORSTAL
BEREAVE	BIGGING	*BLACKLY	BOASTER	BOSCAGE
BERETTA	BIGGISH	BLADDER	BOATING	BOSKAGE
*BERHYME	BIGGITY	BLAMING	BOATMAN	*BOSQUET
BERLINE	BIGHEAD	BLANKET	*BOBBERY	BOSSDOM
BEROBED	BIGHORN	*BLANKLY	BOBBIES	BOSSIER
BERSEEM	BIGNESS	BLARNEY	BOBBING	BOSSIES
BERSERK	BIGOTED	BLASTER	*BOBECHE	BOSSISM
BESCOUR	BIGOTRY	BLASTIE	BOBSLED	BOTANIC
BESEECH	*BIKEWAY	BLATANT	BOBSTAY	BOTCHER
BESHAME	BILIARY	BLATHER	BOBTAIL	BOTONEE
BESHOUT	BILIOUS	BLATTED	*BOFFOLA	BOTTLER
*BESHREW	BILLBUG	BLATTER	BOGBEAN	BOTULIN
BESIDES	BILLIES	*BLAUBOK	BOGGIER	BOUDOIR
BESIEGE	BILLING	*BLEAKLY	BOGGING	BOULDER
BESLIME	BILLION	BLEATER	BOGGISH	BOUNCER
BESMEAR	*BILLOWY	BLEEDER	BOGGLER	BOUNDEN
BESMILE	BILOBED	BLELLUM	BOGWOOD	BOUNDER
*BESMOKE	BILSTED	BLEMISH	*BOGYISM	*BOUQUET
*BESPEAK	BILTONG	BLENDER	*BOGYMAN	BOURBON
BESTEAD	BIMETAL	*BLESBOK	BOHEMIA	BOURDON
BESTIAL	BIMODAL	BLESSED	BOLETUS	BOURREE
BESTREW	BINDERY	BLESSER	BOLIVAR	*BOWHEAD
BESTROW	BINDING	BLETHER	BOLIVIA	*BOWKNOT
BESWARM	BINNING	*BLIGHTY	BOLLARD	BOWLDER
BETAINE	BINOCLE	BLINDER	BOLOGNA	BOWLESS
*BETAXED	BIOCIDE	BLINDLY	BOLONEY	*BOWLFUL
*BETHANK	BIOGENY	BLINKER	BOLSTER	*BOWLIKE
*BETHINK	BIOHERM	*BLINTZE	BOMBARD	BOWLINE
BETHORN	BIOLOGY	BLISTER	BOMBAST	BOWLING
*BETHUMP	BIOMASS	BLITHER	*BONANZA	*BOWSHOT
BETIMES	BIONICS	BLOATER	BONDAGE	*BOXFISH
BETOKEN	BIONOMY	*BLOCKER	BONDMAN	*BOXHAUL
BETROTH	BIOTICS	BLOOMER	BONESET	*BOXIEST
BETTING	BIOTITE	BLOOPER	BONFIRE	*BOXLIKE
BETWEEN	BIOTOPE	BLOSSOM	BONIEST	*BOXWOOD
*BETWIXT	BIOTRON	*BLOTCHY	BONKERS	BOYCOTT
BEVELER	BIOTYPE	BLOTTED	*BONNOCK	*BOYHOOD
BEVOMIT	BIPARTY	BLOTTER	*BOODLER	BRABBLE
*BEWEARY	BIPLANE	BLOUSON	BOOKEND	BRACERO
BEWITCH	BIPOLAR	*BLOWFLY	BOOKING	BRACHET
*BEWORRY	BIRCHEN	BLOWGUN	*BOOKISH	BRACING
*BEZIQUE	BIRDMAN	BLOWIER	BOOKLET	*BRACKEN
*BEZZANT	BIRETTA	*BLOWOFF	*BOOKMAN	*BRACKET
*BHEESTY	BIRLING	BLOWOUT	BOOMIER	BRADAWL
BHISTIE	BISCUIT	BLOWSED	*BOOMKIN	BRADOON
*BIAXIAL	BISMUTH	*BLOWZED	BOOMLET	BRAGGER
BIBASIC	BISNAGA	BLUBBER	BOONIES	BRAIDER
*BIBBERY	BISTATE	BLUCHER	BOORISH	BRAILLE
BIBBING	BISTORT	BLUECAP	BOOSTER	BRAKING
*BIBCOCK	BITABLE	BLUEFIN	BOOTERY	BRAMBLE
BIBELOT	BITTERN	BLUEGUM	BOOTIES	*BRAMBLY
BIBLESS	BITTIER	BLUEING	BOOTLEG	*BRANCHY
*BIBLIKE	BITTING	BLUEISH	BORACES	BRANDER
BICOLOR	*BITTOCK	*BLUEJAY	BORACIC	BRANNED
BICORNE	BITUMEN	*BLUFFER	*BORAZON	BRANNER

BRASIER	BROKAGE	BULLACE	*BUTTOCK	BALDNESS
BRASSIE	BROMATE	BULLATE	BUTTONY	BALDPATE
BRATTLE	BROMIDE	BULLBAT	BUTYRAL	*BALDRICK
BRAVADO	BROMINE	BULLDOG	BUTYRIC	BALEFIRE
*BRAVERY	BROMISM	BULLIED	BUTYRIN	BALISAUR
BRAVEST	BRONCHI	BULLIER	*BUTYRYL	BALKLINE
BRAVING	BRONCHO	BULLIES	*BUZZARD	BALLISTA
BRAVURA	*BRONZER	BULLION	*BUZZWIG	BALLONET
BRAWLER	BROODER	BULLISH	BYLINER	BALLONNE
BRAWLIE	BROTHEL	*BULLOCK	*BABBLING	BALLOTER
*BRAZIER	BROTHER	BULLOUS	BABIRUSA	BALLROOM
*BRAZING	BROTHER	BULLPEN	*BABUSHKA	*BALLYHOO
BREADTH	BROUGHT	BULRUSH	*BABYHOOD	BALLYRAG
BREAKER	BROWNIE	*BULWARK	BACCARAT	BALMORAL
*BREAKUP	BROWSER	BUMBLER	*BACCATED	BALSAMIC
*BREATHY	BRUCINE	BUMBOAT	*BACCHANT	BALUSTER
BRECCIA	BRUISER	BUMMING	*BACCHIUS	BANALITY
*BRECHAM	BRUITER	*BUMPKIN	*BACHELOR	BANAUSIC
BRECHAN	BRULYIE	BUNDIST	BACILLAR	BANDAGER
BREEDER	*BRULZIE	BUNDLER	BACILLUS	BANDANNA
BREVIER	BRUSHER	BUNGLER	*BACKACHE	BANDEROL
*BREVITY	BRUSHUP	BUNTING	*BACKBEND	BANDITRY
BREWAGE	*BRUSQUE	BUOYAGE	*BACKBITE	BANDSMAN
*BREWERY	BRUTELY	BUOYANT	*BACKBONE	BANGTAIL
BREWING	*BRUTIFY	BURBLER	*BACKDOOR	BANISHER
BRIBERY	BRUTING	*BURDOCK	*BACKDROP	BANISTER
BRIBING	BRUTISH	BURETTE	*BACKFILL	*BANJOIST
*BRICKLE	BRUTISM	BURGAGE	*BACKFIRE	*BANKBOOK
BRICOLE	*BRUXISM	BURGEON	*BACKHAND	BANKNOTE
BRIDLER	BUBALIS	BURGESS	*BACKLASH	BANKROLL
BRIDOON	BUBBIES	BURGHER	*BACKLESS	*BANKRUPT
BRIEFER	BUBBLER	BURGLAR	*BACKLIST	*BANKSIDE
*BRIEFLY	BUBINGA	BURGOUT	*BACKMOST	BANNERET
BRIGADE	BUBONIC	BURKITE	*BACKPACK	BANNEROL
BRIGAND	*BUCKEEN	BURLESK	*BACKREST	BANTERER
BRIMFUL	*BUCKEYE	BURNING	*BACKSEAT	BANTLING
BRIMMED	*BUCKISH	BURNISH	*BACKSIDE	BAPTISIA
BRIMMER	*BUCKLER	BURNOUS	*BACKSLAP	*BAPTIZER
BRINDED	*BUCKRAM	BURNOUT	*BACKSLID	BARATHEA
BRINDLE	*BUCKSAW	BURRIER	*BACKSPIN	BARBARIC
BRINGER	BUCOLIC	BURRING	*BACKSTAY	BARBASCO
BRINIER	BUDDIES	BURSARY	*BACKSTOP	BARBECUE
BRINIES	BUDDING	BURSATE	*BACKWARD	*BARBERRY
BRINISH	BUDGING	BURSEED	*BACKWASH	BARBETTE
BRIOCHE	BUDLESS	BURSTER	*BACKWOOD	BARBICAN
*BRIQUET	BUDLIKE	BURTHEN	*BACKYARD	BARBICEL
BRISKET	*BUFFALO	BURWEED	BACTERIA	BARBITAL
*BRISKLY	*BUFFIER	BUSHIDO	BACTERIN	BARBLESS
BRISTLE	*BUFFOON	BUSHIER	BACULINE	*BARBWIRE
BRISTLY	BUGABOO	*BUSHILY	*BADGERLY	*BAREBACK
BRISTOL	BUGBANE	BUSHING	BADINAGE	BAREFOOT
BRITSKA	BUGBEAR	BUSHMAN	*BADMOUTH	BAREHEAD
BRITTLE	BUGGERY	BUSHTIT	*BAGPIPER	BARENESS
*BRITZKA	BUGGING	BUSIEST	BAGUETTE	BARESARK
*BROADAX	BUGLOSS	BUSSING	*BAIDARKA	BARGEMAN
BROADEN	BUGSEED	BUSTARD	BAILMENT	BARGHEST
BROADLY	BUILDER	BUTANOL	BAILSMAN	BARGUEST
BROCADE	BUILDUP	BUTCHER	*BAKEMEAT	BARITONE
*BROCKET	BUIRDLY	BUTLERY	*BAKESHOP	BARKLESS
BROCOLI	BULBOUS	BUTTALS	*BAKSHISH	BARLEDUC
BROIDER	BULIMIA	BUTTERY	BALANCER	BARNACLE
BROILER	BULKAGE	BUTTIES	*BALDHEAD	BARNYARD

BAROGRAM	*BEAMLIKE	*BEHAVIOR	BETATRON	*BIMETHYL
BARONAGE	BEANBALL	*BEHEMOTH	BETATTER	BINAURAL
BARONESS	BEANLIKE	BEHOLDEN	BETELNUT	*BINDWEED
BARONIAL	BEANPOLE	BEHOLDER	BETRAYAL	BINNACLE
*BAROUCHE	BEARLIKE	*BEJUMBLE	BETRAYER	BINOMIAL
BARRABLE	BEARSKIN	*BEKNIGHT	BEUNCLED	BIOASSAY
BARRANCA	*BEATIFIC	BELABOUR	BEVATRON	BIOCLEAN
BARRANCO	BEATLESS	BELIEVER	BEVELLER	*BIOCYCLE
BARRATER	*BEAUTIFY	*BELIQUOR	BEVERAGE	BIOGENIC
BARRATOR	*BEBOPPER	BELITTLE	BEWAILER	BIOLOGIC
BARRATRY	BECARPET	BELLBIRD	BEWILDER	BIOLYSIS
BARRETOR	*BECHAMEL	BELLOWER	*BEWINGED	*BIOMETRY
BARRETRY	*BECHANCE	BELLPULL	*BEWRAYER	BIOPLASM
BARRETTE	*BECKONER	BELLWORT	BHEESTIE	BIOSCOPE
BARSTOOL	BECLAMOR	*BELLYFUL	*BIACETYL	*BIOSCOPY
BARTERER	*BECLOTHE	BELTLESS	BIANNUAL	BIOTICAL
BARTISAN	*BECOMING	BELTLINE	BIASNESS	BIOVULAR
*BARTIZAN	*BECOWARD	BEMADDEN	BIATHLON	BIPAROUS
BARYTONE	BECUDGEL	BEMINGLE	BIBULOUS	BIPARTED
BASALTES	*BEDABBLE	BEMUDDLE	*BICHROME	*BIPHENYL
BASEBALL	*BEDARKEN	BEMURMUR	*BICKERER	BIRACIAL
BASEBORN	*BEDAZZLE	*BEMUZZLE	BICOLOUR	BIRADIAL
BASELESS	*BEDCHAIR	*BENDWAYS	*BICONVEX	BIRAMOSE
BASELINE	*BEDCOVER	BENDWISE	*BICUSPID	BIRAMOUS
BASEMENT	BEDEAFEN	*BENEDICK	BICYCLER	*BIRDBATH
BASENESS	BEDESMAN	BENEDICT	*BICYCLIC	BIRDCAGE
*BASICITY	*BEDFRAME	*BENEFICE	*BIDARKEE	BIRDCALL
BASIDIUM	BEDIAPER	BENJAMIN	BIDDABLE	*BIRDFARM
BASIFIER	*BEDIMPLE	BENTWOOD	BIDENTAL	*BIRDLIKE
BASILARY	*BEDMAKER	*BENZIDIN	BIENNIAL	BIRDLIME
BASILICA	BEDOTTED	*BENZOATE	BIENNIUM	BIRDSEED
BASILISK	BEDPLATE	*BEPIMPLE	*BIFACIAL	BIRDSEYE
*BASKETRY	*BEDQUILT	*BEQUEATH	*BIFIDITY	BIRRETTA
*BASOPHIL	*BEDRENCH	BERASCAL	BIFORATE	*BIRTHDAY
BASSINET	BEDRIVEL	BERBERIN	*BIFORKED	BISECTOR
BASSNESS	BEDSONIA	BERCEUSE	*BIFORMED	*BISEXUAL
BASSWOOD	BEDSTAND	BEREAVER	BIGAMIES	BISTOURY
BASTARDY	BEDSTEAD	BERGAMOT	BIGAMIST	*BITCHERY
BASTILLE	BEDSTRAW	BERIBERI	BIGAMOUS	BITEWING
*BATHETIC	*BEDWARDS	BERINGED	BIGAROON	BITINGLY
BATHLESS	BEEBREAD	BERNICLE	*BIGEMINY	*BITSTOCK
*BATHROBE	*BEECHNUT	BEROUGED	*BIGMOUTH	BITTIEST
*BATHROOM	*BEEFCAKE	BERRETTA	BIGNONIA	BIVALENT
BATTALIA	BEEFIEST	*BESCORCH	*BIHOURLY	BIVALVED
BATTENER	BEEFLESS	BESCREEN	*BIJUGATE	*BIWEEKLY
BATTERIE	*BEEFWOOD	BESETTER	*BIJUGOUS	*BIYEARLY
BATTIEST	BEESWING	*BESHADOW	BILABIAL	*BLACKBOY
*BAUDEKIN	BEETROOT	*BESHIVER	BILANDER	*BLACKCAP
BAUDRONS	BEFINGER	BESHROUD	*BILBERRY	*BLACKFIN
BAWDIEST	*BEFLOWER	BESIEGER	BILINEAR	*BLACKFLY
BAYADEER	BEFOULER	BESLAVED	BILLETER	*BLACKGUM
BAYADERE	BEFRIEND	*BESMIRCH	BILLFISH	*BLACKING
*BAYBERRY	BEFRINGE	*BESMOOTH	BILLFOLD	*BLACKISH
BDELLIUM	*BEFUDDLE	BESMUDGE	BILLHEAD	*BLACKLEG
*BEACHBOY	BEGETTER	BESOOTHE	*BILLHOOK	*BLACKOUT
BEADIEST	*BEGGARLY	BESOUGHT	BILLIARD	*BLACKTOP
*BEADLIKE	BEGINNER	BESPOUSE	*BILLYCAN	BLAMABLE
BEADROLL	BEGIRDLE	BESPREAD	BILOBATE	*BLAMEFUL
BEADSMAN	BEGORRAH	BESPRENT	BIMANOUS	*BLANCHER
*BEADWORK	BEGOTTEN	BESTIARY	BIMANUAL	BLANDISH
BEAMIEST	BEGRUDGE	BESTOWAL	BIMENSAL	BLASTEMA
BEAMLESS	BEGUILER	BESTRIDE	BIMESTER	BLASTIER

BLASTING
*BLASTOFF
BLASTOMA
BLASTULA
*BLATANCY
BLATTING
*BLAZONER
BLAZONRY
*BLEACHER
*BLEAKISH
BLEEDING
*BLENCHER
*BLESBUCK
BLESSING
BLINDAGE
*BLINKARD
BLISTERY
*BLIZZARD
*BLOCKADE
*BLOCKAGE
*BLOCKISH
BLONDISH
BLOODFIN
BLOODIED
BLOODIER
BLOODIES
BLOODILY
BLOODING
BLOODRED
*BLOOMERY
*BLOSSOMY
BLOTLESS
BLOTTIER
BLOTTING
*BLOWBACK
*BLOWFISH
*BLOWHARD
*BLOWHOLE
BLOWIEST
*BLOWPIPE
*BLOWTUBE
*BLUBBERY
BLUDGEON
BLUEBALL
BLUEBELL
BLUEBILL
BLUEBIRD
*BLUEBOOK
BLUECOAT
*BLUEFISH
BLUEGILL
BLUEHEAD
*BLUEJACK
BLUELINE
BLUENESS
BLUENOSE
BLUESMAN
BLUESTEM
BLUEWEED
BLUEWOOD
*BLUSHFUL
BLUSTERY

BOARDING
BOARDMAN
*BOARFISH
BOASTFUL
BOATBILL
BOATLOAD
BOATSMAN
BOATYARD
BOBBINET
*BOBOLINK
*BOBWHITE
*BOCACCIO
BODEMENT
BODILESS
*BODINGLY
*BODYSURF
*BODYWORK
*BOEHMITE
*BOGEYMAN
BOGGIEST
*BOHEMIAN
*BOLDFACE
BOLDNESS
*BOLLWORM
BOLTHEAD
BOLTONIA
BOLTROPE
*BOMBLOAD
*BOMBYCID
BONDMAID
BONDSMAN
*BONEFISH
BONEHEAD
BONELESS
BONEYARD
BONGOIST
*BONHOMIE
*BONIFACE
BONINESS
BONSPELL
BONSPIEL
*BONTEBOK
*BOOGYMAN
*BOOKCASE
BOOKLORE
*BOOKMARK
*BOOKRACK
BOOKREST
*BOOKSHOP
*BOOKWORM
BOOMIEST
*BOOMTOWN
*BOOTJACK
BOOTLACE
BOOTLESS
*BOOTLICK
BORACITE
BORDELLO
BORDERER
BORECOLE
BORINGLY
BORROWER

*BOSCHBOK
*BOSHVARK
BOTANIES
BOTANISE
BOTANIST
*BOTANIZE
*BOTCHERY
BOTONNEE
BOTRYOID
BOTRYOSE
BOTTOMER
*BOTTOMRY
BOTULISM
*BOUFFANT
*BOUGHPOT
BOUGHTEN
BOUILLON
BOUNDARY
BOURGEON
BOURTREE
BOUSOUKI
*BOUTIQUE
*BOUZOUKI
*BOVINELY
*BOVINITY
*BOWFRONT
*BOWINGLY
*BOWLLIKE
*BOWSPRIT
*BOXBERRY
*BOXINESS
*BOXTHORN
*BOYARISM
BRABBLER
BRACELET
*BRACHIAL
*BRACHIUM
*BRACKISH
BRACTLET
BRAGGART
BRAGGEST
BRAGGING
BRAIDING
BRAINIER
BRAINILY
BRAINISH
BRAINPAN
*BRAKEAGE
*BRAKEMAN
*BRANCHIA
BRANDISH
BRANNING
BRANTAIL
BRASILIN
BRASSAGE
BRASSARD
BRASSART
BRASSICA
BRASSISH
BRATTICE
BRAUNITE
*BRAZENLY

*BRAZILIN
*BREACHER
BREADNUT
*BREAKAGE
*BREAKING
BREAKOUT
BREATHER
BREEDING
BRETHREN
*BREVETCY
*BREVIARY
*BRICKBAT
BRIDALLY
BRIDGING
BRIEFING
BRIGHTEN
*BRIMFULL
BRIMLESS
*BRIMMING
BRINDLED
BRINIEST
BRISANCE
BRISLING
*BRITCHES
*BRITZSKA
*BROACHER
*BROADAXE
BROADISH
BROCATEL
BROCCOLI
*BROCHURE
*BROCKAGE
BROGUERY
BROGUISH
BROIDERY
BROMELIN
*BROMIDIC
*BRONCHIA
*BRONCHUS
*BRONZING
BROOKITE
BROOKLET
*BROUGHAM
*BROUHAHA
*BROWBEAT
BROWLESS
BROWNIER
*BROWNISH
BROWNOUT
BRUCELLA
BRUNETTE
*BRUNIZEM
BRUSHIER
*BRUSHOFF
BRYOLOGY
*BRYOZOAN
BUBALINE
*BUCKAROO
*BUCKAYRO
*BUCKBEAN
*BUCKEROO
*BUCKSHEE

*BUCKSHOT
*BUCKSKIN
*BUCKTAIL
BUDDLEIA
BUDGETER
*BUFFETER
*BUFFIEST
BUGHOUSE
*BUHLWORK
BUILDING
*BULKHEAD
*BULLDOZE
BULLETIN
BULLFROG
BULLHEAD
BULLHORN
BULLIEST
*BULLNECK
BULLNOSE
BULLPOUT
BULLRING
BULLRUSH
BULLSHIT
BULLWEED
*BULLWHIP
*BULLYBOY
BULLYRAG
*BUMBLING
*BUNCOMBE
BUNDLING
BUNGALOW
BUNGHOLE
BUNGLING
*BUNKMATE
BUNTLINE
*BUOYANCE
*BUOYANCY
BURDENER
BURGLARY
BURGONET
BURGRAVE
*BURGUNDY
BURNOOSE
BURRIEST
BURROWER
BURSITIS
BURSTONE
*BUSHBUCK
BUSHELER
*BUSHFIRE
BUSHGOAT
BUSHIEST
BUSHLAND
BUSHLESS
*BUSHLIKE
BUSINESS
BUSULFAN
*BUSYBODY
BUSYNESS
*BUSYWORK
BUTANONE
*BUTCHERY

BUTTONER	FI B RIL	NE B ULE	*SU B FIX	CA B ILDO
BUTTRESS	FI B RIN	NE B ULY	SU B GUM	CA B INET
BUTYLATE	FI B ULA	NI B BLE	SU B ITO	CA B OOSE
BUTYLENE	GA B BED	NO B ODY	SU B LET	CI B OULE
BUTYRATE	GA B BER	NU B BIN	SU B MIT	CO B BIER
BUTYROUS	GA B BLE	NU B BLE	SU B ORN	CO B BLER
*BUZZWORD	GA B BRO	NU B BLY	SU B PAR	CU B BAGE
BYSTREET	GA B IES	NU B ILE	SU B SET	CU B BING
	GA B ION	PE B BLE	SU B TLE	*CU B BISH
	GA B OON	*PE B BLY	SU B URB	CU B ICAL
M B IRA	GI B BER	PU B LIC	SU B WAY	CU B ICLE
NO B LE	GI B BET	RA B ATO	TA B ARD	*CU B ICLY
BA B BLE	GI B BON	RA B BET	TA B BED	DA B BLER
BA B IED	GI B LET	RA B BIN	TA B BIS	DA B STER
BA B IES	GO B ANG	RA B BIT	TA B LET	DE B ACLE
BA B OOL	GO B BED	RA B BLE	TA B OUR	DE B ASER
BA B OON	GO B BET	RA B IES	TU B ATE	DE B ATER
BI B BED	GO B BLE	RE B AIT	TU B BED	*DE B AUCH
BI B BER	GO B IES	RE B ATE	TU B BER	DE B ONER
BO B BER	GO B LET	RE B ATO	TU B FUL	*DE B OUCH
BO B BIN	GO B LIN	RE B ECK	TU B ULE	DE B RIEF
BO B BLE	GO B ONY	RE B ILL	VI B IST	DI B ASIC
BO B CAT	HA B ILE	RE B IND	VI B RIO	DI B BING
BU B ALE	HO B BLE	RE B OIL	WA B BLE	DI B BLER
BU B BLE	*HU B BUB	RE B ORN	*WA B BLY	DO B BIES
*BU B BLY	*HU B CAP	*RE B OZO	*WE B FED	DU B BING
CA B ALA	HU B RIS	RE B UFF	WO B BLE	DU B IETY
CA B ANA	*HY B RID	RE B UKE	*WO B BLY	DU B IOUS
CA B BIE	HY B RIS	RE B URY	YA B BER	FA B LIAU
CA B LET	*JA B BER	RI B ALD	*ZE B ECK	FA B LING
CA B MAN	*JA B IRU	RI B AND	*ZI B ETH	FA B ULAR
CE B OID	*JI B BER	RI B BED	BA B ASSU	FE B RILE
CO B ALT	*JO B BER	RI B BER	BA B BITT	FI B ROID
CO B BER	*JU B BAH	RI B BON	BA B BLER	FI B ROIN
CO B BLE	*JU B HAH	RI B LET	BA B ESIA	FI B ROMA
CO B NUT	*JU B ILE	RI B OSE	*BA B ICHE	FI B ROUS
*CO B WEB	*KA B AKA	RO B ALO	*BA B YISH	GA B BARD
CU B ISM	KA B ALA	RO B AND	BE B EERU	GA B BART
CU B IST	*KA B AYA	RO B BED	BE B LOOD	GA B BING
CU B OID	*KA B IKI	RO B BER	BI B ASIC	GA B BLER
CY B ORG	*KA B UKI	RO B BIN	*BI B BERY	GA B ELLE
DA B BER	KE B BIE	RO B UST	BI B BING	GA B FEST
DA B BLE	*KE B LAH	RU B ACE	*BI B COCK	GI B BOSE
DE B ARK	KI B BLE	RU B ATO	BI B ELOT	GI B BOUS
DE B ASE	*KI B ITZ	RU B BED	BI B LESS	GO B BING
DE B ATE	*KI B LAH	RU B BER	*BI B LIKE	GO B BLER
DE B ONE	*KI B OSH	RU B BLE	*BO B BERY	GO B IOID
DE B RIS	KO B OLD	RU B BLY	BO B BIES	GO B ONEE
DE B TOR	LA B IAL	RU B IED	BO B BING	HA B ITAN
DE B UNK	LA B ILE	RU B IER	*BO B ECHE	HA B ITAT
DI B BER	LA B IUM	RU B IES	BO B SLED	HA B ITUS
DI B BLE	LA B OUR	RU B IGO	BO B STAY	HE B ETIC
*DI B BUK	LA B RET	RU B RIC	BO B TAIL	*HI B ACHI
DO B BER	LA B RUM	SA B BAT	BU B ALIS	HO B BIES
DO B BIN	LI B BER	SA B BED	BU B BIES	HO B BLER
DO B LON	LI B IDO	SA B INE	BU B BLER	HO B BNOB
DU B BER	LO B ATE	SO B BER	BU B INGA	*HO B LIKE
DU B BIN	LO B BED	SO B EIT	BU B ONIC	HO B NAIL
*DY B BUK	LO B ULE	SO B FUL	CA B ARET	HO B OISM
FA B LER	LU B BER	SU B BED	CA B BAGE	*JA B BING
FA B RIC	LU B RIC	SU B DEB	CA B BALA	
FI B BER	NE B ULA	SU B DUE	*CA B EZON	

*JI B BING	RI B WORT	SU B SIDE	BER B ERIN	*DUM B BELL
*JI B BOOM	RO B BERY	SU B SIDY	*BIL B ERRY	DUM B NESS
*JO B BERY	RO B BING	SU B SIST	*BLU B BERY	FAU B OURG
*JO B BING	RO B OTRY	SU B SOIL	BOB B INET	*FEE B LISH
*JO B LESS	RU B ASSE	SU B SUME	*BOM B LOAD	FLA B ELLA
*JU B ILEE	RU B BING	SU B TEEN	*BOM B YCID	*FOG B OUND
*KA B ALAH	RU B BISH	SU B TEND	*BOX B ERRY	FOR B IDAL
*KE B BOCK	RU B DOWN	*SU B TEXT	BRA B BLER	FOR B ORNE
*KE B BUCK	RU B ELLA	SU B TILE	*BUM B LING	*FRI B BLER
*KI B BUTZ	RU B IEST	SU B TONE	*CAB B ALAH	*FUR B ELOW
LA B ARUM	RU B IOUS	SU B TYPE	*CAM B OGIA	GAL B ANUM
LA B ELER	SA B ATON	SU B UNIT	*CAR B AMIC	GAM B ESON
LA B ELLA	SA B BATH	SU B VENE	*CAR B AMYL	GAM B USIA
LA B IATE	SA B BING	SU B VERT	*CAR B ARYL	*GAR B ANZO
LA B ORER	SE B ACIC	*SU B ZONE	CAR B INOL	GAR B LESS
LA B ROID	SE B ASIC	TA B ANID	*CAR B ONYL	GAR B OARD
LI B ELEE	SI B LING	TA B ARET	*CAR B OXYL	GER B ILLE
LI B ELER	SO B ERLY	TA B BIED	CAR B URET	GIB B SITE
LI B ERAL	SU B ACID	TA B BIES	CAT B RIER	GLA B ELLA
LI B ERTY	SU B ADAR	TA B BING	*CHU B ASCO	GLA B RATE
LI B RARY	SU B ALAR	TA B ETIC	CLU B ABLE	GLA B ROUS
LI B RATE	SU B AREA	TA B LEAU	*CLU B BING	GLI B NESS
LO B ATED	SU B ARID	TA B LING	*CLU B FOOT	GLO B ATED
LO B BING	SU B ATOM	TA B LOID	*CLU B HAND	GLO B ULAR
LO B BYER	SU B BASE	TA B ORER	*CLU B HAUL	GLO B ULIN
LO B EFIN	SU B BASS	TA B ORET	CLU B ROOT	GOM B ROON
LO B ELIA	SU B BING	TA B ORIN	COB B IEST	GOR B ELLY
LO B STER	SU B CELL	TA B ULAR	COM B ATER	*GOR B LIMY
LO B WORM	SU B CLAN	TO B ACCO	COM B INER	GRA B BIER
*MO B BISH	SU B COOL	TU B BING	*COM B INGS	GRA B BING
MO B ILIS	SU B DEAN	*TU B IFEX	*COM B LIKE	GRA B BLER
MO B OCRA	SU B DUAL	TU B LIKE	*COW B ERRY	*GRU B WORM
NE B BISH	SU B DUCE	TU B ULAR	*CRA B WISE	GUM B OTIL
NI B BLER	SU B DUCT	VE B ROSE	*CRI B BAGE	*HAG B ERRY
*NI B LICK	SU B DUER	VI B RANT	*CRI B BING	HAR B ORER
NI B LIKE	SU B ECHO	VI B RATE	*CRI B BLED	HER B ARIA
NO B BIER	SU B EDIT	VI B RATO	CRI B ROUS	HER B IEST
NO B BILY	SU B ERIC	VI B RION	*CRI B WORK	HER B LESS
NO B BLER	SU B ERIN	WA B BLER	CUM B ERER	*HER B LIKE
NO B LEST	SU B FUSC	*WE B BING	CUM B ROUS	*HOB B YIST
NU B BIER	SU B HEAD	*WE B FOOT	*CUP B OARD	HOT B LOOD
NU B BLES	SU B IDEA	WE B LESS	*CYM B ALER	*HUM B LEST
PA B ULUM	SU B ITEM	WE B STER	*CYM B LING	*HUM B LING
*PI B ROCH	*SU B JECT	*WE B LIKE	DAB B LING	*JAB B ERER
PU B ERTY	*SU B JOIN	*WE B WORM	*DAY B REAK	*JAM B OREE
PU B LISH	SU B LATE	WO B BLER	*DEW B ERRY	*KAB B ALAH
RA B BLER	SU B LIME	*ZE B RASS	DIA B ETES	*KEY B OARD
RA B BONI	SU B MISS	*ZE B RINE	DIA B ETIC	LAM B ASTE
RE B ATER	SU B ORAL	*ZE B ROID	DIA B LERY	*LAM B ENCY
RE B IRTH	SU B OVAL	*BAB B LING	DIA B OLIC	*LAM B KILL
RE B LOOM	SU B PART	BAR B ARIC	DIO B OLON	*LAM B LIKE
RE B OANT	SU B PENA	BAR B ASCO	DIS B OSOM	*LAM B SKIN
RE B OARD	SU B PLOT	BAR B ECUE	DIS B URSE	LAP B OARD
RE B OUND	SU B RACE	*BAR B ERRY	*DOG B ERRY	LAR B OARD
RE B UILD	SU B RENT	BAR B ETTE	DOU B LING	LEE B OARD
RE B UKER	SU B RING	BAR B ICAN	DOU B LOON	LIM B IEST
RI B BAND	SU B RULE	BAR B ICEL	DOU B LURE	LIM B LESS
RI B BIER	SU B SALE	BAR B ITAL	DOU B TFUL	*LOB B YGOW
RI B BING	SU B SECT	BAR B LESS	DRA B NESS	*LOB B YISM
RI B BONY	SU B SERE	*BAR B WIRE	DRI B BLER	*LOB B YIST
RI B LESS		*BAY B ERRY	DRI B BLET	LUM B ERER
RI B LIKE		BEE B READ	DRU B BING	*MOP B OARD

*MOR B IFIC	SNO B BIER	VER B OTEN	SNI B	HOBNO B
*MUL B ERRY	*SNO B BILY	*WAX B ERRY	SNO B	*HUBBU B
*MYO B LAST	*SNO B BISH	*ZAI B ATSU	SNU B	MIDRI B
NOB B IEST	SNO B BISM	*ZOM B IISM	SOR B	PREFA B
NON B ASIC	SNU B NESS		STA B	RECOM B
NON B EING	SOM B RERO		STO B	RESOR B
NUB B IEST	SOM B ROUS	BAR B	STU B	REVER B
NUM B ERER	SOR B ITOL	BIB B	SWA B	SCARA B
*NUM B FISH	*SOW B ELLY	BLA B	SWO B	SERDA B
NUM B NESS	SOW B READ	BLE B	TOM B	SKIBO B
NUT B ROWN	STA B LEST	BLO B	VER B	SUBDE B
PEG B OARD	STA B LING	BOM B	WOM B	SUBUR B
PLE B EIAN	STA B LISH	BOO B	BLUR B	SUPER B
*POT B ELLY	STI B NITE	BUL B	CABO B	BATHTU B
PRE B ASAL	STU B BIER	CHU B	CARO B	CORNCO B
PRE B LESS	*STU B BILY	CLU B	CELE B	COULOM B
PRE B OUND	STU B BING	COB B	CHIM B	*COWHER B
PRO B ABLE	STU B BORN	COM B	CLIM B	*COXCOM B
PUR B LIND	SUB B REED	CRA B	CLOM B	DISTUR B
*QUI B BLER	*SUN B AKED	CRI B	COOM B	*FLUBDU B
RAB B ITER	SUN B ATHE	CUR B	CRUM B	MINICA B
*RAB B ITRY	SUN B URST	DAR B	CUBE B	PEDICA B
RAM B UTAN	*SWA B BING	DAU B	DEMO B	PERTUR B
RAW B ONED	*SYM B IONT	DRA B	KABA B	POTHER B
REA B SORB	*SYM B IOTE	DRI B	KABO B	PROVER B
*RED B RICK	*SYM B OLIC	DRU B	KEBA B	RHUBAR B
*REO B JECT	TAG B OARD	DUM B	KEBO B	*SUCCUM B
REO B TAIN	TAM B OURA	FLA B	NABO B	TAXICA B
*RHA B DOME	TAR B OOSH	FLU B	NAWA B	*WASHTU B
RIB B IEST	TEA B ERRY	FOR B	PLUM B	*CATACOM B
RUB B ABOO	TEA B OARD	GAM B	RHOM B	*CHORIAM B
RUM B LING	THE B AINE	GAR B	RHUM B	CORNCRI B
SAB B ATIC	TOL B OOTH	GLI B	SAHI B	*DOORJAM B
SAW B ONES	TOM B LESS	GLO B	SCRU B	*DOORKNO B
*SCA B BARD	*TOM B LIKE	GRA B	SHRU B	*FIREBOM B
SCA B IOSA	TRA B EATE	GRU B	SLUR B	*FORELIM B
SCA B IOUS	TRI B ASIC	HER B	*SQUA B	*HECATOM B
*SCA B LIKE	*TRI B RACH	*JAM B	*SQUI B	*MEMSAHI B
SCA B ROUS	TRI B UNAL	*JIB B	THRO B	REABSOR B
*SEA B EACH	TUB B ABLE	KER B	THUM B	SILLABU B
SEA B OARD	TUM B LING	KNO B	BAOBA B	SILLIBU B
SEA B ORNE	TUR B INAL	LAM B	BEDAU B	SPARERI B
*SKY B ORNE	TUR B OCAR	LIM B	BEDUM B	*SUBSHRU B
*SLA B BERY	TUR B OFAN	NUM B	BENUM B	*SYLLABU B
SLA B BING	*TUR B OJET	PLE B	BICAR B	*WELLCUR B
*SLO B BERY	*VAM B RACE	SCA B	CHERU B	
*SLO B BISH	*VER B ALLY	SIB B	*COBWE B	
SLU B BING	*VER B ATIM	SLA B	CONFA B	
SLY B OOTS	VER B IAGE	SLO B	*CORYM B	
*SNO B BERY	VER B LESS	SLU B	DESOR B	

C

CADE	CAIN	CALX	CAPH	CARN
CADI	CAKE	CAME	CAPO	CARP
CAFE	CALF	CAMP	CARD	CART
CAGE	CALK	CANE	CARE	CASA
CAGY	CALL	CANT	CARK	CASE
CAID	CALM	CAPE	CARL	CASH

CASK	COAX	CRIS	CANER	CHAIR
CAST	COBB	CROP	CANNA	CHALK
CATE	COCA	CROW	CANNY	CHAMP
CAUL	COCK	CRUD	CANOE	CHANG
CAVE	COCO	CRUS	CANON	CHANT
CAVY	CODA	CRUX	CANSO	CHAOS
CEDE	CODE	CUBE	CANST	CHAPE
CEDI	COED	CUFF	CANTO	CHAPT
CEIL	COFF	CUIF	CANTY	CHARD
CELL	COFT	CUKE	CAPER	CHARE
CELT	COHO	CULL	CAPON	CHARK
CENT	COIL	CULM	CAPUT	CHARM
CERE	COIN	CULT	CARAT	CHARR
CERO	COIR	CUNT	CARER	CHART
CESS	COKE	CURB	CARET	CHARY
CETE	COLA	CURD	CAREX	CHASE
CHAD	COLD	CURE	CARGO	CHASM
CHAM	COLD	CURF	CARLE	CHEAP
CHAP	COLE	CURL	CARNY	CHEAT
CHAR	COLT	CURN	CAROB	CHEEK
CHAT	COLY	CURR	CAROL	CHEEP
CHAW	COMA	CURT	CAROM	CHEER
CHEF	COMA	CUSK	CARPI	CHELA
CHEW	COMB	CUSP	CARRY	CHERT
*CHEZ	COME	CUSS	CARSE	CHESS
CHIA	COMP	CUTE	CARTE	CHEST
CHIC	CONE	CYAN	CARVE	CHETH
CHIN	CONI	CYMA	CASED	*CHEVY
CHIP	CONK	CYME	CASKY	*CHEWY
CHIT	CONN	CYST	CASTE	CHIAO
CHON	CONY	*CZAR	CASUS	*CHICK
CHOP	COOF	CABAL	CATCH	CHICO
CHOW	COOK	CABBY	CATER	CHIDE
CHUB	COOL	CABER	CATTY	CHIEF
CHUG	COON	CABIN	CAULD	CHIEF
CHUM	COOP	CABLE	CAULK	CHIEL
CIAO	COOT	CABOB	CAUSE	CHILD
CINE	COPE	CACAO	CAVED	CHILE
CION	COPY	CACHE	CAVER	CHILI
CIST	CORD	CADDY	CAVIE	CHILL
CITE	CORE	CADET	CAVIL	CHIMB
CITY	CORK	CADGE	CEASE	CHIME
CLAD	CORM	CADGY	CEBID	CHIMP
CLAG	CORN	CADRE	CECUM	CHINA
CLAM	COSH	CAGEY	CEDAR	CHINE
CLAN	COSS	CAHOW	CEDER	CHINK
CLAP	COST	CAIRD	CEIBA	CHINO
CLAW	COSY	CAIRN	CELEB	CHIRK
CLAY	COTE	CAJON	CELLA	CHIRM
CLEF	COUP	CALIF	CELLO	CHIRO
CLEW	COVE	CALIX	CELOM	CHIRP
CLIP	COWL	CALLA	CENSE	CHIRR
CLOD	COWY	CALVE	CENTO	CHIVE
CLOG	COXA	*CALYX	CEORL	*CHIVY
CLON	*COZY	CAMAS	CERED	*CHOCK
CLOP	CRAB	CAMEL	CERIA	CHOIR
CLOT	CRAG	CAMEO	CERIC	CHOKE
CLOY	CRAM	CAMPI	CESTA	*CHOKY
CLUB	CRAP	CAMPO	CESTI	CHOMP
CLUE	CRAW	CAMPY	CHAFE	CHORD
COAL	CREW	CANAL	*CHAFF	CHORE
COAT	CRIB	CANDY	CHAIN	CHOSE

CHOTT	CLOOT	CONTE	CRAVE	CULTI
*CHUCK	CLOSE	CONTO	CRAWL	CUMIN
CHUFA	CLOTH	CONUS	*CRAZE	CUPEL
*CHUFF	CLOUD	COOCH	*CRAZY	CUPID
CHUMP	CLOUR	COOEE	CREAK	CUPPA
CHUNK	CLOUT	COOER	CREAM	CUPPY
CHURL	CLOVE	COOEY	CREDO	CURCH
CHURN	CLOWN	COOKY	CREED	CURDY
CHURR	*CLOZE	COOLY	CREEK	CURER
CHUTE	CLUCK	COOMB	CREEL	CURET
CHYLE	CLUMP	COOPT	CREEP	CURIA
*CHYME	CLUNG	COPAL	CREME	CURIE
CIBOL	CLUNK	COPEN	CREPE	CURIO
CIDER	COACH	COPER	CREPT	CURLY
CIGAR	COACT	COPRA	CREPY	CURRY
CILIA	COALA	COPSE	CRESS	CURSE
CIRCA	COAPT	CORAL	CREST	CURST
CIRRI	COAST	CORBY	CRICK	CURVE
CISCO	COATI	CORER	CRIED	CURVY
CITER	COBBY	CORGI	CRIER	CUSEC
CIVET	COBIA	CORKY	CRIES	CUSHY
CIVIC	COBLE	CORNU	CRIME	CUSSO
CIVIE	COBRA	CORNY	CRIMP	CUTCH
CIVIL	COCCI	CORPS	CRISP	CUTES
*CIVVY	*COCKY	CORSE	CROAK	CUTEY
CLACH	COCOA	COSEC	CROCI	CUTIE
CLACK	CODEN	COSET	CROCK	CUTIN
CLAIM	CODER	COSEY	CROFT	CUTIS
CLAMP	*CODEX	COSIE	CRONE	CUTTY
CLANG	CODON	COSTA	CRONY	CUTUP
CLANK	COGON	COTAN	CROOK	CYANO
CLARO	COHOG	COTTA	CROON	CYCAD
CLARY	COIGN	COUCH	CRORE	CYCAS
CLASH	COLIC	COUDE	CROSS	CYCLE
CLASP	COLIN	COUGH	CROUP	CYCLO
CLASS	COLOG	COULD	CROWD	CYDER
CLAST	COLON	COUNT	CROWN	*CYLIX
CLAVE	COLON	COUPE	*CROZE	CYMAR
CLEAN	COLOR	COURT	CRUDE	CYMOL
CLEAR	*COLZA	COUTH	CRUEL	CYNIC
CLEAT	COMAL	COVEN	CRUET	CYTON
CLEEK	COMBE	COVER	CRUMB	CABALA
CLEFT	COMBO	COVET	CRUMP	CABANA
CLEPE	COMER	COVEY	CRUOR	CABBIE
CLERK	COMET	COWER	CRUSE	CABLET
CLICK	*COMFY	COWRY	CRUSH	CABMAN
CLIFF	COMIC	COYLY	CRUST	CACHET
CLIFT	COMMA	COYPU	CRWTH	CACHOU
CLIMB	COMMY	*COZEN	CRYPT	CACKLE
CLIME	COMPO	*COZEY	CUBBY	CACTUS
CLINE	COMPT	*COZIE	CUBEB	CADDIE
CLING	COMTE	CRAAL	CUBER	CADDIS
CLINK	CONCH	CRACK	CUBIC	CADENT
CLIPT	CONEY	CRAFT	CUBIT	CADGER
CLOAK	CONGA	CRAKE	CUDDY	CAECUM
CLOCK	CONGE	CRAMP	CUING	CAEOMA
CLOMB	CONGO	CRANE	CUISH	CAFTAN
CLOMP	CONGO	CRANK	CULCH	CAGIER
CLONE	CONIC	CRAPE	CULET	CAGILY
CLONK	CONIN	CRASH	CULEX	CAGING
	CONKY	CRASS	CULLY	CAHIER
		CRATE	CULPA	CAHOOT

CAIMAN	CANVAS	CASKET	CEREUS	CHIASM
*CAIQUE	CANYON	*CASQUE	CERING	CHIAUS
*CAJOLE	CAPFUL	CASSIA	CERIPH	*CHICHI
CALAMI	CAPIAS	CASSIS	CERISE	CHICLE
CALASH	CAPITA	CASTER	CERITE	*CHICLY
CALCAR	CAPLIN	CASTLE	CERIUM	CHIDER
CALCES	CAPOTE	CASTOR	CERMET	CHIELD
CALCIC	CAPPED	CASUAL	CEROUS	CHIGOE
CALESA	CAPPER	CATALO	CERTES	CHILDE
CALICO	CAPRIC	*CATCHY	CERUSE	CHILLI
CALIPH	CAPSID	CATENA	*CERVIX	CHILLY
CALKER	CAPTAN	CATGUT	CESIUM	CHIMAR
CALKIN	CAPTOR	CATION	CESTOS	CHIMER
CALLAN	CARACK	CATKIN	CESTUS	CHIMLA
CALLER	CARAFE	CATLIN	CESURA	*CHINCH
CALLET	CARATE	CATNAP	CETANE	*CHINKY
CALLOW	CARBON	CATNIP	*CHABUK	CHINTS
CALLUS	CARBOY	CATSUP	*CHACMA	*CHINTZ
CALORY	CARCEL	CATTED	CHAETA	*CHIPPY
CALPAC	CARDER	CATTIE	CHAFER	*CHIRPY
*CALQUE	CARDIA	CATTLE	*CHAFFY	CHIRRE
CALVES	CAREEN	CAUCUS	CHAINE	CHISEL
CAMAIL	CAREER	CAUDAD	CHAISE	CHITAL
CAMASS	CARESS	CAUDAL	CHALAH	CHITIN
CAMBER	CARFUL	*CAUDEX	CHALEH	CHITON
CAMBIA	CARHOP	CAUDLE	CHALET	CHITTY
CAMERA	CARIBE	CAUGHT	*CHALKY	*CHIVVY
CAMION	CARIES	CAULES	CHALLY	CHOICE
CAMISA	CARINA	CAULIS	CHALOT	*CHOKER
CAMISE	CARING	CAUSAL	*CHAMMY	*CHOKEY
CAMLET	CARLIN	CAUSER	*CHAMPY	CHOLER
CAMPER	CARMAN	CAUSEY	CHANCE	CHOLLA
CAMPUS	CARNAL	CAVEAT	*CHANCY	CHOOSE
CANAPE	CARNEY	CAVERN	CHANGE	CHOOSY
CANARD	CARNIE	CAVIAR	CHANTY	CHOPIN
CANARY	CAROCH	CAVIES	CHAPEL	*CHOPPY
CANCAN	CAROLI	CAVING	CHARAS	CHORAL
CANCEL	CARPAL	CAVITY	CHARGE	CHOREA
CANCER	CARPEL	CAVORT	CHARRO	CHORIC
CANCHA	CARPER	CAYMAN	CHARRY	CHORUS
CANDID	CARPET	CAYUSE	CHASER	CHOSEN
CANDLE	CARPUS	CEBOID	CHASSE	*CHOUGH
CANDOR	CARREL	CEDING	CHASTE	CHOUSE
CANFUL	CARROM	CEDULA	CHATTY	CHOUSH
CANGUE	CARROT	CEILER	CHAUNT	CHOWSE
CANINE	CARTEL	CELERY	CHAWER	CHRISM
CANING	CARTER	CELIAC	*CHAZAN	CHROMA
CANKER	CARTON	CELLAR	*CHEBEC	CHROME
CANNED	CARTOP	CEMENT	CHEDER	CHROMO
CANNEL	CARVEL	CENOTE	*CHEEKY	*CHUBBY
CANNER	CARVEN	CENSER	CHEERY	*CHUCKY
CANNIE	CARVER	CENSOR	CHEESE	*CHUFFY
CANNON	CASABA	CENSUS	CHEESY	*CHUKAR
CANNOT	CASAVA	CENTAL	CHEGOE	*CHUKKA
CANOPY	CASEFY	CENTER	*CHEMIC	*CHUMMY
CANTER	CASEIN	CENTRA	*CHEQUE	*CHUNKY
CANTIC	CASERN	CENTRE	CHERRY	*CHURCH
CANTLE	CASHAW	CENTUM	CHERTY	*CHYMIC
CANTON	CASHEW	CERATE	CHERUB	CICADA
CANTOR	CASHOO	CERCIS	CHESTY	CICALA
CANTUS	CASING	CERCUS	CHETAH	CICELY
CANULA	CASINO	CEREAL	CHEWER	CICERO

CILICE	CLOTTY	COLDLY	COOMBE	COTTON
CILIUM	CLOUDY	COLEUS	COOPER	COTYPE
CINDER	CLOUGH	COLIES	COOTIE	COUGAR
CINEMA	CLOVEN	COLLAR	COPALM	COULEE
CINEOL	CLOVER	COLLET	*COPECK	COUNTY
*CINQUE	*CLUBBY	COLLIE	COPIED	COUPLE
CIPHER	*CLUMPY	COLLOP	COPIER	COUPON
CIRCLE	CLUMSY	COLONI	COPIES	COURSE
CIRCUS	CLUTCH	COLONY	COPING	COUSIN
*CIRQUE	COALER	COLOUR	COPLOT	COUTER
CIRRUS	COARSE	COLTER	COPPED	COVERT
CITHER	COATEE	COLUGO	COPPER	COVING
CITIED	COATER	COLUMN	COPPRA	COWAGE
CITIES	*COAXAL	COLURE	COPRAH	COWARD
CITIFY	*COAXER	COMATE	COPTER	*COWBOY
CITING	COBALT	COMBAT	COPULA	COWIER
CITOLA	COBBER	COMBER	*COQUET	COWMAN
CITOLE	COBBLE	COMEDO	CORBAN	COWPAT
CITRAL	COBNUT	COMEDY	CORBEL	COWPEA
CITRIC	*COBWEB	COMELY	CORBIE	*COWPOX
CITRIN	COCAIN	COMETH	CORDER	COWRIE
CITRON	COCCAL	COMFIT	CORDON	COYISH
CITRUS	COCCIC	COMING	CORING	COYOTE
CIVICS	COCCID	COMITY	CORIUM	COYPOU
CIVISM	COCCUS	COMMIE	CORKER	*COZIER
*CLAMMY	*COCCYX	COMMIT	CORMEL	*COZIES
CLAMOR	COCHIN	*COMMIX	CORNEA	*COZZES
*CLAQUE	COCKER	COMMON	CORNEL	*CRABBY
CLARET	COCKLE	COMOSE	CORNER	*CRACKY
CLASSY	*COCKUP	COMOUS	CORNET	CRADLE
CLAUSE	COCOON	COMPEL	CORNUS	CRAFTY
CLAVER	CODDER	*COMPLY	CORODY	CRAGGY
CLAWER	CODDLE	CONCHA	CORONA	CRAMBE
*CLAXON	CODEIA	*CONCHY	CORPSE	CRAMBO
CLAYEY	CODEIN	CONCUR	CORPUS	CRANCH
CLEAVE	CODGER	CONDOM	CORRAL	CRANIA
CLENCH	*CODIFY	CONDOR	CORRIE	*CRANKY
CLEOME	CODING	CONFAB	CORSAC	CRANNY
CLERGY	CODLIN	CONFER	CORSET	*CRAPPY
CLERIC	COELOM	CONGEE	*CORTEX	CRASES
CLERID	COEMPT	CONGER	CORTIN	CRASIS
CLEVER	COERCE	CONGOU	CORVEE	CRATCH
CLEVIS	COEVAL	CONIES	CORVES	CRATER
CLICHE	COFFEE	CONINE	CORVET	CRATON
CLIENT	COFFER	CONING	*CORYMB	CRAVAT
*CLIFFY	COFFIN	CONIUM	*CORYZA	CRAVEN
*CLIMAX	COFFLE	CONKER	COSHER	CRAVER
CLINAL	COGENT	CONNED	COSIER	CRAWLY
CLINCH	COGGED	CONNER	COSIES	CRAYON
CLINGY	COGITO	CONOID	COSIGN	*CREAKY
CLINIC	COGNAC	CONSOL	COSILY	CREAMY
*CLIQUE	*COGWAY	CONSUL	COSINE	CREASE
*CLIQUY	COHEIR	CONTRA	COSMIC	CREASY
CLOACA	COHERE	*CONVEX	COSMOS	CREATE
CLOCHE	COHORT	CONVEY	COSSET	CRECHE
CLODDY	COHOSH	CONVOY	COSTAR	CREDAL
CLOGGY	COHUNE	COOKER	COSTER	CREDIT
CLONIC	COIFFE	*COOKEY	COSTLY	CREEPY
CLONUS	COIGNE	COOKIE	COTEAU	CREESE
CLOSER	COILER	COOLER	COTING	*CREESH
CLOSET	COINER	COOLIE	COTTAR	CRENEL
CLOTHE	COITUS	COOLLY	COTTER	CREOLE

CREPEY	CUPOLA	CYPRES	CALTRAP	CAPPING
CRESOL	CUPPED	CYPRUS	CALTROP	CAPRICE
CRESYL	CUPPER	CYSTIC	CALUMET	CAPRINE
CRETIC	CUPRIC	CABARET	CALUMNY	*CAPSIZE
CRETIN	CUPRUM	CABBAGE	*CALVARY	CAPSTAN
CREWEL	CUPULA	CABBALA	CALYCES	CAPSULE
*CRIMPY	CUPULE	*CABEZON	CALYCLE	CAPTAIN
CRINGE	CURACY	CABILDO	CALYPSO	CAPTION
CRINUM	CURAGH	CABINET	CAMBIAL	CAPTIVE
CRISIS	CURARA	CABOOSE	*CAMBISM	CAPTURE
CRISPY	CURARE	*CACHEXY	CAMBIST	*CAPUCHE
CRISTA	CURARI	*CACHING	*CAMBIUM	CARABAO
CRITIC	CURATE	*CACIQUE	*CAMBRIC	CARABID
*CROAKY	CURBER	*CACKLER	CAMELIA	CARABIN
CROCUS	CURDLE	*CACODYL	CAMISIA	CARACAL
*CROJIK	CURFEW	CADAVER	CAMORRA	CARACOL
CROSSE	CURING	CADDICE	*CAMPHOL	CARACUL
CROTCH	CURITE	CADDISH	*CAMPHOR	CARAMEL
CROTON	CURIUM	CADELLE	CAMPIER	*CARAPAX
CROUCH	CURLER	CADENCE	*CAMPILY	CARAVAN
CROUPE	CURLEW	*CADENCY	CAMPING	CARAVEL
CROUPY	CURRAN	*CADENZA	CAMPION	*CARAWAY
CROUSE	CURRIE	CADMIUM	CAMPONG	CARBARN
*CROWDY	CURSED	CAESIUM	CANAKIN	CARBIDE
CROWER	CURSER	CAESTUS	CANASTA	CARBINE
CRUCES	CURTAL	CAESURA	CANDELA	CARBORA
CRUDDY	CURTLY	*CAFFEIN	CANDENT	CARCASE
CRUISE	CURTSY	CAGIEST	CANDIDA	CARCASS
*CRUMBY	CURULE	CAISSON	CANDIED	CARDIAC
*CRUMMY	CURVEY	*CAITIFF	CANDIES	CARDING
CRUNCH	CUSCUS	*CAJAPUT	CANDLER	CARDOON
CRURAL	CUSHAT	*CAJOLER	CANDOUR	CAREFUL
CRUSET	CUSHAW	*CAJUPUT	CANELLA	CARFARE
CRUSTY	CUSPID	CALAMAR	CANIKIN	CARIBOU
CRUTCH	CUSPIS	CALAMUS	CANNERY	CARICES
CRYPTO	CUSSER	CALANDO	CANNIER	CARIOCA
CUBAGE	CUSTOM	*CALCIFY	CANNILY	CARIOLE
CUBING	CUSTOS	CALCINE	CANNING	CARIOUS
CUBISM	CUTEST	CALCITE	CANNULA	CARLESS
CUBIST	CUTESY	CALCIUM	CANONRY	CARLINE
CUBOID	CUTLAS	CALDERA	CANSFUL	CARLING
CUCKOO	CUTLER	CALDRON	CANTALA	CARLISH
CUDDIE	CUTLET	CALECHE	CANTATA	CARLOAD
CUDDLE	CUTOFF	CALENDS	CANTDOG	CARMINE
CUDDLY	CUTOUT	CALIBER	CANTEEN	CARNAGE
CUDGEL	CUTTER	CALIBRE	CANTHUS	CARNIES
CUESTA	CUTTLE	CALICES	CANTINA	*CARNIFY
CUISSE	CYANIC	CALICHE	CANTRAP	CAROACH
CULLAY	CYANID	CALICLE	CANTRIP	CAROCHE
CULLER	CYANIN	CALIPEE	CANVASS	CAROLER
CULLET	CYBORG	CALIPER	*CANZONA	CAROLUS
CULLIS	CYCLER	CALLANT	*CANZONE	CAROTID
CULTCH	*CYCLIC	CALLBOY	CAPABLE	CAROTIN
CULTUS	CYESIS	CALLING	CAPELAN	CAROUSE
CULVER	CYGNET	CALLOSE	CAPELET	CARPALE
CUMBER	*CYMBAL	CALLOUS	CAPELIN	CARPING
CUMMER	CYMENE	CALOMEL	CAPERER	CARPORT
CUMMIN	CYMLIN	CALORIC	CAPERER	*CARRACK
CUNDUM	CYMOID	CALORIE	CAPITAL	CARRELL
CUNEAL	CYMOSE	CALOTTE	CAPITOL	CARRIED
CUNNER	CYMOUS	CALOYER	CAPLESS	CARRIER
CUPFUL	*CYPHER	*CALPACK	CAPORAL	CARRIES
			*CAPOUCH	

CARRION	*CAVALRY	*CHAMPAC	CHEROOT	CHOUSER
CARROCH	CAVEMAN	*CHAMPAK	*CHERVIL	*CHOWDER
CARROTY	CAVETTO	*CHAMPER	*CHEVIED	CHRISOM
CARRYON	CAVIARE	CHANCEL	*CHEVIES	*CHRISTY
*CARSICK	CAVILER	CHANCRE	*CHEVIOT	*CHROMIC
CARTAGE	CAYENNE	CHANGER	*CHEVRON	*CHROMYL
CARTOON	*CAZIQUE	CHANNEL	*CHEWINK	CHRONIC
CARVING	CEDILLA	CHANSON	CHIASMA	CHRONON
CASCADE	CEILING	CHANTER	*CHIBOUK	*CHUCKLE
CASCARA	CELADON	*CHANTEY	CHICANE	*CHUDDAH
CASEASE	CELESTA	CHANTOR	*CHICKEN	CHUDDAR
CASEATE	CELESTE	*CHANTRY	*CHICORY	CHUDDER
CASEOSE	CELLIST	CHAPEAU	*CHIEFLY	CHUGGER
CASEOUS	CELLULE	CHAPLET	*CHIFFON	*CHUKKAR
CASERNE	CEMBALO	*CHAPMAN	CHIGGER	CHUNTER
CASETTE	CENACLE	*CHAPPED	CHIGNON	*CHURCHY
*CASHBOX	CENSUAL	CHAPTER	*CHILDLY	CHURNER
CASHIER	CENSURE	CHARADE	CHILIAD	CHUTIST
CASSABA	CENTARE	CHARGER	CHILLER	CHUTNEE
CASSAVA	CENTAUR	CHARIER	CHILLUM	*CHUTNEY
CASSINO	CENTAVO	*CHARILY	*CHIMBLY	*CHUTZPA
*CASSOCK	CENTILE	CHARING	CHIMERA	*CHYMIST
CASTING	CENTIME	CHARIOT	CHIMERE	*CHYMOUS
*CASTOFF	CENTIMO	CHARISM	*CHIMING	CIBOULE
CASUIST	CENTNER	*CHARITY	*CHIMLEY	*CICHLID
CATALOG	CENTRAL	*CHARKHA	*CHIMNEY	CICOREE
CATALPA	CENTRIC	CHARMER	*CHINCHY	CIGARET
CATARRH	CENTRUM	CHARNEL	CHINNED	CILIARY
CATBIRD	CENTURY	CHARPAI	CHINONE	CILIATE
CATBOAT	CERAMAL	*CHARPOY	*CHINOOK	CINDERY
CATCALL	CERAMIC	*CHARQUI	*CHINTZY	CINEAST
CATCHER	CERATED	CHARRED	*CHIPPED	CINEOLE
*CATCHUP	CERATIN	CHARTER	*CHIPPER	CINERIN
CATECHU	CEROTIC	CHASING	*CHIPPIE	*CIPHONY
CATERAN	CERTAIN	CHASSIS	CHIRPER	CIPOLIN
CATERER	*CERTIFY	CHASTEN	CHIRRUP	CIRCLER
CATFACE	CERUMEN	CHATEAU	CHITLIN	CIRCLET
CATFALL	CERVINE	CHATTEL	CHITTER	CIRCUIT
*CATFISH	CESSION	CHATTER	*CHIVARI	CIRRATE
CATHEAD	CESSPIT	*CHAUFER	*CHLAMYS	CIRROSE
CATHECT	CESTODE	*CHAYOTE	CHLORAL	CIRROUS
CATHODE	CESTOID	*CHAZZEN	CHLORIC	CIRSOID
CATLIKE	*CHABOUK	CHEAPEN	CHLORID	CISSOID
CATLING	*CHAFFER	CHEAPIE	CHLORIN	CISTERN
CATMINT	*CHAFING	*CHEAPLY	*CHOKING	CISTRON
CATSPAW	CHAGRIN	CHEATER	CHOLATE	CITABLE
CATTAIL	*CHALAZA	*CHECKER	CHOLERA	CITADEL
CATTALO	*CHALCID	*CHECKUP	CHOLINE	CITHARA
CATTIER	CHALICE	CHEDDAR	CHOOSER	CITHERN
CATTILY	*CHALLAH	CHEDITE	*CHOOSEY	CITHREN
CATTING	CHALLIE	CHEEPER	CHOPINE	*CITIZEN
CATTISH	CHALLIS	CHEERER	*CHOPPED	CITRATE
*CATWALK	CHALLOT	CHEERIO	*CHOPPER	CITRINE
CAUDATE	CHALONE	*CHEETAH	CHORALE	CITROUS
CAULINE	*CHALOTH	*CHEFDOM	CHORDAL	CITTERN
CAULKER	*CHALUTZ	CHELATE	CHORIAL	*CIVILLY
CAUSING	*CHAMADE	CHELOID	CHORINE	*CLABBER
CAUSTIC	*CHAMBER	CHEMISE	CHORING	CLACHAN
CAUTERY	*CHAMFER	*CHEMISM	CHORION	*CLACKER
CAUTION	CHAMISE	CHEMIST	*CHORIZO	CLADODE
CAVALLA	CHAMISO	*CHEQUER	CHOROID	CLAIMER
*CAVALLY	CHAMOIS	*CHERISH	CHORTLE	CLAMANT

CLAMBER	CLYSTER	COINTER	COMPORT	CONTEST
CLAMMED	COACHER	COITION	COMPOSE	*CONTEXT
CLAMOUR	COADMIT	COLDISH	COMPOST	CONTORT
CLAMPER	COAEVAL	COLICIN	COMPOTE	CONTOUR
CLAPPER	COAGENT	*COLICKY	COMPUTE	CONTROL
*CLAQUER	COALBIN	COLITIS	COMRADE	CONTUSE
CLARIES	*COALBOX	COLLAGE	CONATUS	CONVECT
*CLARIFY	*COALIFY	COLLARD	CONCAVE	CONVENE
CLARION	COALPIT	COLLATE	CONCEAL	CONVENT
CLARITY	COAMING	COLLECT	CONCEDE	CONVERT
CLARKIA	*COANNEX	COLLEEN	CONCEIT	CONVICT
CLASHER	COARSEN	COLLEGE	CONCENT	*CONVOKE
CLASPER	COASTAL	COLLIDE	CONCEPT	*COOKERY
CLASSER	COASTER	COLLIED	CONCERN	COOKIES
CLASSES	COATING	COLLIER	CONCERT	COOKING
CLASSIC	*COAXIAL	COLLIES	CONCISE	COOKOUT
CLASSIS	COBBIER	COLLINS	CONCOCT	COOLANT
CLASTIC	COBBLER	COLLOID	CONCORD	COOLIES
CLATTER	COCAINE	COLLUDE	CONCUSS	COOLISH
CLAUCHT	COCCOID	COLOGNE	CONDEMN	COONCAN
CLAUGHT	COCHAIR	COLONEL	CONDIGN	COONTIE
CLAVATE	COCHLEA	COLONIC	CONDOLE	COOPERY
CLAVIER	*COCKADE	COLONUS	CONDONE	COPAIBA
*CLAYISH	*COCKEYE	COLORED	CONDUCE	COPEPOD
CLAYPAN	*COCKIER	COLORER	CONDUCT	COPIHUE
CLEANER	*COCKILY	COLUMEL	CONDUIT	COPILOT
CLEANLY	*COCKISH	*COMAKER	CONDYLE	COPIOUS
CLEANSE	*COCKNEY	COMATIC	CONFECT	*COPPERY
CLEANUP	*COCKPIT	*COMATIK	CONFESS	*COPPICE
CLEARER	*COCKSHY	COMBINE	CONFIDE	COPPING
CLEARLY	COCOMAT	COMBUST	CONFINE	*COPYBOY
CLEAVER	COCONUT	COMEDIC	CONFIRM	*COPYCAT
CLEMENT	COCONUT	COMETIC	*CONFLUX	COPYIST
CLERISY	COCOTTE	COMFIER	CONFORM	*COQUINA
*CLERKLY	CODABLE	COMFORT	CONFUSE	*COQUITO
*CLICKER	CODDLER	*COMFREY	CONFUTE	CORACLE
CLIMATE	CODEINA	COMICAL	CONGEAL	CORANTO
CLIMBER	CODEINE	COMITIA	CONGEST	CORBEIL
CLINGER	*CODFISH	COMMAND	CONGIUS	CORBINA
CLINKER	CODICES	COMMATA	CONICAL	CORDAGE
CLIPPER	CODICIL	COMMEND	CONIFER	CORDATE
*CLIQUEY	CODLING	COMMENT	CONIINE	CORDIAL
CLIVERS	COELIAC	COMMIES	*CONJOIN	CORDOBA
CLOBBER	COELOME	COMMODE	*CONJURE	COREIGN
*CLOCKER	COENACT	*COMMOVE	CONNATE	CORKAGE
CLONISM	COENURE	COMMUNE	CONNECT	CORKIER
CLOSEST	*COEQUAL	COMMUTE	CONNING	CORNCOB
CLOSING	COERCER	*COMPACT	CONNIVE	CORNFED
CLOSURE	COERECT	*COMPANY	CONNOTE	CORNICE
CLOTTED	*COEXERT	COMPARE	*CONQUER	CORNIER
CLOTURE	*COEXIST	COMPART	CONSENT	CORNILY
CLOUTER	*COFFING	COMPASS	CONSIGN	CORNUTE
CLOWDER	*COFFRET	COMPEER	CONSIST	CORNUTO
CLUBBER	*COGENCY	COMPEND	CONSOLE	COROLLA
CLUBMAN	COGGING	COMPERE	CONSORT	CORONAL
CLUMBER	COGNATE	COMPETE	CONSULT	CORONEL
CLUNKER	COGNISE	COMPILE	CONSUME	CORONER
CLUPEID	*COGNIZE	*COMPLEX	CONTACT	CORONET
CLUSTER	COHABIT	COMPLIN	CONTAIN	CORPORA
*CLUTCHY	COHERER	COMPLOT	CONTEMN	CORRADE
CLUTTER	COINAGE	COMPONE	CONTEND	CORRECT
CLYPEUS	COINFER	*COMPONY	CONTENT	CORRECT

CORRIDA	COWIEST	CRIPPLE	CUDDIES	*CUTAWAY
CORRODE	*COWLICK	CRISPEN	CUDWEED	*CUTBACK
CORRODY	COWLING	CRISPER	CUIRASS	CUTDOWN
CORRUPT	*COWPOKE	CRISPLY	CUISINE	CUTICLE
CORRUPT	*COWSHED	CRISSUM	CUITTLE	CUTLASS
CORSAGE	*COWSKIN	CRITTER	CULICID	CUTLERY
CORSAIR	COWSLIP	CRITTUR	CULLIED	CUTLINE
CORSLET	*COXALGY	CROAKER	CULLIES	CUTOVER
CORTEGE	*COXCOMB	CROCEIN	CULLION	CUTTAGE
CORVINA	COYNESS	CROCHET	CULOTTE	CUTTING
CORVINE	*COZENER	CROCINE	CULPRIT	*CUTWORK
COSIEST	CRABBER	*CROCKET	CULTISM	CUTWORM
COSMISM	*CRACKER	CROFTER	CULTIST	CUVETTE
COSMIST	*CRACKLE	CROOKED	CULTURE	CYANATE
*COSSACK	*CRACKLY	CROONER	CULVERT	CYANIDE
COSTARD	*CRACKUP	CROPPED	CUMARIN	CYANINE
COSTATE	CRADLER	CROPPER	*CUMQUAT	CYANITE
COSTIVE	CRAMMED	*CROQUET	*CUMSHAW	CYCASIN
COSTREL	CRAMMER	*CROQUIS	CUMULUS	CYCLASE
COSTUME	CRAMPIT	CROSIER	CUNEATE	*CYCLING
COTERIE	CRAMPON	CROSSER	CUNNING	CYCLIST
COTHURN	CRANIAL	CROUTON	*CUPCAKE	*CYCLIZE
COTIDAL	CRANING	CROWBAR	CUPELER	*CYCLOID
COTTAGE	CRANIUM	CROWDER	*CUPLIKE	CYCLONE
COTTIER	CRANKLE	CROWDIE	CUPPING	*CYCLOPS
COTTONY	*CRANKLY	CROWNER	CUPRITE	*CYMLING
COUCHER	CRANNOG	CROWNET	CUPROUS	CYNICAL
COUGHER	CRAPPER	*CROZIER	CUPSFUL	CYPRESS
COULDST	CRAPPIE	CRUCIAL	CUPULAR	CYPRIAN
COULOIR	CRASHER	CRUCIAN	CURABLE	CYPSELA
COULOMB	CRAUNCH	*CRUCIFY	CURACAO	CYSTEIN
COULTER	CRAVING	CRUDITY	CURACOA	CYSTINE
COUNCIL	CRAWDAD	CRUELTY	CURATOR	CYSTOID
COUNSEL	CRAWLER	CRUISER	CURBING	*CZARDAS
COUNTER	CREAMER	CRULLER	CURCUMA	*CZARDOM
COUNTRY	CREASER	CRUMBER	CURDIER	*CZARINA
COUPLER	CREATIN	CRUMBLE	CURDLER	*CZARISM
COUPLET	CREATOR	*CRUMBLY	CURETTE	*CZARIST
COURAGE	CREDENT	CRUMMIE	CURIOSA	CABALISM
COURANT	CREEPER	CRUMPET	CURIOUS	CABALIST
COURIER	CREEPIE	CRUMPLE	CURLING	CABALLED
COURLAN	CREMATE	*CRUMPLY	CURRACH	*CABBALAH
COURSER	CRENATE	*CRUNCHY	CURRAGH	CABESTRO
COURTLY	CREOSOL	CRUNODE	CURRANT	*CABEZONE
COUTEAU	CRESSET	CRUPPER	CURRENT	*CABLEWAY
COUTHIE	CRESTAL	CRUSADE	CURRIED	*CABOCHED
COUTURE	CREVICE	CRUSADO	CURRIER	*CABOCHON
COUVADE	CREWMAN	CRUSHER	CURRISH	CABOODLE
COVERER	CRIBBER	CRUSILY	CURSING	*CABOSHED
COVETER	*CRICKET	CRUSTAL	CURSIVE	CABOTAGE
COWBANE	CRICOID	*CRUZADO	CURSORY	CABRESTA
COWBELL	CRIMMER	*CRYBABY	CURTAIL	CABRESTO
*COWBIND	CRIMPER	CRYOGEN	CURTAIN	CABRETTA
*COWBIRD	CRIMPLE	*CRYPTIC	CURTATE	CABRILLA
*COWEDLY	CRIMSON	CRYSTAL	CURTESY	CABRIOLE
*COWFISH	CRINGER	CTENOID	CURTSEY	CABSTAND
COWGIRL	CRINGLE	*CUBBISH	CURVING	*CACHALOT
*COWHAGE	CRINITE	CUBICAL	CUSHIER	*CACHEPOT
*COWHAND	CRINKLE	CUBICLE	*CUSHILY	*CACHEXIA
*COWHERB	*CRINKLY	*CUBICLY	CUSHION	*CACHUCHA
*COWHERD	CRINOID	*CUCKOLD	CUSTARD	*CACOMIXL
*COWHIDE	CRIOLLO	CUDBEAR	CUSTODY	CADASTER

CADASTRE	CAMPOREE	CARASSOW	CASTRATO	CENSURER
CADUCEUS	CAMPSITE	*CARBAMIC	CASUALLY	CENTAURY
*CADUCITY	*CAMSHAFT	*CARBAMYL	CASUALTY	CENTESIS
CADUCOUS	CANAILLE	*CARBARYL	*CATACOMB	CENTIARE
*CAFFEINE	CANALISE	CARBINOL	CATALASE	CENTRING
CAGELING	*CANALIZE	*CARBONYL	CATALYST	CENTRISM
CAGINESS	CANALLED	*CARBOXYL	*CATALYZE	CENTRIST
*CAJOLERY	CANALLER	CARBURET	CATAMITE	CENTROID
*CAJOLING	CANCELER	*CARCAJOU	CATAPULT	CENTUPLE
*CAKEWALK	CANCROID	CARCANET	CATARACT	*CEPHALAD
*CALABASH	*CANDIDLY	*CARDAMOM	CATBRIER	*CEPHALIC
CALADIUM	CANEWARE	CARDAMON	*CATCHALL	*CEPHALIN
*CALAMARY	CANFIELD	*CARDAMUM	*CATCHFLY	CERAMIST
CALAMINE	CANINITY	CARDCASE	*CATECHIN	CERASTES
CALAMINT	CANISTER	CARDIGAN	*CATECHOL	CERATOID
CALAMITE	CANITIES	CARDINAL	CATEGORY	CERCARIA
*CALAMITY	CANNABIC	CARDIOID	CATENARY	CEREBRAL
CALATHOS	CANNABIN	CARDITIS	CATENATE	CEREBRUM
CALATHUS	CANNABIS	CAREENER	CATENOID	CEREMENT
CALCANEA	CANNELON	CAREERER	CATERESS	*CEREMONY
CALCANEI	CANNIBAL	CAREFREE	CATHEDRA	CERNUOUS
CALCEATE	CANNIEST	CARELESS	CATHETER	*CEROTYPE
*CALCIFIC	CANNIKIN	CARESSER	*CATHEXIS	CERULEAN
CALCSPAR	CANNONRY	CAREWORN	*CATHOLIC	CERUSITE
*CALCTUFA	CANOEIST	CARILLON	CATHOUSE	CERVELAT
*CALCTUFF	CANONESS	CARINATE	CATNAPER	*CERVICAL
CALCULUS	CANONISE	*CARMAKER	CATTIEST	CESAREAN
CALENDAL	CANONIST	CARNAUBA	CATTLEYA	CESARIAN
CALENDAR	*CANONIZE	CARNIVAL	CAUDATED	CESSPOOL
CALENDER	CANOROUS	CAROLLED	CAUDILLO	CETACEAN
*CALFSKIN	CANTICLE	CAROTENE	CAULDRON	CETOLOGY
CALIFATE	CANTONAL	CAROUSAL	CAULICLE	*CHACONNE
*CALIPASH	CANTRAIP	CAROUSEL	*CAULKING	*CHADARIM
CALISAYA	CANULATE	CAROUSER	CAUSABLE	*CHAINMAN
*CALLBACK	CANVASER	CARRIAGE	CAUSALLY	*CHAIRMAN
CALLIOPE	*CANZONET	CARRIOLE	CAUSERIE	CHALDRON
CALLIPEE	*CAPACITY	*CARRITCH	*CAUSEWAY	CHALLIES
CALLIPER	*CAPESKIN	CARROTIN	CAUTIOUS	*CHALLOTH
CALMNESS	*CAPEWORK	CARRYALL	CAVALERO	*CHAMBRAY
*CALTHROP	CAPITATE	CARRYOUT	CAVALIER	*CHAMFRON
CALUTRON	CAPITULA	CARTLOAD	CAVATINA	*CHAMPION
CALVADOS	*CAPMAKER	*CARTOUCH	CAVEATOR	CHANCERY
CALVARIA	CAPONIER	CARUNCLE	*CAVEFISH	*CHANCIER
*CALYCATE	*CAPONIZE	CARYATID	*CAVELIKE	*CHANCILY
*CALYCEAL	*CAPRICCI	CARYOTIN	*CAVICORN	*CHANCING
*CALYCINE	*CAPRIFIG	CASCABEL	*CAVITARY	CHANDLER
*CALYCULI	CAPRIOLE	CASCABLE	CAVITATE	*CHANFRON
*CALYPTER	CAPSICIN	*CASEBOOK	CAVORTER	CHANTAGE
*CALYPTRA	*CAPSICUM	CASEMATE	CEINTURE	CHANTIES
*CAMBOGIA	CAPSTONE	CASEMENT	CELERIAC	*CHAPBOOK
CAMELEER	CAPSULAR	*CASEWORK	CELERITY	*CHAPERON
CAMELLIA	CAPTIOUS	*CASEWORM	*CELIBACY	*CHAPITER
CAMISADE	CAPTURER	*CASHBOOK	CELIBATE	*CHAPLAIN
CAMISADO	*CAPUCHIN	CASHLESS	CELLARER	*CHAPPING
CAMISOLE	*CAPYBARA	*CASHMERE	CELLARET	*CHAQUETA
CAMOMILE	CARABINE	CASIMERE	CELLULAR	*CHARACID
*CAMPAGNA	CARACARA	CASIMIRE	CEMENTER	*CHARACIN
*CAMPAIGN	CARACOLE	CASSETTE	CEMENTUM	*CHARCOAL
*CAMPFIRE	CARAGANA	CASTANET	*CEMETERY	CHARIEST
*CAMPHENE	CARAGEEN	*CASTAWAY	CENOBITE	*CHARISMA
*CAMPHINE	CARANGID	CASTEISM	*CENOTAPH	*CHARLADY
CAMPIEST	CARAPACE	CASTRATE	CENSURER	*CHARLOCK

*CHARMING	CHLORIDE	CITATION	*CLUBHAUL	COERCION
CHARRIER	CHLORINE	CITEABLE	CLUBROOT	*COERCIVE
CHARRING	CHLORITE	CITREOUS	*CLUMPISH	*COEVALLY
CHARTIST	CHLOROUS	*CITYFIED	CLUPEOID	*COEXTEND
CHASSEUR	*CHOIRBOY	*CITYWARD	CLUSTERY	*COFACTOR
CHASTISE	*CHOLERIC	*CIVICISM	*COACHMAN	COGITATE
*CHASTITY	CHOOSING	CIVILIAN	COACTION	*COGNIZER
*CHASUBLE	*CHOPPING	CIVILISE	*COACTIVE	COGNOMEN
CHATTING	CHORAGUS	*CIVILITY	COADMIRE	COGNOVIT
*CHAUFFER	*CHORALLY	*CIVILIZE	*COAGENCY	*COGWHEEL
CHAUNTER	CHORDATE	CLADDING	COAGULUM	COHERENT
CHAUSSES	CHOREGUS	CLAIMANT	COALESCE	COHERING
*CHEAPISH	*CHOREMAN	*CLAMBAKE	*COALFISH	COHESION
*CHECHAKO	CHOREOID	*CLAMMING	COALHOLE	*COHOBATE
*CHECKOFF	*CHORIAMB	CLAMORER	COALLESS	*COIFFEUR
*CHECKOUT	CHORIOID	*CLAMWORM	*COALSACK	*COIFFURE
*CHECKROW	CHORTLER	CLANGOUR	COALSHED	COINCIDE
*CHEDDITE	CHOUSING	CLANNISH	COALYARD	COINHERE
*CHEEKFUL	*CHOWCHOW	CLANSMAN	COAPPEAR	COINMATE
*CHEERFUL	*CHOWTIME	CLAPTRAP	COASSIST	COINSURE
CHEERIER	CHRESARD	CLARENCE	COASSUME	COISTREL
*CHEERILY	*CHRISMON	CLARINET	COASTING	COISTRIL
CHELATOR	CHRISTEN	CLASSIER	COATLESS	COLANDER
*CHEMICAL	CHRISTIE	*CLASSIFY	*COATRACK	COLDNESS
CHEMURGY	*CHROMATE	CLATTERY	COATROOM	COLESEED
CHENILLE	*CHROMIDE	*CLAVICLE	COATTAIL	COLESLAW
*CHENOPOD	*CHROMING	CLAWLESS	COATTEND	COLESSEE
*CHESSMAN	*CHROMITE	*CLAYBANK	COATTEST	COLESSOR
CHESTFUL	*CHROMIUM	*CLAYLIKE	COAUTHOR	COLEWORT
CHESTNUT	*CHROMIZE	*CLAYMORE	COBBIEST	COLICINE
*CHEVALET	*CHROMOUS	*CLAYWARE	*COBWEBBY	*COLIFORM
*CHEVERON	*CHRONAXY	CLEANSER	*COCCIDIA	COLINEAR
*CHIASMUS	*CHTHONIC	CLEARING	COCINERA	COLINIES
*CHICANER	*CHUBASCO	CLEAVAGE	*COCKATOO	COLISEUM
*CHICCORY	*CHUCKIES	CLEMATIS	*COCKBILL	COLISTIN
*CHICKPEA	*CHUCKLER	*CLEMENCY	*COCKBOAT	COLLAGEN
*CHICNESS	*CHUMSHIP	CLERICAL	*COCKCROW	COLLAPSE
*CHIEFDOM	*CHURCHLY	*CLERIHEW	*COCKEREL	COLLARET
CHIGETAI	CHURNING	*CLERKDOM	*COCKIEST	COLLATOR
*CHILDBED	*CHUTZPAH	*CLERKISH	*COCKLIKE	COLLEGER
*CHILDING	*CHYMOSIN	CLEVEITE	*COCKLOFT	COLLEGIA
*CHILDISH	CIBORIUM	CLINALLY	*COCKSHUT	COLLIERY
CHILDREN	*CICATRIX	*CLINCHER	*COCKSPUR	COLLOGUE
*CHILIASM	CICERONE	*CLIPPING	*COCKSURE	*COLLOQUY
CHILIAST	CICISBEO	*CLIQUISH	*COCKTAIL	COLLUDER
*CHILOPOD	CILANTRO	CLITELLA	COCOBOLA	COLLUVIA
*CHIMAERA	CILIATED	CLITORIS	COCOBOLO	COLLYRIA
*CHIMBLEY	*CINCHONA	CLODPATE	COCREATE	COLOCATE
*CHIMERIC	CINCTURE	CLODPOLE	CODEBTOR	COLONIAL
*CHINBONE	CINEASTE	CLODPOLL	CODELESS	COLONISE
CHINLESS	CINERARY	CLOISTER	CODERIVE	COLONIST
CHINNING	CINGULUM	CLOSEOUT	CODIFIER	*COLONIZE
*CHIPMUCK	CINNABAR	CLOTHIER	*CODPIECE	*COLOPHON
*CHIPMUNK	CINNAMON	CLOTHING	COEDITOR	COLORADO
*CHIPPING	*CINNAMYL	CLOTTING	*COEFFECT	COLORANT
CHISELER	CIRCLING	CLOUDLET	*COEMBODY	COLORFUL
*CHITCHAT	*CIRCUITY	*CLOWNERY	*COEMPLOY	COLORING
CHITLING	CIRCULAR	*CLOWNISH	COENAMOR	COLORISM
*CHIVALRY	CIRRIPED	CLUBABLE	COENDURE	COLORIST
*CHIVAREE	CISLUNAR	*CLUBBING	COENURUS	COLOSSAL
CHLORATE	CISTERNA	*CLUBFOOT	*COENZYME	COLOSSUS
CHLORDAN		*CLUBHAND	*COEQUATE	*COLOTOMY

COLOURER	CONFLATE	*COPPERAH	*COUCHANT	CREDIBLE
COLPITIS	*CONFLICT	COPPERAS	*COUCHING	CREDITOR
COLUBRID	*CONFOCAL	COPREMIA	COULDEST	CREEPAGE
*COLUMBIC	CONFOUND	COPULATE	COULISSE	CREMAINS
COMATOSE	CONFRERE	*COPYBOOK	COUMARIN	CREMATOR
COMATULA	CONFRONT	*COPYDESK	COUMAROU	CRENATED
COMBATER	CONFUTER	*COPYHOLD	COUNTESS	CRENELLE
COMBINER	CONGENER	*COQUETRY	COUNTIAN	CREODONT
*COMBINGS	CONGLOBE	*COQUETTE	COUPLING	CREOSOTE
*COMBLIKE	CONGRESS	*COQUILLE	COURANTE	CRESCENT
*COMEBACK	*CONICITY	CORACOID	COURANTO	*CRESCIVE
COMEDIAN	CONIDIUM	CORDLESS	COURSING	CRESTING
COMEDIES	*CONJUGAL	*CORDLIKE	COURTESY	*CRESYLIC
*COMEDOWN	*CONJUNCT	CORDOVAN	COURTIER	CRETONNE
*COMETHER	*CONJURER	CORDUROY	COUSCOUS	CREVALLE
*COMFIEST	*CONJUROR	CORDWAIN	COUSINRY	CREVASSE
*COMMANDO	CONNIVER	*CORDWOOD	COVALENT	CREWLESS
*COMMENCE	CONODONT	COREDEEM	COVENANT	*CRIBBAGE
*COMMERCE	*CONQUEST	CORELATE	COVERAGE	*CRIBBING
COMMONER	*CONQUIAN	CORELESS	COVERALL	*CRIBBLED
*COMMONLY	CONSERVE	COREMIUM	COVERING	CRIBROUS
COMMUNAL	CONSIDER	CORKIEST	COVERLET	*CRIBWORK
COMMUTER	CONSOLER	*CORKLIKE	COVERLID	CRICETID
*COMPADRE	CONSOMME	*CORKWOOD	*COVERTLY	CRIMINAL
COMPARER	CONSPIRE	CORNBALL	COVETOUS	CRIPPLER
COMPILER	CONSTANT	*CORNCAKE	*COWARDLY	CRISPATE
COMPLAIN	CONSTRUE	CORNCRIB	*COWBERRY	CRISTATE
COMPLEAT	CONSUMER	CORNEOUS	COWINNER	CRITERIA
*COMPLECT	CONTAGIA	*CORNETCY	*COWORKER	*CRITIQUE
COMPLETE	CONTEMPT	*CORNHUSK	*COXALGIA	CROCEINE
*COMPLICE	CONTINUA	*CORNICHE	*COXSWAIN	*CROCKERY
*COMPLIED	CONTINUE	CORNICLE	*COZENAGE	CROCOITE
COMPLIER	CONTINUO	CORNIEST	*COZINESS	*CROMLECH
COMPLIES	CONTRACT	CORNMEAL	*CRABWISE	*CRONYISM
COMPLINE	CONTRAIL	CORNUTED	*CRACKING	CROPLAND
COMPOSER	CONTRARY	*CORONACH	*CRACKNEL	CROPLESS
*COMPOUND	CONTRAST	CORONARY	*CRACKPOT	*CROPPING
COMPRESS	CONTRITE	COROTATE	CRAGSMAN	CROSSARM
COMPRISE	CONTRIVE	CORPORAL	*CRAMMING	CROSSBAR
*COMPRIZE	CONVENER	CORPSMAN	*CRAMOISY	*CROSSBOW
COMPUTER	CONVERGE	CORRIDOR	CRAMPOON	CROSSCUT
CONATION	CONVERSE	CORRIVAL	CRANIATE	CROSSING
CONCEDER	*CONVEXLY	CORSELET	CRANKIER	CROSSLET
*CONCEIVE	CONVEYER	CORTISOL	*CRANKILY	CROSSTIE
CONCERTO	*CONVEYOR	CORUNDUM	CRANKOUS	*CROSSWAY
*CONCHOID	*CONVINCE	CORVETTE	*CRANKPIN	*CROTCHET
*CONCLAVE	*CONVOKER	*CORYPHEE	CRANNIED	CROUPIER
CONCLUDE	*CONVOLVE	COSECANT	CRANNIES	CROUPOUS
CONCRETE	CONVULSE	COSIGNER	CRANNOGE	*CROWFOOT
CONDENSE	COOINGLY	COSINESS	*CRAPPING	*CROWSTEP
CONDOLER	*COOKBOOK	COSMETIC	*CRAVENLY	CRUCIATE
CONDONER	COOKLESS	COSMICAL	*CRAWFISH	CRUCIBLE
CONDUCER	*COOKSHOP	COSTLESS	*CRAWLWAY	*CRUCIFER
CONELRAD	*COOKWARE	*COSTMARY	*CRAYFISH	*CRUCIFIX
CONENOSE	COOLNESS	COSTUMER	*CREAMERY	CRUMBIER
CONEPATE	COONSKIN	*COSTUMEY	CREATINE	*CRUNCHER
CONEPATL	COOPTION	COTENANT	CREATION	CRUSADER
CONFEREE	COPARENT	COTHURNI	CREATIVE	CRUSTOSE
*CONFERVA	COPASTOR	COTILLON	CREATURE	*CRUZEIRO
CONFETTO	COPATRON	*COTQUEAN	CREDENCE	*CRYOGENY
CONFIDER	COPEMATE	COTTAGER	CREDENDA	CRYOLITE
CONFINER	COPLANAR	COTYLOID	*CREDENZA	*CRYONICS

CRYOSTAT	CUTWATER	S C HMO	CO C AIN	FU C OID
CRYOTRON	*CYANAMID	S C HUL	CO C CAL	FU C OSE
CTENIDIA	CYANOGEN	S C HWA	CO C CIC	FU C OUS
CUBATURE	CYANOSIS	S C ION	CO C CID	*HA C KEE
*CUBICITY	*CYCLAMEN	S C OFF	CO C CUS	*HA C KER
CUBICULA	*CYCLECAR	S C OLD	*CO C CYX	*HA C KIE
*CUBIFORM	*CYCLICAL	S C ONE	CO C HIN	*HA C KLE
*CUCUMBER	*CYCLITOL	S C OOP	CO C KER	*HA C KLY
CUCURBIT	CYLINDER	S C OOT	CO C KLE	*HE C KLE
CUDGELER	*CYMATIUM	S C OPE	*CO C KUP	HE C TIC
*CUFFLESS	*CYMBALER	S C ORE	COSIGN	HE C TOR
CULICINE	*CYMBLING	S C ORN	CU C KOO	*HI C CUP
CULINARY	*CYMOGENE	S C OUR	CY C LER	*HI C KEY
CULPABLE	*CYNICISM	S C OUT	*CY C LIC	*HO C KER
CULTIGEN	CYNOSURE	S C OWL	DA C KER	*HO C KEY
CULTIVAR	*CYPRINID	S C RAG	DA C OIT	*HU C KLE
CULTRATE	CYSTEINE	S C RAM	DA C TYL	*JA C ANA
CULTURAL	CYSTITIS	S C RAP	DE C ADE	*JA C KAL
CULVERIN	CYTASTER	S C REE	DE C AMP	*JA C KER
CUMBERER	CYTIDINE	S C REW	DE C ANE	*JA C KET
CUMBROUS	*CYTOGENY	S C RIM	DE C ANT	*JO C KEY
CUMULATE	*CYTOLOGY	S C RIP	DE C ARE	*JO C OSE
CUNEATED	CYTOSINE	S C ROD	DE C EIT	*JO C UND
CUNEATIC	*CZAREVNA	S C RUB	DE C ENT	*KE C KLE
*CUNIFORM	*CZARITZA	S C RUM	DE C ERN	*KI C KER
*CUPBOARD		S C UBA	DE C IDE	*KI C KUP
CUPELLER		S C UDO	DE C ILE	*KU C HEN
*CUPIDITY	S C AB	S C UFF	DE C KEL	LA C HES
CUPREOUS	S C AD	S C ULK	DE C KER	LA C IER
CUPULATE	S C AG	S C ULL	DE C KLE	LA C ILY
CURARINE	S C AM	S C ULP	DE C OCT	LA C ING
*CURARIZE	S C AN	S C URF	DE C ODE	LA C KER
CURASSOW	S C AR	S C UTA	DE C REE	*LA C KEY
CURATIVE	S C AT	S C UTE	DE C URY	LA C TAM
CURCULIO	S C OP	BA C KER	DI C AST	LA C TIC
CURDIEST	S C OT	*BA C KUP	DI C IER	LA C UNA
CURELESS	S C OW	BE C ALM	DI C ING	LA C UNE
CURLICUE	S C UD	BE C AME	DI C KER	LE C HER
*CURLYCUE	S C UM	BE C KET	*DI C KEY	LE C TOR
*CURRENCY	S C UP	BE C KON	DI C KIE	LI C HEE
CURRICLE	S C UT	BE C LOG	DI C TUM	LI C HEN
CURRIERY	S C ALD	BE C OME	DO C ENT	LI C KER
CURRYING	S C ALE	BI C ARB	DO C ILE	LI C TOR
*CURTALAX	S C ALL	BI C EPS	DO C KER	LO C ALE
CURTNESS	S C ALP	BI C KER	DO C KET	LO C ATE
CUSHIEST	S C ALY	BI C RON	DO C TOR	LO C HIA
*CUSHIONY	S C AMP	BO C CIA	DU C KER	LO C KER
CUSPIDAL	S C ANT	BO C CIE	DU C KIE	LO C KET
CUSPIDOR	S C APE	BU C CAL	FA C ADE	LO C KUP
CUSSEDLY	S C ARE	BU C KER	FA C ETE	LO C ULE
CUSSWORD	S C ARP	BU C KET	FA C EUP	LO C UST
CUSTODES	S C ART	BU C KLE	FA C IAL	LU C ENT
CUSTOMER	S C ARY	BU C KRA	FA C IES	LU C ERN
CUSTUMAL	S C ATT	CA C HET	FA C ILE	LU C KIE
*CUTCHERY	S C AUP	CA C HOU	FA C ING	LY C EUM
CUTENESS	S C AUR	CA C KLE	FA C TOR	LY C HEE
CUTGRASS	S C ENA	CA C TUS	FA C ULA	*MI C KEY
CUTICULA	S C END	CI C ADA	FE C IAL	*MO C KUP
CUTINISE	S C ENE	CI C ALA	*FE C KLY	NE C TAR
*CUTINIZE	S C ENT	CI C ELY	FE C ULA	NI C ETY
CUTPURSE	S C HAV	CI C ERO	FE C UND	NI C KEL
CUTTABLE			*FI C KLE	NI C KER

NI C KLE	RE C USE	VA C ANT	*CO C KNEY	DU C TULE
NO C ENT	RI C HEN	VA C ATE	*CO C KPIT	FA C IEND
NU C HAL	RI C HES	VA C UUM	*CO C KSHY	FA C TION
NU C LEI	RI C HLY	VE C TOR	CO C OMAT	*FA C TORY
*PA C IFY	RI C ING	VI C ING	CO C ONUT	FA C TUAL
PA C ING	*RI C KEY	VI C TIM	CO C ONUT	FA C TURE
PA C KER	RI C RAC	VI C TOR	CO C OTTE	*FA C ULTY
PA C KET	RO C HET	VI C UNA	CONSIGN	FI C TILE
*PA C KLY	RO C KER	*WI C KED	*CU C KOLD	FI C TION
PE C HAN	RO C KET	*WI C KER	CYCASIN	*FI C TIVE
PE C KER	RO C OCO	*WI C KET	*CY C LASE	*FO C ALLY
PE C TEN	RU C KUS	*WI C OPY	*CY C LING	FO C USER
PE C TIN	SA C BUT	*ZE C HIN	CY C LIST	*FU C HSIA
PI C ARA	SA C HEM	BA C CARA	*CY C LIZE	*FU C HSIN
PI C ARO	SA C HET	BA C CATE	CY C LOID	*HA C HURE
*PI C KAX	SA C KER	*BA C CHIC	CY C LONE	*HA C KBUT
PI C KER	*SA C QUE	*BA C KHOE	*CY C LOPS	*HA C KLER
PI C KET	SA C RAL	*BA C KING	DA C OITY	*HA C KMAN
PI C KLE	SA C RED	*BA C KLIT	DE C ANAL	*HA C KNEY
*PI C KUP	SA C RUM	*BA C KLOG	DE C APOD	*HA C KSAW
PI C NIC	SA C ULE	*BA C KOUT	DE C AYER	*HE C KLER
PI C RIC	SE C ANT	*BA C KSAW	DE C EASE	HE C TARE
PO C KET	SE C EDE	*BA C KSET	DE C EIVE	*HI C KORY
PU C KER	SE C ERN	BE C AUSE	*DE C ENCY	*JA C AMAR
RA C EME	SE C OND	*BE C HALK	DE C IARE	*JA C INTH
RA C HET	SE C PAR	*BE C HARM	DE C IBEL	*JA C KASS
RA C HIS	SE C RET	BE C LASP	DE C IDER	*JA C KDAW
RA C IAL	SE C TOR	*BE C LOAK	DE C IDUA	*JA C KIES
RA C IER	SE C UND	BE C LOUD	DE C IMAL	*JA C KLEG
RA C ILY	SE C URE	BE C LOWN	*DE C KING	*JA C KPOT
RA C ING	SI C CAN	BE C RAWL	DE C LAIM	*JA C OBIN
RA C ISM	SI C KEN	BE C RIME	DE C LARE	*JA C OBUS
RA C IST	SI C KLE	*BE C ROWD	DE C LASS	*JA C ONET
RA C KER	SO C AGE	BE C RUST	DE C LINE	*JO C ULAR
RA C KET	SO C CER	BE C URSE	DE C ODER	*KA C HINA
RA C KLE	SO C IAL	BI C OLOR	DE C OLOR	*KI C KOFF
RA C OON	SO C KET	BI C ORNE	DE C ORUM	LA C IER
RE C ALL	SO C MAN	*BI C YCLE	DE C OYER	LA C ONIC
RE C ANE	SU C CAH	*BU C KEEN	DE C REER	*LA C QUER
RE C ANT	SU C COR	*BU C KEYE	DE C RIAL	*LA C QUEY
RE C AST	SU C KER	*BU C KISH	DE C RIED	LA C TARY
RE C EDE	SU C KLE	*BU C KLER	DE C RIER	LA C TASE
RE C ENT	TA C KER	*BU C KRAM	DE C ROWN	LA C TATE
RE C EPT	TA C KET	*BU C KSAW	*DE C RYPT	LA C TEAL
RE C ESS	*TA C KEY	BU C OLIC	DE C UMAN	LA C TEAN
RE C IPE	TA C KLE	*CA C HEXY	DE C UPLE	LA C TONE
RE C ITE	TA C TIC	*CA C HING	DE C URVE	LA C TOSE
RE C KON	TE C HED	*CA C IQUE	DI C IEST	LA C UNAR
RE C LAD	TE C TAL	*CA C KLER	DI C KENS	*LE C HERY
RE C OAL	TE C TUM	*CA C ODYL	DI C LINY	LE C TERN
RE C OCK	TI C KER	*CI C HLID	DI C OTYL	LE C TION
RE C OIL	TI C KET	CI C OREE	DI C TATE	LE C TURE
RE C OIN	TI C KLE	CO C AINE	DI C TION	LI C ENCE
RE C OMB	TI C TAC	CO C COID	*DI C YCLY	LI C ENSE
RE C OOK	TI C TOC	CO C COON	DO C ETIC	*LI C HTLY
RE C OPY	TO C HER	CO C HAIR	*DO C KAGE	LI C KING
RE C ORD	TO C SIN	CO C HLEA	DU C HESS	LO C ALLY
RE C OUP	TU C HUN	*CO C KADE	DU C KIER	LO C ATER
RE C TAL	TU C KER	*CO C KEYE	DU C KIES	LO C ATOR
RE C TOR	TU C KET	*CO C KIER	*DU C KPIN	*LO C KAGE
RE C TUM	TY C OON	*CO C KILY	DU C TILE	*LO C KBOX
RE C TUS		*CO C KISH	DU C TING	*LO C KJAW

LO C KNUT	PI C OLIN	*SA C KFUL	VI C OMTE	*CAL C IFIC
LO C KOUT	PI C OTEE	SA C KING	*VI C TORY	CAL C SPAR
*LO C KRAM	*PI C QUET	SA C LIKE	VI C TUAL	*CAL C TUFA
LO C OISM	PI C RATE	SA C RIST	VI C UGNA	*CAL C TUFF
LO C ULAR	PI C RITE	SE C EDER	VO C ABLE	CAL C ULUS
LO C ULUS	PI C TURE	SE C LUDE	*VO C ABLY	CAN C ELER
LO C USTA	*PO C HARD	SE C ONDE	VO C ALIC	CAN C ROID
LU C ARNE	PO C OSIN	SE C ONDO	*VO C ALLY	*CAR C AJOU
LU C ENCE	PS C HENT	SE C RECY	VO C ODER	CAR C ANET
LU C ENCY	PU C COON	SE C RETE	*WI C KAPE	CAS C ABEL
LU C ERNE	*PU C KERY	SE C TARY	*WI C KING	CAS C ABLE
LU C IFER	*PU C KISH	SE C TILE	*WI C KIUP	*CAT C HALL
*LY C HNIS	RA C COON	SE C TION	*WI C KYUP	*CAT C HFLY
*LY C OPOD	RA C EMIC	SE C ULAR	*YA C HTER	CER C ARIA
*MA C AQUE	*RA C EWAY	SE C URER	*ZA C ATON	*CHA C ONNE
*MA C CHIA	RA C IEST	*SI C KBAY	*ZE C CHIN	*CHE C HAKO
*MA C HZOR	*RA C KETY	*SI C KBED	BAC C ARAT	*CHE C KOFF
*MI C RIFY	*RA C QUET	*SI C KISH	*BAC C ATED	*CHE C KOUT
*MI C ROHM	RE C ARRY	SO C AGER	*BAC C HANT	*CHE C KROW
*MO C KERY	RE C EIPT	SO C CAGE	*BAC C HIUS	*CHI C ANER
*MU C KIER	RE C EIVE	SO C IETY	*BEA C HBOY	*CHI C CORY
*MU C KILY	RE C ENCY	*SO C KEYE	*BED C HAIR	*CHI C KPEA
NA C ELLE	RE C HART	*SO C KMAN	*BED C OVER	*CHI C NESS
NE C KING	RE C HEAT	SU C CEED	*BEE C HNUT	*CHU C KIES
NE C KTIE	*RE C HECK	SU C CESS	BER C EUSE	*CHU C KLER
NE C ROSE	RE C ITAL	SU C CORY	*BES C ORCH	*CIN C HONA
NE C TARY	RE C ITER	SU C COTH	BES C REEN	CIN C TURE
NI C OTIN	RE C LAIM	SU C COUR	*BIA C ETYL	CIR C LING
NI C TATE	RE C LAME	SU C CUBA	BIO C LEAN	*CIR C UITY
NO C TUID	RE C LASP	*SU C CUMB	*BIO C YCLE	CIR C ULAR
NO C TULE	RE C LEAN	SU C CUSS	*BIT C HERY	*COA C HMAN
NO C TURN	RE C LINE	SU C KLER	*BLA C KBOY	*COA C TIVE
NO C UOUS	RE C LUSE	SU C RASE	*BLA C KCAP	*COC C IDIA
NU C LEAL	RE C OLOR	SU C ROSE	*BLA C KFIN	CON C EDER
NU C LEAR	RE C OUNT	SU C TION	*BLA C KFLY	*CON C EIVE
NU C LEIN	RE C OUPE	SY C OSIS	*BLA C KGUM	CON C ERTO
NU C LEON	RE C OVER	TA C HISM	*BLA C KING	*CON C HOID
NU C LEUS	RE C RATE	TA C HIST	*BLA C KISH	*CON C LAVE
NU C LIDE	RE C ROSS	TA C KIER	*BLA C KLEG	CON C LUDE
PA C HISI	RE C ROWN	*TA C KIFY	*BLA C KOUT	CON C RETE
*PA C HUCO	RE C RUIT	*TA C KILY	*BLA C KTOP	COSECANT
*PA C IFIC	*RE C TIFY	TA C KLER	*BLO C KADE	COSIGNER
*PA C KAGE	RE C TORY	TA C NODE	*BLO C KAGE	COSINESS
*PA C KING	*RE C TRIX	TA C TFUL	*BLO C KISH	*COU C HANT
*PA C KMAN	RE C URVE	TA C TILE	*BOS C HBOK	*COU C HING
*PA C KWAX	RE C YCLE	TA C TION	*BOT C HERY	*CRA C KING
PA C TION	RI C CTUS	TA C TUAL	BRA C ELET	*CRA C KNEL
PE C CANT	RI C INUS	TE C HNIC	*BRA C HIAL	*CRA C KPOT
PE C CARY	RI C KETS	*TE C TRIX	*BRA C HIUM	CRI C ETID
*PE C CAVI	*RI C KETY	TI C KING	*BRA C KISH	CRO C EINE
PE C TASE	*RI C KSHA	TI C KLER	BRA C TLET	*CRO C KERY
PE C TATE	RI C OTTA	TO C CATA	*BRI C KBAT	CRO C OITE
*PE C TIZE	*RO C KABY	*VA C ANCY	BRO C ATEL	CRU C IATE
*PI C ACHO	*RO C KERY	VA C CINA	BRO C COLI	*CRU C IBLE
PI C ADOR	RO C KIER	VA C CINE	*BRO C HURE	*CRU C IFER
PI C COLO	RO C KOON	*VA C UITY	*BRO C KAGE	*CRU C IFIX
PI C EOUS	RU C HING	VA C UOLE	BRU C ELLA	CUR C ULIO
*PI C KAXE	RU C TION	VA C UOUS	*BUN C OMBE	*CUT C HERY
*PI C KEER	SA C ATON	*VI C ARLY	*BUT C HERY	*DAB C HICK
*PI C KIER	SA C CATE	*VI C EROY	CAL C ANEA	DEA C ONRY
*PI C KING	SA C CATE	VI C INAL	CAL C ANEI	DES C RIBE
*PI C KOFF	*SA C KBUT	VI C IOUS	CAL C EATE	

DES C RIER	GRA C IOSO	PAN C REAS	REA C CUSE	SUB C LASS
DIA C ETYL	GRA C IOUS	PAR C ENER	REA C TANT	*SUB C LERK
DIA C ONAL	GUA C HARO	*PAY C HECK	REA C TION	SUB C UTIS
DIE C IOUS	*HAT C HECK	*PEA C EFUL	REA C TIVE	SUC C INCT
DIO C ESAN	*HAT C HERY	*PEA C OCKY	*REO C CUPY	SUC C INIC
DIS C IPLE	*HAT C HING	*PEC C ABLE	RES C REEN	*SUC C INYL
DIS C LAIM	*HAT C HWAY	*PEC C ANCY	RES C RIPT	SUC C ORER
*DIS C LIKE	*HEN C HMAN	PEN C HANT	SAC C ULAR	SUC C UBUS
DIS C LOSE	HER C ULES	PEN C ILER	SAC C ULUS	SUI C IDAL
DIS C OLOR	*HIC C OUGH	*PER C EIVE	*SAN C TIFY	SUL C ATED
DIS C OUNT	*HOA C TZIN	PIA C ULAR	SAN C TION	SUR C EASE
DIS C OVER	*HOT C HPOT	PIE C RUST	SAN C TITY	*SYN C ARPY
DIS C REET	*HYA C INTH	*PIL C HARD	SAR C ENET	SYN C LINE
DIS C RETE	*JUN C TION	*PIN C HBUG	*SAU C EBOX	*SYN C YTIA
DIS C ROWN	*JUN C TURE	*PIN C HECK	SAU C EPAN	TEA C HING
DRA C AENA	*KER C HIEF	PIS C ATOR	SEA C OAST	TEO C ALLI
DRA C ONIC	*KNA C KERY	PLA C ABLE	SEA C RAFT	TER C ELET
DUE C ENTO	*KNI C KERS	PLA C ATER	*SEE C ATCH	*THI C KISH
DUL C ETLY	*KNO C KOFF	PLA C EMAN	SEI C ENTO	*THI C KSET
DUL C IANA	*KNO C KOUT	PLA C ENTA	SEL C OUTH	TIE C LASP
DUL C IMER	*KNU C KLER	PLE C TRON	*SHA C KLER	TIN C TURE
DUL C INEA	LAN C ELET	PLE C TRUM	*SHU C KING	TOP C ROSS
*DUT C HMAN	LAN C IERS	PLI C ATED	*SMO C KING	TOR C HERE
FAL C ATED	LAR C ENER	POA C EOUS	*SNI C KERY	TOR C HIER
*FAL C HION	*LAT C HKEY	*POE C HORE	SOO C HONG	TRA C HEID
FAL C ONER	LEA C HATE	PRA C TICE	SOR C ERER	*TRA C HOMA
FAL C ONET	LEU C EMIA	PRA C TISE	SOU C HONG	*TRA C HYTE
*FAL C ONRY	*LIN C HPIN	*PRE C HECK	SPA C EMAN	*TRA C KAGE
*FAN C IFUL	LUN C HEON	*PRE C HILL	SPA C IOUS	*TRA C KING
*FAR C ICAL	LUS C IOUS	*PRE C IEUX	SPE C IATE	*TRA C KMAN
*FAS C ICLE	*LYN C HING	PRE C INCT	*SPE C IFIC	TRA C TATE
*FEN C IBLE	MA C ARONI	PRE C IOUS	SPE C IMEN	TRA C TILE
*FIS C ALLY	MA C AROON	PRE C ITED	SPE C IOUS	TRA C TION
FLE C TION	*MAC C ABAW	PRE C LEAN	SPE C TATE	TRE C ENTO
*FLI C HTER	*MAC C ABOY	PRE C LUDE	SPE C TRAL	TRI C HINA
*FLI C KERY	*MAC C OBOY	PRI C IEST	SPE C TRUM	TRI C HITE
*FOR C EFUL	MA C ERATE	*PRI C KIER	SPE C ULUM	TRI C HOID
*FOR C IBLE	MA C RURAN	PRO C AINE	SPI C CATO	*TRI C HOME
*FOR C IPES	MA C ULATE	*PRO C HAIN	SPI C IEST	*TRI C KERY
FRA C TION	*MAR C HESA	*PRO C HEIN	SPI C ULUM	TRI C KIER
FRA C TURE	*MAR C HESE	PRO C LAIM	STA C CATO	*TRI C KILY
FRI C ANDO	*MAT C HBOX	PRO C URAL	*STI C KFUL	*TRI C KISH
FRI C TION	ME C ONIUM	PRO C URER	STI C KIER	TRI C OLOR
*FRU C TIFY	*MER C HANT	*PUN C HEON	*STI C KILY	TRI C ORNE
FRU C TOSE	*MER C IFUL	PUN C TATE	STI C KIER	TRI C TRAC
FUN C TION	MI C ROBAR	PUN C TUAL	*STI C KMAN	*TRI C YCLE
FUR C RAEA	MI C ROBUS	PUN C TURE	STI C KOUT	*TRO C HAIC
*FUR C ULUM	*MIS C ARRY	*PUR C HASE	*STI C KPIN	TRO C HILI
*GIM C RACK	*MIS C HIEF	*QUA C KERY	STO C CADO	TRO C HLEA
GLA C IATE	MO C CASIN	*QUA C KISH	STO C CATA	TRO C HOID
GLU C AGON	*MOS C HATE	*QUA C KISM	*STO C KADE	*TRU C KAGE
GLU C INUM	*MOU C HOIR	*QUI C KSET	*STO C KCAR	*TRU C KING
GLY C ERIN	MU C ILAGE	RAN C HERO	STO C KIER	TRU C KLER
GLY C EROL	*MUT C HKIN	*RAN C HMAN	*STO C KILY	*TRU C KMAN
*GLY C ERYL	NAR C EINE	RAS C ALLY	STO C KING	*VAC C INIA
*GLY C OGEN	NAR C ISSI	REA C CEDE	*STO C KISH	VAS C ULAR
*GLY C ONIC	NAR C OSIS	REA C CENT	STO C KIST	*VAS C ULUM
*GLY C OSYL	NAR C OTIC	REA C CEPT	*STO C KMAN	*VIN C IBLE
*GOD C HILD	NAS C ENCE		*STO C KPOT	*VIN C ULUM
GOL C ONDA	*NAS C ENCY		STU C COER	*VIS C ACHA
GRA C EFUL	NES C IENT		SUB C AUSE	VIS C ERAL
GRA C ILIS	*NEW C OMER		*SUB C HIEF	VIS C OUNT

*VIZ C ACHA	HAVO C	CLINI C	PARSE C	CHLORI C
*VOI C EFUL	HEMI C	CLONI C	PELVI C	*CHROMI C
*VOL C ANIC	HUMI C	COCCI C	PEPTI C	CHRONI C
*VUL C ANIC	LILA C	COGNA C	PHATI C	CLASSI C
*WAH C ONDA	LINA C	CORSA C	PHONI C	CLASTI C
*WAR C RAFT	LOTI C	COSMI C	PHOTI C	COELIA C
*WAT C HCRY	LYRI C	CRETI C	*PHYSI C	COLONI C
*WAT C HDOG	LYTI C	CRITI C	PICNI C	COMATI C
*WAT C HEYE	MAFI C	CUPRI C	PICRI C	COMEDI C
*WAT C HFUL	MAGI C	CYANI C	POETI C	COMETI C
*WAT C HMAN	MALI C	CYSTI C	PUBLI C	*CRYPTI C
*WAT C HOUT	MANI C	DEIFI C	*PYKNI C	DEICTI C
*WEL C OMER	MEDI C	DYADI C	*QUINI C	DEMONI C
*WIT C HERY	MELI C	FABRI C	RICRA C	DEMOTI C
*WIT C HING	MESI C	FENNE C	RUBRI C	DIBASI C
*WRA C KFUL	MIMI C	FERRI C	RUSTI C	DIMERI C
*WRE C KAGE	MUSI C	FILMI C	SCENI C	DINERI C
*WRE C KFUL	PANI C	FISTI C	SEPTI C	DISOMI C
*WRE C KFUL	PUBI C	FORMI C	SORBI C	DOCETI C
*ZEC C HINO	PUDI C	FROLI C	STATI C	DRASTI C
*ZIN C KING	PYRI C	FUNGI C	STERI C	*DYNAMI C
*ZIR C ONIA	RABI C	FUSTI C	SYNDI C	FANATI C
*ZIR C ONIC	REBE C	GALYA C	TACTI C	FARADI C
*ZOO C HORE	RELI C	GARLI C	TAMBA C	FATIDI C
*ZUC C HINI	RUNI C	GEODI C	TANNI C	FRANTI C
	SALI C	GESTI C	TANRE C	FUMARI C
	SERA C	GNOMI C	TARMA C	*FUTHAR C
BLO C	SONI C	GOTHI C	TENRE C	*FUTHOR C
CHI C	STOI C	GUAIA C	THETI C	GASTRI C
DIS C	SUMA C	GWEDU C	THORI C	GENERI C
FIS C	TARO C	HAEMI C	*THYMI C	GENETI C
FLI C	TELI C	HAPTI C	TICTA C	GEORGI C
HUI C	TONI C	HECTI C	TICTO C	*GLYPTI C
LAI C	TOPI C	HELIA C	TOLUI C	GNATHI C
MAR C	TORI C	HERDI C	TOMBA C	GNOSTI C
NAR C	TOXI C	HEROI C	TRAGI C	*GRAPHI C
PYI C	TUNI C	*HYDRI C	TROPI C	*GYNECI C
SPI C	TYPI C	*HYPNI C	VIATI C	HAGADI C
SYN C	VATI C	LACTI C	VITRI C	*HALAKI C
TAL C	VINI C	LENTI C	*ZINCI C	HEBETI C
TOR C	*XEBE C	LIMBI C	*ZODIA C	HEDONI C
*ZIN C	XENI C	LIMNI C	*BACCHI C	HEMATI C
*ZOI C	XERI C	LITHI C	BALDRI C	HEPATI C
BARI C	YOGI C	LUBRI C	BASILI C	HERETI C
BASI C	*ZEBE C	LUETI C	*BAWDRI C	*JURIDI C
BORI C	BARDI C	MANIA C	BENEFI C	*KERAMI C
BRON C	BEYLI C	MANIO C	BENTHI C	KINETI C
CERI C	BIOTI C	MANTI C	BIBASI C	LACONI C
CIVI C	BONDU C	MASTI C	BIVOUA C	LUNATI C
COLI C	BROMI C	METRI C	BORACI C	MALEFI C
COMI C	BUSTI C	MIOTI C	BOTANI C	MASONI C
CONI C	CALCI C	MOSAI C	BUBONI C	MELANI C
COSE C	CALPA C	MUCLU C	BUCOLI C	MELODI C
CUBI C	CANTI C	MYOTI C	BUTYRI C	METOPI C
CUSE C	CAPRI C	MYSTI C	CALORI C	MOLLUS C
CYNI C	CELIA C	*MYTHI C	*CAMBRI C	*MORPHI C
DARI C	*CHEBE C	NASTI C	CARDIA C	MOTIVI C
DOMI C	*CHEMI C	NITRI C	CAUSTI C	MOTORI C
DURO C	CHORI C	NOETI C	CENTRI C	*MUNTJA C
FRAN C	*CHYMI C	NOSTO C	CERAMI C	NEMATI C
GAMI C	CITRI C		CEROTI C	NEPHRI C
GENI C	CLERI C		*CHAMPA C	NERITI C

NUMERI C	TEREBI C	DIDACTI C	MERISTI C	*RHYTHMI C
*PACIFI C	TETANI C	DIETETI C	MESMERI C	ROMANTI C
PARETI C	THERIA C	*DIHYDRI C	METALLI C	RUTHENI C
PARODI C	THERMI C	DIMETRI C	*METHODI C	SABBATI C
PAROTI C	THIONI C	DIOPTRI C	MNEMONI C	*SALVIFI C
PELAGI C	TITANI C	*DIPHASI C	*MOLYBDI C	SANDARA C
PHALLI C	*TRAFFI C	DIURETI C	MONASTI C	SANTALI C
PHRENI C	TRIADI C	DOMESTI C	*MORBIFI C	SARDONI C
PIRATI C	TROPHI C	DRACONI C	*MYOGENI C	SEMANTI C
PLASTI C	VENATI C	DRAMATI C	NARCOTI C	SEMIOTI C
*PLUMBI C	VERIDI C	*DYSGENI C	NEOTERI C	SIMONIA C
POLEMI C	*VIVIFI C	FARADAI C	NEURITI C	*SIPHONI C
POLITI C	VOCALI C	*FEBRIFI C	NEUROTI C	*SLIVOVI C
POTAMI C	*XANTHI C	FORENSI C	*NICKELI C	*SPAGYRI C
PRACTI C	*YASHMA C	FRENETI C	NITROLI C	*SPECIFI C
PRIAPI C	BALSAMI C	*FULMINI C	NONBASI C	SPONDAI C
PROSAI C	BANAUSI C	GALACTI C	NONIONI C	SPORADI C
PRUSSI C	BARBARI C	GALVANI C	*NONTOXI C	STOMATI C
PSALMI C	BARLEDU C	GEODESI C	*PACHALI C	SUBOPTI C
*PSYCHI C	*BATHETI C	GEODETI C	PALLADI C	*SUBPUBI C
PYRETI C	*BEATIFI C	GEOPONI C	*PANDEMI C	SUBSONI C
*PYRRHI C	*BICYCLI C	GERMANI C	PANOPTI C	SUBTONI C
*QUADRI C	BIOGENI C	GERONTI C	*PARHELI C	SUBTOPI C
*QUANTI C	BIOLOGI C	GIGANTI C	*PASHALI C	SUBTUNI C
*QUARTI C	*BROMIDI C	*GLYCONI C	*PATHETI C	SUCCINI C
*QUINTI C	*CALCIFI C	*HABBINI C	PENTOMI C	SULFONI C
RACEMI C	CANNABI C	*HAEMATI C	PERIODI C	SULFURI C
*RHOMBI C	*CARBAMI C	*HAGGADI C	PERIOTI C	*SYLLABI C
*SAPPHI C	*CATHOLI C	*HARMONI C	PERISAR C	*SYLVATI C
SATANI C	CELERIA C	HERALDI C	PETROLI C	*SYMBOLI C
SCALDI C	*CEPHALI C	HERMETI C	*PHENETI C	SYNDETI C
SCEPTI C	*CHIMERI C	HIERATI C	*PHENOLI C	*SYNECTI C
SCIATI C	*CHOLERI C	HISTORI C	*PHONETI C	*SYSTEMI C
SEBACI C	*CHTHONI C	*HOLOZOI C	*PHREATI C	TALMUDI C
SEBASI C	*COLUMBI C	*HORRIFI C	*PHTHALI C	TECTONI C
SELENI C	COSMETI C	*HYDRONI C	*PHTHISI C	TELLURI C
SEMATI C	*CRESYLI C	*HYDROPI C	PLATINI C	TERRIFI C
SHELLA C	CUNEATI C	*HYLOZOI C	PLATONI C	*THEMATI C
SHOEPA C	*DACTYLI C	*HYPNOTI C	POLLINI C	TOREUTI C
SILICI C	DALMATI C	*HYPOTHE C	*POLYZOI C	TRIBASI C
*SKEPTI C	DALTONI C	*HYSTERI C	*PONTIFI C	TRICTRA C
SMECTI C	DEMONIA C	LEPROTI C	POPLITI C	TRISOMI C
SPASTI C	DESERTI C	*LEUKEMI C	POTASSI C	*TROCHAI C
SPATHI C	DEUTERI C	LIMNETI C	*PREMEDI C	TURMERI C
SPHENI C	DIABETI C	LOGISTI C	*PROLIFI C	*TYMPANI C
SPHERI C	DIABOLI C	MAGNETI C	*PROXEMI C	TYRANNI C
SPLENI C	DIALOGI C	*MAGNIFI C	PULMONI C	VILLATI C
STANNI C	DIALYTI C	MAIEUTI C	PURPURI C	*VOLCANI C
STROBI C	DIATOMI C	*MAJESTI C	*PYOGENI C	*VULCANI C
STYPTI C	DIATONI C	MANGANI C	*QUIDNUN C	*ZIRCONI C
SUBERI C	*DICHOTI C	MARGARI C	*QUIXOTI C	*ZOOGENI C
SUBFUS C	*DICHROI C	*MECHANI C	REPUBLI C	
TABETI C	DICROTI C	MEDALLI C	*RHEMATI C	
TECHNI C	*DICYCLI C	*MELLIFI C	RHETORI C	

D

DACE	**DHOW**	DOTY	DAISY	DEPOT
DADA	**DIAL**	DOUR	DALLY	**DEPTH**
DADO	**DICK**	DOVE	DAMAN	DERAT
DAFF	DIDO	DOWN	DAMAR	DERAY
DAFT	DIDY	*DOXY	DANCE	**DERBY**
DAGO	DIED	**DOZE**	**DANDY**	DERMA
DAIS	DIEL	*DOZY	DANIO	DERRY
DALE	DIES	DRAB	DARER	**DESEX**
DAME	DIET	DRAG	DARIC	DETER
DAMN	DIKE	DRAM	**DARKY**	DEVEL
DAMP	DILL	DRAT	**DASHY**	DEVIL
DANG	DIME	DRAW	DATER	DEVON
DANK	DINE	DRAY	DATTO	DEWAN
DARB	DING	DREE	DATUM	*DEWAX
DARE	DINK	DREG	DAUBE	DHOLE
DARK	DINT	DREK	**DAUBY**	DHOTI
DART	DIOL	DREW	DAUNT	DHUTI
DASH	DIPT	DRIB	DAVEN	DIARY
DATA	DIRE	DRIP	DAVIT	*DIAZO
DATE	DIRK	DROP	DAWEN	DICER
DATO	DIRL	DRUB	DEAIR	**DICEY**
DAUB	DIRT	DRUM	DEALT	*DICKY
DAUT	DISC	DUAD	DEARY	DICOT
DAVY	DISH	DUAL	DEASH	DICTA
DAWK	DITA	DUCE	DEATH	DIDST
DAWN	DITE	DUCI	DEAVE	DIENE
DAWT	DIVA	**DUCK**	DEBAR	**DIGHT**
DAZE	DIVE	DUCT	DEBIT	DIGIT
DEAD	**DJIN**	DUDE	DEBUG	**DIKER**
DEAF	DOAT	DUEL	DEBUT	DILDO
DEAL	**DOCK**	DUET	**DEBYE**	DILLY
DEAN	DODO	**DUFF**	DECAL	DIMER
DEAR	DOER	DUKE	**DECAY**	**DIMLY**
DEBT	DOES	DULL	**DECOY**	DINAR
DECK	**DOFF**	DULY	**DECRY**	DINER
DEED	DOGE	DUMA	DEDAL	DINGO
DEEM	DOGY	DUMB	DEFAT	**DINGY**
DEEP	DOIT	DUMP	DEFER	**DINKY**
DEER	**DOJO**	DUNE	**DEFOG**	DIODE
DEFI	DOLE	DUNG	DEGAS	**DIPPY**
DEFT	DOLL	DUNT	DEGUM	DIRER
DEFY	DOLT	DUPE	DEICE	DIRGE
DEIL	DOME	DURA	**DEIFY**	DIRTY
DEKE	DONA	DURE	DEIGN	DISCI
DELE	DONE	DURN	DEISM	DISCO
DELF	DONG	DURO	DEIST	**DISHY**
DELL	DOOM	DURR	DEITY	DISME
DEME	DOOR	DUSK	DELAY	**DITCH**
DEMO	DOPA	DUTY	DELLY	DITTO
DEMY	DOPE	DYAD	DELTA	DITTY
DENE	**DOPY**	DYER	DELVE	DIVAN
DENT	DORM	**DYKE**	DEMIT	DIVOT
DENY	DORR	DYNE	**DEMOB**	*DIVVY
DERE	DORY	**DACHA**	DEMON	DIWAN
DERM	DOSE	**DADDY**	DEMOS	**DIXIT**
DESK	DOSS	*DAFFY	DEMUR	*DIZEN
DEVA	DOST	DAILY	DENIM	*DIZZY
DEWY	DOTE	DAIRY	DENSE	DJINN
DHAK	DOTH			**DOBBY**

DOBIE	DRAWN	DACOIT	**DAWTIE**	**DEGERM**
DOBLA	DREAD	**DACTYL**	**DAYBED**	DEGREE
DOBRA	DREAM	DADDLE	***DAYFLY**	DEGUST
DODGE	DREAR	DAEDAL	***DAZZLE**	**DEHORN**
DODGY	DRESS	DAEMON	DEACON	**DEHORT**
DOEST	DREST	DAGGER	DEADEN	DEICER
DOETH	DRIED	DAGGLE	**DEADLY**	**DEIFIC**
DOGEY	DRIER	**DAGOBA**	**DEAFEN**	***DEJECT**
DOGGO	DRIES	DAHLIA	**DEAFLY**	**DEKARE**
DOGGY	DRIFT	**DAHOON**	DEARIE	DELATE
DOGIE	DRILL	**DAIKER**	**DEARLY**	DELEAD
DOGMA	DRILY	DAIMEN	**DEARTH**	DELETE
DOILY	**DRINK**	DAIMIO	DEASIL	DELICT
DOING	DRIPT	DAIMON	**DEATHY**	DELIME
DOLCE	DRIVE	**DAIMYO**	**DEBARK**	DELIST
DOLLY	DROIT	**DAINTY**	DEBASE	DELUDE
DOMAL	DROLL	**DAKOIT**	DEBATE	DELUGE
DOMIC	DRONE	**DALASI**	DEBONE	**DELUXE**
DONEE	DROOL	**DALETH**	DEBRIS	**DELVER**
DONNA	DROOP	DALLES	DEBTOR	**DEMAND**
DONOR	DROPT	**DAMAGE**	**DEBUNK**	**DEMARK**
DONSY	DROSS	**DAMASK**	**DECADE**	DEMAST
DONUT	**DROUK**	**DAMMAR**	**DECAMP**	DEMEAN
DOOLY	DROVE	**DAMMED**	DECANE	DEMENT
*DOOZY	DROWN	**DAMMER**	DECANT	DEMIES
DOPER	DRUID	**DAMNED**	DECARE	DEMISE
DOPEY	DRUNK	DAMNER	DECEIT	**DEMODE**
DORMY	DRUPE	**DAMPEN**	DECENT	DEMOTE
DORSA	DRUSE	**DAMPER**	DECERN	DEMURE
DORTY	**DRYAD**	**DAMPLY**	**DECIDE**	**DENARY**
DOSER	DRYER	DAMSEL	DECILE	DENGUE
DOTAL	**DRYLY**	DAMSON	**DECKEL**	DENIAL
DOTER	**DUCHY**	DANCER	**DECKER**	DENIED
DOTTY	***DUCKY**	DANDER	**DECKLE**	DENIER
DOUCE	**DUDDY**	DANDLE	**DECOCT**	DENIES
DOUGH	DULIA	DANGER	**DECODE**	DENNED
DOUMA	DULLY	DANGLE	DECREE	DENOTE
DOURA	DULSE	**DAPHNE**	**DECURY**	DENTAL
DOUSE	**DUMKA**	**DAPPED**	DEDANS	DENTIL
DOVEN	**DUMMY**	**DAPPER**	**DEDUCE**	DENTIN
DOWDY	**DUMPY**	**DAPPLE**	**DEDUCT**	DENUDE
DOWEL	DUNCE	DARING	***DEEJAY**	DEODAR
DOWER	**DUNCH**	**DARKEN**	DEEPEN	DEPART
DOWIE	**DUNGY**	**DARKEY**	**DEEPLY**	**DEPEND**
DOWNY	DUOMO	**DARKIE**	**DEEWAN**	**DEPERM**
DOWRY	DUPER	**DARKLE**	DEFACE	**DEPICT**
DOWSE	DUPLE	**DARKLY**	**DEFAME**	**DEPLOY**
DOXIE	DURAL	DARNED	**DEFEAT**	DEPONE
DOYEN	DUROC	DARNEL	**DEFECT**	DEPORT
DOYLY	DURRA	DARNER	**DEFEND**	DEPOSE
*DOZEN	DURST	DARTER	**DEFIED**	DEPUTE
*DOZER	DURUM	DARTLE	**DEFIER**	**DEPUTY**
DRAFF	DUSTY	**DASHER**	**DEFIES**	DERIDE
DRAFT	**DUTCH**	DASSIE	**DEFILE**	**DERIVE**
DRAIL	**DWARF**	**DATARY**	**DEFINE**	DERMIS
DRAIN	DWELL	**DATCHA**	**DEFLEA**	DERRIS
DRAKE	DWELT	DATING	**DEFOAM**	DESALT
DRAMA	DWINE	**DATIVE**	**DEFORM**	DESAND
DRANK	**DYING**	DATURA	**DEFRAY**	**DESCRY**
DRAPE	DABBER	DAUBER	**DEFUSE**	DESERT
DRAVE	**DABBLE**	**DAUBRY**	***DEFUZE**	DESIGN
DRAWL	**DACKER**	DAUTIE	DEGAGE	DESIRE

DESIST	**DIGGED**	***DJINNY**	DOTAGE	DRUDGE
DESMID	DIGGER	DOABLE	DOTARD	**DRUMLY**
DESORB	DIGLOT	**DOBBER**	DOTIER	**DRYLOT**
DESPOT	***DIKDIK**	**DOBBIN**	DOTING	**DUALLY**
DETACH	DIKTAT	DOBIES	DOTTED	**DUBBER**
DETAIL	DILATE	DOBLON	DOTTEL	**DUBBIN**
DETAIN	DILUTE	DOCENT	DOTTER	**DUCKER**
DETECT	**DIMITY**	DOCILE	DOTTLE	**DUCKIE**
DETENT	**DIMMED**	**DOCKER**	DOUBLE	DUDDIE
DETEST	**DIMMER**	**DOCKET**	**DOUBLY**	DUDEEN
DETICK	DIMOUT	DOCTOR	DOUCHE	**DUDISH**
DETOUR	**DIMPLE**	DODDER	**DOUGHT**	DUELER
DEVEIN	**DIMPLY**	DODGER	**DOUGHY**	**DUELLI**
DEVEST	**DIMWIT**	DOFFER	**DOURAH**	DUELLO
DEVICE	DINDLE	**DOGDOM**	**DOURLY**	DUENDE
DEVISE	DINERO	**DOGGED**	DOUSER	DUENNA
DEVOID	**DINGEY**	DOGGER	**DOVISH**	**DUFFEL**
DEVOIR	**DINGHY**	DOGIES	**DOWERY**	**DUFFER**
DEVOTE	DINGLE	DOGLEG	**DOWNER**	**DUFFLE**
DEVOUR	DINGUS	**DOGNAP**	**DOWSER**	DUGONG
DEVOUT	DINING	DOILED	**DOYLEY**	**DUIKER**
DEWIER	**DINKEY**	DOITED	***DOZILY**	DULCET
DEWILY	**DINKLY**	DOLING	***DOZING**	**DUMDUM**
DEWLAP	**DINKUM**	DOLLAR	**DRABLY**	**DUMPER**
DEWOOL	DINNED	DOLLOP	**DRACHM**	DUNITE
DEWORM	DINNER	DOLMAN	**DRAFFY**	DUNLIN
DEXIES	DIOBOL	DOLMEN	**DRAFTY**	DUNNED
DEXTER	***DIOXID**	DOLOUR	DRAGEE	DUNNER
DEXTRO	***DIPLEX**	DOMAIN	**DRAGGY**	DUOLOG
*DEZINC	DIPLOE	DOMINE	DRAPER	**DUPERY**
DHARMA	**DIPODY**	**DOMING**	**DRAWEE**	**DUPING**
DHARNA	DIPOLE	DOMINO	**DRAWER**	***DUPLEX**
DHOOLY	DIPPED	DONATE	**DRAWLY**	DUPPED
DHOORA	**DIPPER**	**DONJON**	DREAMT	DURBAR
DHOOTI	DIPSAS	DONKEY	**DREAMY**	DURESS
DHURNA	***DIQUAT**	DONNED	**DREARY**	DURIAN
DIACID	**DIRDUM**	DONNEE	**DREGGY**	DURING
DIADEM	DIRECT	DONSIE	**DREICH**	DURION
DIALER	**DIRELY**	***DONZEL**	DREIDL	DURNED
DIALOG	DIREST	DOODAD	**DREIGH**	DUSTER
DIAMIN	**DIRHAM**	DOOLEE	**DRENCH**	DUSTUP
DIAPER	DIRNDL	DOOLIE	**DRESSY**	**DYABLE**
DIAPIR	DISARM	***DOOZER**	DRIEST	**DYADIC**
DIATOM	DISBAR	DOPANT	**DRIFTY**	***DYBBUK**
*DIAZIN	**DISBUD**	DOPIER	**DRIPPY**	DYEING
DIBBER	DISCUS	**DOPING**	**DRIVEL**	**DYNAST**
DIBBLE	DISMAL	DORADO	**DRIVEN**	**DYNODE**
*DIBBUK	**DISMAY**	DORBUG	**DRIVER**	**DYVOUR**
DICAST	DISOWN	DORIES	DROGUE	**DABBLER**
DICIER	DISPEL	DORMER	**DROLLY**	**DABSTER**
DICING	DISTAL	DORMIE	DROMON	**DACOITY**
DICKER	DISTIL	DORMIN	DRONER	**DADAISM**
*DICKEY	DISUSE	DORPER	DRONGO	**DADAIST**
DICKIE	DITHER	DORSAD	**DROOPY**	***DAGLOCK**
DICTUM	DIURON	DORSAL	**DROPSY**	***DAKOITY**
DIDACT	**DIVERT**	DORSER	**DROSKY**	**DALAPON**
DIDDLE	**DIVEST**	DORSUM	**DROSSY**	DALLIER
DIDIES	**DIVIDE**	DOSAGE	**DROUTH**	**DAMAGER**
DIETER	**DIVINE**	DOSSAL	**DROVER**	**DAMMING**
DIFFER	**DIVING**	DOSSEL	DROWND	***DAMNIFY**
DIGAMY	***DJEBEL**	DOSSER	**DROWSE**	**DAMOSEL**
DIGEST	**DJINNI**	DOSSIL	**DROWSY**	***DAMOZEL**

*DAMPISH	DECIDUA	DEMOTIC	DEVIOUS	DIGRESS
DANDIER	DECIMAL	DEMOUNT	DEVISAL	DILATER
DANDIES	*DECKING	DENDRON	DEVISEE	DILATOR
DANDILY	DECLAIM	*DENIZEN	DEVISER	DILUENT
DANDLER	DECLARE	DENNING	DEVISOR	DILUTER
DANGLER	DECLASS	DENSIFY	DEVOICE	DILUTOR
DANSEUR	DECLINE	DENSITY	DEVOLVE	DILUVIA
DAPHNIA	DECODER	DENTINE	DEVOTEE	DIMERIC
DAPPING	DECOLOR	DENTIST	DEWATER	DIMETER
DARBIES	DECORUM	DENTOID	*DEWCLAW	DIMMEST
DAREFUL	DECOYER	DENTURE	DEWDROP	DIMMING
DARESAY	DECREER	DENUDER	DEWFALL	DIMNESS
DARIOLE	DECRIAL	DEODAND	DEWIEST	*DIMORPH
DARKIES	DECRIED	DEODARA	DEWLESS	DINERIC
*DARKISH	DECRIER	DEPAINT	*DEXTRAL	DINETTE
DARNING	DECROWN	DEPLANE	*DEXTRAN	DINGBAT
DASHEEN	*DECRYPT	DEPLETE	*DEXTRIN	DINGILY
DASHIER	DECUMAN	DEPLORE	DHOOTIE	DINKIER
*DASHIKI	DECUPLE	DEPLUME	DHOURRA	DINKIES
DASHPOT	DECURVE	DEPOSAL	DIABASE	DINNING
DASTARD	DEERFLY	DEPOSER	DIABOLO	DIOCESE
DASYURE	DEFACER	DEPOSIT	DIAGRAM	DIOPTER
DATABLE	DEFAMER	DEPRAVE	DIALECT	DIOPTRE
DATEDLY	DEFAULT	DEPRESS	DIALING	DIORAMA
DAUBERY	DEFENCE	DEPRIVE	DIALIST	DIORITE
DAUNDER	DEFENSE	DEPSIDE	DIALLED	*DIOXANE
DAUNTER	DEFIANT	DERAIGN	DIALLEL	*DIOXIDE
DAUPHIN	DEFICIT	DERIDER	DIALYSE	DIPHASE
*DAYBOOK	DEFILER	DERIVER	*DIALYZE	DIPLOID
*DAYGLOW	DEFINER	DERMOID	DIAMIDE	DIPLOMA
DAYLILY	DEFLATE	DERNIER	DIAMINE	DIPNOAN
DAYLONG	DEFLECT	DERRICK	DIAMOND	DIPPING
DAYMARE	DEFORCE	DERVISH	DIAPSID	DIPTERA
DAYROOM	DEFRAUD	DESCANT	*DIARCHY	*DIPTYCA
DAYSIDE	*DEFROCK	DESCEND	DIARIES	*DIPTYCH
DAYSMAN	DEFROST	DESCENT	DIARIST	DIREFUL
DAYSTAR	DEFUNCT	DESERVE	DIASTER	DISABLE
DAYTIME	DEGAUSS	DESIRER	*DIAZINE	DISAVOW
*DAZZLER	*DEGLAZE	DESMOID	*DIAZOLE	DISBAND
DEADEYE	DEGRADE	DESPAIR	DIBASIC	DISCANT
DEADPAN	DEHISCE	DESPISE	DIBBING	DISCARD
DEAFISH	DEICIDE	DESPITE	DIBBLER	DISCASE
DEALING	DEICTIC	DESPOIL	DICIEST	DISCEPT
DEANERY	DEIFIED	DESPOND	DICKENS	DISCERN
DEARIES	DEIFIER	DESSERT	DICLINY	DISCOID
DEATHLY	DEIFORM	DESTAIN	DICOTYL	DISCORD
DEBACLE	*DEJECTA	DESTINE	DICTATE	DISCUSS
DEBASER	DELAINE	DESTINY	DICTION	DISDAIN
DEBATER	DELATOR	DESTROY	*DICYCLY	DISEASE
*DEBAUCH	DELAYER	DESUGAR	DIDDLER	DISEUSE
DEBONER	DELIGHT	DETENTE	*DIEBACK	DISGUST
*DEBOUCH	DELIMIT	DETERGE	DIEHARD	DISHELM
DEBRIEF	DELIVER	DETINUE	DIESTER	DISHFUL
DECANAL	DELOUSE	DETRACT	DIETARY	DISHIER
DECAPOD	DELTOID	DETRAIN	DIFFUSE	DISHPAN
DECAYER	DELUDER	DETRUDE	DIGAMMA	DISHRAG
DECEASE	DEMAGOG	*DEUTZIA	DIGGING	*DISJECT
DECEIVE	DEMERIT	DEVALUE	DIGITAL	*DISJOIN
*DECENCY	DEMESNE	DEVELOP	*DIGNIFY	DISLIKE
DECIARE	DEMIGOD	DEVIANT	DIGNITY	DISLIMN
DECIBEL	DEMIREP	DEVIATE	*DIGOXIN	DISMAST
DECIDER	DEMONIC	DEVILRY	DIGRAPH	DISMISS

DISOBEY	DOLEFUL	DRAYMAN	DUNNAGE	DANKNESS
DISOMIC	DOLLIED	DREAMER	DUNNESS	DANSEUSE
DISPART	DOLLIES	DREDGER	DUNNEST	DARINGLY
DISPEND	DOLLISH	DREIDEL	DUNNING	DARKENER
DISPLAY	DOLPHIN	DRESSER	DUNNITE	DARKNESS
DISPORT	DOMICAL	DRIBBLE	DUOPOLY	*DARKROOM
DISPOSE	DOMICIL	DRIBLET	DUOTONE	*DARKSOME
DISPUTE	DOMINIE	DRIFTER	DUPPING	DARNDEST
DISRATE	DONATOR	DRILLER	DUPTRAG	DASHIEST
DISROBE	DONGOLA	DRINKER	DURABLE	DATELESS
DISROOT	DONNERD	DRIPPER	DURAMEN	DATELINE
DISRUPT	DONNERT	*DRIZZLY	DURANCE	DAUGHTER
DISSAVE	DONNING	DROMOND	DURMAST	DAUPHINE
DISSEAT	DONNISH	DRONING	*DUSKISH	*DAWNLIKE
DISSECT	DOOMFUL	DRONISH	DUSTBIN	*DAYBREAK
DISSENT	DOORMAN	DROPLET	DUSTIER	*DAYDREAM
DISSERT	DOORMAT	DROPOUT	DUSTILY	*DAYLIGHT
DISTAFF	DOORWAY	DROPPED	DUSTMAN	DEACONRY
DISTAIN	DOPIEST	DROPPER	DUSTPAN	DEADBEAT
DISTANT	*DORHAWK	DROSERA	DUTEOUS	DEADENER
DISTEND	DORMANT	*DROSHKY	DUTIFUL	DEADFALL
DISTENT	DORMICE	DROUGHT	DUUMVIR	DEADHEAD
DISTICH	DORNECK	DROUTHY	DUVETYN	DEADLIER
DISTILL	DORNICK	DROWNER	DWARVES	DEADLINE
DISTOME	DOSSIER	DRUBBER	DWELLER	*DEADLOCK
DISTORT	DOTIEST	DRUDGER	DWINDLE	DEADNESS
DISTURB	DOTTIER	DRUGGET	*DYARCHY	DEADWOOD
*DISYOKE	DOTTILY	DRUMBLE	DYEABLE	DEAERATE
DITCHER	DOTTING	DRUMLIN	*DYEWEED	DEAFNESS
DITHERY	DOTTREL	DRUMMED	*DYEWOOD	*DEALFISH
DITHIOL	DOUBLER	DRUMMER	*DYNAMIC	DEANSHIP
DITTANY	DOUBLET	DRUNKEN	DYNASTY	DEARNESS
DIURNAL	DOUCEUR	DRYNESS	DYSPNEA	*DEATHBED
DIVERSE	*DOUGHTY	DUALISM	DYSURIA	*DEATHCUP
DIVIDER	DOURINE	DUALIST	DABBLING	*DEATHFUL
DIVINER	DOVECOT	DUALITY	*DABCHICK	DEBILITY
DIVISOR	*DOVEKEY	*DUALIZE	*DACTYLIC	DEBONAIR
DIVORCE	*DOVEKIE	DUBBING	DACTYLUS	*DEBOUCHE
DIVULGE	DOWABLE	DUBIETY	*DAFFODIL	DEBRUISE
DOCETIC	DOWAGER	DUBIOUS	DAFTNESS	*DEBUNKER
*DOCKAGE	DOWNIER	DUCHESS	*DAHABEAH	DEBUTANT
DODDERY	DOYENNE	DUCKIER	*DAHABIAH	DECADENT
DODGERY	*DOZENTH	DUCKIES	*DAHABIEH	DECANTER
DODGING	DRABBET	*DUCKPIN	*DAHABIYA	DECEDENT
DODOISM	DRABBLE	DUCTILE	*DAIQUIRI	DECEIVER
DOESKIN	*DRACHMA	DUCTING	*DAISHIKI	*DECEMVIR
DOGBANE	DRAFTEE	DUCTULE	*DAKERHEN	DECENARY
DOGCART	DRAFTER	DUDGEON	DALESMAN	DECENNIA
DOGEDOM	DRAGGER	DUELIST	DALMATIC	DECENTER
DOGFACE	DRAGGLE	DUELLED	DALTONIC	DECENTRE
*DOGFISH	DRAGNET	DUELLER	DAMEWORT	DECIGRAM
DOGGERY	DRAGOON	DUENESS	DAMNABLE	DECIMATE
DOGGIES	DRAINER	*DUKEDOM	DAMNDEST	*DECIPHER
DOGGING	DRAMMED	*DULCIFY	DAMPENER	DECISION
DOGGISH	DRAPERY	DULLARD	DAMPNESS	DECISIVE
DOGGONE	DRAPING	DULLISH	*DANDRIFF	*DECKHAND
DOGGREL	DRASTIC	DULNESS	*DANDRUFF	DECLARER
DOGLIKE	DRAUGHT	DUMPIER	*DANDYISH	DECLASSE
DOGSLED	DRAWBAR	*DUMPILY	*DANDYISM	DECLINER
DOGTROT	DRAWING	DUMPING	DANEGELD	DECORATE
DOGVANE	DRAWLER	*DUMPISH	DANEWEED	DECOROUS
DOGWOOD	DRAYAGE	DUNGEON	DANEWORT	DECREASE

DECREPIT	DEMONIAN	DETACHER	DIATOMIC	DIOECISM
DECRETAL	DEMONISE	DETAILER	DIATONIC	DIOICOUS
DECURION	DEMONISM	DETAINEE	DIATRIBE	DIOLEFIN
DEDICATE	DEMONIST	DETAINER	*DIAZEPAM	DIOPSIDE
DEEDLESS	*DEMONIZE	*DETECTER	DICHASIA	DIOPTASE
DEEMSTER	DEMOTICS	DETECTOR	*DICHOTIC	DIOPTRIC
DEEPENER	DEMOTING	DETERGER	*DICHROIC	*DIPHASIC
DEEPNESS	DEMOTION	DETERRED	DICROTAL	*DIPHENYL
DEERSKIN	DEMOTIST	DETERRER	DICROTIC	DIPLEGIA
DEERWEED	DEMPSTER	DETESTER	DICTATOR	*DIPLOIDY
DEERYARD	DEMURRAL	DETHRONE	*DICYCLIC	DIPLOMAT
DEFECTOR	DEMURRED	*DETICKER	DIDACTIC	DIPLOPOD
DEFENDER	DEMURRER	DETONATE	*DIDACTYL	DIPLOSIS
DEFERENT	DENARIUS	*DETOXIFY	DIDAPPER	*DIPPABLE
DEFERRAL	DENATURE	DETRITUS	*DIDYMIUM	*DIPSTICK
DEFERRED	*DENAZIFY	DEUTERIC	*DIDYMOUS	DIPTERAL
DEFERRER	DENDRITE	DEUTERON	*DIDYNAMY	DIPTERAN
DEFIANCE	DENDROID	DEVELOPE	DIECIOUS	DIPTERON
DEFILADE	DENIABLE	DEVIANCE	DIELDRIN	DIRECTOR
DEFINITE	DENOUNCE	*DEVIANCY	*DIEMAKER	DIRENESS
DEFLATOR	DENTALIA	DEVIATOR	DIERESIS	DIRIMENT
*DEFLEXED	DENTATED	*DEVILISH	*DIESTOCK	DISABUSE
*DEFLOWER	DENTICLE	*DEVILKIN	DIESTRUM	DISAGREE
DEFOAMER	DENUDATE	DEVILLED	DIESTRUS	DISALLOW
DEFOGGER	DEPICTER	*DEVILTRY	DIETETIC	DISANNUL
DEFOREST	DEPICTOR	DEVISING	*DIFFRACT	DISARMER
DEFORMER	DEPILATE	DEVOTION	*DIFFUSER	DISARRAY
*DEFRAYAL	DEPLORER	DEVOURER	*DIFFUSOR	DISASTER
*DEFRAYER	DEPOLISH	*DEWBERRY	DIGAMIST	DISBOSOM
DEFTNESS	DEPONENT	*DEXTRINE	DIGESTER	DISBURSE
DEGASSER	DEPORTEE	*DEXTROSE	DIGESTOR	DISCIPLE
DEGRADER	DEPRAVER	*DEXTROUS	DIGGINGS	DISCLAIM
DEGREASE	DEPRIVAL	DIABETES	DIGITATE	*DISCLIKE
DEHORNER	DEPRIVER	DIABETIC	*DIGITIZE	DISCLOSE
DEIFICAL	DEPURATE	DIABLERY	DIHEDRAL	DISCOLOR
*DEIONIZE	*DEPUTIZE	DIABOLIC	DIHEDRON	DISCOUNT
*DEJEUNER	DERELICT	DIACETYL	*DIHYBRID	DISCOVER
*DEKAGRAM	DERINGER	DIACONAL	*DIHYDRIC	DISCREET
DELATION	DERISION	DIAGNOSE	DILATANT	DISCRETE
*DELEGACY	DERISIVE	DIAGONAL	DILATATE	DISCROWN
DELEGATE	DERISORY	*DIAGRAPH	DILATION	DISENDOW
DELETION	DERIVATE	DIALLAGE	DILATIVE	*DISFAVOR
*DELICACY	DEROGATE	DIALLIST	DILATORY	*DISFROCK
DELICATE	DERRIERE	DIALOGER	DILIGENT	DISGORGE
DELIRIUM	DESALTER	DIALOGIC	DILUTION	DISGRACE
*DELIVERY	DESCRIBE	DIALOGUE	DILUTIVE	DISGUISE
DELUSION	DESCRIER	DIALYSER	DILUVIAL	DISHERIT
DELUSIVE	DESELECT	DIALYSIS	DILUVIAN	*DISHEVEL
DELUSORY	DESERTER	DIALYTIC	DILUVION	DISHIEST
DELUSTER	DESERTIC	*DIALYZER	DILUVIUM	*DISHLIKE
*DEMAGOGY	DESERVER	DIAMETER	DIMERISM	DISHONOR
DEMANDER	DESIGNEE	DIANTHUS	*DIMERIZE	DISHWARE
*DEMARCHE	DESIGNER	DIAPASON	DIMEROUS	DISINTER
DEMEANOR	DESILVER	DIAPAUSE	*DIMETHYL	*DISJOINT
DEMENTIA	DESINENT	DIAPHONE	DIMETRIC	*DISJUNCT
*DEMIJOHN	DESIROUS	*DIAPHONY	DIMINISH	DISLIKER
DEMILUNE	DESOLATE	DIARRHEA	*DIMMABLE	DISLODGE
DEMIURGE	*DESPATCH	DIASPORA	DINGDONG	DISLOYAL
DEMIVOLT	DESPISER	DIASPORE	DINKIEST	DISMOUNT
DEMOCRAT	DESTRIER	DIASTASE	DINOSAUR	DISORDER
DEMONESS	DESTRUCT	DIASTEMA	DIOBOLON	*DISPATCH
DEMONIAC	DESULFUR	DIASTOLE	DIOCESAN	DISPENSE

DISPERSE	DOCUMENT	DOUGHIER	DROPPING	*DUVETYNE
DISPIRIT	DODDERER	DOUGHNUT	DROPSHOT	*DWARFISH
DISPLACE	*DOGBERRY	DOURNESS	DROPWORT	*DWARFISM
DISPLANT	*DOGESHIP	*DOUZEPER	*DROUGHTY	DWELLING
DISPLODE	*DOGFIGHT	DOVECOTE	DRUBBING	*DYESTUFF
DISPLUME	*DOGGEDLY	*DOVELIKE	DRUDGERY	*DYNAMISM
DISPOSAL	DOGGEREL	DOVETAIL	DRUGGIST	DYNAMIST
DISPOSER	DOGGIEST	DOWNBEAT	DRUIDESS	DYNATRON
DISPREAD	DOGGONED	DOWNCAST	DRUIDISM	*DYSGENIC
*DISPRIZE	DOGHOUSE	*DOWNCOME	DRUMBEAT	*DYSLEXIA
DISPROOF	DOGNAPER	DOWNFALL	DRUMFIRE	*DYSPEPSY
DISPROVE	*DOGSBODY	*DOWNHAUL	*DRUMFISH	DYSPNOEA
DISPUTER	DOGTOOTH	*DOWNHILL	*DRUMHEAD	*DYSTAXIA
*DISQUIET	*DOGWATCH	DOWNIEST	DRUMLIER	DYSTOCIA
DISROBER	DOLDRUMS	*DOWNPLAY	*DRUMLIKE	DYSTONIA
DISSEISE	DOLERITE	DOWNPOUR	DRUMROLL	DYSTOPIA
*DISSEIZE	DOLESOME	DOWNTROD	DRUNKARD	
DISSERVE	DOLOMITE	DOWNTURN	DRUPELET	BA D DIE
DISSUADE	DOLOROUS	*DOWNWARD	DRUTHERS	BA D GER
DISTANCE	*DOMELIKE	*DOWNWIND	DRYPOINT	BA D MAN
DISTASTE	*DOMESDAY	DOWSABEL	DUBONNET	BE D AMN
DISTAVES	DOMESTIC	*DOXOLOGY	*DUCKBILL	BE D AUB
DISTINCT	DOMICILE	*DOZINESS	*DUCKIEST	BE D BUG
DISTRACT	DOMINANT	DRABNESS	*DUCKLING	BE D DED
DISTRAIN	DOMINATE	DRACAENA	*DUCKTAIL	BE D DER
DISTRAIT	DOMINEER	DRACONIC	*DUCKWEED	*BE D ECK
DISTRESS	*DOMINICK	*DRAFFISH	DUCTLESS	BE D ELL
DISTRICT	DOMINION	DRAFTING	*DUDISHLY	BE D LAM
DISTRUST	DOMINIUM	DRAGGIER	DUECENTO	BE D PAN
DISULFID	DONATION	DRAGGING	DUELLING	BE D RID
DISUNION	DONATIVE	DRAGLINE	DUELLIST	BE D RUG
DISUNITE	DONENESS	DRAGONET	DUETTIST	BE D UIN
DISUNITY	DONNERED	DRAGROPE	DULCETLY	BE D UMB
DISVALUE	*DOOMSDAY	DRAGSTER	DULCIANA	BI D DEN
DITHEISM	DOOMSTER	DRAINAGE	DULCIMER	BI D DER
DITHEIST	DOORBELL	DRAMATIC	DULCINEA	BO D EGA
DIURESIS	*DOORJAMB	DRAMMING	DULLNESS	BO D ICE
DIURETIC	*DOORKNOB	*DRAMMOCK	*DUMBBELL	BO D IED
DIVAGATE	DOORLESS	*DRAMSHOP	DUMBNESS	BO D IES
DIVALENT	DOORNAIL	*DRAUGHTY	*DUMFOUND	BO D ILY
DIVERTER	DOORPOST	*DRAWBACK	*DUMMKOPF	BO D ING
DIVIDEND	DOORSILL	DRAWBORE	*DUMPCART	BO D KIN
DIVIDING	DOORSTEP	*DRAWDOWN	DUMPIEST	BU D DER
DIVIDUAL	DOORSTOP	DRAWTUBE	DUMPLING	BU D DLE
DIVINING	DOORYARD	DREADFUL	DUNELAND	BU D GER
DIVINISE	DOPAMINE	DREAMFUL	DUNGAREE	BU D GET
*DIVINITY	DOPESTER	DREDGING	DUNGHILL	BU D GIE
*DIVINIZE	DOPINESS	DRENCHER	DUODENUM	CA D DIE
DIVISION	*DORMANCY	DRESSAGE	DUOLOGUE	CA D DIS
*DIVISIVE	DORMIENT	DRESSING	DUOPSONY	CA D ENT
DIVORCEE	DORMOUSE	DRIBBLER	*DUPLEXER	CA D GER
DIVORCER	DORSALLY	DRIBBLET	DURABLES	CE D ING
DIVULGER	DOSSERET	DRIFTAGE	DURATION	CE D ULA
*DIZYGOUS	DOTATION	DRIFTPIN	DURATIVE	CO D DER
*DJELLABA	DOTINGLY	DRILLING	DURATIVE	CO D DLE
DOCILITY	DOTTEREL	DRIPLESS	DUSTHEAP	CO D EIA
*DOCKHAND	DOTTIEST	DRIPPING	DUSTIEST	CO D EIN
*DOCKLAND	DOUBLING	DRIVELER	DUSTLESS	CO D GER
*DOCKSIDE	DOUBLOON	*DRIVEWAY	DUSTLIKE	*CO D IFY
*DOCKYARD	DOUBLURE	DROLLERY	*DUTCHMAN	CO D ING
DOCTORAL	DOUBTFUL	*DROPHEAD	DUTIABLE	CO D LIN
DOCTRINE	*DOUGHBOY	*DROPKICK	DUVETINE	

CU D DIE	LO D GER	RE D DLE	WA D MEL	CO D EINA
CU D DLE	MA D RAS	RE D EAR	WA D MOL	CO D EINE
CU D DLY	MA D URO	RE D EEM	WA D SET	*CO D FISH
CU D GEL	ME D IAL	RE D EFY	WE D DER	CO D ICES
DA D DLE	ME D IAN	RE D ENY	WE D ELN	CO D ICIL
DE D ANS	*ME D ICK	RE D EYE	WE D GIE	CO D LING
DE D UCE	ME D LAR	RE D FIN	WI D DER	CU D BEAR
DE D UCT	MI D AIR	RE D LEG	WI D DIE	CU D DIES
DI D ACT	*MI D WAY	RE D OCK	WI D DLE	CU D WEED
DI D DLE	MO D ERN	RE D OUT	WI D EST	DA D AISM
DI D IES	MO D EST	RE D OWA	WI D GET	DA D AIST
DO D DER	*MO D IFY	RE D RAW	WI D ISH	DEPAINT
DO D GER	MO D ULE	RE D TOP	YO D LER	DI D DLER
DU D DIE	MO D ULO	RE D UCE	*ZA D DIK	DO D DERY
DU D EEN	NI D GET	RI D DED	*ZO D IAC	DO D GERY
DU D ISH	NI D IFY	RI D DEN	BA D GING	DO D GING
FE D ORA	NI D ING	RI D DER	BA D LAND	DO D OISM
FI D DLE	NO D DED	RI D DLE	BA D NESS	DU D GEON
FI D GET	NO D DER	RI D ENT	BE D DING	FA D ABLE
FO D DER	NO D DLE	RI D GEL	BE D EMAN	FA D DIER
FO D GEL	NO D OSE	RI D GIL	BE D EVIL	FA D DING
FU D DLE	NO D OUS	RI D ING	BE D FAST	*FA D DISH
GA D DED	NO D ULE	RI D LEY	BE D GOWN	FA D DISM
GA D DER	NU D EST	RO D ENT	BE D IGHT	FA D DIST
GA D FLY	NU D GER	RO D MAN	BE D IRTY	FE D AYEE
GA D GET	NU D ISM	RU D DER	*BE D IZEN	FE D ERAL
GA D OID	NU D IST	RU D DLE	BE D LAMP	FI D DLER
GI D DAP	NU D ITY	RU D EST	BE D LESS	FI D EISM
GO D DAM	NU D NIK	SA D DEN	BE D LIKE	*FI D GETY
GO D DED	PA D AUK	SA D DHU	BE D MATE	FI D GING
GO D OWN	PA D DLE	SA D DLE	BE D OUIN	GA D DING
GO D SON	PA D NAG	SA D ISM	BE D POST	GA D ROON
GO D WIT	PA D OUK	SA D IST	BE D RAIL	GA D WALL
*HA D JEE	PE D ANT	SE D ATE	BE D RAPE	GO D DAMN
HA D RON	PE D ATE	SE D ILE	*BE D ROCK	GO D DESS
HE D DLE	PE D DLE	SE D UCE	BE D ROLL	GO D DING
HE D GER	PE D LAR	SI D DUR	BE D ROOM	GO D HEAD
HI D DEN	PI D DLE	SI D ING	BE D SIDE	GO D HOOD
HI D ING	PI D GIN	SI D LER	BE D SORE	GO D LESS
HO D DEN	PO D ITE	SO D DED	BE D TICK	GO D LIER
HO D DIN	PO D IUM	SO D DEN	BE D TIME	GO D LIKE
HU D DLE	PO D SOL	SO D IUM	BE D UNCE	GO D LING
HY D RIA	*PO D ZOL	SO D OMY	BE D WARD	GO D ROON
*HY D RIC	PU D DLE	SU D ARY	*BE D WARF	GO D SEND
HY D RID	PU D DLY	SU D DEN	BI D ARKA	GO D SHIP
*JA D ISH	RA D DLE	SU D SER	BI D DING	GU D GEON
*JU D DER	RA D IAL	TE D DER	BU D DIES	HA D ARIM
*JU D GER	RA D IAN	TE D IUM	BU D DING	HA D DEST
*JU D OKA	RA D ISH	TI D BIT	BU D GING	*HA D DOCK
*KE D DAH	RA D IUM	TI D DLY	BU D LESS	HE D GING
KI D DER	RA D IUS	TI D IER	BU D LIKE	HE D ONIC
KI D DIE	RA D OME	TI D IES	CA D AVER	HI D ABLE
KI D NAP	RA D ULA	TI D ILY	CA D DICE	HI D ALGO
KI D NEY	RE D ACT	TI D ING	CA D DISH	HI D EOUS
LA D DER	RE D ATE	TO D DLE	CA D ELLE	HI D EOUT
LA D DIE	RE D BAY	VA D OSE	CA D ENCE	*HO D ADDY
LA D IES	RE D BUD	WA D DER	*CA D ENCY	HU D DLER
LA D ING	RE D BUG	WA D DIE	*CA D ENZA	*HY D ATID
LA D INO	RE D CAP	WA D DLE	CA D MIUM	HY D RANT
LA D LER	RE D DED	WA D DLY	CE D ILLA	HY D RASE
LA D RON	RE D DEN	WA D MAL	CO D ABLE	HY D RATE
LE D GER	RE D DER		CO D DLER	

*HY D RIDE	RA D IANT	TO D DLER	*CAN D IDLY	*FEE D BACK
*HY D ROID	RA D IATE	VE D ALIA	*CAR D AMOM	FEL D SPAR
*HY D ROPS	RA D ICAL	VE D ETTE	CAR D AMON	*FOL D AWAY
HY D ROUS	RA D ICEL	VI D ETTE	*CAR D AMUM	FOL D BOAT
*HY D ROXY	RA D ICES	VI D ICON	CAR D CASE	FOL D EROL
*JA D EITE	RA D ICLE	VI D UITY	CAR D IGAN	FON D LING
*JO D HPUR	RE D BAIT	WA D ABLE	CAR D INAL	FON D NESS
*JU D OIST	RE D BIRD	WA D DIED	CAR D IOID	FOR D LESS
*KA D DISH	RE D BONE	WA D DIES	CAR D ITIS	GAR D ENER
KI D DIES	RE D COAT	WA D DING	CAU D ATED	GAR D ENIA
KI D DING	RE D DEST	WA D DLER	CAU D ILLO	GAR D YLOO
*KI D DISH	RE D DING	WA D MAAL	*CHA D ARIM	GEN D ARME
*KI D DUSH	RE D DISH	WA D MOLL	*CHE D DITE	GEO D ESIC
*KI D LIKE	RE D FISH	WE D DING	CLA D DING	GEO D ETIC
*KI D SKIN	RE D HEAD	*WE D LOCK	CLO D PATE	GIL D HALL
LA D ANUM	RE D NECK	WI D ENER	CLO D POLE	GLA D DEST
LA D RONE	RE D NESS	WI D GEON	CLO D POLL	GLA D DING
LA D YBUG	RE D OUBT	WI D OWER	COA D MIRE	GLA D IATE
LA D YISH	RE D OUND	YO D ELER	COE D ITOR	GLA D IEST
*LA D YKIN	RE D POLL	*ZE D OARY	COL D NESS	GLA D IOLA
LI D LESS	RE D RAFT	*BAI D ARKA	CON D ENSE	GLA D IOLI
LO D GING	RE D RESS	*BAL D HEAD	CON D OLER	GLA D NESS
LY D DITE	RE D RIED	BAL D NESS	CON D ONER	GLA D SOME
MA D HOUS	RE D RIES	BAL D PATE	CON D UCER	GOA D LIKE
MA D RIGA	RE D RILL	*BAL D RICK	COR D LESS	*GOL D FISH
*MA D ZOON	RE D RIVE	BAN D AGER	*COR D LIKE	GOO D NESS
ME D DUSA	RE D ROOT	BAN D ANNA	COR D OVAN	*GOO D WIFE
*ME D IACY	RE D SKIN	BAN D EROL	COR D UROY	GOO D WILL
MI D LING	RE D UCER	BAN D ITRY	COR D WAIN	GRA D IENT
*MI D RIFF	RE D WARE	BAN D SMAN	*COR D WOOD	GRA D UAND
*MI D SHIP	RE D WING	*BAU D EKIN	CRE D ENCE	GRA D UATE
*MI D WEEK	RE D WOOD	BAU D RONS	CRE D ENDA	GRI D IRON
*MI D WIFE	RI D ABLE	BAW D IEST	*CRE D ENZA	GUI D ANCE
MO D ISTE	RI D DING	BEA D IEST	CRE D IBLE	*HAB D ALAH
*MU D FISH	RI D DLER	*BEA D LIKE	CRE D ITOR	HAN D BALL
*MU D ROCK	RI D GIER	BEA D ROLL	CUR D IEST	HAN D BILL
NO D DIES	RI D GING	BEA D SMAN	*DAN D RIFF	*HAN D BOOK
NO D DING	RI D OTTO	*BEA D WORK	*DAN D RUFF	HAN D CART
NO D ICAL	RO D LESS	*BEN D WAYS	*DAN D YISH	*HAN D CUFF
NU D NICK	RO D LIKE	BEN D WISE	*DAN D YISM	*HAN D FAST
PA D DIES	RO D SMAN	BID D ABLE	*DAY D REAM	*HAN D GRIP
PA D DING	RU D DIER	*BIN D WEED	DEA D BEAT	*HAN D HOLD
PA D DLER	RU D DILY	*BIR D BATH	DEA D ENER	*HAN D ICAP
*PA D DOCK	*RU D DOCK	BIR D CAGE	DEA D FALL	HAN D IEST
*PA D LOCK	RU D ERAL	BIR D CALL	DEA D HEAD	HAN D LING
PA D RONE	RU D ESBY	*BIR D FARM	DEA D LIER	HAN D LIST
*PA D SHAH	SA D DLER	*BIR D LIKE	DEA D LINE	HAN D LOOM
PE D AGOG	SA D IRON	BIR D LIME	*DEA D LOCK	*HAN D MADE
PE D DIES	SA D NESS	BIR D SEED	DEA D NESS	*HAN D MAID
PE D ICAB	SE D ARIM	BIR D SEYE	DEA D WOOD	*HAN D PICK
PE D ICEL	SE D UCER	BLU D GEON	DEE D LESS	HAN D RAIL
PE D ICLE	SI D EARM	*BOL D FACE	DEN D RITE	*HAN D SEWN
PE D LARY	SI D ECAR	BOL D NESS	DEN D ROID	HAN D SFUL
PE D OCAL	SI D EMAN	BON D MAID	DOD D ERER	HAN D SOME
PI D DLER	SI D EWAY	BON D SMAN	DOL D RUMS	*HAN D WORK
*PI D DOCK	SO D DING	BOR D ELLO	DRE D GING	*HAN D WRIT
PO D AGRA	TA D POLE	BOR D ERER	DRU D GERY	*HAN D YMAN
PO D ESTA	TE D IOUS	BRI D ALLY	DUO D ENUM	*HAR D BACK
PU D DING	TI D ERIP	BRI D GING	FAD D IEST	HAR D BALL
PU D DLER	TI D EWAY	BUD D LEIA	FAL D ERAL	HAR D BOOT
*PU D ENCY	TI D IEST	BUN D LING	FAL D EROL	HAR D CASE
RA D IALE	TO D DIES	BUR D ENER	FAN D ANGO	HAR D CORE

HAR D ENER	LAN D SLIP	*PAN D EMIC	SAN D LING	TOA D YISM
*HAR D HACK	LAN D SMAN	PAN D ERER	SAN D PEEP	TRA D ITOR
*HAR D HEAD	LAN D SMAN	*PAN D OWDY	SAN D PILE	TRA D UCER
HAR D IEST	LAN D WARD	PAR D ONER	SAN D SOAP	TRU D GEON
HAR D NESS	LAR D IEST	*PED D LERY	*SAN D WICH	TRU D GING
*HAR D SHIP	LAR D LIKE	PED D LING	SAN D WORM	TWA D DLER
*HAR D TACK	LAU D ABLE	*PEN D ENCY	SAN D WORT	TWI D DLER
*HAR D WARE	LAU D ANUM	PEN D ULUM	SAR D ONIC	VEN D ETTA
*HAR D WOOD	LAU D ATOR	PIE D FORT	*SAR D ONYX	VEN D IBLE
*HAV D ALAH	LEA D IEST	PIE D MONT	SEA D ROME	*VEN D IBLY
*HEA D ACHE	LEA D LESS	PIN D LING	*SEE D CAKE	*VER D ANCY
*HEA D ACHY	LEA D SMAN	PLE D GEOR	SEE D CASE	VER D ERER
*HEA D BAND	*LEA D WORK	PLE D GING	SEE D IEST	VER D EROR
HEA D GATE	LEA D WORT	PON D ERER	SEE D LESS	VER D ITER
HEA D GEAR	LEW D NESS	*PON D WEED	SEE D LIKE	VOI D ANCE
*HEA D HUNT	LOA D STAR	POW D ERER	SEE D LING	VOI D NESS
HEA D IEST	LOR D LESS	PRE D ATOR	SEE D SMAN	WAN D ERER
*HEA D LAMP	LOR D LIER	PRI D EFUL	SEE D TIME	WAN D EROO
HEA D LAND	LOR D LIKE	PRO D IGAL	*SHA D BLOW	*WAR D ENRY
HEA D LESS	LOR D LING	PRO D ROME	*SHA D BUSH	WAR D RESS
HEA D LINE	LOR D OSIS	PRO D UCER	*SHA D CHAN	WAR D ROBE
*HEA D LOCK	LOR D SHIP	PRU D ENCE	*SHA D DOCK	WAR D ROOM
HEA D LONG	LOU D NESS	PUD D LING	SHA D IEST	*WAR D SHIP
HEA D MOST	*MAI D HOOD	PUN D ITRY	*SHA D OWER	WEE D IEST
HEA D NOTE	*MAN D RAKE	*PYO D ERMA	*SHA D RACH	WEE D LESS
HEA D RACE	ME D ALIST	*QUA D RANS	SHE D ABLE	*WEE D LIKE
HEA D REST	ME D ALLIC	*QUA D RANT	SHE D DING	WEL D LESS
HEA D ROOM	ME D IALLY	*QUA D RATE	*SHU D DERY	WEL D MENT
HEA D SAIL	ME D IANLY	*QUA D RIGA	*SKY D IVER	*WHO D UNIT
*HEA D SHIP	ME D IATOR	*QUA D ROON	SLE D DING	*WIL D FIRE
HEA D SMAN	ME D ICAID	*QUI D DITY	*SLI D EWAY	*WIL D FOWL
*HEA D STAY	ME D ICARE	*QUI D NUNC	SMI D GEON	*WIL D LIFE
*HEA D WIND	ME D ICATE	RAN D OMLY	SOD D ENLY	WIL D LING
*HEA D WORD	ME D ICINE	REA D DICT	SOL D ERER	WIL D NESS
*HEA D WORK	ME D ICATE	REA D IEST	SOL D IERY	*WIL D WOOD
*HEB D OMAD	ME D IEVAL	*REA D JUST	SPA D EFUL	WIN D BURN
HEE D LESS	ME D IOCRE	REE D BIRD	SPA D ICES	*WIN D FALL
HER D LIKE	ME D ITATE	*REE D BUCK	SPA D ILLE	*WIN D FLAW
HER D SMAN	ME D USOID	REE D IEST	STE D FAST	WIN D GALL
HIN D ERER	MI D BRAIN	REE D LING	*STU D BOOK	WIN D IEST
HIN D MOST	MI D POINT	REN D ERER	STU D DING	WIN D LASS
*HOL D BACK	MI D RANGE	REN D IBLE	*STU D FISH	WIN D LESS
*HOL D FAST	MI D STORY	*REN D ZINA	STU D IOUS	WIN D LING
*HOL D OVER	MO D ALITY	RHO D AMIN	*STU D WORK	WIN D MILL
HOO D LESS	MO D ELING	RID D ANCE	SUB D EPOT	*WIN D PIPE
*HOO D LIKE	MO D ELLED	ROA D LESS	SUN D ERER	*WIN D SOCK
*HOO D WINK	MO D ELLER	ROA D SIDE	SUN D RIES	*WIN D WARD
KIN D LESS	MO D ERATE	ROA D STER	SUN D ROPS	WON D ERER
KIN D LING	MO D ERATO	*ROA D WORK	*SVE D BERG	WON D ROUS
KIN D NESS	MO D IFIED	RON D ELET	SYN D ESIS	*WOO D BIND
LAB D ANUM	MO D IOLUS	RON D ELLE	SYN D ETIC	WOO D BINE
LAN D FALL	MO D ULATE	*ROW D YISH	SYN D ROME	*WOO D CHAT
LAN D FILL	*MOL D WARP	*ROW D YISM	TEN D ANCE	*WOO D COCK
LAN D FORM	*MOR D ANCY	RUD D IEST	TEN D ENCE	WOO D IEST
LAN D LADY	MU D DIEST	SAD D LERY	TEN D ENCY	WOO D LAND
LAN D LESS	MU D GUARD	SAD D LING	TEN D ERER	*WOO D LARK
LAN D LORD	MU D STONE	SAN D ARAC	TEN D ERLY	WOO D LESS
*LAN D MARK	NEE D IEST	*SAN D BANK	*TOA D FISH	WOO D LORE
LAN D MASS	NEE D LESS	SAN D BURR	*TOA D FLAX	WOO D NOTE
LAN D SIDE	NEE D LING	*SAN D FISH	TOA D LESS	WOO D PILE
*LAN D SKIP	NON D AIRY	SAN D IEST	TOA D LIKE	*WOO D RUFF
LAN D SLID	PAD D LING	SAN D LIKE	*TOA D YISH	*WOO D SHED
	PAN D ANUS			

WOO D SMAN
*WOO D WIND
*WOO D WORK
*WOO D WORM
*WOR D BOOK
WOR D IEST
WOR D LESS
*WOR D PLAY
*YAR D BIRD
*YAR D WAND

BAL D	GOO D	SAR D	BOAR D	HOAR D
BAN D	GOW D	SCA D	BORE D	**HODA D**
BAR D	GRA D	SCU D	**BOVI D**	**HOME D**
BAU D	GRI D	SEE D	BRAI D	HOUN D
BAW D	GUI D	SEN D	BRAN D	**HUMI D**
BEA D	HAN D	SHA D	BREA D	**HYOI D**
BEN D	HAR D	SHE D	BREE D	***JEHA D**
BIN D	HEE D	SHO D	BROA D	**JERI D**
BIR D	HEL D	SIL D	BROO D	***JIHA D**
BOL D	HER D	SKI D	BUIL D	**KNEA D**
BON D	HIN D	SLE D	CAIR D	LAIR D
BRA D	HOL D	SNE D	CASE D	**LAKE D**
BRE D	HOO D	SOL D	CAUL D	LAME D
BUN D	KIN D	SOR D	**CAVE D**	LATE D
BUR D	LAI D	SPE D	**CEBI D**	LIAR D
CAI D	LAN D	SPU D	CERE D	**LIKE D**
CAR D	LAR D	STU D	**CHIL D**	LINE D
CHA D	LAU D	SUD D	**CHOR D**	LIPI D
CLA D	LEA D	SUR D	CLOU D	LIVI D
CLO D	LEN D	TEN D	COUL D	LOVE D
COE D	LEU D	THU D	CREE D	LUCI D
COL D	LEW D	TIE D	CRIE D	LURI D
COR D	LIE D	TOA D	**CROW D**	LUTE D
CRU D	LOA D	TOL D	**CUPI D**	LYAR D
CUR D	LOR D	TRA D	**CYCA D**	MAUN D
DEA D	LOU D	TRO D	DREA D	MENA D
DEE D	MAI D	TUR D	DRIE D	MONA D
DIE D	MEA D	VEL D	DRUI D	**MOPE D**
DUA D	MEE D	VEN D	**DRYA D**	MOUL D
DYA D	MEL D	VOI D	FARA D	MOUN D
FAR D	MEN D	WAN D	FAUL D	**MOVE D**
FEE D	MIL D	WAR D	FELI D	**MUCI D**
FEN D	MOL D	WEE D	FETI D	MURI D
FEO D	MOO D	WEL D	FIEL D	**MYOI D**
FEU D	NAR D	WEN D	FIEN D	NAIA D
FIN D	NEE D	**WHI D**	FIOR D	**NAKE D**
FLE D	PAI D	WIL D	FIRE D	NALE D
FOL D	PAR D	WIN D	***FJEL D**	NITI D
FON D	PEN D	WOA D	***FJOR D**	NOMA D
FOO D	PIE D	WOL D	FLIE D	NOSE D
FOR D	PLE D	WOO D	FLUI D	NOTE D
FUN D	PLO D	WOR D	FOUN D	PAGE D
GAU D	PON D	**WYN D**	FRAU D	PAGO D
GEL D	POO D	YAL D	FREE D	**PAVI D**
GIL D	PRO D	YAR D	**FREM D**	PILE D
GIR D	**QAI D**	YAU D	FRIE D	PINE D
GLA D	**QUA D**	YEL D	FRON D	PLAI D
GLE D	**QUI D**	YIR D	GADI D	PLEA D
GOA D	**QUO D**	YON D	GELI D	PLIE D
GOL D	RAI D	BASE D	GEOI D	POIN D
	RAN D	BEAR D	GLAN D	POLE D
	REA D	BIEL D	GLEE D	POUN D
	RED D	**BIFI D**	GONA D	PRIE D
	REE D	**BIPE D**	GOUR D	PROU D
	REN D	**BIPO D**	GRAN D	**PYOI D**
	RIN D	BLAN D	GREE D	RABI D
	ROA D	BLEE D	GRIN D	RANI D
	ROO D	BLEN D	GUAR D	RAPI D
	RUD D	BLIN D	GUIL D	READ D
	RYN D	BLON D	HALI D	REBI D
	SAI D	BLOO D	***HEXA D**	REDI D
	SAN D	BLUE D		RESI D

RIGI D	WEAL D	**COGGE D**	**FUNNE D**	**KITTE D**
ROSE D	WEIR D	**CONNE D**	**FURRE D**	**KOBOL D**
ROUN D	WIEL D	**CONOI D**	**GABBE D**	LAGEN D
ROUN D	WISE D	**COPIE D**	**GADDE D**	LAGGE D
SALA D	WOAL D	**COPPE D**	GADOI D	**LAMME D**
SAPI D	WORL D	**COWAR D**	**GAGGE D**	**LAMPA D**
SARO D	WOUL D	**CUBOI D**	**GAMME D**	**LAPPE D**
SAYI D	WOUN D	**CUPPE D**	GANOI D	*LAZIE D*
SCAL D	WRIE D	**CURSE D**	**GAPPE D**	**LEAVE D**
SCEN D	YAIR D	**CUSPI D**	GARRE D	LEGEN D
SCOL D	YAUL D	**CYANI D**	GASSE D	**LEGGE D**
SCRO D	YIEL D	**CYMOI D**	GELLE D	**LETTE D**
SHAR D	*ZOOI D*	**DAMME D**	**GEMME D**	**LEVIE D**
SHEN D	**BABIE D**	**DAMNE D**	GERUN D	LIGAN D
SHER D	**BAGGE D**	**DAPPE D**	**GIGGE D**	LILIE D
SHIE D	**BALLA D**	DARNE D	GINNE D	**LIMPI D**
SHRE D	**BANNE D**	**DAYBE D**	**GOBBE D**	LIPOI D
SIDE D	**BARRE D**	**DEFEN D**	**GODDE D**	**LIPPE D**
SKAL D	**BATTE D**	**DEFIE D**	**GRAVI D**	*LIQUI D*
SKIE D	**BAYAR D**	DELEA D	**GROUN D**	*LIZAR D*
SLOI D	**BEDDE D**	**DEMAN D**	**GUMME D**	**LOBBE D**
SLOJ D	**BEDRI D**	DENIE D	GUNNE D	**LOGGE D**
SLOY D	**BEGGE D**	DENNE D	**GUTTE D**	**LOOSE D**
SNOO D	**BEGIR D**	**DEPEN D**	**HAGGE D**	**LOPPE D**
SOLE D	**BEGLA D**	DESAN D	**HAIRE D**	LOTTE D
SOLI D	**BEHEA D**	**DESMI D**	**HALOI D**	**LUGGE D**
SOLI D	**BEHEL D**	**DEVOI D**	**HAMME D**	**MADDE D**
SOUN D	**BEHIN D**	**DIACI D**	**HAPPE D**	**MAENA D**
SPEE D	**BEHOL D**	**DIGGE D**	**HATRE D**	**MALFE D**
SPEN D	**BELAU D**	**DIMME D**	**HATTE D**	MALTE D
SPIE D	**BESTU D**	DINNE D	*HAZAR D*	**MANNE D**
SQUA D	**BETTE D**	*DIOXI D*	**HEMME D**	MANTI D
SQUI D	**BEYON D**	**DIPPE D**	**HEMOI D**	**MAPPE D**
STAI D	**BIBBE D**	**DISBU D**	**HEPTA D**	MARAU D
STAN D	**BIFOL D**	**DOGGE D**	**HERAL D**	MARRE D
STEA D	**BINNE D**	DOILE D	**HIPPE D**	*MASJI D*
STEE D	**BITTE D**	DOITE D	**HISPI D**	**MATTE D**
STIE D	**BODIE D**	DONNE D	**HOGGE D**	*MAZAR D*
STOO D	**BOGGE D**	DOODA D	**HOLAR D**	**MEDIA D**
SWAR D	**BOYAR D**	DORSA D	**HONIE D**	MELOI D
SWOR D	**BRIAR D**	DOTAR D	**HOOPE D**	**METHO D**
SYNO D	**BROMI D**	DOTTE D	**HORRI D**	**MILOR D**
TABI D	**BUGGE D**	**DROWN D**	**HOTBE D**	**MISAD D**
TEII D	**BUMME D**	DUNNE D	**HOTRO D**	MONIE D
TEIN D	**BURIE D**	**DUPPE D**	**HOTTE D**	**MOPPE D**
TEPI D	**BURRE D**	DURNE D	**HUGGE D**	**MORBI D**
THIR D	**BUSIE D**	**FANNE D**	**HUMME D**	**MUCOI D**
TIMI D	**BUSSE D**	**FANTO D**	**HUTTE D**	**MUGGE D**
TIRE D	**BYROA D**	**FATTE D**	*HYBRI D*	**MUMME D**
TREA D	*BYWOR D*	**FECUN D**	**HYDRI D**	**MUSCI D**
TREN D	CANAR D	**FERVI D**	*JAGGE D*	*MUSJI D*
TRIA D	**CANDI D**	**FETTE D**	*JAMME D*	**MYRIA D**
TRIE D	CANNE D	**FINNE D**	JARRE D	*MYXOI D*
TRUE D	**CAPPE D**	**FITTE D**	JASSI D	**NAPPE D**
TUMI D	**CAPSI D**	**FOETI D**	**JEREE D**	**NAVAI D**
TWEE D	**CATTE D**	**FOGGE D**	JERRI D	**NEREI D**
TYPE D	**CAUDA D**	**FORBI D**	**JETTE D**	**NETTE D**
VALI D	**CEBOI D**	**FRIEN D**	*JOCUN D*	**NIMME D**
VAPI D	**CHIEL D**	**FRIGI D**	*JUGGE D*	**NIMRO D**
VIAN D	CITIE D	**FUCOI D**	**KELOI D**	**NITRI D**
VIRI D	**CLERI D**	**FUGGE D**	**KENNE D**	**NODDE D**
VIVI D	**COCCI D**	**FULGI D**	*KEPPE D*	**NORME D**

NUTTE D	RESAI D	SUNNE D	**BANDIE D**	***CHOPPE D**
PALLE D	RESEE D	**SUPPE D**	**BARMAI D**	**CHOROI D**
PALLI D	RESEN D	**SWOUN D**	**BARTEN D**	***CICHLI D**
PANNE D	RESOL D	TABAR D	**BASTAR D**	**CIRSOI D**
PARRE D	RETAR D	**TABBE D**	**BAUSON D**	**CISSOI D**
PATTE D	RETOL D	TAGGE D	***BAYWOO D**	**CLAMME D**
PEGGE D	RETTE D	TANNE D	**BEBLOO D**	**CLOTTE D**
PENNE D	**REVVE D**	**TAPPE D**	**BECLOU D**	**CLUPEI D**
PENTA D	**REWAR D**	TARRE D	***BECROW D**	**COCCOI D**
PEPPE D	**REWEL D**	TATTE D	**BEDWAR D**	**COLLAR D**
PEPTI D	**REWIN D**	TECHE D	**BELACE D**	**COLLIE D**
PERIO D	**REWOR D**	TETRA D	**BELATE D**	**COLLOI D**
PETAR D	RIBAL D	**THREA D**	**BELLIE D**	**COLORE D**
PETTE D	RIBAN D	TIDIE D	**BELOVE D**	**COMMAN D**
PIGGE D	**RIBBE D**	TINEI D	**BEROBE D**	**COMMEN D**
PINNE D	RIDDE D	TINNE D	**BESTEA D**	**COMPEN D**
PIPPE D	RIGGE D	**TIPPE D**	**BIGHEA D**	**CONCOR D**
PITIE D	**RIMME D**	TOGGE D	**BIGOTE D**	**CONTEN D**
PITTE D	**RIPPE D**	TOLUI D	**BILOBE D**	**COPEPO D**
PLACI D	RITAR D	**TOMCO D**	**BILSTE D**	**CORNFE D**
PLATE D	ROBAN D	**TOPPE D**	**BLATTE D**	**COSTAR D**
PLEIA D	**ROBBE D**	TOROI D	**BLESSE D**	***COWBIN D**
PONGI D	ROTTE D	TORPI D	**BLOTTE D**	***COWBIR D**
PONIE D	ROTUN D	TORRI D	**BLOWSE D**	***COWHAN D**
POPPE D	**RUBBE D**	TOTTE D	***BLOWZE D**	***COWHER D**
POTTE D	RUBIE D	**TOWAR D**	**BOBSLE D**	***COWSHE D**
PREME D	RUGGE D	TREPI D	**BOGWOO D**	**CRAMME D**
PSOCI D	RUTTE D	**TRIFI D**	**BOLLAR D**	**CRAWDA D**
PUGGE D	**SABBE D**	TRIPO D	**BOMBAR D**	**CRICOI D**
PUNNE D	SACRE D	**TUBBE D**	**BOOKEN D**	**CRINOI D**
PUPPE D	SAGGE D	TUNNE D	***BOWHEA D**	**CROOKE D**
PURRE D	**SAIYI D**	**TUPPE D**	***BOXWOO D**	**CROPPE D**
PUTRI D	SALPI D	TURBI D	***BOYHOO D**	**CTENOI D**
RAGGE D	**SAPPE D**	TURGI D	**BRANNE D**	***CUCKOL D**
RAMME D	**SAYYI D**	TUTTE D	**BRIGAN D**	**CUDWEE D**
RAMRO D	SCREE D	**VARIE D**	**BRIMME D**	**CULICI D**
RANCI D	SEABE D	**VATTE D**	**BRINDE D**	**CULLIE D**
RAPPE D	SECON D	**VAWAR D**	**BUGSEE D**	**CURRIE D**
RATTE D	SECUN D	**VERBI D**	**BULLIE D**	**CUSTAR D**
REBIN D	**SHAIR D**	**VESPI D**	**BURSEE D**	***CYCLOI D**
RECLA D	**SHALE D**	**VETTE D**	**BURWEE D**	**CYSTOI D**
RECOR D	**SHIEL D**	VISAR D	**BUSTAR D**	DASTAR D
REDBU D	**SHOUL D**	VISCI D	***BUZZAR D**	**DECAPO D**
REDDE D	**SHREW D**	***VIZAR D**	**CANDIE D**	**DECRIE D**
REFEE D	**SHROU D**	WAGGE D	**CARABI D**	**DEFRAU D**
REFFE D	**SINNE D**	WANNE D	**CARLOA D**	**DEIFIE D**
REFIN D	**SIPPE D**	WARRE D	**CAROTI D**	**DELTOI D**
REFOL D	SODDE D	***WEBFE D**	**CARRIE D**	**DEMIGO D**
REFUN D	SOGGE D	WETTE D	**CATBIR D**	**DENTOI D**
REGAR D	SOLAN D	***WICKE D**	**CATHEA D**	**DEODAN D**
REGIL D	**SOPPE D**	WIGGE D	**CERATE D**	**DERMOI D**
RELEN D	SORDI D	WINNE D	**CESTOI D**	**DESCEN D**
RELIE D	SPARI D	WITTE D	***CHALCI D**	**DESMOI D**
RELOA D	SPREA D	***WIZAR D**	***CHAPPE D**	**DESPON D**
REMAN D	STOLI D	WONNE D	**CHARRE D**	**DIALLE D**
REMEN D	STOUN D	***XYLOI D**	**CHELOI D**	**DIAMON D**
REMIN D	STRAN D	**YAPPE D**	***CHEVIE D**	**DIAPSI D**
REMOL D	STROU D	**YESSE D**	**CHILIA D**	**DIEHAR D**
REPAI D	STUPI D	**YIPPE D**	**CHINNE D**	**DIPLOI D**
REPAN D	**SUBBE D**	***ZONKE D**	***CHIPPE D**	**DISBAN D**
REPPE D	**SULFI D**	**BADLAN D**	**CHLORI D**	**DISCAR D**
REREA D	**SUMME D**			**DISCOI D**

DISCOR D	HAEMOI D	MANGOL D	PLASMI D	SAGGAR D
DISPEN D	HAGGAR D	MANHOO D	PLASTI D	SALLIE D
DISTEN D	HALBER D	MANKIN D	PLATTE D	SAPHEA D
DOGSLE D	HALYAR D	MANSAR D	PLEOPO D	SAPWOO D
DOGWOO D	HAPLOI D	MANWAR D	PLOTTE D	SARCOI D
DOLLIE D	HARRIE D	MARRIE D	*PLYWOO D	SATYRI D
DONNER D	HATBAN D	MASTOI D	*POCHAR D	SCANNE D
DRAMME D	HAYSEE D	MATTOI D	POLLAR D	SCARRE D
DROMON D	*HAYWAR D	*MAYWEE D	*POLYPO D	SCATTE D
DROPPE D	HELIPA D	*MAZZAR D	PONIAR D	SCUMME D
DRUMME D	HISTOI D	MEGAPO D	*POPEYE D	SEABIR D
DUELLE D	*HOGWEE D	MERMAI D	POPPIE D	SEAFOO D
DULLAR D	HOLLAN D	MIDLAN D	PORTEN D	SEAWAR D
*DYEWEE D	HOMINI D	MINUEN D	POTHEA D	SEAWEE D
*DYEWOO D	*HOPHEA D	MISBIN D	POULAR D	SEEDBE D
FACIEN D	HOPTOA D	MISDEE D	PREAGE D	SEEDPO D
FANCIE D	HOTHEA D	MISLEA D	PREBEN D	*SHAMME D
FANFOL D	HUNDRE D	MISREA D	PREBIN D	SHINNE D
FATBIR D	HUSBAN D	MISSEN D	PREPAI D	*SHIPPE D
FATHEA D	HYALOI D	MISSHO D	PREPPE D	*SHOPPE D
FERRIE D	*HYDATI D	MISTEN D	PRESOL D	SHOTTE D
FIBROI D	*HYDROI D	MISWOR D	PRETEN D	SIALOI D
FLACDI D	*HYPNOI D	MONACI D	PRIMME D	*SICKBE D
*FLAMME D	*JAYBIR D	MONEYE D	PROBAN D	SIGANI D
*FLAPPE D	*JEOPAR D	MUDDIE D	PROCEE D	SIGMOI D
FLATBE D	*JERREE D	MUMMIE D	PROPEN D	SILURI D
FLATTE D	*JETBEA D	MUSTAR D	PROPPE D	SIMIOI D
*FLIPPE D	*JETTIE D	MYELOI D	PROTEI D	*SIXFOL D
FLUORI D	*JOLLIE D	NEGROI D	PROTEN D	SKINNE D
FOOTPA D	*JUGHEA D	NEUROI D	PSYLLI D	*SKIPPE D
FORFEN D	*KATYDI D	NIGGAR D	PUTTIE D	*SKYWAR D
FORWAR D	*KEYWOR D	NOCTUI D	PYRALI D	SLAPPE D
FOULAR D	KILORA D	NONACI D	*PYRAMI D	SLATTE D
FRACTE D	KINDRE D	NONFOO D	*QUERIE D	SLIMME D
FRETTE D	KNEEPA D	NONSKE D	*QUINOI D	SLIPPE D
FRITTE D	LABROI D	NONSKI D	*QUITTE D	SLITTE D
FROGGE D	LAGGAR D	NORLAN D	RAGWEE D	SLOPPE D
FROSTE D	LALLAN D	NUTWOO D	RALLIE D	SLOTTE D
FROWAR D	LANATE D	PAGURI D	READIE D	SLUGGE D
FUNGOI D	LANGUI D	PANDIE D	REBOAR D	SLUMME D
GABBAR D	LANIAR D	PAROTI D	REBOUN D	SLURRE D
GARLAN D	*LANYAR D	PARRIE D	REBUIL D	SMARAG D
*GIZZAR D	LATERA D	PARTIE D	REDBIR D	SMUTTE D
GLENOI D	LEEWAR D	PAYLOA D	REDHEA D	SNAPPE D
GLOBOI D	LENTOI D	PEASCO D	REDOUN D	SNIPPE D
GLOCHI D	LEOPAR D	PERACI D	REDRIE D	SPANNE D
GLORIE D	LEOTAR D	PERCOI D	REDWOO D	SPAROI D
GLUTTE D	LEPORI D	*PEROXI D	REFLOO D	SPARRE D
GNARRE D	LIANOI D	PERPEN D	REFOUN D	SPATTE D
GOBIOI D	LIMITE D	*PHASMI D	REGRIN D	SPIROI D
GODHEA D	LINGCO D	*PHYTOI D	RESCIN D	SPITTE D
GODHOO D	LINSEE D	PIEBAL D	RESOUN D	SPOROI D
GODSEN D	LITHOI D	PIGWEE D	RESPON D	SPURRE D
GOLIAR D	LOBATE D	PINFOL D	RETREA D	*SQUALI D
GORMAN D	LOGWOO D	PINGUI D	REWOUN D	STAGGE D
GRANDA D	LOWBRE D	PINHEA D	REYNAR D	STARRE D
GRINNE D	LOWLAN D	PINWEE D	*RHIZOI D	STEMME D
GRIPPE D	LUNATE D	PITHEA D	RIBBAN D	STEPPE D
GUISAR D	*LYCOPO D	PLACAR D	RIMLAN D	STEROI D
GUMWEE D	LYRATE D	PLACOI D	RIPCOR D	STEWAR D
GUMWOO D	MALLAR D	PLAFON D	ROADBE D	STIPEN D
GURNAR D		PLANNE D	ROSEBU D	STIRRE D

STOPPE D	WARLOR D	*BLIZZAR D	*CONCHOI D	FILARII D
STORIE D	*WAXWEE D	BLOODIE D	CONELRA D	*FILMCAR D
STUDIE D	*WAYWAR D	BLOODRE D	CONFOUN D	FILMLAN D
STUMME D	WEARIE D	*BLOWHAR D	*COPYHOL D	FIREBIR D
STUNNE D	WEASAN D	BLUEBIR D	CORACOI D	*FIREWEE D
STYLOI D	*WEAZAN D	BLUEHEA D	*CORDWOO D	*FIREWOO D
SUBACI D	*WEEKEN D	BLUEWEE D	*CORKWOO D	*FISHPON D
SUBARI D	WERGEL D	BLUEWOO D	CORNUTE D	FISSIPE D
SUBHEA D	WERGIL D	BOATLOA D	COTYLOI D	*FIVEFOL D
SUBTEN D	WESSAN D	BOATYAR D	COVERLI D	FLANCAR D
SUCCEE D	WETLAN D	BOLTHEA D	CRANNIE D	*FLATHEA D
SULPHI D	*WHIPPE D	*BOMBLOA D	CRENATE D	FLATLAN D
SUMMAN D	WHIRRE D	*BOMBYCI D	*CRIBBLE D	*FLAXSEE D
SUNBIR D	*WHIZZE D	BONDMAI D	CRICETI D	*FOGBOUN D
SUNLAN D	WILLIE D	BONEHEA D	CROPLAN D	*FOOTHOL D
SUNWAR D	WORRIE D	BONEYAR D	CUNEATE D	FORELAN D
SUSPEN D	WORSTE D	BOTRYOI D	*CUPBOAR D	FORESAI D
SWAGGE D	*XIPHOI D	BRASSAR D	CUSSWOR D	*FOREWOR D
SWANNE D	*YCLEPE D	BRINDLE D	*CYANAMI D	*FOREYAR D
SWATTE D	*ZEBROI D	*BULKHEA D	*CYPRINI D	*FOURFOL D
*SYLPHI D	*ZINCKE D	BULLHEA D	DANEGEL D	*FOXHOUN D
*SYRPHI D	*ZINCOI D	BULLWEE D	DANEWEE D	*FREEHAN D
TABANI D	*ZONATE D	BUSHLAN D	DEADHEA D	*FREEHOL D
TABBIE D	*BABYHOO D	*BUZZWOR D	DEADWOO D	FREELOA D
TABLOI D	*BACCATE D	CABALLE D	DEERWEE D	FURIBUN D
TALIPE D	*BACKBEN D	*CABOCHE D	DEERYAR D	GALLIAR D
TALLIE D	*BACKHAN D	*CABOSHE D	DEFERRE D	GANGLAN D
TANKAR D	*BACKSLI D	CABSTAN D	DEMURRE D	GAPESEE D
TANYAR D	*BACKWAR D	CANALLE D	DENDROI D	GARBOAR D
TARRIE D	*BACKWOO D	CANCROI D	*DEFLEXE D	GASIFIE D
TARWEE D	*BACKYAR D	CANFIEL D	DENTATE D	GATEFOL D
*TAXPAI D	*BALDHEA D	CARANGI D	DETERRE D	GEEPOUN D
TELFOR D	BAREHEA D	CARDIOI D	DEVILLE D	GILTHEA D
TENFOL D	BARNYAR D	CAROLLE D	*DIHYBRI D	GIRLHOO D
TETCHE D	BASSWOO D	CARTLOA D	DIPLOPO D	GLOBATE D
THEROI D	*BECOWAR D	CARYATI D	DISPREA D	GOATHER D
THINNE D	BEDOTTE D	CATENOI D	DISULFI D	*GODCHIL D
THYROI D	BEDSTAN D	CAUDATE D	DIVIDEN D	GOURMAN D
TIERCE D	BEDSTEA D	CENTROI D	*DOCKHAN D	GRADUAN D
TOADIE D	BEEBREA D	*CEPHALA D	*DOCKLAN D	GRANDDA D
TOEHOL D	*BEEFWOO D	CERATOI D	*DOCKYAR D	GROUPOI D
TOGATE D	BEFRIEN D	*CHARACI D	DOGGONE D	GRUELLE D
TOWHEA D	BELLBIR D	*CHENOPO D	DONNERE D	*GULFWEE D
TOWMON D	BENTWOO D	*CHILDBE D	DOORYAR D	GUTTATE D
TRAMME D	BERINGE D	*CHILOPO D	DOWNTRO D	*GYNECOI D
TRAPPE D	BEROUGE D	CHOREOI D	*DOWNWAR D	HAIRBAN D
TRIACI D	BESHROU D	CHORIOI D	*DOWNWIN D	HALLIAR D
TRICLA D	BESLAVE D	CHRESAR D	*DROPHEA D	*HANDHOL D
TRIFOL D	BESPREA D	CILIATE D	*DRUMHEA D	*HANDMAI D
TRIMME D	BEUNCLE D	CIRRIPE D	DRUNKAR D	*HANGBIR D
*TRIOXI D	*BEWINGE D	*CITYFIE D	*DUCKWEE D	*HARDHEA D
TRIPPE D	*BICUSPI D	*CITYWAR D	*DUMFOUN D	*HARDWOO D
TROLAN D	*BIFORKE D	*CLUBHAN D	DUNELAN D	*HAULYAR D
TROTTE D	*BIFORME D	CLUPEOI D	FACETTE D	*HAWKWEE D
TWINNE D	BILLFOL D	COALSHE D	*FAHLBAN D	*HEADBAN D
TWITTE D	BILLHEA D	COALYAR D	FAIRLEA D	HEADLAN D
TWOFOL D	BILLIAR D	COATTEN D	FALCATE D	*HEADWIN D
*TYPHOI D	*BINDWEE D	*COEXTEN D	*FARMHAN D	*HEADWOR D
VANWAR D	BIPARTE D	COLESEE D	FARMLAN D	*HEBDOMA D
VISCOI D	BIRDSEE D	COLUBRI D	*FARMYAR D	
WADDIE D	*BIVALVE D	*COMPLIE D	FARMLAN D	
WARHEA D	*BLINKAR D	*COMPOUN D	*FARMYAR D	

HELICOI D	*MAGICKE D	PARODIE D	REEDBIR D	SLIPSHO D
HEMATOI D	*MAIDHOO D	PAROTOI D	REFERRE D	SLUGABE D
*HEMPWEE D	MAINLAN D	PASSBAN D	REMANNE D	SLUGGAR D
*HIGHBRE D	MALPOSE D	PASSWOR D	REPETEN D	SLUMLOR D
*HIGHLAN D	MANIFOL D	PEASECO D	RERECOR D	SNAPWEE D
*HIGHROA D	*MANYFOL D	PEDALLE D	REREWAR D	SNOWBIR D
HOGSHEA D	MARIGOL D	PEGBOAR D	RESINOI D	SNOWLAN D
*HOMEBRE D	MASTHEA D	PELLUCI D	RESPREA D	*SNOWSHE D
HOMELAN D	MEATHEA D	PENNATE D	RETHREA D	*SOFTHEA D
*HOMEWAR D	MEDICAI D	PERIODI D	REVEREN D	*SOFTWOO D
HOMINOI D	MEDUSOI D	PETALOI D	REVULSE D	SOLENOI D
HONORAN D	MELANOI D	*PHOSPHI D	*RHIZOPO D	*SOLIQUI D
HOTBLOO D	METALLE D	*PHYLLOI D	*RHOMBOI D	SONGBIR D
HUMANOI D	*MIDFIEL D	*PILCHAR D	RICEBIR D	SOREHEA D
*HUMIFIE D	*MILKMAI D	PILEATE D	*RICHWEE D	SOURWOO D
*HYDRACI D	*MILKWEE D	PINEWOO D	RIVERBE D	SOWBREA D
*HYPOACI D	*MILKWOO D	PINNATE D	*ROCKWEE D	SPHENOI D
*HYRACOI D	MILLEPE D	PINNIPE D	ROOTHOL D	SPHEROI D
*JACQUAR D	MILLIAR D	PLASMOI D	ROSEWOO D	*SPHINGI D
*JAILBIR D	MILLIPE D	PLAYLAN D	RUBICUN D	SPLENDI D
*JEREMIA D	MILLPON D	PLICATE D	RUNROUN D	*SQUIFFE D
*JIGGERE D	MISAWAR D	*PLOWHEA D	SALMONI D	STAGGAR D
*JUNKYAR D	MISBRAN D	PLOWLAN D	SARABAN D	STANDAR D
*KAILYAR D	MISBUIL D	*PLUMIPE D	SASSWOO D	STEADIE D
*KALEYAR D	MISFIEL D	*POKEWEE D	SATINPO D	STENOSE D
*KEESHON D	MISPLEA D	POLEWAR D	SAUROPO D	STINKAR D
KERATOI D	MISSOUN D	*POLYBIR D	*SCABBAR D	STRIPPE D
*KEYBOAR D	MISSPEN D	*POLYPOI D	*SCAFFOL D	SUBACRI D
*KINGBIR D	MODELLE D	*PONDWEE D	*SCAPHOI D	SUBBREE D
*KINGHOO D	*MONKHOO D	*PORKWOO D	*SCHIZOI D	SUBFIEL D
*KINGWOO D	MONOACI D	POSTCAR D	SCIAENI D	SUBFLUI D
*KNAPWEE D	MOONSEE D	POSTPAI D	SCIUROI D	*SUBHUMI D
*KNOTWEE D	MOONWAR D	POTSHAR D	SCLEREI D	SULCATE D
LABELLE D	MOORLAN D	POTSHER D	SCLEROI D	*SUMPWEE D
LABIATE D	*MOPBOAR D	PREBOUN D	SCOREPA D	*SUNBAKE D
LACERTI D	MORIBUN D	PRECITE D	*SCRAPPE D	SUNSCAL D
LACEWOO D	MUDGUAR D	PRESCIN D	SCURRIE D	SUPERAD D
*LADYBIR D	MULTIFI D	PRETTIE D	SEABOAR D	SURFBIR D
*LADYHOO D	MULTIPE D	PRISMOI D	*SELFHOO D	SURROUN D
*LAMPYRI D	MURAENI D	PROFOUN D	*SELFWAR D	*SWANHER D
LANDLOR D	MURIATE D	PROPOUN D	SEMIARI D	SYNERGI D
LANDSLI D	MUTINIE D	PROTOPO D	SEMIBAL D	TACHINI D
LANDWAR D	*MYRIAPO D	*PROTOXI D	SEMIHAR D	TAGBOAR D
LAPBOAR D	*MYRIOPO D	PTEROPO D	SEMIWIL D	TAILSKI D
LARBOAR D	NAILFOL D	*PULPWOO D	*SERFHOO D	TAILWIN D
LATEWOO D	NAILHEA D	PURBLIN D	SERRANI D	TAMARIN D
LEEBOAR D	NEATHER D	PUREBRE D	SESAMOI D	TEABOAR D
*LEFTWAR D	*NECKBAN D	PYRENOI D	*SHAMMIE D	*TEAKWOO D
LEMUROI D	*NEWFOUN D	RACEMOI D	*SHEETFE D	TEENAGE D
LIBELLE D	*NEWLYWE D	RADICAN D	*SHEPHER D	TETRACI D
LIMULOI D	NINEBAR D	RAILBIR D	SHETLAN D	TETRAPO D
LINEATE D	NINEFOL D	RAILHEA D	SHIPLOA D	*TETROXI D
LINEBRE D	NONFLUI D	RAILROA D	*SHIPYAR D	THEROPO D
LIVERIE D	NONRATE D	RAINBAN D	SIDEBAN D	THINCLA D
LOANWOR D	NONRIGI D	RAINBIR D	SIDEWAR D	THOUSAN D
LOCOWEE D	NONSOLI D	RAPESEE D	*SILKWEE D	*THYREOI D
LONGHAN D	NOSEBAN D	RAVELLE D	SILUROI D	*TICKSEE D
LONGHEA D	*PACIFIE D	RAWBONE D	SINUSOI D	TIDELAN D
LOPSIDE D	PALMATE D	REARWAR D	SISTROI D	*TIGHTWA D
LOVEBIR D	PANELLE D	REASCEN D	*SKEWBAL D	TILTYAR D
*LUNKHEA D	PARANOI D	REDEMAN D	*SKINHEA D	TIMECAR D
LYREBIR D	*PARKLAN D	REDUVII D		TOOLHOL D

TOOLSHE D	TROLLIE D	WATERBE D	*WILLYAR D	*WORKLOA D
TOTALLE D	TUBEROI D	*WAVEBAN D	*WINDWAR D	WORMSEE D
TRACHEI D	*VAGABON D	*WELLHEA D	*WITHHOL D	*WORMWOO D
TRAMROA D	VANGUAR D	WEREGIL D	*WOODBIN D	*WRETCHE D
TRICHOI D	VERECUN D	*WESTWAR D	WOODLAN D	*YARDBIR D
TRILOBE D	VILIPEN D	*WHIPCOR D	*WOODSHE D	
TRIPLOI D	*VINEYAR D	*WIFEHOO D	*WOODWIN D	
TROCHOI D	*VIVERRI D	*WILDWOO D	*WOOLSHE D	

F

FACE	FIEF	FOND	FYCE	*FEEZE
FACT	FIFE	FONT	FYKE	FEIGN
FADE	FILA	FOOD	FABLE	FEINT
FADO	FILE	FOOL	FACER	FEIST
FAIL	FILL	FOOT	FACET	FELID
FAIN	FILM	FORA	FACIA	FELLA
FAIR	FIND	FORB	FADDY	FELLY
FAKE	FINE	FORD	FADER	FELON
FALL	FINK	FORE	FADGE	FEMME
FAME	FIRE	FORK	FAENA	FEMUR
FANE	FIRM	FORM	FAERY	FENCE
FANG	FIRN	FORT	FAGIN	FENNY
FANO	FISC	FOSS	FAGOT	FEOFF
FARD	FISH	FOUL	FAINT	FERAL
FARE	FIST	FOUR	FAIRY	FERIA
FARL	FIVE	FOWL	FAITH	FERLY
FARM	FIXT	*FOXY	FAKER	FERMI
FARO	*FIZZ	*FOZY	FAKIR	FERNY
FART	FLAB	FRAE	FALSE	FERRY
FASH	FLAG	FRAG	FANCY	FESSE
FAST	FLAK	FRAP	FANGA	FETAL
FATE	FLAM	FRAT	FANNY	FETCH
FAUN	FLAN	FRAY	FANON	FETID
FAWN	FLAP	FREE	FANUM	FETOR
*FAZE	FLAT	FRET	*FAQIR	FETUS
FEAL	FLAW	FRIG	FARAD	FEUAR
FEAR	FLAX	FRIT	FARCE	FEVER
FEAT	FLAY	*FRIZ	FARCI	FIBER
FECK	FLEA	FROE	FARCY	FIBRE
FEED	FLED	FROG	FARER	FICHE
FEEL	FLEE	FROM	FARLE	FICHU
FEET	FLEW	FROW	FATAL	FICIN
FELL	FLEX	FRUG	FATLY	FIDGE
FELT	FLEY	FUCI	FATSO	FIELD
FEME	FLIC	FUCK	FATTY	FIEND
FEND	FLIP	FUEL	FAUGH	FIERY
FEOD	FLOW	FUJI	FAULD	FIFER
FERE	FLUB	FULL	FAULT	FIFTH
FERN	FLUE	FUME	FAUNA	FIFTY
FESS	FLUX	FUMY	FAUVE	FIGHT
FETA	FOAL	FUND	FAVOR	FILAR
FETE	FOAM	FUNK	FAVUS	FILCH
FEUD	FOGY	FURL	FAWNY	FILER
FIAR	FOHN	FURY	FEASE	FILET
FIAT	FOIL	FUSE	FEAST	FILLE
FICE	FOIN	FUSS	*FEAZE	FILLY
FICO	FOLD	*FUZE	FECAL	FILMY
FIDO	FOLK	*FUZZ	FECES	FILTH

FILUM	FLYER	FROST	FALTER	FENNEL
FINAL	FLYTE	FROTH	FAMILY	FERBAM
FINCH	FOAMY	FROWN	FAMINE	FERINE
FINER	FOCAL	*FROZE	FAMING	FERITY
FINIS	FOCUS	FRUIT	FAMISH	FERLIE
FINNY	FOEHN	FRUMP	FAMOUS	FERREL
FIORD	FOGEY	FRYER	FANDOM	FERRET
*FIQUE	FOGGY	FUBSY	FANEGA	FERRIC
FIRED	FOGIE	FUCUS	FANION	FERRUM
FIRER	FOIST	FUDGE	*FANJET	FERULA
FIRRY	FOLIA	FUGAL	FANNED	FERULE
FIRST	FOLIO	FUGGY	FANNER	FERVID
FIRTH	FOLLY	FUGIO	FANTOD	FERVOR
FISHY	FONDU	FUGLE	FANTOM	FESCUE
FITCH	FOOTY	FUGUE	*FAQUIR	FESTAL
FITLY	FORAM	FULLY	FARCER	FESTER
FIVER	FORAY	FUMER	FARCIE	FETIAL
*FIXER	FORBY	FUMET	FARDEL	FETICH
*FIZZY	FORCE	FUNGI	FARFAL	FETING
*FJELD	FORDO	FUNGO	FARFEL	FETISH
*FJORD	FORGE	*FUNKY	FARINA	FETTED
FLACK	FORGO	FUNNY	FARING	FETTER
FLAIL	*FORKY	FURAN	FARMER	FETTLE
FLAIR	FORME	FUROR	FARROW	FEUDAL
FLAKE	FORTE	FURRY	FASCES	FIACRE
*FLAKY	FORTH	*FURZE	FASCIA	FIASCO
FLAME	FORTY	*FURZY	FASTEN	FIBBER
FLAMY	FORUM	FUSEE	FATHER	FIBRIL
FLANK	FOSSA	FUSEL	FATHOM	FIBRIN
FLARE	FOSSE	FUSIL	FATING	FIBULA
FLASH	FOUND	FUSSY	FATTED	*FICKLE
FLASK	FOUNT	FUSTY	FATTEN	FIDDLE
FLAWY	FOVEA	*FUZEE	FATTER	FIDGET
*FLAXY	FOYER	*FUZIL	FAUCAL	FIERCE
FLEAM	FRAIL	*FUZZY	FAUCES	FIESTA
FLECK	FRAME	FYTTE	FAUCET	FIGURE
FLEER	FRANC	FABLER	FAULTY	FILIAL
FLEET	FRANK	FABRIC	FAVELA	FILING
FLESH	FRAUD	FACADE	FAVOUR	FILLER
FLICK	FREAK	FACETE	FAWNER	FILLET
FLIED	FREED	FACEUP	FEALTY	FILLIP
FLIER	FREER	FACIAL	FEARER	FILMIC
FLIES	FREMD	FACIES	FECIAL	FILOSE
FLING	FRENA	FACILE	*FECKLY	FILTER
FLINT	FRERE	FACING	FECULA	*FILTHY
FLOUR	FRESH	FACTOR	FECUND	FIMBLE
FLOUT	FRIAR	FACULA	FEDORA	FINALE
FLOWN	FRIED	FADING	FEEBLE	FINDER
FLUFF	FRIER	FAECES	FEEDER	FINELY
FLUID	FRIES	FAERIE	FEELER	FINERY
FLUKE	FRILL	FAGGOT	FEIRIE	FINEST
*FLUKY	FRISE	FAILLE	FEISTY	FINGER
FLUME	FRISK	FAIRLY	FELINE	FINIAL
FLUMP	FRITH	FAKEER	FELLAH	FINISH
FLUNG	FRITT	*FAKERY	FELLER	FINITE
FLUNK	*FRIZZ	FAKING	FELLOE	FINNED
FLUOR	FROCK	FALCON	FELLOW	FIPPLE
FLUSH	FROND	FALLAL	FELONY	FIRING
FLUTE	FRONS	FALLEN	FEMALE	FIRKIN
FLUTY	FRONT	FALLER	FENCER	FIRMAN
FLUYT	FRORE	FALLOW	FENDER	FIRMER
*FLYBY	FROSH	FALSIE	FENNEC	FIRMLY

FISCAL	*FLYWAY	*FOXILY	FUNEST	FANFARE
FISHER	FOAMER	*FOXING	FUNGAL	FANFOLD
*FISHLY	FODDER	FRACAS	FUNGIC	FANLIKE
FISTIC	FODGEL	FRAISE	FUNGUS	FANNING
*FITCHY	FOEMAN	FRAMER	FUNKER	FANTAIL
FITFUL	FOETAL	FRAPPE	FUNKIA	FANTASM
FITTED	FOETID	FRATER	FUNNED	FANTAST
FITTER	FOETOR	*FREAKY	FUNNEL	FANTASY
*FIXATE	FOETUS	FREELY	FURANE	FANWISE
*FIXITY	*FOGBOW	FREEST	FURFUR	FANWORT
*FIXURE	FOGDOG	*FREEZE	FURIES	FARADAY
*FIZGIG	FOGGED	FRENCH	FURLER	FARADIC
*FIZZER	FOGGER	FRENUM	FURORE	*FARAWAY
*FIZZES	FOIBLE	*FRENZY	FURRED	FARCEUR
*FIZZLE	FOISON	FRESCO	FURROW	FARCING
*FLABBY	FOLATE	FRETTY	FUSAIN	FARINHA
FLACON	FOLDER	FRIARY	FUSILE	FARMING
FLAGGY	FOLIAR	FRIDGE	FUSING	FARNESS
FLAGON	FOLIUM	FRIEND	FUSION	FARRAGO
FLAKER	*FOLKSY	*FRIEZE	FUSSER	FARRIER
FLAMBE	FOLLIS	FRIGHT	FUSTIC	FARTHER
FLAMEN	FOLLOW	FRIGID	FUTILE	FASCINE
FLAMER	FOMENT	*FRIJOL	FUTURE	FASCISM
FLANGE	FONDLE	FRILER	*FUZING	FASCIST
*FLAPPY	FONDLY	FRILLY	*FYLFOT	FASHION
*FLASHY	FONDUE	FRINGE	FABLIAU	FASTING
FLATLY	FOOTER	FRINGY	FABLING	FATALLY
FLATUS	FOOTLE	*FRISKY	FABULAR	*FATBACK
FLAUNT	*FOOZLE	FRIVOL	FACIEND	FATBIRD
FLAVIN	FORAGE	*FRIZER	FACTION	FATEFUL
FLAVOR	FORBAN	*FRIZZY	*FACTORY	FATHEAD
*FLAXEN	FORBID	FROGGY	FACTUAL	FATIDIC
FLAYER	FORBYE	FROLIC	FACTURE	FATIGUE
FLECHE	FORCER	FROSTY	*FACULTY	FATLESS
*FLECKY	FOREBY	*FROTHY	FADABLE	FATLIKE
FLEDGE	FOREDO	*FROUZY	FADDIER	FATLING
FLEDGY	FOREGO	*FROWSY	*FADDISM	FATNESS
FLEECE	FOREST	*FROWZY	FADDIST	FATTEST
FLEECH	FORGAT	*FROZEN	FAGOTER	FATTIER
FLEECY	FORGER	FRUGAL	FAIENCE	FATTIES
FLENCH	FORGET	FRUITY	FAILING	FATTILY
FLENSE	FORGOT	*FRUMPY	FAILURE	FATTING
*FLESHY	FORINT	FRUSTA	FAINTER	FATTISH
FLETCH	FORKER	FRYPAN	FAINTLY	FATUITY
FLEURY	FORMAL	FUCOID	FAIRIES	FATUOUS
*FLEXOR	FORMAT	FUCOSE	FAIRING	FAUCIAL
FLIEST	FORMEE	FUCOUS	FAIRISH	FAUTEIL
FLIGHT	FORMER	FUDDLE	*FAIRWAY	*FAUVISM
FLIMSY	FORMIC	FUELER	FAITOUR	FAUVIST
FLINCH	FORMOL	FUGATO	FALBALA	FAVORER
FLINTY	FORMYL	FUGGED	FALCATE	*FAZENDA
FLOURY	*FORNIX	FUHRER	*FALLACY	FEARFUL
FLOWER	FORRIT	FULFIL	*FALLOFF	FEASTER
FLUENT	FORTIS	FULGID	FALLOUT	FEATHER
*FLUFFY	*FORWHY	FULHAM	*FALSIFY	FEATURE
*FLUKEY	FOSSIL	FULLAM	FALSITY	FEBRILE
*FLUNKY	FOSTER	FULLER	FAMULUS	FEDAYEE
FLURRY	FOUGHT	FULMAR	FANATIC	FEDERAL
FLUTER	FOULLY	FUMBLE	FANCIED	FEEDBAG
FLYING	FOURTH	FUMIER	FANCIER	*FEEDBOX
FLYMAN	FOWLER	FUMING	FANCIES	FEEDLOT
*FLYSCH	*FOXIER	FUNDUS		FEELESS

FEELING	FIGWORT	*FIXEDLY	FLUTIST	*FOREBYE
FEIGNER	FILAREE	*FIXINGS	FLUTTER	FOREGUT
FELLIES	FILARIA	*FIXTUTE	FLUVIAL	FOREIGN
FELONRY	FILBERT	FLACDID	*FLUXION	FORELEG
FELSITE	*FILCHER	FLAGGER	*FLYABLE	FOREMAN
FELSPAR	FILEMOT	FLAGMAN	*FLYAWAY	*FOREPAW
FELTING	FILIATE	FLAMBEE	*FLYBELT	FORERUN
FELUCCA	FILIBEG	FLAMEAU	*FLYBLOW	FORESEE
FELWORT	FILLIES	FLAMIER	*FLYBOAT	FORETOP
FEMINIE	FILLING	FLAMING	*FLYLEAF	FOREVER
FEMORAL	*FILMDOM	*FLAMMED	*FLYOVER	FORFEIT
FENAGLE	FILMIER	FLANEUR	*FLYPAST	FORFEND
FENCING	*FILMILY	FLANGER	FLYTIER	FORGAVE
FEODARY	FILMSET	FLANKER	FLYTING	FORGERY
*FEOFFEE	FIMBRIA	FLANNEL	*FLYTRAP	FORGING
*FEOFFER	FINABLE	*FLAPPED	FOAMIER	FORGIVE
*FEOFFOR	FINAGLE	FLAPPER	*FOAMILY	FORGOER
FERMATA	FINALIS	FLASHER	*FOCALLY	*FORKFUL
FERMENT	FINALLY	FLASKET	FOCUSER	FORKIER
FERMION	FINANCE	FLATBED	FOGGAGE	FORLORN
FERMIUM	*FINBACK	FLATCAP	FOGGING	FORMANT
FERNERY	FINDING	FLATCAR	FOGHORN	FORMATE
FERRATE	FINESSE	FLATLET	FOGLESS	*FORMFUL
FERRETY	*FINFISH	FLATTED	*FOGYISM	FORMULA
FERRIED	FINFOOT	FLATTEN	FOLACIN	FORSAKE
FERRIES	FINICAL	FLATTER	FOLDOUT	FORTIES
FERRITE	*FINICKY	FLATTOP	FOLIAGE	*FORTIFY
FERROUS	FINIKIN	FLAUNTY	FOLIATE	FORTUNE
FERRULE	FINLESS	FLAVINE	FOLIOSE	FORWARD
FERTILE	FINLIKE	FLAVONE	FOLIOUS	FORWENT
FERVENT	*FINMARK	*FLAVORY	*FOLKISH	FORWORN
FERVOUR	FINNIER	FLAVOUR	*FOLKMOT	*FOSSICK
FESTIVE	FINNING	FLEABAG	*FOLKWAY	FOULARD
FESTOON	FIREARM	FLEECER	FOLLIES	FOULING
*FETCHER	*FIREBOX	*FLEMISH	FONDANT	FOUNDER
*FETLOCK	FIREBUG	FLENSER	FONDLER	FOUNDRY
FETTING	FIREDOG	FLESHER	FONTINA	FOURGON
FEUDARY	*FIREFLY	*FLESHLY	FOOLERY	FOVEOLA
FEUDIST	FIREMAN	*FLEXILE	FOOLISH	FOVEOLE
FEWNESS	FIREPAN	*FLEXION	FOOTAGE	FOWLING
FEYNESS	FIRSTLY	*FLEXURE	*FOOTBOY	*FOWLPOX
FIANCEE	*FISHERY	*FLICKER	FOOTIER	*FOXFIRE
FIBROID	*FISHEYE	*FLIGHTY	FOOTING	*FOXFISH
FIBROIN	*FISHGIG	FLINDER	FOOTLER	*FOXHOLE
FIBROMA	FISHIER	FLINGER	FOOTMAN	*FOXIEST
FIBROUS	FISHING	*FLIPPED	FOOTPAD	*FOXLIKE
FICTILE	FISHNET	FLIPPER	FOOTSIE	*FOXSKIN
FICTION	*FISHWAY	FLOUTER	*FOOTWAY	*FOXTAIL
*FICTIVE	FISSATE	FLOWAGE	*FOOZLER	FRACTED
FIDDLER	FISSILE	*FLOWERY	*FOPPERY	FRACTUR
FIDEISM	FISSION	*FLUBDUB	*FOPPISH	FRAENUM
FIDEIST	FISSURE	*FLUENCY	FORAGER	FRAGILE
*FIDGETY	FISTFUL	FLUIDLY	FORAMEN	FRAILTY
FIDGING	FISTULA	*FLUMMOX	FORAYER	FRAKTUR
*FIEFDOM	*FITCHEE	FLUNKER	FORBADE	FRANKER
FIELDER	*FITCHET	*FLUNKEY	FORBEAR	*FRANKLY
FIFTEEN	*FITCHEW	FLUORID	FORBODE	FRANTIC
*FIFTHLY	FITMENT	FLUORIN	FORBORE	FRAUGHT
FIGHTER	FITNESS	FLUSHER	FORCEPS	FRAYING
FIGMENT	FITTEST	FLUSTER	FORCING	*FRAZZLE
FIGURAL	FITTING	FLUTIER	FOREARM	*FRECKLE
FIGURER	*FIXATIF	FLUTING	*FOREBAY	*FRECKLY

FREEBEE	FUNERAL	FALLIBLE	FELDSPAR	*FILMCARD
FREEBIE	FUNFAIR	FALSETTO	*FELICITY	FILMGOER
FREEDOM	FUNGOID	FALTBOAT	FELINELY	FILMIEST
FREEMAN	FUNGOUS	FALTERER	FELINITY	FILMLAND
FREESIA	FUNICLE	FAMELESS	FELLABLE	FILTERER
*FREEWAY	FUNNING	FAMILIAL	FELLATIO	FILTRATE
*FREEZER	*FURBISH	FAMILIAR	FELLNESS	FINAGLER
FREIGHT	FURCATE	*FANCIFUL	*FELLOWLY	FINALISM
FRESHEN	FURCULA	FANDANGO	FELSTONE	FINALIST
FRESHET	FURIOSO	FANEGADA	*FEMINACY	FINALITY
*FRESHLY	FURIOUS	FANFARON	FEMININE	*FINALIZE
FRESNEL	FURLESS	*FANLIGHT	FEMINISE	FINEABLE
FRETFUL	FURLONG	FANTASIA	*FEMINISM	FINENESS
FRETSAW	*FURMETY	FANTASIE	FEMINIST	FINESPUN
FRETTED	*FURMITY	FARADAIC	*FEMINITY	FINGERER
FRIABLE	FURNACE	FARADISE	*FEMINIZE	*FINICKIN
FRIBBLE	FURNISH	FARADISM	*FENCIBLE	*FINIKING
FRIGATE	FURRIER	*FARADIZE	FENESTRA	FINISHER
*FRIJOLE	FURRILY	*FARCICAL	*FERACITY	FINITELY
FRISEUR	FURRING	FAREWELL	FERETORY	FINITUDE
FRISKER	*FURROWY	FARINOSE	*FEROCITY	*FINNICKY
FRISKET	FURTHER	*FARMHAND	FERREOUS	FINNIEST
FRISSON	FURTIVE	FARMLAND	FERRETER	*FINNMARK
FRITTED	FUSCOUS	*FARMYARD	FERRIAGE	*FINOCHIO
FRITTER	FUSIBLE	FARNESOL	FERRITIN	FIREBALL
*FRIZZER	FUSSPOT	*FAROUCHE	*FERRYMAN	FIREBIRD
*FRIZZLE	FUSTIAN	FARRIERY	*FERVENCY	FIREBOAT
*FRIZZLY	*FUTHARC	FARTHEST	FESSWISE	*FIREBOMB
FROGEYE	*FUTHARK	*FARTHING	FESTIVAL	FIREBRAT
FROGGED	*FUTHORC	*FASCICLE	FETATION	*FIRECLAY
FROGMAN	*FUTHORK	FASHIOUS	FETERITA	*FIREDAMP
FROMAGE	*FUTTOCK	*FASTBACK	FETIALIS	*FIREFANG
FRONTAL	FABULIST	FASTBALL	FETICIDE	FIREHALL
FRONTES	FABULOUS	FASTENER	*FETOLOGY	FIRELESS
FRONTON	*FACEDOWN	FASTNESS	FETTERER	*FIRELOCK
FROSTED	FACELESS	FASTUOUS	FETTLING	*FIREPINK
FROUNCE	FACETIAE	FATALISM	*FEVERFEW	FIREPLUG
FROWARD	FACETTED	FATALIST	FEVERISH	FIREROOM
FROWNER	*FACIALLY	FATALITY	FEVEROUS	FIRESIDE
*FROWSTY	*FACILITY	*FATHERLY	*FIBERIZE	FIRETRAP
FRUITER	FACTIOUS	*FATSTOCK	FIBRILLA	*FIREWEED
FRUSTUM	*FACTOTUM	FATTENER	FIBROSIS	*FIREWOOD
*FUCHSIA	FADDIEST	FATTIEST	*FIDELITY	*FIREWORK
*FUCHSIN	*FADEAWAY	FAUBOURG	FIDGETER	*FIREWORM
FUEHRER	FADELESS	FAVONIAN	FIDUCIAL	FIRMNESS
FUELLER	FAGOTING	FAVORITE	*FIENDISH	*FISCALLY
FUGGING	*FAHLBAND	FAVOURER	FIGEATER	*FISHABLE
FUGUIST	FAINEANT	*FAWNLIKE	*FIGHTING	*FISHBOLT
FULCRUM	FAINTISH	FAYALITE	FIGULINE	*FISHBONE
FULFILL	FAIRLEAD	FEARLESS	FIGURANT	*FISHBOWL
FULGENT	FAIRNESS	FEARSOME	FIGURATE	*FISHHOOK
FULLERY	*FAIRYISM	FEASANCE	FIGURINE	FISHIEST
FULMINE	*FAITHFUL	FEASIBLE	FIGURING	FISHLESS
FULNESS	FALCATED	FEASTFUL	FILAGREE	*FISHLIKE
FULSOME	*FALCHION	*FEATHERY	FILAMENT	FISHLINE
FULVOUS	FALCONER	*FEBRIFIC	FILARIID	*FISHMEAL
FUMARIC	FALCONET	*FECKLESS	FILATURE	*FISHPOLE
FUMBLER	*FALCONRY	FECULENT	*FILEFISH	*FISHPOND
FUMETTE	FALDERAL	*FEDERACY	FILICIDE	FISHTAIL
FUMIEST	FALDEROL	FEDERATE	*FILIFORM	*FISHWIFE
FUMULUS	*FALLBACK	*FEEBLISH	FILIGREE	FISSIPED
FUNCTOR	*FALLFISH	*FEEDBACK	FILISTER	FISTNOTE

FITTABLE	*FLICHTER	*FOOTPACE	FORETIME	FREELOAD
*FIVEFOLD	*FLICKERY	*FOOTPATH	FOREWARN	FREENESS
*FIVEPINS	*FLIMFLAM	FOOTRACE	FOREWENT	FREEWILL
*FIXATION	*FLINCHER	FOOTREST	*FOREWING	FREMITUS
*FIXATIVE	*FLIPPANT	FOOTROPE	*FOREWORD	FRENETIC
FLABELLA	FLOURISH	FOOTSLOG	FOREWORN	FRENULUM
FLAGELLA	FLOWERER	FOOTSORE	*FOREYARD	*FRENZILY
FLAGGING	FLOWERET	FOOTSTEP	*FORGIVER	*FREQUENT
FLAGLESS	FLUERICS	FOOTWALL	*FORJUDGE	FRESCOER
FLAGPOLE	FLUIDICS	FOOTWEAR	*FORKIEST	*FRESHMAN
FLAGRANT	FLUIDISE	*FOOTWORK	*FORKLESS	FRETLESS
*FLAGSHIP	*FLUIDITY	FOOTWORN	*FORKLIFT	FRETSOME
*FLAMENCO	*FLUIDIZE	FORBIDAL	*FORKLIKE	FRETTING
FLAMEOUT	FLUIDRAM	FORBORNE	*FORKSFUL	*FRETWORK
FLAMIEST	*FLUMMERY	*FORCEFUL	FORMALIN	*FRIBBLER
FLAMINES	FLUORENE	*FORCIBLE	*FORMALLY	FRICANDO
FLAMINGO	FLUORIDE	*FORCIPES	*FORMERLY	FRICTION
*FLAMMING	FLUORINE	FORDLESS	FORMLESS	*FRIENDLY
FLANCARD	FLUORITE	FOREBEAR	FORRADER	*FRIGHTEN
FLANERIE	FLUTIEST	FOREBODE	*FORSAKER	FRILLING
*FLAPJACK	FLUTTERY	*FOREBODY	FORSOOTH	*FRIPPERY
FLAPLESS	*FLYPAPER	*FOREBOOM	FORSPENT	FRISETTE
*FLAPPING	*FLYSPECK	FORECAST	FORSWEAR	FRITTING
*FLASHGUN	*FLYWHEEL	FOREDATE	FORTIETH	FRIVOLER
*FLASHING	FOAMIEST	*FOREDECK	FORTRESS	*FRIZZIER
FLATBOAT	FOAMLESS	FOREDOOM	FORTUITY	*FRIZZIER
*FLATFISH	*FOAMLIKE	*FOREFACE	*FORZANDO	*FRIZZILY
FLATFOOT	FOCALISE	FOREFEEL	FOSSETTE	*FRIZZLER
*FLATHEAD	*FOCALIZE	*FOREFEND	FOSTERER	*FROGFISH
FLATIRON	*FOGBOUND	FOREFOOT	*FOUGHTEN	FROGGING
FLATLAND	*FOGFRUIT	FOREGOER	FOULNESS	*FROGLIKE
FLATLING	FOILSMAN	*FOREHAND	FOUNTAIN	*FROMENTY
FLATNESS	*FOLDAWAY	*FOREHEAD	*FOURCHEE	FRONDEUR
FLATTERY	FOLDBOAT	*FOREHOOF	*FOURFOLD	FRONTAGE
FLATTEST	FOLDEROL	*FOREKNOW	FOURSOME	FRONTIER
FLATTING	*FOLKLIKE	FORELADY	FOURTEEN	FRONTLET
FLATTISH	*FOLKLORE	FORELAND	*FOURTHLY	FROSTBIT
FLATWARE	*FOLKMOOT	*FORELIMB	FOVEOLET	FROSTING
*FLATWASH	*FOLKMOTE	*FORELOCK	*FOXGLOVE	FROTTAGE
*FLATWAYS	*FOLKTALE	FOREMAST	*FOXHOUND	FROTTEUR
FLATWISE	FOLLICLE	*FOREMILK	*FOXINESS	FROUFROU
*FLATWORK	FOLLOWER	FOREMOST	*FOZINESS	*FRUCTIFY
*FLATWORM	FOMENTER	FORENAME	FRACTION	FRUCTOSE
FLAUNTER	FONDLING	FORENOON	FRACTURE	FRUITAGE
FLAVONOL	FONDNESS	FORENSIC	FRAGGING	FRUITFUL
FLAVORER	FONTANEL	FOREPART	FRAGMENT	FRUITIER
*FLAVOURY	*FOOFARAW	FOREPAST	FRAGRANT	FRUITION
FLAWLESS	*FOOLFISH	*FOREPEAK	*FRANCIUM	FRUITLET
*FLAXSEED	*FOOLSCAP	*FOREPLAY	*FRANKEST	*FRUMENTY
FLEABANE	FOOTBALL	*FORERANK	*FRANKLIN	FRUSTULE
FLEABITE	*FOOTBATH	FORESAID	FRAULEIN	*FUCHSINE
FLEAWORT	FOOTFALL	FORESAIL	*FREAKIER	FUELLING
FLECTION	FOOTGEAR	FORESEER	*FREAKILY	FUGACITY
FLEECING	FOOTHILL	*FORESHOW	*FREAKISH	*FUGITIVE
FLESHIER	*FOOTHOLD	FORESIDE	*FREAKOUT	FUGLEMAN
*FLESHING	FOOTIEST	*FORESKIN	FREEBOOT	*FULLBACK
*FLESHPOT	FOOTLESS	FORESTAL	FREEBORN	*FULLFACE
*FLETCHER	*FOOTLIKE	FORESTAY	FREEDMAN	FULLNESS
*FLEXIBLE	FOOTLING	FORESTER	*FREEFORM	*FULMINIC
*FLEXUOSE	*FOOTMARK	FORESTRY	*FREEHAND	FUMARASE
*FLEXUOUS	FOOTNOTE	FORETELL	*FREEHOLD	FUMARATE

FUMAROLE	DE F EAT	*RU F FLY	*HA F NIUM	*BUF F ETER
*FUMATORY	DE F ECT	RU F OUS	*HU F FISH	*BUF F IEST
FUMELESS	DE F END	SA F ARI	LE F TISM	*CAF F EINE
*FUMELIKE	DE F IED	SA F EST	LE F TIST	*CAL F SKIN
FUMIGANT	DE F IER	SA F ETY	*LI F EFUL	CAN F IELD
FUMIGATE	DE F IES	SA F ROL	*LI F EWAY	*COE F FECT
*FUMITORY	DE F ILE	SI F TER	LI F TMAN	*COI F FEUR
FUNCTION	DE F INE	SO F FIT	*LI F TOFF	*COI F FURE
FUNERARY	DE F LEA	SO F TEN	LO F TILY	*COM F IEST
FUNEREAL	DE F OAM	SO F TIE	*MA F FICK	CON F EREE
FUNGIBLE	DE F ORM	SO F TLY	*MU F FLER	*CON F ERVA
FUNICULI	DE F RAY	SU F FER	*PU F FERY	CON F ETTO
*FUNNYMAN	DE F USE	*SU F FIX	RA F FISH	CON F IDER
FURANOSE	*DE F UZE	TA F FIA	RA F FLER	CON F INER
*FURBELOW	DI F FER	TI F FIN	RE F FING	CON F LATE
FURCRAEA	DO F FER	TO F FEE	RE F IGHT	*CON F LICT
*FURCULUM	DU F FEL	TU F FET	RE F INER	*CON F OCAL
FURFURAL	DU F FER	TU F TER	RE F LATE	CON F OUND
FURFURAN	DU F FLE	*WA F FERY	RE F LECT	CON F RERE
FURIBUND	GA F FER	*WA F FIE	RE F LIES	*CON F RONT
*FURLOUGH	GO F FER	*WA F FLE	RE F LOAT	CON F UTER
*FURMENTY	*GU F FAW	WA F TER	RE F LOOD	*CUF F LESS
FURRIERY	HA F TER	*WI F FLY	RE F OCUS	*DAF F ODIL
FURRIEST	HE F TER	WI F ING	RE F ORGE	DEA F NESS
FURRINER	*KA F FIR	*ZA F FAR	RE F OUND	DEI F ICAL
FURROWER	KA F TAN	*ZA F FER	RE F RACT	*DIF F RACT
FURTHEST	LI F TER	*ZA F FIR	RE F RAIN	*DIF F USER
FURUNCLE	LO F TER	*ZA F FRE	RE F RAME	*DIF F USOR
FUSELAGE	NI F FER	*ZA F TIG	RE F RESH	*DIS F AVOR
FUSELESS	PI F FLE	*ZO F TIG	RE F RONT	*DIS F ROCK
*FUSIFORM	PU F FER	*BA F FIES	RE F UGEE	*DOG F IGHT
FUSILEER	PU F FIN	*BA F FLER	RE F USAL	*DRA F FISH
FUSILIER	RA F FIA	*BE F LECK	RE F USER	DRA F TING
FUTILITY	RA F FLE	BI F ILAR	RE F UTAL	DRI F TAGE
FUTURISM	RA F TER	BI F OCAL	RE F UTER	DRI F TPIN
FUTURIST	RE F ACE	*BO F FOLA	RI F FLER	*DUM F OUND
FUTURITY	RE F ALL	*BU F FALO	RI F FLER	FAN F ARON
	RE F ECT	*BU F FIER	RI F FLERY	*FOG F RUIT
	RE F EED	*BU F FOON	RU F FIAN	*FOO F ARAW
BA F FLE	RE F ELL	*CA F FEIN	RU F FLER	FUR F URAL
BE F ALL	RE F FED	*CO F FING	SA F FRON	FUR F URAN
BE F LAG	RE F ILE	*CO F FRET	SA F ROLE	GON F ALON
BE F LEA	RE F ILL	DE F ACER	SI F TING	GON F ANON
BE F OOL	RE F ILM	DE F AMER	SO F TIES	GOO F BALL
BE F ORE	RE F IND	DE F AULT	SU F FARI	*GRA F FITO
BE F OUL	RE F INE	DE F ENCE	*SU F FICE	GRA F TAGE
BE F RET	RE F IRE	DE F ENSE	SU F FUSE	*GRU F FIER
BI F FIN	RE F LET	DE F IANT	TA F FETA	*GRU F FILY
*BI F LEX	RE F LEW	DE F ICIT	*TI F FANY	*GRU F FISH
BI F OLD	*RE F LEX	DE F ILER	WA F TAGE	GUL F IEST
BI F ORM	RE F LOW	DE F INER	WA F TURE	*GUL F LIKE
BO F FIN	*RE F LUX	DE F LATE	*WI F EDOM	*GUL F WEED
BU F FER	RE F OLD	DE F LECT	*BED F RAME	*GUN F IGHT
BU F FET	RE F ORM	DE F ORCE	*BEE F CAKE	GUN F LINT
CA F TAN	RE F UEL	DE F RAUD	BEE F IEST	*HAL F BACK
CO F FEE	RE F UGE	*DE F ROCK	BEE F LESS	*HAL F BEAK
CO F FER	RE F UND	DE F ROST	*BEE F WOOD	*HAL F LIFE
CO F FIN	RE F USE	DE F UNCT	*BOU F FANT	HAL F NESS
CO F FLE	RE F UTE	DI F FUSE	*BOW F RONT	*HAL F TIME
DE F ACE	RI F FLE	FI F TEEN		HAL F TONE
DE F AME	RU F FLE	*FI F THLY		*HAW F INCH

*HOO F BEAT	*SNI F FILY	CUI F	CHIE F	SCRUF F
HOO F LESS	*SNI F FISH	CUR F	*CHUF F	SETOF F
*HOO F LIKE	SNI F FLER	DAF F	CLIF F	SHADU F
*KAF F IYEH	*SNU F FBOX	DEA F	DRAF F	SHARI F
*KIN F OLKS	SNU F FIER	DEL F	DWAR F	SHERI F
LEA F IEST	*SNU F FILY	DOF F	FEOF F	*SHROF F
LEA F LESS	SNU F FLER	DUF F	FLUF F	TARIF F
*LEA F LIKE	SOL F EGGI	FIE F	GANE F	TIPOF F
*LEA F WORM	*SPI F FING	GAF F	GANO F	*BAILIF F
*MEN F OLKS	*STI F FISH	GOL F	GLIF F	*BEDWAR F
*MID F IELD	*STU F FING	GOO F	GONI F	*BLOWOF F
*MIS F AITH	SUB F IELD	GUF F	GONO F	*CAITIF F
*MIS F RAME	SUB F LOOR	GUL F	GRIE F	*CASTOF F
*MOF F ETTE	SUB F LUID	HAA F	GRIF F	DEBRIE F
*MOU F FLON	SUF F ERER	HAL F	GRUF F	DISTAF F
*NEW F OUND	*SUF F ICER	HOO F	*HOWF F	*FALLOF F
NON F LUID	*SUF F IXAL	HOW F	KALI F	*FIXATI F
NON F OCAL	SUF F LATE	HUF F	KENA F	*FLYLEA F
*PAR F LESH	*SUF F RAGE	*JIF F	KLOO F	*HANDOF F
*PAR F OCAL	SUL F INYL	KAI F	MOTI F	HERSEL F
*PER F ECTA	SUL F ONAL	KEE F	PILA F	*HIMSEL F
*PER F ECTO	SUL F ONIC	KER F	POUF F	HISSEL F
*PER F ORCE	SUL F ONYL	KIE F	PROO F	*JUMPOF F
*PER F UMER	SUL F URET	LEA F	*QUAF F	*KICKOF F
PIL F ERER	SUL F URIC	LIE F	*QUIF F	LEADOF F
*PRE F ACER	SUL F URYL	LOA F	SCAR F	*LIFTOF F
*PRE F IXAL	SUR F ACER	LOO F	SCOF F	*MASTIF F
*PRE F OCUS	SUR F BIRD	LUF F	SCUF F	*MIDRIF F
*PRE F RANK	SUR F BOAT	MIF F	SCUR F	*PICKOF F
PRO F ANER	*SUR F FISH	MUF F	SERI F	*PLAYOF F
PRO F ILER	SUR F IEST	NAI F	SHEA F	*PONTIF F
PRO F ITER	*SUR F LIKE	NEI F	SHEL F	*RAKEOF F
PRO F OUND	TAF F AREL	PEL F	*SKIF F	REPROO F
*PUF F BALL	TAF F EREL	POU F	SLUF F	RESTAF F
PUR F LING	TAF F RAIL	PRO F	SNIF F	RESTUF F
*REA F FIRM	TRI F LING	PUF F	SNUF F	SENDOF F
*RIF F RAFF	TRI F OCAL	RAF F	SPOO F	SHADOO F
ROO F LESS	TRI F ORIA	REE F	STAF F	SHEREE F
*ROO F LIKE	TUR F IEST	REI F	STIF F	*SHERIF F
ROO F LINE	TUR F LESS	RIF F	STUF F	*SHOWOF F
ROO F TREE	*TUR F LIKE	ROO F	SWAR F	*SHUTOF F
*RUF F LIKE	WAR F ARIN	RUF F	THIE F	*SPINOF F
*RUF F LING	*WAY F ARER	SEL F	WHAR F	SUNROO F
*SCA F FOLD	*WHI F FLER	SER F	*WHIF F	*TAKEOF F
*SCO F FLAW	*WOL F FISH	SUR F	BEGUL F	THEREO F
*SCU F FLER	*WOL F LIKE	TEF F	BEHAL F	*THYSEL F
SEA F ARER		TIF F	BEHOO F	TURNOF F
SEA F LOOR		TOF F	BELIE F	*WAVEOF F
SEA F RONT	BAF F	TRE F	CUTOF F	*WERWOL F
SEL F HEAL	BAR F	TUF F	HEREO F	*WHEREO F
*SEL F HOOD	BEE F	TUR F	*KHALI F	WITLOO F
SEL F LESS	BIF F	WAF F	*LAYOF F	*BLASTOF F
SEL F NESS	BOF F	WAI F	MASSI F	*BODYSUR F
SEL F SAME	BUF F	WOL F	MYSEL F	*BRUSHOF F
*SEL F WARD	BUM F	WOO F	*PAYOF F	*CALCTUF F
*SER F HOOD	CAL F	YAF F	PILAF F	*CHECKOF F
*SER F LIKE	CHE F	*ZAR F	PUTOF F	*DANDRIF F
*SHA F TING	CLE F	BLUF F	REBUF F	*DANDRUF F
*SHU F FLER	COF F	BRIE F	RELIE F	DISPROO F
SIF F LEUR	COO F	CALI F	RUNOF F	*DUMMKOP F
SNI F FIER	CUF F	*CHAF F	SCLAF F	*DYESTUF F

*FOREHOO F	LANGLAU F	*RIFFRAF F	*STANDOF F	*WETPROO F
*HANDCUF F	LONGLEA F	SANSERI F	*SUBCHIE F	*WOODRUF F
*KERCHIE F	*MISCHIE F	SEMIDEA F	*TIPSTAF F	YOURSEL F
*KNOCKOF F	*MOONCAL F	SHINLEA F	*WEREWOL F	

G

GABY	GIMP	GRAD	GAMEY	GESTE
GADI	GINK	GRAM	GAMIC	GETUP
GAFF	GIRD	GRAT	GAMIN	GHAST
GAGA	GIRL	GRAY	GAMIN	GHAUT
GAGE	GIRN	GREE	GAMMA	*GHAZI
GAIN	GIRO	GREW	GAMUT	GHOST
GAIT	GIRT	GREY	GANEF	GHOUL
GALA	GIST	GRID	GANEV	GHYLL
GALE	GIVE	GRIG	GANJA	GIANT
GALL	GLAD	GRIM	GANOF	GIBER
GAMB	GLED	GRIN	GAPER	GIDDY
GAME	GLEE	GRIP	GAPPY	GIGAS
GAMP	GLEG	GRIT	GARTH	GIGHE
GAMY	GLEN	GROG	GASSY	GIGOT
GANE	GLEY	GROT	GAUDY	GIGUE
GANG	GLIB	GROW	GAUGE	GILLY
GAOL	GLIM	GRUB	GAULT	GIMEL
GAPE	GLOB	GRUM	GAUNT	GIMPY
GAPY	GLOM	GUAN	GAUSS	GINNY
GARB	GLOP	GUAR	*GAUZE	GIPON
GASH	GLOW	GUCK	*GAUZY	GIPSY
GASP	GLUE	GUDE	GAVEL	GIRLY
GAST	GLUM	GUFF	GAVOT	GIRON
GATE	GLUT	GUID	GAYAL	GIRSH
GAUD	GNAR	GULF	GAYLY	GIRTH
GAUM	GNAT	GULL	*GAZER	GISMO
GAUN	GNAW	GULP	GECKO	GIVEN
GAUR	GOAD	GUNK	GEESE	GIVER
GAVE	GOAL	GURU	GEEST	*GIZMO
GAWK	GOAT	GUSH	GELEE	GLACE
GAZE	GOBO	GUST	GELID	GLADE
GEAR	GOBY	GYBE	GEMMA	GLADY
GECK	GOER	GYRE	GEMMY	GLAIR
GEEK	GOGO	GYRI	GEMOT	GLAND
GELD	GOLD	GYRO	GENET	GLANS
GELT	GOLF	GYVE	GENIC	GLARE
GENE	GONE	GABBY	GENIE	GLARY
GENS	GONG	GABLE	GENII	GLASS
GENT	GOOD	GADDI	GENIP	*GLAZE
GENU	GOOF	GADID	GENOA	*GLAZY
GERM	GOOK	GAFFE	GENOM	GLEAM
GEST	GOON	GAGER	GENRE	GLEAN
GEUM	GOOP	GAILY	GENRO	GLEBA
GHAT	GORE	GALAH	GENUS	GLEBE
GHEE	GORY	GALAX	GEODE	GLEDE
GIBE	GOSH	GALEA	GEOID	GLEED
GIFT	GOUT	GALLY	GERAH	GLEEK
GIGA	GOWD	GALOP	GERMY	GLEET
GILD	GOWK	GAMBA	GESSO	GLIAL
GILL	GOWN	GAMBE		GLIDE
GILT	GRAB	GAMER		GLIFF

GLIME	GRASP	**GUMMY**	GAMIER	GELATE
GLINT	GRASS	GUNNY	**GAMILY**	GELDER
GLINT	GRATE	**GUPPY**	GAMINE	GELLED
GLOAM	GRAVE	GURGE	**GAMING**	**GEMMED**
GLOAT	**GRAVY**	GURRY	**GAMMED**	GEMOTE
GLOBE	*****GRAZE**	GURSH	**GAMMER**	GENDER
GLOGG	GREAT	**GUSHY**	**GAMMON**	GENERA
GLOOM	GREBE	GUSTO	GANDER	**GENEVA**
GLORY	GREED	GUSTY	GANGER	GENIAL
GLOSS	**GREEK**	GUTSY	GANGLY	GENIUS
GLOST	GREEN	GUTTA	GANGUE	GENTES
GLOUT	GREET	GUTTY	GANNET	GENTIL
GLOVE	GREGO	GUYOT	GANOID	GENTLE
*****GLOZE**	GRIDE	**GYPSY**	**GANTRY**	**GENTRY**
GLUER	GRIEF	GYRAL	GAOLER	**GEODIC**
GLUEY	**GRIFF**	GYRON	**GAPING**	GERBIL
GLUME	GRIFT	GYRUS	**GAPPED**	GERENT
GLYPH	GRILL	**GABBED**	GARAGE	GERMAN
GNARL	GRIME	**GABBER**	GARBLE	GERMEN
GNARR	**GRIMY**	**GABBLE**	GARCON	GERUND
GNASH	GRIND	**GABBRO**	GARDEN	GESTIC
GNAWN	GRIPE	GABIES	GARGET	GETTER
GNOME	GRIPT	GABION	GARGLE	**GEWGAW**
GOBAN	**GRIPY**	GABOON	**GARISH**	**GEYSER**
GODLY	GRIST	**GADDED**	GARLIC	**GHARRI**
GOING	GRITH	GADDER	GARNER	**GHARRY**
GOLEM	GROAN	**GADFLY**	GARNET	**GHERAO**
GOLLY	GROIN	GADGET	GAROTE	**GHETTO**
GOMBO	GROOM	GADOID	GARRED	**GHIBLI**
GONAD	GROPE	**GAFFER**	GARRET	**GHOSTY**
GONER	GROSS	**GAGGED**	GARRON	GIAOUR
GONIA	*****GROSZ**	GAGGER	GARTER	**GIBBER**
GONIF	GROUP	GAGGLE	**GARVEY**	**GIBBET**
GONOF	GROUT	GAGING	**GASBAG**	**GIBBON**
GOODY	GROVE	**GAGMAN**	GASCON	GIBLET
GOOEY	GROWL	**GAIETY**	**GASIFY**	GIDDAP
GOOFY	GROWN	**GAINLY**	**GASKET**	**GIGGED**
GOONY	GRUEL	GAINER	**GASKIN**	GIGGLE
GOOSE	**GRUFF**	GAINST	GASLIT	**GIGGLY**
GOOSY	GRUME	GAITER	GASMAN	GIGLET
GORAL	**GRUMP**	GALAGO	GASPER	GIGLOT
GORGE	GRUNT	*****GALAXY**	GASSED	GIGOLO
GORSE	GUACO	GALENA	GASSER	GILDER
GORSY	GUANO	GALERE	GASSES	GILLER
GOUGE	GUARD	GALIOT	**GATHER**	GILLIE
GOURD	GUAVA	**GALLEY**	GATING	**GIMBAL**
GOUTY	GUESS	GALLON	**GAUCHE**	GIMLET
GOWAN	GUEST	GALLOP	**GAUCHO**	**GIMMAL**
GRAAL	GUIDE	GALLUS	GAUGER	GINGAL
GRACE	GUILD	GALOOT	**GAVAGE**	GINGER
GRADE	GUILE	GALORE	**GAVIAL**	**GINGKO**
GRAFT	GUILT	GALOSH	GAWKER	**GINKGO**
GRAIL	GUIRO	**GALYAC**	GAWSIE	GINNED
GRAIN	GUISE	**GALYAK**	**GAYETY**	GINNER
GRAMA	GULAR	GAMBIA	*****GAZABO**	**GIPPER**
GRAMP	**GULCH**	**GAMBIR**	*****GAZEBO**	GIRDER
GRANA	GULES	**GAMBIT**	*****GAZING**	GIRDLE
GRAND	**GULFY**	**GAMBLE**	**GEEGAW**	GIRLIE
GRANT	GULLY	**GAMBOL**	*****GEEZER**	GITANO
GRAPE	**GULPY**	**GAMELY**	GEISHA	**GIVING**
GRAPH	**GUMBO**	GAMEST	GELADA	GLACIS
GRAPY	**GUMMA**	GAMETE	GELANT	**GLADLY**

GLAIRE	GONION	GRIGRI	**GUSHER**	**GARBOIL**
GLAIRY	GONIUM	GRILLE	GUSSET	GARDANT
GLAIVE	**GONOPH**	GRILSE	GUTTED	**GARFISH**
GLAMOR	GOOBER	**GRIMLY**	GUTTER	GARGLER
GLANCE	**GOODBY**	GRINGO	GUTTLE	GARLAND
GLASSY	**GOODLY**	GRIPER	*GUZZLE	**GARMENT**
*GLAZER	**GOOGLY**	**GRIPPE**	GWEDUC	**GARNISH**
GLEAMY	GOOGOL	**GRIPPY**	**GYPPER**	GAROTTE
GLEETY	GOOIER	GRISLY	**GYPSUM**	**GARPIKE**
GLIDER	**GOONEY**	GRISON	**GYRATE**	GARRING
GLIOMA	GOONIE	**GRITTY**	**GYRENE**	GARROTE
GLITCH	GOORAL	**GRIVET**	**GYRING**	GASEOUS
GLOBAL	**GOOSEY**	GROCER	**GYROSE**	**GASKING**
GLOBIN	**GOPHER**	**GROGGY**	**GABBARD**	GASLESS
GLOMUS	GORGER	**GROOVE**	**GABBART**	GASSING
GLOOMY	GORGET	**GROOVY**	**GABBING**	GASTRAL
GLORIA	GORGON	**GORHEN**	**GABBLER**	GASTREA
GLOSSA	GORIER	GROPER	**GABELLE**	**GASTRIC**
GLOSSY	**GORILY**	GROTTO	**GABFEST**	GASTRIN
GLOVER	GORING	**GROUCH**	**GADDING**	**GATEMAN**
GLOWER	GOSPEL	GROUND	GADROON	**GATEWAY**
GLUING	GOSSAN	GROUSE	**GADWALL**	**GAUDERY**
GLUMPY	GOSSIP	**GROUTY**	**GAGGING**	**GAUFFER**
GLUNCH	**GOTHIC**	**GROVEL**	GAGSTER	**GAUNTRY**
GLUTEI	GOTTEN	**GROWER**	**GAHNITE**	**GAVOTTE**
GLUTEN	GOUGER	**GROWLY**	**GAINFUL**	*GAWKIER
GLYCAN	GOURDE	**GROWTH**	**GAINSAY**	*GAWKIES
GLYCIN	GOVERN	**GROYNE**	GALATEA	*GAWKISH
GLYCOL	**GRABBY**	**GRUBBY**	GALILEE	**GAYNESS**
*GLYCYL	GRABEN	GRUDGE	**GALIPOT**	*GAZELLE
GNARLY	*GRUFFY	GRUGRU	**GALLANT**	*GAZETTE
GNATTY	GRADER	**GRUMPY**	**GALLATE**	*GEARBOX
GNAWER	GRADIN	**GRUTCH**	GALLEIN	GEARING
GNEISS	GRADUS	GUAIAC	GALLEON	GELATIN
GNOMIC	**GRAHAM**	GUANIN	**GALLERY**	**GELDING**
GNOMON	**GRAINY**	GUENON	GALLETA	GELLANT
GNOSIS	**GRAMME**	*GUFFAW	**GALLFLY**	GELLING
GOALIE	GRANGE	GUGGLE	**GALLIUM**	**GEMINAL**
GOATEE	**GRANNY**	GUGLET	GALLNUT	**GEMLIKE**
GOBANG	GRANUM	GUIDER	GALLOON	**GEMMATE**
GOBBED	**GRAPPA**	GUIDON	GALLOOT	**GEMMIER**
GOBBET	**GRASSY**	**GUILTY**	GALLOUS	*GEMMILY
GOBBLE	GRATER	**GUIMPE**	**GALLOWS**	**GEMMING**
GOBIES	GRATIN	GUINEA	**GALOSHE**	**GEMMULE**
GOBLET	GRATIS	GUITAR	*GALUMPH	*GEMSBOK
GOBLIN	**GRAVEL**	GULDEN	**GAMBADE**	GENERAL
GOBONY	**GRAVEN**	GULLET	**GAMBIER**	**GENERIC**
GODDAM	**GRAVER**	**GULLEY**	**GAMBLER**	GENESIS
GODDED	**GRAVID**	GULPER	**GAMBOGE**	**GENETIC**
GODOWN	**GRAYLY**	**GUMMED**	**GAMBREL**	GENETTE
GODSON	*GRAZER	**GUMMER**	**GAMELAN**	**GENIPAP**
GODWIT	GREASE	GUNDOG	**GAMIEST**	GENITAL
GOFFER	**GREASY**	GUNMAN	**GAMMING**	GENITOR
GOGGLE	**GREAVE**	GUNNED	GANGLIA	GENSENG
GOGGLY	**GREEDY**	GUNNEL	GANGREL	GENTEEL
GOGLET	**GREENY**	GUNNEN	*GANGWAY	GENTIAN
GOITER	GREIGE	GUNNER	**GANTLET**	GENTILE
GOITRE	GRELAG	GUNSEL	**GAPOSIS**	GENUINE
GOLDEN	**GREMMY**	GURGLE	**GAPPING**	**GEODESY**
GOLFER	**GREYLY**	GURNET	**GARBAGE**	*GEODUCK
GOLOSH	**GRIEVE**	**GURNEY**	**GARBLER**	**GEOLOGY**
GOMUTI	**GRIFFE**			**GEORGIC**

GERBERA	GLIMPSE	GOODISH	GRAVURE	*GRUFFLY
GERENUK	GLISTEN	GOODMAN	GRAYISH	GRUMBLE
GERMANE	GLISTER	GOOIEST	GRAYLAG	GRUMMER
GERMIER	GLITTER	*GORCOCK	GRAYOUT	GRUMMET
GERMINA	GLOATER	GORGING	*GRAZIER	GRUMOSE
GESTALT	GLOBATE	GORIEST	*GRAZING	GRUMOUS
GESTAPO	GLOBOID	GORILLA	GREASER	*GRUMPHY
GESTATE	GLOBOSE	GORMAND	GREATEN	GRUNION
GESTURE	GLOBOUS	GOSHAWK	GREATLY	GRUNTER
GETAWAY	GLOBULE	GOSLING	*GRECIZE	GRUNTLE
GETTING	GLOCHID	GOSPORT	GREENLY	GRUSHIE
GHASTLY	GLORIED	GOSSIPY	GREENTH	GRUTTEN
*GHERKIN	GLORIES	GOSSOON	GREETER	*GRYPHON
GHILLIE	GLORIFY	GOTHITE	GREISEN	GUANACO
GHOSTLY	GLOSSER	GOUACHE	GREMIAL	GUANASE
GIBBING	GLOTTIS	GOULASH	GREMLIN	GUANINE
GIBBOSE	*GLOWFLY	GOURAMI	GREMMIE	GUARANI
GIBBOUS	GLUCOSE	GOURMET	GRENADE	GUARDER
GIGABIT	GLUTEAL	GRABBER	GREYHEN	GUAYULE
GIGATON	GLUTEUS	GRABBLE	GREYISH	GUDGEON
GIGGING	GLUTTED	GRACILE	GRIBBLE	GUERDON
GIGGLER	GLUTTON	GRACING	GRIDDLE	GUESSER
GILBERT	GLYCINE	GRACKLE	GRIEVER	GUILDER
GILDING	*GLYPTIC	GRADATE	GRIFFIN	GUIPURE
GILLNET	GNARRED	GRADINE	GRIFFON	GUISARD
*GIMMICK	GNATHAL	GRADING	GRIFTER	GULFIER
GINGALL	GNATHIC	GRADUAL	GRILLER	GUMBOIL
GINGELI	GNAWING	GRAFTER	GRIMACE	GUMDROP
GINGELY	*GNOCCHI	GRAINER	GRIMIER	GUMLESS
GINGERY	GNOMISH	GRAMARY	GRIMING	GUMLIKE
GINGHAM	GNOMIST	GRAMMAR	GRIMMER	GUMMIER
GINGILI	GNOSTIC	GRAMPUS	GRINDER	GUMMING
GINGIVA	GOATISH	GRANARY	GRINNED	GUMMITE
GINNING	GOBBING	GRANDAD	GRINNER	GUMMOSE
GINSENG	GOBBLER	GRANDAM	GRIPIER	GUMMOUS
GIPPING	GOBIOID	GRANDEE	GRIPING	GUMSHOE
GIRAFFE	GOBONEE	GRANDLY	GRIPPED	GUMTREE
GIRASOL	GODDAMN	GRANDMA	GRIPPER	GUMWEED
GIRDLER	GODDESS	GRANDPA	GRIPPLE	GUMWOOD
GIRLISH	GODDING	GRANGER	GRISKIN	GUNBOAT
GIROSOL	GODHEAD	GRANITE	GRISTLE	GUNFIRE
GISARME	GODHOOD	GRANNIE	GRISTLY	GUNLESS
GITTERN	GODLESS	GRANTEE	*GRIZZLE	GUNLOCK
*GIZZARD	GODLIER	GRANTER	*GRIZZLY	GUNNERY
*GJETOST	GODLIKE	GRANTOR	GROANER	GUNNING
GLACIAL	GODLING	GRANULE	GROCERY	GUNPLAY
GLACIER	GODROON	GRAPERY	GROGRAM	GUNROOM
GLADDEN	GODSEND	*GRAPHIC	GROMMET	GUNSHIP
GLADDER	GODSHIP	GRAPIER	GROOMER	GUNSHOT
GLADIER	GOGGLER	GRAPLIN	GROOVER	GUNWALE
GLAIKET	GOLDARN	GRAPNEL	GROSSER	GURGLET
GLAIKIT	GOLDBUG	GRAPPLE	GROSSLY	GURNARD
GLAMOUR	GOLDEYE	GRASPER	*GROUCHY	GUSTIER
GLASSIE	GOLDURN	GRATIFY	GROUPER	GUSTILY
*GLAZIER	GOLFING	GRATING	GROUPIE	GUTLESS
*GLAZING	GOLIARD	GRAUPEL	GROUSER	GUTLIKE
GLEANER	GOMERAL	GRAVELY	GROUTER	GUTTATE
GLEEFUL	GOMEREL	GRAVEST	GROWLER	GUTTERY
GLEEMAN	GOMERIL	GRAVIDA	GROWNUP	GUTTIER
GLENOID	GONDOLA	GRAVIES	GRUBBER	GUTTING
GLIADIN	GOODBYE	GRAVING	GRUDGER	GUTTLER
GLIMMER	GOODIES	GRAVITY	GRUELER	*GUZZLER

*GWEDUCK	GASHOUSE	GERBILLE	GLORIOLE	GOURMAND
GYMNAST	GASIFIED	GERMANIC	GLORIOUS	GOVERNOR
GYNECIA	GASIFIER	GERMFREE	GLOSSARY	GOWNSMAN
*GYNECIC	GASIFORM	GERMIEST	GLOSSEME	GRABBIER
GYRATOR	GASLIGHT	GERMINAL	GLOSSIES	GRABBING
GADABOUT	GASOGENE	GERONTIC	GLOSSINA	GRABBLER
GADARENE	GASOLENE	GESTICAL	*GLOWWORM	GRACEFUL
GADGETRY	GASOLIER	GESTURAL	*GLOXINIA	GRACILIS
*GADZOOKS	GASOLINE	*GHASTFUL	GLUCAGON	GRACIOSO
GAINLESS	GASTIGHT	GIANTESS	GLUCINUM	GRACIOUS
GALACTIC	GASTNESS	GIANTISM	GLUELIKE	GRADIENT
GALANGAL	GASTRAEA	GIBBSITE	GLUMNESS	GRADUAND
GALAVANT	GASTRULA	*GIFTEDLY	GLUTELIN	GRADUATE
GALBANUM	*GASWORKS	GIFTLESS	GLUTTING	*GRAECIZE
GALENITE	GATEFOLD	GIGANTIC	GLUTTONY	*GRAFFITO
GALIVANT	GATELESS	GIGAWATT	GLYCERIN	GRAFTAGE
GALLEASS	GATELIKE	GILDHALL	GLYCEROL	GRAMARYE
GALLIARD	GATEPOST	GILTHEAD	*GLYCERYL	*GRAMERCY
GALLOPER	GATHERER	*GIMCRACK	*GLYCOGEN	GRANDAME
GALOPADE	GAUNTLET	*GIMMICKY	*GLYCONIC	GRANDDAD
GALVANIC	*GAVELOCK	GINGELEY	*GLYCOSYL	GRANDEUR
GAMASHES	*GAYWINGS	GINGELLY	GNARRING	GRANDSIR
GAMBESON	*GAZOGENE	GINGERLY	GNATHION	GRANDSON
GAMBUSIA	*GAZPACHO	GIRASOLE	GNATHITE	GRANULAR
*GAMECOCK	GEARCASE	GIRLHOOD	GNATLIKE	*GRAPHEME
GAMENESS	GEARLESS	*GIVEAWAY	GNOMICAL	GRAPHITE
GAMESOME	GEEPOUND	GLABELLA	GOADLIKE	GRAPIEST
GAMESTER	GELATINE	GLABRATE	GOALLESS	GRAPLINE
GAMINESS	GELATION	GLABROUS	GOALPOST	GRAPPLER
GAMMADIA	GELIDITY	GLACIATE	*GOATFISH	GRATEFUL
GAMMONER	GELSEMIA	GLADDEST	GOATHERD	GRATUITY
GAMODEME	GEMINATE	GLADDING	GOATLIKE	GRAVAMEN
GANGLAND	GEMMIEST	GLADIATE	GOATSKIN	GRAVE
GANGLIAL	*GEMOLOGY	GLADIEST	*GODCHILD	*GRAVELLY
GANGLIAR	*GEMSBUCK	GLADIOLA	GODLIEST	GRAVITON
GANGLIER	GEMSTONE	GLADIOLI	GOETHITE	*GRAYBACK
GANGLING	GENDARME	GLADNESS	GOLCONDA	*GRAYFISH
GANGLION	GENERATE	GLADSOME	*GOLDFISH	GRAYLING
*GANGPLOW	GENEROUS	GLANDERS	GOLGOTHA	GRAYNESS
GANGRENE	GENETICS	GLANDULE	GOLLIWOG	*GRAZIOSO
GANGSTER	GENITALS	GLASSFUL	GOMBROON	GREEGREE
GANISTER	GENITIVE	GLASSIER	GONENESS	GREENBUG
GANTLINE	GENITURE	GLASSILY	GONFALON	GREENERY
GANTLOPE	GENOCIDE	GLASSINE	GONFANON	*GREENFLY
*GANYMEDE	GENOTYPE	GLASSMAN	GONGLIKE	GREENIER
GAPESEED	GENTRICE	GLAUCOMA	GONIDIUM	GREENING
*GAPEWORM	GEODESIC	GLAUCOUS	GONOCYTE	GREENISH
*GAPINGLY	GEODETIC	*GLAZIERY	GONOPORE	GREENLET
*GARBANZO	GEOGNOSY	GLEANING	GOODNESS	GREETING
GARBLESS	GEOLOGER	GLEESOME	*GOODWIFE	GREWSOME
GARBOARD	*GEOMANCY	GLEGNESS	GOODWILL	GREYNESS
GARDENER	GEOMETER	GLIADINE	GOOFBALL	GRIDIRON
GARDENIA	GEOMETRY	GLIBNESS	GORBELLY	GRIEVANT
GARDYLOO	*GEOPHAGY	GLIMPSER	*GORBLIMY	GRIEVOUS
GARGANEY	GEOPHONE	GLISSADE	GORGEOUS	GRILLADE
GARGOYLE	*GEOPHYTE	GLITTERY	GORGERIN	GRILLAGE
GAROTTER	GEOPONIC	GLOAMING	GORINESS	GRIMACER
GARRISON	*GEOTAXIS	GLOBATED	GOSPELER	GRIMIEST
GARROTER	GERANIAL	GLOBULAR	GOSSAMER	GRIMMEST
GARROTTE	GERANIOL	GLOBULIN	GOSSIPER	GRIMNESS
GASALIER	GERANIUM	GLOOMFUL	GOSSIPRY	GRINDERY
GASELIER	GERARDIA	GLOOMING	GOSSYPOL	GRINNING

GRIPIEST	GUTTIEST	CO G NAC	*JA G GER	PI G EON
GRIPPIER	GUTTURAL	*CO G WAY	JA G UAR	PI G GED
GRIPPING	*GYMKHANA	CY G NET	*JI G GER	PI G GIE
*GRIPSACK	GYMNASIA	DA G GER	*JI G GLE	PI G GIN
GRISEOUS	GYNAECEA	DA G GLE	*JI G GLY	PI G LET
GRISETTE	GYNAECIA	DA G OBA	*JI G SAW	PI G NUS
*GRIZZLER	*GYNANDRY	DE G AGE	*JO G GER	PI G NUT
GROGGERY	*GYNARCHY	DE G ERM	*JO G GLE	PI G PEN
*GROGSHOP	*GYNECIUM	DE G REE	JU G ATE	PI G STY
GROMWELL	*GYNECOID	DE G UST	*JU G FUL	PO G IES
*GROSBEAK	*GYNIATRY	DI G AMY	*JU G GED	PO G ROM
GROSCHEN	GYNOECIA	DI G EST	*JU G GLE	PU G GED
GROUNDER	GYPSEIAN	DI G GED	JU G ULA	PU G GRY
GROUPING	GYPSEOUS	DI G GER	KE G LER	PU G REE
GROUPOID	*GYPSYDOM	DI G LOT	LA G END	RA G BAG
GROVELER	*GYPSYISH	DO G DOM	LA G GED	RA G GED
*GRUBWORM	*GYPSYISM	DO G GED	LA G GER	RA G GLE
GRUELING	GYRATION	DO G GER	LA G OON	RA G ING
GRUELLED	*GYRATORY	DO G LEG	LA G UNA	RA G LAN
GRUELLER	GYROIDAL	DO G NAP	LA G UNE	RA G MAN
GRUESOME	GYROSTAT	DU G ONG	LE G ACY	RA G OUT
*GRUFFIER		FA G GOT	LE G ATE	RA G TAG
*GRUFFILY		FI G URE	LE G ATO	RE G AIN
*GRUFFISH	N G WEE	*FO G BOW	LE G END	RE G ALE
GRUMBLER	BA G ASS	FO G DOG	LE G GED	RE G ARD
GRUMMEST	BA G FUL	FO G GED	LE G GIN	RE G AVE
*GRUMPHIE	BA G GED	FO G GER	LE G ION	RE G EAR
*GRUMPISH	BA G GIE	FU G ATO	LE G IST	RE G ENT
GUACHARO	BA G MAN	FU G GED	LE G MAN	RE G ILD
GUAIACOL	BA G NIO	GA G GED	LE G UME	RE G IME
GUAIACUM	BA G UET	GA G GER	LI G AND	RE G INA
GUAIOCUM	BA G WIG	GA G GLE	LI G ASE	RE G ION
GUANIDIN	BE G ALL	GA G MAN	LI G ATE	RE G IUS
GUARANTY	*BE G AZE	GI G GED	LI G NIN	RE G IVE
GUARDANT	BE G GAR	GI G GLE	LI G ULA	RE G LET
GUARDIAN	BE G GED	GI G GLY	LI G ULE	RE G LOW
GUERILLA	BE G IRD	GI G LET	LI G URE	RE G LUE
GUERNSEY	BE G LAD	GI G LOT	LO G GED	RE G NAL
GUIDANCE	BE G ONE	GI G OLO	LO G GER	RE G NUM
GUILEFUL	BE G RIM	GO G GLE	LO G GIA	RE G RET
GULFIEST	BE G ULF	GO G GLY	LO G ILY	RE G REW
*GULFLIKE	BI G AMY	GO G LET	LO G ION	RE G ROW
*GULFWEED	BI G EYE	GU G GLE	*LO G JAM	RI G GED
GULLABLE	BI G GER	GU G LET	LO G WAY	RI G GER
GULLIBLE	BI G GIE	HA G BUT	LU G GED	RI G HTO
GULOSITY	BI G GIN	HA G DON	LU G GER	RI G HTY
GUMBOTIL	BI G WIG	HA G GED	LU G GIE	RI G OUR
GUMMIEST	BO G GED	HA G GIS	MA G NET	RU G GED
GUMMOSIS	BO G GLE	HA G GLE	ME G ASS	RU G GER
GUMPTION	BO G IES	HE G ARI	*MI G HTY	RU G OSE
*GUNFIGHT	BU G EYE	HE G IRA	MI G NON	RU G OUS
GUNFLINT	BU G GED	HI G GLE	NA G ANA	SA G BUT
GUNMETAL	BU G GER	*HI G HLY	NA G GER	SA G EST
GUNPAPER	BU G LER	*HI G HTH	NE G ATE	SA G GAR
GUNPOINT	BU G SHA	HO G GED	NI G GER	SA G GED
GUNSMITH	BY G ONE	HO G GER	NI G GLE	SA G GER
*GUNSTOCK	CA G IER	HO G NUT	NO G GIN	SE G GAR
GURUSHIP	CA G ILY	HO G TIE	NU G GET	SI G HER
GUSTABLE	CA G ING	HU G EST	PA G ING	SI G LOS
GUSTIEST	CO G ENT	HU G GED	PA G ODA	SI G NAL
GUSTLESS	CO G GED	HU G GER	*PE G BOX	SI G NER
GUTTATED	CO G ITO	*JA G GED	PE G GED	SI G NET

SI G NOR
SO G GED
SU G ARY
TA G GED
TA G GER
TA G RAG
TE G MEN
TI G HTS
TI G LON
TO G ATE
TO G GED
TO G GLE
TU G GER
TU G RIK
VA G ARY
VA G ILE
VA G INA
VA G ROM
VE G ETE
VI G OUR
WA G GED
WA G GER
WA G GLE
WA G GLY
WA G GON
WI G EON
WI G GED
WI G GLE
WI G GLY
WI G LET
WI G WAG
*WI G WAM
YO G INI
YO G URT
*ZI G ZAG
*ZY G OMA
*ZY G OTE
BA G ASSE
BA G GAGE
BA G GING
BA G PIPE
BA G SFUL
*BA G WORM
BE G GARY
BE G GING
BE G LOOM
BE G ONIA
BE G ORAH
BE G ORRA
BE G RIME
BE G ROAN
BE G UILE
BE G UINE
BI G GEST
BI G GETY
BI G GING
BI G GISH
BI G GITY
BI G HEAD
BI G HORN
BI G NESS
BI G OTED

BI G OTRY
BO G BEAN
BO G GIER
BO G GING
BO G GISH
BO G WOOD
*BO G YISM
*BO G YMAN
BU G ABOO
BU G BANE
BU G BEAR
BU G GERY
BU G GING
BU G LOSS
BU G SEED
CA G IEST
CI G ARET
*CO G ENCY
CO G GING
CO G NATE
CO G NISE
*CO G NIZE
*DA G LOCK
DE G AUSS
*DE G LAZE
DE G RADE
DI G AMMA
DI G GING
DI G ITAL
*DI G NIFY
DI G NITY
*DI G OXIN
DI G RAPH
DI G RESS
DO G BANE
DO G CART
DO G EDOM
DO G FACE
*DO G FISH
DO G GERY
DO G GIES
DO G GING
DO G GISH
DO G GONE
DO G GREL
DO G LIKE
DO G SLED
DO G TROT
DO G VANE
DO G WOOD
FA G OTER
FI G HTER
FI G MENT
FI G URAL
FI G URER
FI G WORT
FO G GAGE
FO G GING
FO G HORN
FO G LESS
*FO G YISM

FU G GING
FU G UIST
GA G GING
GA G STER
GI G ABIT
GI G ATON
GI G GING
GI G GLER
GO G GLER
HA G ADIC
HA G BORN
*HA G BUSH
*HA G FISH
HA G GARD
HA G GING
*HA G GISH
HA G GLER
HA G RIDE
HE G UMEN
*HI G HBOY
*HI G HWAY
*HO G BACK
*HO G FISH
*HO G LIKE
HO G MANE
HO G NOSE
*HO G WASH
*HO G WEED
HU G EOUS
HU G GING
HY G EIST
HY G IENE
*JA G GARY
*JA G GERY
*JA G GING
*JA G LESS
*JI G ABOO
*JI G GING
*JO G GLER
*JU G GING
*JU G GLER
*JU G HEAD
*JU G SFUL
*JU G ULAR
*JU G ULUM
KE G ELER
KE G LING
LA G GARD
LA G GING
LE G ALLY
LE G ATEE
LE G ATOR
LE G GIER
LE G GING
LE G HORN
LE G IBLE
LE G LESS
LE G LIKE
LE G ROOM
LE G UMIN
*LE G WORK
LI G HTEN

LI G HTER
LI G HTLY
LI G NIFY
LI G NITE
LI G ROIN
LO G BOOK
LO G GATS
LO G GETS
LO G GIER
LO G GING
LO G ICAL
LO G IEST
LO G ROLL
LO G WOOD
LU G GAGE
LU G GING
LU G SAIL
LU G WORM
MA G NETO
*MA G NIFY
ME G ALIT
ME G APOD
ME G AVOL
ME G AWAT
ME G ILLA
*ME G ILPH
MI G NONN
MI G RAIN
MU G GIES
*MU G WUMP
NA G GING
NE G ATON
NE G ATOR
NE G ATOR
NE G LECT
NE G LIGE
NE G ROID
NI G GARD
NI G GHTY
NI G GLER
NI G HTIE
NI G HTLY
NI G RIFY
NO G GING
PA G EANT
*PA G EBOY
PA G INAL
PA G URID
PE G GING
PE G LESS
PE G LIKE
*PI G FISH
PI G GERY
PI G GIES
PI G GING
PI G GISH
PI G MENT
PI G SKIN
PI G SNEY
PI G WEED
PO G ONIA

PO G ONIP
PU G AREE
PU G GIER
PU G GING
PU G GISH
*PU G MARK
RA G GING
RA G GING
RA G TIME
RA G WEED
RA G WORT
RE G ALIA
RE G ALLY
RE G ATTA
RE G AUGE
RE G ENCY
RE G IMEN
*RE G LAZE
RE G LOSS
RE G NANT
RE G ORGE
RE G OSOL
RE G RADE
RE G RAFT
RE G RANT
RE G RATE
RE G REET
RE G RESS
RE G RIND
RE G ROUP
RE G ULAR
RE G ULUS
RI G GING
RI G HTER
RI G HTLY
RI G IDLY
RO G UERY
RO G UISH
RU G GING
RU G LIKE
SA G AMAN
SA G GARD
SA G GIER
SA G GING
SA G IEST
SA G UARO
SE G ETAL
SE G MENT
SI G ANID
SI G HTER
SI G HTLY
SI G MOID
SI G NIFY
SI G NIOR
SI G NORA
SI G NORE
SI G NORY
SU G GEST
TA G GING
TA G LIKE
TA G MEME
TE G ULAR

TE G UMEN	CON G RESS	GIN G ELEY	LOD G MENT	RIB G RASS	
TI G HTEN	CRA G SMAN	GIN G ELLY	LON G BOAT	RID G IEST	
TI G RESS	CUD G ELER	GIN G ERLY	LON G ERON	RID G LING	
TI G RISH	CUT G RASS	GLE G NESS	LON G HAIR	*RIN G BARK	
TO G ATED	DAU G HTER	GOL G OTHA	LON G HAND	RIN G BOLT	
TO G GERY	DIA G NOSE	GON G LIKE	LON G HEAD	RIN G BONE	
TO G GING	DIA G ONAL	GOR G EOUS	LON G HORN	RIN G DOVE	
TO G GLER	*DIA G RAPH	GOR G ERIN	LON G LEAF	RIN G HALS	
TU G BOAT	DIG G INGS	GRO G GERY	LON G LINE	RIN G LIKE	
TU G GING	DIN G DONG	*GRO G SHOP	LON G NESS	*RIN G NECK	
TU G LESS	DIS G ORGE	*HAG G ADIC	LON G SHIP	RIN G SIDE	
VA G RANT	DIS G RACE	*HAN G BIRD	LON G SOME	RIN G TAIL	
VE G ETAL	DIS G UISE	*HAN G FIRE	LON G SPUR	RIN G TOSS	
WA G ERER	*DOG G EDLY	HAN G NAIL	LON G TIME	RIN G WORM	
*WA G GERY	DOG G EREL	HAN G NEST	LON G UEUR	ROU G HAGE	
WA G GING	DOG G IEST	*HAN G OVER	*LON G WAYS	*ROU G HDRY	
WA G GING	DOG G ONED	*HED G EHOG	LON G WISE	*ROU G HHEW	
*WA G GISH	*DOU G HBOY	*HED G EHOP	*LUN G FISH	*ROU G HISH	
WA G ONER	DOU G HIER	*HED G EPIG	LUN G WORM	ROU G HLEG	
WA G SOME	DOU G HNUT	*HED G EROW	LUN G WORT	RYE G RASS	
WA G TAIL	DRA G GIER	*HEI G HTEN	MA G ICIAN	SAN G AREE	
*WI G GERY	DRA G GING	*HUG G ABLE	MA G ISTER	SAN G UINE	
WI G GING	DRA G LINE	*JAG G HERY	MA G NESIA	SAR G ASSO	
WI G GLER	DRA G ONET	*JAR G ONEL	MA G NETIC	SEA G OING	
WI G LESS	DRA G ROPE	*JIG G ERED	*MAN G ABEY	SEI G NEUR	
*WI G LIKE	DRA G STER	*JIN G OISM	MI G RATOR	SEI G NIOR	
YE G GMAN	DRU G GIST	*JIN G OIST	*MYO G ENIC	SEI G NORY	
YO G HURT	DUN G AREE	*JON G LEUR	*MYO G RAPH	SER G EANT	
*ZY G OSIS	DUN G HILL	*JUD G MENT	NAR G HILE	*SHA G BARK	
*BAD G ERLY	*DYS G ENIC	*JUG G LERY	NAR G ILEH	SHA G REEN	
BAN G TAIL	FID G ETER	*JUG G LING	NEI G HBOR	SHI G ELLA	
BAR G EMAN	FIN G ERER	KAN G AROO	NIG G LING	SIN G SONG	
BAR G HEST	FLA G ELLA	KED G EREE	NON G ATAL	SIN G ULAR	
BAR G UEST	FLA G GING	*KIN G BIRD	NON G REEN	SLO G GING	
*BEG G ARLY	FLA G LESS	*KIN G BOLT	NON G UILT	SLU G ABED	
BER G AMOT	FLA G POLE	*KIN G FISH	NUT G RASS	SLU G FEST	
BIO G ENIC	FLA G RANT	*KIN G HOOD	PAN G OLIN	SLU G GARD	
BOG G IEST	*FLA G SHIP	KIN G LESS	PEI G NOIR	SLU G GING	
BON G OIST	*FOR G IVER	*KIN G LIKE	PIN G RASS	SLU G GISH	
*BOO G YMAN	*FOU G HTEN	*KIN G POST	PLA G IARY	SMU G GLER	
*BOU G HPOT	FOX G LOVE	*KIN G SHIP	PLA G UING	SMU G NESS	
BOU G HTEN	FRA G GING	KIN G SIDE	PLI G HTER	SNA G LIKE	
BRA G GART	FRA G MENT	*KIN G WOOD	PLU G LESS	SNI G GLER	
BRA G GEST	FRA G RANT	*KNI G HTLY	*PLU G UGLY	SNU G GERY	
BRA G GING	*FRI G HTEN	LAN G LAUF	POI G NANT	SNU G GEST	
BRI G HTEN	*FRO G FISH	LAN G RAGE	PRE G NANT	SNU G GING	
BRO G UERY	FRO G GING	LAN G SHAN	*PRI G GERY	SNU G NESS	
BRO G UISH	*FRO G LIKE	LAN G SYNE	*PRI G GISH	SON G BIRD	
BUD G ETER	FUN G IBLE	LAN G UAGE	PRI G GISM	*SON G BOOK	
BUN G ALOW	GAD G ETRY	LAN G UISH	PRO G GING	SON G FEST	
BUN G HOLE	GAN G LAND	LAR G ESSE	PRO G NOSE	SON G LESS	
BUN G LING	GAN G LIAL	LAU G HING	PRO G RADE	SON G LIKE	
BUR G LARY	GAN G LIAR	LAU G HTER	PRO G RESS	SON G STER	
BUR G ONET	GAN G LIER	*LAW G IVER	PUG G AREE	*SPA G YRIC	
BUR G RAVE	GAN G LING	LEG G IEST	PUG G IEST	SPY G LASS	
*BUR G UNDY	GAN G LION	LIE G EMAN	*PUN G ENCY	STA G GARD	
CHI G ETAI	*GAN G PLOW	LIN G ERER	*PYO G ENIC	STA G GART	
CIN G ULUM	GAN G RENE	LIN G ERIE	*QUA G MIRE	STA G GERY	
*COA G ENCY	GAN G STER	LIN G IEST	*QUA G MIRY	STA G GING	
COA G ULUM	GAR G ANEY	LIN G UINE	RAY G RASS	STA G IEST	
CON G ENER	GAR G OYLE	LIN G UINI	REI G NITE	STA G NANT	
CON G LOBE	GEO G NOSY	LIN G UIST		STA G NATE	

STE G ODON	DON G	TRI G	VYIN G	DOTIN G
SUB G ENUS	DRA G	TUN G	WHAN G	*DOZIN G
SUB G RADE	DRE G	TWI G	WRAN G	DUGON G
SUB G ROUP	DUN G	VAN G	WRIN G	DUOLO G
SUN G LASS	FAN G	VUG G	WRON G	DUPIN G
SUR G ICAL	FLA G	WIN G	WRUN G	DURIN G
SWA G GING	FRA G	YAN G	YOUN G	DYEIN G
TAI G LACH	FRI G	YEG G	BAGWI G	FACIN G
TEI G LACH	FRO G	ZIN G	BAKIN G	FADIN G
*THU G GERY	FRU G	*BEFO G	BALIN G	FAKIN G
*THU G GISH	GAN G	BEIN G	BANDO G	FAMIN G
TON G UING	GLE G	*BEWI G	BANIN G	FARIN G
TOU G HIES	GON G	*BHAN G	BARIN G	FATIN G
*TOU G HISH	GRI G	BOUR G	BARON G	FETIN G
TRA G ICAL	GRO G	BRIN G	BASIN G	FILIN G
TRA G OPAN	HAN G	*CHAN G	BATIN G	FIRIN G
TRI G GEST	HOG G	CLAN G	BECLO G	*FIZGI G
TRI G GING	HON G	CLIN G	BEDBU G	FLYIN G
*TRI G LYPH	HUN G	CLUN G	BEDRU G	FOGDO G
TRI G NESS	JAG G	COHO G	BEFLA G	*FOXIN G
TRI G ONAL	KIN G	COLO G	BELON G	FUMIN G
TRI G RAPH	LAN G	CUIN G	BIDIN G	FUSIN G
TUN G STEN	LIN G	DEBU G	BIGWI G	*FUZIN G
TUR G ENCY	LON G	*DEFO G	BIKIN G	GAGIN G
TWI G LESS	LUN G	DOIN G	BITIN G	GAMIN G
*TWI G LIKE	MIG G	DYIN G	BLUIN G	GAPIN G
VAN G UARD	MUG G	FLIN G	BODIN G	GASBA G
*VEN G EFUL	NOG G	FLUN G	BONIN G	GATIN G
VER G ENCE	PAN G	GLOG G	BORIN G	*GAZIN G
VIR G INAL	PEA G	GOIN G	BOWIN G	GIVIN G
WAG G ONER	PIN G	*HYIN G	BOWLE G	GLUIN G
*WAY G OING	PLU G	KIAN G	*BOXIN G	GOBAN G
WEI G ELIA	PRI G	KLON G	BUSIN G	GORIN G
*WEI G HMAN	PRO G	LIAN G	CAGIN G	GRELA G
*WEI G HTER	PUN G	LYIN G	CANIN G	GUNDO G
*WIN G BACK	QUA G	PIRO G	CARIN G	GYRIN G
WIN G DING	RAN G	PRAN G	CASIN G	HALIN G
*WIN G EDLY	RIN G	PRON G	CAVIN G	HARIN G
WIN G IEST	RUN G	RENI G	CEDIN G	HATIN G
WIN G LESS	SAN G	RUIN G	CERIN G	HAYIN G
*WIN G LIKE	SCA G	SCRA G	CITIN G	*HAZIN G
*WIN G OVER	SHA G	SHRU G	CODIN G	HIDIN G
WIN G SPAN	SHO G	SLAN G	COMIN G	HIRIN G
WRI G GLER	SIN G	SLIN G	CONIN G	HOLIN G
*ZIG G URAT	SKA G	SLUN G	COPIN G	HOMIN G
*ZOO G ENIC	SKE G	SPAN G	CORIN G	HONIN G
*ZOO G LOEA	SLA G	SPRA G	COTIN G	HOPIN G
	SLO G	SPRI G	COVIN G	HOSIN G
	SLU G	SPRU G	CUBIN G	HOTDO G
BAN G	SMO G	*SQUE G	CURIN G	HUMBU G
BER G	SMU G	STAI G	CYBOR G	*JAPIN G
BON G	SNA G	STAN G	DARIN G	*JOKIN G
BRA G	SNU G	STIN G	DATIN G	KALON G
BRI G	SON G	STUN G	DIALO G	KITIN G
BUN G	STA G	SUIN G	DICIN G	LACIN G
BUR G	SUN G	SWAN G	DININ G	LADIN G
CHU G	SWA G	SWIN G	DIVIN G	LAKIN G
CLA G	SWI G	SWUN G	DOGLE G	LAMIN G
CLO G	THU G	THIN G	DOLIN G	LAPDO G
CRA G	TIN G	THON G	DOMIN G	LASIN G
DAN G	TON G	TWAN G	DOPIN G	LAVIN G
DIN G	TRI G	TYIN G	DORBU G	LAWIN G

*LAZIN G	RAPIN G	TININ G	BILLIN G	COOKIN G
LIKIN G	RARIN G	TIRIN G	BILTON G	COPPIN G
LIMIN G	RASIN G	TOLIN G	BINDIN G	COWLIN G
LININ G	RATIN G	TONIN G	BINNIN G	CRANIN G
LIVIN G	RAVIN G	TOPIN G	BIRLIN G	CRANNO G
LOSIN G	*RAZIN G	TOTIN G	BITTIN G	CRAVIN G
LOVIN G	REDBU G	TRUIN G	BLAMIN G	CUNNIN G
LOWIN G	REDIN G	TUBIN G	BLUEIN G	CUPPIN G
LURIN G	REDLE G	TUNIN G	BOATIN G	CURBIN G
LUTIN G	REHAN G	TYPIN G	BOBBIN G	CURLIN G
LYSIN G	REHUN G	VICIN G	BOGGIN G	CURSIN G
MACIN G	RICIN G	VIKIN G	BOOKIN G	CURVIN G
MAKIN G	RIDIN G	VININ G	BOOTLE G	CUTTIN G
MASKE G	RILIN G	VISIN G	BOWLIN G	*CYCLIN G
MATIN G	RIMIN G	VOTIN G	BRACIN G	*CYMLIN G
MAYIN G	RIPIN G	WADIN G	BRAKIN G	DAMMIN G
*MAZIN G	RISIN G	WAGIN G	BRAVIN G	DAPPIN G
METIN G	RIVIN G	WAKIN G	*BRAZIN G	DARNIN G
MIDLE G	ROPIN G	WALIN G	BREWIN G	DAYLON G
MIMIN G	ROSIN G	WANIN G	BRIBIN G	DEALIN G
MININ G	ROVIN G	WARIN G	BRUTIN G	*DECKIN G
MIRIN G	ROWIN G	WAVIN G	BUDDIN G	DEMAGO G
MOPIN G	RULIN G	*WAXIN G	BUDGIN G	DENNIN G
MOVIN G	SANIN G	WIFIN G	BUGGIN G	DIALIN G
MULIN G	SARON G	WIGWA G	BULLDO G	DIBBIN G
MURIN G	SATAN G	WILIN G	BUMMIN G	DIGGIN G
MUSIN G	SATIN G	WININ G	BUNTIN G	DIMMIN G
MUSKE G	SAVIN G	WIPIN G	BURNIN G	DINNIN G
MUTIN G	SAWLO G	WIRIN G	BURRIN G	DIPPIN G
NAMIN G	SAYIN G	WISIN G	BUSHIN G	DISHRA G
NIDIN G	SEABA G	WITIN G	BUSSIN G	DODGIN G
NOSIN G	SEADO G	WIVIN G	*BUZZWI G	DOGGIN G
NOTIN G	SEEIN G	YOKIN G	*CACHIN G	DONNIN G
NUTME G	SERIN G	*ZAFTI G	CALLIN G	DOTTIN G
PACIN G	SEWIN G	*ZIGZA G	CAMPIN G	DRAPIN G
PADNA G	SIDIN G	*ZOFTI G	CAMPON G	DRAWIN G
PAGIN G	SIPIN G	*ZONIN G	CANNIN G	DRONIN G
PALIN G	SIRIN G	*BACKIN G	CANTDO G	DUBBIN G
PARAN G	SITIN G	*BACKLO G	CAPPIN G	DUCTIN G
PARIN G	*SIZIN G	BADGIN G	CARDIN G	DUMPIN G
PAVIN G	SKIIN G	BAGGIN G	CARLIN G	DUNNIN G
PENAN G	SLUIN G	BANKIN G	CARPIN G	DUPPIN G
PHOTO G	SOLIN G	BANNIN G	CARVIN G	DUPTRA G
PIEIN G	SPRAN G	BARGIN G	CASTIN G	FABLIN G
PIKIN G	SPRIN G	BARRIN G	CATALO G	FAILIN G
PILIN G	SPRUN G	BASTIN G	CATLIN G	FAIRIN G
PINAN G	STALA G	BATHIN G	CATTIN G	FANNIN G
PININ G	STRAN G	BATTIN G	CAUSIN G	FARCIN G
PIPIN G	STRIN G	BATWIN G	CEILIN G	FARMIN G
POKIN G	STRON G	BEADIN G	*CHAFIN G	FASTIN G
POLIN G	STRUN G	BEANBA G	CHARIN G	FATLIN G
POSIN G	SUNDO G	BEARIN G	CHASIN G	FATTIN G
PROLE G	TAGRA G	BEATIN G	*CHIMIN G	FEEDBA G
PROLO G	TAKIN G	BEDDIN G	*CHOKIN G	FEELIN G
PULIN G	TAMIN G	BEGGIN G	CHORIN G	FELTIN G
PUTLO G	TAPIN G	BELTIN G	CLOSIN G	FENCIN G
*QUAHO G	TARIN G	BELYIN G	COAMIN G	FETTIN G
RACIN G	TAUTO G	BETTIN G	COATIN G	FIDGIN G
RAGBA G	THRON G	BIBBIN G	CODLIN G	FILIBE G
RAGIN G	TIDIN G	BIDDIN G	*COFFIN G	FILLIN G
RAGTA G	TILIN G	BIGGIN G	COGGIN G	FINDIN G
RAKIN G	TIMIN G	BILLBU G	CONNIN G	FINNIN G

FIREBU G	*HAMBUR G	LADYBU G	MUSTAN G	PULSIN G
FIREDO G	*HAMMIN G	LAGGIN G	NAGGIN G	PUNNIN G
*FISHGI-G	HANDBA G	LAMMIN G	NAPPIN G	PUPPIN G
FISHIN G	HANGDO G	LANCIN G	NECKIN G	PURGIN G
FITTIN G	HANGIN G	LANDIN G	NERVIN G	PURRIN G
FLAMIN G	HANGTA G	LAPPIN G	NETTIN G	PURSIN G
FLEABA G	*HAPPIN G	LAPWIN G	NIMMIN G	PUTTIN G
FLUTIN G	HARPIN G	LASHIN G	NIPPIN G	*QUAHAU G
FLYTIN G	HATTIN G	LASTIN G	NODDIN G	*QUOTIN G
FOGGIN G	*HAWKIN G	LATHIN G	NOGGIN G	RAGGIN G
FOOTIN G	HEADIN G	LEADIN G	NOONIN G	RAILIN G
FORCIN G	HEARIN G	LEANIN G	NOSEBA G	RAISIN G
FORELE G	HEAVIN G	LEASIN G	NOTHIN G	RAMMIN G
FORGIN G	HEDGIN G	LEAVIN G	NURSIN G	RAPPIN G
FOULIN G	HEELIN G	LEGGIN G	NUTTIN G	RATTIN G
FOWLIN G	HELPIN G	LEMMIN G	*PACKIN G	READIN G
FRAYIN G	HEMAGO G	LETTIN G	PADDIN G	REDDIN G
FUGGIN G	*HEMMIN G	LICKIN G	PALLIN G	REDWIN G
FUNNIN G	HERRIN G	LINSAN G	PANNIN G	REEDIN G
FURLON G	HILDIN G	LIPPIN G	PARKIN G	REFFIN G
FURRIN G	*HIPPIN G	LISTIN G	PARLIN G	RETTIN G
GABBIN G	HISSIN G	LOADIN G	PARRIN G	RETYIN G
GADDIN G	HOLDIN G	LOANIN G	PARSIN G	REVVIN G
GAGGIN G	*HOMBUR G	LOBBIN G	PARTIN G	RIBBIN G
GAMMIN G	HOMOLO G	LODGIN G	PASSIN G	RIDDIN G
GAPPIN G	*HOPPIN G	LOGGIN G	PASTIN G	RIDGIN G
GARRIN G	HORSIN G	LONGIN G	PATTIN G	RIFLIN G
GASKIN G	HOTTIN G	LOOSIN G	PEACIN G	RIGGIN G
GASSIN G	HOUSIN G	LOPPIN G	PEDAGO G	RIMMIN G
GEARIN G	HUGGIN G	LORDIN G	PEELIN G	RINNIN G
GELDIN G	*HUMMIN G	LOTTIN G	PEGGIN G	RINSIN G
GELLIN G	HUNTIN G	LUGGIN G	PENNIN G	RIPPIN G
GEMMIN G	HURLIN G	LUNGIN G	PEPPIN G	ROARIN G
GENSEN G	*HUSKIN G	MADDIN G	PERIWI G	ROBBIN G
GETTIN G	HUTTIN G	*MAHJON G	PETTIN G	ROLLIN G
GIBBIN G	*JABBIN G	MAHUAN G	PFENNI G	ROOFIN G
GIGGIN G	*JACKLE G	MAILBA G	PHONIN G	ROTTIN G
GILDIN G	*JAGGIN G	MAILIN G	*PICKIN G	ROUGIN G
GINNIN G	*JAMMIN G	MANNIN G	PIECIN G	ROUTIN G
GINSEN G	*JARRIN G	MAPPIN G	PIGGIN G	RUBBIN G
GIPPIN G	*JESTIN G	MARKIN G	PINKIN G	RUCHIN G
*GLAZIN G	*JETTIN G	MARLIN G	PINNIN G	RUGGIN G
GNAWIN G	*JIBBIN G	MARRIN G	PIPPIN G	RUNNIN G
GOBBIN G	*JIGGIN G	MASKIN G	PITTIN G	RUSHIN G
GODDIN G	*JOBBIN G	MATTIN G	PLACIN G	RUTTIN G
GODLIN G	*JOININ G	MEANIN G	PLANIN G	SABBIN G
GOLDBU G	*JOTTIN G	MEETIN G	PLATIN G	SACKIN G
GOLFIN G	*JUGGIN G	MENDIN G	PLUMIN G	SAGGIN G
GORGIN G	*KAMPON G	MERGIN G	POPPIN G	SAILIN G
GOSLIN G	KARTIN G	METRIN G	POSTBA G	SALVIN G
GRACIN G	KEEPIN G	*MILCHI G	POSTIN G	SANDBA G
GRADIN G	KEGLIN G	MILLIN G	POTTIN G	SANDHO G
GRATIN G	KENNIN G	MOLDIN G	PRATIN G	SAPLIN G
GRAVIN G	*KEPPIN G	MONOLO G	PRICIN G	SAPPIN G
GRAYLA G	KIDDIN G	MOORIN G	PRIMIN G	SAUCIN G
*GRAZIN G	KILLIN G	MOPPIN G	PROBAN G	SCALIN G
GRIMIN G	KILTIN G	MORNIN G	PROLON G	SCARIN G
GRIPIN G	*KIPPIN G	MOUSIN G	PROSIN G	SCORIN G
GUMMIN G	KITLIN G	MUDDIN G	PROVIN G	SEATIN G
GUNNIN G	KITTIN G	MUGGIN G	PRUNIN G	SEEMIN G
GUTTIN G	*KNOWIN G	MUMMIN G	PUDDIN G	SEISIN G
HAGGIN G	*KNOWIN G	MUNTIN G	PUGGIN G	*SEIZIN G

SEMILO G	SWIVIN G	WESTIN G	*CAULKIN G	*FARTHIN G
SENSIN G	SYNAGO G	WETTIN G	CENTRIN G	FAUBOUR G
SERGIN G	TABBIN G	WHALIN G	*CHANCIN G	FETTLIN G
SERVIN G	TABLIN G	WHININ G	*CHAPPIN G	*FIGHTIN G
SETTIN G	TAGGIN G	WHITIN G	*CHARMIN G	FIGURIN G
SHADIN G	TAILIN G	WHORIN G	CHARRIN G	*FINIKIN G
*SHAKIN G	TALKIN G	*WICKIN G	CHATTIN G	*FIREFAN G
SHAMIN G	TANNIN G	WIGGIN G	*CHILDIN G	FIREPLU G
SHAPIN G	TAPPIN G	WILDIN G	CHINNIN G	FLAGGIN G
SHARIN G	TARRIN G	WILLIN G	*CHIPPIN G	*FLAMMIN G
SHAVIN G	TASTIN G	WINCIN G	CHITLIN G	*FLAPPIN G
SHEBAN G	TATTIN G	WINDBA G	CHOOSIN G	*FLASHIN G
SHINDI G	TAUTAU G	WINDIN G	CHOUSIN G	FLATLIN G
SHININ G	*TAXYIN G	WINNIN G	*CHROMIN G	FLATTIN G
SHORIN G	TEASIN G	WITHIN G	CHURNIN G	FLEECIN G
SHOVIN G	TENSIN G	WITLIN G	CIRCLIN G	*FLESHIN G
SHOWIN G	TESTIN G	WITTIN G	CLADDIN G	FONDLIN G
SIAMAN G	THEOLO G	WONNIN G	*CLAMMIN G	FOOTLIN G
SIBLIN G	TICKIN G	WORDIN G	CLEARIN G	FOOTSLO G
SIFTIN G	TINNIN G	*WORKBA G	*CLIPPIN G	*FOREWIN G
SINNIN G	TINTIN G	*WORKIN G	CLOTHIN G	FRAGGIN G
SIPPIN G	TIPPIN G	WRITIN G	CLOTTIN G	FRETTIN G
SITTIN G	TITHIN G	*YAPPIN G	*CLUBBIN G	FRILLIN G
SKATIN G	TOGGIN G	*YAWPIN G	COASTIN G	FRITTIN G
SLATIN G	TOOLIN G	YEALIN G	COHERIN G	FROGGIN G
SLAVIN G	TOPPIN G	YESSIN G	COLORIN G	FROSTIN G
SLIDIN G	TOTTIN G	*YIPPIN G	*COUCHIN G	FUELLIN G
SLIMIN G	TOURIN G	*BABBLIN G	COUPLIN G	GANGLIN G
SMITIN G	TRACIN G	BALLYRA G	COURSIN G	GLADDIN G
SMOKIN G	TREPAN G	BANTLIN G	COVERIN G	GLEANIN G
SOARIN G	TRICIN G	*BECOMIN G	*CRACKIN G	GLOAMIN G
SODDIN G	TUBBIN G	BEESWIN G	*CRAMMIN G	GLOOMIN G
SOLVIN G	TUGGIN G	BITEWIN G	*CRAPPIN G	GLUTTIN G
SOPPIN G	TUNNIN G	*BLACKIN G	CRESTIN G	GNARRIN G
SPACIN G	TUPPIN G	*BLACKLE G	*CRIBBIN G	GOLLIWO G
SPADIN G	TURNIN G	BLASTIN G	*CROPPIN G	GRABBIN G
SPAEIN G	TUTTIN G	BLATTIN G	CROSSIN G	GRAYLIN G
SPARIN G	TWININ G	BLEEDIN G	CURRYIN G	GREENBU G
SPICIN G	VATTIN G	BLESSIN G	*CYMBLIN G	GREENIN G
SPIKIN G	VEILIN G	BLOODIN G	DABBLIN G	GREETIN G
SPILIN G	VEININ G	BLOTTIN G	DEMOTIN G	GRINNIN G
SPIRIN G	VERGIN G	BOARDIN G	DEVISIN G	GRIPPIN G
SPITIN G	VERSIN G	BRAGGIN G	DINGDON G	GROUPIN G
SPUMIN G	VESTIN G	BRAIDIN G	DIVIDIN G	GRUELIN G
STAGIN G	VETTIN G	BRANNIN G	DIVININ G	HANDLIN G
STANIN G	VIEWIN G	*BREAKIN G	DOUBLIN G	*HATCHIN G
STARIN G	VOICIN G	BREEDIN G	DRAFTIN G	HEADLON G
STATIN G	WADDIN G	BRIDGIN G	DRAGGIN G	*HEDGEHO G
STOKIN G	WAGGIN G	BRIEFIN G	DRAMMIN G	*HEDGEPI G
STONIN G	WAITIN G	*BRIMMIN G	DREDGIN G	HIRELIN G
STOPIN G	*WALKIN G	BRISLIN G	DRESSIN G	HOARDIN G
STORIN G	WANNIN G	*BRONZIN G	DRILLIN G	*HUMBLIN G
STYLIN G	WARNIN G	BUILDIN G	DRIPPIN G	*HYDRAGO G
SUBBIN G	WARRIN G	BULLFRO G	DROPPIN G	*JELUTON G
SUBRIN G	WARTHO G	BULLRIN G	DRUBBIN G	*JUGGLIN G
SUITIN G	WASHIN G	BULLYRA G	DRUMMIN G	KAOLIAN G
SUMMIN G	WASHRA G	*BUMBLIN G	*DUCKLIN G	KINDLIN G
SUNNIN G	WASTIN G	BUNDLIN G	DUELLIN G	KNITTIN G
SUPPIN G	*WAXWIN G	BUNGLIN G	DUMPLIN G	LACEWIN G
SURFIN G	*WEBBIN G	CAGELIN G	DWELLIN G	LALLYGA G
SURGIN G	WEDDIN G	*CAJOLIN G	FAGOTIN G	LAUGHIN G
SWAGIN G	WELTIN G	*CAPRIFI G		LAYERIN G

LEAPFRO G	PLEDGIN G	*SHAMMIN G	SPARLIN G	*TORQUIN G
LEARNIN G	PLOTTIN G	SHANTUN G	SPARRIN G	TOWELIN G
*LEFTWIN G	*PLUMBIN G	SHEALIN G	SPATTIN G	*TRACKIN G
LEGATIN G	POLLIWO G	SHEDDIN G	*SPEAKIN G	TRAININ G
LIFELON G	*POLLYWO G	*SHEEPDO G	SPEEDIN G	TRAMMIN G
LIGHTIN G	*PREPPIN G	SHEETIN G	SPEERIN G	TRAPPIN G
LIVELON G	*PRIMMIN G	*SHELVIN G	SPELLIN G	TRAVELO G
LOATHIN G	PRINTIN G	SHIELIN G	SPHERIN G	TRIFLIN G
LOLLYGA G	PROGGIN G	SHILLIN G	*SPIFFIN G	TRIGGIN G
LORDLIN G	*PROPPIN G	*SHIMMIN G	SPINNIN G	TRIMMIN G
LUSTRIN G	PUDDLIN G	SHINNIN G	SPITTIN G	TRIPLIN G
*LYNCHIN G	PURFLIN G	*SHIPPIN G	SPONGIN G	TRIPPIN G
*MAHJONG G	*QUANDAN G	SHIRRIN G	SPOONIN G	TRITHIN G
MANTLIN G	*QUANDON G	SHIRTIN G	SPOTTIN G	TROLLIN G
MANURIN G	*QUANTON G	SHITTIN G	SPURRIN G	TROTTIN G
MARBLIN G	*QUILTIN G	SHOOTIN G	*SQUARIN G	TROUPIN G
*MEALYBU G	*QUISLIN G	*SHOPPIN G	STABLIN G	*TRUCKIN G
MIDDLIN G	*QUITTIN G	SHOTTIN G	STAGGIN G	TRUDGIN G
MINUTIN G	RALLYIN G	*SHRIVIN G	STANDIN G	TRUSSIN G
MISDOIN G	RATTLIN G	*SHUCKIN G	STARLIN G	TUMBLIN G
MISLYIN G	RAVELIN G	SHUTTIN G	STARRIN G	TURTLIN G
MODELIN G	RAVENIN G	SIDELIN G	STEADIN G	TWILLIN G
*MONEYBA G	REEDLIN G	SIDELON G	STEALIN G	TWINNIN G
MOTORIN G	REFININ G	SINGSON G	STEEVIN G	TWISTIN G
MOULDIN G	RESPRIN G	SKILLIN G	STEMMIN G	TWITTIN G
MOUNTIN G	RESTRIN G	*SKIMMIN G	STEPPIN G	VAPORIN G
MOURNIN G	RESTRUN G	SKINNIN G	STERLIN G	VAULTIN G
MUTININ G	RETIRIN G	SKIORIN G	STIRRIN G	WAISTIN G
*MYSTAGO G	REVERIN G	*SKIPPIN G	*STOCKIN G	*WAKENIN G
NAETHIN G	*REVIVIN G	SKIRTIN G	STOPPIN G	*WATCHDO G
NEEDLIN G	RIDGLIN G	SLABBIN G	STRAVAI G	WATERDO G
NESTLIN G	RIPPLIN G	SLAPPIN G	STRIDIN G	WATERIN G
NIDERIN G	*ROCKLIN G	SLASHIN G	STRIPIN G	WATERLO G
NIGGLIN G	ROUGHLE G	SLATTIN G	STUBBIN G	*WAYGOIN G
NONBEIN G	*RUFFLIN G	SLEDDIN G	STUDDIN G	*WEAKLIN G
NONUSIN G	RUMBLIN G	SLEEPIN G	*STUFFIN G	WEANLIN G
NORTHIN G	RUSTLIN G	SLIMMIN G	STUMMIN G	*WEEKLON G
NURSLIN G	SADDLIN G	SLIPPIN G	STUNNIN G	*WHEELIN G
PADDLIN G	SALADAN G	SLITTIN G	*SUCKLIN G	*WHETTIN G
PAINTIN G	SAMPLIN G	SLOGGIN G	*SVEDBER G	*WHIPPIN G
PANELIN G	SANDLIN G	SLOPPIN G	*SWABBIN G	*WHIRRIN G
PARADIN G	SAVAGIN G	SLOTTIN G	SWAGGIN G	*WHIZBAN G
PARASAN G	SCALAWA G	SLUBBIN G	SWANNIN G	*WHIZZIN G
PEDDLIN G	SCANNIN G	SLUGGIN G	SWATTIN G	WILDLIN G
PETTIFO G	SCARRIN G	SLUMMIN G	SWEEPIN G	WINDLIN G
*PHILABE G	SCATTIN G	SLURRIN G	SWEETIN G	WINGDIN G
*PHILIBE G	SCOLDIN G	*SMOCKIN G	SWELLIN G	*WITCHIN G
PHRASIN G	SCOURIN G	SMUTTIN G	*SWIMMIN G	*WRAPPIN G
PILOTIN G	SCOUTIN G	SNAPPIN G	*TACKLIN G	*WRECKIN G
*PINCHBU G	SCRAPIN G	SNIPPIN G	TAGALON G	*WRITHIN G
PINDLIN G	*SCUMMIN G	SNUGGIN G	TEACHIN G	*YACHTIN G
PLAGUIN G	*SCUPPAU G	SOOCHON G	TEETHIN G	YEANLIN G
PLAITIN G	SEAGOIN G	SOOTHIN G	*THIEVIN G	YEARLIN G
*PLANKIN G	SECURIN G	SOUCHON G	*THINKIN G	YEARLON G
PLANNIN G	SEEDLIN G	SOUNDIN G	THINNIN G	YEARNIN G
PLANTIN G	SELADAN G	SOUTHIN G	TINKLIN G	*ZINCKIN G
PLATTIN G	SETTLIN G	*SPANKIN G	TONGUIN G	
PLEADIN G	*SHAFTIN G	SPANNIN G		

H

HAAF	HENT	**HOWL**	**HAWSE**	HOGAN
HAAR	**HERB**	**HUCK**	**HAYER**	**HOICK**
HABU	**HERD**	**HUFF**	*HAZAN	HOISE
HACK	**HERE**	**HUGE**	*HAZEL	HOIST
HADE	HERL	HUIC	*HAZER	*HOKEY
*HADJ	**HERM**	HULA	**HEADY**	*HOKKU
HAEM	**HERN**	**HULK**	**HEART**	HOKUM
HAEN	**HERO**	HULL	**HEAVE**	**HOLEY**
HAET	**HERS**	**HUMP**	**HEAVY**	HOLLA
HAFT	**HEST**	HUNG	HEDER	HOLLO
HAIK	**HETH**	**HUNK**	**HEDGE**	**HOMED**
HAIL	**HICK**	HUNT	**HEDGY**	**HOMER**
HAIR	HIDE	HURL	*HEEZE	**HOMEY**
HAJI	**HIGH**	HURT	**HEFTY**	HONAN
*HAJJ	**HIKE**	**HUSH**	**HEIGH**	HONDA
HAKE	HILA	**HUSK**	HEIST	HONER
HALE	HILI	**HWAN**	HELIO	**HONEY**
HALF	HILL	**HYLA**	*HELIX	*HONKY
HALL	HILT	**HYMN**	HELLO	HONOR
HALM	HIND	**HYPO**	HELOT	**HOOCH**
HALO	HIRE	**HYTE**	**HELVE**	**HOOEY**
HALT	HISN	**HABIT**	HEMAL	**HOOKA**
HAME	HISS	**HACEK**	HEMIC	*HOOKY
HAND	HIST	HADAL	**HEMIN**	**HOOLY**
HANG	**HIVE**	*HADJI	*HEMPY	**HOPER**
HANK	HOAR	HADST	**HENCE**	**HORAH**
HANT	**HOAX**	*HAFIZ	HENNA	HORAL
HARD	**HOCK**	HAIKU	**HENRY**	HORDE
HARE	HOER	**HAIRY**	**HERBY**	**HORNY**
HARL	HOGG	*HAJJI	HERES	HORSE
HARM	**HOKE**	HALER	**HERMA**	HORST
HARP	HOLD	HALID	HERON	**HORSY**
HART	HOLE	HALLO	**HERRY**	HOSEL
HASH	HOLK	**HALVA**	*HERTZ	**HOTCH**
HASP	**HOLP**	**HALVE**	**HEUGH**	HOTEL
HAST	HOLM	**HAMAL**	**HEWER**	**HOTLY**
HATE	HOLT	*HAMMY	*HEXAD	HOUND
HATH	**HOLY**	*HAMZA	*HEXER	HOURI
HAUL	HOME	**HANCE**	*HEXYL	HOUSE
HAVE	HOMO	**HANDY**	HIDER	**HOVEL**
HAWK	**HOMY**	*HANKY	**HIGHT**	**HOVER**
*HAZE	HONE	HANSE	**HIKER**	*HOWFF
*HAZY	HONG	HAOLE	HILAR	**HOYLE**
HEAL	**HONK**	*HAPAX	HILLO	*HUBBY
HEAP	HOOD	**HAPLY**	**HILLY**	*HUFFY
HEAR	HOOF	*HAPPY	**HILUM**	HUGER
HEAT	**HOOK**	HARDS	HILUS	*HULKY
HECK	HOOP	**HARDY**	HINGE	HULLO
HEED	HOOT	**HAREM**	**HINNY**	**HUMAN**
HEEL	HOPE	**HARPY**	HIPPO	HUMIC
HEFT	HORA	**HARRY**	*HIPPY	**HUMID**
HEIL	HOSE	**HARSH**	HIRER	**HUMOR**
HEIR	HOST	HASTE	**HITCH**	*HUMPH
HELD	HOUR	**HATCH**	**HOAGY**	*HUMPY
HELL	**HOVE**	HATER	HOARD	**HUMUS**
HELM	**HOWE**	**HAUGH**	**HOARY**	HUNCH
HELP	**HOWF**	**HAULM**	*HOBBY	*HUNKY
HEME	**HOWK**	HAUNT	**HOCUS**	HURDS
HEMP			**HAVOC**	HODAD	**HURLY**

HURRY	HANGAR	HEAVER	HILLER	*HOOKEY
*HUSKY	HANGER	*HECKLE	HILLOA	*HOOKUP
HUSSY	HANGUP	HECTIC	HINDER	HOOLIE
HUTCH	HANKER	HECTOR	HINGER	HOOPED
*HUZZA	HANKIE	HEDDLE	HIPPED	HOOPER
HYDRA	HANSEL	HEDGER	HIPPER	HOOPLA
HYDRO	HANSOM	HEEDER	HIPPIE	HOOPOE
HYENA	HANTLE	*HEEHAW	HIRING	HOOPOO
HYING	HAPPED	HEELER	HIRPLE	HOORAH
HYMEN	HAPPEN	HEFTER	HIRSEL	HOORAY
HYOID	HAPTEN	HEGARI	HIRSLE	HOOTCH
*HYPHA	HAPTIC	HEGIRA	HISPID	HOOTER
*HYRAX	HARASS	HEIFER	HISSER	HOOVES
HYSON	HARBOR	HEIGHT	HITHER	HOPING
HABILE	HARDEN	HEINIE	HOAGIE	HOPPLE
*HACKEE	HARDLY	*HEJIRA	HOARSE	HORARY
*HACKER	HAREEM	HELIAC	*HOAXER	HORNET
*HACKIE	HARING	HELIUM	HOBBLE	HORRID
*HACKLE	HARLOT	HELLER	HOBNOB	HORROR
*HACKLY	HARMER	HELMET	*HOCKER	HORSEY
*HADJEE	HARMIN	HELPER	*HOCKEY	HORSTE
HADRON	HARPER	HEMMED	HODDEN	HOSIER
HAEMAL	HARPIN	HEMMER	HODDIN	HOSING
HAEMIC	HARROW	HEMOID	HOGGED	HOSTEL
HAEMIN	HARTAL	HEMPEN	HOGGER	HOSTLY
HAERES	HASLET	HEMPIE	HOGNUT	HOTBED
HAFTER	HASSEL	HENBIT	HOGTIE	*HOTBOX
HAGBUT	HASSLE	HEPCAT	HOIDEN	HOTDOG
HAGDON	HASTEN	HEPTAD	HOLARD	HOTROD
HAGGED	*HATBOX	HERALD	HOLDEN	HOTTED
HAGGIS	HATFUL	HERBAL	HOLDER	HOTTER
HAGGLE	HATING	HERDER	HOLDUP	HOUDAH
HAILER	HATPIN	HERDIC	HOLIER	HOURLY
HAIRDO	HATRED	HEREAT	HOLIES	HOUSEL
HAIRED	HATTED	HEREIN	HOLILY	HOUSER
*HAKEEM	HATTER	HEREOF	HOLING	*HOWDAH
HALALA	HAULER	HEREON	HOLISM	HOWLER
HALEST	HAULMY	HERESY	HOLIST	HOWLET
HALIDE	HAUNCH	HERETO	HOLLER	HOYDEN
HALING	HAUSEN	HERIOT	HOLLOA	*HUBBUB
HALITE	HAVIOR	HERMIT	HOLLOO	*HUBCAP
HALLAH	*HAWKER	HERNIA	HOLLOW	HUBRIS
HALLEL	*HAWKEY	HEROIC	HOLPEN	*HUCKLE
HALLOA	*HAWKIE	HEROIN	HOMAGE	HUDDLE
HALLOO	HAWSER	HERPES	HOMBRE	HUGEST
HALLOT	HAYING	HETERO	HOMELY	HUGGED
HALLOW	*HAYMOW	*HEXADE	HOMIER	HUGGER
*HALLUX	*HAZARD	*HEXANE	HOMILY	HULLER
HALOID	*HAZIER	*HEXONE	HOMING	HULLOA
HALTER	*HAZILY	*HEXOSE	HOMINY	HUMANE
*HALUTZ	*HAZING	*HEYDAY	HONCHO	HUMATE
*HALVAH	*HAZZAN	*HEYDEY	HONEST	HUMBLE
HALVES	HEADER	HIATUS	HONIED	*HUMBLY
HAMATE	HEALER	*HICCUP	HONING	HUMBUG
HAMAUL	HEALTH	*HICKEY	HONKER	HUMMED
HAMLET	HEARER	HIDDEN	*HONKEY	HUMMER
HAMMAL	HEARSE	HIDING	HONKIE	HUMOUR
HAMMED	HEARTH	HIEMAL	HONOUR	HUNGER
HAMMER	HEARTY	HIGGLE	HOODIE	HUNGRY
HAMPER	*HEATHY	*HIGHLY	HOODOO	HUNKER
*HAMZAH	HEAUME	*HIGHTH	HOOFER	HUNTER
HANDLE	HEAVEN	*HIJACK	*HOOKAH	HURDLE

HURLER	*HALLWAY	HARVEST	HEELING	*HICKORY
HURLEY	HALOGEN	*HASHISH	HEGUMEN	HIDABLE
HURRAH	HALVERS	*HASSOCK	*HEIGHTH	HIDALGO
HURRAY	HALYARD	HASTATE	HEINOUS	HIDEOUS
HURTER	*HAMBURG	HASTING	HEIRDOM	HIDEOUT
HURTLE	HAMMIER	HATABLE	HEIRESS	*HIGHBOY
HUSKER	*HAMMILY	HATBAND	HEISTER	*HIGHWAY
HUSSAR	*HAMMING	*HATCHEL	HEKTARE	*HIJINKS
HUSTLE	*HAMMOCK	*HATCHER	HELIAST	HILDING
HUTTED	HAMSTER	*HATCHET	HELICAL	HILLIER
*HUTZPA	HAMULUS	HATEFUL	HELICES	*HILLOCK
*HUZZAH	HANAPER	HATLESS	HELICON	HILLTOP
HYAENA	HANDBAG	HATLIKE	HELIPAD	*HIMSELF
*HYBRID	HANDCAR	*HATRACK	*HELLBOX	HINDGUT
HYBRIS	HANDFUL	HATSFUL	HELLCAT	HIPBONE
HYDRIA	HANDGUN	HATTING	HELLERI	HIPLESS
*HYDRIC	HANDIER	*HAUBERK	HELLERY	*HIPLIKE
HYDRID	HANDILY	*HAUGHTY	HELLISH	HIPNESS
HYETAL	HANDLER	HAULAGE	HELLUVA	HIPPEST
HYMNAL	*HANDOFF	HAULIER	HELOTRY	HIPPIER
*HYPHEN	HANDOUT	HAUNTER	*HELPFUL	*HIPPING
*HYPNIC	HANDSAW	*HAUTBOY	HELPING	*HIPPISH
HYSSOP	HANDSEL	HAUTEUR	HEMAGOG	*HIPSHOT
HABITAN	HANDSET	HAVEREL	HEMATAL	HIPSTER
HABITAT	HANGDOG	HAVIOUR	HEMATIC	HIRABLE
HABITUE	HANGING	*HAWKING	HEMATIN	HIRCINE
HABITUS	HANGMAN	*HAWKISH	HEMIOLA	HIRSUTE
*HACHURE	HANGOUT	HAYCOCK	HEMLINE	HIRUDIN
*HACKBUT	HANGTAG	*HAYFORK	*HEMLOCK	HISSELF
*HACKLER	HANUMAN	HAYLAGE	*HEMMING	HISSING
*HACKMAN	HAPLESS	*HAYLOFT	HEMPIER	HISTOID
*HACKNEY	HAPLITE	*HAYRACK	HENBANE	HISTONE
*HACKSAW	HAPLOID	HAYRICK	HENCOOP	HISTORY
HADARIM	HAPLONT	HAYRIDE	HENLIKE	*HITCHER
HADDEST	*HAPPING	HAYSEED	HENNERY	HITLESS
*HADDOCK	HAPTENE	*HAYWARD	*HENPECK	HOARDER
HAEMOID	HARBOUR	HAYWIRE	HEPARIN	HOARIER
*HAFNIUM	HARDHAT	*HAZELLY	HEPATIC	HOARILY
HAGADIC	HARDIER	*HAZIEST	HEPTANE	HOARSEN
HAGBORN	HARDIES	HEADIER	HEPTOSE	*HOATZIN
*HAGBUSH	HARDILY	HEADILY	HERBAGE	HOBBIES
*HAGFISH	HARDPAN	HEADING	HERBIER	HOBBLER
HAGGARD	HARDSET	HEADMAN	HERDMAN	*HOBLIKE
HAGGING	HARDTOP	HEADPIN	HEREDES	HOBNAIL
*HAGGISH	HARELIP	HEADSET	HERETIC	HOBOISM
HAGGLER	HARIANA	*HEADWAY	HERITOR	*HODADDY
HAGRIDE	HARICOT	*HEALTHY	HEROINE	*HOECAKE
HAIRCAP	*HARIJAN	HEARING	HEROISM	HOEDOWN
HAIRCUT	*HARMFUL	HEARKEN	*HEROIZE	HOELIKE
HAIRIER	HARMINE	HEARSAY	HERONRY	*HOGBACK
HAIRPIN	*HARMONY	HEARTEN	HERRING	*HOGFISH
*HALAKIC	HARNESS	HEATHEN	HERSELF	*HOGLIKE
HALALAH	HARPIES	HEATHER	HESSIAN	HOGMANE
*HALAVAH	HARPING	HEAVIER	HESSITE	HOGNOSE
HALBERD	HARPIST	HEAVIES	HETAERA	*HOGWASH
HALBERT	HARPOON	HEAVING	HETAIRA	*HOGWEED
*HALCYON	HARRIED	HEBETIC	*HEXAGON	HOISTER
*HALFWAY	HARRIER	*HECKLER	*HEXAPLA	HOLDALL
HALIBUT	HARRIES	HECTARE	*HEXAPOD	HOLDING
HALIDOM	HARSHEN	HEDGING	*HEXEREI	HOLDOUT
HALITUS	*HARSHLY	HEDONIC	*HEXOSAN	HOLIBUT
HALLOTH	HARSLET	HEEDFUL	*HIBACHI	HOLIDAY

HOLIEST	HUMBLER	*HAFTARAH	*HAPLOIDY	*HEADHUNT
HOLLAND	*HUMDRUM	*HAFTORAH	*HAPTICAL	HEADIEST
HOLMIUM	HUMERAL	HAGADIST	HARANGUE	*HEADLAMP
HOLSTER	HUMERUS	*HAGBERRY	HARASSER	HEADLAND
*HOLYDAY	*HUMIDLY	*HAGGADIC	HARBORER	HEADLESS
HOMAGER	HUMIDOR	HAIRBALL	*HARDBACK	HEADLINE
*HOMBURG	*HUMMING	HAIRBAND	HARDBALL	*HEADLOCK
HOMIEST	*HUMMOCK	HAIRIEST	HARDBOOT	HEADLONG
HOMINID	HUMORAL	HAIRLESS	HARDCASE	HEADMOST
*HOMMOCK	HUNDRED	*HAIRLIKE	HARDCORE	HEADNOTE
HOMOLOG	HUNNISH	HAIRLINE	HARDENER	HEADRACE
*HOMONYM	HUNTING	*HAIRLOCK	*HARDHACK	HEADREST
HONESTY	HURDIES	*HAIRWORK	*HARDHEAD	HEADROOM
HONOREE	HURDLER	*HAIRWORM	HARDIEST	HEADSAIL
HONORER	HURLING	*HALAKIST	HARDNESS	*HEADSHIP
HOODLUM	HURRIER	*HALAKOTH	*HARDSHIP	HEADSMAN
HOOKIER	HURTFUL	HALATION	*HARDTACK	*HEADSTAY
HOOKIES	HUSBAND	HALENESS	*HARDWARE	*HEADWIND
HOOKLET	*HUSHABY	*HALFBACK	*HARDWOOD	*HEADWORD
HOOSGOW	*HUSHFUL	*HALFBEAK	HAREBELL	*HEADWORK
*HOPEFUL	HUSKIER	*HALFLIFE	*HARELIKE	*HEATEDLY
*HOPHEAD	HUSKIES	HALFNESS	HARKENER	HEATLESS
HOPLITE	*HUSKILY	*HALFTIME	HARLOTRY	*HEAVENLY
*HOPPING	*HUSKING	HALFTONE	HARMLESS	*HEAVYSET
*HOPSACK	HUSTLER	HALIDOME	*HARMONIC	*HEBDOMAD
HOPTOAD	*HUSWIFE	HALLIARD	HARRIDAN	HEBETATE
HORDEIN	HUTLIKE	*HALLMARK	HARROWER	HEBETUDE
*HORIZON	HUTMENT	HALLOWER	*HARRUMPH	*HEBRAIZE
HORNIER	HUTTING	*HALOLIKE	HARUSPEX	*HECATOMB
HORNILY	*HUTZPAH	HAMARTIA	*HASHEESH	*HECTICAL
HORNITO	HYALITE	*HAMMERER	HASTEFUL	*HEDGEHOG
HORRENT	HYALOID	*HAMMIEST	HASTENER	*HEDGEHOP
*HORRIFY	*HYDATID	*HAMPERER	*HATCHECK	*HEDGEPIG
HORSIER	HYDRANT	HANDBALL	*HATCHERY	*HEDGEROW
HORSILY	HYDRASE	HANDBILL	*HATCHING	HEDONICS
HORSING	HYDRATE	*HANDBOOK	*HATCHWAY	HEDONISM
HOSANNA	*HYDRIDE	HANDCART	HATEABLE	HEDONIST
HOSIERY	*HYDROID	*HANDCUFF	*HATMAKER	HEEDLESS
HOSPICE	*HYDROPS	*HANDFAST	HATTERIA	HEELBALL
HOSTAGE	HYDROUS	*HANDGRIP	*HAULYARD	HEELLESS
HOSTESS	*HYDROXY	*HANDHOLD	HAUSFRAU	*HEGEMONY
HOSTILE	HYGEIST	*HANDICAP	HAUTBOIS	HEGUMENE
HOSTLER	HYGIENE	HANDIEST	*HAVDALAH	*HEGUMENY
*HOTCAKE	*HYMNARY	HANDLING	*HAVELOCK	*HEIGHTEN
HOTFOOT	*HYMNIST	HANDLIST	*HAVOCKER	HEIRLESS
HOTHEAD	*HYMNODY	HANDLOOM	*HAWFINCH	HEIRLOOM
HOTNESS	*HYPERON	*HANDMADE	*HAWKBILL	*HEIRSHIP
HOTSHOT	*HYPNOID	*HANDMAID	*HAWKLIKE	HELIACAL
HOTSPUR	*HYPOGEA	*HANDPICK	*HAWKMOTH	*HELICITY
HOTTEST	*HYPONEA	HANDRAIL	*HAWKNOSE	HELICOID
HOTTING	*HYPOXIA	*HANDSEWN	*HAWKSHAW	*HELICOPT
HOTTISH	HABANERA	*HANDSFUL	*HAWKWEED	HELIPORT
HOUNDER	*HABBINIC	HANDSOME	*HAWTHORN	HELISTOP
HOUSING	HABITANT	*HANDWORK	*HAYMAKER	HELLBENT
HOVERER	HABITUAL	*HANDWRIT	*HAYSTACK	HELLFIRE
*HOWBEIT	HABITUDE	*HANDYMAN	HAZELNUT	*HELLKITE
*HOWEVER	HACIENDA	*HANGBIRD	*HAZINESS	*HELMINTH
HUDDLER	*HACKWORK	*HANGFIRE	*HEADACHE	HELMLESS
*HUFFISH	HAEMATAL	HANGNAIL	*HEADACHY	*HELMSMAN
HUGEOUS	*HAEMATIC	HANGNEST	*HEADBAND	HELOTAGE
HUGGING	HAEMATIN	*HANGOVER	HEADGATE	HELOTISM
*HUMANLY		*HANKERER	HEADGEAR	HELPLESS

*HELPMATE	*HIGHBROW	HOMINIES	*HOUSEFLY	*HYPOGEUM
*HELPMEET	*HIGHBUSH	HOMININE	HOUSEFUL	*HYPOGYNY
HEMATEIN	*HIGHJACK	HOMINOID	HOUSEMAN	*HYPONOIA
HEMATINE	*HIGHLAND	*HOMOGONY	HOUSETOP	*HYPOPNEA
HEMATITE	*HIGHNESS	*HOMOLOGY	*HOWITZER	*HYPOPYON
HEMATOID	*HIGHROAD	*HOMONYMY	*HUARACHE	*HYPOTHEC
*HEMATOMA	*HIGHTAIL	HONEWORT	*HUARACHO	*HYRACOID
*HEMIPTER	*HIJACKER	*HONEYBEE	*HUCKSTER	HYSTERIA
*HEMOCOEL	HILARITY	*HONEYBUN	HUGENESS	*HYSTERIC
*HEMOCYTE	HILLIEST	*HONEYDEW	*HUGGABLE	
*HEMOLYZE	HILLSIDE	*HONEYFUL	HUMANISE	
HEMOSTAT	HILTLESS	HONORAND	*HUMANISM	B H UT
*HEMPIEST	HIMATION	HONORARY	*HUMANIZE	C H AD
*HEMPWEED	HINDERER	HONOURER	HUMANOID	C H AM
*HENCHMAN	HINDMOST	HOODLESS	*HUMBLEST	C H AP
*HENEQUEN	*HIPPARCH	*HOODLIKE	*HUMBLING	C H AR
HENEQUIN	*HIPPIEST	*HOODWINK	*HUMIDIFY	C H AT
HENHOUSE	HIRAGANA	*HOOFBEAT	*HUMIDITY	C H AW
*HENIQUEN	HIRELING	HOOFLESS	*HUMIFIED	C H EF
*HEPATICA	HISTAMIN	*HOOFLIKE	*HUMILITY	C H EW
*HEPATIZE	HISTIDIN	HOOKIEST	*HUMMABLE	*C H EZ
*HEPATOMA	HISTOGEN	*HOOKLESS	*HUMORFUL	C H IA
HEPTAGON	HISTORIC	*HOOKLIKE	HUMORIST	C H IC
*HEPTARCH	HITHERTO	*HOOKNOSE	HUMOROUS	C H IN
HERALDIC	HIVELESS	*HOOKWORM	*HUMPBACK	C H IP
*HERALDRY	*HOACTZIN	HOOLIGAN	*HUMPLESS	C H IT
HERBARIA	HOARDING	HOOPLESS	HURTLESS	C H ON
HERBIEST	HOARIEST	*HOOPLIKE	*HUSKIEST	C H OP
HERBLESS	*HOBBYIST	HOOPSTER	*HUSKLIKE	C H OW
*HERBLIKE	*HOCKSHOP	*HOOSEGOW	HUSTINGS	C H UB
HERCULES	*HOGMANAY	HOPELESS	*HYACINTH	C H UG
*HERDLIKE	*HOGMENAY	*HORNBEAM	*HYALOGEN	C H UM
HERDSMAN	*HOGSHEAD	HORNBILL	*HYDRACID	D H AK
*HEREDITY	*HOKYPOKY	*HORNBOOK	*HYDRAGOG	D H OW
HEREINTO	*HOLDBACK	HORNFELS	*HYDRANTH	G H AT
*HERETRIX	*HOLDFAST	HORNIEST	*HYDRATOR	G H EE
HEREUNTO	*HOLDOVER	HORNLESS	*HYDROGEL	K H AN
HEREUPON	HOLELESS	*HORNLIKE	*HYDROGEN	K H AT
*HEREWITH	HOLINESS	*HORNPIPE	*HYDROMEL	P H AT
HERITAGE	HOLOGRAM	HORNPOUT	*HYDRONIC	P H EW
*HERITRIX	*HOLOGYNY	HORNTAIL	*HYDROPIC	*P H IZ
*HERMETIC	*HOLOTYPE	*HORNWORM	*HYDROPSY	P H ON
*HERMITRY	*HOLOZOIC	HORNWORT	*HYDROSOL	P H OT
HERNIATE	HOLSTEIN	HOROLOGE	*HYDROXYL	R H EA
HEROICAL	*HOLYTIDE	*HOROLOGY	*HYGIEIST	R H US
HESITANT	*HOMEBODY	HORRIBLE	*HYLOZOIC	S H AD
HESITATE	*HOMEBRED	*HORRIBLY	*HYMENEAL	S H AG
*HEXAGRAM	HOMELAND	*HORRIFIC	*HYMENIUM	S H AH
*HEXAMINE	HOMELESS	HORSECAR	*HYMNBOOK	S H AM
*HEXAPODY	*HOMELIKE	*HORSEFLY	*HYMNLESS	S H AT
*HEXARCHY	*HOMEMADE	HORSEMAN	*HYMNLIKE	S H AW
HIBERNAL	HOMEROOM	HORSIEST	*HYOSCINE	S H AY
*HIBISCUS	*HOMESICK	HOSPITAL	*HYPERGOL	S H EA
*HICCOUGH	HOMESITE	HOSPITIA	*HYPEROPE	S H ED
*HIDEAWAY	*HOMESPUN	HOSPODAR	*HYPHEMIA	S H EW
HIDELESS	*HOMETOWN	HOTBLOOD	*HYPNOSIS	S H IM
HIDROSIS	*HOMEWARD	*HOTCHPOT	*HYPNOTIC	S H IN
*HIERARCH	*HOMEWORK	HOTELIER	*HYPOACID	S H IP
HIERATIC	*HOMICIDE	HOTELMAN	*HYPODERM	S H IT
*HIGHBALL	HOMILIST	HOTHOUSE	*HYPOGEAL	S H IV
*HIGHBORN	HOMINESS	HOTPRESS	*HYPOGEAN	S H MO
*HIGHBRED	HOMINIAN	*HOUSEBOY	*HYPOGENE	S H OD

S H OE	C H ARK	C H YLE	S H ELF	T H ERM
S H OG	C H ARM	*C H YME	S H ELL	T H ESE
S H OO	C H ARR	D H OLE	S H END	T H ETA
S H OP	C H ART	D H OTI	S H EOL	T H ICK
S H OT	C H ARY	D H UTI	S H ERD	T H IEF
S H OW	C H ASE	G H AST	S H IED	T H IGH
S H RI	C H ASM	G H AUT	S H IEL	T H ILL
S H UL	C H EAP	*G H AZI	S H IER	T H INE
S H UN	C H EAT	G H OST	S H IES	T H ING
S H UT	C H EEK	G H OUL	**S H IFT**	**T H INK**
T H AE	C H EEP	G H YLL	S H ILL	T H IOL
T H AN	C H EER	K H ADI	**S H ILY**	T H IRD
T H AT	C H ELA	*K H AKI	S H INE	T H IRL
T H AW	C H ERT	K H EDA	**S H INY**	T H OLE
T H EE	C H ESS	P H AGE	S H IRE	T H ONG
T H EM	C H EST	P H ASE	**S H IRK**	T H ORN
T H EN	C H ETH	P H IAL	S H IRR	T H ORO
T H EW	*C H EVY	*P H LOX	S H IRT	T H ORP
T H EY	*C H EWY	P H ONE	S H IST	T H OSE
T H IN	C H IAO	P H ONO	**S H IVA**	T H RAW
T H IO	*C H ICK	P H ONY	**S H IVE**	T H REE
T H IR	C H ICO	P H OTO	S H OAL	**T H REW**
T H IS	C H IDE	*P H PHT	S H OAT	T H RIP
T H OU	C H IEF	P H YLA	**S H OCK**	T H ROB
T H RO	C H IEL	P H YLE	S H OER	T H ROE
T H RU	C H ILD	R H EUM	*S H OJI	T H ROW
T H UD	C H ILE	R H INO	S H ONE	T H RUM
T H UG	C H ILI	R H OMB	**S H OOK**	*T H UJA
T H US	C H ILL	R H UMB	S H OOL	T H UMB
W H AM	C H IMB	R H YME	S H OON	T H UMP
W H AP	C H IME	R H YTA	S H OOT	T H URL
W H AT	C H IMP	S H ACK	S H ORE	T H UYA
W H EE	C H INA	S H ADE	S H ORL	T H YME
W H EN	C H INE	S H ADY	S H ORN	T H YMI
W H ET	C H INK	S H AFT	**S H ORT**	*T H YMY
W H EW	C H INO	S H AKE	S H OTE	*W H ACK
W H EY	C H IRK	*S H AKY	S H OTT	W H ALE
W H ID	C H IRM	S H ALE	S H OUT	W H ANG
W H IM	C H IRO	S H ALL	**S H OVE**	W H ARF
W H IN	C H IRP	S H ALT	**S H OWN**	W H AUP
W H IP	C H IRR	**S H ALY**	**S H OWY**	W H EAL
W H IR	C H IVE	S H AME	S H RED	W H EAT
W H IT	*C H IVY	S H ANK	**S H REW**	W H EEL
*W H IZ	*C H OCK	S H APE	S H RUB	W H EEN
W H OA	C H OIR	S H ARD	S H RUG	W H EEP
W H OM	C H OKE	S H ARE	**S H UCK**	*W H ELK
W H OP	*C H OKY	S H ARK	S H UNT	W H ELM
B H ANG	C H OMP	S H ARN	**S H USH**	W H ELP
B H OOT	C H ORD	S H ARP	S H UTE	W H ERE
C H AFE	C H ORE	S H AUL	**S H YER**	*W H ICH
*C H AFF	C H OSE	S H AWL	**S H YLY**	*W H IFF
C H AIN	C H OTT	**T H ACK**	W H ILE	
C H AIR	*C H UCK	S H AWM	T H ANE	W H INE
C H ALK	C H UFA	S H AWN	T H ANK	W H INY
C H AMP	*C H UFF	S H EAF	T H ARM	W H IPT
C H ANG	*C H UFF	S H EAL	T H ECA	W H IRL
C H ANT	C H UMP	S H EAR	T H EFT	W H IRR
C H AOS	C H UNK	S H EEN	T H EGN	W H ISH
C H APE	C H URL	S H EEP	T H EIN	*W H ISK
C H APT	C H URN	S H EER	T H EIR	W H IST
C H ARD	C H URR	S H EET	**T H EME**	W H ITE
C H ARE	C H UTE	S H EIK	T H ERE	W H ITY

*W H IZZ	BA H ADUR	*CAS H BOOK	*HIG H ROAD	PAT H LESS
W H OLE	*BE H AVER	CAS H LESS	*HIG H TAIL	PAT H OGEN
*W H OMP	*BE H OOVE	*CAS H MERE	HIT H ERTO	*PHT H ALIC
W H OOP	BO H EMIA	CAT H EDRA	HOT H OUSE	*PHT H ALIN
W H ORE	CO H ABIT	CAT H ETER	*HYP H EMIA	*PHT H ISIC
W H ORL	CO H ERER	*CAT H EXIS	*KAS H RUTH	*PHT H ISIS
W H ORT	DE H ISCE	*CAT H OLIC	*KEP H ALIN	PIT H LESS
W H OSE	GA H NITE	CAT H OUSE	*KYP H OSIS	POT H OUSE
W H OSO	*LE H AYIM	*CEP H ALAD	LAT H ERER	*PRE H UMAN
*W H UMP	MA H ARAN	*CEP H ALIC	LAT H IEST	*PRO H IBIT
BE H ALF	*MA H JONG	*CEP H ALIN	*LAT H WORK	*PUS H BALL
BE H AVE	*PA H LAVI	*CHT H ONIC	*LEC H AYIM	*PUS H CART
BE H ELD	RE H INGE	COT H URNI	LET H ALLY	*PUS H DOWN
BE H ELD	RE H OUSE	CUS H IEST	*LET H ARGY	PUS H IEST
BE H EST	SA H IWAL	*CUS H IONY	LIC H ENIN	*PUS H OVER
BE H IND	SA H UARO	DAS H IEST	*LIG H TISH	RAC H ITIS
BE H OLD	*SC H APPE	DET H RONE	LIG H TING	RAS H NESS
BE H OOF	SC H EMER	DIC H ASIA	*LIG H TISH	REC H ANGE
BE H OVE	*SC H ERZO	*DIC H OTIC	LIT H ARGE	REC H ARGE
BE H OWL	*SC H LEPP	*DIC H ROIC	LIT H EMIA	REC H OOSE
*BO H UNK	*SC H LOCK	*DIP H ASIC	LIT H OSOL	RED H ORSE
CA H IER	*SC H MALZ	*DIP H ENYL	LOT H ARIO	REP H RASE
CA H OOT	SC H MEER	DIS H ERIT	LOT H SOME	RES H APER
CO H EIR	SC H MOOS	*DIS H EVEL	LUS H NESS	RET H READ
CO H ERE	*SC H MUCK	DIS H IEST	*MAC H ISMO	RIC H NESS
CO H ORT	SC H NAPS	*DIS H LIKE	*MEC H ANIC	*RIC H WEED
CO H OSH	*SC H NOOK	DIS H ONOR	*MEP H ITIS	*RIG H TFUL
CO H UNE	SC H OLAR	*DIS H WARE	*MES H WORK	RIG H TIES
DA H LIA	*SC H TICK	DIT H EISM	*MET H INKS	RIG H TISM
DA H OON	SP H ENIC	DIT H EIST	*MET H ODIC	RIG H TIST
DE H ORN	SP H ERAL	DOG H OUSE	*MET H OXYL	RUS H IEST
DE H ORT	SP H ERIC	FAS H IOUS	*MET H YLAL	*RUS H LIKE
FU H RER	ST H ENIA	*FAT H ERLY	*MIS H MASH	RUT H ENIC
*JO H NNY	*VE H ICLE	*FIG H TING	*MIS H MOSH	RUT H LESS
KA H UNA	*BAC H ELOR	*FIS H ABLE	*MOT H BALL	SAW H ORSE
*MA H ZOR	*BAT H ETIC	*FIS H BOLT	*MOT H ERLY	SIG H LESS
RE H ANG	BAT H LESS	*FIS H BONE	*MUC H NESS	*SIG H LIKE
RE H ASH	*BAT H ROBE	*FIS H BOWL	*MUS H ROOM	SIG H TSEE
RE H EAR	*BAT H ROOM	*FIS H HOOK	*MYT H ICAL	SIP H ONAL
RE H EAT	*BEC H AMEL	FIS H IEST	*NAP H THOL	*SIP H ONIC
RE H EEL	*BEC H ANCE	FIS H LESS	*NAP H THYL	SIT H ENCE
RE H IRE	*BES H ADOW	*FIS H LIKE	NAT H LESS	*SUB H UMAN
RE H UNG	*BES H IVER	FIS H LINE	*NEP H RISM	*SUB H UMID
SC H EMA	BES H ROUD	*FIS H MEAL	NEP H RITE	*SUC H LIKE
SC H EME	*BIC H ROME	*FIS H POLE	*NIG H NESS	SUC H NESS
SC H ISM	*BIP H ENYL	*FIS H POND	*NIG H TCAP	*SYP H ILIS
SC H IST	*BOE H MITE	FIS H TAIL	NIG H TIES	TAC H INID
*SC H IZO	*BON H OMIE	*FIS H WIFE	*NIG H TJAR	TAC H ISTE
SC H LEP	*BOS H VARK	*FOX H OUND	*NON H ARDY	TAP H OUSE
SC H MOE	BUG H OUSE	*FUC H SINE	NON H UMAN	TEA H OUSE
SC H OOL	BUS H BUCK	GAS H OUSE	*NUT H ATCH	TEP H RITE
SC H ORL	BUS H ELER	GAT H ERER	NUT H OUSE	*TIG H TWAD
*SC H RIK	*BUS H FIRE	*HAS H EESH	*PAC H ADOM	TIT H ABLE
SC H UIT	BUS H GOAT	HEN H OUSE	*PAC H ALIC	TIT H ONIA
SC H USS	BUS H IEST	*HIG H BALL	*PAC H OULI	TRI H EDRA
SP H ENE	BUS H LAND	*HIG H BORN	*PAN H UMAN	*WAS H ABLE
SP H ERE	BUS H LESS	*HIG H BRED	PAR H ELIA	*WAS H BOWL
SP H ERY	*BUS H LIKE	*HIG H BROW	*PAR H ELIC	WAS H IEST
*SP H INX	*CAC H ALOT	*HIG H BUSH	PAS H ADOM	*WAS H ROOM
TA H SIL	*CAC H EPOT	*HIG H JACK	*PAS H ALIC	*WIS H BONE
VA H INE	*CAC H EXIA	*HIG H LAND	*PAS H ALIK	WIS H LESS
WA H INE	*CAC H UCHA	*HIG H NESS	*PAT H ETIC	*WIT H DRAW

WIT H ERER	*QOP H	COUC H	LAIG H	ROTC H
*WIT H HOLD	RAS H	COUG H	LAIT H	ROUG H
WIT H IEST	RAT H	COUT H	LARC H	ROUT H
*YAC H TING	RES H	CRAS H	LATC H	ROWT H
*YAC H TMAN	RIC H	CRUS H	LAUG H	SAIT H
*YES H IVAH	RUS H	CRWT H	LEAC H	SANG H
*YOG H OURT	RUT H	CUIS H	LEAS H	SAUC H
	SAS H	CULC H	LEEC H	SAUG H
	SHA H	CURC H	LETC H	SELA H
BAC H	SIG H	CUTC H	LOAC H	SHUS H
BAS H	SIN H	DEAS H	LOAT H	*SIXT H
BAT H	SIT H	DEAT H	LOTA H	SLAS H
BET H	SOP H	DEPT H	LOUG H	SLOS H
BLA H	SOT H	DITC H	LUNC H	SLOT H
BOT H	SUC H	DOET H	LURC H	SLUS H
BUS H	SUG H	DOUG H	*LYMP H	SMAS H
CAP H	TAC H	DUNC H	LYNC H	SMIT H
CAS H	TET H	DUTC H	MARC H	SNAS H
DAS H	TOP H	FAIT H	MARS H	SNAT H
DIS H	TOS H	FAUG H	MATC H	SOOT H
DOT H	TUS H	FETC H	MILC H	SOUG H
FAS H	VUG H	FIFT H	MIRT H	SOUT H
FIS H	WAS H	FILC H	MONT H	STAP H
GAS H	WIC H	FILT H	MOOC H	STAS H
GOS H	WIS H	FINC H	MORP H	STIC H
GUS H	WIT H	FIRT H	MOUC H	SUBA H
HAS H	*WYC H	FITC H	MOUT H	SURA H
HAT H	YEA H	FLAS H	MULC H	SWAS H
HET H	YOD H	FLES H	MUNC H	SWAT H
HIG H	YOG H	FLUS H	MUST H	SWIS H
HUS H	BAIT H	FORT H	MUTC H	SWIT H
JOS H	BATC H	FRES H	MYNA H	SYLP H
KAP H	BEAC H	FRIT H	MYRR H	SYNC H
KIT H	BEEC H	FROS H	NEAT H	TEAC H
KOP H	BELC H	FROT H	NEIG H	TEET H
LAK H	BENC H	GALA H	NORT H	TENC H
LAS H	BERT H	GART H	NOTC H	TENT H
LAT H	BIMA H	GERA H	*NYMP H	TEUC H
LEC H	BIRC H	GIRS H	PARC H	TEUG H
LOC H	BIRT H	GIRT H	PATC H	THIG H
LOT H	BITC H	GLYP H	PEAC H	TILT H
LUS H	BLUS H	GNAS H	PERC H	TOOT H
LUS H	BOOT H	GRAP H	PINC H	TORA H
MAC H	BOTC H	GRIT H	PITC H	TORC H
MAS H	BOUG H	GULC H	PLAS H	TOUC H
MAT H	BRAC H	GURS H	PLUS H	TOUG H
MES H	BRAS H	HARS H	POAC H	TRAS H
MOT H	BROT H	HATC H	POOC H	TROT H
MUC H	BRUG H	HAUG H	PORC H	TRUT H
MUS H	BRUS H	HEIG H	POUC H	VETC H
MYT H	BUNC H	HEUG H	*PSYC H	VOUC H
NIG H	BURG H	HITC H	PUNC H	WATC H
NOS H	BUTC H	HOOC H	*QUAS H	WAUG H
PAS H	CATC H	HORA H	*QUOT H	WEIG H
PAT H	CHET H	HOTC H	*QURS H	WELC H
PEC H	CINC H	*HUMP H	*RAJA H	WELS H
PIS H	CLAC H	HUNC H	RANC H	WENC H
PIT H	CLAS H	HUTC H	RATC H	*WHIC H
POO H	CLOT H	KENC H	RAYA H	WHIS H
POS H	COAC H	KETC H	REAC H	WIDT H
PUG H	CONC H	KNIS H	RETC H	WINC H
PUS H	COOC H	LAIC H	ROAC H	WITC H

WOOS H	FELLA H	*MIKVE H	*SHIVA H	WRENC H
WORT H	FETIC H	MINIS H	SIRRA H	WRETC H
WRAT H	FETIS H	MODIS H	SKEIG H	*ZENIT H
WROT H	FINIS H	MOLLA H	*SKETC H	*ZIBET H
YIRT H	FLEEC H	MOLOC H	SLATC H	*ZILLA H
YOUT H	FLENC H	MONIS H	SLEIG H	*ZIZIT H
*ZILC H	FLETC H	MOOLA H	SLEUT H	*BABYIS H
BANIS H	FLINC H	MOPIS H	SLOUC H	BALDIS H
BLANC H	*FLYSC H	MULIS H	SLOUG H	*BATFIS H
BLEAC H	FOURT H	MULLA H	SMIRC H	BEAMIS H
BLENC H	FRENC H	NAUTC H	SMOOC H	BEARIS H
BLOTC H	GALOS H	NEWIS H	SMOOT H	BEGORA H
BLUIS H	GARIS H	NULLA H	SMUTC H	BENEAT H
BORSC H	GLITC H	PAINC H	SNATC H	BESEEC H
BOYIS H	GLUNC H	PALIS H	SNEES H	BETROT H
BRANC H	GOLOS H	PARAP H	SNITC H	*BEWITC H
BREAC H	GONOP H	PARDA H	SPEEC H	BIGGIS H
BREAT H	GROUC H	PARIA H	SPILT H	BISMUT H
BREEC H	GROWT H	PARIS H	SPLAS H	BLEMIS H
BROAC H	GRUTC H	PAUNC H	SPLOS H	BLUEIS H
BROOC H	HALLA H	PERIS H	*SQUAS H	BOARIS H
BRUNC H	*HALVA H	PLANC H	*SQUIS H	BOGGIS H
*BYPAT H	*HAMZA H	PLEAC H	*SQUUS H	*BOOKIS H
CALAS H	HAUNC H	PLINT H	STANC H	BOORIS H
CALIP H	HEALT H	PLOUG H	STARC H	BOROUG H
CAROC H	HEART H	POLIS H	STENC H	*BOXFIS H
CERIP H	*HIGHT H	POPIS H	STITC H	BREADT H
CHALA H	*HOOKA H	POTAS H	STRAT H	BRINIS H
CHALE H	HOORA H	PREAC H	SUCCA H	BRUTIS H
CHETA H	HOOTC H	PRUTA H	*SUKKA H	*BUCKIS H
*CHINC H	HOUDA H	PUNIS H	SUMAC H	BULLIS H
*CHOUG H	*HOWDA H	*PUNKA H	SWART H	BULRUS H
CHOUS H	HURRA H	PURDA H	SWATC H	BURNIS H
*CHURC H	*HUZZA H	PUTSC H	SWITC H	CADDIS H
CLENC H	*JADIS H	*QUAIC H	SWOOS H	*CAPOUC H
CLINC H	*JARRA H	*QUAIG H	TEMPE H	CARLIS H
CLOUG H	*JOSEP H	*QUENC H	TERAP H	CAROAC H
CLUTC H	*JUBBA H	*QUITC H	THATC H	CARROC H
COHOS H	*JUBHA H	*QURUS H	THOUG H	CATARR H
COMET H	*KALIP H	RADIS H	THRAS H	*CATFIS H
COPRA H	*KEBLA H	RAKIS H	THRES H	CATTIS H
COYIS H	*KEDDA H	RAVIS H	THRUS H	*CHALLA H
CRANC H	*KHEDA H	RAWIS H	TONIS H	*CHALOT H
CRATC H	KIAUG H	REHAS H	TOYIS H	*CHEETA H
CREES H	*KIBLA H	RELIS H	TREFA H	*CHERIS H
CROTC H	*KIBOS H	REWAS H	TRENC H	*CHUDDA H
CROUC H	*KIRSC H	RUPIA H	TROUG H	*CLAYIS H
CRUNC H	*KITSC H	SAMEC H	TROWT H	*COCKIS H
CRUTC H	*KLATC H	*SAMEK H	TUSSA H	*CODFIS H
CULTC H	*KVETC H	SCARP H	TUSSE H	COLDIS H
CURAG H	LAMED H	SCORC H	TWITC H	COOLIS H
DALET H	LATIS H	SCOTC H	VANIS H	*COWFIS H
DEART H	LAUNC H	SCOUT H	WALLA H	CRAUNC H
DETAC H	LAVIS H	SCUTC H	WARMT H	*CUBBIS H
DOURA H	LENGT H	SEARC H	WEALT H	CURRAC H
DOVIS H	LOOFA H	SERAP H	*WHIDA H	CURRAG H
DREIC H	LOWIS H	SHAUG H	*WHOOS H	CURRIS H
DREIG H	MARIS H	SHEAT H	*WHYDA H	*DAMPIS H
DRENC H	*MATZA H	*SHEIK H	WIDIS H	*DARKIS H
DROUT H	*MATZO H	SHEUC H	WINIS H	DEAFIS H
DUDIS H	MENSC H	SHEUG H	WRAIT H	*DEBAUC H
FAMIS H	*MIKVA H	SHIBA H	WREAT H	*DEBOUC H

DERVIS H	LADYIS H	RATTIS H	TRIUMP H	*CARRITC H
DIGRAP H	LARGIS H	REBIRT H	TUNDIS H	*CARTOUC H
*DIMORP H	*LAZYIS H	REDDIS H	TURBET H	*CAVEFIS H
*DIPTYC H	LONGIS H	REDFIS H	TURBIT H	*CENOTAP H
DISTIC H	LOUDIS H	REFRES H	TURPET H	*CHALLOT H
*DOGFIS H	LOUTIS H	REMATC H	*TWELFT H	*CHEAPIS H
DOGGIS H	LUMPIS H	RETEAC H	*VAMPIS H	*CHILDIS H
DOLLIS H	MADDIS H	RETOUC H	VARNIS H	*CHUTZPA H
DONNIS H	MANNIS H	REWEIG H	*VERMUT H	CLANNIS H
*DOZENT H	*MATZOT H	ROGUIS H	*WAGGIS H	*CLERKIS H
DRONIS H	*MAWKIS H	ROMPIS H	*WAMPIS H	*CLIQUIS H
DULLIS H	*MAYBUS H	RUBBIS H	*WARMIS H	*CLOWNIS H
*DUMPIS H	*MEGILP H	RUTTIS H	*WARPAT H	*CLUMPIS H
*DUSKIS H	MENORA H	SABBAT H	*WEAKIS H	*COALFIS H
*FADDIS H	MESARC H	SALTIS H	WEARIS H	*COPPERA H
FAIRIS H	MESSIA H	*SAWFIS H	WENNIS H	*CORONAC H
FATTIS H	*MEZUZA H	SCRAIC H	WETTIS H	*CRAWFIS H
*FINFIS H	MIDRAS H	SCRAIG H	*WHITIS H	*CRAYFIS H
*FLEMIS H	*MITSVA H	SCRATC H	*WHORIS H	*CROMLEC H
*FOLKIS H	*MITZVA H	SCREEC H	WILDIS H	*DAHABEA H
FOOLIS H	*MOBBIS H	SCRUNC H	*WISPIS H	*DAHABIA H
*FOPPIS H	MONARC H	SELFIS H	*WOLFIS H	*DAHABIE H
*FOXFIS H	*MONKIS H	SERFIS H	*WORMIS H	*DANDYIS H
*FURBIS H	MOONIS H	SEVENT H	WOTTET H	*DEALFIS H
FURNIS H	MOORIS H	SHANTI H	*XERARC H	DEPOLIS H
*GALUMP H	*MUDFIS H	SHITTA H	*ZANYIS H	*DESPATC H
GARFIS H	NEBBIS H	*SICKIS H	*ZAPTIA H	*DEVILIS H
GARNIS H	NEOLIT H	*SKREEG H	*ZAPTIE H	*DIAGRAP H
*GAWKIS H	NOMARC H	*SKREIG H	*BACKLAS H	DIMINIS H
GIRLIS H	NONCAS H	SLAVIS H	*BACKWAS H	*DISPATC H
GNOMIS H	NONSUC H	SLOWIS H	*BADMOUT H	DOGTOOT H
GOATIS H	NOURIS H	SOTTIS H	*BAKSHIS H	*DOGWATC H
GOODIS H	NUNNIS H	SOURIS H	*BEDRENC H	*DRAFFIS H
GOULAS H	*PADSHA H	SPINAC H	BEGORRA H	*DRUMFIS H
GRAYIS H	*PANFIS H	SPLOTC H	*BEHEMOT H	*DWARFIS H
GREENT H	*PEAKIS H	*SQUELC H	*BEQUEAT H	FAINTIS H
GREYIS H	*PEEVIS H	*SQUINC H	*BESCORC H	*FALLFIS H
*HAGBUS H	*PERKIS H	*SQUOOS H	*BESMIRC H	*FEEBLIS H
*HAGFIS H	PETTIS H	STAUNC H	*BESMOOT H	*FEVERIS H
*HAGGIS H	*PHARAO H	STEALT H	*BIGMOUT H	*FIENDIS H
HALALA H	*PIBROC H	STENGA H	*BILLFIS H	FILEFIS H
*HALAVA H	*PIGFIS H	STOMAC H	*BIRDBAT H	*FLATFIS H
HALLOT H	PIGGIS H	STONIS H	*BLACKIS H	FLATTIS H
*HASHIS H	*PINFIS H	STRETC H	BLANDIS H	*FLATWAS H
*HAWKIS H	*PINKIS H	STYLIS H	*BLEAKIS H	FLOURIS H
*HEIGHT H	PLANIS H	SUCCOT H	*BLOCKIS H	*FOOLFIS H
HELLIS H	PLENIS H	SUNBAT H	BLONDIS H	*FOOTBAT H
*HIPPIS H	POORIS H	SUNFIS H	*BLOWFIS H	*FOOTPAT H
*HOGFIS H	POTLAC H	SWINIS H	*BLUEFIS H	FORSOOT H
*HOGWAS H	*PREWAS H	TALLIS H	*BOARFIS H	FORTIET H
HOTTIS H	PRUDIS H	TALLIT H	*BONEFIS H	*FREAKIS H
*HUFFIS H	PUBLIS H	TANNIS H	*BRACKIS H	*FROGFIS H
HUNNIS H	*PUCKIS H	TARBUS H	BRAINIS H	*FURLOUG H
*HUTZPA H	PUGGIS H	TARNIS H	BRANDIS H	*GOATFIS H
*JACINT H	*PUPFIS H	TARTIS H	BRASSIS H	*GOLDFIS H
*JEWFIS H	*QUAMAS H	TEREFA H	BROADIS H	*GRAYFIS H
*KADDIS H	*RAFFIS H	THROUG H	BROGUIS H	GREENIS H
*KHIRKA H	RAMMIS H	TIGRIS H	*BROWNIS H	*GRUFFIS H
*KIDDIS H	RANKIS H	TOADIS H	BULLRUS H	*GRUMPIS H
*KIDDUS H	RASPIS H	TONNIS H	*CABBALA H	GUNSMIT H
*KLATSC H	RATFIS H	TOWNIS H	*CALABAS H	*GYPSYIS H
*KURBAS H		*TOWPAT H	*CALIPAS H	*HABDALA H

*HAFTARA H	*MISFAIT H	*QUIPPIS H	*SKIRMIS H	TIGERIS H
*HAFTORA H	*MISHMAS H	RAINWAS H	*SKITTIS H	TILEFIS H
*HALAKOT H	*MISHMOS H	REATTAC H	SLAPDAS H	TINSMIT H
*HARRUMP H	*MISMATC H	*REBRANC H	*SLOBBIS H	*TOADFIS H
*HASHEES H	*MISPATC H	REFINIS H	SLUGGIS H	*TOADYIS H
*HAVDALA H	*MISTEAC H	REGOLIT H	SMALLIS H	TOLBOOT H
*HAWFINC H	*MISTOUC H	*REGROWT H	*SNAPPIS H	*TOPNOTC H
*HAWKMOT H	*MONKFIS H	RELAUNC H	*SNIFFIS H	*TOUGHIS H
*HELMINT H	MONOLIT H	REPOLIS H	*SNOBBIS H	*TOVARIC H
*HEPTARC H	MONTEIT H	*REPROAC H	SNOUTIS H	TOVARIS H
*HEREWIT H	*MOONFIS H	RESEARC H	*SNOWBUS H	*TRAMPIS H
*HICCOUG H	*MUSQUAS H	RESMOOT H	*SPARKIS H	*TRIBRAC H
*HIERARC H	*MYOGRAP H	RETRENC H	*SPOOKIS H	*TRICKIS H
*HIGHBUS H	NARGILE H	*ROCKFIS H	*SQUARIS H	*TRIGLYP H
*HIPPARC H	*NEOMORP H	ROSEBUS H	*SQUIRIS H	TRIGRAP H
*HYACINT H	NONESUC H	ROSEFIS H	STABLIS H	*TRIMORP H
*HYDRANT H	NONTRUT H	*ROUGHIS H	STANDIS H	*TRIPTYC H
*JACKFIS H	*NUMBFIS H	ROUNDIS H	STARFIS H	TRISTIC H
*KABBALA H	*NUTHATC H	*ROWDYIS H	*STIFFIS H	*TZITZIT H
*KAFFIYE H	*PADISHA H	SAGANAS H	*STOCKIS H	*VANQUIS H
*KASHRUT H	PAGANIS H	SAILFIS H	STOUTIS H	*VAPORIS H
*KEYPUNC H	*PARASHA H	SALTBUS H	STRAMAS H	*VERANDA H
*KINGFIS H	*PARFLES H	*SANDFIS H	STRENGT H	*VERMOUT H
*KRYOLIT H	*PARRITC H	*SANDWIC H	*STUDFIS H	*VIGORIS H
*LADYFIS H	PEARLAS H	SAVANNA H	*SUBEPOC H	*WARMOUT H
LANGUIS H	*PENTARC H	SAWTOOT H	*SUCKFIS H	WATERIS H
*LIGHTIS H	PERIANT H	*SCAMPIS H	*SURFFIS H	*WEAKFIS H
LIONFIS H	*PIPEFIS H	SEABEAC H	*SWAMPIS H	*WHIPLAS H
LITTLIS H	*PLUMPIS H	*SEECATC H	SWEETIS H	*WOLFFIS H
LIVERIS H	*POLYMAT H	SELCOUT H	TAIGLAC H	*WOMANIS H
*LOGOMAC H	POORTIT H	*SEMIHIG H	TARBOOS H	WOSTTET H
*LUMPFIS H	*POTLATC H	*SHADBUS H	TEIGLAC H	*XENOLIT H
*LUNGFIS H	*PRANKIS H	*SHADRAC H	TETRARC H	*YESHIVA H
*MASTABA H	*PREPUNC H	*SHAMMAS H	*THICKIS H	*YOKELIS H
MEGALIT H	*PRIGGIS H	*SHEEPIS H	*THIEVIS H	*YOUNGIS H
MEGILLA H	*PURPLIS H	SHORTIS H	THINNIS H	*ZOOMORP H
*MIDMONT H	*QUACKIS H	*SHREWIS H	THOROUG H	
*MIDWATC H	*QUALMIS H	SISSYIS H	*THUGGIS H	
*MILKFIS H	*QUEERIS H	*SIXTIET H	*TICKLIS H	

J

*JACK	*JEEZ	JIVE	*JUJU	JALOP
JADE	JEFE	*JOCK	*JUKE	*JAMBE
JAGG	JEHU	JOEY	*JUMP	*JANTY
JAIL	JELL	JOHN	*JUNK	JAPAN
*JAKE	*JERK	JOIN	JUPE	JAPER
*JAMB	JESS	*JOKE	JURA	JAUNT
JANE	JEST	JOLE	JURY	*JAWAN
JAPE	JETE	JOLT	JUST	*JAZZY
JARL	*JIBB	JOSH	JUTE	JEBEL
JATO	JIBE	JOSS	JABOT	*JEHAD
*JAUK	*JIFF	JOTA	JACAL	*JELLY
JAUP	JILL	*JOUK	*JACKY	*JEMMY
JAVA	JILT	JOWL	JAGER	*JENNY
*JAZZ	*JIMP	JUBA	*JAGGY	JERID
JEAN	*JINK	JUBE	JAGRA	*JERKY
JEEP	JINN	JUDO	*JAKES	*JERRY
JEER	*JINX	JUGA	JALAP	JESSE

JETON	JARGON	*JOYFUL	*JAYWALK	*JUGGING
*JETTY	JARINA	*JOYOUS	*JAZZMAN	*JUGGLER
*JEWEL	*JARRAH	*JOYPOP	JEALOUS	*JUGHEAD
JIBER	JARRED	*JUBBAH	*JEEPERS	*JUGSFUL
*JIFFY	*JARVEY	*JUBHAH	*JEJUNAL	*JUGULAR
*JIHAD	*JASPER	*JUBILE	*JEJUNUM	*JUGULUM
*JIMMY	JASSID	*JUDDER	*JELLIFY	*JUJITSU
*JIMPY	*JAUNCE	*JUDGER	*JEMADAR	*JUJUISM
JINGO	*JAYGEE	*JUDOKA	*JEMIDAR	*JUJUIST
JINNI	*JAYVEE	JUGATE	*JEOPARD	*JUJUTSU
*JOCKO	*JAZZER	*JUGFUL	*JERKIES	*JUKEBOX
JOINT	JEERER	*JUGGED	*JERREED	*JUMBLER
JOIST	*JEJUNA	*JUGGLE	JESSANT	*JUMBUCK
*JOKER	*JEJUNE	JUGULA	*JESTFUL	*JUMPOFF
*JOLLY	JENNET	*JUICER	*JESTING	*JUNIPER
*JOLTY	*JERBOA	*JUJUBE	*JETBEAD	*JUNKMAN
JORAM	JEREED	*JUMBLE	*JETPORT	*JURIDIC
JORUM	*JERKER	*JUMPER	*JETTIED	*JURYMAN
*JOTTY	*JERKIN	JUNGLE	JETTIES	*JUSSIVE
JOULE	JERRID	*JUNGLY	*JETTING	*JUSTICE
JOUST	*JERSEY	JUNIOR	*JEWELER	*JUSTIFY
*JOWLY	JESTER	*JUNKER	*JEWELRY	*JUVENAL
JUDAS	JESUIT	*JUNKET	*JEWFISH	*JABBERER
JUDGE	*JETSAM	*JUNKIE	*JEZEBEL	*JACINTHE
JUGAL	*JETSOM	JURANT	*JIBBING	*JACKAROO
*JUGUM	JETTED	JURIES	*JIBBOOM	*JACKBOOT
JUICE	JETTON	JURIST	*JIGABOO	*JACKEROO
*JUICY	*JEZAIL	JUSTER	*JIGGING	*JACKFISH
JULEP	*JIBBER	JUSTLE	JILLION	*JACKSTAY
*JUMBO	*JIGGER	*JUSTLY	*JIMJAMS	*JACQUARD
*JUMPY	*JIGGLE	*JACAMAR	*JIMMINY	*JACULATE
JUNCO	*JIGGLY	*JACINTH	*JINGALL	*JAGGHERY
*JUNKY	*JIGSAW	*JACKASS	*JINGLER	*JAILBAIT
JUNTA	JILTER	*JACKDAW	*JITTERY	*JAILBIRD
JUNTO	*JIMINY	*JACKIES	JOANNES	*JALOUSIE
JUPON	JINGAL	*JACKLEG	*JOBBERY	*JAMBOREE
JURAL	*JINGKO	*JACKPOT	*JOBBING	*JANIFORM
JURAT	JINGLE	*JACOBIN	*JOBLESS	*JANISARY
JUREL	*JINGLY	*JACOBUS	*JOCULAR	*JANIZARY
JUROR	*JINKER	*JACONET	*JODHPUR	*JAPANNER
*JUTTY	JINNEE	*JADEITE	*JOGGLER	*JAPINGLY
*JABBER	*JITNEY	*JAGGARY	*JOINDER	*JAPONICA
*JABIRU	JITTER	*JAGGERY	*JOINERY	*JARGONEL
*JACANA	*JOBBER	*JAGGING	*JOINING	*JAROSITE
*JACKAL	*JOCKEY	*JAGLESS	JOINTER	*JAROVIZE
*JACKER	*JOCOSE	*JALAPIN	*JOINTLY	*JAUNDICE
*JACKET	*JOCUND	*JALOPPY	*JOLLIED	*JAVELINA
*JADISH	*JOGGER	*JAMBEAU	JOLLIER	*JEALOUSY
JAEGER	*JOGGLE	*JAMMING	JOLLIES	*JEJUNITY
*JAGGED	*JOHNNY	*JANGLER	*JOLLIFY	*JELUTONG
*JAGGER	JOINER	JANITOR	*JOLLITY	*JEOPARDY
JAGUAR	*JOJOBA	*JARGOON	JONQUIL	*JEREMIAD
JAILER	*JOKING	*JARLDOM	JOSTLER	*JEROBOAM
JAILOR	JOLTER	*JARRING	*JOTTING	*JERRICAN
*JALOPY	JORDAN	*JARSFUL	JOURNAL	*JERRYCAN
*JAMMED	*JOSEPH	*JASMINE	*JOURNEY	*JESUITRY
*JAMMER	*JOSHER	*JAVELIN	JOUSTER	*JETLINER
JANGLE	JOSTLE	*JAWBONE	*JOYANCE	*JETTISON
*JAPERY	*JOUNCE	*JAWLIKE	*JOYLESS	*JEWELLER
*JAPING	*JOUNCY	*JAWLINE	*JOYRIDE	*JIGGERED
*JARFUL	*JOVIAL	*JAYBIRD	*JUBILEE	*JINGOISM

*JINGOIST	*JUGGLING	*JE J UNA	*JU J UTSU	*JIU J ITSU
*JIPIJAPA	*JUGULATE	*JE J UNE	*KA J EPUT	*JIU J UTSU
*JIUJITSU	*JULIENNE	*JO J OBA	*MA J AGUA	*MAH J ONGG
*JIUJUTSU	*JUNCTION	*JU J UBE	*MA J ESTY	*MIS J UDGE
*JOCOSITY	*JUNCTURE	*PA J AMA	*MA J ORAM	*NON J UROR
*JOHANNES	*JUNKETER	*RE J ECT	*MO J ARRA	*PER J URER
*JOHNBOAT	*JUNKYARD	RE J OIN	*PY J AMAS	*PRE J UDGE
*JOINTURE	*JURATORY	SE J ANT	*RE J OICE	*SER J EANT
*JOKESTER	*JUSTNESS	*BE J EWEL	*RE J UDGE	*SKI J ORER
*JOKINGLY	*JUVENILE	*CA J APUT	SE J EANT	*VER J UICE
*JOLLIEST		*CA J APUT	SO J OURN	
*JONGLEUR		*CA J OLER	*BAN J OIST	
*JOVIALTY	D J IN	*CA J UPUT	*BEN J AMIN	*HAD J
*JOYRIDER	D J INN	*DE J ECTA	*CON J UGAL	*HAJ J
*JOYSTICK	*F J ELD	*HI J INKS	*CON J UNCT	*SVARA J
*JUBILANT	*F J ORD	*JE J UNAL	*CON J URER	*SWARA J
*JUBILATE	*CA J OLE	*JE J UNUM	*CON J UROR	
*JUDGMENT	*DE J ECT	*JU J ITSU	*DIS J OINT	
*JUDICIAL	*HE J IRA	*JU J UISM	*DIS J UNCT	
*JUGGLERY	*HI J ACK	*JU J UIST	*FOR J UDGE	

K

KAAS	KERN	KOAN	KAURY	*KLUTZ
KADI	KETO	KOEL	*KAYAK	*KNACK
KAGU	KHAN	KOHL	*KAZOO	KNAVE
KAIF	KHAT	KOLA	KEBAB	KNEAD
KAIL	KIBE	KOLO	KEBAR	KNEEL
KAIN	KICK	KOOK	KEBOB	KNELT
KAKA	KIEF	KOPH	KEDGE	KNIFE
KAKI	KIKE	KOSS	KEEVE	KNISH
KALE	KIER	KOTO	KEFIR	*KNOCK
KAME	KILL	KRIS	KELPY	KNOLL
KAMI	KILN	KUDO	KEMPT	KNOSP
KANA	KILO	KUDU	KENAF	KNOUT
KANE	KILT	KURU	KENCH	KNOWN
KAON	KIND	KVAS	KENDO	KNURL
KAPA	KINE	KYAR	KERNE	KOALA
KAPH	KING	KYAT	KERRY	KOINE
KARN	KINK	KYTE	KETCH	*KOOKY
KART	KINO	KABAB	KEVEL	*KOPEK
KAVA	KIRK	KABAR	KEVIL	*KOPJE
KAYO	KIRN	KABOB	KHADI	KOPPA
KECK	KISS	KAFIR	KHEDA	KOTOW
KEEF	KIST	KAIAK	KIANG	KRAAL
KEEK	KITE	KALAM	KIBLA	*KRAFT
KEEL	KITH	KALIF	KIDDO	KRAIT
KEEN	KIVA	KALPA	KIDDY	KRAUT
KEEP	KIWI	*KAMIK	KILIM	KRILL
KEET	KNAP	*KANJI	KILTY	KRONA
KEIR	KNAR	*KAPOK	KININ	KRONE
KELP	KNEE	KAPPA	KIOSK	KROON
KEMP	KNEW	KAPUT	KITER	KRUBI
KENO	KNIT	KARAT	KITHE	*KUDZU
KENT	KNOB	KARMA	KITTY	KULAK
KEPI	KNOP	KAROO	KLONG	KUMYS
KEPT	KNOT	KARST	KLOOF	KURTA
KERB	KNOW	KASHA		KUSSO
KERF	KNUR	KAURI		KVASS

*KYACK	*KHAZEN	KOUSSO	*KHAMSIN	*KNUCKLY
*KYLIX	*KHEDAH	*KOWTOW	KHANATE	*KOKANEE
KYRIE	KIAUGH	KRAKEN	*KHEDIVE	*KOLACKY
*KYTHE	KIBBLE	KRATER	*KHIRKAH	*KOLKHOS
*KABAKA	*KIBITZ	KRONOR	*KIBBUTZ	*KOLKHOZ
KABALA	*KIBLAH	KRONUR	*KICKOFF	KOMATIK
*KABAYA	*KIBOSH	KRUBUT	KIDDIES	KOTOWER
*KABIKI	*KICKER	*KUCHEN	KIDDING	KOUMISS
*KABUKI	*KICKUP	KULTUR	*KIDDISH	*KOUMYSS
*KAFFIR	KIDDER	KUMISS	*KIDDUSH	KREMLIN
KAFTAN	KIDDIE	KUMMEL	*KIDLIKE	*KREUZER
KAHUNA	KIDNAP	KURGAN	*KIDSKIN	*KRIMMER
KAINIT	KIDNEY	*KVETCH	KIESTER	KRULLER
KAISER	KILLER	*KWACHA	KILLDEE	*KRYPTON
*KAKAPO	KILTER	*KABBALA	*KILLICK	*KUMQUAT
KALIAN	KILTIE	*KACHINA	KILLING	*KUNZITE
*KALIPH	KIMONO	*KADDISH	*KILLJOY	*KURBASH
KALIUM	KINASE	KAINITE	*KILLOCK	KYANISE
KALMIA	KINDLE	*KAJEPUT	KILOBAR	KYANITE
KALONG	KINDLY	KALENDS	KILOBIT	*KYANIZE
*KALPAK	KINEMA	*KALIMBA	KILORAD	*KABBALAH
KAMALA	KINGLY	*KAMPONG	KILOTON	*KABELJOU
KAMSIN	KIPPEN	KAMSEEN	KILTING	*KAFFIYEH
KANTAR	KIPPER	KANTELE	KINDLER	*KAILYARD
KAOLIN	*KIRSCH	KAOLINE	KINDRED	KAISERIN
KAPUTT	KIRTLE	*KARAKUL	KINESIS	*KAKEMONO
KARATE	*KISHKA	KARTING	KINETIC	*KALEWIFE
KAROSS	*KISHKE	*KASHMIR	KINETIN	*KALEYARD
KARROO	KISMAT	KASHRUT	*KINFOLK	*KALIFATE
KASHER	KISMET	*KATHODE	*KINGCUP	KALLIDIN
KATION	KISSER	*KATYDID	*KINGDOM	*KALYPTRA
KAVASS	KITING	*KAYAKER	KINGLET	KAMAAINA
KAYLES	*KITSCH	*KEBBOCK	KINGPIN	*KAMACITE
KEBBIE	KITTED	*KEBBUCK	*KINSHIP	*KAMIKAZE
*KEBLAH	KITTEL	KEELAGE	KINSMAN	KANGAROO
*KECKLE	KITTEN	KEELSON	*KIPPING	KAOLIANG
*KEDDAH	KITTLE	KEEPING	*KIPSKIN	*KARYOTIN
KEENER	*KLATCH	KEESTER	*KIRKMAN	*KASHRUTH
KEENLY	*KLAXON	KEGELER	KIRMESS	*KATAKANA
KEEPER	*KLEPHT	KEGLING	KISTFUL	KEDGEREE
KEGLER	KLUDGE	KEISTER	*KITCHEN	KEELBOAT
KELOID	*KLUTZY	KEITLOA	KITHARA	*KEELHALE
KELPIE	KNAWEL	KENNING	KITLING	*KEELHAUL
KELSON	KNIFER	KENOSIS	KITTIES	KEELLESS
KELTER	KNIGHT	*KEPPING	KITTING	KEENNESS
KELVIN	KNIVES	*KERAMIC	*KLATSCH	*KEEPSAKE
KENNED	*KNOBBY	KERATIN	KLAVERN	*KEESHOND
KENNEL	KNOLLY	*KERCHOO	KLEAGLE	KENOTRON
*KEPPED	KNOTTY	KERMESS	*KNACKER	*KEPHALIN
KEPPEN	KNOWER	KERNITE	*KNAPPER	KERATOID
KERMES	KNURLY	KEROGEN	*KNAVERY	KERATOMA
KERMIS	KOBOLD	*KERYGMA	KNEADER	KERATOSE
KERNEL	*KOLHOZ	KESTREL	*KNEECAP	*KERCHIEF
KERRIA	*KOLKOZ	*KETCHUP	KNEELER	KEROSENE
KERSEY	KOODOO	KETOSIS	KNEEPAD	KEROSINE
KETENE	KOOKIE	*KEYHOLE	KNITTER	*KERPLUNK
KETONE	*KOPECK	KEYLESS	*KNOCKER	*KEYBOARD
KETOSE	KOPPIE	KEYNOTE	KNOLLER	*KEYNOTER
KETTLE	KORUNA	KEYSTER	KNOTTER	*KEYPUNCH
KEYSET	KOSHER	*KEYWORD	*KNOWING	*KEYSTONE
*KEYWAY	KOUMIS	*KHADDAR	*KNOWING	*KHAMSEEN
*KHALIF	*KOUMYS	*KHALIFA	*KNUCKLE	*KIBITZER

*KICKBACK	S K EW	PI K ING	*BAC K STOP	*DOC K SIDE
*KICKSHAW	S K ID	PO K IER	*BAC K WARD	*DOC K YARD
*KIDNAPER	S K IM	PO K IES	*BAC K WASH	*DUC K BILL
KIELBASA	S K IN	*PO K ILY	*BAC K WOOD	*DUC K IEST
KILLDEER	S K IP	PO K ING	*BAC K YARD	*DUC K LING
*KILOGRAM	S K IT	*PY K NIC	BAL K LINE	*DUC K TAIL
KILOMOLE	S K UA	RA K ING	*BAN K BOOK	*DUC K WEED
*KILOVOLT	KNAVE	RA K ISH	BAN K NOTE	*FEC K LESS
*KILOWATT	S K ALD	RE K NIT	BAN K ROLL	*FOL K LIKE
KINDLESS	S K ATE	*SU K KAH	*BAN K RUPT	*FOL K LORE
KINDLING	S K EAN	TA K AHE	*BAN K SIDE	*FOL K MOOT
KINDNESS	S K EEN	TA K ING	BAR K LESS	*FOL K MOTE
KINESICS	S K EET	TS K TSK	*BAS K ETRY	*FOL K TALE
KINETICS	S K EIN	VA K EEL	BEC K ONER	*FOR K IEST
*KINFOLKS	S K ELP	VI K ING	*BIC K ERER	*FOR K LESS
*KINGBIRD	S K ENE	*WA K IKI	*BOO K CASE	*FOR K LIFT
*KINGBOLT	S K IED	WA K ING	BOO K LORE	*FOR K LIKE
*KINGFISH	S K IER	*WI K IUP	*BOO K MARK	*FOR K SFUL
*KINGHOOD	S K IES	YO K ING	*BOO K RACK	*GYM K HANA
KINGLESS	S K IEY	*BA K LAVA	BOO K REST	*HAC K WORK
*KINGLIKE	*S K IFF	*BA K LAWA	*BOO K SHOP	*HAN K ERER
*KINGPOST	S K ILL	*BI K EWAY	*BOO K WORM	*HAR K ENER
*KINGSHIP	S K IMO	*DA K OITY	*BRA K EAGE	*HAW K BILL
KINGSIDE	S K IMP	*DU K EDOM	*BRA K EMAN	*HAW K LIKE
*KINGWOOD	S K INK	HE K TARE	*BUC K AROO	*HAW K MOTH
*KINKAJOU	S K INT	*JU K EBOX	*BUC K AYRO	*HAW K NOSE
*KINSFOLK	S K IRL	*KO K ANEE	*BUC K BEAN	*HAW K SHAW
KIRIGAMI	S K IRR	LI K ABLE	*BUC K EROO	*HAW K WEED
*KLYSTRON	S K IRT	*PI K EMAN	*BUC K SHEE	*HOC K SHOP
*KNACKERY	S K ITE	PO K IEST	*BUC K SHOT	*HOO K IEST
*KNAPSACK	S K IVE	*RA K EOFF	*BUC K SKIN	*HOO K LESS
*KNAPWEED	S K OAL	RI K ISHA	*BUC K TAIL	*HOO K LIKE
*KNEEHOLE	S K ULK	*RI K SHAW	*BUL K HEAD	*HOO K NOSE
*KNICKERS	S K ULL	SO K EMAN	*BUN K MATE	*HOO K WORM
*KNIGHTLY	S K UNK	*TA K EOFF	*COC K ATOO	*HUC K STER
KNITTING	*S K YEY	TA K EOUT	*COC K BILL	*HUS K IEST
*KNITWEAR	*BA K ERY	TE K TITE	*COC K BOAT	*HUS K LIKE
*KNOCKOFF	BA K ING	*WA K ANDA	*COC K CROW	*JAC K AROO
*KNOCKOUT	BE K ISS	*WA K EFUL	*COC K EREL	*JAC K BOOT
*KNOTHOLE	BE K NOT	WA K ENER	*COC K IEST	*JAC K EROO
KNOTLESS	BI K ING	*ZI K URAT	*COC K LIKE	*JAC K FISH
*KNOTLIKE	BI K INI	*BAC K ACHE	*COC K LOFT	*JAC K STAY
*KNOTWEED	DA K OIT	*BAC K BEND	*COC K SHUT	*JUN K ETER
*KNUCKLER	DE K ARE	*BAC K BITE	*COC K SPUR	*JUN K YARD
*KOHLRABI	*DI K DIK	*BAC K BONE	*COC K SURE	*KIC K BACK
KOLINSKI	DI K TAT	*BAC K DOOR	*COC K TAIL	*KIC K SHAW
*KOLINSKY	FA K EER	*BAC K DROP	*COO K BOOK	*KIN K AJOU
*KOMONDOR	*FA K ERY	*BAC K FILL	COO K LESS	*LAC K ADAY
*KOWTOWER	FA K ING	*BAC K FIRE	*COO K SHOP	LAN K NESS
*KREUTZER	*HA K EEM	*BAC K HAND	*COO K WARE	LAR K IEST
*KRYOLITE	*JO K ING	*BAC K LASH	COR K IEST	LAR K SOME
*KRYOLITH	*KA K APO	*BAC K LESS	*COR K LIKE	LAR K SPUR
KURTOSIS	LA K ING	*BAC K LIST	*COR K WOOD	LEA K LESS
*KYMOGRAM	LI K ELY	*BAC K MOST	DAN K NESS	LEU K EMIA
*KYPHOSIS	LI K EST	*BAC K PACK	DAR K ENER	*LEU K EMIC
	LI K ING	*BAC K REST	DAR K NESS	LEU K OSIS
	LI K UTA	*BAC K SEAT	*DAR K ROOM	*LIC K SPIT
	*MI K VAH	*BAC K SIDE	*DAR K SOME	LIN K SMAN
S K AG	*MI K VEH	*BAC K SLAP	*DEC K HAND	*LIN K WORK
S K AT	*MU K LUK	*BAC K SLID	DIN K IEST	*LOC K STEP
S K EE	NE K TON	*BAC K SPIN	*DOC K HAND	*LOO K DOWN
S K EG	*PI K AKE	*BAC K STAY	*DOC K LAND	*LUN K HEAD
S K EP				

*MAC K EREL	*ROC K FISH	*WOR K SHOP	HEC K	PIC K
*MAC K INAW	ROC K IEST	*WOR K WEEK	HIC K	PIN K
*MAR K DOWN	ROC K LESS	*ZIK K URAT	HOC K	POC K
*MAR K EDLY	*ROC K LIKE		HOL K	POR K
*MAR K HOOR	*ROC K LING		HON K	PUC K
*MAR K SMAN	ROC K ROSE	BAC K	HOO K	PUN K
*MAS K LIKE	*RUC K SACK	BAL K	HOW K	RAC K
*MIL K FISH	*SAC K LIKE	BAN K	HUC K	RAN K
*MIL K MAID	*SAC K SFUL	BAR K	HUL K	REC K
*MIL K WEED	*SHA K EOUT	BAS K	HUN K	REE K
*MIL K WOOD	*SHA K IEST	BEA K	HUS K	RIC K
*MIL K WORT	*SHI K AREE	BEC K	*JAC K	RIN K
*MON K FISH	SIC K ENER	BIL K	*JAU K	RIS K
*MON K HOOD	SIC K NESS	BIR K	*JER K	ROC K
*MUC K IEST	*SIC K ROOM	BIS K	*JIN K	ROO K
*MUC K LUCK	SIL K IEST	BOC K	*JOC K	RUC K
*MUC K RAKE	*SIL K LIKE	BOO K	*JOU K	RUS K
*MUC K WORM	*SIL K WEED	BOS K	*JUN K	SAC K
*MUS K ETRY	*SIL K WORM	BUC K	KEC K	SAN K
*NEC K BAND	*SIN K HOLE	BUL K	KEE K	SAR K
*NEC K LACE	*SMO K EPOT	BUN K	KIC K	SEE K
NEC K LESS	SPI K ELET	BUS K	KIN K	SIC K
*NEC K LIKE	STA K EOUT	CAL K	KIR K	SIL K
NEC K LINE	STO K ESIA	CAR K	KOO K	SIN K
*NEC K WEAR	*SUC K FISH	CAS K	LAC K	SOA K
*NIC K ELIC	SUC K LESS	COC K	LAN K	SOC K
*NIC K NACK	*SUC K LING	CON K	LAR K	SPI K
*NIC K NAME	TAC K IEST	COO K	LEA K	SUC K
*PAC K AGER	TAC K LESS	COR K	LEE K	SUL K
*PAC K NESS	*TAC K LING	CUS K	LIC K	SUN K
*PAC K SACK	TAL K ABLE	DAN K	LIN K	TAC K
*PAR K LAND	*TAS K WORK	DAR K	LOC K	TAL K
*PAR K LIKE	*TEA K WOOD	DAW K	LOO K	TAS K
PEA K IEST	*TIC K LISH	DEC K	LUC K	TEA K
PEA K LESS	*TIC K SEED	DES K	LUN K	TIC K
*PEA K LIKE	TIC K TACK	DIC K	LUR K	TOO K
*PEE K ABOO	*TIC K TOCK	DIN K	MAC K	TRE K
*PEN K NIFE	TIN K ERER	DIR K	MAR K	TUC K
*PIC K ADIL	TIN K LING	DOC K	MAS K	TUS K
*PIC K EREL	*TUC K AHOE	DRE K	MEE K	WAC K
*PIC K ETER	TUS K LESS	DUC K	MER K	WAL K
*PIC K IEST	*TUS K LIKE	DUS K	MIC K	WAR K
*PIC K LOCK	*VAL K YRIE	FEC K	MIL K	WAU K
*PIC K WICK	*WAL K AWAY	FIN K	MIR K	WEA K
PIN K NESS	*WAL K OVER	FLA K	MOC K	WEE K
PIN K ROOT	*WAL K YRIE	FOL K	MON K	WIC K
*POC K ETER	*WEA K ENER	FOR K	MOS K	WIN K
*POC K MARK	*WEA K FISH	FUC K	MUC K	WOR K
POR K IEST	*WEA K LING	FUN K	MUR K	YAC K
*POR K WOOD	*WEA K NESS	GAW K	MUS K	YAN K
*PUC K ERER	*WEE K LONG	GEC K	NAR K	YEL K
*RAC K WORK	*WOR K ABLE	GEE K	NEC K	YER K
RAN K NESS	*WOR K ADAY	GIN K	NIC K	YEU K
REC K LESS	*WOR K BOAT	GOO K	NOC K	YOL K
REC K ONER	*WOR K BOOK	GOW K	NOO K	BATI K
*RIC K RACK	*WOR K FOLK	GUC K	PAC K	BAUL K
*RIC K SHAW	*WOR K LESS	GUN K	PAI K	BLAC K
*ROC K ABYE	*WOR K LOAD	HAC K	PAR K	BLAN K
*ROC K AWAY	*WOR K ROOM	HAI K	PEA K	BLEA K
ROC K ETER		HAN K	PEC K	BLIN K
*ROC K ETRY		HAW K	PEE K	BLOC K
*ROC K FALL			PER K	BRAN K

BREA K	KULA K	STIN K	*MUZJI K	*BULWAR K
BRIC K	*KYAC K	STIR K	NUDNI K	*BURDOC K
BRIN K	*MUJI K	STOC K	PADAU K	BURLES K
BRIS K	PLAC K	STOO K	PADOU K	*BUTTOC K
BROC K	PLAN K	STOR K	REBEC K	*CALPAC K
BROO K	PLIN K	STUC K	RECOC K	*CARRAC K
BRUS K	PLON K	STUN K	RECOO K	*CARSIC K
CAUL K	PLUC K	SWAN K	REDOC K	*CASSOC K
CHAL K	PLUN K	SWIN K	REMAR K	*CATWAL K
CHEE K	PRAN K	TALU K	REPAC K	*CHABOU K
*CHIC K	PRIC K	TARO K	REPER K	*CHAMPA K
CHIN K	PRIN K	THAC K	RESEE K	*CHEWIN K
CHIR K	PULI K	THAN K	RETOO K	*CHIBOU K
CHIR K	*QUAC K	THIC K	REWOR K	*CHINOO K
*CHOC K	*QUAR K	THIN K	*RHEBO K	*COMATI K
*CHUC K	*QUIC K	TORS K	*SANJA K	*COSSAC K
CHUN K	*QUIR K	TRAC K	*SCHRI K	*COWLIC K
CLAC K	SAME K	TRAI K	SCREA K	*CUTBAC K
CLAN K	SCUL K	TRIC K	*SHLOC K	*CUTWOR K
CLEE K	SHAC K	TROA K	SHRAN K	*DAGLOC K
CLER K	SHAN K	TROC K	SHRIE K	*DAYBOO K
CLIC K	SHAR K	TRUC K	SHRIN K	*DEFROC K
CLIN K	SHEI K	TRUN K	SHRUN K	DERRIC K
CLOA K	SHIR K	TUPI K	*SHTIC K	*DIEBAC K
CLOC K	SHOC K	TWEA K	*SQUAW K	*DORHAW K
CLON K	SHOO K	*WHAC K	*SQUEA K	DORNEC K
CLUC K	SHUC K	*WHEL K	STREA K	DORNIC K
CLUN K	SKIN K	*WHIS K	STREE K	*FATBAC K
CRAC K	SKUL K	WRAC K	STRIC K	*FETLOC K
CRAN K	SKUN K	WREA K	STROO K	*FINBAC K
CREA K	SLAC K	WREC K	STRUC K	*FINMAR K
CREE K	SLAN K	YAPO K	SUSLI K	*FOSSIC K
CRIC K	SLEE K	BATTI K	*THWAC K	*FUTHAR K
CROA K	SLIC K	*BEDEC K	TOMBA K	*FUTHOR K
CROC K	SLIN K	*BEMOC K	TSKTS K	*FUTTOC K
CROO K	SLUN K	BETOO K	TUGRI K	*GEMSBO K
DRAN K	SMAC K	*BEYLI K	*YAPOC K	*GEODUC K
DRIN K	SMEE K	*BIPAC K	*YASMA K	GERENU K
DROU K	SMER K	*BOHUN K	*ZADDI K	*GIMMIC K
DRUN K	SMIR K	*BYTAL K	*ZEBEC K	*GORCOC K
FLAC K	SMOC K	*BYWOR K	*BANGKO K	GOSHAW K
FLAN K	SNAC K	CARAC K	*BANNOC K	GUNLOC K
FLAS K	SNAR K	*CHABU K	*BARRAC K	*GWEDUC K
FLEC K	SNEA K	*COPEC K	*BASHLY K	*HADDOC K
FLIC K	SNEC K	*CROJI K	*BAWCOC K	*HAMMOC K
FLUN K	SNIC K	DAMAS K	BEATNI K	*HASSOC K
FRAN K	SNOO K	DEBAR K	*BECHAL K	*HATRAC K
FREA K	SNUC K	DEBUN K	*BECLOA K	*HAUBER K
FRIS K	SPAN K	DEMAR K	*BEDROC K	*HAYCOC K
FROC K	SPAR K	DETIC K	*BEDTIC K	*HAYFOR K
GLEE K	SPEA K	*DIBBU K	*BEFLEC K	*HAYRAC K
GREE K	SPEC K	*DIKDI K	BELLEE K	*HAYRIC K
HACE K	SPIC K	*DYBBU K	BERSER K	*HEMLOC K
HOIC K	SPOO K	GALYA K	*BETHAN K	*HENPEC K
KAIA K	SPUN K	*HIJAC K	*BETHIN K	*HILLOC K
*KAMI K	STAC K	*KALPA K	*BIBCOC K	*HOGBAC K
*KAPO K	STAL K	*KOPEC K	*BITTOC K	*HOMMOC K
*KAYA K	STAN K	MAMLU K	*BLAUBO K	*HOPSAC K
KIOS K	STAR K	*MEDIC K	*BLESBO K	*HUMMOC K
*KNAC K	STEA K	*MOUJI K	BONNOC K	*JAYWAL K
*KNOC K	STEE K	*MUKLU K	*BULLOC K	*JUMBUC K
*KOPE K	STIC K	*MUZHI K		*KEBBOC K

*KEBBUC K	*RUNBAC K	*BULLNEC K	*HAIRLOC K	*PICKWIC K
*KILLIC K	*SAWBUC K	*BUSHBUC K	*HAIRWOR K	*PIGSTIC K
*KILLOC K	*SCHLOC K	*BUSYWOR K	*HALFBAC K	*PINCHEC K
*KINFOL K	*SCHMUC K	*CAKEWAL K	*HALFBEA K	*PINPRIC K
*KOMATI K	*SCHNOO K	*CALLBAC K	*HALLMAR K	*PIROZHO K
*LAVROC K	*SCHTIC K	*CAPEWOR K	*HANDBOO K	*PLAYBAC K
*LEGWOR K	*SEACOC K	*CASEBOO K	*HANDPIC K	*PLAYBOO K
LENTIS K	SEAMAR K	*CASEWOR K	*HANDWOR K	*PLOWBAC K
*LIMBEC K	SEASIC K	*CASHBOO K	*HARDBAC K	*POCKMAR K
LOGBOO K	*SETBAC K	*CHAPBOO K	*HARDHAC K	*POLITIC K
*MAFFIC K	SHASLI K	*CHARLOC K	*HARDTAC K	*POSTMAR K
*MAMMOC K	*SHYLOC K	*CHIPMUC K	*HATCHEC K	*PRECHEC K
*MANPAC K	*SKYHOO K	*CHIPMUN K	*HAVELOC K	*PREFRAN K
*MATTOC K	*SKYJAC K	*CLAYBAN K	*HAYSTAC K	*PRINCOC K
*MENFOL K	*SKYLAR K	*COALSAC K	*HEADLOC K	*PULLBAC K
*MIDWEE K	SPELUN K	*COATRAC K	*HEADWOR K	*RACKWOR K
*MISCOO K	SPUTNI K	*COMEBAC K	*HIGHJAC K	*REAPHOO K
*MISMAR K	*SUNBAC K	*COOKBOO K	*HOLDBAC K	REATTAC K
MISTEU K	TANBAR K	*COPYBOO K	*HOMESIC K	*REDBRIC K
MISTOO K	*TIEBAC K	*COPYDES K	*HOMEWOR K	*REDSHAN K
MUDLAR K	TINWOR K	*CORNHUS K	*HOODWIN K	*REEDBUC K
*MUDROC K	TITLAR K	*CRIBWOR K	*HORNBOO K	*REEMBAR K
*MULLOC K	*TOMBAC K	*DABCHIC K	*HUMPBAC K	RESTRUC K
MULLUS K	*TOPKIC K	*DAYBREA K	*HYMNBOO K	*RICKRAC K
*MUNTJA K	*TOPWOR K	*DEADLOC K	*JOYSTIC K	*RINGBAR K
NETWOR K	*TRIPAC K	*DIESTOC K	*KERPLUN K	*RINGNEC K
*NIBLIC K	TUSSOC K	*DIPSTIC K	*KICKBAC K	*ROADWOR K
*NITPIC K	TUSSUC K	*DISFROC K	*KINSFOL K	*ROCKWOR K
NONBAN K	*TZADDI K	*DOMINIC K	*KNAPSAC K	*ROLLBAC K
NONBOO K	*WAESUC K	*DRAMMOC K	*LACEWOR K	*ROORBAC K
NUDNIC K	*WARLOC K	*DRAWBAC K	*LANDMAR K	*ROPEWAL K
*NUTPIC K	*WARWOR K	*DROPKIC K	*LATHWOR K	*RUCKSAC K
*PADDOC K	*WAXWOR K	*FALLBAC K	*LAVEROC K	*SALTWOR K
*PADLOC K	*WEDLOC K	*FASTBAC K	*LEADWOR K	*SANDBAN K
PARTOO K	*WETBAC K	*FATSTOC K	*LIFEWOR K	*SCATBAC K
*PEACOC K	*WINNOC K	*FEEDBAC K	*LIMERIC K	*SEATWOR K
*PETCOC K	*WRYNEC K	*FINNMAR K	*LINKWOR K	SELAMLI K
*PIDDOC K	*YASHMA K	*FIRELOC K	LINSTOC K	*SHADDOC K
*PINWOR K	*BACKPAC K	*FIREPIN K	*LIPSTIC K	*SHAGBAR K
*POLLAC K	*BALDRIC K	*FIREWOR K	*LOBSTIC K	*SHAMROC K
*POLLOC K	*BANKBOO K	*FISHHOO K	*LOPSTIC K	*SHASHLI K
*POTHOO K	*BAREBAC K	*FLAPJAC K	*LOVELOC K	*SHELDUC K
*POTLUC K	BARESAR K	*FLATWOR K	*LOVESIC K	*SHELLAC K
*PRECOC K	BASILIS K	*FLYSPEC K	*MAVERIC K	*SHERLOC K
PREDUS K	*BEADWOR K	*FOOTMAR K	*MEGABUC K	*SHOEPAC K
*PREPAC K	*BENEDIC K	*FOOTWOR K	*MESHWOR K	*SHOPTAL K
PRESOA K	*BILLHOO K	*FOREDEC K	*MILLWOR K	*SIDEKIC K
*PUGMAR K	*BITSTOC K	*FORELOC K	*MISSPEA K	*SIDEWAL K
RANSAC K	*BLESBUC K	*FOREMIL K	*MISTHIN K	*SITZMAR K
RATFIN K	*BLOWBAC K	*FOREPEA K	*MOSSBAC K	*SKEWBAC K
*RECHEC K	*BLUEBOO K	*FORERAN K	*MUCKLUC K	*SKIPJAC K
REDNEC K	*BLUEJAC K	*FRETWOR K	NAINSOO K	*SLAPJAC K
REITBO K	*BOBOLIN K	*FULLBAC K	*NEWSPEA K	*SLOPWOR K
RESTAC K	*BODYWOR K	*GAMECOC K	*NICKNAC K	*SLOTBAC K
RESTOC K	*BONTEBO K	*GAVELOC K	NONSTIC K	*SNAPBAC K
RETHIN K	*BOOKMAR K	*GEMSBUC K	NOTEBOO K	*SNOWBAN K
RETRAC K	*BOOKRAC K	*GIMCRAC K	*PACKSAC K	*SNOWPAC K
*RIMROC K	*BOOTJAC K	*GRAYBAC K	*PASHALI K	*SOAPBAR K
*ROEBUC K	*BOOTLIC K	*GRIPSAC K	*PASSBOO K	*SOFTBAC K
ROLLIC K	*BOSCHBO K	*GROSBEA K	*PAYCHEC K	*SONGBOO K
*ROWLOC K	*BOSHVAR K	*GUNSTOC K	*PENSTOC K	STEENBO K
*RUDDOC K	*BUHLWOR K	*HACKWOR K	*PICKLOC K	STEINBO K

*STOPCOC K	*TASKWOR K	*TIPSTOC K	*WIREWOR K	*WORKFOL K
*STUDBOO K	*TEAMWOR K	*TOMAHAW K	*WOODCOC K	*WORKWEE K
*STUDWOR K	TELEMAR K	*TOWNFOL K	*WOODLAR K	*YEARBOO K
*SUBCLER K	*TEXTBOO K	*TRAPROC K	*WOODWOR K	ZWIEBAC K
*SWAYBAC K	*TICKTAC K	*TUBEWOR K	*WOOLPAC K	
*TAILBAC K	*TICKTOC K	*WHITRAC K	*WOOLSAC K	
*TAMARAC K	*TIDEMAR K	*WINDSOC K	*WORDBOO K	
TAMARIS K	*TIMEWOR K	*WINGBAC K	*WORKBOO K	

L

LACE	LEHR	LOAN	LULU	LARES
LACK	LEND	LOBE	LUMP	LARGE
LACY	LENO	LOBO	LUNA	LARGO
LADE	LENS	LOCA	LUNE	LARKY
LADY	LENT	LOCH	LUNG	LARUM
LAIC	LESS	LOCI	LUNK	LARVA
LAID	LEST	LOCK	LUNY	LASER
LAIN	LEUD	LOCO	LURE	LASSO
LAIR	LEVO	LODE	LURK	LATCH
LAKE	LEVY	LOFT	LUSH	LATED
LAKH	LEWD	LOGE	LUST	LATEN
LAKY	LIAR	LOGO	LUTE	LATER
LALL	LICE	LOGY	LUXE	LATEX
LAMA	LICK	LOIN	LYNX	LATHE
LAMB	LIDO	LOLL	LYRE	LATHY
LAME	LIED	LONE	LYSE	LAUAN
LAMP	LIEF	LONG	LABEL	LAUGH
LAND	LIEN	LOOF	LABIA	LAURA
LANE	LIER	LOOK	LABOR	LAVER
LANG	LIEU	LOOM	LABRA	LAYER
LANK	LIFE	LOON	LACER	*LAXLY
LARD	LIFT	LOOP	LACEY	LAYER
LARK	LIKE	LOOT	LACEY	LAZAR
LASE	LILT	LOPE	LADEN	LEACH
LASH	LILY	LORD	LADER	LEADY
LASS	LIMA	LORE	LADLE	LEAFY
LAST	LIMB	LORN	LAEVO	LEAKY
LATE	LIME	LORY	LAGAN	LEANT
LATH	LIMN	LOSE	LAGER	LEAPT
LATI	LIMO	LOSS	LAICH	LEARN
LAUD	LIMP	LOST	LAIGH	LEARY
LAVA	LIMY	LOTA	LAIRD	LEASE
LAVE	LINE	LOTH	LAITH	LEASH
LAWN	LING	LOUD	LAITY	LEAST
LAZE	LINK	LOUP	LAKED	LEAVE
*LAZY	LINN	LOUR	LAKER	LEAVY
LEAD	LINO	LOUT	LAMED	LEBEN
LEAF	LINT	LOVE	LAMER	LEDGE
LEAK	LINY	LOWE	LAMIA	LEDGY
LEAL	LION	LOWN	LANAI	LEECH
LEAN	LIRA	LUAU	LANCE	LEERY
LEAP	LISP	LUBE	LAPEL	LEFTY
LEAR	LIST	LUCE	LAPIN	LEGAL
LECH	LITU	LUCK	LAPIS	LEGER
LEEK	LIVE	LUES	LAPSE	LEGES
LEER	LOAD	LUFF	LARCH	LEGGY
LEET	LOAF	LUGE	LARDY	LEGIT
LEFT	LOAM	LULL	LARDY	LEHUA
				LEMAN

LEMMA	**LIPPY**	LOVER	LADLER	LATTER
LEMON	LISLE	LOWER	LADRON	LATTIN
LEMUR	LITAS	**LOWLY**	LAGEND	LAUDER
LENES	LITER	LOWSE	LAGGED	LAUNCE
LENIS	LITHE	LOYAL	LAGGER	**LAUNCH**
LENSE	LITHO	LUCES	LAGOON	LAUREL
LENTO	LITRE	LUCID	LAGUNA	**LAVABO**
LEONE	LIVEN	**LUCKY**	LAGUNE	**LAVAGE**
LEPER	LIVER	LUCRE	**LAKING**	LAVEER
LETCH	LIVES	**LUFFA**	LALLAN	**LAVING**
LETHE	LIVID	LUMEN	**LAMBDA**	**LAVISH**
LETUP	LIVRE	**LUMPY**	**LAMBER**	**LAWFUL**
LEVEE	LLAMA	LUNAR	**LAMBIE**	LAWINE
LEVEL	LLANO	**LUNCH**	**LAMEDH**	**LAWING**
LEVER	**LOACH**	LUNET	**LAMELY**	**LAWMAN**
LEVIN	**LOAMY**	LUNGE	LAMENT	**LAWYER**
LEWIS	LOATH	LUNGI	LAMEST	*LAXITY
LIANA	LOBAR	LUPIN	LAMINA	**LAYMAN**
LIANE	**LOBBY**	LUPUS	LAMING	*LAYOFF
LIANG	LOCAL	**LURCH**	**LAMMED**	*LAZIED
LIARD	LOCUM	LURER	**LAMPAD**	*LAZIER
LIBEL	LOCUS	LURID	**LAMPAS**	*LAZIES
LIBER	LODEN	LUSTY	LANATE	*LAZILY
LIBRA	LODGE	LUSUS	LANCER	*LAZING
LIBRI	LOESS	LUTEA	LANCET	*LAZULI
LICHI	**LOFTY**	LUTED	LANDAU	**LEACHY**
LICHT	**LOGGY**	LYARD	LANDER	**LEADEN**
LICIT	LOGIA	LYART	LANELY	LEADER
LIDAR	LOGOS	LYASE	LANGUE	LEAGUE
LIEGE	LOLLY	**LYCEA**	LANGUR	**LEAKER**
LIEVE	LONER	**LYCEE**	LANNER	LEALTY
LIFER	LONGE	LYING	LANOSE	LEAPER
LIGAN	LOOEY	*LYMPH	LANUGO	LEARNT
LIGHT	**LOOBY**	**LYNCH**	**LAPDOG**	LEASER
LIKED	LOOFA	**LYRIC**	**LAPFUL**	**LEAVED**
LIKEN	LOOIE	LYSIN	**LAPPED**	LEAVEN
LIKER	LOONY	LYSIS	**LAPPER**	LEAVER
LILAC	**LOOPY**	LYSSA	**LAPPET**	LEAVES
LIMAN	LOOSE	**LYTIC**	LAPSER	**LECHER**
LIMBA	LOPER	LYTTA	LAPSUS	LECTOR
LIMBI	**LOPPY**	LAAGER	LARDER	LEDGER
LIMBO	LORAL	LABIAL	LARDON	**LEEWAY**
LIMBY	LORAN	LABILE	LARIAT	**LEGACY**
LIMEN	LORIS	**LABIUM**	LARINE	LEGATE
LIMES	LORRY	LABOUR	**LARKER**	LEGATO
LIMEY	LOSEL	LABRET	LARRUP	LEGEND
LIMIT	LOSER	**LABRUM**	*LARYNX	LEGGED
LINAC	LOSSY	**LACHES**	LASCAR	LEGGIN
LINDY	LOTAH	LACIER	LASHER	LEGION
LINED	LOTIC	**LACILY**	LASING	LEGIST
LINEN	LOTOS	LACING	LASSIE	LEGMAN
LINER	LOTTO	**LACKER**	LASTER	LEGUME
LINEY	LOTUS	*LACKEY	LASTLY	LENDER
LINGA	LOUGH	**LACTAM**	LATEEN	**LENGTH**
LINGO	LOUIE	**LACTIC**	LATELY	LENITY
LINGY	LOUIS	LACUNA	LATENT	LENTEN
LININ	LOUPE	LACUNE	LATEST	LENTIC
LINKY	LOURY	LADDER	LATHER	LENTIL
LINTY	LOUSE	LADDIE	LATIGO	LEPTON
LINUM	LOUSY	LADIES	LATISH	LESION
LIPID	LOVED	LADING	LATRIA	LESSEE
LIPIN	LOVER	LADINO	LATTEN	LESSEN

LESSER	LINNET	LOLLOP	LUPINE	LAMSTER
LESSON	LINSEY	LOMENT	LUPOUS	LANATED
LETHAL	LINTEL	LONELY	LURDAN	**LANCING**
LETTED	LINTER	LONGAN	LURING	LANDING
LETTER	LINTOL	LONGER	**LURKER**	LANDLER
LEUCIN	LIPASE	**LONGLY**	LUSTER	**LANDMAN**
LEUKON	LIPIDE	**LOOFAH**	LUSTRA	**LANDMEN**
LEVANT	LIPOID	**LOOKER**	LUSTRE	LANGREL
LEVIED	**LIPOMA**	**LOOKUP**	LUTEAL	LANGUET
LEVIER	**LIPPED**	LOONEY	LUTEIN	LANGUID
LEVIES	**LIPPEN**	LOOPER	LUTEUM	LANGUOR
LEVITY	**LIPPER**	LOOSED	LUTING	LANIARD
LIABLE	*LIQUID	LOOSEN	LUTIST	**LANIARY**
LIAISE	*LIQUOR	LOOSER	**LUXATE**	LANITAL
LIBBER	LISPER	LOOTER	*LUXURY	LANOLIN
LIBIDO	LISSOM	LOPPED	LYCEUM	LANTANA
LICHEE	LISTEL	LOPPER	LYCHEE	LANTERN
LICHEN	LISTEN	*LOQUAT	LYRATE	**LANYARD**
LICKER	LISTER	**LORDLY**	LYRISM	LAPIDES
LICTOR	LITANY	LOREAL	LYRIST	LAPPING
LIENAL	**LITCHI**	LORICA	LYSATE	**LARCENY**
LIERNE	LITHIA	LOSING	LYSINE	LARDIER
LIFTER	**LITHIC**	LOTION	**LYSING**	LARDOON
LIGAND	LITMUS	LOTTED	**LABARUM**	LARGESS
LIGASE	LITTEN	LOUDEN	LABELER	**LARGISH**
LIGATE	LITTER	**LOUDLY**	LABELLA	**LARKIER**
LIGNIN	LITTLE	LOUNGE	LABIATE	LASAGNA
LIGULA	**LIVELY**	**LOUNGY**	LABORER	LASAGNE
LIGULE	**LIVERY**	LOUVER	**LABROID**	**LASHING**
LIGURE	LIVEST	LOUVRE	LACIEST	**LASHINS**
LIKELY	LIVIER	**LOVAGE**	LACONIC	LASHKAR
LIKEST	**LIVING**	**LOVELY**	*LACQUER	LASSOER
LIKING	**LIVYER**	**LOVING**	*LACQUEY	LASTING
LIKUTA	*LIZARD	**LOWBOY**	**LACTARY**	LATAKIA
LILIED	LOADER	**LOWERY**	LACTASE	**LATCHET**
LIMBER	LOAFER	**LOWING**	LACTATE	**LATENCY**
LIMBER	LOANER	**LOWISH**	LACTEAL	LATERAD
LIMBIC	LOATHE	**LUBBER**	LACTEAN	LATERAL
LIMBUS	LOBATE	**LUBRIC**	LACTONE	**LATHERY**
LIMIER	LOAVES	LUCENT	LACTOSE	**LATHIER**
LIMINA	**LOBBED**	LUCERN	LACUNAR	**LATHING**
LIMING	LOBULE	**LUCKIE**	**LADANUM**	LATICES
LIMMER	LOCALE	LUETIC	LADRONE	LATOSOL
LIMNER	LOCATE	LUGGED	**LADYBUG**	LATRINE
LIMNIC	**LOCHIA**	LUGGER	**LADYISH**	LATTICE
LIMPER	**LOCKER**	LUGGIE	*LADYKIN	LAUGHER
LIMPET	**LOCKET**	LUMBAR	LAGGARD	LAUNDER
LIMPID	**LOCKUP**	**LUMBER**	LAGGING	LAUNDRY
LIMPLY	LOCULE	*LUMMOX	LAICISE	LAUWINE
LIMPSY	LOCUST	**LUMPEN**	LAICISM	*LAVROCK
LINAGE	LODGER	**LUMPER**	*LAICIZE	LAWLESS
LINDEN	LOFTER	LUNACY	LALLAND	LAWLIKE
LINEAL	LOGGED	LUNATE	**LAMBAST**	LAWSUIT
LINEAR	LOGGER	LUNGAN	**LAMBENT**	LAXNESS
LINEUP	LOGGIA	LUNGEE	**LAMBERT**	*LAYAWAY
LINGAM	LOGIER	LUNGER	*LAMBKIN	LAYETTE
LINGER	**LOGILY**	LUNGYI	LAMELLA	LAYOVER
LINGUA	LOGION	LUNIER	**LAMMING**	*LAZARET
LINIER	*LOGJAM	LUNIES	LAMPERS	*LAZIEST
LINING	**LOGWAY**	LUNKER	LAMPION	*LAZYISH
LINKER	LOITER	LUNULA	LAMPOON	LEACHER
LINKUP	LOLLER	LUNULE	**LAMPREY**	

LEADIER	LEVERET	LIPLIKE	LORINER	LABURNUM
LEADING	LEVULIN	LIPPING	LOTTERY	LACELESS
LEADOFF	*LEXICAL	*LIQUATE	LOTTING	LACELIKE
LEAFAGE	*LEXICON	*LIQUEFY	LOUDISH	LACERATE
LEAFIER	LIAISON	*LIQUEUR	LOUTISH	LACERTID
LEAFLET	LIANOID	*LIQUIFY	LOVABLE	LACEWING
LEAGUER	LIBELEE	LISSOME	LOWBORN	LACEWOOD
LEAKAGE	LIBELER	LISTING	LOWBRED	*LACEWORK
LEANING	LIBERAL	LITERAL	*LOWBROW	LACINESS
LEARIER	LIBERTY	LITHIUM	LOWDOWN	*LACKADAY
LEARNER	LIBRARY	LITHOID	LOWLAND	LACONISM
LEASING	LIBRATE	LITORAL	LOWLIFE	LACRIMAL
LEATHER	LICENCE	LITOTES	LOWNESS	LACROSSE
LEAVING	LICENSE	LITTERY	LOYALLY	LACTEOUS
*LECHERY	*LICHTLY	LITURGY	LOYALTY	LACUNOSE
LECTERN	LICKING	LIVABLE	*LOZENGE	LADLEFUL
LECTION	LIDLESS	LIVENER	LUCARNE	*LADYBIRD
LECTURE	LIFEFUL	LOADING	LUCENCE	*LADYFISH
LEEWARD	*LIFEWAY	LOANING	LUCENCY	*LADYHOOD
LEFTISM	LIFTMAN	LOATHER	LUCERNE	*LADYLIKE
LEFTIST	*LIFTOFF	LOATHLY	LUCIFER	*LADYLOVE
LEGALLY	LIGHTEN	LOBATED	LUGGAGE	*LADYPALM
LEGATEE	LIGHTER	LOBBING	LUGGING	*LADYSHIP
LEGATOR	LIGHTLY	LOBBYER	LUGSAIL	LAGNAPPE
LEGGIER	LIGNIFY	LOBEFIN	LUGWORM	LAITANCE
LEGGING	LIGNITE	LOBELIA	LULLABY	LAKEPORT
LEGHORN	LIGROIN	LOBSTER	LUMBAGO	LAKESIDE
LEGIBLE	LIKABLE	LOBWORM	LUMPISH	LALLYGAG
LEGLESS	LIMACON	LOCALLY	LUNATED	LAMASERY
LEGLIKE	LIMBATE	LOCATER	LUNATIC	*LAMBASTE
LEGROOM	*LIMBECK	LOCATOR	LUNCHER	*LAMBENCY
LEGUMIN	LIMBIER	*LOCKBOX	LUNETTE	*LAMBKILL
*LEGWORK	LIMEADE	*LOCKJAW	LUNGING	*LAMBLIKE
*LEHAYIM	LIMIEST	LOCKNUT	LUNIEST	*LAMBSKIN
LEISTER	LIMINAL	LOCKOUT	LUPANAR	LAMENESS
LEISURE	LIMITED	*LOCKRAM	LUPULIN	LAMENTER
LEMMING	LIMITER	LOCOISM	LURCHER	LAMINATE
LEMPIRA	LIMITES	LOCULAR	LUSTFUL	LAMINOSE
LEMURES	*LIMPKIN	LOCULUS	LUSTIER	LAMINOUS
LENGTHY	LIMULUS	LOCUSTA	LUSTILY	LAMISTER
LENIENT	LINABLE	LODGING	LUSTRAL	LAMPPOST
LENTIGO	LINALOL	LOFTILY	LUSTRUM	*LAMPYRID
LENTISK	LINDANE	LOGBOOK	LUTEOUS	LANCELET
LENTOID	LINEAGE	LOGGATS	LUTHERN	LANCIERS
LEONINE	LINEATE	LOGGETS	*LYCHNIS	LANDFALL
LEOPARD	LINECUT	LOGGING	*LYCOPOD	LANDFILL
LEOTARD	LINEMAN	LOGICAL	LYDDITE	LANDFORM
LEPORID	LINGCOD	LOGIEST	LYINGLY	LANDLADY
LEPROSE	LINGIER	LOGROLL	LYNCEAN	LANDLESS
LEPROSY	LINGUAL	LOGWOOD	*LYNCHER	LANDLORD
LEPROUS	LINIEST	LONGBOW	LYRATED	*LANDMARK
LESBIAN	LINKAGE	LONGING	LYRICAL	LANDMASS
LETDOWN	*LINKBOY	LONGISH	LYSOGEN	LANDSIDE
LETTING	LINKMAN	LONGISH	LABDANUM	*LANDSKIP
LETTUCE	LINOCUT	LOOKOUT	LABELLED	LANDSLID
LEUCINE	LINSANG	LOOSEST	LABELLER	LANDSLIP
LEUCITE	LINSEED	LOOSING	LABELLUM	LANDSMAN
LEUCOMA	LINTIER	LOPPING	LABIALLY	LANDWARD
LEUKOMA	LIONESS	LORDING	LABIATED	LANGLAUF
LEVATOR	LIONISE	LORDOMA	LABILITY	LANGRAGE
LEVELER	*LIONIZE	LORGNON	LABORITE	LANGSHAN
LEVELLY	LIPLESS	LORIMER	LABOURER	LANGSYNE

LANGUAGE	*LAZURITE	LEVIABLE	LINALOOL	LOBLOLLY
LANGUISH	LEACHATE	LEVIGATE	*LINCHPIN	*LOBOTOMY
LANKNESS	LEADIEST	LEVIRATE	LINEABLE	*LOBSTICK
LANNERET	LEADLESS	LEVITATE	LINEATED	LOCALISE
LANOLINE	LEADSMAN	*LEVOGYRE	LINEBRED	LOCALISM
LANOSITY	*LEADWORK	LEVULOSE	LINELESS	LOCALIST
LANTHORN	LEADWORT	LEWDNESS	LINELIKE	LOCALITE
LAPBOARD	LEAFIEST	LEWISITE	LINESMAN	LOCALITY
LAPIDARY	LEAFLESS	LEWISSON	LINGERER	*LOCALIZE
LAPIDATE	*LEAFLIKE	LIBATION	LINGERIE	LOCATION
*LAPIDIFY	*LEAFWORM	LIBECCIO	LINGIEST	LOCATIVE
LAPIDIST	LEAKLESS	LIBELANT	LINGUINE	*LOCKSTEP
LAPILLUS	LEANNESS	LIBELIST	LINGUINI	*LOCOFOCO
LARBOARD	LEAPFROG	LIBELLED	LINGUIST	LOCOMOTE
LARCENER	LEARIEST	LIBELLEE	LINIMENT	LOCOWEED
LARDIEST	LEARNING	LIBELLER	LINKSMAN	LOCULATE
LARDLIKE	LEATHERN	LIBELOUS	*LINKWORK	LOCUTION
LARGESSE	LEATHERY	LIBERATE	LINOLEUM	LOCUTORY
LARKIEST	*LECHAYIM	LIBRETTO	LINSTOCK	LODESTAR
LARKSOME	LECITHIN	LICENCEE	LINTIEST	LODGMENT
LARKSPUR	LECTURER	LICENCER	LINTLESS	LODICULE
LARRIGAN	*LECYTHUS	LICENSEE	LIONFISH	LOFTLESS
LARRIKIN	LEEBOARD	LICENSER	LIONISER	LOGICIAN
LARRUPER	LEFTOVER	LICENSOR	*LIONIZER	LOGICISE
*LATCHKEY	*LEFTWARD	LICHENIN	LIONLIKE	*LOGICIZE
LATEENER	*LEFTWING	*LICKSPIT	*LIPOCYTE	LOGINESS
LATENESS	LEGALESE	LICORICE	*LIPSTICK	LOGISTIC
LATENTLY	LEGALISE	LIEGEMAN	*LIQUIDLY	LOGOGRAM
LATERITE	LEGALISM	LIENABLE	LIRIPIPE	*LOGOMACH
LATEWOOD	LEGALIST	LIENTERY	LISTENER	LOGOTYPE
LATHERER	LEGALITY	LIFEBOAT	LISTLESS	*LOGOTYPY
LATHIEST	*LEGALIZE	LIFELESS	LITERACY	LOITERER
*LATHWORK	LEGATINE	*LIFELIKE	LITERARY	LOLLIPOP
LATINITY	LEGATING	LIFELINE	LITERATE	LOLLYGAG
*LATINIZE	LEGATION	LIFELONG	LITERATI	*LOLLYPOP
LATITUDE	LEGENDRY	LIFETIME	LITHARGE	LOMENTUM
LATTERLY	LEGERITY	*LIFEWORK	LITHEMIA	LONENESS
LAUDABLE	LEGGIEST	LIGAMENT	LITHOSOL	LONESOME
LAUDANUM	*LEKYTHOS	LIGATION	LITIGANT	LONGBOAT
LAUDATOR	*LEKYTHUS	LIGATURE	LITIGATE	LONGERON
LAUGHING	LEMNISCI	*LIGHTFUL	LITTERER	LONGHAIR
LAUGHTER	LEMONADE	LIGHTING	LITTLISH	LONGHAND
LAUNCHER	LEMUROID	*LIGHTISH	LITTORAL	LONGHEAD
LAUREATE	LENGTHEN	LIGNEOUS	LIVEABLE	LONGHORN
LAVALAVA	LENIENCE	LIGROINE	LIVELONG	LONGLEAF
LAVALIER	LENIENCY	LIKEABLE	LIVENESS	LONGLINE
*LAVALIKE	LENITIVE	LIKENESS	LIVERIED	LONGNESS
LAVATION	LENTANDO	*LIKEWISE	LIVERISH	LONGSHIP
LAVATORY	LENTICEL	LILLIPUT	LIVETRAP	LONGSOME
LAVENDER	LEPIDOTE	LIMACINE	*LIVIDITY	LONGSPUR
*LAVEROCK	LEPORINE	LIMBIEST	*LIVINGLY	LONGTIME
LAVISHER	LEPROTIC	LIMBLESS	*LIXIVIUM	LONGUEUR
*LAWGIVER	LETHALLY	LIMEKILN	LOADSTAR	*LONGWAYS
*LAWMAKER	*LETHARGY	LIMELESS	LOAMLESS	LONGWISE
*LAXATION	LETTERER	*LIMERICK	LOANWORD	*LOOKDOWN
*LAXATIVE	LEUCEMIA	LIMINESS	LOATHFUL	LOOPHOLE
LAYABOUT	LEUKEMIA	LIMITARY	LOATHING	LOOSENER
LAYERAGE	*LEUKEMIC	LIMNETIC	LOBATION	LOPSIDED
LAYERING	LEUKOSIS	LIMONENE	*LOBBYGOW	*LOPSTICK
*LAYWOMAN	LEVANTER	LIMONITE	*LOBBYISM	LORDLESS
*LAZINESS	LEVELLER	LIMPNESS	*LOBBYIST	LORDLIER
*LAZULITE	LEVERAGE	LIMULOID	LOBELINE	LORDLIKE

LORDLING	*LYRIFORM	G L ED	B L ATE	C L INE
LORDOSIS	*LYSOGENY	G L EE	*B L AZE	C L ING
LORDSHIP	LYSOSOME	G L EG	B L EAK	C L INK
LORICATE	*LYSOZYME	G L EN	B L EAR	C L IPT
LORIKEET		G L EY	B L EAT	C L OAK
LORNNESS		G L IB	B L EED	C L OCK
LOSINGLY	B L AB	G L IM	B L END	C L OMB
LOSTNESS	B L AE	G L OB	B L ENT	C L OMP
LOTHARIO	B L AH	G L OM	B L ESS	C L ONE
LOTHSOME	B L AT	G L OP	B L EST	C L ONK
LOUDNESS	B L AW	G L OW	B L IMP	C L OOT
LOVEABLE	B L EB	G L UE	B L IMY	C L OSE
LOVEBIRD	B L ET	G L UM	B L IND	C L OTH
LOVELESS	B L IN	G L UT	B L INI	C L OUD
LOVELIER	B L IP	P L AN	B L INK	C L OUR
LOVELIES	B L OB	P L AT	B L ISS	C L OUT
LOVELILY	B L OC	P L AY	B L ITE	C L OVE
*LOVELOCK	B L OT	P L EA	*B L ITZ	C L OWN
LOVELORN	B L OW	P L EB	B L OAT	*C L OZE
*LOVESICK	B L UE	P L ED	B L OCK	C L UCK
LOVESOME	B L UR	P L IE	B L OKE	C L UMP
LOVEVINE	C L AD	P L OD	B L OND	C L UNG
*LOVINGLY	C L AG	P L OP	B L OOD	C L UNK
LOYALISM	C L AM	P L OT	B L OOM	F L ACK
LOYALIST	C L AN	P L OW	B L OOP	F L AIL
LUCIDITY	C L AP	P L OY	B L OWN	F L AKE
LUCKLESS	C L AW	P L UG	B L OWY	*F L AKY
LUCULENT	C L AY	P L UM	B L UED	F L AME
*LUKEWARM	C L EF	P L US	B L UER	F L AMY
LUMBERER	C L EW	S L AB	B L UET	F L ANK
LUMINARY	C L IP	S L AG	B L UEY	F L ARE
LUMINIST	C L OD	S L AM	B L UFF	F L ASH
LUMINOUS	C L OG	S L AP	B L UME	F L ASK
*LUMPFISH	C L ON	S L AT	B L UNT	F L AWY
LUNARIAN	C L OP	S L AW	B L URB	*F L AXY
LUNATION	C L OT	S L AY	B L URT	F L EAM
LUNCHEON	C L OY	S L ED	B L USH	F L ECK
*LUNGFISH	C L UB	S L EW	B L YPE	F L EER
LUNGWORM	C L UE	S L IM	C L ACH	F L EET
LUNGWORT	F L AB	S L IP	C L ACK	F L ESH
*LUNKHEAD	F L AG	S L IT	C L AIM	F L ICK
LUSCIOUS	F L AK	S L OB	C L AMP	F L IED
LUSHNESS	F L AM	S L OE	C L ANG	F L IER
LUSTIEST	F L AN	S L OG	C L ANK	F L IES
LUSTRATE	F L AP	S L OP	C L ARO	F L ING
LUSTRING	F L AT	S L OT	C L ARY	F L INT
LUSTROUS	F L AW	S L OW	C L ASH	F L OUR
LUTANIST	F L AX	S L UB	C L ASP	F L OUT
LUTECIUM	F L AY	S L UE	C L ASS	F L OWN
LUTENIST	F L EA	S L UG	C L AST	F L UFF
LUTEOLIN	F L ED	S L UM	C L EAN	F L UID
LUTETIUM	F L EE	S L UR	C L EAR	F L UKE
*LUXATION	F L EW	S L UT	C L EAT	*F L UKY
*LYCOPENE	F L EX	B L ACK	C L EEK	F L UME
*LYMPHOMA	F L EY	B L ADE	C L EFT	F L UMP
*LYNCHING	F L IC	B L AIN	C L EPE	F L UNG
*LYOPHILE	F L IP	B L AME	C L ERK	F L UNK
LYREBIRD	F L OW	B L AND	C L ICK	F L UOR
LYRICISE	F L UB	B L ANK	C L IFF	F L USH
*LYRICISM	F L UE	B L ARE	C L IMB	F L UTE
LYRICIST	F L UX	B L ASE	C L IME	F L UTY
*LYRICIZE	G L AD	B L AST		

F L UYT	*P L AZA	BA L EEN	CE L ERY	FI L LIP
*F L YBY	P L EAD	BA L KER	CE L IAC	FI L MIC
F L YER	P L EAT	BA L LAD	CE L LAR	FI L OSE
F L YTE	P L EBE	BA L LER	CI L ICE	FI L TER
G L ACE	P L ENA	BA L LET	CI L IUM	*FI L THY
G L ADE	P L ICA	BA L LON	CO L DLY	FO L ATE
G L ADY	P L IED	BA L LOT	CO L EUS	FO L DER
G L AIR	P L IER	BA L SAM	CO L LAR	FO L IAR
G L AND	P L IES	BE L ADY	CO L LET	FO L IUM
G L ANS	P L INK	BE L AUD	CO L LIE	*FO L KSY
G L ARE	P L ONK	BE L DAM	CO L LOP	FO L LIS
G L ARY	P L UCK	BE L EAP	CO L ONI	FO L LOW
G L ASS	P L UMB	BE L FRY	CO L ONY	FU L FIL
*G L AZE	P L UME	BE L IED	CO L OUR	FU L GID
*G L AZY	P L UMP	BE L IEF	CO L TER	FU L HAM
G L EAM	P L UMY	BE L IER	CO L UGO	FU L LAM
G L EAN	P L UNK	BE L IES	CO L UMN	FU L LER
G L EBA	P L USH	BE L IKE	CO L URE	FU L MAR
G L EBE	P L YER	BE L IVE	CU L LAY	*FY L FOT
G L EDE	S L ACK	BE L LOW	CU L LER	GA L AGO
G L EED	S L AIN	BE L ONG	CU L LET	*GA L AXY
G L EEK	S L AKE	BE L UGA	CU L LIS	GA L ENA
G L EET	S L ANG	BI L BOA	CU L TCH	GA L ERE
G L IAL	S L ANK	BI L KER	CU L TUS	GA L LEY
G L IDE	S L ANT	BI L LER	CU L VER	GA L LON
G L IFF	S L ASH	BI L LET	DA L ASI	GA L LOP
G L IME	S L ATE	BI L LIE	DA L ETH	GA L LUS
G L OAM	S L ATY	BI L LON	DA L LES	GA L ORE
G L OAT	S L EEK	BI L LOW	DE L ATE	GA L OSH
G L OBE	S L EEP	BO L ERO	DE L EAD	GA L YAK
G L OGG	S L EET	BO L ETE	DE L ETE	GE L ADA
G L OOM	S L EPT	BO L IDE	DE L ICT	GE L ANT
G L ORY	S L ICE	*BO L LIX	DE L IME	GE L ATE
G L OSS	S L ICK	*BO L LOX	DE L IST	GE L DER
G L OST	S L IDE	BO L SON	DE L UDE	GE L LED
G L OUT	S L IER	BO L TER	DE L UGE	GI L DER
G L OVE	S L ILY	BU L BEL	DE L UXE	GI L LER
*G L OZE	S L IME	BU L BIL	DE L VER	GI L LIE
G L UER	S L IMY	BU L BUL	DI L ATE	GO L DEN
G L UEY	S L ING	BU L GER	DI L UTE	GO L FER
G L UME	S L INK	BU L GUR	DO L LAR	GO L OSH
G L YPH	S L IPE	BU L LET	DO L LOP	GU L DEN
K L ONG	S L IPT	BY L INE	DO L MAN	GU L LET
K L OOF	S L OID	CA L AMI	DO L MEN	GU L LEY
*K L UTZ	S L OJD	CA L ASH	DO L OUR	GU L PER
L L AMA	S L OOP	CA L CAR	DU L CET	HA L ALA
L L ANO	S L OPE	CA L CES	FA L CON	HA L EST
P L ACE	S L OSH	CA L CIC	FA L LAL	HA L IDE
P L ACK	S L OTH	CA L ESA	FA L LEN	HA L ING
P L AGE	S L OYD	CA L ICO	FA L LER	HA L ITE
P L AID	S L UFF	CA L IPH	FA L LOW	HA L LAH
P L AIN	S L UMP	CA L KER	FA L SIE	HA L LEL
P L AIT	S L UNG	CA L KIN	FA L TER	HA L LOA
P L ANE	S L UNK	CA L LAN	FE L INE	HA L LOO
P L ANK	S L URB	CA L LER	FE L LAH	HA L LOT
P L ANT	S L URP	CA L LET	FE L LER	HA L LOW
P L ASH	S L USH	CA L LOW	FE L LOE	*HA L LUX
P L ASM	S L YPE	CA L LUS	FE L LOW	HA L OID
P L ATE	*Z L OTY	CA L ORY	FE L ONY	HA L TER
P L ATY	BA L ATA	CA L PAC	FI L IAL	*HA L UTZ
P L ATY	BA L BOA	*CA L QUE	FI L LER	*HA L VAH
P L AYA	BA L DLY	CA L VES	FI L LET	HA L VES

HE L IAC	MI L AGE	PO L EIS	SA L VOR	**TE L EGA**
HE L IUM	MI L DEN	**PO L EYN**	**SC L AFF**	**TE L FER**
HE L LER	MI L IEU	**PO L ICE**	SC L ERA	TE L IAL
HE L MET	MI L LER	**PO L ICY**	SE L DOM	TE L IUM
HE L PER	MI L LET	PO L ING	SE L ECT	**TE L LER**
HI L LER	MI L ORD	**PO L ISH**	SE L LER	TE L OME
HI L LOA	MI L TER	PO L ITE	SE L SYN	TE L SON
HO L ARD	MO L DER	**PO L ITY**	SE L VES	TI L LER
HO L DEN	MO L EST	PO L LEE	***SH L OCK**	TI L TER
HO L DER	MO L INE	PO L LEN	SI L AGE	TO L ANE
HO L DUP	MO L LIE	PO L LER	SI L ANE	TO L EDO
HO L IER	MO L TEN	***PO L LEX**	SI L ENI	TO L LER
HO L IES	MO L TER	**PO L YPI**	SI L ENT	TO L UIC
HO L ILY	MU L ETA	PU L LER	SI L ICA	TO L UID
HO L ING	MU L ING	PU L LET	**SI L KEN**	TO L UOL
HO L ISM	MU L LEN	**PU L LEY**	SI L LER	TO L UYL
HO L IST	MU L LER	**PU L PAL**	SI L VAN	TU L ADI
HO L LER	MU L LET	**PU L PER**	SI L VER	**VA L GUS**
HO L LOA	NE L SON	**PU L PIT**	**SK L ENT**	VA L INE
HO L LOO	NI L GAI	***PU L QUE**	SO L ACE	VA L ISE
HO L LOW	NI L GAU	PU L SAR	SO L AND	**VA L LEY**
HO L PEN	NU L LAH	PU L SER	SO L ANO	VA L OUR
HU L LER	**PA L ACE**	RA L LYE	SO L ATE	VA L UER
HU L LOA	PA L AIS	RE L ACE	SO L DAN	VA L UTA
*JA L OPY	**PA L ATE**	RE L ATE	SO L DER	**VA L VAL**
JI L TER	PA L EST	RE L END	SO L ELY	**VA L VAR**
JO L TER	**PA L ISH**	RE L ENT	SO L EMN	VE L ATE
KA L IAN	PA L LED	RE L ICT	SO L GEL	**VE L LUM**
*KA L IPH	PA L LET	RE L IED	SO L IDI	**VE L OCE**
KA L IUM	PA L LIA	RE L IEF	SO L ING	VE L OUR
KA L MIA	PA L LID	RE L IER	SO L ION	VE L URE
KA L ONG	PA L LOR	RE L IES	SO L UTE	**VE L VET**
*KA L PAK	**PA L MAR**	RE L INE	SO L VER	VI L LUS
KE L OID	**PA L MER**	RE L ISH	**SP L AKE**	VO L ANT
KE L PIE	**PA L PAL**	RE L IST	**SP L ASH**	**VO L ERY**
KE L SON	**PA L PUS**	RE L IVE	**SP L EEN**	**VO L LEY**
KE L TER	PA L TER	RE L OAD	**SP L ENT**	VO L OST
KE L VIN	PE L AGE	RE L OAN	**SP L ICE**	**VO L UME**
KI L LER	PE L ITE	RE L UCT	**SP L INE**	VO L UTE
KI L TER	PE L LET	RE L UME	**SP L INT**	***VO L VOX**
KI L TIE	PE L OTA	RI L LET	**SP L ORE**	**VU L GAR**
*KO L HOZ	PE L TER	RO L LER	**SP L OSH**	**VU L GUS**
*KO L KOZ	**PE L TRY**	RU L ING	SU L CUS	**WA L ING**
KU L TUR	**PE L VIC**	SA L AAM	SU L DAN	**WA L KER**
LA L LAN	**PE L VIS**	SA L AMI	**SU L FID**	***WA L KUP**
LI L IED	**PH L EGM**	SA L ARY	SU L FUR	**WA L LAH**
LO L LER	**PH L OEM**	**SA L IFY**	**SU L KER**	WA L LET
LO L LOP	**PI L AFF**	SA L INA	SU L LEN	WA L LIE
MA L ATE	**PI L EUM**	SA L INE	**SU L PHA**	**WA L LOP**
MA L GRE	**PI L EUP**	SA L IVA	SU L TAN	**WA L LOW**
MA L IGN	**PI L EUS**	SA L LET	SU L TRY	WA L NUT
MA L INE	**PI L FER**	SA L LOW	**SY L VAN**	WA L RUS
MA L LEE	PI L ING	SA L MON	**SY L VIN**	**WE L DER**
MA L LEI	PI L LAR	SA L OON	**TA L CUM**	**WE L DOR**
MA L LET	**PI L LOW**	SA L OOP	TA L ENT	**WE L KIN**
MA L TED	PI L OSE	SA L PID	TA L ION	WE L TER
MA L TOL	PI L OUS	SA L TER	**TA L KER**	**WI L DER**
ME L DER	PI L ULE	SA L TIE	**TA L KIE**	**WI L DLY**
ME L OID	PO L DER	**SA L UKI**	TA L LOL	**WI L FUL**
ME L TER	***PO L EAX**	SA L UTE	**TA L LOW**	WI L IER
ME L TON		SA L VER	**TA L UKA**	**WI L ILY**
MI L ADI		SA L VIA	TE L EDU	**WI L ING**

WI L LER	BU L LBAT	CO L DISH	FA L CATE	GA L LOWS
WI L LET	BU L LDOG	CO L ICIN	*FA L LACY	GA L LYAC
WI L LOW	BU L LIED	*CO L ICKY	*FA L LOFF	GA L OSHE
WO L FER	BU L LIER	CO L ITIS	FA L LOUT	*GA L UMPH
WO L VER	BU L LIES	CO L LAGE	*FA L SIFY	GE L ATIN
WO L VES	BU L LION	CO L LARD	FA L SITY	GE L DING
*XY L ENE	BU L LISH	CO L LECT	FE L LIES	GE L LANT
*XY L OID	*BU L LOCK	CO L LEEN	FE L ONRY	GE L LING
*XY L OSE	BU L LOUS	CO L LEGE	FE L SITE	GI L BERT
YC L EPT	BU L LPEN	CO L LIDE	FE L SPAR	GI L DING
YE L LER	BU L RUSH	CO L LIED	FE L TING	GI L LNET
YE L LOW	*BU L WARK	CO L LIES	FE L UCCA	GO L DARN
YE L LOW	BY L INER	CO L LINS	FE L WORT	GO L DBUG
YE L PER	CA L AMAR	CO L LOID	FI L AREE	GO L DEYE
*ZI L LAH	CA L AMUS	CO L LUDE	FI L ARIA	GO L FING
BA L ANCE	CA L ANDO	CO L OGNE	FI L BERT	GO L IARD
BA L CONY	*CA L CIFY	CO L ONEL	*FI L CHER	GU L FIER
BA L DISH	CA L CINE	CO L ONIC	FI L EMOT	*HA L AKIC
BA L DRIC	CA L CITE	CO L ONUS	FI L IATE	HA L ALAH
BA L EFUL	CA L CIUM	CO L ORED	FI L IBEG	*HA L AVAH
BA L LADE	CA L DERA	CO L ORER	FI L LIES	HA L BERD
BA L LAST	CA L DRON	CO L UMEL	FI L LING	HA L BERT
BA L LING	CA L ECHE	CU L ICID	FI L LING	*HA L CYON
BA L LOON	CA L ENDS	CU L LIED	*FI L MDOM	*HA L FWAY
BA L NEAL	CA L IBER	CU L LIES	FI L MIER	HA L IBUT
BA L ONEY	CA L IBRE	CU L LION	*FI L MILY	HA L IDOM
BE L ABOR	CA L ICES	CU L LOTTE	FI L MSET	HA L ITUS
BE L ACED	CA L ICHE	CU L PRIT	FO L ACIN	HA L LOTH
BE L ATED	CA L ICLE	CU L TISM	FO L DOUT	*HA L LWAY
BE L CHER	CA L IPEE	CU L TIST	FO L IAGE	HA L OGEN
BE L DAME	CA L IPER	CU L TURE	FO L IATE	HA L VERS
BE L IEVE	CA L LANT	CU L VERT	FO L IOSE	HA L YARD
BE L LBOY	CA L LBOY	DA L APON	FO L IOUS	HE L IAST
BE L LEEK	CA L LING	DA L LIER	*FO L KISH	HE L ICAL
BE L LHOP	CA L LOSE	DE L AINE	*FO L KMOT	HE L ICES
BE L LMAN	CA L LOUS	DE L ATOR	*FO L KWAY	HE L ICON
BE L OVED	CA L OMEL	DE L AYER	FO L LIES	HE L IPAD
BE L TING	CA L ORIC	DE L IGHT	FU L CRUM	*HE L LBOX
*BE L TWAY	CA L ORIE	DE L IMIT	FU L FILL	HE L LCAT
BE L YING	CA L OTTE	DE L IVER	FU L GENT	HE L LERI
BI L IARY	CA L OYER	DE L OUSE	FU L LERY	HE L LERY
BI L IOUS	*CA L PACK	DE L TOID	FU L MINE	HE L LISH
BI L LBUG	CA L TRAP	DE L UDER	FU L NESS	HE L LUVA
BI L LIES	CA L TROP	DI L ATER	FU L SOME	HE L OTRY
BI L LING	CA L UMET	DI L ATOR	FU L VOUS	*HE L PFUL
BI L LION	CA L UMNY	DI L UENT	GA L ATEA	HE L PING
*BI L LOWY	*CA L VARY	DI L UTER	GA L ILEE	HI L DING
BI L OBED	CA L YCES	DI L UTOR	GA L IPOT	HI L LIER
BI L STED	CA L YCLE	DI L UVIA	GA L LANT	*HI L LOCK
BI L TONG	CA L YPSO	DO L EFUL	GA L LATE	HI L LTOP
BO L ETUS	CE L ADON	DO L LIED	GA L LEIN	HO L DALL
BO L IVAR	CE L ESTA	DO L LIES	GA L LEON	HO L DING
BO L IVIA	CE L ESTE	DO L LING	GA L LERY	HO L DOUT
BO L LARD	CE L LIST	DO L LISH	GA L LETA	HO L IBUT
BO L OGNA	CE L LULE	DO L PHIN	GA L LFLY	HO L IDAY
BO L ONEY	*CH L AMYS	*DU L CIFY	GA L LIOT	HO L IEST
BO L STER	CH L ORAL	DU L LARD	GA L LIUM	HO L LAND
BU L BOUS	CH L ORIC	DU L LISH	GA L LNUT	HO L MIUM
BU L IMIA	CH L ORID	DU L NESS	GA L LOON	HO L STER
BU L KAGE	CH L ORIN	FA L BALA	GA L LOOT	*HO L YDAY
BU L LACE	CI L IARY		GA L LOOT	*JA L APIN
BU L LATE	CI L IATE		GA L LOUS	

*JA L OPPY	MI L LION	PO L EMIC	*SA L TBOX	SU L FURY
*JE L LIFY	MI L LRUN	PO L ENTA	SA L TERN	SU L LAGE
JI L LION	MI L REIS	PO L ITIC	SA L TIER	SU L PHID
*JO L LIED	MO L LIES	*PO L LACK	SA L TILY	SU L PHUR
JO L LIER	*MO L LIFY	PO L LARD	SA L TINE	SU L TANA
JO L LIES	MU L ATTO	PO L LIST	SA L TIRE	SY L LABI
*JO L LIFY	MU L LEIN	PO L OIST	SA L TISH	*SY L PHID
*JO L LITY	MU L LION	PO L YCOT	SA L TPAN	SY L VINE
KA L ENDS	MU L LITE	PO L YENE	SA L UTER	SY L VITE
*KA L IMBA	*MU L LOCK	PO L YGON	SA L VAGE	TA L ARIA
KI L LDEE	MU L TURE	PO L YMER	SA L VING	TA L IPED
*KI L LICK	NE L UMBO	*PO L YNYA	SE L ENIC	TA L IPES
KI L LING	NI L GHAI	*PO L YPOD	SE L FDOM	TA L IPOT
*KI L LJOY	NI L GHAU	PO L YPUS	SE L FISH	TA L KING
*KI L LOCK	NU L LIFY	*SE L TZER	SE L LOUT	TA L LAGE
KI L OBAR	NU L LITY	SE L VAGE	*SE L TZER	TA L LBOY
KI L OBIT	NY L GHAI	PU L LING	SE L VAGE	TA L LIED
KI L ORAD	NY L GHAU	PU L LMAN	SI L ENCE	TA L LIER
KI L OTON	PA L ABRA	PU L LOUT	SI L ENTS	TA L LIES
KI L TING	PA L ADIN	PU L PIER	SI L ENUS	TA L LISH
*KO L ACKY	PA L ATAL	PU L PILY	SI L ESIA	TA L LITH
*KO L KHOS	PA L AVER	PU L POUS	SI L ICIC	TA L LOWY
*KO L KHOZ	*PA L AZZO	PU L SANT	SI L ICLE	TA L LYHO
LA L LAND	PA L ETOT	PU L SATE	SI L ICON	TA L OOKA
LU L LABY	*PA L ETTE	PU L SING	*SI L IQUA	TE L AMON
MA L AISE	*PA L FREY	PU L SION	*SI L IQUE	TE L EMAN
MA L AMUT	PA L IEST	PY L ORUS	SI L KIER	TE L EOST
MA L APER	PA L IKAR	RA L LIED	SI L KILY	TE L ERAN
MA L APRO	PA L LIAL	RA L LIER	SI L URID	TE L ESIS
MA L ARIA	PA L LIER	RA L LINE	SI L VERN	TE L FORD
*MA L ARKY	PA L LIER	RE L ABEL	SI L VERY	TE L LIES
MA L AROM	PA L LING	RE L APSE	SI L VICS	TE L PHER
MA L EATE	PA L LING	RE L ATER	SO L ACER	TI L APIA
MA L EDIC	PA L LIUM	RE L ATOR	SO L ANIN	TI L BURY
MA L EMIU	PA L MARY	RE L AXER	SO L ANUM	TI L LAGE
MA L EMUT	PA L MATE	RE L AXIN	SO L ARIA	TI L LING
MA L ENES	PA L MIER	RE L EARN	SO L ATIA	TO L IDIN
MA L IGNE	PA L MIST	RE L EASE	SO L DIER	TO L LAGE
MA L IGNL	PA L MYRA	RE L IANT	SO L ERET	TO L LBAR
MA L IHIN	PA L OOKA	RE L IEVE	SO L ICIT	TO L LING
MA L INGE	PA L PATE	RE L IEVO	SO L FEGE	TO L LMAN
MA L ISON	PA L UDAL	RE L IGHT	SO L ICIT	TO L LWAY
MA L LEUS	PE L AGIC	*RE L IQUE	SO L IDLY	TO L UATE
MA L POSE	PE L ICAN	RI L IEVO	SO L IDUS	TO L UENE
MA L TASE	PE L ISSE	RI L LING	SO L OIST	TO L UIDE
MA L TIER	PE L ORIA	RO L LICK	SO L UBLE	TO L UOLE
MA L TIES	PE L ORUS	RO L LING	SO L UBLY	VA L ANCE
MA L TOSE	PE L TAST	RO L LMOP	SO L VATE	VA L ENCE
ME L ANIN	PE L TATE	RO L LOUT	SO L VENT	*VA L ENCY
ME L ILIT	*PH L EGMY	RO L LTOP	SO L VING	VA L IANT
ME L ILOT	PI L EATE	RO L LWAY	*SP L ASHY	VA L IDLY
ME L INIT	PI L EOUS	SA L ABLE	SP L EENY	VA L LATE
ME L ODIE	PI L GRIM	SA L ICIN	SP L ENIA	VA L ONIA
ME L ODIC	PI L LAGE	SA L IENT	SP L ENIC	VA L UATE
*MI L CHIG	*PI L LBOX	SA L LIED	SP L ICER	VA L VATE
*MI L DEWY	PI L LION	SA L LIER	SP L OTCH	VA L VULA
MI L ITIA	PI L LORY	SA L LIES	SP L URGE	VA L VULE
*MI L KILY	*PI L LOWY	SA L LOWY	SP L URGY	VE L AMEN
*MI L KMAN	PI L SNER	SA L PIAN	SU L CATE	VE L IGER
*MI L KSOP	PO L ARON	*SA L PINX	SU L FATE	VE L ITES
MI L LIER	*PO L EAXE	SA L SIFY	SU L FIDE	VE L OUTE
MI L LINE	PO L ECAT	SA L TANT	SU L FITE	VI L AYET
			SU L FONE	

VI L LAGE	*BIL L FISH	COL L ATOR	FEL L ABLE	LAD L EFUL
VI L LAIN	BIL L FOLD	COL L EGER	FEL L ATIO	LAL L YGAG
VI L LEIN	BIL L HEAD	COL L EGIA	FEL L NESS	LIL L IPUT
*VI L LIFY	*BIL L HOOK	COL L IERY	*FEL L OWLY	LOB L OLLY
VO L ANTE	BIL L IARD	COL L OGUE	FOI L SMAN	LOL L IPOP
VO L CANO	*BIL L YCAN	*COL L OQUY	FOL L ICLE	LOL L YGAG
VO L TAGE	BIO L OGIC	COL L UDER	FOL L OWER	*LOL L YPOP
VO L UBLE	BIO L YSIS	COL L UVIA	*FOO L FISH	LUCKLESS
VO L UTIN	*BOL L WORM	COL L YRIA	*FOO L SCAP	LUCULENT
VU L GATE	*BOW L LIKE	COO L NESS	FOU L NESS	MA L LEOLI
VU L PINE	*BUH L WORK	COP L ANAR	FRI L LING	MA L TREAT
VU L TURE	BUI L DING	COU L DEST	FUE L LING	MA L TSTER
*WA L KING	*BUL L DOZE	COU L ISSE	FUG L EMAN	MA L VASIA
WA L KOUT	BUL L ETIN	CUR L ICUE	*FUL L BACK	*MEA L WORM
*WA L KWAY	BUL L FROG	*CUR L YCUE	*FUL L FACE	*MEA L YBUG
*WA L LEYE	BUL L HEAD	*CYC L AMEN	FUL L NESS	ME L AMINE
WA L LIES	BUL L HORN	*CYC L ECAR	*FUR L OUGH	ME L ANIAN
WA L LIES	BUL L IEST	*CYC L ICAL	GAL L EASS	ME L ANISM
*WA L TZER	BUL L NECK	*CYC L ITOL	GAL L IARD	ME L ANITE
*WE L CHER	BUL L NOSE	*DAY L IGHT	GAL L OPER	ME L ANOID
WE L COME	BUL L POUT	*DEA L FISH	GAS L IGHT	ME L ANOMA
WE L FARE	BUL L RING	DEC L ARER	GEO L OGER	ME L ANOUS
WE L SHER	BUL L RUSH	DEC L ASSE	GIR L HOOD	*MEL L IFIC
WE L TING	BUL L SHIT	DEC L INER	GOA L LESS	ME L ODEON
WI L DCAT	BUL L WEED	DEF L ATOR	GOA L POST	ME L ODIST
WI L DING	*BUL L WHIP	*DEF L EXED	GOD L IEST	MI L DNESS
WI L DISH	BUL L YBOY	*DEF L OWER	GOL L IWOG	MI L EPOST
WI L IEST	BUL L YRAG	DEP L ORER	GRI L LADE	MI L ESIMO
WI L LFUL	*CAB L EWAY	DIA L LAGE	GRI L LAGE	MI L IARIA
WI L LIED	*CAL L BACK	DIA L LIST	GUI L EFUL	MI L ITANT
WI L LIES	CAL L IOPE	DIA L OGER	GUL L ABLE	MI L ITARY
WI L LING	CAL L IPEE	DIA L OGIC	GUL L IBLE	MI L ITATE
*WI L LOWY	CAL L IPER	DIA L OGUE	HAL L IARD	MI L KIEST
*WO L FISH	CAU L DRON	DIA L YSER	*HAL L MARK	MI L LEPED
*WO L FRAM	CAU L ICLE	DIA L YSIS	HAL L OWER	MI L LIARD
*XY L IDIN	*CAU L KING	DIA L YTIC	*HAP L OIDY	MI L LIARE
*YC L EPED	CEL L ARER	*DIA L YZER	HAR L OTRY	MI L LIARY
*YE L LOWY	CEL L ARET	DIE L DRIN	*HAU L YARD	MI L LIBAR
*ZE L KOVA	CEL L ULAR	DIO L EFIN	HEE L BALL	MI L LIEME
*ZI L LION	CHA L DRON	DIP L EGIA	HEE L LESS	MI L LIGAL
BAI L MENT	CHA L LIES	*DIP L OIDY	HEL L BENT	*MIL L ILUX
BAI L SMAN	*CHA L LOTH	DIP L OMAT	HEL L FIRE	*MIL L IMHO
BAL L ISTA	CHE L ATOR	DIP L OPOD	*HEL L KITE	MI L LINER
BAL L ONET	*CHI L DBED	DIP L OSIS	HIL L IEST	*MIL L IOHM
BAL L ONNE	*CHI L DING	DIS L IKER	HIL L SIDE	MI L LIREM
BAL L OTER	*CHI L DISH	DIS L ODGE	HOO L IGAN	MI L LPOND
BAL L ROOM	CHI L DREN	DIS L OYAL	*HYA L OGEN	MI L LRACE
*BAL L YHOO	CHI L IASM	*DJE L LABA	*JAI L BAIT	*MIL L WORK
BAL L YRAG	*CHI L OPOD	DRI L LING	*JAI L BIRD	MO L ALITY
BAR L EDUC	*CHO L ERIC	DRO L LERY	*JEA L OUSY	MO L ARITY
BDE L LIUM	CIS L UNAR	DUE L LING	*JET L INER	MO L ASSES
BEC L AMOR	COA L ESCE	DUE L LIST	*JOL L IEST	MO L DIEST
*BEC L OTHE	*COA L FISH	DUL L NESS	*KAI L YARD	MO L ECULE
*BEF L OWER	COA L HOLE	DUO L OGUE	KAL L IDIN	MO L EHILL
BEL L BIRD	COA L LESS	*DUP L EXER	KAO L IANG	MO L ESKIN
BEL L OWER	*COA L SACK	DWE L LING	KEE L BOAT	MO L ESTER
BEL L PULL	COA L SHED	*DYS L EXIA	*KEE L HALE	MU L ETEER
BEL L WORT	COA L YARD	*FAH L BAND	*KEE L HAUL	MU L LIGAN
*BEL L YFUL	COL L AGEN	*FAL L BACK	KEE L LESS	MU L TIFID
BES L AVED	COL L APSE	*FAL L FISH	KIE L BASA	MU L TIPED
BIL L ETER	COL L ARET	FAL L IBLE	KIL L DEER	MU L TIPLY
			*FAN L IGHT	*KOH L RABI	

MY L ONITE	PRO L ABOR	*SHE L LACK	TAL L YMAN	*WIL L YARD
NAI L FOLD	PRO L AMIN	*SHE L VING	TAR L ETAN	WIL L YART
NAI L HEAD	PRO L APSE	SHI L INGI	TEL L TALE	*WIL L YWAW
NEG L IGEE	*PRO L IFIC	SHI L LALA	TEL L URIC	WOO L FELL
*NEW L YWED	PRO L OGUE	SHI L LING	THA L AMUS	WOO L IEST
NIE L LIST	PRO L ONGE	SIL L ABUB	THA L LIUM	WOO L LIER
NOB L EMAN	PSA L MIST	SIL L IBUB	THE L ITIS	WOO L LIES
NOB L ESSE	*PSA L MODY	SKE L ETON	THO L EPIN	*WOO L LIKE
NON L EGAL	PSA L TERY	SKI L LESS	TOI L ETRY	*WOO L PACK
NON L OCAL	PSI L OSIS	*SKI L LFUL	TOI L ETTE	*WOO L SACK
NUC L EASE	PUB L ICAN	SKI L LING	TOI L SOME	*WOO L SHED
NUC L EATE	*PUB L ICLY	*SKU L LCAP	TOI L WORN	*WOO L SKIN
NUC L EOLE	PUL L BACK	*SKY L IGHT	TOL L GATE	WOU L DEST
NUC L EOLI	PUL L OVER	SMA L LAGE	TOO L HEAD	*ZEA L OTRY
PAL L ADIA	PYE L ITIS	SMA L LISH	TOO L LESS	*ZOO L ATER
PAL L ADIC	*QUA L MISH	*SMA L LPOX	TOO L ROOM	*ZOO L ATRY
PAL L ETTE	*QUI L TING	SMA L TINE	TOO L SHED	
PAL L IATE	RAC L ETTE	SMA L TITE	*TOP L OFTY	
PAL L IEST	RAI L BIRD	SME L TERY	TRI L LION	BAA L
PAR L ANCE	RAI L HEAD	SOI L LESS	TRI L LIUM	BAI L
PAR L ANDO	RAI L LERY	SOL L ERET	TRI L OBAL	BAL L
PAR L ANTE	RAI L ROAD	SPA L PEEN	TRI L OBED	BAW L
PAR L EYER	RAL L YING	SPE L AEAN	TRO L LIED	BEL L
PAU L DRON	RAL L YIST	SPE L LING	TRO L LIES	BIL L
PEL L AGRA	REA L ISER	SPI L IKIN	TRO L LING	BIR L
PEL L ETAL	*REA L IZER	SPI L LAGE	TUL L IBEE	BOI L
PEL L ICLE	REA L NESS	*SPI L LWAY	*TWE L VEMO	BOL L
PEL L MELL	REC L INER	SPO L IATE	*TWI L IGHT	BOW L
PEL L UCID	REC L OTHE	STA L LION	TWI L LING	BUH L
PEN L IGHT	*REF L EXLY	STA L WART	*VA L KYRIE	BUL L
PER L UDER	REF L OWER	STE L LATE	VAR L ETRY	BUR L
PHA L ANGE	REF L UENT	STE L LIFY	VAU L TING	BYR L
*PHA L LISM	REP L ACER	STI L BENE	*VEI L EDLY	CAL L
PHA L LIST	REP L EDGE	STI L BITE	*VEI L LIKE	CAR L
PHE L ONIA	REP L EVIN	STI L ETTO	VEL L EITY	CAU L
*PHI L ABEG	REP L UNGE	STI L LMAN	VIL L ADOM	CEI L
*PHI L IBEG	RIF L EMAN	STU L TIFY	VIL L AGER	CEL L
*PHI L OMEL	ROL L AWAY	STY L ISER	VIL L AINY	COA L
*PHY L AXIS	*ROL L BACK	*STY L IZER	VIL L ATIC	COI L
*PHY L ESIS	*ROL L ICKY	SUB L EASE	VIO L ABLE	COO L
*PHY L LARY	ROL L OVER	SUB L EVEL	VIO L ATER	COW L
*PHY L LITE	ROU L ETTE	SUB L IMER	VIO L ATOR	CUL L
*PHY L LODE	SAI L BOAT	SUN L IGHT	VIO L ENCE	CUR L
*PHY L LOID	SAI L FISH	SWE L LING	VOL L EYER	DEA L
*PHY L LOME	SCA L ABLE	*SYL L ABIC	WAI L SOME	DEI L
PIC L ORAM	SCA L AWAG	SYL L ABLE	WAL L AROO	DEL L
PIL L AGER	SCA L ENUS	*SYL L ABUB	WAL L OPER	DIA L
POL L INIA	SCA L EPAN	SYL L ABUS	WAL L OWER	DIE L
POL L INIC	SCA L IEST	TAB L EFUL	*WAY L AYER	DIL L
POL L IWOG	SCA L LION	TAB L ETOP	*WEL L ADAY	DIO L
POL L STER	SCI L ICET	*TAI L BACK	*WEL L AWAY	DIR L
POL L UTER	SCO L DING	TAI L BONE	WEL L BORN	DOL L
*POL L YWOG	SCO L IOMA	TAI L COAT	*WEL L CURB	DUA L
POO L HALL	SCU L LERY	TAI L GATE	WEL L DOER	DUE L
POO L ROOM	SCU L LION	TAI L LESS	*WEL L HEAD	DUL L
POP L ITIC	SCU L PTOR	TAI L LIKE	WEL L HOLE	FAI L
*POT L ACHE	SEA L LIKE	TAI L PIPE	WEL L NESS	FAL L
*POT L ATCH	SEA L SKIN	TAI L RACE	WEL L SITE	FAR L
POU L ARDE	SHA L IEST	TAI L SKID	*WHA L EMAN	FEA L
POU L TICE	SHA L LOON	TAI L SPIN	WIL L IWAU	FEE L
PRE L EGAL	*SHE L DUCK	TAI L WIND	*WIL L IWAW	FEL L
PRE L IMIT	*SHE L FFUL	TAL L NESS	WIL L OWER	FIL L

FOA L	PAW L	BAGE L	FUGA L	NASA L
FOI L	PEA L	BANA L	FUSE L	NATA L
FOO L	PEE L	BASA L	FUSI L	NAVA L
FOU L	PIA L	BASI L	*FUZI L	NAVE L
FOW L	PIL L	BEDE L	GAVE L	NERO L
FUE L	POL L	**BERY L**	GAYA L	NEWE L
FUL L	POO L	BETE L	GHOU L	NICO L
FUR L	PUL L	**BEVE L**	**GHYL L**	NIDA L
GAL L	PUR L	*BEZE L	GIME L	NIHI L
GAO L	RAI L	*BEZI L	GLIA L	NIVA L
GIL L	REA L	BINA L	GNAR L	NODA L
GIR L	REE L	BOTE L	GORA L	NOPA L
GOA L	RIA L	**BOWE L**	GRAA L	NOTA L
GUL L	RIE L	BRAI L	GRAI L	NOVE L
HAI L	RIL L	**BRAW L**	GRIL L	PANE L
HAL L	ROI L	BRIL L	GROW L	PAPA L
HAR L	ROL L	BROI L	GRUE L	PARO L
HAU L	ROT L	BUBA L	GYRA L	PEAR L
HEA L	SAI L	**BUTY L**	HADA L	PEDA L
HEE L	SAL L	CABA L	**HAMA L**	PENA L
HEI L	SAU L	CAME L	*HAZE L	PERI L
HEL L	SEA L	CANA L	**HEMA L**	PETA L
HER L	SEE L	CARO L	*HEXY L	PHIA L
HIL L	SEL L	**CAVI L**	HORA L	PICA L
HOW L	SHU L	CEOR L	HOSE L	PICU L
HUL L	SIA L	**CHIE L**	HOTE L	PIPA L
HUR L	SIL L	**CHIL L**	**HOVE L**	PRIL L
JAI L	SOI L	**CHUR L**	JACA L	**PROW L**
JAR L	SOU L	CIBO L	JEBE L	PUPI L
JEL L	TAE L	**CIVI L**	*JEWE L	**QUAI L**
JIL L	TAI L	COMA L	**JUGA L**	**QUEL L**
JOW L	TAL L	COPA L	**JURA L**	**QUIL L**
KAI L	TEA L	CORA L	**JURE L**	RATA L
KEE L	TEL L	CRAA L	**KEVE L**	RATE L
KIL L	TIL L	**CRAW L**	**KEVI L**	RAVE L
KOE L	TIR L	CREE L	KNEE L	REBE L
KOH L	TOI L	CRUE L	KNOL L	REFE L
LAL L	TOL L	CUPE L	KNUR L	REGA L
LEA L	TOO L	**CYMO L**	KRAA L	RENA L
LOL L	VAI L	DECA L	KRIL L	REOI L
LUL L	VEA L	DEDA L	LABE L	REPE L
MAI L	VEI L	DEVE L	LAPE L	REVE L
MAL L	VIA L	DEVI L	LEGA L	RIVA L
MAR L	VIL L	DOMA L	LEVE L	RIYA L
MAU L	VIO L	DOTA L	LIBE L	ROWE L
MEA L	VIR L	DOWE L	LOCA L	ROYA L
MEL L	WAI L	DRAI L	LORA L	RURA L
MER L	WAL L	DRAW L	LOSE L	SALO L
MEW L	WAU L	DRIL L	LOYA L	SCAL L
MIL L	**WAW L**	DROL L	MAIL L	**SCHU L**
MOI L	WEA L	DROO L	MEDA L	**SCOW L**
MOL L	WEE L	DURA L	META L	SCUL L
MOO L	WEL L	DWEL L	MIAU L	SEPA L
MUL L	WIL L	FATA L	MODA L	SERA L
NAI L	WOO L	**FECA L**	MODE L	SHAL L
NIL L	**YAW L**	FERA L	MOGU L	SHAU L
NOE L	YEL L	FETA L	**MOHE L**	**SHAW L**
NOI L	YIL L	FINA L	MOLA L	SHEA L
NUL L	**YOW L**	FLAI L	MORA L	SHEL L
NUR L	**ZEA L**	FOCA L	MORE L	SHEO L
PAI L	BABE L	FRAI L	MOTE L	SHIE L
PAL L	BABU L	FRIL L	MURA L	SHIL L

SHOA L	VAKI L	CARNA L	DOTTE L	HOSTE L
SHOO L	VENA L	CARPA L	DREID L	HOUSE L
SHOR L	*VEXI L	CARPE L	DRIVE L	HYETA L
SIBY L	VIGI L	CARRE L	DUFFE L	HYMNA L
SIGI L	VINA L	CARTE L	FACIA L	*JACKA L
SISA L	VINY L	CARVE L	FALLA L	*JARFU L
SKIL L	VIRA L	CASUA L	FARDE L	*JEZAI L
SKIR L	VITA L	CAUDA L	FARFA L	JINGA L
SKOA L	VOCA L	CAUSA L	FARFE L	*JOVIA L
SKUL L	VOWE L	CENTA L	FAUCA L	*JOYFU L
SMAL L	WEDE L	CEREA L	FECIA L	*JUGFU L
SMEL L	WHEA L	CHAPE L	FENNE L	KENNE L
SNAI L	WHEE L	CHISE L	FERRE L	KERNE L
SNAR L	WHIR L	CHITA L	FESTA L	KITTE L
SNEL L	WHOR L	CHORA L	FETIA L	KNAWE L
SNOO L	WOFU L	CINEO L	FEUDA L	KUMME L
SORE L	*XYLO L	CITRA L	FIBRI L	LABIA L
SOTO L	*XYLY L	CLINA L	FILIA L	LAPFU L
SPAI L	YODE L	*COAXA L	FINIA L	LAURE L
SPAL L	YOKE L	COCCA L	FISCA L	LAWFU L
SPEE L	ZONA L	COEVA L	FITFU L	LENTI L
SPEI L	ZORI L	COMPE L	FODGE L	LETHA L
SPEL L	BABOO L	CONSO L	FOETA L	LIENA L
SPIE L	BAGFU L	CONSU L	FORMA L	LINEA L
SPIL L	BARBA L	CORBE L	FORMO L	LINTE L
SPOI L	BARBE L	CORME L	FORMY L	LINTO L
SPOO L	BARRE L	CORNE L	FOSSI L	LISTE L
STAL L	BEDEL L	CORRA L	*FRIJO L	LOREA L
STEA L	BEFAL L	CREDA L	FRIVO L	LUTEA L
STEE L	BEFOO L	CRENE L	FRUGA L	MALTO L
STIL L	BEFOU L	CRESO L	FULFI L	MAMMA L
STOO L	BEGAL L	CRESY L	FUNGA L	MANFU L
STUL L	BEHOW L	CREWE L	FUNNE L	MANGE L
SURA L	*BENZA L	CRURA L	GAMBO L	MANTE L
SWAI L	*BENZO L	CUDGE L	GAVIA L	MANUA L
SWEL L	*BENZY L	CUNEA L	GENIA L	MARCE L
SWIL L	BETHE L	CUPFU L	GENTI L	MARVE L
SWIR L	BEWAI L	CURTA L	GERBI L	MEDIA L
TAMA L	*BIAXA L	*CYMBA L	GIMBA L	MENIA L
TEPA L	BOATE L	DACTY L	GIMMA L	MENSA L
THIL L	BORDE L	DAEDA L	GINGA L	MENTA L
THIO L	BOREA L	DAMSE L	GLOBA L	MESCA L
THIR L	*BOXFU L	DARNE L	GLYCO L	MESIA L
THUR L	BRASI L	DEASI L	*GLYCY L	METHY L
TICA L	*BRAZI L	DECKE L	GOOGO L	*MEZCA L
TIDA L	BRIDA L	DENIA L	GOORA L	MICEL L
TOLY L	BROMA L	DENTA L	GOSPE L	MISKA L
TONA L	BRUMA L	DENTI L	GRAVE L	MISSA L
TOTA L	BRUTA L	DETAI L	GROVE L	MISSE L
TOWE L	BUCCA L	DEWOO L	GUNNE L	MITRA L
TRAI L	BULBE L	DIOBO L	GUNSE L	MONGO L
TRAW L	BULBI L	DIRND L	HAEMA L	MORSE L
TRIA L	BULBU L	DISMA L	HALLE L	MORTA L
TRIL L	BURIA L	DISPE L	HAMAU L	MUSSE L
TRIO L	BUSHE L	DISTA L	HAMMA L	MUTUA L
TROL L	CAMAI L	DISTI L	HANSE L	MUTUE L
TRUL L	CANCE L	*DJEBE L	HARTA L	NARWA L
TUBA L	CANFU L	*DONZE L	HASSE L	NICKE L
TWIL L	CANNE L	DORSA L	HATFU L	NITRI L
TWIR L	CAPFU L	DOSSA L	HERBA L	NORMA L
TYPA L	CARCE L	DOSSE L	HIEMA L	NUCHA L
VAGA L	CARFU L	DOSSI L	HIRSE L	

PALPA L	REPEA L	STIPE L	WILFU L	CHANNE L
PANFU L	REROL L	STOMA L	WITHA L	CHARNE L
PARCE L	RESAI L	STROL L	WITTO L	CHATTE L
PARRA L	RESEA L	SWIVE L	*WOEFU L	*CHERVI L
PARRE L	RESEL L	SYMBO L	WORMI L	CHLORA L
PASSE L	RETAI L	TAHSI L	BABBOO L	CHORDA L
PASTE L	RETEL L	TALLO L	BAGSFU L	CHORIA L
PASTI L	RETIA L	TARNA L	BALEFU L	*CHROMY L
PATRO L	RETOO L	TARSA L	BALNEA L	CITADE L
PAUSA L	RETRA L	TASSE L	BANEFU L	COAEVA L
PEEPU L	REVEA L	TEASE L	BARBEL L	COASTA L
PENCE L	RHINA L	*TEAZE L	*BASHFU L	CODICI L
PENCI L	RIDGE L	TECTA L	*BATFOW L	*COAXIA L
PENSI L	RIDGI L	TELIA L	*BATHYA L	COLONE L
PENTY L	RITUA L	TENAI L	BECRAW L	COLUME L
PETRE L	RONDE L	TERCE L	BEDEVI L	COMICA L
PETRO L	RONNE L	TERGA L	BEDRAI L	CONCEA L
PEYOT L	RUEFU L	TETRY L	BEDROL L	CONGEA L
PHENO L	RUNNE L	THENA L	BENTHA L	CONICA L
PHENY L	SACRA L	THRAL L	*BENZOY L	CONTRO L
PHONA L	SAFRO L	THRIL L	BESTIA L	CORBEI L
PINEA L	SAMIE L	THYMO L	*BIAXIA L	CORDIA L
PINNA L	SANDA L	TIMBA L	BIFOCA L	CORONA L
PISTI L	SANTO L	TINCA L	BIMETA L	CORONE L
PISTO L	SAURE L	TINFU L	BIMODA L	COSTRE L
PLAGA L	SCHOO L	TINSE L	*BIVINY L	COTIDA L
PLURA L	SCHOR L	TOLUO L	BOBTAI L	COUNCI L
PODSO L	SCRAW L	TOLUY L	BORNEO L	COUNSE L
*PODZO L	SCROL L	TOMBA L	BORSTA L	COWBEL L
POMME L	SEIDE L	TONSI L	*BOWLFU L	COWGIR L
PONTI L	SENDA L	TOPFU L	*BOXHAU L	CRANIA L
PORTA L	SEPTA L	TRAME L	BRADAW L	CREOSO L
POSTA L	*SEQUE L	TRAVE L	BRIMFU L	CRESTA L
POTFU L	SERAI L	TRIBA L	BRISTO L	CRUCIA L
PRIMA L	SERIA L	TRINA L	BROTHE L	CRUSTA L
PROPE L	SERVA L	TROTY L	BUTANO L	CRYSTA L
PROPY L	SEXUA L	TROWE L	BUTYRA L	CUBICA L
PROTY L	SHEKE L	TUBFU L	*BUTYRY L	CUPSFU L
PULPA L	SHOVE L	TUNNE L	*CACODY L	CURTAI L
PUMME L	SHRIL L	TUSSA L	CALOME L	CYNICA L
PYRRO L	SHRIL L	TWIBI L	CAMBIA L	DAMOSE L
*QUEZA L	SHTET L	TYMBA L	*CAMPHO L	*DAMOZE L
*QUINO L	SIGNA L	VAKEE L	CANSFU L	DAREFU L
RACIA L	SIMNE L	VALVA L	CAPITA L	DECANA L
RADIA L	SINFU L	VANDA L	CAPITO L	DECIBE L
RAMTI L	SKATO L	VASSA L	CAPORA L	DECIMA L
RAPPE L	SNIVE L	VATFU L	CARACA L	DECRIA L
RASCA L	SOBFU L	VEINA L	CARACO L	DEPOSA L
REBIL L	SOCIA L	VENIA L	CARACU L	DESPOI L
REBOI L	SOLGE L	VERBA L	CARAME L	DEVISA L
RECAL L	SORRE L	VERNA L	CARAVE L	DEWFAL L
RECOA L	SPINA L	VERSA L	CAREFU L	*DEXTRA L
RECOI L	SPINE L	VESSE L	CARREL L	DIALLE L
RECTA L	SPIRA L	VESTA L	CATCAL L	DICOTY L
REFAL L	SPITA L	VINEA L	CATFAL L	DIGITA L
REFEL L	SPORA L	VISUA L	CATTAI L	DIREFU L
REFIL L	SPRAW L	WADMA L	CENSUA L	DISHFU L
REFUE L	*SQUAL L	WADME L	CENTRA L	DISTIL L
REGNA L	*SQUEA L	WADMO L	CERAMA L	DITHIO L
REHEE L	*SQUIL L	WAEFU L	CHANCE L	DIURNA L
REMAI L	STATA L	WEASE L		DOGGRE L
RENTA L	STERO L	WEEVI L		

DOLEFU L	*HELPFU L	MONOFI L	*QUETZA L	SPONSA L
DOMICA L	HEMATA L	MUDSIL L	*QUINTA L	SPOUSA L
DOMICI L	HOBNAI L	MUSEFU L	RADICA L	STAMME L
DOOMFU L	HOLDAL L	MUSICA L	RADICE L	STENCI L
DOTTRE L	*HOPEFU L	NAPHTO L	RATTAI L	STERNA L
DREIDE L	HUMERA L	NARWHA L	RECITA L	STIBIA L
DUTIFU L	HUMORA L	NEEDFU L	REDPOL L	STRATA L
FACTUA L	HURTFU L	NEUTRA L	REDRIL L	STRIGI L
FANTAI L	*HUSHFU L	NODICA L	*REEXPE L	STROBI L
FATEFU L	*JARSFU L	NOMBRI L	REFUSA L	STRUDE L
FAUCIA L	*JEJUNA L	NOMINA L	REFUTA L	SUBCEL L
FAUTEI L	*JESTFU L	NOSTRI L	REGOSO L	SUBCOO L
FEARFU L	*JEZEBE L	NUCLEA L	RELABE L	SUBDUA L
FEDERA L	*JINGAL L	NUMERA L	REMODE L	SUBORA L
FEMORA L	*JONQUI L	NUPTIA L	REMOVA L	SUBOVA L
FIGURA L	JOURNA L	NUTGAL L	RENEWA L	SUBSOI L
FINICA L	*JUGSFU L	PAGINA L	REPOSA L	SUNDIA L
FISTFU L	*JUVENA L	PAILFU L	RESPEL L	SURREA L
FLANNE L	*KARAKU L	PAINFU L	RESTFU L	SURVEI L
FLUVIA L	KESTRE L	PALATA L	RETINA L	SUTURA L
*FORKFU L	KISTFU L	PALLIA L	RETINO L	*SWAYFU L
*FORMFU L	LACTEA L	PALUDA L	RETRIA L	TACTFU L
*FOXTAI L	LANGRE L	PARASO L	REVISA L	TACTUA L
FRESNE L	LANITA L	PARBOI L	REVIVA L	TANKFU L
FRETFU L	LATERA L	PARTIA L	ROOMFU L	TEABOW L
FRONTA L	LATOSO L	PASCHA L	*RORQUA L	TEARFU L
FULFIL L	LEXICA L	*PASQUI L	ROSTRA L	TEENFU L
FUNERA L	LIBERA L	PAYROL L	ROUNDE L	TENDRI L
GADWAL L	LIFEFU L	*PEAFOW L	RUDERA L	TERTIA L
GAINFU L	LIMINA L	PEDICE L	RUTHFU L	TETANA L
GAMBRE L	LINALO L	PEDOCA L	*SACKFU L	TEXTUA L
GANGRE L	LINGUA L	PENICI L	SAHIWA L	THEELO L
GARBOI L	LITERA L	PERORA L	SATCHE L	THERMA L
GASTRA L	LITORA L	PERUSA L	SAWBIL L	THERME L
GEMINA L	LOGICA L	PEYTRA L	SAWMIL L	*THIAZO L
GENERA L	LOGROL L	PEYTRE L	SCALPE L	THIONY L
GENITA L	LUGSAI L	PHRASA L	SCANDA L	TIERCE L
GENTEE L	LUSTFU L	PINBAL L	SCRIBA L	TIMBRE L
GINGAL L	LUSTRA L	PINTAI L	SCURRI L	TINFOI L
GIRASO L	LYRICA L	PIPEFU L	SEAFOW L	TISSUA L
GIROSO L	MAGICA L	PITFAL L	SEAWAL L	TOENAI L
GLACIA L	MANDRE L	PITIFU L	SEGETA L	TOILFU L
GLEEFU L	MANDRI L	PIVOTA L	SEMINA L	TOMFOO L
GLUTEA L	MARITA L	*PLAYFU L	SENSUA L	TOPFUL L
GNATHA L	MARSHA L	PLIMSO L	SEVERA L	TOPSAI L
GOMERA L	MARTIA L	PLUVIA L	SHRIVE L	TOPSOI L
GOMERE L	MATINA L	POITRE L	SHTETE L	*TOXICA L
GOMERI L	*MAXIMA L	POTBOI L	SKILFU L	TRAMEL L
GRADUA L	*MAXWEL L	POUNDA L	SKINFU L	TRAMME L
GRAPNE L	MEDICA L	POUTFU L	SKYSAI L	TRAVAI L
GRAUPE L	MENTHO L	PREANA L	SNORKE L	TRAYFU L
GREMIA L	MILFOI L	PREBIL L	SONGFU L	TREFOI L
GUMBOI L	MIMICA L	PREBOI L	SORORA L	TRENAI L
HANDFU L	MINDFU L	PRECOO L	SOULFU L	TRESSE L
HANDSE L	MINERA L	PREDIA L	SPACIA L	TRIVIA L
*HARMFU L	MINIMA L	PRESEL L	SPANCE L	TROCHA L
*HATCHE L	MISBIL L	*PRETZE L	SPANIE L	TROCHI L
HATEFU L	MISCAL L	PREVAI L	SPATIA L	TROMME L
HATSFU L	MISDEA L	*PUSHFU L	SPECIA L	TRUNNE L
HAVERE L	MISTRA L	*QUANTA L	SPECIA L	TRYSAI L
HEEDFU L	MOANFU L	*QUANTA L	SPHERA L	TUMBRE L
HELICA L	MONGRE L	*QUARRE L	SPIEGE L	TUMBRI L

TUNEFU L	BIRACIA L	*CONJUGA L	FAMILIA L	HAIRBAL L
TURMOI L	BIRADIA L	CONTRAI L	*FANCIFU L	HANDBAL L
TWIBIL L	BIRDCAL L	CORNBAL L	*FARCICA L	HANDBIL L
TYPICA L	*BISEXUA L	CORNMEA L	FAREWEL L	HANDRAI L
VATICA L	*BLAMEFU L	CORPORA L	FARNESO L	*HANDSFU L
VEGETA L	BLUEBAL L	CORRIVA L	FASTBAL L	HANGNAI L
VENTAI L	BLUEBEL L	CORTISO L	FEASTFU L	*HAPTICA L
VENTRA L	BLUEBIL L	COSMICA L	FESTIVA L	HARDBAL L
VERMEI L	BLUEGIL L	COVERAL L	FIDUCIA L	HAREBEL L
VICINA L	*BLUSHFU L	*CRACKNE L	FIREBAL L	HASTEFU L
VICTUA L	BOASTFU L	CRIMINA L	FIREHAL L	*HAWKBIL L
VIRTUA L	BOATBIL L	CULTURA L	*FISHBOW L	HEADSAI L
VITRIO L	BONSPEL L	CUSPIDA L	*FISHMEA L	*HECTICA L
WADMAA L	BONSPIE L	CUSTUMA L	FISHTAI L	HEELBAL L
WADMOL L	*BRACHIA L	*CYCLICA L	FLAVONO L	HELIACA L
WAGTAI L	BRANTAI L	*CYCLITO L	*FLYWHEE L	*HEMOCOE L
WAILFU L	*BRIMFUL L	*DAFFODI L	FOLDERO L	HEROICA L
*WAKEFU L	BROCATE L	DEADFAL L	FONTANE L	HIBERNA L
*WAMEFU L	*BUCKTAI L	*DEATHFU L	FOOTBAL L	*HIGHBAL L
WASSAI L	CALENDA L	DECRETA L	FOOTFAL L	*HIGHTAI L
WASTRE L	*CALYCEA L	DEFERRA L	FOOTHIL L	*HONEYFU L
*WAXBIL L	CANNIBA L	*DEFRAYA L	FOOTWAL L	HORNBIL L
*WAYBIL L	CANTONA L	DEIFICA L	FORBIDA L	HORNTAI L
WILLFU L	*CARBAMY L	DEMURRA L	*FORCEFU L	HOSPITA L
*WISHFU L	*CARBARY L	DEPRIVA L	FOREFEE L	HOUSEFU L
WISTFU L	CARBINO L	DIACETY L	FORESAI L	*HUMORFU L
*ZESTFU L	*CARBONY L	DIACONA L	FORESTA L	*HYDROGE L
*BACKFIL L	*CARBOXY L	DIAGONA L	FORETEL L	*HYDROME L
BALMORA L	CARDINA L	DICROTA L	*FORKSFU L	*HYDROSO L
BANDERO L	CARNIVA L	*DIDACTY L	FREEWIL L	*HYDROXY L
BANGTAI L	CAROUSA L	DIHEDRA L	FRUITFU L	*HYMENEA L
BANKROL L	CAROUSE L	DILUVIA L	FUNEREA L	*HYPERGO L
BANNERO L	CARRYAL L	*DIMETHY L	FURFURA L	*HYPOGEA L
BARBICE L	CASCABE L	*DIPHENY L	GALANGA L	*JARGONE L
BARBITA L	*CATCHAL L	DIPTERA L	GANGLIA L	*JUDICIA L
BARONIA L	*CATECHO L	DISANNU L	GERANIA L	*KEELHAU L
BARSTOO L	CEREBRA L	*DISHEVE L	GERANIO L	LACRIMA L
BASEBAL L	*CERVICA L	DISLOYA L	GERMINA L	LADLEFU L
*BASOPHI L	CESSPOO L	DISPOSA L	GESTICA L	*LAMBKIL L
BEADROL L	*CHARCOA L	DIVIDUA L	GESTURA L	LANDFAL L
BEANBAL L	*CHEEKFU L	DOCTORA L	*GHASTFU L	LANDFIL L
*BECHAME L	*CHEERFU L	DOGGERE L	GILDHAL L	LENTICE L
BECUDGE L	*CHEMICA L	DOORBEL L	GLASSFU L	*LIGHTFU L
BEDRIVE L	*CHESTFU L	DOORNAI L	GLOOMFU L	LINALOO L
BELLPUL L	*CINNAMY L	DOORSIL L	GLYCERO L	LITHOSO L
*BELLYFU L	CLERICA L	DOTTERE L	*GLYCERY L	LITTORA L
BERASCA L	CLODPOL L	DOUBTFU L	*GLYCOSY L	LOATHFU L
BESTOWA L	*CLUBHAU L	DOVETAI L	GNOMICA L	*MACKERE L
BETRAYA L	COATTAI L	*DOWNFAL L	GOODWIL L	MACRURA L
*BIACETY L	*COCKBIL L	*DOWNHAU L	GOOFBAL L	MADRIGA L
BIANNUA L	*COCKERE L	*DOWNHIL L	GOSSYPO L	MAINSAI L
BIDENTA L	*COCKTAI L	DOWSABE L	GRACEFU L	MANDRIL L
BIENNIA L	*COGWHEE L	DREADFU L	GRATEFU L	MANGONE L
*BIFACIA L	COISTRE L	DREAMFU L	GROMWEL L	MANNITO L
BILABIA L	COISTRI L	DRUMROL L	GUAIACO L	MANURIA L
BIMANUA L	COLONIA L	*DUCKBIL L	GUILEFU L	MARGINA L
BIMENSA L	COLORFU L	*DUCKTAI L	GUMBOTI L	MARSHAL L
*BIMETHY L	COLOSSA L	*DUMBBEL L	GUNMETA L	MATERIA L
BINAURA L	COMMUNA L	DUNGHIL L	GUTTURA L	MATERIE L
BINOMIA L	CONEPAT L	*FAITHFU L	GYROIDA L	MATERNA L
BIOTICA L	*CONFOCA L	FALDERA L	HABITUA L	MEATBAL L
*BIPHENY L		FALDERO L	HAEMATA L	MEDIEVA L

MEMORIA L	NUDICAU L	*PROXIMA L	SNEERFU L	*THANKFU L
MENSEFU L	NUMSKUL L	*PUFFBAL L	SNOWBAL L	THETICA L
MENSURA L	NUTSHEL L	PUNCTUA L	SNOWBEL L	TRAGICA L
*MERCIFU L	PALATIA L	*PUSHBAL L	SNOWFAL L	TRAINFU L
*MESOPHY L	PARALLE L	RAINFAL L	SOFTBAL L	*TRANQUI L
METHANO L	PARENTA L	*RAKEHEL L	SOMEDEA L	TRAPBAL L
*METHOXY L	*PARFOCA L	RASORIA L	SORBITO L	TREENAI L
*METHYLA L	PARIETA L	RATIONA L	SOURBAL L	*TRIAXIA L
METRICA L	PASTORA L	REASSAI L	SPADEFU L	TRIBUNA L
MILLIGA L	PASTURA L	REBURIA L	SPANDRE L	TRIETHY L
MINSTRE L	PATERNA L	REBUTTA L	SPANDRI L	TRIFOCA L
MISENRO L	PECTORA L	REFERRA L	SPECTRA L	TRIGONA L
MISLABE L	PEDESTA L	REGIONA L	SPITBAL L	TRILOBA L
MISSPEL L	PELLETA L	REMEDIA L	SPITEFU L	TRINODA L
MISTRIA L	PELLMEL L	REMITTA L	SPLENIA L	TRIPEDA L
MOISTFU L	PENONCE L	REPRISA L	SPOONFU L	TRISTFU L
MOLEHIL L	PERONEA L	REPROVA L	SPORTFU L	TROOPIA L
*MONACHA L	PERSONA L	*REQUITA L	SPRINGA L	TROUPIA L
MONAURA L	PETRONE L	RESIDUA L	SPURGAL L	TRUSTFU L
*MONAXIA L	PETROSA L	RESTORA L	*SQUIRRE L	TRUTHFU L
MONOFUE L	PHENETO L	REVERSA L	STAUMRE L	TURBINA L
MONOMIA L	*PHILOME L	REVIEWA L	STAYSAI L	TURNHAL L
MONORAI L	*PHYSICA L	*RHEOPHI L	STERICA L	TURRICA L
MOONSAI L	*PICKADI L	*RIGHTFU L	*STICKFU L	TUTORIA L
*MOORFOW L	*PICKERE L	RINGTAI L	STOMATA L	*TYMPANA L
*MOTHBAL L	*PINWHEE L	*ROCKFAL L	STREUSE L	VAUNTFU L
MOTIONA L	PLANOSO L	ROTOTIL L	STRONGY L	VENEREA L
MOURNFU L	PLATEFU L	*SACKSFU L	STUNSAI L	*VENGEFU L
*MOUTHFU L	*PLAYBIL L	SAGITTA L	*SUBAXIA L	VERTICA L
MUSCADE L	PLAYGIR L	SAPROPE L	SUBLEVE L	VERTICI L
MUSCATE L	PLIMSOL L	SCENICA L	SUBNASA L	VESPERA L
*MYSTICA L	POETICA L	SCEPTRA L	SUBNODA L	VESTURA L
*MYTHICA L	PONYTAI L	*SCOOPFU L	SUBTOTA L	VIATICA L
*NAPHTHO L	POOLHAL L	SCORNFU L	SUBVIRA L	VICARIA L
*NAPHTHY L	POSTANA L	SCRANNE L	*SUBVOCA L	VIRGINA L
NATIONA L	POSTORA L	SEASHEL L	SUCCINY L	VISCERA L
NAUTICA L	POSTURA L	SEASONA L	*SUFFIXA L	VISIONA L
NEWSREE L	*POWERFU L	SECTORA L	SUICIDA L	*VOICEFU L
NITROSY L	PRAEDIA L	SELFHEA L	SULFINY L	WARRAGA L
*NONEQUA L	PRANDIA L	SENSEFU L	SULFONA L	WARRIGA L
NONFOCA L	PRATFAL L	SENTINE L	SULFONY L	*WASHBOW L
NONGATA L	*PREAXIA L	SESSPOO L	SULFURY L	WASTEFU L
NONIDEA L	PREBASA L	*SHAMEFU L	SUPERNA L	*WATCHFU L
NONLEGA L	*PRECHIL L	SHEENFU L	SUPPOSA L	WEARIFU L
NONLOCA L	*PREFIXA L	*SHELFFU L	SURGICA L	*WHIMBRE L
NONMETA L	PRELEGA L	SHLEMIE L	SURROYA L	*WHIPTAI L
NONMODA L	PRENATA L	SHOEBIL L	SURVIVA L	*WILDFOW L
NONMORA L	PRERENA L	SHOPGIR L	TABLEFU L	*WINDFAL L
NONNAVA L	PRIDEFU L	*SHOWGIR L	TAFFERE L	WINDGAL L
NONPAPA L	*PRIMEVA L	SHRAPNE L	TAFFERE L	WINDMIL L
NONRIVA L	PROCURA L	SHRIEVA L	TAFFRAI L	WOOLFEL L
NONROYA L	PRODIGA L	SIDEHIL L	TASTEFU L	*WORTHFU L
NONRURA L	PROPENO L	SIDEREA L	TEETOTA L	*WRACKFU L
NONTIDA L	*PROPENY L	SIDEWAL L	TEGMINA L	*WRATHFU L
NONVIRA L	PROPOSA L	SILVICA L	TEMPORA L	*WRECKFU L
NONVOCA L	PROTOCO L	SIPHONA L	TERMINA L	*WRONGFU L
NOTARIA L	PROUDFU L	*SKILLFU L	TERPINO L	*WROTHFU L
NOVERCA L		SLOTHFU L	*TEXTURA L	*YOUTHFU L

M

MAAR	MERL	MONY	MAILL	*MAZER
MACE	MESA	MOOD	MAIST	MEALY
MACH	MESH	MOOL	*MAIZE	MEANT
MACK	MESS	MOON	MAJOR	MEANY
MADE	META	MOOR	MAKAR	MEATY
MAGE	METE	MOOT	MAKER	MECCA
MAGI	MEWL	MOPE	MALAR	MEDAL
MAID	MICA	MORA	MALIC	MEDIA
MAIL	MICE	MORE	MALMY	MEDIC
MAIM	MICK	MORN	MALTY	MEDII
MAIN	MIDI	MORT	MAMBA	MEINY
MAIR	MIEN	MOSK	MAMBO	MELEE
MAKE	MIFF	MOSS	MAMEY	MELIC
MAKO	MIGG	MOST	MAMIE	MELON
MALE	MIKE	MOTE	MAMMA	MENAD
MALL	MILD	MOTH	MAMMY	MENSA
MALM	MILE	MOTT	MANGE	MENSE
MALT	MILK	MOUE	MANGO	MENTA
MAMA	MILL	MOVE	MANGY	MERCY
MANA	MILO	MOXA	MANIA	MERGE
MANE	MILT	*MOZO	MANIC	MERIT
MANO	MIME	MUCH	MANNA	MERLE
MANY	MINA	MUCK	MANOR	MERRY
MARC	MIND	MUFF	MANSE	MESHY
MARE	MINE	MUGG	MANTA	MESIC
MARK	MINI	MULE	MANUS	MESNE
MARL	MINK	MULL	MAPLE	MESON
MART	MINT	MUMM	*MAQUI	MESSY
MASH	MINX	MUMP	MARCH	METAL
MASK	MIRE	MUON	MARGE	METER
MASS	MIRI	MURA	MARIA	METIS
MAST	MIRK	MURE	MARLY	METRE
MATE	MIRY	MURK	MARRY	METRO
MATH	MISE	MURR	MARSE	*MEZZO
MATT	MISO	MUSE	MARSH	MIAOU
MAUL	MISS	MUSH	MASER	MIAOW
MAUN	MIST	MUSK	MASHY	MIASM
MAUT	MITE	MUSS	MASON	MIAUL
MAXI	MITT	MUST	MASSA	MICRA
MAYA	MITY	MUTE	MASSE	MICRO
*MAZE	MIXT	MUTT	MASSY	MIDDY
*MAZY	MOAN	MYNA	MATCH	MIDGE
MEAD	MOAT	MYTH	MATER	MIDST
MEAL	MOCK	MACAW	MATEY	*MIFFY
MEAN	MODE	MACER	MATIN	MIGHT
MEAT	MODI	MACHO	MATTE	MILCH
MEED	MOIL	MACLE	MAUND	MILER
MEEK	MOKE	MACRO	MAUVE	MILIA
MEET	MOLA	MADAM	MAVEN	MILKY
MELD	MOLD	MADLY	MAVIE	MILLE
MELL	MOLE	MADRE	MAVIN	MILPA
MELT	MOLL	MAFIA	MAVIS	MILTY
MEMO	MOLT	MAFIC	*MAXIM	MIMER
MEND	MOLY	MAGIC	MAYBE	MIMIC
MENO	MOME	MAGMA	MAYOR	MINCE
MENU	MOMI	MAGOT	MAYST	MINCY
MEOW	MONK	MAGUS		MINER
MERE	MONO	MAHOE		MINGY
MERK	MONS	MAILE		

MINIM	MOSSY	MYOID	MANAGE	MASHIE
MINNY	MOSTE	MYOMA	MANANA	*MASJID
MINOR	MOTEL	MYOPE	MANCHE	MASKEG
MINTY	MOTET	*MYOPY	MANEGE	MASKER
MINUS	MOTEY	MYRRH	MANFUL	*MASQUE
MIREX	MOTHY	MACACO	MANGEL	MASSIF
MIRKY	MOTIF	MACING	MANGER	MASTER
MIRTH	MOTOR	MACKLE	MANGEY	MASTIC
*MIRZA	MOTTE	MACRON	MANGLE	*MASTIX
MISDO	MOTTO	MACULA	MANIAC	MATING
MISER	MOUCH	MACULE	MANILA	MATRES
MISSY	MOULD	MADAME	MANIOC	*MATRIX
MISTY	MOULT	MADCAP	MANITO	MATRON
MITER	MOUND	MADDED	MANITU	MATTED
MITIS	MOUNT	MADDEN	MANNAN	MATTER
MITRE	MOURN	MADDER	MANNED	MATTIN
MIXER	MOUSE	MADMAN	MANNER	MATURE
*MIXUP	MOUSY	MADRAS	*MANQUE	*MATZAH
*MIZEN	MOUTH	MADURO	MANTEL	*MATZOH
MOCHA	MOVED	MAENAD	MANTES	*MATZOT
MODAL	MOVER	MAFFIA	MANTIC	MAUGER
MODEL	MOVIE	MAFTIR	MANTID	MAUGRE
MODUS	MOWER	MAGGOT	MANTIS	MAULER
MOGUL	MOXIE	MAGILP	MANTLE	MAUMET
MOHEL	MUCID	MAGNET	MANTRA	MAUNDY
MOHUR	MUCIN	MAGNUM	MANTUA	*MAXIMA
MOIRA	*MUCKY	MAGPIE	MANUAL	*MAXIXE
MOIRE	MUCOR	MAGUEY	MANURE	*MAYDAY
MOIST	MUCRO	MAHOUT	MAPPED	MAYEST
MOLAL	MUCUS	*MAHZOR	MAPPER	*MAYFLY
MOLAR	MUDDY	MAIDEN	*MAQUIS	*MAYHAP
MOLDY	MUDRA	MAIGRE	MARACA	*MAYHEM
MOLLY	MUFTI	MAIHEM	MARBLE	MAYING
MOLTO	MUGGY	MAILER	MARBLY	*MAYPOP
MOMMA	MUHLY	MAIMER	MARCEL	MAYVIN
MOMMY	*MUJIK	MAINLY	MARGAY	*MAZARD
MOMUS	MULCH	MAKEUP	MARGIN	*MAZIER
MONAD	MULCT	MAKING	MARINA	*MAZILY
MONAS	MULEY	MAKUTA	MARINE	*MAZING
MONDE	MULLA	MALADY	MARISH	*MAZUMA
MONDO	MUMMY	MALATE	MARKER	MEADOW
MONEY	MUNCH	MALFED	MARKET	MEAGER
MONGO	MUNGO	MALGRE	*MARKKA	MEAGRE
MONIE	MURAL	MALICE	MARKUP	MEALIE
MONTE	MUREX	MALIGN	MARLIN	MEANER
MONTH	MURID	MALINE	MARMOT	MEANIE
MOOCH	MURKY	MALKIN	MAROON	MEANLY
MOODY	MURRA	MALLEE	*MARQUE	MEASLE
MOOLA	MURRE	MALLEI	MARRAM	MEASLY
MOONY	MURRY	MALLET	MARRED	MEATUS
MOORY	MUSCA	MALLOW	MARRER	MEDAKA
MOOSE	MUSER	MALTED	MARRON	MEDDLE
MOPED	MUSHY	MALTHA	MARROW	MEDIAD
MOPER	MUSIC	MALTOL	MARSHY	MEDIAL
MORAL	MUSKY	MAMLUK	MARTEN	MEDIAN
MORAY	MUSSY	MAMMAL	MARTIN	*MEDICK
MOREL	MUSTH	MAMMEE	MARTYR	MEDICO
MORON	MUSTY	MAMMER	MARVEL	MEDIUM
MORPH	MUTCH	MAMMET	MASCON	MEDLAR
MORRO	MUTER	*MAMMEY	MASCOT	MEDLEY
MOSEY	*MUZZY	MAMMIE	MASHER	MEDUSA
MOSSO	MYNAH	MAMMON		MEETER

MEETLY	MIDGET	MISLIT	MORALE	MUMBLE
MEGASS	MIDGUT	MISPEN	MORALS	MUMMED
MEGILP	MIDLEG	MISSAL	MORASS	MUMMER
MEGOHM	MIDRIB	MISSAY	MORBID	MUMPER
MEGRIM	*MIDWAY	MISSEL	MOREEN	MUNTIN
MEIKLE	MIGGLE	MISSIS	MORGEN	MURDER
MEINIE	*MIGHTY	MISSUS	MORGUE	MUREIN
MELDER	MIGNON	MISTER	MORION	MURINE
MELLOW	MIKADO	MISUSE	MOROSE	MURING
MELODY	MIKRON	MITHER	MORPHO	MURMUR
MELOID	*MIKVAH	MITIER	MORRIS	*MURPHY
MELTER	*MIKVEH	MITRAL	MORROW	MURREY
MELTON	MILADI	MITTEN	MORSEL	MURRHA
MEMBER	MILADY	*MIZZEN	MORTAL	MUSCAT
MEMOIR	MILAGE	*MIZZLE	MORTAR	MUSCID
MEMORY	MILDEN	*MIZZLY	MORULA	MUSCLE
MENACE	MILDEW	MOBBER	MOSAIC	MUSCLY
MENAGE	MILIEU	MOBCAP	MOSHAV	MUSEUM
MENDER	MILIUM	MOBILE	*MOSQUE	MUSHER
MENHIR	MILKER	MOCKER	MOSSER	MUSING
MENIAL	MILLER	*MOCKUP	MOSTLY	*MUSJID
*MENINX	MILLET	MODERN	MOTHER	MUSKEG
MENSAL	MILORD	MODEST	MOTILE	MUSKET
MENSCH	MILTER	*MODIFY	MOTION	MUSKIE
MENTAL	MIMBAR	MODISH	MOTIVE	MUSKIT
MENTOR	MIMING	MODIST	MOTLEY	MUSLIN
MENTUM	MIMOSA	MODULE	MOTMOT	MUSSEL
MERCER	MINCER	MODULO	MOTTLE	MUSTEE
MERGER	MINDER	MOHAIR	*MOUJIK	MUSTER
MERINO	MINGLE	MOIETY	MOULDY	MUTANT
MERLIN	MINIFY	MOLDER	MOULIN	MUTASE
MERLON	MINIMA	MOLEST	MOUSER	MUTATE
MERMAN	MINING	MOLIES	MOUSEY	MUTEST
MESCAL	MINION	MOLINE	MOUSSE	MUTINE
MESIAL	MINISH	MOLLAH	MOUTHY	MUTING
MESIAN	MINIUM	MOLLIE	MOUTON	MUTINY
MESSAN	MINNOW	MOLOCH	MOVING	MUTISM
MESTEE	MINTER	MOLTEN	MUCKER	MUTTER
METAGE	MINUET	MOLTER	MUCKLE	MUTTON
METATE	MINUTE	MOMENT	MUCLUC	MUTUAL
METEOR	MINYAN	MOMISM	MUCOID	MUTUEL
METEPA	MIOLER	MONGER	MUCOSA	MUTULE
METHOD	MIOSIS	MONGOE	MUCOSE	MUUMUU
METHYL	MIOTIC	MONGOL	MUCOUS	*MUZHIK
METIER	MIRAGE	MONGST	MUDCAP	*MUZJIK
METING	MIRIER	MONIED	MUDDER	*MUZZLE
METOPE	MIRING	MONIES	MUDDLE	MYASIS
METRIC	MIRROR	MONISH	MUFFIN	MYCELE
METTLE	MISACT	MONISM	MUFFLE	MYELIN
METUMP	MISADD	MONIST	MUGGAR	MYOPIA
MEWLER	MISAIM	*MONKEY	MUGGED	MYOSIN
*MEZCAL	MISATE	MONODY	MUGGER	MYOSIS
*MEZUZA	MISCUE	MONTES	MUGGUR	MYOTIC
MIASMA	MISCUT	MOOLAH	*MUKLUK	MYRIAD
MICELL	MISEAT	MOOLEY	MULETA	MYRICA
*MICKEY	MISERY	MOOTER	MULING	MYRTLE
MICKLE	MISFIT	MOPING	MULISH	MYSELF
MICRON	MISHAP	MOPISH	MULLAH	MYSOST
MIDAIR	MISHIT	MOPOKE	MULLEN	MYSTIC
MIDDAY	MISKAL	MOPPED	MULLER	*MYTHIC
MIDDEN	MISLAY	MOPPER	MULLET	MYTHOS
MIDDLE	MISLIE	MOPPET	MULLEY	*MYXOID

*MYXOMA	MANAGER	MARMITE	MEATILY	METRIST
MACABER	MANAKIN	MARPLOT	MEATMAN	*MEZQUIT
MACABRE	MANATEE	*MARQUEE	MEDDLER	*MEZUZAH
MACADAM	MANCHET	*MARQUIS	MEDIANT	MICELLA
*MACAQUE	MANDALA	MARRIED	*MEDIACY	MICELLE
*MACCHIA	MANDATE	MARRIER	MEDIANT	*MICRIFY
MACHETE	MANDOLA	MARRIES	MEDIATE	MICROBE
MACHINE	MANDREL	MARRING	MEDICAL	*MICROHM
MACHREE	MANDRIL	*MARROWY	MEDULLA	MIDDIES
*MACHZOR	*MANGABY	MARSHAL	MEDUSAN	MIDDLER
MACRAME	MANGIER	MARTIAL	MEETING	MIDIRON
MADDEST	MANGILY	MARTIAN	MEGABAR	MIDLAND
MADDING	MANGLER	MARTINI	MEGABIT	MIDLINE
MADDISH	MANGOLD	MARTLET	MEGAPOD	MIDMOST
MADEIRA	MANHOLE	*MARTYRY	MEGASSE	MIDNOON
MADNESS	MANHOOD	MASCARA	MEGATON	MIDRASH
MADONNA	MANHUNT	MASKING	*MEGILPH	*MIDRIFF
MADRONA	MANIHOT	MASONIC	MEIOSIS	*MIDSHIP
MADRONE	MANIKIN	MASONRY	MELANGE	MIDTERM
MADRONO	MANILLA	*MASQUER	MELANIC	MIDTOWN
MADWORT	MANILLE	MASSAGE	MELANIN	*MIDWEEK
*MADZOON	MANIOCA	MASSEUR	MELILOT	*MIDWIFE
MAESTRO	MANIPLE	MASSIER	MELISMA	MIDYEAR
*MAFFICK	MANITOU	MASSIVE	MELODIA	MIGRANT
MAFIOSO	MANKIND	MASTABA	MELODIC	MIGRATE
MAGENTA	MANLESS	MASTERY	MELTAGE	*MILCHIG
MAGICAL	MANLIKE	*MASTIFF	MEMENTO	*MILDEWY
MAGNATE	MANMADE	MASTOID	MENACER	MILEAGE
MAGNETO	MANNING	MATADOR	MENDIGO	MILFOIL
*MAGNIFY	MANNISH	MATCHER	MENDING	MILIARY
MAHATMA	MANNITE	MATILDA	*MENFOLK	MILITIA
*MAHJONG	MANNOSE	MATINAL	MENORAH	MILKIER
MAHONIA	*MANPACK	MATINEE	MENTHOL	*MILKILY
MAHUANG	MANROPE	MATLESS	MENTION	*MILKMAN
MAILBAG	MANSARD	MATRASS	MERCERY	*MILKSOP
*MAILBOX	MANSION	MATTERY	MERCIES	MILLAGE
MAILING	MANTEAU	MATTING	MERCURY	MILLDAM
MAILLOT	MANTLET	*MATTOCK	MERGING	MILLIER
MAILMAN	MANTRAP	MATTOID	MERISIS	MILLIME
MAINTOP	MANUARY	*MATZOON	MERMAID	MILLINE
*MAJAGUA	MANUMIT	*MATZOTH	MEROPIA	MILLING
*MAJESTY	MANURER	MAUDLIN	MESALLY	MILLION
*MAJORAM	MANWARD	MAUNDER	MESARCH	MILLRUN
MALAISE	MANWISE	*MAWKISH	MESEEMS	MILREIS
MALARIA	MAPPING	*MAXILLA	*MESQUIT	MIMESIS
*MALARKY	MARABOU	*MAXIMAL	MESSAGE	MIMICAL
MALEATE	MARANTA	*MAXIMIN	MESSIAH	*MIMICRY
MALEFIC	MARASCA	*MAXIMUM	MESSIER	MINABLE
MALISON	MARBLER	*MAXWELL	MESSILY	MINARET
MALLARD	MARCHEN	*MAYBUSH	MESSMAN	MINDFUL
MALLEUS	MARCHER	MAYPOLE	MESTESO	MINERAL
MALMSEY	MAREMMA	*MAYWEED	MESTINO	MINGIER
MALODOR	MARGENT	*MAZIEST	*MESTIZA	MINGLER
MALTASE	MARIMBA	*MAZURKA	*MESTIZO	MINIBUS
MALTIER	MARINER	*MAZZARD	METAMER	MINICAB
MALTOSE	MARITAL	MEALIER	METHANE	MINICAR
*MAMMARY	*MARKHOR	MEANDER	*METHOXY	MINIKIN
MAMMATE	MARKING	MEANEST	METISSE	MINIMAL
MAMMIES	MARLIER	MEANIES	METONYM	*MINIMAX
*MAMMOCK	MARLINE	MEANING	METOPIC	MINIMUM
*MAMMOTH	MARLING	MEASURE	METOPON	MINIVER
MANACLE	MARLITE	MEATIER	*METRIFY	MINORCA

MINSTER	MISSTEP	MONOLOG	MUDDIER	MYELOMA
MINTAGE	MISSTOP	MONOMER	MUDDIES	MYIASIS
MINUEND	MISSUIT	MONSOON	MUDDILY	*MYNHEER
MINUTIA	MISTAKE	MONSTER	MUDDING	*MYOLOGY
MIRACLE	MISTBOW	MONTAGE	MUDDLER	MYOSOTE
MIRADOR	MISTEND	MONTANE	*MUDFISH	MYOTOME
MIRIEST	MISTERM	MONTERO	MUDLARK	*MYSTERY
MISALLY	MISTEUK	*MONTHLY	*MUDROCK	*MYSTIFY
MISAVER	MISTIER	MONURON	MUDROOM	MACARONI
MISBIAS	MISTILY	MOOCHER	MUDSILL	MACAROON
MISBILL	MISTIME	MOONBOW	MUEDDIN	*MACCABAW
MISBIND	MISTOOK	MOONEYE	*MUEZZIN	*MACCABOY
MISCALL	MISTRAL	MOONIER	*MUFFLER	*MACCOBOY
MISCAST	MISTUNE	MOONILY	MUGGIER	MACERATE
MISCITE	MISTYPE	MOONISH	MUGGILY	*MACHISMO
MISCOIN	MISUSER	MOONLET	MUGGING	*MACKEREL
*MISCOOK	MISWORD	MOONLIT	MUGGINS	*MACKINAW
*MISCOPY	*MISYOKE	MOONSET	MUGWORT	MACRURAL
MISDATE	MITERER	MOORAGE	*MUGWUMP	MACRURAN
MISDEAL	MITIEST	MOORHEN	MULATTO	MACULATE
MISDEED	MITOGEN	MOORIER	MULLEIN	MADHOUSE
MISDEEM	MITOSIS	MOORING	MULLION	MADRIGAL
MISDOER	*MITSVAH	MOORISH	MULLITE	*MADWOMAN
MISDONE	*MITZVAH	MOPPING	*MULLOCK	MAESTOSO
MISDRAW	*MIXTURE	MORAINE	MULLUSK	MAGAZINE
MISEASE	MOANFUL	MORCEAU	MULTURE	MAGICIAN
MISEDIT	*MOBBISH	MORDANT	MUMBLER	*MAGICKED
MISERLY	MOBSTER	MORDENT	*MUMMERY	MAGISTER
MISFILE	MOCHILA	MORELLE	MUMMIED	MAGNESIA
MISFIRE	*MOCKERY	MORELLO	MUMMIES	MAGNETIC
MISFORM	MODELER	MORNING	*MUMMIFY	MAGNETON
MISGIVE	MODESTY	MOROCCO	MUMMING	*MAGNIFIC
MISGROW	MODICUM	MORPHIA	MUNCHER	MAGNOLIA
MISHEAR	MODULAR	*MORPHIC	MUNDANE	*MAHARAJA
*MISJOIN	MODULUS	MORPHIN	MUNNION	MAHARANI
*MISKEEP	MOFETTE	MORRION	MUNSTER	*MAHJONGG
*MISKNOW	MOIDORE	MORTARY	MUNTING	*MAHOGANY
MISLAIN	MOISTEN	MORTICE	*MUNTJAC	*MAIDHOOD
MISLEAD	MOISTLY	*MORTIFY	*MUNTJAK	MAIEUTIC
MISLIKE	*MOJARRA	MORTISE	MURIATE	MAILLESS
MISLIVE	MOLDIER	MOSSIER	MURICES	MAINLAND
*MISMARK	MOLDING	*MOTHERY	MURRAIN	MAINLINE
MISMATE	MOLLIES	MOTIVIC	MURRINE	MAINMAST
MISMEET	*MOLLIFY	MOTORIC	MURTHER	MAINSAIL
MISMOVE	MOLLUSC	MOTTLER	MUSEFUL	MAINSTAY
MISNAME	MOMENTA	MOUFLON	MUSETTE	MAINTAIN
MISPAGE	MOMENTO	MOUILLE	MUSICAL	MAIOLICA
MISPART	MONACID	MOULAGE	MUSKIER	*MAJESTIC
MISPLAY	MONADES	MOULDER	*MUSKILY	*MAJOLICA
MISRATE	MONARCH	MOULTER	MUSKRAT	*MAJORITY
MISREAD	MONARDA	MOUNTER	*MUSPIKE	*MAKEBATE
MISRELY	MONEYED	MOURNER	MUSTANG	*MAKEFAST
MISRULE	MONEYER	MOUSIER	MUSTARD	*MAKIMONO
MISSEAT	MONGREL	MOUSILY	MUTABLE	MALAMUTE
MISSEND	MONIKER	MOUSING	MUTAGEN	MALAPERT
MISSHOD	MONITOR	MOUTHER	*MUZZIER	MALAPROP
MISSIES	*MONKERY	MOVABLE	*MUZZILY	*MALARKEY
MISSILE	*MONKISH	*MOVABLY	*MUZZLER	MALAROMA
MISSION	MONOCLE	*MOZETTA	MYALGIA	MALEDICT
MISSIVE	MONOCOT	*MUCKIER	MYCOSIS	MALEMIUT
MISSORT	MONOECY	*MUCKILY	MYELINE	MALEMUTE
MISSOUT	MONOFIL	MUDDIED	MYELOID	MALENESS

MALIGNER	MARIGOLD	*MAZAEDIA	*MENFOLKS	*MICROMHO
MALIGNLY	MARINADE	*MAZELIKE	MENHADEN	*MICRURGY
MALIHINI	MARINARA	*MAZINESS	MENIALLY	MIDBRAIN
MALINGER	MARINATE	*MAZOURKA	MENISCUS	MIDDLING
MALLEOLI	MARIPOSA	MEALIEST	MENOLOGY	*MIDFIELD
MALPOSED	MARITIME	MEALLESS	MENSEFUL	*MIDMONTH
MALTIEST	*MARKDOWN	MEALTIME	MENSTRUA	*MIDNIGHT
MALTREAT	*MARKEDLY	*MEALWORM	MENSURAL	MIDPOINT
MALTSTER	MARKETER	*MEALYBUG	MENSWEAR	MIDRANGE
MALVASIA	*MARKHOOR	MEANNESS	MENTHENE	*MIDSHIPS
*MAMELUKE	*MARKSMAN	MEANTIME	*MEPHITIS	*MIDSPACE
MAMMATUS	MARLIEST	MEASURER	MERCAPTO	MIDSTORY
MAMMILLA	MARMOSET	MEATBALL	*MERCHANT	*MIDWATCH
MAMMITIS	*MARQUESS	MEATHEAD	*MERCIFUL	MIGNONNE
MANCIPLE	*MARQUISE	MEATIEST	MERENGUE	MIGRAINE
MANDAMUS	MARRIAGE	MEATLESS	MERGENCE	MIGRATOR
MANDARIN	MARSHALL	*MECHANIC	MERIDIAN	*MIJNHEER
MANDATOR	MARSUPIA	MECONIUM	MERINGUE	MILDNESS
MANDIBLE	MARTAGON	MEDALIST	MERISTEM	MILEPOST
MANDIOCA	MARTINET	MEDALLIC	MERISTIC	MILESIMO
MANDOLIN	*MARTYRLY	MEDIALLY	MESDAMES	MILIARIA
*MANDRAKE	*MARZIPAN	MEDIANLY	*MESHWORK	MILITANT
MANDRILL	*MASKLIKE	MEDIATOR	MESMERIC	MILITARY
MANEUVER	MASSACRE	MEDICAID	MESNALTY	MILITATE
*MANGABEY	MASSAGER	MEDICARE	MESOCARP	*MILKFISH
MANGANIC	MASSEDLY	MEDICATE	MESODERM	MILKIEST
MANGIEST	MASSETER	MEDICINE	MESOGLEA	*MILKMAID
MANGONEL	MASSEUSE	MEDIEVAL	MESOMERE	*MILKWEED
MANGROVE	MASSICOT	MEDIOCRE	*MESOPHYL	*MILKWOOD
MANICURE	MASSIEST	MEDITATE	MESOSOME	*MILKWORT
MANIFEST	MASSLESS	MEDUSOID	MESOTRON	MILLEPED
MANIFOLD	*MASTABAH	MEEKNESS	*MESQUITE	MILLIARD
MANNERLY	MASTERLY	MEETNESS	MESSIEST	MILLIARE
MANNIKIN	MASTHEAD	*MEGABUCK	MESSMATE	MILLIARY
MANNITOL	*MASTICHE	*MEGADYNE	MESSUAGE	MILLIBAR
*MANPOWER	MASTITIS	MEGALITH	METALISE	MILLIEME
MANTELET	MASTLESS	MEGAPODE	METALIST	MILLIGAL
MANTILLA	MASTLIKE	MEGAVOLT	*METALIZE	*MILLILUX
MANTISSA	MASTODON	MEGAWATT	METALLED	*MILLIMHO
MANTLING	MASURIUM	MEGILLAH	METALLIC	MILLINER
MANUALLY	*MATCHBOX	MELAMINE	METAMERE	*MILLIOHM
MANUBRIA	MATELESS	MELANIAN	*METAPHOR	MILLIPED
MANURIAL	MATELOTE	MELANISM	*METAZOAN	MILLIREM
MANURING	MATERIAL	MELANIST	*METAZOON	MILLPOND
MANWARDS	MATERIEL	MELANITE	METERAGE	MILLRACE
*MANYFOLD	MATERNAL	*MELANIZE	METHADON	*MILLWORK
*MAPMAKER	*MATESHIP	MELANOID	METHANOL	MIMETITE
*MAPPABLE	MATINESS	MELANOMA	*METHINKS	*MIMICKER
*MAQUETTE	MATTEDLY	MELANOUS	*METHODIC	*MINACITY
MARABOUT	MATTRASS	MELILITE	*METHOXYL	MINATORY
MARASMUS	MATTRESS	MELINITE	*METHYLAL	MINDLESS
MARATHON	MATURATE	*MELLIFIC	*METONYMY	MINEABLE
MARAUDER	MATURITY	MELODEON	METRICAL	MINGIEST
MARAVEDI	*MAUMETRY	MELODIES	METRITIS	*MINIBIKE
MARBLING	MAUSOLEA	MELODISE	MEUNIERE	MINIMISE
*MARCHESA	*MAVERICK	MELODIST	*MEZEREON	*MINIMIZE
*MARCHESE	*MAXICOAT	*MELODIZE	*MEZEREUM	MINISTER
MARGARIC	*MAXIMISE	MEMBRANE	*MEZQUITE	MINISTRY
MARGARIN	*MAXIMITE	MEMORIAL	*MICAWBER	MINORITY
MARGINAL	*MAXIMIZE	*MEMORIZE	MICROBAR	MINSTREL
MARGRAVE	*MAYAPPLE	*MEMSAHIB	MICROBUS	MINUTING
*MARIACHI	MAYORESS	*MENARCHE	*MICROLUX	*MIQUELET

MIRINESS	MISRAISE	MOLEHILL	MOONSAIL	MOUSSAKA
MISADAPT	MISREFER	MOLESKIN	MOONSEED	*MOUTHFUL
MISAGENT	MISSENSE	MOLESTER	MOONSHOT	*MOVEABLE
MISALTER	*MISSHAPE	*MOLYBDIC	MOONWARD	*MOVEABLY
*MISAPPLY	MISSILRY	*MOMENTLY	MOONWORT	MOVELESS
MISASSAY	MISSOUND	MOMENTUM	*MOORFOWL	*MOVEMENT
MISATONE	MISSPACE	*MONACHAL	MOORIEST	*MOVIEDOM
MISAWARD	*MISSPEAK	MONADISM	MOORLAND	*MOVINGLY
MISBEGIN	MISSPELL	MONANDRY	MOORWORT	*MOZZETTA
MISBEGOT	MISSPEND	*MONARCHY	*MOPBOARD	MRIDANGA
MISBRAND	*MISSPOKE	MONASTIC	*MOPINGLY	*MUCHNESS
MISBUILD	MISSTART	MONAURAL	*MOQUETTE	*MUCIDITY
*MISCARRY	MISSTATE	*MONAXIAL	MORALISE	MUCILAGE
*MISCHIEF	MISSTEER	*MONAZITE	MORALISM	*MUCKIEST
MISCIBLE	MISSTYLE	MONECIAN	MORALIST	*MUCKLUCK
MISCLAIM	MISTAKER	MONETARY	MORALITY	*MUCKRAKE
MISCLASS	*MISTEACH	MONETISE	*MORALIZE	*MUCKWORM
MISCOLOR	*MISTHINK	*MONETIZE	MORATORY	*MUCOSITY
MISCOUNT	*MISTHROW	*MONEYBAG	*MORBIFIC	MUDDIEST
MISDOING	MISTIEST	MONGEESE	MORBILLI	MUDGUARD
MISDOUBT	MISTITLE	MONGOOSE	*MORDANCY	*MUDPUPPY
MISDRIVE	*MISTOUCH	*MONICKER	MOREOVER	MUDSTONE
MISENROL	MISTRACE	MONITION	*MORESQUE	MUENSTER
MISENTER	MISTREAT	MONITIVE	MORIBUND	MUGGIEST
MISENTRY	MISTRESS	MONITORY	MORONISM	*MULBERRY
MISERERE	MISTRIAL	*MONKFISH	MORONITY	MULETEER
MISEVENT	MISTRUST	*MONKHOOD	MOROSITY	MULLIGAN
*MISFAITH	MISTRYST	MONOACID	*MORPHEME	MULTIFID
MISFIELD	MISTUTOR	MONOCARP	*MORPHINE	MULTIPED
*MISFRAME	MISUNION	MONOCRAT	MORTALLY	MULTIPLE
MISGAUGE	MISUSAGE	*MONOCYTE	MORTGAGE	*MULTIPLY
MISGRAFT	MISVALUE	MONODIST	MORTISER	MUNDUNGO
MISGUESS	MISWRITE	MONOFUEL	MORTMAIN	MUNGOOSE
MISGUIDE	MITICIDE	*MONOGAMY	MORTUARY	MUNIMENT
*MISHMASH	MITIGATE	MONOGENY	*MOSCHATE	MUNITION
*MISHMOSH	MITTIMUS	MONOGERM	*MOSQUITO	MURAENID
MISINFER	*MIXOLOGY	MONOGRAM	*MOSSBACK	MURALIST
MISINTER	MNEMONIC	*MONOGYNY	MOSSIEST	MURDEREE
*MISJUDGE	MOATLIKE	MONOLITH	MOSSLIKE	MURDERER
MISLABEL	MOBILISE	MONOLOGY	*MOTHBALL	MURIATED
MISLAYER	*MOBILITY	MONOMIAL	*MOTHERLY	MURICATE
MISLEARN	*MOBILIZE	MONOPODE	MOTILITY	MURMURER
MISLIGHT	MOBOCRAT	*MONOPODY	MOTIONAL	MURRELET
MISLIKER	MOCCASIN	MONOPOLE	MOTIONER	MUSCADEL
MISLODGE	MODALITY	*MONOPOLY	MOTIVATE	MUSCATEL
MISLYING	MODELING	MONORAIL	*MOTIVITY	MUSCULAR
*MISMATCH	MODELLED	MONOSOME	MOTORBUS	*MUSHROOM
MISNOMER	MODELLER	MONOTINT	MOTORCAR	MUSICALE
*MISOGAMY	MODERATE	MONOTONE	MOTORING	MUSICIAN
*MISOGYNY	MODERATO	MONOTONY	MOTORISE	MUSINGLY
MISOLOGY	MODIFIER	*MONOTYPE	MOTORIST	*MUSKETRY
MISPAINT	MODIOLUS	*MONOXIDE	*MOTORIZE	MUSKIEST
MISPARSE	MODULATE	MONSIEUR	MOTORMAN	MUSQUASH
*MISPATCH	*MOFFETTE	MONTEITH	*MOTORWAY	*MUSTACHE
MISPLACE	MOISTFUL	MONUMENT	*MOUCHOIR	MUTATION
MISPLANT	MOISTURE	MOONBEAM	*MOUFFLON	*MUTCHKIN
MISPLEAD	MOLALITY	*MOONCALF	MOULDING	MUTENESS
MISPOINT	MOLARITY	*MOONFISH	MOUNTAIN	MUTICOUS
MISPOISE	MOLASSES	MOONIEST	MOUNTING	MUTILATE
MISPRINT	MOLDIEST	MOONLESS	MOURNFUL	MUTINEER
*MISPRIZE	*MOLDWARP	MOONLIKE	MOURNING	MUTINIED
*MISQUOTE	MOLECULE	MOONRISE	MOUSIEST	MUTINIES

MUTINIES	BU M BLE	DE M IES	HE M MER	LU M PEN
MUTINING	BU M KIN	DE M ISE	HE M OID	LU M PER
MUTINOUS	BU M MED	DE M ODE	HE M PEN	*MA M MEY
MUTTERER	BU M MER	DE M OTE	HE M PIE	NA M ELY
*MUZZIEST	BU M PER	DE M URE	HO M AGE	NA M ING
*MYCELIUM	CA M AIL	DI M ING	HO M BRE	NI M BLE
*MYCETOMA	CA M ASS	DI M ITY	HO M ELY	NI M BUS
*MYCOLOGY	CA M BER	DI M MED	HO M IER	NI M MED
MYELITIS	CA M BIA	DI M MER	HO M ILY	NI M ROD
MYLONITE	CA M ERA	DI M OUT	HO M ING	NO M ISM
*MYOBLAST	CA M ION	DI M PLE	HO M INY	NU M BER
*MYOGENIC	CA M ISA	DI M PLY	HU M ANE	NU M BLY
*MYOGRAPH	CA M ISE	DI M WIT	HU M ATE	NU M INA
*MYOPATHY	CA M LET	DO M AIN	HU M BLE	*NY M PHA
*MYOSCOPE	CA M PER	DO M INE	HU M BLE	*NY M PHO
MYOSOTIS	CA M PUS	DO M ING	*HU M BLY	PA M PER
MYOTONIA	CE M ENT	DO M INO	HU M BUG	PI M PLE
*MYRIAPOD	CO M ATE	DU M DUM	HU M MED	*PI M PLY
*MYRIOPOD	CO M BAT	DU M PER	HU M MER	PO M ACE
*MYRMIDON	CO M BER	FA M ILY	HU M OUR	PO M ADE
*MYSTAGOG	CO M EDO	FA M INE	HY M NAL	PO·M ELO
*MYSTICAL	CO M EDY	FA M ING	*JA M MED	PO M MEE
*MYSTICLY	CO M ELY	FA M ISH	*JA M MER	PO M MEL
*MYSTIQUE	CO M ETH	FA M OUS	*JI M INY	PO M POM
*MYTHICAL	CO M FIT	FE M ALE	*JU M BLE	PO M PON
*MYXEDEMA	CO M ING	FI M BLE	*JU M PER	PU M ELO
*MYXOCYTE	CO M ITY	FO M ENT	KA M ALA	PU M ICE
	CO M MIE	FU M BLE	KA M SIN	PU M MEL
	CO M MIT	FU M IER	KI M ONO	PU M PER
S M EW	*CO M MIX	FU M ING	KU M ISS	RA M ATE
S M OG	CO M MON	GA M BIA	KU M MEL	RA M BLE
S M UG	CO M MON	GA M BIR	LA M BDA	RA M IFY
S M UT	CO M OSE	GA M BIT	LA M BER	*RA M JET
S M ACK	CO M OUS	GA M BLE	LA M BIE	RA M MED
S M ALL	CO M PEL	GA M BOL	LA M EDH	RA M MER
S M ALT	*CO M PLY	GA M ELY	LA M ELY	RA M OSE
S M ARM	CU M BER	GA M EST	LA M ENT	RA M OUS
S M ART	CU M MER	GA M ETE	LA M EST	RA M ROD
S M ASH	CU M MIN	GA M IER	LA M INA	RA M SON
*S M AZE	*CY M BAL	GA M ILY	LA M ING	RA M TIL
S M EAR	CY M ENE	GA M INE	LA M MED	RE M AIL
S M EEK	CY M LIN	GA M ING	LA M PAD	RE M AIN
S M ELL	CY M OID	GA M MED	LA M PAS	RE M AKE
S M ELT	CY M OSE	GA M MER	LI M BER	RE M AND
S M ERK	CY M OUS	GA M MON	LI M BER	RE M ARK
S M ILE	DA M AGE	GE M MED	LI M BUS	RE M EDY
S M IRK	DA M ASK	GE M OTE	LI M IER	RE M EET
S M ITE	DA M MAR	GI M BAL	LI M INA	RE M ELT
S M ITH	DA M MED	GI M LET	LI M MED	RE M END
S M OCK	DA M MED	GI M MAL	LI M MER	RE M IND
S M OKE	DA M MER	GO M UTI	LI M MIC	RE M INT
S M OKY	DA M NER	GU M MED	LI M NER	RE M ISE
S M OLT	DA M PEN	GU M MER	LI M NIC	RE M ISS
S M OTE	DA M PER	HA M ATE	LI M PER	RE M OLD
BE M EAN	DA M PLY	HA M AUL	LI M PET	RE M ORA
BE M IRE	DA M SEL	HA M LET	LI M PID	RE M OTA
BE M IST	DA M SON	HA M MAL	LI M PLY	RE M OVE
BE M OAN	DE M AND	HA M MED	LI M PSY	RE M UDA
*BE M OCK	DE M ARK	HA M MER	LO M ENT	RI M IER
BE M USE	DE M AST	HA M PER	LU M BAR	RI M ING
BO M BER	DE M EAN	*HA M ZAH	LU M BER	RI M MED
*BO M BYX	DE M ENT	HE M MED	*LU M MOX	RI M MER

RI M OSE	TI M BER	CO M ATIC	DE M OUNT	HA M STER
RI M OUS	TI M BRE	*CO M ATIK	DI M ERIC	HA M ULUS
RI M PLE	TI M ELY	CO M BINE	DI M ETER	HE M AGOG
RO M ANO	TI M ING	CO M BUST	DI M MEST	HE M ATAL
RO M PER	TO M ATO	CO M BUST	DI M NESS	HE M ATIC
RU M BLE	TO M BAC	CO M EDIC	*DI M ORPH	HE M ATIN
RU M BLY	TO M BAK	CO M ETIC	DO M ICAL	HE M IOLA
RU M MER	TO M BAL	CO M FIER	DO M ICIL	HE M LINE
RU M MER	TO M BOY	CO M FORT	DO M INIE	*HE M LOCK
RU M OUR	TO M CAT	CO M ICAL	DU M PIER	*HE M MING
RU M PLE	TO M COD	CO M ITIA	*DU M PILY	HE M PIER
RU M PLY	TO M TIT	CO M MAND	DU M PING	*HI M SELF
RU M PUS	TU M BLE	CO M MATA	*DU M PISH	HO M AGER
SA M ARA	TU M EFY	CO M MEND	FA M ULUS	*HO M BURG
SA M BAR	TU M OUR	CO M MENT	FE M INIE	HO M IEST
SA M BUR	TU M ULI	CO M MIES	FE M ORAL	HO M INID
SA M ECH	TU M ULT	CO M MODE	FI M BRIA	*HO M MOCK
*SA M EKH	TY M BAL	*CO M MOVE	FU M ARIC	HO M OLOG
SA M IEL	TY M PAN	CO M MUNE	FU M BLER	*HO M ONYM
SA M ITE	VA M OSE	CO M MUTE	FU M ETTE	*HU M ANLY
SA M LET	VA M PER	CO M PACT	FU M IEST	HU M BLER
SA M PAN	VO M ICA	*CO M PACT	FU M ULUS	*HU M DRUM
SA M PLE	VO M ITO	*CO M PANY	GA M BADE	HU M ERAL
SA M SHU	WA M BLE	CO M PARE	GA M BADO	HU M ERUS
SE M EME	*WA M BLY	CO M PART	GA M BIER	*HU M IDLY
SE M INA	WA M MUS	CO M PASS	GA M BLER	HU M IDOR
SE M PLE	*WA M PUM	CO M PEER	GA M BOGE	*HU M MING
SE M PRE	WA M PUS	CO M PEND	GA M BREL	*HU M MOCK
SI M IAN	WI M BLE	CO M PERE	GA M ELAN	HU M ORAL
SI M ILE	WI M PLE	CO M PETE	GA M IEST	*HY M NARY
SI M LIN	WO M BAT	CO M PILE	GA M MING	*HY M NIST
SI M MER	WO M ERA	*CO M PLEX	GE M INAL	*HY M NODY
SI M NEL	YA M MER	*CO M PLEX	GE M LIKE	*JA M BEAU
SI M ONY	*ZO M BIE	CO M PLIN	GE M MATE	*JA M MING
SI M OOM	*ZY M ASE	CO M PLOT	GE M MIER	*JE M ADAR
SI M OON	BA M BINO	CO M PONE	*GE M MILY	*JE M IDAR
SI M PER	BE M ADAM	*CO M PONY	GE M MING	*JI M JAMS
SI M PLE	BI M ETAL	CO M PORT	GE M MULE	*JI M MINY
SO M BER	BI M ODAL	CO M POSE	*GE M SBOK	*JU M BLER
SO M BRE	BO M BARD	CO M POST	*GI M MICK	*JU M BUCK
SO M ITE	BO M BAST	CO M POTE	GO M ERAL	*JU M POFF
SU M ACH	BU M BLER	CO M PUTE	GO M EREL	*KA M PONG
SU M MED	BU M BOAT	CO M RADE	GO M ERIL	KA M SEEN
SU M MER	BU M MING	CU M ARIN	GU M BOIL	*KO M ATIK
SU M MIT	*BU M PKIN	*CU M QUAT	GU M DROP	*KU M QUAT
SU M MON	CA M BIAL	*CU M SHAW	GU M LESS	LA M BAST
SY M BOL	*CA M BISM	CU M ULUS	GU M LIKE	LA M BENT
TA M ALE	CA M BIST	*CY M LING	GU M MIER	LA M BERT
TA M BAC	*CA M BIUM	DA M AGER	GU M MITE	*LA M BKIN
TA M BUR	*CA M BRIC	DA M MING	GU M MING	LA M ELLA
TA M EIN	CA M ELIA	*DA M NIFY	GU M MOSE	LA M MING
TA M ELY	CA M ISIA	DA M OSEL	GU M MOUS	LA M PERS
TA M EST	CA M ORRA	*DA M OZEL	GU M SHOE	LA M PION
TA M ING	*CA M PHOL	*DA M PISH	GU M TREE	LA M POON
TA M MIE	*CA M PHOR	DE M AGOG	GU M WEED	LA M PREY
TA M PAN	CA M PIER	DE M ERIT	GU M WOOD	LA M STER
TA M PER	*CA M PILY	DE M ESNE	GY M NAST	LE M MING
TA M PON	CA M PION	DE M IGOD	*HA M BURG	LE M PIRA
TE M PEH	CA M PONG	DE M IREP	HA M MIER	LE M URES
TE M PER	CE M BALO	DE M ONIC	*HA M MILY	LI M ACON
TE M PLE	*CO M AKER	DE M OTIC	*HA M MING	LI M BATE
TI M BAL			*HA M MOCK	*LI M BECK

LI M BIER	RE M OVAL	TA M BURA	*BRI M MING	*DRU M HEAD
LI M EADE	RE M OVER	TA M PALA	BRO M ELIN	DRU M LIER
LI M IEST	RI M FIRE	TA M PION	*BRO M IDIC	*DRU M LIKE
LI M INAL	RI M IEST	TE M PERA	CAL M NESS	*DRU M ROLL
LI M ITED	RI M LAND	TE M PEST	*CAP M AKER	*DUM M KOPF
LI M ITER	RI M LESS	TE M PLAR	*CAR M AKER	*FAR M HAND
LI M ITES	RI M MING	TE M PLET	*CHA M BRAY	FAR M LAND
*LI M PKIN	RO M AINE	TE M PTER	*CHA M FRON	*FAR M YARD
LI M ULUS	RO M ANCE	TE M PURA	*CHA M PION	*FIL M CARD
LU M BAGO	RO M AUNT	TI M ARAU	*CHE M ICAL	FIL M GOER
LU M PISH	RO M PISH	TI M BALE	*CHE M URGY	FIL M IEST
*MA M MARY	RU M BLER	TI M BREL	*CHI M AERA	FIL M LAND
*MA M MOCK	RU M MAGE	TI M EOUS	*CHI M BLEY	FIR M NESS
*MA M MOTH	SA M BHAR	TI M EOUT	*CHI M ERIC	*FLA M ENCO
*MAXIMIN	SA M BHUR	TI M PANO	*CHU M SHIP	FLA M EOUT
*MI M ICRY	SA M BUCA	*TO M BACK	*CHY M OSIN	FLA M IEST
MISFILE	*SA M BUKE	TO M BOLO	*CLA M BAKE	FLA M INES
*MU M MERY	SA M ISEN	TO M FOOL	*CLA M MING	FLA M INGO
*MU M MIFY	SA M OVAR	TO M PION	CLA M ORER	*FLA M MING
NE M ATIC	SA M PLER	TU M BLER	*CLA M WORM	*FLI M FLAM
NE M ESIS	SA M SARA	TU M BREL	CLE M ATIS	*FLU M MERY
NI M IETY	SA M URAI	TU M BRIL	*CLE M ENCY	FOA M IEST
NI M MING	SE M ATIC	TU M ULAR	*CLU M PISH	FOA M LESS
NO M ARCH	SE M IDRY	TU M ULUS	*COE M BODY	*FOA M LIKE
NO M BLES	SE M IFIT	TY M PANA	*COE M PLOY	FOR M ALIN
NO M BRIL	SE M ILOG	TY M PANI	*COM M ANDO	*FOR M ALLY
NO M INAL	SE M IMAT	*TY M PANY	*COM M ENCE	*FOR M ERLY
NO M INEE	SE M INAL	VA M OOSE	*COM M ERCE	FOR M LESS
NU M ERAL	SE M INAR	VA M PIRE	COM M ONER	FRE M ITUS
NU M ERIC	SE M IPRO	*VA M PISH	*COM M ONLY	*FRO M ENTY
NU M MARY	SE M IRAW	VO M ITER	COM M UNAL	*FRU M ENTY
*NY M PHET	SI M ILAR	VO M ITUS	COM M UTER	*FUL M INIC
PA M PEAN	SI M IOID	*WA M EFOU	COS M ETIC	*FUR M ENTY
PA M PERO	SI M IOUS	*WA M EFUL	COS M ICAL	GAM M ADIA
PE M BINA	SI M ITAR	*WA M PISH	COU M ARIN	GAM M ONER
PE M ICAN	*SI M PLEX	*WO M ANLY	COU M AROU	GEM M IEST
*PE M PHIX	SI M ULAR	WO M MERA	*CRA M MING	*GEO M ANCY
PI M ENTO	SO M EDAY	*ZA M ARRA	*CRA M OISY	GEO M ETER
PO M ATUM	*SO M EHOW	*ZA M ARRO	CRA M POON	GEO M ETRY
PO M PANO	*SO M EWAY	*ZE M STVO	CRE M AINS	GER M ANIC
PO M POUS	SU M LESS	*ZY M OGEN	CRE M ATOR	GER M FREE
PU M ICER	SU M MAND	*ZY M OSIS	CRI M INAL	GER M IEST
*PU M PKIN	SU M MARY	*ZY M URGY	*CRO M LECH	GER M INAL
RA M BLER	SU M MATE	*BAD M OUTH	CRU M BIER	*GIM M ICKY
RA M EKIN	SU M MERY	BAL M ORAL	DAL M ATIC	GLI M PSER
RA M ILIE	SU M MING	BEA M IEST	DEE M STER	GLU M NESS
RA M MIER	SU M MONS	BEA M LESS	DIA M ETER	GNO M ICAL
RA M MING	SU M PTER	*BEA M LIKE	*DIE M AKER	GRA M ARYE
RA M MISH	SY M BION	*BED M AKER	*DIM M ABLE	*GRA M ERCY
RA M PAGE	SY M BIOT	*BES M IRCH	DIS M OUNT	GRI M ACER
RA M PANT	*SY M PTOM	*BES M OOTH	*DOO M SDAY	GRI M IEST
RA M PART	TA M ABLE	BES M UDGE	DOO M STER	GRI M MEST
*RA M PIKE	TA M ANDU	*BIG M OUTH	*DOR M ANCY	GRI M NESS
RA M PION	TA M ARAO	*BIO M ETRY	DOR M IENT	GRO M WELL
RA M POLE	TA M ARAU	BLA M ABLE	DOR M OUSE	GRU M BLER
RE M ARRY	TA M ARIN	*BLA M EFUL	DRA M ATIC	GRU M MEST
RE M ATCH	TA M ASHA	BOO M IEST	DRA M MING	*GRU M PHIE
RE M ERGE	TA M BALA	*BOO M TOWN	*DRA M MOCK	*GRU M PISH
RE M NANT	TA M BOUR	*BRI M FULL	*DRA M SHOP	GUM M IEST
RE M ODEL		BRI M LESS	DRU M BEAT	GUM M OSIS
RE M ORSE			DRU M FIRE	GUN M ETAL
RE M OUNT			*DRU M FISH	

HAE M ATAL	*PLU M BISM	*SHA M ABLE	TRA M LESS	FIL M
*HAE M ATIC	PLU M BOUS	*SHA M EFUL	TRA M LINE	FIR M
HAE M ATIN	PLU M ELET	*SHA M MASH	TRA M MING	FLA M
*HAM M ERER	PLU M IEST	*SHA M MIED	*TRA M PISH	FOA M
*HAM M IEST	*PLU M IPED	*SHA M MIES	TRA M PLER	FOR M
HAR M LESS	*PLU M LIKE	*SHA M MING	TRA M ROAD	FRO M
*HAR M ONIC	*PLU M PISH	*SHA M OSIM	TRE M BLER	GAU M
*HAT M AKER	*PRE M EDIC	*SHA M ROCK	TRI M ARAN	GER M
*HAY M AKER	PRE M IERE	*SHI M MERY	TRI M ETER	GEU M
*HEL M INTH	PRE M OLAR	*SHI M MING	TRI M MEST	GLI M
HEL M LESS	PRE M ORSE	*SKI M MING	TRI M MING	GLO M
*HEL M SMAN	*PRI M EVAL	SLI M IEST	TRI M NESS	GLU M
*HER M ETIC	PRI M MEST	SLI M MEST	*TRI M ORPH	GRA M
*HER M ITRY	*PRI M MING	SLI M MING	TRI M OTOR	GRI M
*HOG M ANAY	PRI M NESS	SLI M NESS	TRO M BONE	GRU M
*HOG M ENAY	PRI M ROSE	*SLU M BERY	*TRU M PERY	HAE M
*HUM M ABLE	PRO M ISEE	SLU M LORD	TUR M ERIC	HAL M
*KHA M SEEN	PRO M ISER	SLU M MING	VER M OULU	HAR M
*LAW M AKER	PRO M ISOR	SPU M IEST	*VER M OUTH	HEL M
LOA M LESS	PRO M OTER	STA M PEDE	*VIO M YCIN	HER M
MA M MATUS	PRO M PTER	STE M LESS	*WAR M AKER	HOL M
MA M MILLA	*PRO M PTLY	STE M LIKE	WAR M NESS	LOA M
MA M MITIS	PRO M ULGE	*STE M MERY	*WAR M OUTH	LOO M
*MAP M AKER	PSA M MITE	STE M MING	*WHI M BREL	MAI M
*MAU M ETRY	PTO M AINE	STE M WARE	*WHO M EVER	MAL M
ME M BRANE	PUL M ONIC	STI M ULUS	*WIG M AKER	**MUM M**
ME M ORIAL	PUL M OTOR	*STO M ACHY	*WOR M HOLE	NEE M
*MID M ONTH	*PYG M YISM	STO M ATAL	WOR M IEST	NEU M
MI M ETITE	*QIO M TAIN	STO M ATIC	*WOR M LIKE	NOR M
*MINACITY	RAM M IEST	STO M ODEA	WOR M ROOT	PAL M
*MINIMIZE	*REE M BARK	STU M BLER	WOR M SEED	PER M
*MIS M ATCH	*REE M BODY	STU M MING	*WOR M WOOD	PLU M
MO M ENTUM	REE M ERGE	STU M PAGE	*YAM M ERER	POE M
*MYR M IDON	*REE M PLOY	SUB M ERGE	*YAR M ELKE	PRA M
*NAU M ACHY	REI M PORT	SUB M ERSE	*YAR M ULKE	PRI M
*NEO M ORPH	REI M POSE	SUM M ABLE	*YAW M ETER	PRO M
*NEO M YCIN	RES M OOTH	*SUM M ERLY	*YEO M ANRY	REA M
NON M ETAL	RHA M NOSE	*SUM M ITRY	*ZOO M ANIA	ROA M
NON M ODAL	*RHE M ATIC	SUM M ONER	*ZOO M ETRY	ROO M
NON M ONEY	*RHO M BOID	SUR M ISER	*ZOO M ORPH	SCA M
NON M ORAL	ROO M ETTE	SUR M OUNT		SCU M
*NOR M ALCY	ROO M MATE	*SWA M PISH		SEA M
NOR M ALLY	RUM M AGER	*SWI M MING	BAL M	SEE M
NOR M LESS	SAL M ONID	SWI M SUIT	BAR M	SHA M
NOU M ENON	SAR M ENTA	*SYM M ETRY	BEA M	SHI M
NUM M ULAR	*SCA M MONY	TAL M UDIC	BER M	**SKI M**
PAL M ATED	*SCA M PISH	TEA M AKER	BOO M	SLA M
PAL M ETTE	*SCH M ALTZ	TEA M MATE	BRI M	SLI M
PAL M ETTO	*SCH M ALZY	TEA M STER	CAL M	SLU M
PAL M IEST	*SCH M ELZE	*TEA M WORK	CHA M	STE M
PAL M ITIN	*SCH M OOSE	TEG M ENTA	CHU M	STU M
*PAL M LIKE	*SCH M OOZE	TEG M INAL	CLA M	SWA M
*PAN M IXIA	SCI M ETAR	TER M INAL	COR M	SWI M
*PEM M ICAN	SCI M ITAR	TER M INUS	CRA M	SWU M
PER M EASE	SCI M ITER	TER M LESS	CUL M	TEA M
PER M EATE	*SCU M LIKE	TER M TIME	DEE M	TEE M
*PHI M OSIS	*SCU M MING	*THE M ATIC	DER M	TER M
PLI M SOLE	SEA M IEST	*THU M BKIN	DOO M	THE M
PLI M SOLL	SEA M LESS	*THU M BNUT	DOR M	TOO M
*PLU M BAGO	SEA M LIKE	*THY M IEST	DRA M	TRA M
*PLU M BERY	SEA M OUNT	TIT M OUSE	DRU M	TRI M
*PLU M BING	SEA M STER	*TOM M YROT	FAR M	WAR M

WHA M	REAR M	CURIU M	MUSEU M	TECTU M
WHI M	REHE M	CUSTO M	MUTIS M	TEDIU M
WHO M	RETE M	DEFOA M	NANIS M	TELIU M
WOR M	RHEU M	DEFOR M	NAPAL M	TERGU M
*ZOO M	SAGU M	DEGER M	NOMIS M	THAIR M
BEDI M	SATE M	DEPER M	NONCO M	THEIS M
BEGU M	SCRA M	DEWOR M	NUDIS M	THIRA M
BESO M	SCRI M	DIADE M	PASSI M	TRUIS M
BLOO M	SCRU M	DIATO M	PAYNI M	VACUU M
BOSO M	SEBU M	DICTU M	PEPLU M	VAGRO M
BREA M	SEDU M	DINKU M	PHENO M	VELLU M
BROO M	SEIS M	DIRDU M	PHLEG M	VERIS M
*BUXO M	SERU M	DIRHA M	PHLOE M	VICTI M
CARO M	SHAW M	DISAR M	*PHYLU M	*WAMPU M
CECU M	SMAR M	DOGDO M	PILEU M	WHILO M
CELO M	SOLU M	DORSU M	PLENU M	*WIGWA M
CHAS M	SPAS M	DRACH M	PODIU M	WISDO M
CHIR M	SPER M	DUMDU M	POGRO M	BAALIS M
CLAI M	STEA M	FANDO M	POMPO M	*BAGWOR M
CREA M	STOR M	FANTO M	PORIS M	BAPTIS M
DATU M	STRU M	FATHO M	POSSU M	BARROO M
DEGU M	SWAR M	FERBA M	PREAR M	*BECHAR M
DEIS M	THAR M	FERRU M	PRELI M	BEDROO M
DENI M	THER M	FOLIU M	PURIS M	BEGLOO M
DREA M	THRU M	FRENU M	*QUORU M	BEMADA M
DURU M	TOTE M	FULHA M	RACIS M	BERSEE M
FANU M	VELU M	FULLA M	RADIU M	BESWAR M
FILU M	VENO M	GODDA M	RANDO M	BIOHER M
FLEA M	VROO M	GONIU M	RANSO M	BLELLU M
FORA M	WHEL M	GRAHA M	RECTU M	BLOSSO M
FORU M	*XYLE M	GRANU M	REDEE M	BLUEGU M
GENO M	*ZIRA M	GYPSU M	REFIL M	*BOGYIS M
GLEA M	BALSA M	*HAKEE M	REFOR M	BOREDO M
GLOA M	BANTA M	HANSO M	REGNU M	BOSSDO M
GLOO M	BARIU M	HAREE M	RETRI M	BOSSIS M
GOLE M	BECAL M	HELIU M	REWAR M	*BRECHA M
GROO M	BEDLA M	HOLIS M	*RHYTH M	BROMIS M
HARE M	BEGRI M	*JETSA M	SACHE M	BRUTIS M
HAUL M	BELDA M	*JETSO M	SACRU M	*BRUXIS M
HILU M	BESEE M	KALIU M	SADIS M	*BUCKRA M
HOKU M	BEWOR M	LABIU M	SALAA M	CADMIU M
JORA M	BIFOR M	LABRU M	SCHIS M	CAESIU M
JORU M	BOTTO M	LACTA M	SCREA M	CALCIU M
*JUGU M	BUNKU M	LINGA M	SCUTU M	*CAMBIS M
KALA M	CAECU M	LISSO M	SELDO M	*CAMBIU M
KILI M	CARRO M	*LOGJA M	SENSU M	CENTRU M
LARU M	CENTU M	LUTEU M	SEPTU M	CHARIS M
LINU M	CERIU M	LYCEU M	*SEXIS M	*CHEFDO M
LOCU M	CESIU M	LYRIS M	SHALO M	*CHEMIS M
MADA M	CHIAS M	MAGNU M	SHOLO M	CHILLU M
*MAXI M	CHRIS M	MAIHE M	SIMOO M	CHRISO M
MIAS M	CILIU M	MARRA M	SLALO M	CLONIS M
MINI M	CIVIS M	*MAYHE M	SODIU M	CONFIR M
NOTU M	COELO M	MEDIU M	SPIRE M	CONFOR M
*NUZA M	CONDO M	MEGOH M	SPUTU M	COSMIS M
PLAS M	CONIU M	MEGRI M	*SQUIR M	CRANIU M
PRAA M	COPAL M	MENTU M	STREA M	CRISSU M
PRIS M	CORIU M	MILIU M	SUBGU M	CULTIS M
PROE M	CRINU M	MINIU M	SYNCO M	CUTWOR M
PSAL M	CUBIS M	MISAI M	SYSTE M	*CZARDO M
*QUAL M	CUNDU M	MOMIS M	TALCU M	*CZARIS M
REAL M	CUPRU M	MONIS M	TANDE M	DADAIS M

DAYROO M	*MICROH M	SOLANU M	*BOOKWOR M	*FAIRYIS M
DECLAI M	MIDTER M	SOPHIS M	BOTULIS M	FARADIS M
DECORU M	MILLDA M	SORGHU M	*BOYARIS M	FATALIS M
DEIFOR M	MINIMU M	STADIU M	*BRACHIU M	*FEMINIS M
DIAGRA M	MISDEE M	STANNU M	*BROUGHA M	FILIFOR M
DISHEL M	MISFOR M	STARDO M	*BRUNIZE M	FINALIS M
DODOIS M	MISTER M	STATIS M	CABALIS M	FIREROO M
DOGEDO M	MODICU M	STERNU M	CALADIU M	*FIREWOR M
DUALIS M	MUDROO M	STEWBU M	*CAPSICU M	*FLATWOR M
*DUKEDO M	NARCIS M	STIBIU M	*CARDAMO M	*FLIMFLA M
FADDIS M	NATRIU M	*STICKU M	*CARDAMU M	FLUIDRA M
FANTAS M	NIOBIU M	STRATU M	*CASEWOR M	*FOREBOO M
FASCIS M	NONFAR M	SUBATO M	CASTEIS M	FOREDOO M
*FAUVIS M	NOSTRU M	SUBITE M	CEMENTU M	*FRANCIU M
FERMIU M	PABULU M	SUNBEA M	CENTRIS M	*FREEFOR M
FIDEIS M	PALLIU M	SUNROO M	CEREBRU M	FRENULU M
*FIEFDO M	PANICU M	*SYMPTO M	*CHADARI M	*FURCULU M
*FILMDO M	PANTOU M	*SYNONY M	*CHIEFDO M	*FUSIFOR M
FIREAR M	PARONY M	TACHIS M	*CHILIAS M	FUTURIS M
*FOGYIS M	PEONIS M	TANGRA M	*CHROMIU M	GALBANU M
FOREAR M	PERFOR M	TANTRU M	CIBORIU M	*GAPEWOR M
FREEDO M	PHANTO M	TAPETU M	CINGULU M	GASIFOR M
FRUSTU M	PHELLE M	TAPROO M	*CIVICIS M	GERANIU M
FULCRU M	PIANIS M	TEAROO M	*CLAMWOR M	GIANTIS M
GALLIU M	PIETIS M	TERAOH M	*CLERKDO M	*GLOWWOR M
GINGHA M	PILGRI M	TERBIU M	COAGULU M	GLUCINU M
GRANDA M	PINETU M	TETOTU M	COATROO M	GONIDIU M
GROGRA M	PINWOR M	THEORE M	*COLIFOR M	*GRUBWOR M
GUNROO M	PLENIS M	THORIU M	COLISEU M	GUAIACU M
HADARI M	*PLUMBU M	THULIU M	COLORIS M	GUAIOCU M
*HAFNIU M	POMATU M	TOPONY M	CONIDIU M	*GYNECIU M
HALIDO M	POPEDO M	TOURIS M	COREDEE M	*GYPSYDO M
HEIRDO M	PREFOR M	TRANGA M	COREMIU M	*GYPSYIS M
HEROIS M	PREMIU M	TRANSO M	CORUNDU M	*HAIRWOR M
HOBOIS M	PREWAR M	TRIDUU M	*CRONYIS M	HANDLOO M
HOLMIU M	PROBLE M	TRIFOR M	CROSSAR M	HEADROO M
*HOMONY M	PROGRA M	TRITIU M	*CUBIFOR M	HEDONIS M
HOODLU M	PROTIU M	TRIVIU M	*CUNIFOR M	HEIRLOO M
*HUMDRU M	*QUANTU M	TROPIS M	*CYMATIU M	HELOTIS M
*JARLDO M	*QUONDA M	TSARDO M	CYNICIS M	*HEXAGRA M
*JEJUNU M	REALIS M	TSARIS M	*DANDYIS M	HOLOGRA M
*JIBBOO M	REBLOO M	*TZARDO M	*DARKROO M	*HOMEROO M
*JUGULU M	RECLAI M	*TZARIS M	*DAYDREA M	*HOOKWOR M
*JUJUIS M	*REQUIE M	*WAXWOR M	DECIGRA M	*HORNBEA M
*KINGDO M	*RHABDO M	*WEBWOR M	*DEKAGRA M	*HORNWOR M
LABARU M	RHENIU M	*WHOLIS M	DELIRIU M	HUMANIS M
LADANU M	RHODIU M	*WIFEDO M	DEMONIS M	*HYMENIU M
LAICIS M	ROSTRU M	*WOLFRA M	*DIAZEPA M	*HYPODER M
LEFTIS M	SANCTU M	YARDAR M	*DIDYMIU M	*HYPOGEU M
LEGROO M	SARCAS M	YTTRIU M	DIESTRU M	*JANIFOR M
*LEHAYI M	SCROTU M	*ZOARIU M	DILUVIU M	*JEROBOA M
LITHIU M	SEDARI M	BALLROO M	DIMERIS M	*JINGOIS M
LOBWOR M	SELFDO M	BAROGRA M	DIOECIS M	*KILOGRA M
*LOCKRA M	SERFDO M	BASIDIU M	DISBOSO M	*KYMOGRA M
LOCOIS M	*SHAHDO M	*BATHROO M	DISCLAI M	LABDANU M
LUGWOR M	SHITTI M	BDELLIU M	DITHEIS M	LABELLU M
LUSTRU M	SIDEAR M	BIENNIU M	DOMINIU M	LABURNU M
MACADA M	SISTRU M	BIOPLAS M	DRUIDIS M	LACONIS M
*MAJORA M	SKELLU M	*BIRDFAR M	DUODENU M	*LADYPAL M
*MAXIMU M	*SKOOKU M	*BLACKGU M	*DWARFIS M	LANDFOR M
METONY M	SLUMGU M	BLUESTE M	*DYNAMIS M	LAUDANU M
	SMEDDU M	*BOLLWOR M	FACTOTU M	*LEAFWOR M

*LECHAYI M	NOBELIU M	PRONOTU M	SEDILIU M	TITANIS M
LEGALIS M	NOMADIS M	PROSAIS M	SEISMIS M	TITANIU M
LINOLEU M	NOMOGRA M	*PTYALIS M	SELENIU M	TOADYIS M
*LIXIVIU M	*PACHADO M	PUDENDU M	*SERAPHI M	TOKENIS M
*LOBBYIS M	*PACIFIS M	PUGILIS M	SERIATI M	TOMENTU M
LOCALIS M	PAEANIS M	PUPARIU M	SETIFOR M	TOMOGRA M
LOGOGRA M	PAGANDO M	*PUPPYDO M	*SHAMOSI M	TOOLROO M
LOMENTU M	PAGANIS M	*PYGIDIU M	*SHEIKDO M	TOTALIS M
LOYALIS M	PALUDIS M	*PYGMYIS M	*SHIPWOR M	TOTEMIS M
*LUKEWAR M	PARADIG M	*PYRIFOR M	*SHKOTZI M	TRIADIS M
LUNGWOR M	*PARAFOR M	*PYXIDIU M	*SHOWROO M	TRILLIU M
LUTECIU M	PARECIS M	*QUACKIS M	*SICKROO M	TRITICU M
LUTETIU M	*PAROXYS M	*QUIETIS M	*SIEROZE M	*TUBIFOR M
*LYRICIS M	*PASHADO M	RACEMIS M	SILICIU M	*TYMPANU M
*LYRIFOR M	PATAGIU M	RAMENTU M	*SILKWOR M	VANADIU M
MASURIU M	PECULIU M	*RAMIFOR M	SIMPLIS M	*VARIFOR M
*MEALWOR M	*PEDIFOR M	*REAFFIR M	SINAPIS M	VARIORU M
MECONIU M	PENDULU M	REBELDO M	*SKIAGRA M	*VASCULU M
MELANIS M	PEPONIU M	REFUGIU M	*SLIPFOR M	*VASIFOR M
MERISTE M	PERIBLE M	REINFOR M	*SLOWWOR M	VEGANIS M
MESODER M	PERIDER M	RENIFOR M	SNOBBIS M	VELARIU M
*MEZEREU M	PERIDIU M	RENOGRA M	SOLARIS M	VERATRU M
*MILLIOH M	PERINEU M	RESIDUU M	SOLARIU M	*VERBATI M
MILLIRE M	*PHALLIS M	RETIFOR M	SOLATIU M	*VEXILLU M
MISCLAI M	*PHANTAS M	RIGHTIS M	SOLECIS M	*VIATICU M
MOMENTU M	PICLORA M	RIGORIS M	*SPANWOR M	*VIBURNU M
MONADIS M	*PICOGRA M	RINGWOR M	SPECTRU M	VILLADO M
MONOGER M	*PILIFOR M	ROBOTIS M	SPECULU M	*VINCULU M
MONOGRA M	PIPESTE M	ROSARIU M	*SPHAGNU M	VIRILIS M
MOONBEA M	*PISIFOR M	ROTIFOR M	SPICULU M	VITALIS M
MORALIS M	*PLANFOR M	*ROWDYIS M	SPLENIU M	*VIVARIU M
MORONIS M	PLASTRU M	ROYALIS M	STOICIS M	*VOCALIS M
*MOVIEDO M	*PLATFOR M	RUBIDIU M	SUDARIU M	VOLTAIS M
*MUCKWOR M	PLATINU M	RURALIS M	*SYCONIU M	WARDROO M
*MUSHROO M	*PLAYROO M	SAINTDO M	TALEYSI M	WAREROO M
*MYCELIU M	PLECTRU M	SALEROO M	TANTALU M	*WASHROO M
NABOBIS M	PLEONAS M	SAMARIU M	*TAPEWOR M	*WAVEFOR M
NANOGRA M	*PLUMBIS M	SANDWOR M	TAUTONY M	*WHIPWOR M
*NAPIFOR M	POLONIU M	*SAPPHIS M	TEETOTU M	*WHOREDO M
NATIVIS M	POPULIS M	SATANIS M	TELEFIL M	*WIREWOR M
NEOPLAS M	POOLROO M	SAVAGIS M	TELEGRA M	*WOODWOR M
*NEPHRIS M	*POSTFOR M	SCANDIU M	TERATIS M	*WORKROO M
NEPOTIS M	PRIAPIS M	*SCHOLIU M	THALLIU M	*YAHOOIS M
NEWSROO M	PRIGGIS M	SCIOLIS M	THRALDO M	*ZOMBIIS M
NIHILIS M	PROCLAI M	SECUNDU M	TIMPANU M	*ZOOSPER M

N

NAIF	**NAVY**	NENE	**NICK**	NODI
NAIL	**NAZI**	NEON	NIDE	NOEL
NAME	NEAP	NESS	NIDI	NOGG
NANA	NEAR	NEST	NIGH	NOIL
NAOS	NEAT	NETT	NILL	NOIR
NAPE	**NECK**	NEUM	NINE	NOLO
NARC	NEED	NEVE	NIPA	NOMA
NARD	NEEM	NEWS	NISI	NOME
NARK	NEEP	NEWT	**NIXY**	NONA
NARY	NEIF	**NEXT**	**NOCK**	NONE
NAVE	NEMA	NICE	NODE	NOOK

NOON	NIGHT	NEBULE	NOTARY	*NEWSBOY
NOPE	NIHIL	NECTAR	NOTATE	*NIBLICK
NORM	NINNY	NEEDER	NOTICE	NICOTIN
NOSE	NINON	NEEDLE	NOTING	NICTATE
NOSH	NINTH	NEGATE	NOTION	NIGGLER
NOSY	NISEI	NELSON	NOUGAT	NINEPIN
NOTA	NISUS	NEREID	NOVENA	*NITPICK
NOTE	NITER	NEREIS	NOWISE	NITRATE
NOUN	NITID	NEROLI	*NOZZLE	NITRIDE
NOUS	NITON	NESTER	NUANCE	NITRILE
NOVA	NITRE	NESTLE	NUBILE	NITRITE
NOWT	NITRO	NESTOR	NUBLES	NITROSO
NUDE	NITTY	NETHER	NUCLEI	NITROUS
NULL	NIVAL	NETTED	NUDEST	NOBLEST
NUMB	NOBLE	NETTER	NUDGER	NOCTULE
NURL	NODAL	NETTLE	NUDISM	NOCTURN
NABIS	NODUS	NETTLY	NUDIST	NOCUOUS
NABOB	NOISE	NEURAL	NUGGET	NODDIES
NACRE	NOISY	NEURON	NULLAH	NOISOME
NADIR	NOMAD	NEUTER	NUMINA	NOMINAL
NAIAD	NOMEN	NEWTON	NUNCIO	NOMINEE
NAIVE	NOMOS	NIACIN	NUNCLE	NONAGON
NAKED	NONCE	NIDGET	NURSER	NONPLUS
NALED	NOOSE	NIDING	NUTANT	NONPROS
NAMER	NOPAL	NIELLO	NUTATE	NONSLIP
NANCE	NORIA	NIGGER	NUTLET	NONSTOP
NANNY	NORTH	NIGGLE	NUTMEG	NONSUIT
NAPPE	NOSED	NILGAI	NUTRIA	NONUPLE
NAPPY	NOSEY	NILGAU	NUTTED	NONUSER
NARCO	NOTAL	NIMROD	NUTTER	*NONZERO
NARES	NOTED	NINETY	*NUZZLE	NOONING
NARIS	NOTER	NITRIC	*NYMPHA	NORLAND
NASAL	NOTUM	NITRID	*NYMPHO	NOSIEST
NASTY	NOVEL	NITRIL	NARCOSE	NOSTRIL
NATAL	NUBIA	NITWIT	NARGILE	NOSTRUM
NATES	NUDER	NOBLER	NARRATE	NOTABLE
NATTY	NUDGE	NOCENT	NASCENT	*NARTHEX
NAVAL	NUDIE	NODDED	NASTIUM	NUCLEAL
NAVAR	NUMEN	NODDER	NATRIUM	NUCLEAR
NAVEL	NURSE	NODDLE	NATURAL	NUCLEIN
NEATH	NUTTY	NODOSE	NECROSE	NUCLEON
NEEDY	NYALA	NODOUS	NEEDIER	NUCLEUS
NEGRO	NYLON	NODULE	NEEDLER	NUMERAL
NEGUS	*NYMPH	NOESIS	NEGATON	NUPTIAL
NEIGH	NARROW	NOETIC	NEGATOR	NURSING
NEIST	NARWAL	NOGGIN	NEGLIGE	NURTURE
NEROL	NASION	NONAGE	NEGROID	NUTGALL
NERTS	NASTIC	NONEGO	NEMESIS	*NUTPICK
NERVE	NATANT	NONFAT	NEONATE	NUTMEAT
NETOP	NATION	NONMAN	NERITIC	NUTTING
NETTY	NATIVE	NONPAR	NESTLER	*NYMPHET
NEUME	NATRON	NONUSE	NETLESS	NARRATER
NEVER	NATTER	NOODLE	NETTIER	NARRATOR
NEVUS	NATURE	NOOSER	NETTING	NASALISE
NEWEL	NAUSEA	NORITE	NETTLER	*NASALIZE
NGWEE	NAVIES	NORMAL	NEUROID	*NASCENCY
NICOL	*NAZIFY	NORMED	NEUROMA	NATATION
NIDAL	NEARLY	NOSHER	NEURONE	NATIONAL
NIDUS	NEATEN	NOSIER	NEUSTON	*NAUMACHY
NIECE	NEATLY	NOSILY	NEUTRAL	NAUSEANT
NIEVE	NEBULA	NOSING	NEUTRON	NAUSEATE
		NOSTOC	*NEWMOWN	NAUSEOUS
				NAUTILUS

NEARNESS	NOONTIDE	**K N OSP**	BI N ATE	CE N TRE
NEATNESS	*NORMALCY	K N OUT	BI N DER	**CE N TUM**
*NEBULIZE	NOSELESS	**K N OWN**	BI N DLE	CI N DER
*NECKBAND	NOSINESS	K N URL	BI N NED	**CI N EMA**
*NECKLACE	NOTARIAL	**S N ACK**	**BO N ACI**	CI N EOL
*NECKLIKE	*NOTARIZE	S N AFU	**BO N BON**	*CI N QUE
*NECKWEAR	NOTATION	S N AIL	BO N DER	CO N CHA
*NECROPSY	NOTELESS	S N AKE	**BO N DUC**	*CO N CHY
NEEDIEST	NOTORNIS	**S N AKY**	BO N IER	CO N CUR
NEEDLESS	NOTTURNO	S N ARE	BO N ING	CO N DOM
NEGATION	*NOVELIZE	S N ARK	BO N ITA	CO N DOR
NEGATRON	*NOWADAYS	S N ARL	BO N ITO	CO N FAB
*NEOMORPH	NUDENESS	S N ASH	BO N NET	CO N FER
*NEOMYCIN	*NUMBFISH	S N ATH	BO N NIE	CO N GEE
*NEOPHYTE	NURSLING	S N EAK	BO N SAI	CO N GER
*NEPHRISM	NURTURER	S N EAP	*BO N ZER	CO N GOU
NESTLING	NUTATION	**S N ECK**	*BU N CHY	CO N IES
NETTIEST	NUTGRASS	S N EER	BU N GLE	CO N INE
*NEURAXON	*NUTHATCH	S N ELL	BU N ION	CO N ING
NEURITIS	NUTRIENT	**S N ICK**	**BU N KER**	CO N IUM
NEUROSIS		S N IDE	**BU N KUM**	**CO N KER**
NEUTRINO		**S N IFF**	BU N TER	CO N NED
		S N IPE	**BY N AME**	CO N NER
*NEWCOMER	G N AR	S N OOD	**CA N APE**	CO N OID
*NEWFOUND	G N AT	S N OOK	CA N ARD	CO N SOL
*NEWLYWED	G N AW	S N OOL	CA N ARY	CO N SUL
*NEWSPEAK	**K N AP**	S N OOP	**CA N CAN**	CO N TRA
*NEXTDOOR	K N AR	S N OOT	CA N CEL	*CO N VEX
*NICKELIC	K N EE	S N ORE	CA N CER	CO N VEY
*NICKNACK	**K N EW**	S N ORT	CA N CHA	CO N VOY
*NICKNAME	K N IT	S N OUT	CA N DID	CU N DUM
NIELLIST	**K N OB**	**S N OWY**	CA N DLE	CU N EAL
*NIGHTCAP	**K N OP**	**S N UCK**	CA N DOR	CU N NER
*NIGHTJAR	K N OT	S N UFF	**CA N FUL**	DA N CER
NIGROSIN	**K N OW**	BA N ANA	CA N GUE	DA N DER
NINETEEN	K N UR	BA N DER	CA N INE	DA N DLE
NITRATOR	S N AG	BA N DIT	CA N ING	DA N GER
NITROGEN	S N AP	**BA N DOG**	**CA N KER**	DA N GLE
*NIZAMATE	S N AW	BA N GER	CA N NED	DE N ARY
*NOMARCHY	S N ED	BA N GLE	CA N NEL	DE N GUE
NONADULT	S N IB	BA N IAN	CA N NER	DE N IAL
*NONEMPTY	S N IP	**BA N ISH**	CA N NIE	DE N IED
*NONEQUAL	S N IT	**BA N KER**	CA N NON	DE N IER
NONGATAL	S N OB	BA N NED	CA N NOT	DE N IES
NONGREEN	S N OT	BA N NER	**CA N OPY**	DE N NED
NONGUILT	S N OW	BA N NET	CA N TER	DE N OTE
*NONHARDY	S N UB	**BA N TAM**	**CA N TIC**	DE N TAL
NONIDEAL	S N UG	BA N TER	CA N TLE	DE N TIL
*NONJUROR	S N YE	BA N YAN	CA N TON	DE N TIN
NONLEGAL	G N ARL	*BA N ZAI	CA N TOR	DE N UDE
*NONQUOTA	G N ARR	**BE N AME**	CA N TUS	DI N DLE
NONRATED	G N ASH	BE N DAY	CA N ULA	DI N ERO
NONRURAL	G N AWN	BE N DEE	**CA N VAS**	**DI N GEY**
NONSENSE	G N OME	BE N DER	**CA N YON**	**DI N GHY**
NONSOLAR	J N ANA	BE N IGN	CE N OTE	DI N GLE
NONSOLID	*K N ACK	BE N NET	CE N SER	DI N GUS
NONSUGAR	**K N EAD**	**BE N UMB**	CE N SOR	DI N ING
NONTIDAL	K N EEL	*BE N ZAL	CE N SUS	**DI N KEY**
NONTITLE	K N ELT	*BE N ZIN	CE N TAL	**DI N KLY**
*NONTOXIC	**K N IFE**	*BE N ZOL	CE N TER	**DI N KUM**
NONUNION	K N ISH	*BE N ZYL	CE N TRA	DI N NED
NONUSING	*K N OCK	**BI N ARY**		DI N NER
*NONWOODY	K N OLL			

DO N ATE	GE N TIL	KI N DLY	MA N NER	PE N CEL
DO N ERD	GE N TLE	KI N EMA	*MA N QUE	PE N CIL
DO N ERT	GE N TRY	KI N GLY	MA N TEL	PE N MAN
DO N JON	GI N GAL	LA N ATE	MA N TES	PE N NED
DO N KEY	GI N GER	LA N CER	MA N TID	PE N NER
DO N NED	GI N GKO	LA N CET	MA N TIS	PE N NON
DO N NEE	GI N KGO	LA N DAU	MA N TLE	PE N SEE
DO N SIE	GI N NED	LA N DER	MA N TRA	PE N SIL
*DO N ZEL	GI N NER	LA N ELY	MA N TUA	PE N TAD
DU N ITE	GO N ION	LA N GUE	MA N UAL	PE N TYL
DU N LIN	GO N IUM	LA N GUR	ME N AGE	PE N ULT
DU N NED	GO N OPH	LA N NER	ME N DER	PE N URY
DU N NER	GU N DOG	LA N OSE	*ME N INX	PI N ANG
DY N AST	GU N MAN	LA N UGO	ME N SAL	PI N ATA
DY N ODE	GU N NED	LE N DER	ME N TAL	PI N CER
FA N DOM	GU N NEL	LE N GTH	ME N TOR	PI N DER
FA N EGA	GU N NEN	LE N ITY	MI N DER	PI N EAL
FA N ION	GU N NER	LE N TEN	MI N GLE	PI N ENE
*FA N JET	GU N SEL	LE N TIC	MI N ING	PI N ERY
FA N NED	HA N DLE	LE N TIL	MI N ION	PI N GER
FA N NER	HA N GAR	LI N AGE	MI N TER	PI N IER
FA N TOD	HA N GER	LI N DEN	MI N UET	PI N ING
FA N TOM	HA N GUP	LI N EAL	MI N UTE	PI N ION
FE N CER	HA N KER	LI N EAR	MO N GER	PI N ITE
FE N DER	HA N KIE	LI N EUP	MO N GOE	PI N KIE
FE N NEC	HA N SEL	LI N GAM	MO N GOL	*PI N KLY
FE N NEL	HA N SOM	LI N GER	MO N GST	PI N NAE
FI N ALE	HA N TLE	LI N GUA	MO N IED	PI N NAL
FI N DER	HE N BIT	LI N IER	MO N IES	PI N NED
FI N ELY	HI N DER	LI N ING	MO N IST	PI N NER
FI N ERY	HI N GER	LI N KER	*MO N KEY	PI N OLE
FI N EST	HO N CHO	LI N KUP	MO N TES	PI N TLE
FI N GER	HO N EST	LI N NET	MU N TIN	PI N YON
FI N IAL	HO N IED	LI N SEY	NA N DIN	PO N CHO
FI N ING	HO N ING	LI N TEL	NA N ISM	PO N DER
FI N ISH	HO N KER	LI N TER	NA N KIN	PO N ENT
FI N ITE	*HO N KEY	LI N TOL	NA N NIE	PO N GEE
FI N NED	HO N KIE	LO N ELY	NI N ETY	PO N GID
FO N DLE	HO N OUR	LO N GAN	NO N AGE	PO N IED
FO N DLY	HU N GER	LO N GER	NO N COM	PO N IES
FO N DUE	HU N GRY	LO N GLY	NO N EGO	PO N TIL
FU N DUS	HU N KER	LU N ACY	NO N FAT	PO N TON
FU N GAL	HU N TER	LU N ATE	NO N MAN	*PU N CHY
FU N GIC	JA N GLE	LU N GAN	NO N PAR	PU N DIT
FU N`GUS	JE N NET	LU N GEE	NO N TAX	PU N IER
FU N KER	JI N GAL	LU N GER	NO N USE	PU N ILY
FU N KIA	*JI N GKO	LU N GYI	NU N CIO	PU N ISH
FU N NED	JI N GLE	LU N IER	NU N CLE	*PU N KAH
FU N NEL	*JI N GLY	LU N IES	PA N ADA	*PU N KEY
GA N DER	*JI N KER	LU N KER	PA N DER	PU N KIE
GA N GER	JI N NEE	LU N ULA	PA N DIT	PU N KIN
GA N GLY	JU N GLE	LU N ULE	PA N FUL	PU N NED
GA N GUE	*JU N GLY	MA N AGE	PA N GEN	PU N NER
GA N NET	JU N IOR	MA N ANA	PA N IER	PU N TER
GA N OID	*JU N KER	MA N EGE	PA N NED	*QI N DAR
GA N TRY	*JU N KET	MA N GEL	PA N TIE	*QI N TAR
GE N DER	*JU N KIE	MA N GER	PA N TRY	RA N CHO
GE N ERA	KA N TAR	MA N GLE	*PA N ZER	RA N CID
GE N EVA	KE N NED	MA N ILA	PE N ANG	RA N COR
GE N IAL	KE N NEL	MA N ITU		RA N DAN
GE N IUS	KI N ASE	MA N NAN		RA N DOM
GE N TES	KI N DLE	MA N NED		RA N GER

RA N KER	SH N APS	TI N DER	WA N TER	BE N EATH
RA N KLE	SI N EWY	TI N EID	WA N TON	BE N EFIC
RA N KLY	SI N FUL	TI N FUL	WI N CER	BE N EFIT
RA N SOM	SI N GER	TI N GLE	WI N CEY	BE N EMPT
RA N TER	SI N GLE	TI N GLY	WI N DER	BE N ISON
RA N ULA	SI N GLY	TI N IER	WI N DLE	BE N THAL
RE N AME	SI N KER	TI N ILY	WI N DOW	BE N THIC
RE N DER	SI N NED	TI N ING	WI N DUP	BE N THOS
RE N EGE	SI N NER	TI N KER	WI N ERY	*BE N ZENE
RE N NET	SI N TER	TI N KLE	WI N GER	*BE N ZINE
RE N NIN	SO N ANT	TI N KLY	WI N IER	*BE N ZOIN
RE N OWN	SO N ATA	TI N MAN	WI N ING	*BE N ZOLE
RE N TAL	SO N DER	TI N NED	WI N ISH	*BE N ZOYL
RE N TER	SO N ICS	TI N NER	WI N KER	BI N DERY
RE N VOI	SO N NET	TI N SEL	WI N KLE	BI N DING
RI N GER	SO N SIE	TI N TER	WI N NED	BI N NING
RI N SER	SU N BOW	TO N EME	WI N NER	BI N OCLE
RO N DEL	SU N DAE	TO N GER	WI N NOW	*BO N ANZA
RO N ION	SU N DER	TO N GUE	WI N TER	BO N DAGE
RO N NEL	SU N DEW	TO N IER	WI N TLE	BO N DMAN
RO N YON	SU N DOG	TO N ING	WI N TRY	BO N ESET
RU N DLE	SU N DRY	TO N ISH	WO N DER	BO N FIRE
RU N KLE	SU N KEN	TO N LET	WO N NED	BO N IEST
RU N LET	SU N KET	TO N NER	WO N NER	BO N KERS
RU N NEL	SU N LIT	TO N SIL	WO N TON	*BO N NOCK
RU N NER	SU N NED	TU N DRA	*YA N QUI	BU N DIST
RU N OFF	SU N SET	TU N ICA	YO N DER	BU N DLER
RU N OUT	SU N TAN	TU N ING	YO N KER	BU N GLER
RU N WAY	SY N COM	TU N NED	*ZA N ANA	BU N TING
SA N CTA	SY N DET	TU N NEL	*ZA N DER	CA N AKIN
SA N DAL	SY N DIC	VA N DAL	*ZA N IER	CA N ASTA
SA N DER	*SY N TAX	VA N ISH	*ZA N IES	CA N DELA
SA N DHI	SY N URA	VA N ITY	*ZE N ANA	CA N DENT
SA N EST	TA N DEM	VA N MAN	*ZE N ITH	CA N DIDA
SA N GAR	TA N GLE	VE N DEE	*ZI N CIC	CA N DIED
SA N GER	TA N GLY	VE N DER	*ZI N CKY	CA N DIES
SA N IES	TA N IST	VE N DOR	*ZI N NIA	CA N DLER
SA N ING	TA N KER	VE N DUE	*ZO N ARY	CA N DOUR
SA N ITY	TA N NER	VE N EER	*ZO N ATE	CA N ELLA
*SA N JAK	TA N NIC	VE N ERY	*ZO N ING	CA N IKIN
SA N NOP	TA N NIN	VE N IAL	*ZO N KED	CA N NERY
SA N NUP	TA N REC	VE N INE	*ZO N ULA	CA N NIER
SA N SAR	TA N TRA	VE N IRE	*ZO N ULE	CA N NILY
SA N SEI	TE N ACE	VE N OSE	BA N DAGE	CA N NING
SA N TIR	TE N AIL	VE N OUS	BA N DANA	CA N NULA
SA N TOL	TE N ANT	VE N TER	*BA N DBOX	CA N ONRY
SE N ARY	TE N DER	VE N ULE	BA N DEAU	CA N SFUL
SE N ATE	TE N DON	VI N EAL	BA N DIED	CA N TALA
SE N DAL	TE N IST	VI N IER	BA N DIES	CA N TATA
SE N DER	TE N NER	VI N ING	BA N DORA	CA N TDOG
SE N ECA	TE N NIS	VI N OUS	BA N DORE	CA N TEEN
SE N EGA	TE N OUR	WA N DER	BA N EFUL	CA N THUS
SE N HOR	TE N PIN	WA N DLE	*BA N GKOK	CA N TINA
SE N ILE	TE N REC	WA N GAN	BA N KING	CA N TRAP
SE N IOR	TE N SOR	WA N GLE	BA N KSIA	CA N TRIP
SE N ITI	TE N TER	WA N GUN	BA N NING	CA N VASS
SE N NET	TE N TIE	WA N IER	BA N NING	*CA N ZONA
SE N NIT	TE N UIS	WA N ING	*BA N NOCK	*CA N ZONE
SE N ORA	TE N URE	WA N ION	*BA N QUET	CE N ACLE
SE N SUM	TE N UTO	WA N NED	BA N SHEE	CE N SUAL
SE N TRY	TI N CAL	WA N NER	BA N SHIE	CE N SURE
			BE N CHER	CE N TARE

CE N TAUR	CO N SORT	FA N FARE	GI N GERY
CE N TAVO	CO N SULT	FA N FOLD	GI N GHAM
CE N TILE	CO N SUME	FA N LIKE	GI N GILI
CE N TIME	CO N TACT	FA N NING	GI N GIVA
CE N TIMO	CO N TAIN	FA N TAIL	GI N NING
CE N TNER	CO N TEMN	FA N TASM	GI N SENG
CE N TRAL	CO N TEND	FA N TAST	GO N DOLA
CE N TRAL	CO N TENT	FA N TASY	GU N BOAT
CE N TRIC	CO N TEST	FA N WISE	GU N FIRE
CE N TRUM	*CO N TEXT	FA N WORT	GU N LESS
CE N TURY	CO N TORT	FE N AGLE	GU N LOCK
CI N DERY	CO N TOUR	FE N CING	GU N NERY
CI N EAST	CO N TROL	FI N ABLE	GU N NING
CI N EOLE	CO N TUSE	FI N AGLE	GU N PLAY
CI N ERIN	CO N VECT	FI N ALIS	GU N ROOM
CO N ATUS	CO N VENE	FI N ALLY	GU N SHIP
CO N CAVE	CO N VENT	FI N ANCE	GU N SHOT
CO N CEAL	CO N VERT	FI N ANCE	GU N WALE
CO N CEDE	CO N VICT	*FI N BACK	GY N ECIA
CO N CEIT	*CO N VOKE	FI N DING	*GY N ECIC
CO N CENT	CU N EATE	FI N ESSE	HA N APER
CO N CEPT	CU N NING	*FI N FISH	HA N DBAG
CO N CERN	CY N ICAL	*FI N FOOT	HA N DCAR
CO N CERT	DA N DIER	FI N ICAL	HA N DFUL
CO N CISE	DA N DIES	*FI N ICKY	HA N DGUN
CO N COCT	DA N DILY	FI N IKIN	HA N DIER
CO N CORD	DA N DLER	FI N LESS	HA N DILY
CO N CUSS	DA N GLER	FI N LIKE	HA N DLER
CO N DEMN	DA N SEUR	*FI N MARK	*HA N DOFF
CO N DIGN	DE N DRON	FI N NIER	HA N DOUT
CO N DOLE	*DE N IZEN	FI N NING	HA N DSAW
CO N DONE	DE N NING	FO N DANT	HA N DSEL
CO N DUCE	DE N SIFY	FO N DLER	HA N DSET
CO N DUCT	DE N SITY	FO N TINA	HA N GDOG
CO N DUIT	DE N TINE	FU N CTOR	HA N GING
CO N DYLE	DE N TIST	FU N ERAL	HA N GMAN
CO N FECT	DE N TOID	FU'N FAIR	HA N GOUT
CO N FESS	DE N TURE	FU N GOID	HA N GTAG
CO N FIDE	DE N UDER	FU N GOUS	HA N UMAN
CO N FINE	DI N ERIC	FU N ICLE	HE N BANE
CO N FIRM	DI N ETTE	FU N NEST	HE N COOP
*CO N FLUX	DI N GBAT	FU N NING	HE N LIKE
CO N FORM	DI N GILY	GA N GLIA	HE N NERY
CO N FUSE	DI N KIER	GA N GREL	*HE N PECK
CO N FUTE	DI N KIES	*GA N GWAY	HI N DGUT
CO N GEAL	DI N NING	GA N TLET	HO N ESTY
CO N GEST	DO N ATOR	GE N ERAL	HO N OREE
CO N GIUS	DO N GOLA	GE N ERIC	HO N ORER
CO N ICAL	DO N NING	GE N ESIS	HU N DRED
CO N IFER	DO N NISH	GE N ETIC	HU N NISH
CO N IINE	DU N GEON	GE N ETTE	HU N TING
*CO N JOIN	DU N NAGE	GE N IPAP	*JA N GLER
*CO N JURE	DU N NESS	GE N ITAL	JA N ITOR
CO N NATE	DU N NEST	GE N ITOR	*JI N GALL
CO N NECT	DU N NING	GE N SENG	*JI N GLER
CO N NING	DU N NITE	GE N TEEL	*JO N QUIL
CO N NIVE	*DY N AMIC	GE N TIAN	*JU N IPER
CO N NOTE	DY N ASTY	GE N TILE	*JU N KMAN
*CO N QUER	FA N ATIC	GE N UINE	KA N TELE
CO N SENT	FA N CIED	GI N GALL	KE N NING
CO N SIST	FA N CIER	GI N GELI	KE N OSIS
CO N SOLE	FA N CIES	GI N GELY	KI N DLER

KI N DRED
KI N ESIS
KI N ETIC
KI N ETIN
*KI N FOLK
*KI N GCUP
*KI N GDOM
KI N GLET
KI N GPIN
*KI N SHIP
KI N SMAN
*KU N ZITE
LA N ATED
LA N CING
LA N DING
LA N DLER
LA N DMAN
LA N DMEN
LA N GREL
LA N GUET
LA N GUID
LA N GUOR
LA N IARD
LA N IARY
LA N ITAL
LA N OLIN
LA N TANA
LA N TERN
LA N YARD
LE N GTHY
LE N IENT
LE N TIGO
LE N TISK
LE N TOID
LI N ABLE
LI N ALOL
LI N DANE
LI N EAGE
LI N EATE
LI N ECUT
LI N EMAN
LI N GCOD
LI N GIER
LI N GUAL
LI N IEST
LI N KAGE
*LI N KBOY
LI N KMAN
LI N OCUT
LI N SANG
LI N SEED
LI N TIER
LO N GBOW
LO N GING
LO N GISH
LU N ATED
LU N ATIC
LU N CHER
LU N ETTE
LU N GING
LU N IEST
LY N CEAN

*LY N CHER	NU N LIKE	PI N HOLE	SA N DIER	*SY N ONYM
MA N ATEE	NU N NERY	PI N IEST	SA N DLOT	SY N OVIA
MA N DRIL	NU N NISH	*PI N KEYE	SA N DMAN	SY N TONY
*MA N GABY	PA N ACEA	PI N KIES	SA N DPIT	TA N AGER
MA N ILLA	PA N ACHE	PI N KING	SA N GRIA	TA N BARK
MA N ILLE	*PA N CAKE	*PI N KISH	SA N ICLE	TA N GELO
MA N ITOU	*PA N CHAX	PI N NACE	SA N TIMS	TA N GENT
MA N ITOU	PA N DECT	PI N NATE	SA N TOUR	TA N GIER
MA N LESS	PA N DIED	PI N NING	SE N ATOR	TA N GLER
MA N NITE	PA N DIES	PI N NULA	SE N DOFF	TA N GRAM
MA N NOSE	PA N DOOR	PI N NULE	SE N ECIO	TA N KAGE
*MA N PACK	PA N DORA	PI N OCLE	SE N HORA	TA N KARD
MA N SION	PA N DORE	PI N TADA	SE N OPIA	TA N KFUL
MA N TEAU	PA N DOUR	PI N TADO	SE N SATE	TA N NAGE
MA N TLET	PA N DURA	PI N TAIL	SE N SING	TA N NATE
MA N URER	*PA N FISH	PI N TANO	SE N SORY	TA N NERY
MA N WARD	*PA N ICKY	PI N WALE	SE N SUAL	TA N NEST
*ME N FOLK	PA N ICLE	PI N WEED	SI N CERE	TA N NING
ME N TION	PA N ICUM	*PI N WORK	SI N GLET	TA N NISH
MI N ARET	PA N NIER	PI N WORM	SI N KAGE	TA N TARA
MI N ERAL	PA N NING	PO N IARD	SI N LESS	TA N TIVY
*MI N IMAX	PA N OCHA	*PO N TIFF	SI N NING	TA N TRUM
MI N STER	PA N OCHE	PO N TINE	SI N OPIA	TA N YARD
MI N UTIA	PA N OPLY	PO N TOON	SI N SYNE	TE N ABLE
MO N ITOR	PA N PIPE	PU N CHER	SI N UATE	TE N ANCY
*MO N KERY	PA N THER	PU N GENT	SI N UOUS	TE N DRIL
*MO N KISH	PA N TIES	PU N IEST	SO N ANCE	TE N FOLD
MO N SOON	PA N TILE	PU N NING	SO N GFUL	TE N ONER
MO N STER	PA N TOUM	PU N STER	SO N LESS	TE N SILE
MO N TANE	PE N ALLY	RA N CHER	SO N LIKE	TE N SING
MO N TERO	PE N ALTY	RA N COUR	*SO N OVOX	TE N SION
*MO N THLY	PE N ANCE	RA N DIES	SO N SHIP	TE N SITY
MO N URON	PE N ATES	RA N KISH	*SU N BACK	TE N SIVE
MU N NION	PE N DANT	RA N PIKE	SU N BATH	TE N TAGE
MU N STER	PE N DENT	RA N SACK	SU N BEAM	TE N THLY
*MU N TJAC	PE N GUIN	RE N EGER	SU N BIRD	TE N TIER
*MU N TJAK	PE N ICIL	RE N EWAL	SU N BURN	TE N UITY
*MY N HEER	PE N LITE	RE N EWER	SU N DIAL	TE N UOUS
NA N KEEN	PE N NAME	RE N NASE	SU N DOWN	TI N AMOU
NI N EPIN	PE N NANT	RE N TIER	SU N FAST	TI N FOIL
NI N THLY	PE N NATE	RI N GENT	SU N FISH	TI N GLER
NO N ACID	PE N NIES	RI N GLET	SU N GLOW	TI N HORN
NO N AGON	PE N NINE	RI N GTAW	SU N LAMP	TI N IEST
NO N BANK	PE N NING	RI N NING	SU N LAND	TI N LIKE
NO N BOOK	PE N OCHE	RI N SING	SU N LESS	TI N NIER
NO N CASH	PE N SILE	RO N DEAU	SU N LIKE	TI N NILY
NO N FARM	PE N SION	RO N DURE	SU N NING	TI N NING
NO N FOOD	PE N SIVE	RO N TGEN	SU N RISE	TI N TING
NO N GAME	PE N STER	RU N AWAY	SU N ROOF	TI N TYPE
NO N HERO	PE N TANE	*RU N BACK	SU N ROOM	TI N WARE
NO N LIFE	PE N TOSE	RU N DLET	SU N SPOT	TI N WORK
NO N PLUS	PE N UCHE	RU N DOWN	SU N SUIT	TO N ETTE
NO N PROS	PE N UCHI	RU N LESS	SU N WARD	TO N GMAN
NO N SKED	PI N BALL	RU N NING	SU N WISE	TO N IEST
NO N SKID	PI N BONE	RU N OVER	SY N AGOG	TO N IGHT
NO N SLIP	PI N CHER	SA N CTUM	SY N APSE	TO N NAGE
NO N STOP	PI N ESAP	SA N DBAG	SY N CARP	TO N NEAU
NO N SUCH	PI N ETUM	SA N DBAR	*SY N CHRO	TO N NISH
NO N SUIT	PI N FOLD	*SA N DBOX	SY N COPE	TO N SURE
NO N UPLE	PI N GUID	SA N DFLY	SY N ERGY	TO N TINE
NO N USER	PI N HEAD	SA N DHOG	SY N ESIS	TU N ABLE
*NO N ZERO			*SY N GAMY	TU N DISH

TU N EFUL	*ZI N GANO	*CHI N BONE	DOW N CAST	*HOR N PIPE
TU N ICLE	*ZI N GARA	CHI N LESS	*DOW N COME	HOR N POUT
TU N NAGE	*ZI N GARO	CHI N NING	*DOW N FALL	HOR N TAIL
TU N NING	*ZI N KIFY	CIN N ABAR	*DOW N HAUL	*HOR N WORM
*VA N DYKE	*ZO N ATED	CIN N AMON	*DOW N HILL	HOR N WORT
VA N ILLA	BAN N ERET	CLA N GOUR	DOW N IEST	*HYM N BOOK
VA N TAGE	BAN N EROL	CLA N NISH	*DOW N PLAY	*HYM N LESS
VA N WARD	BAR N ACLE	CLA N SMAN	DOW N POUR	*HYM N LIKE
VE N ATIC	BAR N YARD	CLI N ALLY	DOW N TROD	*HYP N OSIS
VE N DACE	BEA N BALL	*CLI N CHER	DOW N TURN	*HYP N OTIC
VE N ISON	BEA N LIKE	COE N AMOR	*DOW N WARD	*JAU N DICE
VE N OMER	BEA N POLE	COE N DURE	*DOW N WIND	*JOH N BOAT
VE N TAGE	*BEK N IGHT	COE N URUS	DRE N CHER	*JOI N TURE
VE N TAIL	BER N ICLE	*COE N ZYME	DRU N KARD	KEE N NESS
VE N TRAL	BEU N CLED	*COG N IZER	FAI N EANT	*KEY N OTER
VE N TURE	BIA N NUAL	COG N OMEN	FAI N TISH	*KID N APER
VE N TURI	BIE N NIAL	COG N OVIT	FAR N ESOL	LAG N APPE
VI N ASSE	BIE N NIUM	COI N CIDE	*FAW N LIKE	LAN N ERET
VI N EGAR	BIG N ONIA	COI N HERE	*FIE N DISH	LAU N CHER
VI N IEST	BIN N ACLE	COI N MATE	*FIN N ICKY	LEA N NESS
VI N TAGE	*BLA N CHER	COI N SURE	FIN N IEST	LEM N ISCI
VI N TNER	BLA N DISH	CON N IVER	*FIN N MARK	LIE N ABLE
WA N GLER	*BLE N CHER	COO N SKIN	FLA N CARD	LIE N TERY
WA N IEST	BLI N DAGE	COR N BALL	FLA N ERIE	LIG N EOUS
WA N IGAN	*BLI N KARD	*COR N CAKE	*FLI N CHER	LIM N ETIC
WA N NESS	BLO N DISH	COR N CRIB	FOU N TAIN	LIO N FISH
WA N NEST	BOU N DARY	COR N EOUS	*FRA N CIUM	LIO N ISER
WA N NING	*BRA N CHIA	*COR N ETCY	*FRA N KEST	*LIO N IZER
WA N TAGE	BRA N DISH	*COR N HUSK	*FRA N KLIN	LIO N LIKE
*WE N CHER	BRA N NING	*COR N ICHE	FRE N ETIC	LOA N WORD
WE N DIGO	BRA N TAIL	COR N ICLE	FRE N ULUM	LOR N NESS
WE N NISH	BRI N DLED	COR N IEST	*FRE N ZILY	*MAG N IFIC
*WI N CHER	BRI N IEST	COR N MEAL	FRO N DEUR	MA N CIPLE
WI N CING	*BRO N CHIA	COR N UTED	FRO N TAGE	MA N DAMUS
WI N DAGE	*BRO N CHUS	COU N TESS	FRO N TIER	MA N DARIN
WI N DBAG	*BRO N ZING	COU N TIAN	FRO N TLET	MA N DATOR
WI N DIER	BRU N ETTE	CRA N IATE	*FUN N YMAN	MA N DIBLE
WI N DIGO	*BRU N IZEM	CRA N KIER	GAI N LESS	MA N DIOCA
WI N DILY	BUR N OOSE	*CRA N KILY	GAU N TLET	MA N DOLIN
WI N DING	CAN N ABIC	CRA N KOUS	GIA N TESS	MA N EUVER
WI N DROW	CAN N ABIN	CRA N NIED	GIA N TISM	MA N GANIC
*WI N DWAY	CAN N ABIS	CRA N NIES	GLA N DERS	MA N GIEST
WI N ESOP	CAN N ELON	CRA N NOGE	GLA N DULE	MA N GONEL
*WI N GBOW	CAN N IBAL	CRE N ATED	GOW N SMAN	MA N GROVE
WI N GIER	CAN N IEST	CRE N ELLE	GRA N DAME	MA N ICURE
WI N GLET	CAN N IKIN	*CRO N YISM	GRA N DDAD	MA N IFEST
WI N GMAN	CAN N ONRY	*CRU N CHER	GRA N DEUR	MA N IFOLD
WI N IEST	CAR N AUBA	CTE N IDIA	GRA N DSIR	MA N NERLY
WI N NING	CAR N IVAL	*CYA N AMID	GRA N DSON	MA N NIKIN
*WI N NOCK	CAT N APER	CYA N OGEN	GRA N ULAR	MA N NITOL
WI N SOME	CEI N TURE	CYA N OSIS	GRI N DERY	MA N TELET
WI N TERY	CER N UOUS	DAM N ABLE	GRI N NING	MA N TILLA
WO N NING	*CHA N CERY	DAM N DEST	GUA N IDIN	MA N TISSA
*XA N THIC	*CHA N CIER	DAR N DEST	GYM N ASIA	MA N TLING
*XA N THIN	*CHA N CILY	*DAW N LIKE	HER N IATE	MA N UALLY
*ZA N YISH	*CHA N CING	DEA N SHIP	*HOR N BEAM	MA N UBRIA
*ZI N CATE	CHA N DLER	DIA N THUS	HOR N BILL	MA N URIAL
*ZI N CIFY	CHA N TIES	DOG N APER	*HOR N BOOK	MA N URING
*ZI N CITE	CHE N ILLE	DON N ERED	HOR N FELS	ME N HADEN
*ZI N CKED	*CHE N OPOD	DOW N BEAT	HOR N IEST	ME N IALLY
*ZI N COID			*HOR N LIKE	ME N ISCUS
*ZI N COUS				ME N OLOGY

ME N SEFUL	PAN N IKIN	RAI N BAND	SIG N IORY	*SWI N EPOX
ME N STRUA	*PAW N SHOP	RAI N BIRD	SIG N POST	TAN N ABLE
ME N SURAL	PEN N ATED	RAI N COAT	*SKI N HEAD	TEE N AGED
ME N SWEAR	*PHA N TASM	RAI N DROP	SKI N LESS	TEE N AGER
ME N THENE	PHA N TAST	RAI N FALL	*SKI N LIKE	THA N ATOS
*MID N IGHT	*PHA N TASY	RAI N IEST	SKI N NING	*THA N KFUL
*MIJ N HEER	*PHE N AZIN	RAI N LESS	*SOU N DBOX	THI N CLAD
MI N ATORY	*PHE N ETIC	RAI N WASH	SOU N DING	*THI N DOWN
MI N DLESS	PHE N ETOL	RAI N WEAR	SPA N DREL	*THI N KING
MI N EABLE	*PHE N OLIC	REA N OINT	SPA N DRIL	THI N NESS
MI N GIEST	*PHO N ETIC	REE N GAGE	*SPA N KING	THI N NEST
MI N IMISE	PHO N IEST	REE N LIST	SPA N LESS	THI N NING
MI N ISTER	*PIC N ICKY	REG N ANCY	SPA N NING	THI N NISH
MI N ISTRY	PIN N ACLE	REI N CITE	*SPA N WORM	*THU N DERY
MI N ORITY	PIN N ATED	REI N DEER	SPI N ALLY	TIN N IEST
MI N STREL	PIN N IPED	REI N DUCE	SPI N DLER	TIN N ITUS
MI N UTING	PLA N ARIA	REI N DUCT	SPI N ELLE	*TOP N OTCH
MO N ADISM	*PLA N CHET	REI N FECT	*SPI N IFEX	TOR N ILLO
MO N ANDRY	*PLA N FORM	REI N FORM	SPI N LESS	*TOW N FOLK
MO N ASTIC	PLA N GENT	REI N FUSE	SPI N NERY	TOW N LESS
MO N AURAL	*PLA N KING	*REI N JURE	SPI N NING	*TOW N SHIP
MO N ECIAN	PLA N KTER	REI N LESS	SPI N STER	TOW N SMAN
MO N ETARY	PLA N KTON	REI N SERT	SPO N DAIC	TOW N WEAR
MO N ETISE	PLA N LESS	REI N SMAN	SPO N GIER	*TRA N QUIL
MO N GEESE	PLA N NING	REI N SURE	SPO N GILY	TRA N SACT
MO N GOOSE	PLA N OSOL	REI N VENT	SPO N GING	TRA N SECT
MO N ITION	PLA N TAIN	REI N VEST	SPO N SION	TRA N SEPT
MO N ITIVE	PLA N TING	REI N VITE	SPO N TOON	TRA N SFER
MO N ITORY	POI N TMAN	*REI N VOKE	STA N CHER	*TRA N SFIX
MO N OACID	POU N DAGE	REU N ITER	*STA N CHLY	TRA N SHIP
MO N OCARP	PRA N DIAL	RHI N ITIS	STA N DARD	TRA N SMIT
MO N OCRAT	*PRA N KISH	*RHO N CHUS	STA N DING	TRA N SUDE
MO N ODIST	PRE N ATAL	ROE N TGEN	STA N DISH	TRE N CHER
MO N OFUEL	PRE N OMEN	ROU N DISH	*STA N DOFF	TRI N KUMS
MO N OGENY	PRE N TICE	ROU N DLET	STA N DOUT	TRI N ODAL
MO N OGERM	*PRI N CELY	SAI N FOIN	STA N DPAT	TRU N CATE
MO N OGRAM	PRI N CESS	SAI N TDOM	STA N HOPE	TRU N DLER
MO N OLITH	PRI N CIPE	SAN N YASI	STA N NARY	TRU N NION
MO N OLOGY	*PRI N COCK	SCA N DENT	STA N NITE	TUN N ELER
MO N OMIAL	PRI N TERY	SCA N DIUM	STA N NOUS	TUR N COAT
MO N OPODE	PRI N TING	SCA N NING	STE N OSED	*TUR N DOWN
MO N OPOLY	PRI N TOUT	SCA N SION	STE N OSIS	TUR N HALL
MO N ORAIL	PRO N ATOR	SCA N TIER	STI N GILY	TUR N OVER
MO N OSOME	PRO N OTUM	SCA N TIES	STI N GRAY	TUR N PIKE
MO N OTINT	PRU N ELLA	SCE N ARIO	STI N KARD	TUR N SOLE
MO N OTONE	PRU N ELLE	SCE N ICAL	*STI N KBUG	TUR N SPIT
MO N OTONY	PRU N ELLO	*SCH N APPS	STI N KIER	TWA N GIER
MO N SIEUR	*PYC N IDIA	*SCH N ECKE	STI N KPOT	TWA N GLER
MO N TEITH	*QUA N DANG	SCI N COID	STO N EFLY	TWI N BORN
MO N UMENT	*QUA N DARY	SEN N IGHT	STO N IEST	TWI N IEST
*MOO N CALF	*QUA N DONG	*SHA N GHAI	STU N NING	*TWI N IGHT
*MOO N RISE	*QUA N TIFY	SHA N TIES	STU N SAIL	*TWI N KLER
MU N DUNGO	*QUA N TITY	SHA N TUNG	SUB N ASAL	TWI N NING
MU N GOOSE	*QUA N TIZE	SHI N BONE	SUB N ODAL	*TWI N SHIP
MU N IMENT	*QUA N TONG	SHI N GLER	SUR N AMER	VAI N NESS
MU N ITION	*QUE N CHER	SHI N IEST	*SWA N HERD	*VAR N ISHY
NAI N SOOK	*QUE N ELLE	SHI N LEAF	*SWA N LIKE	VAU N TFUL
NON N AVAL	*QUI N CUNX	SHI N NERY	SWA N NERY	VEI N IEST
NOO N TIDE	*QUI N ELLA	SHI N NING	SWA N NING	VEI N LESS
NOO N TIME	*QUI N IELA	*SHU N PIKE	*SWA N SKIN	*VEI N LIKE
PAI N LESS	*QUI N OLIN	SIG N ALER	SWI N DLER	VEI N ULET
PAI N TING	*QUI N TILE	SIG N ALLY		VER N ACLE

VER N ICLE	GUA N	SCA N	BRAI N	GNAW N	
VIG N ETTE	HAE N	SEE N	**BRAW N**	GOBA N	
WAI N SCOT	HER N	SEW N	**BROW N**	GOWA N	
WAN N IGAN	HIS N	SHI N	BRUI N	GRAI N	
WEA N LING	HWA N	SHU N	BURA N	GREE N	
*WHE N EVER	HYM N	SIG N	BURI N	GROA N	
*WHI N CHAT	JEA N	SKI N	CABI N	GROI N	
WHI N IEST	JIN N	SOO N	CAIR N	GROW N	
WIN N ABLE	JOH N	SOR N	CAJO N	GYRO N	
WIN N OWER	JOI N	SOW N	CANO N	*HAZA N	
WOR N NESS	KAI N	SPA N	CAPO N	HEMI N	
WRA N GLER	KAO N	SPI N	CHAI N	HERO N	
*WRO N GFUL	KAR N	SPU N	CHUR N	HOGA N	
YEA N LING	KEE N	STU N	CLEA N	HONA N	
*YOU N GISH	KER N	SUN N	CLOW N	HUMA N	
*ZOO N OSIS	KHA N	SWA N	CODE N	HYME N	
	KIL N	TAI N	CODO N	HYSO N	
	KIR N	TAR N	COGO N	JAPA N	
BAR N	KOA N	TEE N	COIG N	*JAWA N	
BEA N	LAI N	TER N	COLI N	JETO N	
BEE N	LAW N	THA N	COLO N	JUPO N	
BLI N	LEA N	THE N	CONI N	KINI N	
BOO N	LIE N	THI N	COPE N	KNOW N	
BOR N	LIM N	TOO N	COTA N	KROO N	
BRA N	LIN N	TOR N	COVE N	LADE N	
BRI N	LIO N	TOW N	*COZE N	LAGA N	
BUN N	LOA N	TUR N	CROO N	LAPI N	
BUR N	LOI N	TWI N	CROW N	LATE N	
CAI N	LOO N	VAI N	CUMI N	LAUA N	
CAR N	LOR N	VEI N	CUTI N	LEAR N	
CHI N	LOW N	WAI N	CYTO N	LEBE N	
CHO N	MAI N	WAR N	DAMA N	LEMA N	
CIO N	MAU N	WEA N	DAVE N	LEMO N	
CLA N	MEA N	WEE N	DAWE N	LEVI N	
CLO N	MIE N	WHE N	DEIG N	LIGA N	
COI N	MOA N	WHI N	DEMO N	LIKE N	
CON N	MOO N	WOR N	DEVO N	LIMA N	
COO N	MOR N	WRE N	DEWA N	LIME N	
COR N	MUO N	WYN N	DIVA N	LINE N	
CUR N	NEO N	YAR N	DIWA N	LINI N	
CYA N	NOO N	YAW N	*DIZE N	LIPI N	
DAM N	NOU N	YEA N	DJIN N	LIVE N	
DAW N	PAI N	YUA N	DOVE N	LODE N	
DEA N	PAW N	ZEI N	DOYE N	LOGA N	
DJI N	PEA N	ZOO N	*DOZE N	LORA N	
DOW N	PEE N	BACO N	DRAI N	LUME N	
DUR N	PEI N	BAIR N	DRAW N	LUPI N	
FAI N	PEO N	BARO N	DROW N	LYSI N	
FAU N	PHO N	BASI N	FAGI N	MASO N	
FAW N	PIA N	BATO N	FANO N	MATI N	
FER N	PIO N	BEGA N	FEIG N	MAVE N	
FIR N	PIR N	BEGI N	FELO N	MAVI N	
FLA N	PLA N	BEGU N	FICI N	MELO N	
FOH N	POO N	BETO N	FLOW N	MESO N	
FOI N	POR N	BISO N	FOEH N	*MIZE N	
GAI N	PYI N	BLAI N	FROW N	MORO N	
GAU N	RAI N	BLOW N	FURA N	MOUR N	
GIR N	REI N	BOGA N	GAMI N	MUCI N	
GLE N	ROA N	BORO N	GIPO N	NINO N	
GOO N	RUI N	BOSO N	GIRO N	NITO N	
GOW N	SAI N	BOSU N	GIVE N	NOME N	
GRI N	SAW N	BOUR N	GLEA N	NUME N	

NYLO N	SEME N	**WOKE N**	BUNIO N	CURRA N
PAEA N	SERI N	**WOMA N**	BURDE N	**CYANI N**
PAEO N	SETO N	**WOME N**	BURTO N	**CYMLI N**
PAGA N	SEVE N	**WOVE N**	**BUSKI N**	DAEMO N
PATE N	SEWA N	XENO N	**BUSMA N**	DAIME N
PATI N	SHAR N	*XYLA N	BUTTO N	DAIMO N
PAVA N	**SHAW N**	**YAME N**	**CABMA N**	**DAMPE N**
PAVI N	SHEE N	**YAMU N**	**CAFTA N**	DAMSO N
PECA N	SHOO N	**YAPO N**	**CAIMA N**	**DARKE N**
PEKA N	SHOR N	YEAR N	**CALKI N**	DEACO N
PEKI N	**SHOW N**	YOGI N	CALLA N	DEADE N
PELO N	SIRE N	YOUR N	**CAMIO N**	**DEAFE N**
PINO N	SKEA N	YULA N	CANCA N	DECER N
PITO N	SKEE N	**YUPO N**	CANNO N	DEEPE N
PLAI N	SKEI N	*ZAYI N	CANTO N	**DEEWA N**
PRAW N	SLAI N	**BABOO N**	CANYO N	**DEHOR N**
PREE N	SOLA N	**BADMA N**	**CAPLI N**	DEMEA N
PURI N	SOLO N	**BAGMA N**	**CAPTA N**	DENTI N
PUTO N	**SOZI N**	BALEE N	**CARBO N**	DESIG N
PYLO N	**SPAW N**	BALLO N	CAREE N	DETAI N
PYRA N	SPEA N	BANIA N	CARLI N	**DEVEI N**
QUEA N	SPOO N	**BANYA N**	**CARMA N**	DIAMI N
QUEE N	SPUR N	**BARMA N**	CARTO N	*DIAZI N
QUER N	STAI N	BARRE N	**CARVE N**	**DISOW N**
QUOI N	STEI N	**BARYO N**	CASEI N	DIURO N
RACO N	STER N	**BATMA N**	CASER N	**DOBBI N**
RADO N	SWAI N	BATTE N	CATIO N	DOBLO N
RATA N	SWOO N	**BEACO N**	**CATKI N**	DOLMA N
RAVE N	SWOR N	**BECKO N**	CATLI N	DOLME N
RAVI N	SWOU N	**BEDAM N**	**CAVER N**	DOMAI N
RAYO N	SYRE N	**BEDPA N**	**CAYMA N**	**DONJO N**
RECO N	TAKI N	**BEMEA N**	*CHAZA N	DORMI N
REDA N	TALO N	**BEMOA N**	**CHITI N**	**DRIVE N**
REIG N	**TAXO N**	BENIG N	**CHITO N**	DROMO N
REMA N	TENO N	*BENZI N	**CHOPI N**	**DUBBI N**
RENI N	THEG N	BERLI N	**CHOSE N**	DUDEE N
REPI N	THEI N	**BICOR N**	CITRI N	DUNLI N
RERA N	THOR N	**BICRO N**	CITRO N	DURIA N
RERU N	TIGO N	**BIDDE N**	*CLAXO N	DURIO N
RESI N	TITA N	**BIFFI N**	**CLOVE N**	**FALCO N**
REWA N	TOKE N	**BIGGI N**	COCAI N	FALLE N
REWI N	TOLA N	BILLO N	COCHI N	FANIO N
REWO N	TOMA N	BIOGE N	COCOO N	FASTE N
RICI N	**TOXI N**	BIOTI N	CODEI N	FATTE N
RIPE N	TOYO N	BITTE N	CODLI N	**FIBRI N**
ROBI N	TRAI N	*BLAZO N	**COFFI N**	**FIRKI N**
ROMA N	TWAI N	**BOBBI N**	**COLUM N**	**FIRMA N**
ROSI N	TWEE N	**BODKI N**	**COMMO N**	**FLACO N**
ROUE N	VEGA N	**BOFFI N**	**CORBA N**	**FLAGO N**
ROVE N	VENI N	BOLSO N	CORDO N	**FLAME N**
ROWA N	**VIME N**	**BONBO N**	CORTI N	**FLAVI N**
ROWE N	*VIXE N	BOSTO N	COSIG N	*FLAXE N
RUME N	VODU N	**BOWFI N**	COTTO N	**FLYMA N**
SABI N	WAGO N	**BOWMA N**	COUPO N	**FOEMA N**
SALO N	**WAKE N**	*BRAZE N	COUSI N	FOISO N
SARI N	*WAXE N	BROGA N	**COWMA N**	**FORBA N**
SASI N	**WHEE N**	**BROKE N**	CRATO N	*FROZE N
SATI N	WIDE N	**BROMI N**	**CRAVE N**	**FRYPA N**
SAVI N	WIGA N	**BRUCI N**	**CRAYO N**	FUSAI N
SCIO N	WITA N	**BUMKI N**	CRETI N	FUSIO N
SCOR N	WITE N		CROTO N	GABIO N
SEDA N	*WIZE N		**CUMMI N**	

GABOO N	HOYDE N	MALIG N	**NUBBI N**	**RABBI N**
GAGMA N	*HYPHE N	**MALKI N**	PAISA N	RACOO N
GALLO N	**JARGO N**	**MAMMO N**	PANGE N	RADIA N
GAMMO N	*JERKI N	MANNA N	**PAPAI N**	RAGLA N
GARCO N	**JETTO N**	MARGI N	PARDO N	RAGMA N
GARDE N	**JORDA N**	MARLI N	PARIA N	RAISI N
GARRO N	**KAFTA N**	MAROO N	PARSO N	RAMSO N
GASCO N	KALIA N	MARRO N	PARTA N	RANDA N
GASKI N	**KAMSI N**	MARTE N	PARTO N	**RAPPE N**
GASMA N	**KAOLI N**	MARTI N	PATRO N	RATIO N
GERMA N	**KATIO N**	**MASCO N**	PATTE N	RATLI N
GERME N	**KELSO N**	MATRO N	PAULI N	RATOO N
GIBBO N	**KELVI N**	MATTI N	**PEAHE N**	RATTA N
GLOBI N	**KEPPE N**	**MAYVI N**	PECHA N	RATTE N
GLUTE N	*KHAZE N	MEDIA N	**PECTE N**	RATTO N
GLYCA N	**KIPPE N**	MELTO N	**PECTI N**	REAGI N
GLYCI N	**KITTE N**	MERLI N	PENMA N	REASO N
GNOMO N	*KLAXO N	MERLO N	PENNO N	REBOR N
GOBLI N	**KRAKE N**	MESIA N	PERRO N	**RECKO N**
GODOW N	*KUCHE N	MESSA N	PERSO N	RECOI N
GODSO N	**KURGA N**	**MICRO N**	PHONO N	REDDE N
GOLDE N	LADRO N	**MIDDE N**	PHOTO N	**REDFI N**
GONIO N	LAGOO N	MIGNO N	PHYLO N	REEAR N
GORGO N	LALLA N	**MIKRO N**	PHYTI N	REGAI N
GORHE N	LARDO N	MILDE N	PHYTO N	REGIO N
GOSSA N	LATEE N	MINIO N	**PIDGI N**	**REJOI N**
GOTTE N	LATTE N	**MINYA N**	PIGEO N	RELOA N
GOVER N	LATTI N	**MISPE N**	**PIGGI N**	REMAI N
GRABE N	**LAWMA N**	MITTE N	**PIGPE N**	RENNI N
GRADI N	**LAYMA N**	MODER N	PINIO N	RENOW N
GRATI N	LEADE N	MOLTE N	**PINYO N**	REOPE N
GRAVE N	LEAVE N	MOREE N	**PIPKI N**	REPLA N
GRISO N	LEGGI N	MORGE N	**PIPPI N**	REPUG N
GUANI N	LEGIO N	MORIO N	PISTO N	*REQUI N
GUENO N	LEGMA N	MOTIO N	**PITMA N**	RESEE N
GUIDO N	LENTE N	MOULI N	PLATA N	RESIG N
GULDE N	LEPTO N	MOUTO N	PLATE N	RETAI N
GUNMA N	LESIO N	**MUFFI N**	PLUTO N	RETUR N
GUNNE N	LESSE N	MULLE N	POISO N	**RHYTO N**
HADRO N	LESSO N	MUNTI N	**POLEY N**	**RIBBO N**
HAEMI N	LEUCI N	MUREI N	POLLE N	**RICHE N**
HAGDO N	**LEUKO N**	MUSLI N	**POMPO N**	RIDDE N
HAPPE N	**LICHE N**	MUTTO N	PONTO N	**ROBBI N**
HAPTE N	LIGNI N	**MYELI N**	**POPGU N**	RODMA N
HARDE N	LINDE N	**MYOSI N**	POPLI N	RONIO N
HARMI N	**LIPPE N**	**NANDI N**	POSTI N	RONYO N
HARPI N	LISTE N	**NANKI N**	POTEE N	ROTTE N
HASTE N	LITTE N	**NAPKI N**	POTIO N	RURBA N
HATPI N	LOGIO N	NASIO N	**POTMA N**	SADDE N
HAUSE N	LONGA N	NATIO N	**PREMA N**	SALMO N
*HAZZA N	LOOSE N	NATRO N	**PREME N**	SALOO N
HEAVE N	LOTIO N	NEATE N	PRISO N	**SAMPA N**
HEMPE N	LOUDE N	**NEKTO N**	PROLA N	SARSE N
HEREI N	LUCER N	NELSO N	PROTO N	SATEE N
HEREO N	**LUMPE N**	NEURO N	PTERI N	SCREE N
HEROI N	LUNGA N	NEWTO N	PTISA N	SEAMA N
HIDDE N	LURDA N	NIACI N	**PUFFI N**	SEASO N
HODDE N	LUTEI N	NOGGI N	**PUNKI N**	SEAWA N
HODDI N	**MACRO N**	NONMA N	PURLI N	SECER N
HOIDE N	MADDE N	NOTIO N	**PYTHO N**	SEISI N
HOLDE N	**MADMA N**		*QUINI N	*SEIZI N
HOLPE N	MAIDE N			SELSY N

*SEQUI N	*TAXMA N	*ZEATI N	CAMPIO N	CONTAI N
SEREI N	TEGME N	*ZECHI N	CANAKI N	CONTEM N
SERMO N	TELSO N	*ZIRCO N	CANIKI N	COONCA N
SEXTA N	TENDO N	BALLOO N	CANTEE N	COREIG N
SEXTO N	TENPI N	BARGAI N	CAPELA N	COTHUR N
SHAIR N	TEOPA N	BASEMA N	CAPELI N	COURLA N
SHAMA N	TESTO N	BASSOO N	CAPSTA N	*COWSKI N
SHOGU N	THORO N	BASTIO N	CAPTAI N	CRAMPO N
SHORA N	THRAW N	BATSMA N	CAPTIO N	CREATI N
SICCA N	TIEPI N	BEADMA N	CARABI N	CREWMA N
SICKE N	TIFFI N	BECLOW N	CARAVA N	CRIMSO N
SILKE N	TIGLO N	BEDEMA N	CARBAR N	CRISPE N
SILVA N	TINMA N	BEDGOW N	CARDOO N	CROCEI N
SIMIA N	TITIA N	BEDOUI N	CAROTI N	CROUTO N
SIMLI N	TITMA N	BEGROA N	CARRIO N	CRUCIA N
SIMOO N	TOCSI N	BELLMA N	CARRYO N	CRYOGE N
SIPHO N	TOUCA N	BENISO N	CARTOO N	CULLIO N
SISKI N	TRAPA N	*BENZOI N	CATERA N	CUMARI N
SITTE N	TREPA N	BETHOR N	CAUTIO N	CURTAI N
*SKYMA N	TRIGO N	BETOKE N	CAVEMA N	CUSHIO N
SLOGA N	TRITO N	BETWEE N	CELADO N	CUTDOW N
SLOVE N	TROGO N	BIGHOR N	CERATI N	CYCASI N
SOCMA N	TROPI N	BILLIO N	CERTAI N	CYPRIA N
SODDE N	TUCHU N	BIOTRO N	CERUME N	CYSTEI N
SOFTE N	TURBA N	BIRCHE N	CESSIO N	DALAPO N
SOLDA N	TUREE N	BIRDMA N	CHAGRI N	DASHEE N
SOLEM N	TYCOO N	BITTER N	CHANSO N	DAUPHI N
SOLIO N	TYMPA N	BITUME N	*CHAPMA N	DAYSMA N
SOUDA N	TYPHO N	*BLACKE N	CHASTE N	DEADPA N
SOVRA N	VANMA N	BLOUSO N	*CHAZZE N	DECROW N
SPAVI N	VERDI N	BLOWGU N	CHEAPE N	DECUMA N
SPLEE N	VERMI N	BLUEFI N	*CHEVRO N	DENDRO N
SPOKE N	VIOLI N	BOATMA N	*CHICKE N	*DENIZE N
SPRAI N	VIRGI N	BOGBEA N	*CHIFFO N	DERAIG N
STAME N	VIRIO N	*BOGYMA N	CHIGNO N	DESTAI N
STOLE N	VISIO N	BONDMA N	CHITLI N	DETRAI N
STOLO N	WAGGO N	*BOOKMA N	CHLORI N	*DEXTRA N
STRAI N	WANGA N	*BOOMKI N	CHORIO N	*DEXTRI N
SUBOR N	WANGU N	*BORAZO N	CHRONO N	DICTIO N
SUDDE N	WANIO N	BOTULI N	CINERI N	*DIGOXI N
SULDA N	WANTO N	BOUNDE N	CIPOLI N	DIPNOA N
SULLE N	WARDE N	BOURBO N	CISTER N	DISCER N
SULTA N	WARRE N	BOURDO N	CISTRO N	DISDAI N
SUMMO N	WEAKE N	*BRACKE N	CITHER N	DISHPA N
SUNKE N	WEAPO N	BRADOO N	CITHRE N	*DISJOI N
SUNTA N	WEASO N	BRECHA N	*CITIZE N	DISLIM N
SWEVE N	WEDEL N	BRIDOO N	CITTER N	DISTAI N
SYLVA N	WELKI N	BROADE N	CLACHA N	DOESKI N
SYLVI N	WHITE N	*BUCKEE N	CLARIO N	DOLPHI N
SYPHO N	WIGEO N	*BUFFOO N	CLAYPA N	DOORMA N
TAIPA N	WITHI N	BULLIO N	CLUBMA N	DRAGOO N
TALIO N	WIVER N	BULLPE N	COALBI N	DRAYMA N
TAMEI N	*WIZZE N	*BUMPKI N	COARSE N	DRUMLI N
TAMPA N	WONTO N	BURGEO N	COITIO N	DRUNKE N
TAMPO N	WOODE N	BURTHE N	COLICI N	*DUCKPI N
TANNI N	WOOLE N	BUSHMA N	COLLEE N	DUDGEO N
TARPA N	WORSE N	BUTYRI N	COMPLI N	DUNGEO N
TARPO N	*WYVER N	*CABEZO N	CONCER N	DURAME N
TARTA N	YAUPO N	*CAFFEI N	CONDEM N	DUSTBI N
*TARZA N	YEELI N	CAISSO N	CONDIG N	DUSTMA N
TAUTE N	YEOMA N	CALDRO N	*CONJOI N	DUSTPA N
TAVER N	YOUPO N		CONSIG N	DUVETY N

FACTIO N	GRIFFI N	KLAVER N	MISCOI N	PLOSIO N
FASHIO N	GRIFFO N	KREMLI N	*MISJOI N	PLOWMA N
FERMIO N	GRISKI N	*KRYPTO N	MISLAI N	PLUMPE N
FESTOO N	GRUNIO N	LACTEA N	MISSIO N	POCOSI N
FIBROI N	GRUTTE N	*LADYKI N	*LADYKI N	POLARO N
FICTIO N	*GRYPHO N	*LAMBKI N	MITOGE N	POLYGO N
FIFTEE N	GUDGEO N	LAMPIO N	MOISTE N	PONTOO N
FINIKI N	GUERDO N	LAMPOO N	MONSOO N	POPCOR N
FIREMA N	HABITA N	LANDMA N	MONURO N	PORTIO N
FIREPA N	*HACKMA N	LANDME N	MOORHE N	POSTEE N
FISSIO N	HAGBOR N	LANOLI N	MORPHI N	POSTER N
FLAGMA N	HAIRPI N	LANTER N	MORRIO N	POSTMA N
FLATTE N	*HALCYO N	LARDOO N	MOUFLO N	POTHEE N
*FLEXIO N	HALOGE N	LECTER N	MUEDDI N	POTTEE N
*FLUXIO N	HANDGU N	LECTIO N	*MUEZZI N	PREDAW N
FOGHOR N	HANGMA N	LEGHOR N	MULLEI N	PREPLA N
FOLACI N	HANUMA N	LEGUMI N	MULLIO N	PRETEE N
FOOTMA N	HARDPA N	LESBIA N	MUNNIO N	PREWAR N
FORAME N	*HARIJA N	LETDOW N	MURRAI N	PRONOU N
FOREIG N	HARPOO N	LEVULI N	MUTAGE N	PROPMA N
FOREMA N	HARSHE N	*LEXICO N	NANKEE N	PROTEA N
FORERU N	HEADMA N	LIAISO N	NARCEI N	PROTEI N
FORLOR N	HEADPI N	LIFTMA N	NEGATO N	PTOMAI N
FORWOR N	HEARKE N	LIGHTE N	NEPHRO N	PTYALI N
FOURGO N	HEARTE N	LIGROI N	NEUSTO N	PUCCOO N
*FOXSKI N	HEATHE N	LIMACO N	NEUTRO N	PULLMA N
FREEMA N	HEGUME N	*LIMPKI N	NEWBOR N	PULSIO N
FRESHE N	HELICO N	LINEMA N	*NEWMOW N	*PUMPKI N
FRISSO N	HEMATI N	LINKMA N	NEWSMA N	PURITA N
FROGMA N	HEPARI N	LOBEFI N	NICOTI N	PURLOI N
FRONTO N	HERDMA N	LORGNO N	NINEPI N	PUSHPI N
*FUCHSI N	HESSIA N	LOWBOR N	NOCTUR N	PUTAME N
FUSTIA N	*HEXAGO N	LOWDOW N	NONAGO N	PYROGE N
GADROO N	*HEXOSA N	LUPULI N	NOVATI N	*QUARTA N
GALLEI N	HIRUDI N	LUTHER N	NUCLEI N	*QUASSI N
GALLEO N	HOARSE N	LYNCEA N	NUCLEO N	*QUICKE N
GALLOO N	*HOATZI N	LYSOGE N	*PACKMA N	*QUIETE N
GAMELA N	HOEDOW N	*MADZOO N	PACTIO N	*QUINTA N
GASTRI N	HORDEI N	MAILMA N	PALADI N	*QUINTI N
GATEMA N	*HORIZO N	MALISO N	PAMPEA N	RACCOO N
GELATI N	*HYPERO N	MANAKI N	PAPHIA N	RAMEKI N
GENTIA N	*JACOBI N	MANIKI N	PARAGO N	RAMPIO N
*GHERKI N	*JALAPI N	MANSIO N	PASSIO N	RATTEE N
GIGATO N	*JARGOO N	MARCHE N	PASTER N	RATTOO N
GITTER N	*JAVELI N	MARTIA N	PATROO N	RAVELI N
GLADDE N	*JAZZMA N	*MATZOO N	PATTER N	READOR N
GLEEMA N	JILLIO N	MAUDLI N	PEEBEE N	REALIG N
GLIADI N	*JUNKMA N	*MAXIMI N	PELICA N	RECLEA N
GLISTE N	*JURYMA N	MEATMA N	PEMICA N	RECROW N
GLUTTO N	KAMSEE N	MEDUSA N	PENGUI N	REDSKI N
GODDAM N	KEELSO N	MEGATO N	PENSIO N	REFRAI N
GODROO N	KERATI N	MELANI N	PERIGO N	REGIME N
GOLDAR N	KEROGE N	MENTIO N	PERTAI N	RELAXI N
GOLDUR N	*KHAMSI N	MESSMA N	PHAETO N	RELEAR N
GOODMA N	*KIDSKI N	METOPO N	PICOLI N	RETRAI N
GOSSOO N	KILOTO N	MIDIRO N	PIGSKI N	REUNIO N
GRAPLI N	KINETI N	MIDNOO N	*PIKEMA N	REWAKE N
GREATE N	KINGPI N	MIDTOW N	PILLIO N	REWIDE N
GREISE N	KINSMA N	*MILKMA N	PLASMI N	REWOKE N
GREMLI N	*KIPSKI N	MILLIO N	PLASMO N	REWOVE N
GREYHE N	*KIRKMA N	MILLRU N	PLATOO N	ROCKOO N
	*KITCHE N	MINIKI N	PLAYPE N	RODSMA N
			PLEURO N	

RONTGE N	STATIO N	TRUDGE N	**BEDEAFE N**	***CAVICOR N**	
ROUGHE N	STEARI N	**TRYPSI N**	**BEDESMA N**	***CEPHALI N**	
RUBDOW N	**STEEPE N**	TUITIO N	**BEGOTTE N**	**CERULEA N**	
RUCTIO N	STEMSO N	**TURFMA N**	**BEHOLDE N**	**CESAREA N**	
RUFFIA N	STEPSO N	TWIGGE N	**BEMADDE N**	**CESARIA N**	
RUNDOW N	STETSO N	***TYPHOO N**	***BENJAMI N**	**CETACEA N**	
SABATO N	**STEWPA N**	VELAME N	***BENZIDI N**	***CHAINMA N**	
SACATO N	**STIFFE N**	VENISO N	**BERBERI N**	***CHAIRMA N**	
SADIRO N	STOLLE N	VERMIA N	**BESCREE N**	**CHALDRO N**	
SAFFRO N	STOUTE N	VERSIO N	**BETATRO N**	***CHAMFRO N**	
SAGAMA N	**STYGIA N**	VERVAI N	**BEVATRO N**	***CHAMPIO N**	
SALICI N	SUASIO N	VETERA N	**BIATHLO N**	***CHANFRO N**	
SALPIA N	**SUBCLA N**	VIBRIO N	**BIGAROO N**	***CHAPERO N**	
SALTER N	**SUBDEA N**	VIDICO N	***BILLYCA N**	***CHAPLAI N**	
SALTPA N	SUBERI N	VILLAI N	**BIOCLEA N**	***CHARACI N**	
SAMISE N	***SUBJOI N**	VILLEI N	***BLACKFI N**	***CHESSMA N**	
SANDMA N	SUBTEE N	VITAMI N	**BLOODFI N**	***CHEVERO N**	
SAPONI N	SUCTIO N	VOLUTI N	**BLUDGEO N**	**CHILDRE N**	
SAURIA N	SUNBUR N	WANIGA N	**BLUESMA N**	**CHLORDA N**	
*SAXHOR N	**SUNDOW N.**	WARISO N	**BOARDMA N**	***CHOREMA N**	
SCULPI N	SURGEO N	WARWOR N	**BOATSMA N**	***CHRISMO N**	
SECTIO N	SUSTAI N	***WAYWOR N**	***BOGEYMA N**	**CHRISTE N**	
SEEDMA N	**SWAGMA N**	WESTER N	***BOHEMIA N**	***CHYMOSI N**	
SERICI N	**SWANPA N**	WHEATE N	**BONDSMA N**	**CINNAMO N**	
SESSIO N	**SWEETE N**	WHEREI N	***BOOGYMA N**	***CINQUAI N**	
SEXTAI N	**SWOLLE N**	WHEREO N	***BOOMTOW N**	**CITATIO N**	
SHAITA N	**SYMBIO N**	WIDGEO N	**BOUGHTE N**	**CIVILIA N**	
SHARPE N	TABORI N	**WINGMA N**	**BOUILLO N**	**CLANSMA N**	
SHEBEA N	TACTIO N	**WIREMA N**	**BOURGEO N**	***COACHMA N**	
SHEBEE N	TAMARI N	WOODBI N	***BOXTHOR N**	**COACTIO N**	
SHEITA N	TAMPIO N	WOODHE N	**BRAINPA N**	**COERCIO N**	
SHIPMA N	***TAXIMA N**	**WOODMA N**	***BRAKEMA N**	**COGNOME N**	
SHIPPE N	**TEGUME N**	WOOLLE N	**BRASILI N**	**COHESIO N**	
SHIPPO N	TELAMO N	**WOOLMA N**	***BRAZILI N**	**COLISTI N**	
SHODDE N	TELEMA N	***WORKMA N**	**BRETHRE N**	**COLLAGE N**	
SHOPMA N	TELERA N	WRITHE N	**BRIGHTE N**	***COLOPHO N**	
SHORTE N	TENSIO N	WRITTE N	**BROMELI N**	**COMEDIA N**	
SHOTGU N	TERNIO N	***XANTHI N**	***BRYOZOA N**	***COMEDOW N**	
SHOTTE N	TERRAI N	***XYLIDI N**	***BUCKBEA N**	**COMPLAI N**	
*SHOWMA N	TERREE N	**YARDMA N**	***BUCKSKI N**	**CONATIO N**	
SIDEMA N	TERTIA N	YATAGA N	**BULLETI N**	***CONQUIA N**	
SILICO N	TESTOO N	**YEGGMA N**	**BULLHOR N**	**COONSKI N**	
SILVER N	**THEELI N**	YESTER N	**BUSULFA N**	**COOPTIO N**	
SIRLOI N	**THEREI N**	***YOYTHE N**	***CABOCHO N**	**COPATRO N**	
SIXTEE N	**THEREO N**	***ZACATO N**	***CALFSKI N**	**CORDOVA N**	
SLACKE N	THIAMI N	***ZECCHI N**	**CALUTRO N**	**CORDWAI N**	
SLEEKE N	***THIAZI N**	***ZILLIO N**	***CAMPAIG N**	**CORPSMA N**	
SMARTE N	***THICKE N**	***ZITHER N**	**CANNABI N**	**COTILLO N**	
SMIDGE N	THIONI N	***ZYMOGE N**	**CANNELO N**	***COTQUEA N**	
SMIDGI N	**TIGHTE N**	***BACKSPI N**	**CANNIKI N**	**COUMARI N**	
SMITTE N	**TINHOR N**	BACTERI N	***CAPESKI N**	**COUNTIA N**	
SNOWMA N	TOLIDI N	**BAILSMA N**	**CAPSICI N**	**COXSWAI N**	
*SOCKMA N	TOLLMA N	**BANDSMA N**	***CAPUCHI N**	**CRAGSMA N**	
SOJOUR N	TOMPIO N	BARBICA N	**CARAGEE N**	**CRAMPOO N**	
SOKEMA N	**TONGMA N**	**BARGEMA N**	**CARDAMO N**	***CRANKPI N**	
SOLANI N	**TORCHO N**	BARTISA N	**CARDIGA N**	**CREATIO N**	
SOUPCO N	TORSIO N	***BARTIZA N**	**CAREWOR N**	**CRYOTRO N**	
SOYBEA N	**TOUGHE N**	**BASEBOR N**	**CARILLO N**	**CULTIGE N**	
SPELEA N	TREASO N	***BAUDEKI N**	**CARROTI N**	**CULVERI N**	
SPONGI N	***TRIAZI N**	**BEADSMA N**	**CARYOTI N**	**CYANOGE N**	
SPONSO N	TRICOR N	BEARSKI N	***CATECHI N**	***CYCLAME N**	
SPORRA N	TRODDE N	***BEDARKE N**	**CAULDRO N**	***DAKERHE N**	

DALESMA N	FOURTEE N	HISTOGE N	MACAROO N	PAGURIA N
DECISIO N	FRACTIO N	*HOACTZI N	MACRURA N	PALMITI N
DECURIO N	*FRANKLI N	HOLSTEI N	*MADWOMA N	PANGOLI N
DEERSKI N	FRAULEI N	*HOMESPU N	MAGICIA N	*PANHUMA N
DELATIO N	FREEBOR N	HOMETOW N	MAGNETO N	PANNIKI N
DELETIO N	FREEDMA N	HOMINIA N	MAINTAI N	PANTHEO N
DELUSIO N	*FRESHMA N	HONEYBU N	MANDARI N	PAPILLO N
*DEMIJOH N	FRICTIO N	HOOLIGA N	MANDOLI N	*PARAFFI N
DEMONIA N	*FRIGHTE N	HORSEMA N	MANNIKI N	PARTISA N
DEMOTIO N	FRUITIO N	HOTELMA N	MARATHO N	*PARTIZA N
DERISIO N	FUGLEMA N	HOUSEMA N	MARGARI N	PARVOLI N
DEUTERO N	FUNCTIO N	*HYALOGE N	*MARKDOW N	PATHOGE N
*DEVILKI N	*FUNNYMA N	*HYDROGE N	MARKSMA N	*PATTYPA N
DEVOTIO N	FURFURA N	*HYPOGEA N	MARTAGO N	PAULDRO N
DIAPASO N	GAMBESO N	*HYPOPYO N	*MARZIPA N	PAVILIO N
DIELDRI N	GANGLIO N	*JERRICA N	MASTODO N	PEARMAI N
DIHEDRO N	GARRISO N	*JERRYCA N	MELANIA N	*PEMMICA N
DILATIO N	GELATIO N	*JETTISO N	MELODEO N	PENTAGO N
DILUTIO N	GLASSMA N	*JUNCTIO N	MENHADE N	PENTOSA N
DILUVIA N	GLOBULI N	KAISERI N	MERIDIA N	PEREGRI N
DILUVIO N	GLUCAGO N	*KARYOTI N	MESOTRO N	PETITIO N
DIOBOLO N	GLUTELI N	KENOTRO N	*METAZOA N	*PHENAZI N
DIOCESA N	GLYCERI N	*KEPHALI N	*METAZOO N	*PHOSPHI N
DIOLEFI N	*GLYCOGE N	*KHAMSEE N	METHADO N	*PHTHALI N
DIPTERA N	GNATHIO N	*KLYSTRO N	*MEZEREO N	PICAROO N
DIPTERO N	GOATSKI N	*LAMBSKI N	MISLEAR N	*PITCHMA N
DISCROW N	GOMBROO N	LANDSMA N	MISUNIO N	PLACEMA N
DISTRAI N	GONFALO N	LANGSHA N	MOCCASI N	PLANKTO N
DISUNIO N	GONFANO N	LANTHOR N	MOLESKI N	PLANTAI N
DIVISIO N	GORGERI N	LARRIGA N	MONECIA N	PLASTRO N
DOMINIO N	GOWNSMA N	LARRIKI N	MONITIO N	*PLAYDOW N
DONATIO N	GRANDSO N	LAVATIO N	MORTMAI N	PLEBEIA N
DOTATIO N	GRAVAME N	*LAXATIO N	MOTORMA N	PLECTRO N
DOUBLOO N	GRAVITO N	*LAYWOMA N	*MOUFFLO N	PLEUSTO N
DOWNTUR N	GRIDIRO N	LEADSMA N	MOUNTAI N	POINTMA N
*DRAWDOW N	GROSCHE N	LEATHER N	MULLIGA N	POLTROO N
DRIFTPI N	GUANIDI N	LECITHI N	MUNITIO N	*POLYZOA N
DURATIO N	GUARDIA N	LEGATIO N	MUSICIA N	POSITIO N
DYNATRO N	GUMPTIO N	LENGTHE N	MUTATIO N	POSITRO N
*DUTCHMA N	GYPSEIA N	LEWISSO N	*MUTCHKI N	POTATIO N
*FACEDOW N	GYRATIO N	LIBATIO N	*MYRMIDO N	*POZZOLA N
*FALCHIO N	HAEMATI N	LICHENI N	NAPOLEO N	PRECLEA N
FANFARO N	HALATIO N	LIEGEMA N	NATATIO N	*PREHUMA N
FAVONIA N	*HANDSEW N	LIGATIO N	NEGATIO N	PRENOME N
FERRITI N	*HANDYMA N	LIMEKIL N	NEGATRO N	PRESSMA N
*FERRYMA N	HARRIDA N	*LINCHPI N	*NEOMYCI N	PRESSRU N
FETATIO N	*HAWTHOR N	LINESMA N	*NEURAXO N	PREUNIO N
FINESPU N	HEADSMA N	LINKSMA N	NIGROSI N	PRIAPEA N
*FINICKI N	*HEIGHTE N	LOBATIO N	NINETEE N	*PROCHAI N
*FIXATIO N	*HELMSMA N	LOCATIO N	NITROGE N	*PROCHEI N
*FLASHGU N	HEMATEI N	LOCUTIO N	NOBLEMA N	PROLAMI N
FLATIRO N	*HENCHMA N	LOGICIA N	NONGREE N	*PROPYLO N
FLECTIO N	*HENEQUE N	LONGERO N	NONHUMA N	PROTAMI N
FOILSMA N	*HENEQUI N	LONGHOR N	NONPAGA N	PROUNIO N
FOOTWOR N	*HENIQUE N	*LOOKDOW N	NONUNIO N	PUBLICA N
FORENOO N	HEPTAGO N	LOVELOR N	NONURBA N	*PUNCHEO N
*FORESKI N	HERDSMA N	LUNARIA N	NONWOVE N	PUNITIO N
FOREWAR N	HEREUPO N	LUNATIO N	NORTHER N	PUPATIO N
FOREWOR N	*HIGHBOR N	LUNCHEO N	NOTATIO N	PURPURI N
FORMALI N	HIMATIO N	LUTEOLI N	NOUMENO N	*PUSHDOW N
*FOUGHTE N	HISTAMI N	*LUXATIO N	NUTATIO N	*QIOMTAI N
FOUNTAI N	HISTIDI N		NUTBROW N	*QUADROO N

*QUARTER N	ROUTEMA N	SONARMA N	TALESMA N	TURBOFA N
*QUATRAI N	SAFRANI N	SORPTIO N	TALISMA N	TURNDOW N
*QUESTIO N	SAINFOI N	SOUTHER N	TALLYMA N	TWINBOR N
*QUINOLI N	SALESMA N	SOUTHRO N	TARLATA N	VACATIO N
RADIOMA N	SANCTIO N	SPACEMA N	TARLETA N	VALERIA N
RAFTSMA N	SANTONI N	SPALPEE N	TARRAGO N	VANILLI N
RAMBUTA N	SAUCEPA N	SPEARMA N	*TAXATIO N	VENATIO N
*RAMEQUI N	SCALEPA N	SPECIME N	TEARDOW N	VENETIA N
RAMSHOR N	SCALLIO N	SPELAEA N	TEASPOO N	VERATRI N
*RANCHMA N	SCANSIO N	SPILIKI N	TELETHO N	VERBOTE N
RATAPLA N	*SCARFPI N	SPITTOO N	TERRAPI N	VERSEMA N
REACTIO N	SCISSIO N	SPONSIO N	TETRAGO N	VESUVIA N
REASSIG N	SCORPIO N	SPONTOO N	THEREMI N	*VEXATIO N
REATTAI N	SCULLIO N	*SQUADRO N	THERMIO N	*VIOMYCI N
*REAWAKE N	SEALSKI N	*SQUIREE N	THESPIA N	VIRIDIA N
REBUTTO N	SEATRAI N	STALLIO N	*THINDOW N	VITELLI N
RECISIO N	SECRETI N	STASIMO N	*THIOPHE N	VOCATIO N
REDESIG N	SEDATIO N	STEAPSI N	THIRTEE N	VOLITIO N
REFASTE N	SEDITIO N	STEGODO N	THOLEPI N	VOLUTIO N
REHARDE N	SEEDSMA N	STERNSO N	THREATE N	WANNIGA N
REINSMA N	*SHADCHA N	*STICKMA N	*THROMBI N	WARFARI N
RELATIO N	SHAGREE N	*STICKPI N	*THUMBKI N	*WATCHMA N
RELIGIO N	SHALLOO N	STILLMA N	*THYROXI N	WATERMA N
REMOTIO N	*SHEEPMA N	*STOCKMA N	TIMEWOR N	*WEIGHMA N
REOBTAI N	SHOEHOR N	STRAITE N	TOBOGGA N	WELLBOR N
REORDAI N	*SHOPWOR N	STRICKE N	TOILWOR N	*WHALEMA N
REPLEVI N	*SHOWDOW N	STRUCKE N	TOLUIDI N	*WHEELMA N
RESCREE N	*SHRUNKE N	STUBBOR N	TOWNSMA N	WHORESO N
RESORCI N	*SHUTDOW N	STURGEO N	*TRACKMA N	WINDBUR N
RESTRAI N	*SHWANPA N	*SUBHUMA N	TRACTIO N	*WINESKI N
RESUMMO N	SIDESPI N	SUBURBA N	TRAGOPA N	WINGSPA N
REVISIO N	SIMOLEO N	SUDATIO N	TRAINMA N	WOODSMA N
RHODAMI N	SIRENIA N	SUPERMA N	TRAPPEA N	*WOOLSKI N
RIFLEMA N	SKELETO N	*SUZERAI N	TRASHMA N	*XANTHEI N
RIGADOO N	SLATTER N	*SWANSKI N	TRILLIO N	*YACHTMA N
RIGAUDO N	*SLOWDOW N	SWORDMA N	TRIMARA N	*YATAGHA N
RIPARIA N	SMIDGEO N	*SYRPHIA N	*TRUCKMA N	YESTREE N
ROENTGE N	SMOOTHE N	TACITUR N	TRUDGEO N	*ZEPPELI N
ROGATIO N	SOLATIO N	TAILSPI N	TRUEBOR N	*ZONATIO N
ROSARIA N	SOLUTIO N	*TAKEDOW N	TRUNNIO N	
ROTATIO N	*SOMEWHE N	TALAPOI N	TUNGSTE N	

P

PACA	PANE	PATH	PEEN	PERM
PACE	PANG	PATY	PEEP	PERT
PACK	PANT	PAVE	PEER	PESO
PACT	PAPA	PAWL	PEIN	PEST
PAGE	PARA	PAWN	**PEKE**	PHAT
PAID	PARD	PEAG	PELE	**PHEW**
PAIK	PARE	**PEAK**	PELF	*PHIZ
PAIL	**PARK**	PEAL	PELT	PHON
PAIN	PARR	PEAN	PEND	PHOT
PAIR	PART	PEAR	PENT	PIAL
PALE	PASE	PEAT	PEON	PIAN
PALL	PASH	**PECH**	PEPO	PICA
PALM	PASS	**PECK**	PERE	PICE
PALP	PAST	**PEEK**	PERI	**PICK**
PALY	PATE	PEEL	**PERK**	PIED

PIER	POOR	PADLE	**PAVER**	**PHONY**
PIKA	POPE	PADRE	**PAVID**	**PHOTO**
PIKE	PORE	PAEAN	**PAVIN**	*PHPHT
PILE	**PORK**	PAEON	**PAVIS**	**PHYLA**
PILI	PORN	PAGAN	**PAWER**	**PHYLE**
PILL	PORT	PAGED	*PAWKY	PIANO
PILY	POSE	PAGOD	**PAYEE**	PICAL
PIMA	POSH	PAINT	**PAYER**	*PICKY
PIMP	POST	PAISA	**PAYOR**	PICOT
PINA	POSY	PAISE	PEACE	PICUL
PINE	POUF	PALEA	**PEACH**	PIECE
PING	POUR	PALER	PEAGE	PIETA
PINK	POUT	PALET	**PEAKY**	PIETY
PINT	PRAM	**PALLY**	PEARL	**PIGGY**
PINY	PRAO	**PALMY**	PEART	**PIGMY**
PION	PRAT	**PALSY**	PEASE	**PIKER**
PIPE	PRAU	**PAMPA**	**PEATY**	PILAF
PIPY	PRAY	**PANDA**	**PEAVY**	PILAR
PIRN	PREE	**PANDY**	PECAN	PILAU
PISH	PREP	PANEL	*PECKY	**PILAW**
PISS	**PREX**	PANGA	PEDAL	PILEA
PITA	PREY	PANIC	PEDES	PILED
PITH	PRIG	PANNE	PEDRO	PILEI
PITY	PRIM	**PANSY**	**PEERY**	PILOT
*PIXY	PROA	**PANTY**	**PEEVE**	PILUS
PLAN	PROD	PAPAL	PEISE	**PINCH**
PLAT	PROF	**PAPAW**	**PEKAN**	PINED
PLAY	PROG	PAPER	**PEKIN**	**PINEY**
PLEA	PROM	**PAPPI**	**PEKOE**	PINGO
PLEB	PROP	**PAPPY**	PELON	**PINKO**
PLED	PROW	**PARCH**	PENAL	**PINKY**
PLIE	PSST	PARDI	PENCE	PINNA
PLOD	PUCE	**PARDY**	PENES	PINON
PLOP	**PUCK**	PARER	PENGO	PINTA
PLOT	**PUFF**	PAREU	PENIS	PINTO
PLOW	**PUGH**	PARGE	PENNA	PINUP
PLOY	**PUKE**	PARGO	PENNI	PIOUS
PLUG	PULE	PARIS	**PENNY**	PIPAL
PLUM	PULI	**PARKA**	**PEONY**	PIPER
PLUS	PULL	PARLE	**PEPPY**	PIPET
POCK	PULP	PAROL	**PERCH**	PIPIT
POCO	PUMA	**PARRY**	PERDU	*PIQUE
POEM	**PUMP**	PARSE	**PERDY**	PIROG
POET	PUNA	**PARTY**	PERIL	**PITCH**
POGY	PUNG	**PARVE**	**PERKY**	**PITHY**
POKE	**PUNK**	PASEO	**PERRY**	PITON
POKY	PUNT	**PASHA**	PERSE	**PIVOT**
POLE	PUNY	PASSE	**PESKY**	**PIXIE**
POLL	PUPA	PASTA	PETAL	*PIZZA
POLO	PURE	PASTE	PETER	PLACE
POLY	PURI	**PASTY**	PETIT	**PLACK**
POME	PURL	**PASTY**	PETTI	**PLAGE**
POMP	PURR	**PATCH**	PETTO	PLAID
POND	PUSH	PATEN	**PETTY**	PLAIN
PONE	PUSS	PATER	PEWEE	PLAIT
PONS	PUTT	PATIN	PEWIT	PLANE
PONY	**PYIC**	PATIO	**PHAGE**	**PLANK**
POOD	PYIN	**PATLY**	**PHASE**	PLANT
POOH	PYRE	**PATSY**	PHIAL	**PLASH**
POOL	PACER	**PATTY**	*PHLOX	PLASM
POON	**PACHA**	PAUSE	**PHONE**	PLATE
POOP	**PADDY**	PAVAN	**PHONO**	**PLATY**

PLATY	PRAAM	*PUFFY	PALMAR	PARURE
PLAYA	PRAHU	PUGGY	PALMER	PARVIS
*PLAZA	PRANG	*PUKKA	PALPAL	PASSEE
PLEAD	PRANK	PULER	PALPUS	PASSEL
PLEAT	PRASE	PULIK	PALTER	PASSER
PLEBE	PRATE	PULPY	PALTRY	PASSIM
PLENA	PRAWN	PULSE	PAMPER	PASSUS
PLICA	PREEN	PUNCH	PANADA	PASTEL
PLIED	PRESA	PUNKA	PANAMA	PASTER
PLIER	PRESE	PUNKY	PANDER	PASTIL
PLIES	PRESS	PUNNY	PANDIT	PASTOR
PLINK	PREST	PUNTO	PANFUL	PASTRY
PLONK	*PREXY	PUNTY	PANGEN	PATACA
PLUCK	PRICE	PUPIL	PANIER	*PATCHY
PLUMB	PRICK	PUPPY	PANNED	PATENT
PLUME	PRICY	PURDA	PANTIE	PATHOS
PLUMP	PRIDE	PUREE	PANTRY	PATINA
PLUMY	PRIED	PURER	*PANZER	PATINE
PLUNK	PRIER	PURGE	*PAPACY	PATOIS
PLUSH	PRIES	PURIN	PAPAIN	PATROL
PLYER	PRILL	PURSE	PAPAYA	PATRON
POACH	PRIMA	PURSY	PAPERY	PATTED
*POCKY	PRIME	PUSHY	PAPIST	PATTEE
PODGY	PRIMI	PUSSY	PAPPUS	PATTEN
PODIA	PRIMO	PUTON	PAPULA	PATTER
POESY	PRIMP	PUTTY	PAPULE	PATTIE
POGEY	PRINK	*PYGMY	PARADE	PAULIN
POILU	PRINT	PYLON	PARANG	PAUNCH
POIND	PRIOR	PYOID	PARAPH	PAUPER
POINT	PRISE	PYRAN	PARCEL	PAUSAL
POISE	PRISM	PYRIC	PARDAH	PAUSER
POKER	PRISS	*PYXIE	PARDEE	PAVANE
POKEY	PRIVY	*PYXIS	PARDIE	PAVING
POLAR	*PRIZE	*PACIFY	PARDON	PAVIOR
POLED	PROBE	PACING	PARENT	PAVISE
POLER	PROEM	PACKER	PARIAH	PAWNEE
POLIO	PROLE	PACKET	PARIAN	PAWNER
POLIS	PRONE	*PACKLY	PARIES	PAWNOR
POLKA	PRONG	PADAUK	PARING	*PAWPAW
POLYP	PROOF	PADDLE	PARISH	*PAXWAX
PONCE	PROSE	PADNAG	PARITY	*PAYDAY
POOCH	PROSO	PADOUK	PARKER	PAYNIM
POORI	PROST	PAELLA	PARLAY	*PAYOFF
POPPA	PROSY	PAGING	PARLEY	PAYOLA
POPPY	PROUD	PAGODA	PARLOR	*PEACHY
PORCH	PROVE	PAINCH	PAROLE	PEAHEN
PORGY	PROWL	PAINTY	PAROUS	PEANUT
PORKY	*PROXY	PAISAN	PARRAL	PEARLY
PORNO	PRUDE	*PAJAMA	PARRED	PEAVEY
POSER	PRUNE	PALACE	PARREL	PEBBLE
POSIT	PRUTA	PALAIS	PARROT	*PEBBLY
POSSE	PRYER	PALATE	PARSEC	PECHAN
POTSY	PSALM	PALELY	PARSER	PECKER
POTTO	PSHAW	PALEST	PARSON	PECTEN
POTTY	PSOAS	PALIER	PARTAN	PECTIN
POUCH	*PSYCH	PALING	PARTLY	PEDANT
POUFF	PUBES	PALISH	PARTON	PEDATE
POULT	PUBIC	PALLED	PARURA	PEDDLE
POUND	PUBIS	PALLET	PARURA	PEDLAR
POUTY	PUCKA	PALLIA		PEDLER
POWER	PUDGY	PALLID		PEELER
POYOU	PUDIC	PALLOR		PEEPER

PEEPUL	PHASIS	PILLAR	PLANER	POLITE
PEERIE	PHATIC	**PILLOW**	PLANET	**POLITY**
PEEWEE	*PHENIX	PILOSE	*PLAQUE	POLLEE
PEEWIT	PHENOL	PILOUS	**PLASHY**	POLLEN
*PEGBOX	**PHENOM**	PILULE	**PLASMA**	POLLER
PEGGED	PHENYL	**PIMPLE**	PLATAN	*POLLEX
PELAGE	**PHLEGM**	*PIMPLY	PLATED	POLYPI
PELITE	PHLOEM	PINANG	PLATEN	POMACE
PELLET	PHOBIA	PINATA	PLATER	POMADE
PELOTA	PHOEBE	PINCER	**PLAYER**	POMELO
PELTER	PHONAL	PINDER	PLEACH	POMMEE
PELTRY	PHONEY	PINEAL	PLEASE	POMMEL
PELVIC	PHONIC	PINENE	PLEDGE	POMPOM
PELVIS	PHONON	**PINERY**	PLEIAD	POMPON
PENANG	**PHOOEY**	PINGER	**PLENTY**	PONCHO
PENCEL	PHOTIC	PINIER	**PLENUM**	PONDER
PENCIL	PHOTOG	PINING	PLEURA	PONENT
PENMAN	PHOTON	PINION	PLIANT	PONGEE
PENNED	PHRASE	PINITE	**PLIGHT**	PONGID
PENNER	PHYLAE	**PINKIE**	PLINTH	PONIED
PENNON	PHYLAR	PINNAE	*PLISKY	PONIES
PENSEE	PHYLON	PINNAL	PLISSE	PONTIL
PENSIL	*PHYLUM	PINNED	**PLOIDY**	PONTON
PENTAD	PHYSES	PINNER	**PLOTTY**	POODLE
PENTYL	*PHYSIC	PINOLE	**PLOUGH**	**POORLY**
PENULT	PHYSIS	PINTLE	**PLOVER**	POPERY
PENURY	PHYTIN	PINYON	**PLOWER**	POPGUN
PEOPLE	PHYTON	PIOLET	*PLUCKY	POPISH
PEPLOS	PIAFFE	**PIPAGE**	*PLUMMY	POPLAR
PEPLUM	*PIAZZA	PIPIER	PLUNGE	POPLIN
PEPLUS	PICARA	**PIPING**	PLURAL	POPPED
PEPPED	PICARO	PIPKIN	**PLUSHY**	POPPER
PEPPER	*PICKAX	PIPPED	PLUTON	POPPET
PEPSIN	PICKER	PIPPIN	PNEUMA	POPPLE
PEPTIC	PICKET	*PIQUET	*POACHY	PORISM
PEPTID	PICKLE	PIRACY	**POCKET**	PORKER
PERDIE	*PICKUP	PIRANA	PODITE	POROSE
PERDUE	PICNIC	PIRATE	**PODIUM**	POROUS
PERIOD	PICRIC	PIRAYA	PODSOL	PORTAL
PERISH	PIDDLE	PISTIL	*PODZOL	PORTER
PERMIT	PIDGIN	PISTOL	**POETIC**	**PORTLY**
PERRON	PIECER	PISTON	**POETRY**	POSADA
PERSON	PIEING	*PITCHY	POGIES	POSEUR
PERUKE	PIERCE	PITIED	POGROM	POSIES
PERUSE	PIFFLE	PITIER	POINTE	POSING
PESADE	PIGEON	PITIES	**POINTY**	POSSET
PESETA	PIGGED	**PITMAN**	POISER	**POSSUM**
PESEWA	PIGGIE	PITSAW	POISON	POSTAL
PESTER	PIGGIN	PITTED	POKIER	POSTER
PESTLE	PIGLET	*PIZAZZ	POKIES	POSTIN
PETARD	PIGNUS	*PIZZLE	*POKILY	POTAGE
PETITE	PIGNUT	PLACER	POKING	**POTASH**
PETREL	PIGPEN	PLACET	POLDER	POTATO
PETROL	PIGSTY	PLACID	POLEIS	POTBOY
PETTED	*PIKAKE	PLAGAL	POLEYN	POTEEN
PETTER	PIKING	PLAGUE	POLICE	POTENT
PETTLE	PILAFF	PLAGUY	**POLICY**	POTFUL
PEWTER	PILEUM	PLAICE	POLING	POTHER
PEYOTE	PILEUP	PLAINT	**POLISH**	POTION
PEYOTL	PILEUS	PLANAR		POTMAN
PHALLI	PILFER	PLANCH		POTPIE
PHAROS	PILING			POTSIE

POTTED	PROMPT	PUPPET	*PAHLAVI	PAPRICA
POTTER	PRONTO	PURANA	PAILFUL	*PAPRIKA
POTTLE	PROPEL	PURDAH	PAINFUL	PAPYRUS
*POUCHY	PROPER	PURELY	PAINTER	PARABLE
POUFFE	PROPYL	PUREST	PAISANO	PARADER
POUNCE	PROSER	PURFLE	PAISLEY	PARADOS
POURER	PROSIT	PURGER	PALABRA	*PARADOX
POUTER	PROTEA	PURIFY	PALADIN	PARAGON
POWDER	PROTEI	PURINE	PALATAL	PARAPET
POWTER	PROTON	PURISM	PALAVER	PARASOL
*POWWOW	PROTYL	PURIST	*PALAZZO	PARBOIL
PRAISE	PROVER	PURITY	PALETOT	PARDINE
PRANCE	PROWAR	PURLIN	PALETTE	PARDNER
PRATER	PRUNER	PURPLE	*PALFREY	PAREIRA
*PRAXIS	PRUTAH	PURPLY	PALIEST	PARESIS
PRAYER	PSEUDO	PURRED	PALIKAR	PARETIC
PREACH	PSOCID	PURSER	PALLIAL	PARFAIT
PREACT	*PSYCHE	PURSUE	PALLIER	PARKING
PREAMP	*PSYCHO	PURVEY	PALLING	*PARKWAY
PREARM	PSYLLA	PUSHER	PALLIUM	PARLING
PRECIS	PTERIN	PUSHUP	PALMARY	PARLOUR
PREFAB	PTISAN	PUSLEY	PALMATE	PARLOUS
PREFER	PTOSIS	PUSSLY	PALMIER	PARODIC
*PREFIX	PUBLIC	PUTLOG	PALMIST	PARODOS
PRELIM	PUCKER	PUTOFF	PALMYRA	PAROLEE
PREMAN	PUDDLE	PUTOUT	PALOOKA	PARONYM
PREMED	PUDDLY	PUTRID	PALPATE	PAROTIC
PREMEN	PUEBLO	PUTSCH	PALUDAL	PAROTID
PREMIE	PUFFER	PUTTEE	PAMPEAN	*PARQUET
*PREMIX	PUFFIN	PUTTER	PAMPERO	PARRIED
PREPAY	PUGGED	*PUZZLE	PANACEA	PARRIES
PRESET	PUGGRY	PYEMIA	PANACHE	PARRING
PRESTO	PUGREE	*PYKNIC	*PANCAKE	PARROTY
*PRETAX	PUISNE	PYOSIS	*PANCHAX	PARSING
PRETOR	PULING	PYRENE	PANDECT	PARSLEY
PRETTY	PULLER	PYRITE	PANDIED	PARSNIP
PREVUE	PULLET	PYROLA	PANDIES	PARTAKE
PREWAR	PULLEY	PYRONE	PANDOOR	PARTIAL
PREYER	PULPAL	PYROPE	PANDORA	PARTIED
PRIAPI	PULPER	PYRROL	PANDORE	PARTIES
PRICER	PULPIT	PYTHON	PANDOUR	PARTING
PRICEY	*PULQUE	PYURIA	PANDURA	PARTITA
*PRICKY	PULSAR	PABULUM	*PANFISH	PARTITE
PRIEST	PULSER	PACHISI	*PANICKY	PARTLET
PRIMAL	PUMELO	*PACHUCO	PANICLE	PARTNER
PRIMER	PUMICE	*PACIFIC	PANICUM	PARTOOK
PRIMLY	PUMMEL	*PACKAGE	PANNIER	*PARTWAY
PRIMUS	PUMPER	*PACKING	PANNING	PARVENU
PRINCE	*PUNCHY	*PACKMAN	PANOCHA	PARVISE
PRIORY	PUNDIT	*PACKWAX	PANOCHE	PASCHAL
PRISON	PUNIER	PACTION	PANOPLY	*PASQUIL
PRISSY	PUNILY	PADDIES	PANPIPE	PASSADE
PRIVET	PUNISH	PADDING	PANTHER	PASSADO
*PRIZER	*PUNKAH	PADDLER	PANTIES	PASSAGE
PROBER	*PUNKEY	*PADDOCK	PANTILE	PASSANT
PROBIT	PUNKIE	*PADLOCK	PANTOUM	PASSING
PROFIT	PUNKIN	PADRONE	PAPERER	PASSION
*PROJET	PUNNED	*PADSHAH	PAPHIAN	PASSIVE
PROLAN	PUNNER	PAGEANT	PAPILLA	*PASSKEY
PROLEG	PUNTER	*PAGEBOY	PAPOOSE	PASTERN
*PROLIX	PUPATE	PAGINAL	PAPPIER	PASTIER
PROLOG	PUPPED	PAGURID	PAPPIES	PASTIES

PASTIME	PELTAST	PERLITE	PIANISM	PINHOLE
PASTINA	PELTATE	**PERMUTE**	PIANIST	PINIEST
PASTING	**PEMBINA**	PERORAL	**PIASABA**	*PINKEYE
PASTURE	**PEMICAN**	*PEROXID	**PIASAVA**	PINKIES
PATAMAR	*PEMPHIX	PERPEND	PIASTER	PINKING
PATCHER	PENALLY	PERPENT	PIASTRE	*PINKISH
PATELLA	**PENALTY**	*PERPLEX	*PIBROCH	PINNACE
PATENCY	PENANCE	PERSALT	*PICACHO	PINNATE
*PATHWAY	PENATES	PERSIST	**PICADOR**	PINNING
PATIENT	PENDANT	PERSONA	PICCOLO	PINNULA
PATNESS	PENDENT	PERSONA	PICEOUS	PINNULE
PATRIOT	PENGUIN	PERTAIN	*PICKAXE	PINOCLE
PATROON	PENICIL	PERTURB	*PICKEER	PINTADA
PATTERN	PENLITE	PERUSAL	*PICKIER	PINTADO
PATTING	**PENNAME**	PERUSER	**PICKING**	PINTAIL
PAUCITY	PENNANT	PERVADE	*PICKOFF	PINTANO
*PAUGHTY	PENNATE	PERVERT	PICOLIN	PINWALE
*PAUNCHY	PENNIES	PESSARY	PICOTEE	PINWEED
PAVIOUR	PENNINE	PETASOS	*PICQUET	*PINWORK
PAVISER	PENNING	PETASUS	PICRATE	PINWORM
PAWNAGE	PENOCHE	*PETCOCK	PICRITE	PIONEER
PAYABLE	PENSILE	PETIOLE	PICTURE	PIOSITY
PAYLOAD	PENSION	*PETRIFY	PIDDLER	PIPEAGE
PAYMENT	PENSIVE	PETROUS	*PIDDOCK	PIPEFUL
PAYROLL	PENSTER	PETTIER	PIEBALD	PIPETTE
PEACHER	PENTANE	PETTILY	PIECING	PIPIEST
PEACING	PENTOSE	PETTING	PIEFORT	PIPPING
PEACOAT	PENUCHE	PETTISH	PIERCER	*PIQUANT
*PEACOCK	PENUCHI	PETUNIA	PIERROT	PIRAGUA
*PEAFOWL	PEONAGE	PEYTRAL	PIETIES	PIRANHA
PEAKIER	PEONISM	PEYTREL	PIETISM	PIRATIC
*PEAKISH	PEOPLER	PFENNIG	PIETIST	PIROGUE
PEALIKE	*PEPPERY	PHAETON	PIGBOAT	*PIROQUE
PEARLER	PEPPING	*PHALANX	*PIGFISH	PISCARY
PEASANT	PEPSINE	PHALLIC	PIGGERY	PISCINA
PEASCOD	PEPTIDE	PHALLUS	PIGGIES	PISCINE
PECCANT	*PEPTIZE	PHANTOM	PIGGING	PISMIRE
*PECCARY	PEPTONE	*PHARAOH	PIGGISH	PISSANT
*PECCAVI	PERACID	*PHARYNX	PIGMENT	PISSOIR
PECTASE	PERCALE	*PHASMID	PIGSKIN	PISTOLE
PECTATE	PERCENT	PHELLEM	PIGSNEY	PITAPAT
*PECTIZE	PERCEPT	PHILTER	PIGWEED	PITCHER
PEDAGOG	PERCHER	PHILTRE	*PIKEMAN	PITEOUS
PEDDLER	PERCOID	*PHLEGMY	PILEATE	PITFALL
PEDICAB	PERCUSS	PHOCINE	PILEOUS	PITHEAD
PEDICEL	PERFECT	*PHOENIX	PILGRIM	PITIFUL
PEDICLE	*PERFIDY	PHONATE	PILLAGE	PITTING
PEDLARY	PERFORM	PHONEME	*PILLBOX	PIVOTAL
PEDOCAL	PERFUME	PHONICS	PILLION	PLACARD
PEEBEEN	PERFUSE	PHONIER	PILLORY	PLACATE
PEELING	PERGOLA	PHONIES	*PILLOWY	PLACEBO
PEERAGE	PERHAPS	*PHONILY	PILSNER	PLACING
PEERESS	PERIAPT	PHONING	PIMENTO	*PLACKET
*PEEVISH	PERIDOT	PHORATE	PINBALL	PLACOID
PEGGING	PERIGEE	PHOTICS	PINBONE	PLAFOND
PEGLESS	PERIGON	PHRASAL	PINCHER	PLAGUER
PEGLIKE	PERILLA	*PHRATRY	PINESAP	PLAGUEY
PELAGIC	*PERIQUE	PHRENIC	PINETUM	PLAITER
PELICAN	PERIWIG	*PHRENSY	*PINFISH	PLANATE
PELISSE	*PERJURE	*PHYTANE	PINFOLD	PLANCHE
PELORIA	*PERJURY	*PHYTOID	PINGUID	PLANING
PELORUS	*PERKISH	*PIAFFER	PINHEAD	PLANISH

PLANNED	PLUMIER	POPULAR	PRAWNER	PRETEEN
PLANNER	PLUMING	PORCINE	*PREACHY	PRETEND
PLANTAR	PLUMMET	PORKIER	PREAGED	PRETEST
PLANULA	PLUMOSE	PORKIES	PREANAL	*PRETEXT
PLASHER	PLUMPEN	*PORKPIE	PREAVER	*PRETZEL
PLASMID	PLUMPER	PORRECT	PREBEND	PREVAIL
PLASMIN	*PLUMPLY	PORTAGE	PREBILL	PREVENT
PLASMON	PLUMULE	PORTEND	PREBIND	*PREVIEW
PLASTER	PLUNDER	PORTENT	PREBOIL	PREVISE
PLASTIC	PLUNGER	PORTICO	PRECAST	PREWARM
PLASTID	PLUNKER	PORTION	PRECAVA	PREWARN
PLATANE	PLUSSES	PORTRAY	PRECEDE	*PREWASH
PLATEAU	PLUVIAL	POSSESS	PRECENT	PREWRAP
PLATIER	*PLYWOOD	POSTAGE	PRECEPT	PRIAPIC
PLATIES	POACHER	POSTBAG	PRECESS	PRIAPUS
PLATINA	*POCHARD	*POSTBOX	PRECIPE	PRICIER
PLATING	POCOSIN	POSTBOY	PRECISE	*PRICKER
PLATOON	PODAGRA	POSTEEN	*PRECOOK	*PRICKET
PLATTED	PODESTA	POSTERN	PRECOOL	*PRICKLE
PLATTER	POETESS	*POSTFIX	PRECURE	*PRICKLY
PLAUDIT	POETICS	POSTING	PREDATE	*PRIMACY
PLAYACT	POETISE	POSTMAN	PREDAWN	PRIMAGE
*PLAYBOY	*POETIZE	POSTURE	PREDIAL	PRIMARY
*PLAYDAY	POGONIA	POSTWAR	PREDICT	PRIMATE
*PLAYFUL	POGONIP	POTABLE	PREDUSK	PRIMELY
PLAYLET	POINTER	POTAMIC	PREEMIE	PRIMERO
*PLAYOFF	POITREL	POTBOIL	PREEMPT	PRIMINE
PLAYPEN	POKIEST	POTENCE	PREENER	PRIMING
PLEADER	POLARON	POTENCY	PREFACE	PRIMMED
PLEASER	*POLEAXE	POTHEAD	PREFECT	PRIMMER
PLEATER	POLECAT	POTHEEN	PREFORM	PRIMSIE
PLEDGEE	POLEMIC	POTHERB	PREGAME	PRIMULA
PLEDGER	POLENTA	POTHOLE	PREHEAT	*PRINCOX
PLEDGET	POLITIC	*POTHOOK	PRELACY	PRINKER
PLEDGOR	*POLLACK	POTICHE	PRELATE	PRINTER
PLENARY	POLLARD	POTLACH	PRELECT	PRIORLY
PLENISH	POLLIST	POTLIKE	PRELUDE	PRISERE
PLENISM	*POLLOCK	*POTLUCK	PREMIER	*PRITHEE
PLENIST	POLLUTE	POTSHOT	PREMISE	*PRIVACY
PLEOPOD	POLOIST	POTTEEN	PREMISS	PRIVATE
PLESSOR	POLYCOT	POTTAGE	PREMIUM	PRIVIER
PLEURON	POLYENE	POTTERY	PREMUNE	PRIVIES
PLIABLE	POLYGON	POTTIER	PRENAME	*PRIVITY
PLIANCY	POLYMER	POTTIES	*PREPACK	PROBAND
PLICATE	*POLYNYA	POTTING	PREPAID	PROBANG
PLIMSOL	*POLYPOD	POULARD	PREPARE	PROBATE
PLINKER	POLYPUS	POULTRY	PREPLAN	PROBITY
PLISKIE	POMATUM	POUNCER	PREPPED	PROBLEM
PLODDER	POMPANO	POUNDAL	PREPPIE	PROCARP
PLOSION	POMPOUS	POUNDER	PREPUCE	PROCEED
PLOSIVE	PONIARD	POUSSIE	PRESAGE	PROCESS
PLOTTED	*PONTIFF	POUTFUL	PRESELL	PROCTOR
PLOTTER	PONTINE	*POVERTY	PRESENT	PROCURE
*PLOWBOY	PONTOON	*POWDERY	*PRESHOW	PRODDER
PLOWMAN	POORISH	PRACTIC	PRESIDE	PRODIGY
*PLUCKER	POPCORN	PRAETOR	PRESIFT	PRODUCE
PLUGGER	POPEDOM	PRAIRIE	PRESOAK	PRODUCT
PLUMAGE	*POPEYED	PRAISER	PRESOLD	PROETTE
PLUMATE	POPOVER	PRALINE	PRESSER	PROFANE
PLUMBER	POPPIED	PRANCER	PRESSOR	PROFESS
*PLUMBIC	POPPIES	PRATING	PRESTER	*PROFFER
*PLUMBUM	POPPING	PRATTLE	PRESUME	

PROFILE	PSALTER	PUSHPIN	PALMATED	PARASITE
PROFUSE	PSALTRY	PUSSIER	PALMETTE	PARAVANE
PROGENY	PSCHENT	PUSSIES	PALMETTO	PARCENER
PROGGER	*PSYCHIC	PUSSLEY	PALMIEST	PARDONER
PROGRAM	PSYLLID	PUSTULE	PALMITIN	PARECISM
*PROJECT	PTERYLA	PUTAMEN	*PALMLIKE	PARENTAL
PROLATE	PTOMAIN	*PUTREFY	PALOMINO	*PARFLESH
PROLINE	PTYALIN	PUTTIED	PALPABLE	*PARFOCAL
PROLONG	PUBERTY	PUTTIER	PALPATOR	PARHELIA
PROMISE	PUBLISH	PUTTING	PALPEBRA	*PARHELIC
PROMOTE	PUCCOON	*PUZZLER	PALTERER	PARIETAL
PRONATE	*PUCKERY	PYAEMIA	PALUDISM	*PARKLAND
PRONOUN	*PUCKISH	*PYJAMAS	PAMPERER	*PARKLIKE
PROOFER	PUDDING	PYLORUS	*PAMPHLET	PARLANCE
PROPANE	PUDDLER	PYRALID	PANATELA	PARLANDO
PROPEND	PUDENCY	*PYRAMID	PANCREAS	PARLANTE
PROPENE	PUERILE	PYRETIC	PANDANUS	PARLEYER
PROPHET	*PUFFERY	*PYREXIA	*PANDEMIC	PARODIED
PROPINE	PUGAREE	PYROGEN	PANDERER	PARODIES
*PROPJET	PUGGIER	PYROSIS	*PANDOWDY	PARODIST
PROPMAN	PUGGING	*PYRRHIC	PANELING	*PAROQUET
PROPONE	PUGGISH	PYRROLE	PANELIST	PAROTOID
PROPOSE	PUGGREE	*PYXIDES	PANELLED	*PAROXYSM
PROPPED	*PUGMARK	*PACHADOM	PANETELA	PARRIDGE
PRORATE	PULLMAN	*PACHALIC	PANGOLIN	*PARRITCH
PROSAIC	PULLOUT	*PACHOULI	*PANHUMAN	PARROKET
PROSECT	PULPIER	*PACIFIED	*PANMIXIA	PARROTER
PROSIER	PULPILY	*PACIFIER	PANNIKIN	PARTAKER
PROSILY	PULPOUS	*PACIFIES	PANOPTIC	PARTERRE
PROSING	PULSANT	*PACIFISM	PANORAMA	PARTIBLE
PROSODY	PULSATE	*PACIFIST	*PANSOPHY	PARTICLE
PROSOMA	PULSING	*PACKAGER	PANTHEON	PARTISAN
PROSPER	PULSION	*PACKNESS	PANTOFLE	*PARTIZAN
PROTEAN	PUMICER	*PACKSACK	PANTSUIT	PARVENUE
PROTECT	*PUMPKIN	PADDLING	*PAPERBOY	PARVOLIN
PROTEGE	PUNCHER	*PADISHAH	PAPILLON	*PASHADOM
PROTEID	PUNGENT	PADUASOY	*PAPISTRY	*PASHALIC
PROTEIN	PUNIEST	PAEANISM	PAPPIEST	*PASHALIK
PROTEND	PUNNING	PAGANDOM	PAPPOOSE	PASSABLE
PROTEST	PUNSTER	PAGANISE	PARABOLA	PASSBAND
PROTEUS	*PUPFISH	PAGANISH	*PARACHOR	*PASSBOOK
PROTIST	PUPILAR	PAGANISM	PARADIGM	*PASSERBY
PROTIUM	PUPPING	PAGANIST	PARADING	PASSIBLE
PROTYLE	PURGING	*PAGANIZE	PARADISE	PASSLESS
PROVERB	PURITAN	PAGINATE	PARADROP	PASSOVER
PROVIDE	PURLIEU	PAGURIAN	*PARAFFIN	PASSPORT
PROVING	PURLINE	PAINLESS	*PARAFORM	PASSWORD
PROVISO	PURLOIN	PAINTING	PARAGOGE	PASTICCI
*PROVOKE	PURPORT	PALATIAL	PARAKEET	*PASTICHE
PROVOST	PURPOSE	PALATINE	*PARALLAX	PASTIEST
PROWESS	PURPURA	*PALEFACE	PARALLEL	PASTILLE
PROWLER	PURPURE	PALENESS	PARALYSE	PASTNESS
*PROXIES	PURRING	PALESTRA	*PARALYZE	PASTORAL
*PROXIMO	PURSIER	*PALEWAYS	PARAMENT	PASTRAMI
PRUDENT	PURSILY	PALEWISE	PARAMOUR	PASTROMI
PRUDERY	PURSING	PALINODE	PARANOEA	PASTURAL
PRUDISH	PURSUER	PALISADE	PARANOIA	PASTURER
PRUNING	PURSUIT	PALLADIA	PARANOID	PATAGIUM
PRURIGO	*PURVIEW	PALLADIC	*PARAQUAT	PATENTEE
PRUSSIC	*PUSHFUL	PALLETTE	*PARAQUET	PATENTLY
*PRYTHEE	PUSHIER	PALLIATE	PARASANG	PATENTOR
PSALMIC	*PUSHILY	PALLIEST	*PARASHAH	PATERNAL

*PATHETIC	PENALISE	PERVADER	*PHYSICAL	PIRARUCU
PATHLESS	PENALITY	PERVERSE	*PHYSIQUE	*PIROZHOK
PATHOGEN	*PENALIZE	PERVIOUS	PIACULAR	PISCATOR
PATIENCE	*PENCHANT	PESTERER	PIASSABA	*PISIFORM
PATTAMAR	PENCILER	PESTHOLE	PIASSAVA	PISOLITE
PATTERER	*PENDENCY	PETALINE	PICAROON	*PISTACHE
*PATTYPAN	PENDULUM	PETALODY	*PICAYUNE	*PITCHIER
PATULENT	PENITENT	PETALOID	*PICKADIL	*PITCHILY
PATULOUS	*PENKNIFE	PETALOUS	*PICKEREL	*PITCHMAN
PAULDRON	PENLIGHT	*PETECHIA	*PICKETER	*PITCHOUT
*PAVEMENT	PENNATED	PETIOLAR	*PICKIEST	PITHLESS
PAVILION	PENOLOGY	PETITION	*PICKLOCK	PITIABLE
PAVONINE	PENONCEL	PETROLIC	*PICKWICK	PITILESS
*PAWNSHOP	PENPOINT	PETRONEL	PICLORAM	PITTANCE
*PAYCHECK	PENSIONE	PETROSAL	*PICNICKY	*PIXINESS
*PEACEFUL	*PENSTOCK	PETTEDLY	*PICOGRAM	*PIZZERIA
*PEACOCKY	PENTACLE	PETTIEST	PICOLINE	PLACABLE
PEAKIEST	PENTAGON	PETTIFOG	PIECRUST	PLACATER
PEAKLESS	*PENTARCH	PETULANT	PIEDFORT	PLACEMAN
*PEAKLIKE	PENTOMIC	PETUNTSE	PIEDMONT	PLACENTA
PEARLASH	PENTOSAN	PEWTERER	PIEPLANT	PLAGIARY
PEARLITE	*PENUCHLE	PHALANGE	*PIGSTICK	PLAGUING
PEARMAIN	*PENUCKLE	*PHALLISM	PILASTER	PLAISTER
PEASECOD	PENUMBRA	PHALLIST	*PILCHARD	PLAITING
*PECCABLE	PEPERONI	*PHANTASM	PILEATED	PLANARIA
*PECCANCY	PEPONIDA	PHANTAST	PILEWORT	*PLANCHET
PECTORAL	PEPONIUM	*PHANTASY	PILFERER	*PLANFORM
PECULATE	PEPPERER	PHARISEE	*PILIFORM	PLANGENT
PECULIAR	*PEPTIZER	*PHARMACY	PILLAGER	*PLANKING
PECULIUM	*PERCEIVE	PHASEOUT	PILOSITY	PLANKTER
*PEDAGOGY	PEREGRIN	PHEASANT	PILOTAGE	PLANKTON
PEDALFER	*PERFECTA	PHELONIA	PILOTING	PLANLESS
PEDALIER	*PERFECTO	*PHENAZIN	PILSENER	PLANNING
PEDALLED	*PERFORCE	*PHENETIC	PIMIENTO	PLANOSOL
PEDANTRY	*PERFUMER	PHENETOL	PINAFORE	PLANTAIN
*PEDDLERY	PERIANTH	*PHENOLIC	PINASTER	PLANTING
PEDDLING	PERIBLEM	*PHILABEG	*PINCHBUG	PLASMOID
PEDERAST	PERICARP	*PHILIBEG	*PINCHECK	PLASTERY
PEDESTAL	PERICOPE	*PHILOMEL	PINDLING	PLASTRON
PEDICURE	PERIDERM	PHIMOSIS	PINECONE	PLASTRUM
*PEDIFORM	PERIDIUM	*PHONETIC	PINELIKE	PLATEFUL
PEDIGREE	*PERIGYNY	PHONIEST	PINEWOOD	PLATELET
PEDIMENT	PERILOUS	PHOSGENE	PINGRASS	*PLATFORM
*PEDIPALP	PERILUNE	*PHOSPHID	PINKNESS	*PLATIEST
*PEDOLOGY	PERINEUM	*PHOSPHIN	PINKROOT	PLATINIC
PEDUNCLE	PERIODIC	*PHOSPHOR	PINNACLE	PLATINUM
*PEEKABOO	PERIODID	*PHOTOMAP	PINNATED	PLATONIC
*PEEPHOLE	PERIOTIC	*PHOTOPIA	PINNIPED	PLATTING
*PEEPSHOW	*PERIPETY	PHOTOSET	*PINOCHLE	*PLATYPUS
PEERLESS	PERIPTER	PHRASING	PINPOINT	PLAUSIVE
*PEESWEEP	PERISARC	*PHREATIC	*PINPRICK	*PLAYBACK
PEETWEET	*PERJURER	*PHTHALIC	*PINSCHER	*PLAYBILL
PEGBOARD	PERLUDER	*PHTHALIN	*PINTSIZE	*PLAYBOOK
PEIGNOIR	PERMEASE	*PHTHISIC	*PINWHEEL	*PLAYDOWN
PELERINE	PERMEATE	*PHTHISIS	PIPEFISH	PLAYGIRL
PELLAGRA	PERONEAL	*PHYLAXIS	PIPELESS	PLAYGOER
PELLETAL	PERORATE	*PHYLESIS	*PIPELIKE	PLAYLAND
PELLICLE	*PEROXIDE	*PHYLLARY	PIPELINE	PLAYLESS
PELLMELL	PERSONAL	*PHYLLITE	PIPERINE	*PLAYLIKE
PELLUCID	PERSPIRE	*PHYLLODE	PIPESTEM	*PLAYMATE
*PEMMICAN	PERSUADE	*PHYLLOID	*PIPINGLY	*PLAYROOM
PEMOLINE	PERTNESS	*PHYLLOME	*PIQUANCY	PLAYSUIT

*PLAYTIME	*POLARIZE	*PORPHYRY	PRATFALL	PRESTAMP
*PLAYWEAR	POLELESS	PORPOISE	*PRATIQUE	PRESTIGE
PLEADING	POLEMIST	PORRIDGE	PRATTLER	PRESUMER
PLEASANT	*POLEMIZE	PORTABLE	*PREACHER	PRETASTE
PLEASURE	POLESTAR	*PORTABLY	PREADAPT	PRETENCE
PLEBEIAN	POLEWARD	PORTANCE	PREADMIT	PRETENSE
PLECTRON	POLISHER	PORTHOLE	PREADOPT	PRETERIT
PLECTRUM	*POLITICK	PORTIERE	PREADULT	PRETREAT
PLEDGEOR	POLITICO	PORTLESS	PREALLOT	PRETTIED
PLEDGING	POLITICS	PORTRAIT	PREAMBLE	PRETTIER
PLEONASM	POLLINIA	PORTRESS	*PREAXIAL	PRETTIES
PLETHORA	POLLINIC	POSINGLY	PREBASAL	*PRETTIFY
PLEURISY	POLLIWOG	POSITION	PREBLESS	PREUNION
PLEUSTON	POLLSTER	POSITIVE	PREBOUND	PREUNITE
PLICATED	POLLUTER	POSITIVE	*PRECHECK	PREVIOUS
PLIGHTER	*POLLYWOG	POSITRON	*PRECHILL	PREVISOR
PLIMSOLE	POLONIUM	POSOLOGY	*PRECIEUX	PRIAPEAN
PLIMSOLL	POLTROON	POSSIBLE	PRECINCT	PRIAPISM
PLOTLESS	*POLYBIRD	POSTALLY	PRECIOUS	PRICIEST
PLOTTAGE	POLYGALA	POSTANAL	PRECITED	*PRICKIER
PLOTTIER	*POLYGAMY	POSTCARD	PRECLEAN	PRIDEFUL
PLOTTIES	POLYGENE	*POSTCAVA	PRECLUDE	PRIEDIEU
PLOTTING	POLYGLOT	POSTDATE	PREDATOR	PRIESTLY
PLOUGHER	*POLYGONY	*POSTFACE	PREELECT	*PRIGGERY
*PLOWBACK	*POLYGYNY	*POSTFORM	PREENACT	*PRIGGISH
*PLOWHEAD	*POLYMATH	POSTHOLE	*PREEXIST	PRIGGISM
PLOWLAND	*POLYPARY	*POSTICHE	*PREFACER	*PRIMEVAL
PLUGLESS	*POLYPIDE	*POSTIQUE	*PREFIXAL	PRIMMEST
*PLUGUGLY	*POLYPNEA	POSTLUDE	*PREFOCUS	*PRIMMING
*PLUMBAGO	*POLYPODY	*POSTMARK	*PREFRANK	PRIMNESS
*PLUMBERY	*POLYPOID	POSTORAL	PREGNANT	PRIMROSE
*PLUMBING	*POLYPORE	POSTPAID	*PREHUMAN	*PRINCELY
*PLUMBISM	*POLYPOUS	POSTPONE	*PREJUDGE	PRINCESS
PLUMBOUS	*POLYSEMY	POSTURAL	PRELEGAL	PRINCIPE
PLUMELET	*POLYSOME	POSTURER	PRELIMIT	*PRINCOCK
PLUMIEST	POLYTENE	POTASSIC	*PREMEDIC	PRINTERY
*PLUMPED	*POLYTENY	POTATION	PREMIERE	PRINTING
*PLUMLIKE	*POLYTYPE	POTATORY	PREMOLAR	PRINTOUT
*PLUMPISH	POLYURIA	*POTBELLY	PREMORSE	PRIORATE
PLURALLY	*POLYZOAN	POTHOUSE	PRENATAL	PRIORESS
PLUSSAGE	*POLYZOIC	*POTLACHE	PRENOMEN	PRIORIES
PLUVIOSE	POMANDER	*POTLATCH	PRENTICE	PRIORITY
PLUVIOUS	*POMOLOGY	POTSHARD	PREPARER	PRISMOID
POACEOUS	PONDERER	POTSHERD	PREPENSE	PRISONER
*POCKETER	*PONDWEED	POTSTONE	PREPLACE	PRISTANE
*POCKMARK	*PONTIFEX	POTTERER	PREPLANT	PRISTINE
PODIATRY	*PONTIFIC	POTTIEST	*PREPPING	PROBABLE
PODOMERE	PONYTAIL	POULARDE	PREPRINT	PROCAINE
*POECHORE	POOLHALL	POULTICE	*PREPUNCH	*PROCHAIN
POETICAL	POOLROOM	POUNDAGE	PRERENAL	*PROCHEIN
POETISER	POORNESS	POWDERER	PRESAGER	PROCLAIM
*POETIZER	POORTITH	*POWERFUL	PRESCIND	PROCURAL
POETLESS	*POPINJAY	*POXVIRUS	PRESCORE	PROCURER
POETLIKE	POPLITIC	*POZZOLAN	PRESENCE	PRODIGAL
POIGNANT	POPULACE	PRACTICE	PRESERVE	PRODROME
POINTMAN	POPULATE	PRACTISE	*PRESHAPE	PRODUCER
POISONER	POPULISM	PRAECIPE	PRESIDER	PROFANER
POKEROOT	POPULIST	PRAEDIAL	PRESIDIA	PROFILER
*POKEWEED	POPULOUS	PRAELECT	PRESIDIO	PROFITER
POKINESS	PORKIEST	PRANDIAL	PRESSMAN	PROFOUND
POLARISE	*PORKWOOD	*PRANKISH	PRESSRUN	PROGGING
POLARITY	POROSITY		PRESSURE	PROGNOSE

PROGRADE	PRUINOSE	PURBLIND	S P ACE	S P ORE
PROGRESS	PRUNELLA	*PURCHASE	S P ADE	S P ORT
*PROHIBIT	PRUNELLE	PUREBRED	S P ADO	S P OUT
PROLABOR	PRUNELLO	PURENESS	S P AHI	S P RAG
PROLAMIN	PRURIENT	PURFLING	S P AIL	S P RAT
PROLAPSE	PRURITUS	PURIFIER	S P AIT	‡S P RAY
*PROLIFIC	PSALMIST	*PURPLISH	S P AKE	S P REE
PROLOGUE	*PSALMODY	PURPURIC	S P ALE	S P RIG
PROLONGE	PSALTERY	PURPURIN	S P ALL	S P RIT
PROMISEE	PSAMMITE	PURSIEST	S P ANG	S P RUE
PROMISER	*PSEPHITE	PURSLANE	S P ANK	S P RUG
PROMISOR	PSILOSIS	PURSUANT	S P ARE	S P UME
PROMOTER	PSORALEA	PURULENT	S P ARK	S P UMY
PROMPTER	PTEROPOD	*PURVEYOR	S P ASM	S P UNK
*PROMPTLY	PTOMAINE	*PUSHBALL	S P ATE	S P URN
PROMULGE	*PTYALISM	*PUSHCART	S P AWN	S P URT
PRONATOR	PUBLICAN	*PUSHDOWN	S P EAK	S P UTA
PRONOTUM	*PUBLICLY	PUSHIEST	S P EAN	*BI P ACK
PROPENOL	*PUCKERER	*PUSHOVER	S P EAR	BO P PER
PROPENSE	PUDDLING	PUSSIEST	S P ECK	BY P ASS
*PROPENYL	PUDENDUM	PUSSLIKE	S P ECS	BY P AST
*PROPERTY	*PUFFBALL	*PUSSYCAT	S P EED	*BY P ATH
*PROPHAGE	PUGGAREE	PUTATIVE	S P EEL	*BY P LAY
*PROPHASE	PUGGIEST	PUTTERER	S P EER	CA P FUL
*PROPHECY	PUGILISM	*PYCNIDIA	S P EIL	CA P IAS
*PROPHESY	PUGILIST	PYELITIS	S P EIR	CA P ITA
PROPOLIS	PUISSANT	*PYGIDIUM	S P ELL	CA P LIN
PROPOSAL	PULICENE	*PYGMYISM	S P ELT	CA P OTE
PROPOSER	PULICIDE	*PYODERMA	S P END	CA P PED
PROPOUND	PULINGLY	*PYOGENIC	S P ENT	CA P PER
*PROPPING	*PULLBACK	*PYORRHEA	S P ERM	CA P RIC
*PROPYLON	PULLOVER	PYRANOSE	S P ICA	CA P SID
PROROGUE	PULMONIC	PYRENOID	S P ICE	CA P TAN
PROSAISM	PULMOTOR	PYRIDINE	S P ICK	CA P TOR
PROSAIST	PULPIEST	*PYRIFORM	S P ICY	CI P HER
PROSIEST	PULPLESS	*PYROLOGY	S P IED	CO P ALM
PROSPECT	*PULPWOOD	*PYROLYZE	S P IEL	*CO P ECK
PROSTATE	PULSATOR	PYRONINE	S P IER	CO P IED
PROSTYLE	*PULSEJET	PYROSTAT	·S P IES	CO P IER
PROTAMIN	*PULSOJET	*PYROXENE	S P IKE	CO P IES
PROTASIS	PULVILLI	*PYRUVATE	S P IKY	CO P ING
PROTEASE	PULVINUS	*PYXIDIUM	S P ILE	CO P LOT
PROTEGEE	PUMICITE		S P ILL	CO P PED
PROTEIDE	PUMPLESS		S P ILT	CO P PER
PROTEOSE	*PUMPLIKE	S P AE	S P INE	CO P PRA
PROTOCOL	*PUNCHEON	S P AN	S P INY	CO P RAH
PROTOPOD	PUNCTATE	S P AR	S P IRE	CO P TER
*PROTOXID	PUNCTUAL	S P AT	S P IRT	CO P ULA
*PROTOZOA	PUNCTURE	S P AY	S P IRY	CU P FUL
PROTRACT	PUNDITRY	S P ED	S P ITE	CU P OLA
PROTRUDE	*PUNGENCY	S P EW	*S P ITZ	CU P PED
PROUDFUL	PUNINESS	S P IC	S P LAT	CU P PER
PROUNION	PUNISHER	S P IK	S P LAY	CU P RIC
*PROVENLY	PUNITION	S P IN	S P LIT	CU P RUM
PROVIDER	PUNITIVE	S P IT	S P ODE	CU P ULA
*PROVINCE	PUNITORY	S P IV	S P OIL	CU P ULE
PROVIRUS	PUPARIUM	S P OT	S P OKE	*CY P HER
*PROVOKER	PUPATION	S P RY	S P OOF	CY P RES
*PROXEMIC	PUPILAGE	S P UD	S P OOK	CY P RUS
*PROXIMAL	*PUPILARY	S P UE	S P OOL	DA P HNE
*PRTUNTZE	*PUPPETRY	S P UN	S P OON	DA P PED
PRUDENCE	*PUPPYDOM	S P UR	S P OOR	DA P PER

DA P PLE	LI P ASE	RA P PEL	SY P HON	CA P SULE
DE P ART	LI P IDE	RA P PEN	TA P ALO	CA P TAIN
DE P END	LI P OID	RA P PER	TA P PED	CA P TION
DE P ERM	LI P OMA	RA P TOR	TA P PER	CA P TIVE
DE P ICT	LI P PED	RE P ACK	TA P PET	CA P TURE
DE P LOY	LI P PEN	RE P AID	TE P EFY	*CA P UCHE
DE P ONE	LI P PER	RE P AIR	TE P HRA	*CI P HONY
DE P ORT	LO P PED	RE P AND	TI P CAT	CI P OLIN
DE P OSE	LO P PER	RE P ASS	TI P OFF	CO P AIBA
DE P UTE	LU P INE	RE P AST	TI P PED	CO P EPOD
DE P UTY	LU P OUS	RE P AVE	TI P PER	CO P IHUE
*DI P LEX	NA P ALM	RE P EAL	TI P PET	CO P ILOT
DI P LOE	NA P ERY	RE P EAT	TI P PLE	CO P IOUS
DI P ODY	NA P KIN	RE P ENT	TI P TOE	*CO P PERY
DI P OLE	NA P PED	RE P ERK	TI P TOP	*CO P PICE
DI P PED	NA P PER	RE P INE	TO P FUL	CO P PING
DI P PER	NA P PIE	RE P LAN	TO P HUS	*CO P YBOY
DI P SAS	NE P HEW	RE P LAY	TO P ING	*CO P YCAT
DO P ANT	NI P PER	RE P ORT	TO P PED	CO P YIST
DO P IER	NI P PLE	RE P OSE	TO P PER	*CU P CAKE
DO P ING	*PA P ACY	RE P OUR	TO P PLE	CU P ELER
DU P ERY	PA P AIN	RE P PED	TU P ELO	*CU P LIKE
DU P ING	PA P AYA	RE P UGN	TU P PED	CU P PING
*DU P LEX	PA P ERY	RE P UTE	TY P HON	CU P RITE
DU P PED	PA P IST	RI P EST	TY P HUS	CU P ROUS
FI P PLE	PA P PUS	RI P ING	TY P IER	CU P SFUL
GA P ING	PA P ULA	RI P OST	*TY P IFY	CU P ULAR
GA P PED	PA P ULE	RI P PED	TY P ING	CY P RESS
GI P PER	PE P LOS	RI P PER	TY P IST	CY P RIAN
GO P HER	PE P LUM	RI P PLE	VA P ORY	CY P SELA
GY P PER	PE P LUS	RI P PLY	VA P OUR	DA P HNIA
GY P SUM	PE P PED	RI P RAP	WI P ING	DA P PING
HA P PED	PE P PER	RI P SAW	*YA P OCK	DE P LANE
HA P PEN	PE P SIN	RO P ERY	YA P PED	DE P LETE
HA P TEN	PE P TIC	RO P IER	YA P PER	DE P LORE
HA P TIC	PE P TID	RO P ILY	YI P PED	DE P LUME
HE P CAT	PI P AGE	RO P ING	YI P PEE	DE P OSAL
HE P TAD	PI P IER	RU P IAH	YI P PIE	DE P OSER
HI P'PED	PI P ING	SA P OTA	*ZE P HYR	DE P OSIT
HI P PER	PI P KIN	SA P OUR	*ZI P PER	DE P RAVE
HI P PIE	PI P PED	SA P PED	BA P TISE	DE P RESS
HO P ING	PI P PIN	SA P PER	BA P TISM	DE P RIVE
HO P PLE	PO P ERY	SE P SIS	BA P TIST	DE P SIDE
*HY P HEN	PO P GUN	SE P TAL	*BA P TIZE	DI P HASE
*HY P NIC	PO P ISH	SE P TET	BI P ARTY	DI P LOID
*JA P ERY	PO P LAR	SE P TIC	BI P LANE	DI P LOMA
*JA P ING	PO P LIN	SE P TUM	BI P OLAR	DI P LOMA
KA P UTT	PO P PED	SI P HON	CA P ABLE	DI P NOAN
*KE P PED	PO P PER	SI P ING	CA P ELAN	DI P PING
KE P PEN	PO P PET	SI P PED	CA P ELET	DI P TERA
KI P PEN	PO P PLE	SI P PER	CA P ELIN	*DI P TYCA
KI P PER	PU P ATE	SI P PET	CA P ERER	*DI P TYCH
*KO P ECK	PU P PED	SO P ITE	CA P ITAL	DO P IEST
KO P PIE	PU P PET	SO P PED	CA P ITOL	DU P PING
LA P DOG	RA P HIA	SU P ERB	CA P LESS	DU P TRAG
LA P FUL	RA P HIS	SU P INE	CA P ORAL	*FO P PERY
LA P PED	RA P IER	SU P PED	*CA P OUCH	*FO P PISH
LA P PER	RA P INE	SU P PER	CA P PING	GA P OSIS
LA P PET	RA P ING	SU P PLE	CA P RICE	GA P PING
LA P SER	RA P IST	SU P PLE	CA P RINE	GI P PING
LA P SUS	RA P PED	SU P PLY	*CA P SIZE	HA P LESS
LE P TON	RA P PEE	SY P HER	CA P STAN	HA P LITE

HA P LOID	*PA P RIKA	RU P TURE	*TY P HOON	*COP P ERAH
HA P LONT	PA P YRUS	*SA P AJOU	*TY P HOSE	COP P ERAS
*HA P PING	*PE P PERY	SA P HEAD	TY P ICAL	COR P ORAL
HA P TENE	PE P PING	SA P HENA	TY P IEST	COR P SMAN
HE P ARIN	PE P SINE	SA P IENS	VA P ORER	COU P LING
HE P ATIC	PE P TIDE	SA P IENT	*VA P OURY	*CRA P PING
HE P TANE	*PE P TIZE	SA P LESS	WA P PITI	CRI P PLER
HE P TOSE	PE P TONE	SA P LING	WI P EOUT	CRO P LAND
HI P BONE	PI P EAGE	SA P ONIN	*XI P HOID	CRO P LESS
HI P LESS	PI P EFUL	*SA P PHIC	*YA P PING	*CRO P PING
*HI P LIKE	PI P ETTE	SA P PING	*YI P PING	CUL P ABLE
HI P NESS	PI P IEST	SA P ROBE	*ZA P ATEO	CUS P IDAL
HI P PEST	PI P PING	SA P SAGO	*ZA P TIAH	CUS P IDOR
HI P PIER	PO P CORN	SA P WOOD	*ZA P TIEH	CUT P URSE
*HI P PING	*PO P EYED	*SE P PUKU	*BAG P IPER	DAM P ENER
*HI P PISH	PO P OVER	SE P TATE	BED P LATE	DAM P NESS
*HI P SHOT	PO P PIED	SE P TIME	BES P OUSE	DAU P HINE
HI P STER	PO P PIES	SI P PING	BES P READ	DEE P ENER
*HO P EFUL	PO P PING	SO P HIES	BES P RENT	DEE P NESS
*HO P HEAD	PO P ULAR	SO P HISM	BIO P LASM	DEM P STER
HO P LITE	*PU P FISH	SO P HIST	*CAM P AGNA	*DES P ATCH
*HO P PING	PU P ILAR	SO P PING	*CAM P AIGN	DES P ISER
*HO P SACK	PU P PING	SO P RANO	*CAM P FIRE	DIA P ASON
HO P TOAD	RA P HIDE	SU P PING	*CAM P HENE	DIA P AUSE
*HY P ERON	RA P PING	SU P PORT	*CAM P HINE	DIA P HONE
*HY P NOID	RA P PINI	SU P POSE	CAM P IEST	*DIA P HONY
*HY P OGEA	RA P PORT	SU P REME	CAM P OREE	DIO P SIDE
*HY P ONEA	RA P TURE	TA P ERER	CAM P SITE	DIO P TASE
*HY P OXIA	RE P APER	TA P ETUM	*CHA P BOOK	DIO P TRIC
*KE P PING	RE P INER	TA P HOLE	*CHA P ERON	*DIP P ABLE
*KI P PING	RE P LACE	TA P IOCA	*CHA P ITER	*DIS P ATCH
*KI P SKIN	RE P LANT	TA P PING	*CHA P LAIN	DIS P ENSE
LA P IDES	RE P LATE	TA P ROOM	*CHA P PING	DIS P ERSE
LA P PING	RE P LETE	TA P ROOT	*CHI P MUCK	DIS P IRIT
LA P WING	*RE P LEVY	TA P STER	*CHI P MUNK	DIS P LACE
LE P ORID	RE P LICA	TI P CART	*CHI P PING	DIS P LANT
LE P ROSE	RE P LIER	TI P LESS	*CHO P PING	DIS P LODE
LE P ROSY	RE P OSAL	TI P PIER	CLA P TRAP	DIS P LUME
LE P ROUS	RE P OSER	TI P PING	*CLI P PING	DIS P OSAL
LI P LESS	RE P OSIT	TI P PLER	CLU P EOID	DIS P OSER
LI P LIKE	RE P OWER	TI P SIER	COA P PEAR	DIS P READ
LI P PING	RE P RESS	TI P SILY	*COD P IECE	*DIS P RIZE
LO P PING	RE P RICE	TI P STER	COL P ITIS	DIS P ROOF
LU P ANAR	RE P RINT	TO P COAT	*COM P ADRE	DIS P ROVE
LU P ULIN	RE P RISE	TO P FULL	COM P ARER	DIS P UTER
*NA P HTHA	RE P ROBE	TO P IARY	COM P ILER	DRI P LESS
NA P HTOL	RE P ROOF	*TO P KICK	COM P LAIN	DRI P PING
NA P LESS	RE P ROVE	TO P KNOT	*COM P LEAT	*DRO P HEAD
NA P PING	RE P TANT	TO P LESS	*COM P LECT	*DRO P KICK
NE P HRIC	RE P TILE	TO P MAST	COM P LETE	DRO P SHOT
NE P HRON	RE P ULSE	TO P MOST	*COM P LICE	DRO P WORT
NI P PIER	RI P CORD	TO P ONYM	*COM P LIED	DRU P ELET
NI P PILY	RI P ENER	TO P PING	COM P LIER	DRY P OINT
NI P PING	RI P IENO	TO P SAIL	COM P LIES	*DUM P CART
NU P TIAL	RI P OSTE	TO P SIDE	COM P LINE	DUM P IEST
PA P ERER	RI P PING	TO P SOIL	COM P OSER	DUM P LING
PA P HIAN	RI P PLER	*TO P WORK	*COM P OUND	DUO P SONY
PA P ILLA	RI P PLET	TU P PING	COM P RESS	*DYS P EPSY
PA P OOSE	RI P TIDE	TY P EBAR	COM P RISE	DYS P NOEA
PA P PIER	*RO P EWAY	TY P ESET	*COM P RIZE	*FLA P JACK
PA P PIES	RO P IEST	*TY P HOID	COM P UTER	FLA P LESS
PA P RICA			COO P TION	

*FLA P PING	*MYO P ATHY	*RAM P ANCY	SLI P WARE	TEM P ORAL
*FLI P PANT	NAU P LIUS	RAP P AREE	SLO P PING	TEN P ENCE
*FLY P APER	*NEO P HYTE	*REA P HOOK	*SLO P WORK	TEN P ENNY
*FRI P PERY	NEO P LASM	REA P PEAR	*SNA P BACK	TER P INOL
*GAZ P ACHO	NEO P RENE	REO P POSE	SNA P LESS	TIM P ANUM
GEE P OUND	NIP P IEST	RES P ONSA	*SNA P PIER	TIN P LATE
*GEO P HAGY	NON P AGAN	RES P ONSE	SNA P PING	TIP P ABLE
GEO P HONE	NON P APAL	RES P READ	*SNA P PISH	TIP P IEST
*GEO P HYTE	NON P ARTY	RES P RING	SNA P SHOT	TOE P IECE
GEO P ONIC	NON P OLAR	RHA P SODE	*SNA P WEED	TOE P LATE
GOS P ELER	PAL P ABLE	*RHA P SODY	*SNI P PETY	TOR P IDLY
*GRA P HEME	PAL P ATOR	RIP P ABLE	SNI P PING	TRA P BALL
GRA P HITE	PAL P EBRA	RIP P LING	*SOA P BARK	TRA P DOOR
GRA P IEST	PAM P ERER	*SAM P HIRE	SOA P IEST	*TRA P EZIA
GRA P PLER	PAP P IEST	SAM P LING	SOA P LESS	TRA P LIKE
GRI P IEST	PAP P OOSE	*SAP P HIRE	SOA P SUDS	TRA P NEST
GRI P PIER	*PEE P HOLE	*SAP P HISM	SOA P WORT	TRA P PEAN
GRI P PING	*PEE P SHOW	*SAP P HIST	SOR P TION	TRA P PING
*GRI P SACK	PEN P OINT	*SCA P HOID	STA P EDES	TRA P POSE
GUM P TION	PEP P ERER	SCA P ULAR	STA P ELIA	TRA P POUS
GUN P APER	PIE P LANT	SCE P TRAL	STE P DAME	*TRA P ROCK
GUN P OINT	PIN P OINT	*SCU P PAUG	STE P LIKE	TRA P UNTO
*HAM P ERER	*PIN P RICK	*SCY P HATE	STE P PING	TRE P HINE
HEL P LESS	*POR P HYRY	SEA P IECE	STE P WISE	TRI P EDAL
*HEL P MATE	POR P OISE	SEA P LANE	STI P PLER	TRI P HASE
*HEL P MEET	PRE P ARER	SEM P LICE	*STO P COCK	TRI P LANE
*HEM P IEST	PRE P ENSE	*SHE P HERD	STO P OVER	TRI P LING
*HEM P WEED	PRE P LACE	SHI P LOAD	STO P PAGE	TRI P LITE
*HIP P ARCH	PRE P LANT	*SHI P MATE	STO P PING	TRI P LOID
*HIP P IEST	*PRE P PING	*SHI P MENT	*SUB P HYLA	TRI P PING
HOO P LESS	PRE P RINT	*SHI P PING	SUB P OENA	TRI P TANE
*HOO P LIKE	*PRE P UNCH	SHI P SIDE	SUB P OLAR	*TRI P TYCA
HOO P STER	PRO P ENOL	*SHI P WORM	*SUB P UBIC	*TRI P TYCH
HOS P ITAL	*PRO P ENYL	*SHI P YARD	SUL P HATE	TUM P LINE
HOS P ITIA	*PRO P ERTY	SHO P GIRL	SUL P HIDE	TUP P ENCE
HOS P ODAR	*PRO P HAGE	*SHO P LIFT	SUL P HITE	*TUP P ENNY
HOT P RESS	*PRO P HASE	*SHO P PING	SUL P HONE	*TWO P ENCE
*HUM P BACK	*PRO P HECY	*SHO P TALK	*SUL P HURY	*TWO P ENNY
*HUM P LESS	*PRO P HESY	*SHO P WORN	*SUM P WEED	*TYM P ANAL
*JEO P ARDY	PRO P OLIS	SIM P ERER	SUP P LANT	*TYM P ANIC
*KEE P SAKE	PRO P OSAL	*SIM P LIFY	SUP P LIER	*TYM P ANUM
*KER P LUNK	PRO P OSER	SIM P LISM	SUP P OSER	VES P ERAL
*KEY P UNCH	PRO P OUND	*SIX P ENCE	SUP P RESS	*VES P IARY
*KNA P SACK	*PRO P PING	*SIX P ENNY	SUR P LICE	VOL P LANE
*KNA P WEED	*PRO P YLON	*SKI P JACK	SUR P RINT	WAR P LANE
LAM P POST	*PSE P HITE	SKI P LANE	SUR P RISE	*WAR P OWER
*LAM P YRID	PUL P IEST	*SKI P PING	*SUR P RIZE	*WAR P WISE
LEA P FROG	PUL P LESS	SLA P DASH	SUS P ENSE	*WAX P LANT
LIM P NESS	PUM P LESS	*SLA P JACK	*SYM P ATHY	*WEA P ONRY
LOO P HOLE	*PUL P WOOD	SLA P PING	*SYM P ATRY	*WET P ROOF
*LUM P FISH	*PUM P LIKE	SLI P CASE	*SYM P HONY	*WHI P CORD
*LYM P HOMA	*PUP P ETRY	*SLI P FORM	*SYM P ODIA	*WHI P LASH
*LYO P HILE	*PUP P YDOM	SLI P KNOT	*SYM P OSIA	*WHI P LIKE
*MAN P OWER	*PUR P LISH	SLI P LESS	*SYR P HIAN	*WHI P PIER
*MAP P ABLE	PUR P URIC	SLI P OVER	TAM P ERER	*WHI P PING
*MIS P ATCH	PUR P URIN	SLI P PAGE	TAR P APER	*WHI P TAIL
*MIS P RIZE	*QUI P PISH	*SLI P PERY	*TAX P AYER	*WHI P WORM
*MOR P HEME	*QUI P STER	SLI P PING	TEM P ERER	WIS P IEST
*MOR P HINE	RAM P AGER	SLI P SHOD	TEM P LATE	*WIS P LIKE
*MUD P UPPY		SLI P SLOP		*WRA P PING
		SLI P SOLE		*ZEP P ELIN

*ZOO P HILE	MUM P	YAW P	SIRU P	DOLLO P
*ZOO P HYTE	NEA P	YEL P	SKEL P	DUSTU P
	NEE P	BEBO P	SKIM P	FACEU P
	PAL P	BECA P	SLEE P	FILLI P
	PEE P	BLIM P	SLOO P	GALLO P
BEE P	PIM P	BLOO P	SLUM P	GIDDA P
BLI P	PLO P	CHAM P	SLUR P	GOSSI P
BUM P	POM P	CHEA P	SNEA P	HANGU P
BUR P	POO P	CHEE P	SNOO P	*HICCU P
CAM P	PRE P	CHIM P	STAM P	HOLDU P
CAR P	PRO P	CHIR P	STEE P	*HOOKU P
CHA P	PUL P	CHOM P	STIR P	*HUBCA P
CHI P	PUM P	CHUM P	STOM P	HYSSO P
CHO P	*QUI P	CLAM P	STOO P	*JOYPO P
CLA P	RAM P	CLAS P	STOU P	*KICKU P
CLI P	RAS P	CLOM P	STOW P	KIDNA P
CLO P	REA P	CLUM P	STRA P	LARRU P
COM P	REP P	CRAM P	STRE P	LINEU P
COO P	ROM P	CREE P	STRI P	LINKU P
COU P	ROU P	CRIM P	STRO P	LOCKU P
CRA P	RUM P	CRIS P	STUM P	LOLLO P
CRO P	SAL P	CROU P	SUNU P	LOOKU P
CUS P	SAM P	CRUM P	SWAM P	MADCA P
DAM P	SCO P	CUTU P	SWEE P	MAGIL P
DEE P	SCU P	DROO P	SWOO P	MAKEU P
DRI P	SEE P	FLUM P	SYRU P	MARKU P
DRO P	SHI P	FRUM P	THOR P	*MAYHA P
DUM P	SHO P	GALO P	THRI P	*MAYPO P
FLA P	SIM P	GENI P	THUM P	MEGIL P
FLI P	SKE P	GETU P	TRAM P	METUM P
FRA P	SKI P	GRAM P	TROM P	MISHA P
GAM P	SLA P	GRAS P	TROO P	MOBCA P
GAS P	SLI P	GROU P	TRUM P	*MOCKU P
GIM P	SLO P	GRUM P	TULI P	MUDCA P
GLO P	SNA P	JALA P	TWER P	*PICKU P
GOO P	SNI P	JALO P	TWIR P	PILEU P
GRI P	SOA P	JULE P	WATA P	PREAM P
GUL P	SOU P	KNOS P	WHAU P	PUSHU P
HAR P	STE P	LETU P	WHEE P	RECOU P
HAS P	STO P	*MIXU P	WHEL P	REDCA P
HEA P	SUM P	NETO P	*WHOM P	REDTO P
HEL P	SWA P	PINU P	WHOO P	RESHI P
HEM P	SWO P	PLUM P	*WHUM P	REVAM P
HOL P	TAM P	POLY P	*BACKU P	REWRA P
HOO P	TAR P	PRIM P	BARHO P	RIPRA P
HUM P	TRA P	REBO P	BELEA P	SALOO P
JAU P	TRI P	RECA P	BEWEE P	SANNO P
JEE P	TRO P	REDI P	BEWRA P	SANNU P
*JIM P	TUM P	REMA P	BISHO P	SATRA P
*JUM P	TYP P	SALE P	BLOWU P	SCHLE P
KEE P	VAM P	SCAL P	BURLA P	SCRIM P
KEL P	VEE P	SCAM P	CARHO P	SCROO P
KEM P	WAR P	SCAR P	CARTO P	SHRIM P
KNA P	WAS P	SCAU P	CATNA P	*SKYCA P
KNO P	WEE P	SCOO P	CATNI P	SLIPU P
LAM P	WHA P	SCRA P	CATSU P	TEACU P
LEA P	WHI P	SCRI P	*COCKU P	THREA P
LIM P	WHO P	SCUL P	COLLO P	THREE P
LIS P	WIS P	SETU P	DECAM P	TIPTO P
LOO P	WRA P	SHAR P	DEWLA P	TITTU P
LOU P	YAU P	SHEE P	DOGNA P	TOECA P
LUM P				

TOSSU P
TURNI P
TURNU P
*WALKU P
WALLO P
WARMU P
*WIKIU P
WINDU P
*WORKU P
*BARKEE P
BECLAS P
BEDLAM P
BELLHO P
*BETHUM P
BLUECA P
*BREAKU P
BRUSHU P
BUILDU P
CALTRA P
CALTRO P
CANTRA P
CANTRI P
*CATCHU P
*CHECKU P
CHIRRU P
CLEANU P
COWSLI P
*CRACKU P
DEMIRE P
DEVELO P
DEWDRO P
FLATCA P
FLATTO P
*FLYTRA P
FORETO P
GENIPA P
GODSHI P
GROWNU P

GUMDRO P
GUNSHI P
HAIRCA P
HARDTO P
HARELI P
HENCOO P
HILLTO P
*KETCHU P
*KINGCU P
*KINSHI P
*KNEECA P
MAINTO P
MANTRA P
*MIDSHI P
*MILKSO P
*MISKEE P
MISSTE P
MISSTO P
*MUGWUM P
NONSLI P
NONSTO P
PARSNI P
PINESA P
POGONI P
PREWRA P
PROCAR P
RATTRA P
RECLAS P
*REEQUI P
REGROU P
RESTAM P
ROLLMO P
ROLLTO P
ROOFTO P
ROUNDU P
SCALLO P
*SCHLEP P
SCOLLO P

*SHAKEU P
SHALLO P
SHAPEU P
SHIPLA P
SMASHU P
SNOWCA P
SONSHI P
SOURSO P
SPEEDU P
STANDU P
*STICKU P
STIRRU P
STOPGA P
SUNLAM P
SYNCAR P
TEASHO P
TIDERI P
TOUCHU P
TREETO P
TROLLO P
*WARSHI P
*WICKIU P
*WICKYU P
WINESO P
WIRETA P
*WORSHI P
*BACKDRO P
*BACKSLA P
*BACKSTO P
*BAKESHO P
*BLACKCA P
*BLACKTO P
*BOOKSHO P
*BULLWHI P
*CALTHRO P
CANTRAI P
*CHUMSHI P
CLAPTRA P

*COOKSHO P
*CROWSTE P
DEANSHI P
*DEATHCU P
*DOGESHI P
DOORSTE P
DOORSTO P
*DRAMSHO P
DUSTHEA P
*FIREDAM P
FIRETRA P
*FLAGSHI P
*FOOLSCA P
FOOTSTE P
*GROGSHO P
GURUSHI P
*HANDGRI P
*HANDICA P
*HARDSHI P
*HEADLAM P
*HEADSHI P
*HEDGEHO P
*HEIRSHI P
HELISTO P
*HOCKSHO P
HOUSETO P
*KINGSHI P
*LADYSHI P
*LANDSKI P
LANDSLI P
LIVETRA P
*LOCKSTE P
LOLLIPO P
*LOLLYPO P
LONGSHI P
LORDSHI P
MALAPRO P
*MATESHI P

MESOCAR P
*MOLDWAR P
MONOCAR P
*NIGHTCA P
NONTRUM P
PARADRO P
*PAWNSHO P
*PEDIPAL P
*PEESWEE P
PERICAR P
*PHOTOMA P
PRESTAM P
RAINDRO P
SANDPEE P
SANDSOA P
SIDESLI P
SIDESTE P
*SKULLCA P
SLIPSLO P
SNOWDRO P
SUBGROU P
SWEETSO P
TABLETO P
*TANKSHI P
TEARDRO P
TIECLAS P
*TOWNSHI P
TRANSHI P
*TWINSHI P
*WARDSHI P
WHITECA P
*WINESHO P
*WORKSHO P
*XYLOCAR P

Q

QAID
*QOPH
QUAD
QUAG
QUAI
*QUAY
*QUEY
QUID
*QUIP
QUIT
*QUIZ
QUOD
*QUACK
*QUAFF
QUAIL
*QUAKE
*QUAKY
QUALE

*QUALM
QUANT
QUARE
*QUARK
QUART
*QUASH
QUASI
QUASS
QUATE
QUEAN
QUEEN
QUEER
QUELL
QUERN
*QUERY
QUEST
QUEUE
*QUICK

QUIET
*QUIFF
QUILL
QUILT
QUINT
*QUIPU
QUIRE
*QUIRK
QUIRT
QUITE
QUOIN
QUOIT
QUOTA
QUOTE
*QUOTH
*QURSH
*QINDAR
*QINTAR

*QIVIUT
*QUAERE
*QUAGGA
*QUAGGY
*QUAHOG
*QUAICH
*QUAIGH
*QUAINT
*QUAKER
*QUALMY
*QUANTA
*QUARRY
*QUARTE
*QUARTO
*QUARTZ
*QUASAR
*QUATRE
*QUAVER

*QUEASY
*QUEAZY
*QUENCH
*QUEUER
*QUEZAL
*QUICHE
*QUINCE
*QUINIC
*QUININ
*QUINOA
*QUINOL
*QUINSY
*QUIPPU
*QUIRKY
*QUITCH
*QUIVER
*QUORUM
*QUOTER

*QUOTHA	*QUIETER	*QUAGMIRE	*QUISLING	*PI Q UANT
*QURUSH	*QUIETLY	*QUAGMIRY	*QUITRENT	*RE Q UEST
*QUADRAT	*QUIETUS	*QUALMISH	*QUITTING	*RE Q UIEM
*QUADRIC	*QUILLAI	*QUANDANG	*QUIVERER	*RE Q UIRE
*QUAFFER	*QUILLET	*QUANDARY	*QUIXOTIC	*RE Q UIRE
*QUAHAUG	*QUILTER	*QUANDONG	*QUIXOTRY	*SE Q UELA
*QUALIFY	*QUINARY	*QUANTIFY	*QUOTIENT	*SE Q UENT
*QUALITY	*QUINATE	*QUANTITY		*SE Q UOIA
*QUAMASH	*QUININA	*QUANTIZE		*TE Q UILA
*QUANTAL	*QUININE	*QUANTONG	*S Q UAB	*VA Q UERO
*QUANTIC	*QUINNAT	*QUARRIER	*S Q UAD	*BED Q UILT
*QUANTUM	*QUINOID	*QUARTERN	S Q UAT	*CHA Q UETA
*QUARREL	*QUINONE	*QUARTILE	*S Q UAW	*CIN Q UAIN
*QUARTAN	*QUINTAL	*QUATORZE	*S Q UEG	*CLI Q UISH
*QUARTER	*QUINTAN	*QUATRAIN	*S Q UIB	*COE Q UATE
*QUARTET	*QUINTAR	*QUAVERER	*S Q UID	*CON Q UEST
*QUARTIC	*QUINTET	*QUAYSIDE	*BU Q SHA	*CON Q UIAN
*QUASSIA	*QUINTIC	*QUEERISH	*CO Q UET	*COT Q UEAN
*QUASSIN	*QUINTIN	*QUENCHER	*DI Q UAT	*DAI Q UIRI
*QUAVERY	*QUITTED	*QUENELLE	*FA Q UIR	*DIS Q UIET
*QUAYAGE	*QUITTER	*QUERCINE	*LI Q UID	*FRE Q UENT
*QUEENLY	*QUITTOR	*QUESTION	*LI Q UOR	*FRE Q UENT
*QUEERLY	*QUIVERY	*QUIBBLER	*LO Q UAT	*JAC Q UARD
*QUELLER	*QUIXOTE	*QUICKSET	*MA Q UIS	*MAR Q UESS
*QUERIDA	*QUIZZER	*QUIDDITY	*PI Q UET	*MAR Q UISE
*QUERIED	*QUOMODO	*QUIDNUNC	*RE Q UIN	*MES Q UITE
*QUERIER	*QUONDAM	*QUIETISM	*RO Q UET	*MEZ Q UITE
*QUERIES	*QUOTING	*QUIETIST	*SE Q UEL	*MIS Q UOTE
*QUERIST	*QIOMTAIN	*QUIETUDE	*SE Q UIN	*MOS Q UITO
*QUESTER	*QUACKERY	*QUILTING	*TO Q UET	*MUS Q UASH
*QUESTOR	*QUACKISH	*QUINCUNX	*BE Q UEST	*NON Q UOTA
*QUETZAL	*QUACKISM	*QUINELLA	*CO Q UINA	*SEA Q UAKE
*QUIBBLE	*QUADRANS	*QUINIELA	*CO Q UITO	*TOR Q UATE
*QUICKEN	*QUADRANT	*QUINOLIN	*LI Q UATE	*TOR Q UING
*QUICKIE	*QUADRATE	*QUINTILE	*LI Q UEFY	*TUR Q UOIS
*QUICKLY	*QUADRIGA	*QUIPPISH	*LI Q UEUR	*VAN Q UISH
*QUIETEN	*QUADROON	*QUIPSTER	*LI Q UIFY	

R

RACE	RANG	REAM	RESH	RING
RACK	RANI	REAP	REST	RINK
RACY	RANK	REAR	RETE	RIOT
RAFF	RANT	**RECK**	RHEA	RIPE
RAFT	RAPE	REDD	RHUS	RISE
RAGA	RAPT	REDE	RIAL	RISK
RAGE	RARE	REDO	RICE	RITE
RAGI	RASE	REED	RICH	**RITZ**
RAIA	RASH	REEF	**RICK**	RIVE
RAID	RASP	REEK	RIDE	ROAD
RAIL	RATE	REEL	RIEL	ROAM
RAIN	RATH	REFT	RIFE	ROAN
RAJA	RATO	REIF	**RIFF**	ROAR
RAKE	RAVE	REIN	RIFT	ROBE
RAKI	RAYA	REIS	RILE	**ROCK**
RALE	**RAZE**	RELY	RILL	RODE
RAMI	***RAZZ**	REND	RIME	ROIL
RAMP	READ	RENT	RIMY	ROLE
RAND	REAL	REPP	RIND	ROLL

ROMP	**RAMMY**	REDYE	REWAN	ROUEN
ROOD	RAMUS	REEDY	*REWAX	ROUGE
ROOF	RANCE	**REEFY**	REWIN	ROUGH
ROOK	**RANCH**	**REEKY**	REWON	ROUND
ROOM	RANDY	REEST	**RHEUM**	**ROUPY**
ROOT	RANEE	REEVE	RHINO	ROUSE
ROPE	RANGE	REFEL	**RHOMB**	ROUST
ROPY	RANGY	REFER	**RHUMB**	ROUTE
ROSE	RANID	REFIT	**RHYME**	ROUTH
ROSY	RAPER	*REFIX	**RHYTA**	ROVEN
ROTA	**RAPHE**	**REFLY**	RIANT	ROVER
ROTE	RAPID	**REFRY**	RIATA	ROWAN
ROTL	RARER	REGAL	**RIBBY**	**ROWDY**
ROTO	RASER	REGES	RIBES	ROWEL
ROUE	RATAL	REGMA	RICER	ROWEN
ROUP	RATAN	REGNA	RICIN	ROWER
ROUX	**RATCH**	**REHEM**	RIDER	**ROWTH**
ROVE	RATEL	**REIFY**	RIDGE	ROYAL
RUBE	RATER	REIGN	**RIDGY**	RUBLE
RUBY	RATHE	REIVE	RIFLE	RUBUS
RUCK	RATIO	**REKEY**	RIGHT	**RUCHE**
RUDD	RATTY	**RELAX**	RIGID	**RUDDY**
RUDE	RAVEL	RELAY	RIGOR	**RUFFE**
RUER	RAVEN	RELET	RILEY	**RUGBY**
RUFF	RAVER	RELIC	RILLE	RUING
RUGA	RAVIN	RELIT	RIMER	RULER
RUIN	**RAWLY**	REMAN	RINSE	RUMBA
RULE	**RAYAH**	REMAP	RIPEN	RUMEN
RUMP	RAYON	REMET	RIPER	**RUMMY**
RUNE	**RAZEE**	**REMEX**	RISER	RUMOR
RUNG	**RAZER**	REMIT	RISHI	RUNIC
RUNT	**RAZOR**	**REMIX**	**RISKY**	RUNNY
RUSE	**REACH**	RENAL	RISUS	RUNTY
RUSH	REACT	RENEW	*RITZY	RUPEE
RUSK	READD	RENIG	RIVAL	RURAL
RUST	READY	RENIN	RIVER	**RUSHY**
RUTH	REALM	RENTE	RIVET	RUSTY
RYKE	REARM	REOIL	RIYAL	RUTTY
RYND	REATA	**REPAY**	**ROACH**	RABATO
RYOT	REAVE	REPEL	ROAST	**RABBET**
RABBI	REBBE	REPIN	ROBIN	**RABBIN**
RABIC	REBEC	**REPLY**	ROBLE	**RABBIT**
RABID	REBEL	REPRO	ROBOT	**RABBLE**
RACER	REBID	RERAN	**ROCKY**	RABIES
RACON	REBOP	RERUN	RODEO	**RACEME**
RADAR	REBUS	RESAW	ROGER	**RACHET**
RADII	REBUT	RESAY	ROGUE	**RACHIS**
RADIO	RECAP	RESEE	ROILY	RACIAL
RADIX	RECON	RESET	ROMAN	RACIER
RADON	RECTA	RESEW	RONDO	**RACILY**
RAGEE	RECTI	RESID	**ROOKY**	RACING
RAGGY	RECTO	RESIN	**ROOMY**	**RACISM**
RAINY	RECUR	RESOW	ROOSE	RACIST
RAISE	RECUT	**RETCH**	ROOST	**RACKER**
*RAJAH	REDAN	RETEM	ROOTY	**RACKET**
RAKEE	REDIA	RETIA	ROPER	**RACKLE**
RAKER	REDID	RETIE	ROSED	RACOON
RALLY	REDIP	RETRY	ROSET	RADDLE
RAMEE	REDLY	REUSE	ROSIN	RADIAL
RAMET	**REDOX**	REVEL	**ROTCH**	RADIAN
RAMIE	REDRY	REVET	ROTOR	**RADISH**
		REVUE		RADIUM

RADIUS	RASCAL	RECITE	*REFLEX	REMARK
RADOME	RASHER	**RECKON**	**REFLOW**	**REMEDY**
RADULA	**RASHLY**	RECLAD	*REFLUX	REMEET
RAFFIA	RASING	RECOAL	**REFOLD**	REMELT
RAFFLE	RASPER	**RECOCK**	**REFORM**	REMEND
RAFTER	RASSLE	RECOIL	REFUEL	REMIND
RAGBAG	RASTER	RECOIN	**REFUGE**	REMINT
RAGGED	RASURE	**RECOMB**	**REFUND**	REMISE
RAGGLE	RATANY	**RECOOK**	REFUSE	REMISS
RAGING	RATHER	**RECOPY**	REFUTE	REMOLD
RAGLAN	**RATIFY**	RECORD	REGAIN	REMORA
RAGMAN	RATINE	**RECOUP**	REGALE	REMOTE
RAGOUT	RATING	RECTAL	REGARD	**REMOVE**
RAGTAG	RATION	RECTOR	**REGAVE**	REMUDA
RAIDER	RATITE	**RECTUM**	REGEAR	RENAME
RAILER	RATLIN	RECTUS	REGENT	RENDER
RAISER	RATOON	RECUSE	REGILD	RENEGE
RAISIN	RATTAN	REDACT	REGIME	RENNET
RAKING	RATTED	REDATE	REGINA	RENNIN
RAKISH	RATTEN	**REDBAY**	REGION	RENOWN
RALLYE	RATTER	**REDBUD**	REGIUS	RENTAL
RAMATE	RATTLE	**REDBUG**	**REGIVE**	RENTER
RAMBLE	RATTLY	**REDCAP**	REGLET	RENVOI
RAMIFY	RATTON	REDDED	**REGLOW**	REOPEN
*RAMJET	**RAVAGE**	REDDEN	REGLUE	**REPACK**
RAMMED	RAVINE	REDDER	REGNAL	REPAID
RAMMER	**RAVING**	REDDLE	REGNUM	REPAIR
RAMOSE	**RAVISH**	REDEAR	REGRET	REPAND
RAMOUS	**RAWISH**	REDEEM	**REGREW**	REPASS
RAMROD	*RAZING	**REDEFY**	**REGROW**	REPAST
RAMSON	READER	**REDENY**	**REHANG**	**REPAVE**
RAMTIL	REAGIN	**REDEYE**	**REHASH**	REPEAL
RANCHO	REALIA	**REDFIN**	REHEAR	REPEAT
RANCID	REALLY	REDING	REHEAT	REPENT
RANCOR	REALTY	REDLEG	REHEEL	**REPERK**
RANDAN	REAMER	**REDOCK**	REHIRE	REPINE
RANDOM	REAPER	REDOUT	**REHUNG**	REPLAN
RANGER	REARER	**REDOWA**	REIVER	**REPLAY**
RANKER	REASON	**REDRAW**	*REJECT	REPORT
RANKLE	REAVER	REDTOP	**REJOIN**	REPOSE
RANKLY	**REAVOW**	REDUCE	**REKNIT**	REPOUR
RANSOM	REBAIT	REEARN	RELACE	**REPPED**
RANTER	REBATE	**REECHO**	RELATE	REPUGN
RANULA	REBATO	REEDIT	RELEND	REPUTE
RAPHIA	**REBECK**	REEFER	RELENT	*REQUIN
RAPHIS	REBILL	**REEKER**	RELICT	REREAD
RAPIER	REBIND	REELER	RELIED	RERISE
RAPINE	REBOIL	REEMIT	RELIEF	REROLL
RAPING	REBORN	**REFACE**	RELIER	RESAID
RAPIST	*REBOZO	REFALL	RELIES	RESAIL
RAPPED	**REBUFF**	**REFECT**	RELINE	RESALE
RAPPEE	**REBUKE**	**REFEED**	RELISH	RESCUE
RAPPEL	**REBURY**	REFELL	RELIST	RESEAL
RAPPEN	RECALL	**REFFED**	RELIVE	RESEAT
RAPPER	RECANE	REFILE	RELOAD	RESEAU
RAPTOR	RECANT	REFILL	RELOAN	RESECT
RAREFY	RECAST	**REFILM**	RELUCT	RESEDA
RARELY	RECEDE	**REFIND**	RELUME	RESEED
RAREST	RECENT	REFINE	REMAIL	**RESEEK**
RARIFY	**RECEPT**	REFIRE	REMAIN	RESEEN
RARING	RECESS	REFLET	**REMAKE**	RESELL
RARITY	**RECIPE**	**REFLEW**	REMAND	RESEND

RESENT	REWIRE	RIPEST	ROTTEN	**RABBONI**
RESHIP	**REWOKE**	RIPING	ROTTER	**RACCOON**
RESHOE	**REWORD**	RIPOST	ROTUND	**RACEMIC**
RESHOW	**REWORK**	RIPPED	ROUBLE	*RACEWAY
RESIDE	**REWOVE**	**RIPPER**	**ROUCHE**	RACIEST
RESIFT	**REWRAP**	**RIPPLE**	ROUPET	*RACKETY
RESIGN	*REZONE	**RIPPLY**	ROUSER	*RACQUET
RESILE	**RHAPHE**	**RIPSAW**	ROUTER	RADIALE
RESINY	*RHEBOK	RISING	**ROVING**	RADIANT
RESIST	RHESUS	**RISKER**	**ROWING**	RADIATE
*RESIZE	RHETOR	*RISQUE	*ROZZER	RADICAL
RESOLD	**RHEUMY**	RITARD	**RUBACE**	**RADICEL**
RESOLE	RHINAL	RITTER	RUBATO	**RADICES**
RESORB	**RHOMBI**	RITUAL	**RUBBED**	**RADICLE**
RESORT	**RHUMBA**	RIVAGE	**RUBBER**	*RAFFISH
RESTER	**RHYMER**	RIVING	**RUBBLE**	**RAFFLER**
RESULT	*RHYTHM	ROAMER	**RUBBLY**	**RAGGEDY**
RESUME	**RHYTON**	ROARER	RUBIED	**RAGGING**
RETAIL	RIALTO	ROBALO	RUBIER	**RAGTIME**
RETAIN	RIBALD	ROBAND	RUBIES	**RAGWEED**
RETAKE	RIBAND	**ROBBED**	RUBIGO	**RAGWORT**
RETARD	**RIBBED**	**ROBBER**	**RUBRIC**	RAILING
RETELL	**RIBBER**	**ROBBIN**	**RUCKUS**	**RAILWAY**
RETENE	**RIBBON**	ROBUST	RUDDER	RAIMENT
RETEST	RIBLET	**ROCHET**	RUDDLE	**RAINBOW**
RETIAL	RIBOSE	**ROCKER**	RUDEST	RAINIER
RETIME	**RICHEN**	**ROCKET**	RUEFUL	**RAINILY**
RETINA	**RICHES**	ROCOCO	**RUFFLE**	RAINOUT
RETINT	**RICHLY**	RODENT	*RUFFLY	RAISING
RETIRE	RICING	RODMAN	RUFOUS	*RAKEOFF
RETOLD	*RICKEY	ROLLER	RUGGED	RALLIED
RETOOK	**RICRAC**	ROMANO	RUGGER	RALLIER
RETOOL	RICTUS	**ROMPER**	RUGOSE	RALLINE
RETORT	RIDDED	RONDEL	RUGOUS	**RAMBLER**
RETRAL	RIDDEN	RONION	RUINER	**RAMEKIN**
RETRIM	RIDDER	RONNEL	RULING	RAMILIE
RETTED	RIDDLE	RONYON	**RUMBLE**	**RAMMIER**
RETUNE	RIDENT	ROOFER	**RUMBLY**	**RAMMING**
RETURN	RIDGEL	ROOKIE	**RUMMER**	**RAMMISH**
RETUSE	RIDGIL	ROOMER	RUMOUR	**RAMPAGE**
RETYPE	RIDING	ROOSER	**RUMPLE**	**RAMPANT**
REVAMP	**RIDLEY**	ROOTER	**RUMPLY**	**RAMPART**
REVEAL	RIEVER	**ROPERY**	**RUMPUS**	*RAMPIKE
REVERB	**RIFFLE**	ROPIER	RUNDLE	**RAMPION**
REVERE	RIFLER	**ROPILY**	RUNLET	**RAMPOLE**
REVERS	RIGGED	ROPING	RUNNEL	**RANCHER**
REVERT	RIGGER	*ROQUET	RUNNER	RANCOUR
REVERY	**RIGHTO**	ROSARY	**RUNOFF**	RANDIES
REVEST	**RIGHTY**	ROSCOE	RUNOUT	**RANKISH**
REVIEW	RIGOUR	ROSERY	**RUNWAY**	**RANPIKE**
REVILE	RILING	ROSIER	**RUPIAH**	**RANSACK**
REVISE	RILLET	ROSILY	RURBAN	**RAPHIDE**
REVIVE	RIMIER	ROSING	RUSHEE	**RAPPING**
REVOKE	RIMING	ROSINY	RUSHER	**RAPPINI**
REVOLT	**RIMMED**	ROSTER	RUSINE	**RAPPORT**
REVVED	**RIMMER**	ROSTRA	RUSSET	RAPTURE
REWAKE	RIMOSE	ROTARY	RUSTIC	RAREBIT
REWARD	RIMOUS	ROTATE	RUSTLE	RASBORA
REWARM	**RIMPLE**	**ROTCHE**	RUTILE	**RASPISH**
REWASH	RINGER	ROTGUT	RUTTED	RATABLE
REWELD	RINSER	ROTTED	**RABBLER**	**RATAFEE**
REWIND	RIOTER	ROTTEN	**RABBONI**	**RATAFIA**

RATATAT	RECARRY	REENTER	RELATER	*RESEIZE
RATCHET	**RECEIPT**	**REENTRY**	RELATOR	**RESERVE**
RATFINK	**RECEIVE**	*REEQUIP	**RELAXER**	**RESHAPE**
RATFISH	**RECENCY**	REERECT	**RELAXIN**	**RESHOOT**
RATHOLE	**RECHART**	**REEVOKE**	RELEARN	RESIDER
RATLIKE	**RECHEAT**	REFFING	RELEASE	RESIDUA
RATLINE	*RECHECK	**REFEREE**	**RELIANT**	RESIDUE
RATTEEN	**RECITAL**	**REFIGHT**	**RELIEVE**	**RESMELT**
RATTIER	RECITER	REFINER	**RELIEVO**	**RESOJET**
RATTING	**RECLAIM**	**REFLATE**	**RELIGHT**	**RESOLVE**
RATTISH	**RECLAME**	**REFLECT**	*RELIQUE	RESOUND
RATTLER	**RECLASP**	**REFLIES**	**REMARRY**	**RESPECT**
RATTOON	RECLEAN	**REFLOAT**	**REMATCH**	RESPELL
RATTRAP	RECLINE	**REFLOOD**	**REMERGE**	RESPIRE
RAUCITY	RECLUSE	**REFOCUS**	REMNANT	RESPITE
RAUCOUS	RECOLOR	**REFORGE**	**REMODEL**	**RESPOND**
*RAUNCHY	RECOUNT	**REFOUND**	REMORSE	**RESTACK**
RAVAGER	RECOUPE	**REFRACT**	REMOUNT	**RESTAFF**
RAVELER	**RECOVER**	**REFRAIN**	**REMOVAL**	RESTAGE
RAVELIN	RECRATE	**REFRAME**	**REMOVER**	**RESTAMP**
RAVELLY	RECROSS	**REFRESH**	RENEGER	RESTART
RAVENER	**RECROWN**	**REFRONT**	**RENEWAL**	RESTATE
RAVIOLI	RECRUIT	**REFUGEE**	**RENEWER**	**RESTFUL**
RAWHIDE	*RECTIFY	**REFUSAL**	RENNASE	**RESTIVE**
RAWNESS	**RECTORY**	**REFUSER**	RENTIER	**RESTOCK**
RAYLESS	*RECTRIX	**REFUTAL**	**REOCCUR**	RESTORE
REACHER	**RECURVE**	**REFUTER**	**REOFFER**	**RESTUDY**
REACTOR	**RECYCLE**	REGALIA	REORDER	**RESTUFF**
READAPT	**REDBAIT**	**REGALLY**	REPAINT	**RESTYLE**
READIED	**REDBIRD**	REGATTA	**REPAPER**	RESUMER
READIER	**REDBONE**	REGAUGE	REPINER	RESURGE
READIES	REDCOAT	**REGENCY**	**REPLACE**	RETABLE
READILY	REDDEST	**REGIMEN**	REPLANT	**RETAKER**
READING	REDDING	*REGLAZE	REPLATE	RETASTE
READMIT	**REDDISH**	REGLOSS	REPLETE	**RETEACH**
READOPT	REDFISH	REGNANT	*REPLEVY	**RETHINK**
READORN	REDHEAD	REGORGE	**REPLICA**	**RETIARY**
READOUT	**REDNECK**	REGOSOL	REPLIER	RETICLE
*REAFFIX	REDNESS	REGRADE	REPOSAL	RETINAL
REAGENT	**REDOUBT**	REGRAFT	REPOSER	RETINOL
REALGAR	REDOUND	REGRANT	REPOSIT	RETINUE
REALIGN	**REDPOLL**	REGRATE	**REPOWER**	RETIREE
REALISE	**REDRAFT**	REGREET	REPRESS	RETIRER
REALISM	REDRESS	REGRESS	**REPRICE**	RETITLE
REALIST	REDRIED	REGRIND	REPRINT	**RETOUCH**
REALITY	REDRIES	**REGROUP**	REPRISE	RETRACE
*REALIZE	REDRILL	REGULAR	**REPROBE**	**RETRACK**
REALLOT	**REDRIVE**	REGULUS	**REPROOF**	RETRACT
REALTER	REDROOT	**REHINGE**	**REPROVE**	RETRAIN
REANNEX	**REDSKIN**	**REHOUSE**	REPTANT	RETREAD
REAPPLY	**REDUCER**	**REIFIER**	REPTILE	RETREAT
REARGUE	**REDWARE**	**REIMAGE**	REPULSE	RETRIAL
REAWAKE	**REDWING**	REINCUR	*REQUEST	RETSINA
REBATER	**REDWOOD**	REINTER	*REQUIEM	RETTING
REBIRTH	REEDIER	*REINDEX	*REQUIRE	**RETWIST**
REBLOOM	REEDIFY	REINTER	*REQUITE	**RETYING**
REBOANT	REEDING	REISSUE	REREDOS	**REUNIFY**
REBOARD	*REEJECT	**REITBOK**	REROUTE	REUNION
REBOUND	REELECT	*REJOICE	RESCALE	REUNITE
REBUILD	REENACT	*REJUDGE	**RESCIND**	REUTTER
REBUKER	**REENDOW**	RELABEL	RESCORE	**REVALUE**
	*REENJOY	RELAPSE	RESCUER	**REVELER**

REVELRY	RIGGING	ROMPISH	RUDERAL	RAINFALL
REVENGE	RIGHTER	RONDEAU	RUDESBY	RAINIEST
REVENUE	RIGHTLY	RONDURE	RUFFIAN	RAINLESS
REVERER	RIGIDLY	RONTGEN	RUFFLER	RAINWASH
REVERIE	RIKISHA	ROOFING	RUGGING	RAINWEAR
REVERSE	*RIKSHAW	ROOFTOP	RUGLIKE	RAISONNE
REVERSO	RILIEVO	ROOKERY	RUINATE	*RAKEHELL
REVILER	RIMFIRE	ROOMFUL	RUINOUS	RALLYING
REVISAL	RIMIEST	ROOSTER	RUMBLER	RALLYIST
REVISER	RIMLAND	ROOTAGE	RUMMAGE	RAMBUTAN
REVISIT	RIMLESS	ROOTIER	RUMMEST	RAMENTUM
REVISOR	RIMMING	ROOTLET	RUNAWAY	*RAMEQUIN
REVIVAL	*RIMROCK	*ROPEWAY	*RUNBACK	RAMIFORM
REVIVER	RINGENT	ROPIEST	RUNDLET	RAMILLIE
REVOICE	RINGLET	*RORQUAL	RUNDOWN	RAMMIEST
REVOKER	RINGTAW	ROSARIA	RUNLESS	RAMOSITY
REVOLVE	RINNING	ROSEATE	RUNNING	RAMPAGER
REVUIST	RINSING	ROSEBAY	RUNOVER	*RAMPANCY
REVVING	RIOTOUS	ROSEBUD	RUPTURE	RAMSHORN
REWAKEN	RIPCORD	ROSELLE	RURALLY	RAMULOSE
REWEAVE	RIPENER	ROSEOLA	RUSHIER	RAMULOUS
REWEIGH	RIPIENO	ROSETTE	RUSHING	RANCHERO
REWIDEN	RIPOSTE	ROSIEST	RUSSIFY	*RANCHMAN
REWOKEN	RIPPING	ROSOLIO	RUSTIER	RANDOMLY
REWOUND	RIPPLER	ROSTRAL	RUSTILY	RANKNESS
REWOVEN	RIPPLET	ROSTRUM	RUSTLER	RANSOMER
REWRITE	RIPTIDE	ROTATOR	RUTHFUL	*RAPACITY
REYNARD	RISIBLE	ROTIFER	RUTTIER	RAPESEED
*RHABDOM	RISOTTO	ROTTING	RUTTILY	RAPIDITY
*RHACHIS	RISSOLE	ROTUNDA	RUTTING	RAPPAREE
RHAMNUS	RIVALRY	ROUGHEN	RUTTISH	RAPTNESS
RHATANY	RIVETER	ROUGHER	RABBITER	RAREFIER
RHENIUM	RIVIERA	ROUGHLY	*RABBITRY	RARENESS
*RHIZOID	RIVIERE	ROUGING	RABIDITY	RARERIPE
*RHIZOMA	RIVULET	ROULADE	RACEMATE	RASCALLY
*RHIZOME	ROADBED	ROULEAU	RACEMISM	RASHNESS
RHODIUM	ROADWAY	ROUNDEL	*RACEMIZE	RASORIAL
RHODORA	ROARING	ROUNDER	RACEMOID	RATAPLAN
*RHOMBIC	ROASTER	ROUNDLY	RACEMOSE	RATEABLE
RHOMBUS	ROBBERY	ROUNDUP	RACEMOUS	RATICIDE
RHUBARB	ROBBING	ROUSTER	RACHITIS	RATIFIER
RIBBAND	ROBOTRY	ROUTINE	RACINESS	RATIONAL
RIBBIER	*ROCKABY	ROUTING	*RACKWORK	RATOONER
RIBBING	*ROCKERY	ROWBOAT	RACLETTE	RATSBANE
RIBBONY	ROCKIER	*ROWLOCK	RADIABLE	RATTENER
RIBLESS	ROCKOON	ROYALLY	RADIALLY	RATTIEST
RIBLIKE	RODLESS	ROYALTY	RADIANCE	RATTLING
RIBWORT	RODLIKE	ROYSTER	RADIANCY	RAVELING
RICINUS	RODSMAN	RUBABOO	RADIATOR	RAVELLED
RICKETS	*ROEBUCK	RUBASSE	RADICAND	RAVELLER
*RICKETY	ROGUERY	RUBBING	RADICATE	RAVENING
*RICKSHA	ROGUISH	RUBBISH	RADIOMAN	RAVENOUS
RICOTTA	ROISTER	RUBDOWN	RAFTSMAN	RAVIGOTE
RIDABLE	ROLLICK	RUBELLA	RAGINGLY	*RAVINGLY
RIDDING	ROLLING	RUBEOLA	RAILBIRD	RAVISHER
RIDDLER	ROLLMOP	RUBIEST	RAILHEAD	RAWBONED
RIDGIER	ROLLOUT	RUBIOUS	RAILLERY	RAYGRASS
RIDGING	ROLLTOP	RUCHING	RAILROAD	REABSORB
RIDOTTO	ROLLWAY	RUCTION	RAINBAND	REACCEDE
RIFFLER	ROMAINE	RUDDIER	RAINBIRD	REACCENT
RIFLERY	ROMANCE	RUDDILY	RAINCOAT	REACCEPT
RIFLING	ROMAUNT	*RUDDOCK	RAINDROP	REACCUSE

REACTANT	REDACTOR	REGROOVE	REMOLADE	RESEMBLE
REACTION	REDARGUE	*REGROWTH	REMOTION	RESERVER
REACTIVE	*REDBRICK	REGULATE	RENATURE	RESETTER
READDICT	REDEEMER	*REHAMMER	RENDERER	RESETTLE
READIEST	REDEFEAT	REHANDLE	RENDIBLE	RESHAPER
*READJUST	REDEFINE	REHARDEN	*RENDZINA	RESIDENT
*REAFFIRM	REDEMAND	REHEARSE	RENEGADE	RESIDUAL
REALISER	REDEPLOY	REHEATER	RENEGADO	RESIDUUM
*REALIZER	REDESIGN	REIGNITE	RENIFORM	RESIGNER
REALNESS	REDHORSE	REIMPORT	RENITENT	RESILVER
REANOINT	REDIGEST	REIMPOSE	RENOGRAM	RESINATE
*REAPHOOK	REDIRECT	REINCITE	RENOTIFY	RESINIFY
REAPPEAR	REDIVIDE	REINDEER	RENOUNCE	RESINOID
REARMICE	REDOLENT	REINDUCE	RENOVATE	RESINOUS
REARMOST	REDOUBLE	REINDUCT	RENUMBER	RESISTER
REAROUSE	REDRAWER	REINFECT	*REOBJECT	RESISTOR
REARREST	*REDSHANK	REINFORM	REOBTAIN	RESMOOTH
REARWARD	REDSHIRT	REINFUSE	*REOCCUPY	RESOLDER
REASCEND	REDSTART	*REINJURE	REOPPOSE	RESOLUTE
REASCENT	REDUVIID	REINLESS	REORDAIN	RESOLVER
REASONER	REEDBIRD	REINSERT	REORIENT	RESONANT
REASSAIL	*REEDBUCK	REINSMAN	REOVIRUS	RESONATE
REASSERT	REEDIEST	REINSURE	*REPACIFY	RESORCIN
REASSESS	REEDLING	REINVENT	REPAIRER	RESORTER
REASSIGN	*REEMBARK	REINVEST	REPARTEE	RESOUGHT
REASSORT	*REEMBODY	REINVITE	REPEALER	RESOURCE
REASSUME	REEMERGE	*REINVOKE	REPEATER	RESPONSA
REASSURE	*REEMPLOY	REISSUER	REPELLER	RESPONSE
REATTACH	REENGAGE	*REJECTEE	REPENTER	RESPREAD
REATTACK	REENLIST	*REJECTER	REPEOPLE	RESPRING
REATTAIN	*REEXPORT	*REJECTOR	REPETEND	RESTLESS
*REAWAKEN	REFASTEN	*REJIGGER	REPHRASE	RESTORAL
REBELDOM	REFERENT	*REJOICER	REPLACER	RESTORER
*REBRANCH	REFERRAL	REKINDLE	REPLEDGE	RESTRAIN
REBURIAL	REFERRED	RELAPSER	REPLEVIN	RESTRICT
REBUTTAL	REFERRER	RELATION	REPLUNGE	RESTRIKE
REBUTTER	REFIGURE	RELATIVE	REPOLISH	RESTRING
REBUTTON	REFILTER	RELAUNCH	REPORTER	RESTRIVE
RECALLER	REFINERY	*RELAXANT	REPOUSSE	RESTRUCK
RECANTER	REFINING	RELEASER	REPRIEVE	RESTRUNG
RECEIVER	REFINISH	RELEGATE	REPRISAL	RESUBMIT
RECEPTOR	*REFLEXLY	RELETTER	*REPROACH	RESUMMON
RECHANGE	REFLOWER	RELEVANT	REPROVAL	RESUPINE
RECHARGE	REFLUENT	RELIABLE	REPROVER	*RESUPPLY
RECHOOSE	REFOREST	RELIANCE	REPUBLIC	RESURVEY
RECIRCLE	REFORMAT	RELIEVER	REPULSER	RETAILER
RECISION	REFORMER	RELIGION	*REPURIFY	RETAILOR
RECKLESS	*REFOUGHT	RELOADER	REPURSUE	RETAINER
RECKONER	*REFREEZE	RELOCATE	*REQUIRER	RETARDER
RECLINER	REFUGIUM	RELUCENT	*REQUITAL	RETHREAD
RECLOTHE	REFUNDER	RELUMINE	*REQUITER	RETIARII
*RECODIFY	REGAINER	REMANENT	RERECORD	RETICENT
RECOILER	REGALITY	REMANNED	REREMICE	RETICULA
RECOMMIT	REGATHER	REMARKER	REREWARD	RETICULE
*RECONVEY	REGELATE	*REMARQUE	REROLLER	RETIFORM
RECORDER	REGICIDE	REMEDIAL	RESADDLE	RETINENE
RECOUPLE	REGIMENT	REMEMBER	RESALUTE	RETINITE
RECOURSE	REGIONAL	REMINDER	RESAMPLE	RETINULA
*RECOVERY	REGISTER	REMITTAL	RESCREEN	RETIRANT
RECREANT	REGISTRY	REMITTER	RESCRIPT	RETIRING
RECREATE	REGNANCY	REMITTOR	RESEARCH	RETORTER
RECUSANT	REGOLITH	*REMODIFY	RESELLER	RETRENCH

RETRIEVE	RICEBIRD	*ROCKFISH	ROUTEMAN	B R IN
RETROACT	RICERCAR	ROCKIEST	ROUTEWAY	B R IO
RETROFIT	RICHNESS	ROCKLESS	*ROVINGLY	B R IT
RETRORSE	*RICHWEED	*ROCKLIKE	*ROWDYISH	B R OO
RETURNEE	*RICKRACK	*ROCKLING	*ROWDYISM	B R OW
RETURNER	*RICKSHAW	ROCKROSE	ROYALISM	B R UT
REUNITER	*RICOCHET	*ROCKWEED	ROYALIST	C R AB
REUSABLE	RIDDANCE	*ROCKWORK	RUBAIYAT	C R AG
*REVAMPER	RIDEABLE	ROENTGEN	RUBBABOO	C R AM
*REVANCHE	RIDGIEST	ROGATION	RUBICUND	C R AP
REVEALER	RIDGLING	ROGATORY	RUBIDIUM	C R AW
REVEHENT	RIDICULE	ROLAMITE	*RUBYLIKE	C R EW
REVEILLE	RIFENESS	ROLLAWAY	*RUCKSACK	C R IB
REVELLER	*RIFFRAFF	*ROLLBACK	RUCTIOUS	C R IS
REVENANT	RIFLEMAN	*ROLLICKY	RUDDIEST	C R OP
REVENGER	RIFTLESS	ROLLOVER	RUDENESS	C R OW
REVENUER	RIGADOON	ROMANCER	RUDIMENT	C R UD
REVEREND	RIGATONI	*ROMANIZE	*RUFFLIKE	C R US
REVERENT	RIGAUDON	ROMANTIC	*RUFFLING	C R UX
REVERIES	*RIGHTFUL	RONDELET	RUGOSITY	D R AB
*REVERIFY	RIGHTIES	RONDELLE	RUGULOSE	D R AG
REVERING	RIGHTISM	ROOFLESS	RULELESS	D R AM
REVERSAL	RIGHTIST	*ROOFLIKE	RUMBLING	D R AT
REVERSER	*RIGIDIFY	ROOFLINE	RUMINANT	D R AW
REVERTER	RIGIDITY	ROOFTREE	RUMINATE	D R AY
REVIEWAL	RIGORISM	ROOMETTE	RUMMAGER	D R EE
REVIEWER	RIGORIST	ROOMMATE	RUNABOUT	D R EG
REVISION	RIGOROUS	*ROORBACK	RUNAGATE	D R EK
REVISORY	RIMESTER	ROOTHOLD	RUNROUND	D R EW
*REVIVIFY	RIMOSITY	ROOTIEST	RURALISE	D R IB
*REVIVING	*RINGBARK	ROOTLESS	*RURALISM	D R IP
REVOLTER	RINGBOLT	ROOTLIKE	RURALIST	D R OP
REVOLUTE	RINGBONE	*ROPEWALK	RURALITE	D R UB
REVOLVER	RINGDOVE	ROPINESS	RURALITY	D R UM
REVULSED	RINGHALS	ROSARIAN	*RURALIZE	F R AE
REWARDER	RINGLIKE	ROSARIUM	RUSHIEST	F R AG
REWINDER	*RINGNECK	ROSEBUSH	*RUSHLIKE	F R AP
REWRITER	RINGSIDE	ROSEFISH	RUSTICLY	F R AT
*RHABDOME	RINGTAIL	ROSELIKE	RUSTIEST	F R AY
RHAMNOSE	RINGTOSS	ROSEMARY	RUSTLESS	F R EE
RHAPSODE	RINGWORM	ROSEROOT	RUSTLING	F R ET
*RHAPSODY	RIPARIAN	ROSEWOOD	RUTABAGA	F R IG
*RHEMATIC	RIPENESS	ROSINESS	RUTHENIC	F R IT
RHEOBASE	RIPPABLE	ROSINOUS	RUTHLESS	*F R IZ
*RHEOLOGY	RIPPLING	ROSTELLA	RUTILANT	F R OE
*RHEOPHIL	RISIBLES	ROSTRATE	RUTTIEST	F R OG
RHEOSTAT	RITUALLY	ROSULATE	RYEGRASS	F R OM
RHETORIC	RIVERBED	ROTATION		F R OW
RHINITIS	RIVERINE	ROTATORY		F R UG
*RHIZOBIA	ROADLESS	ROTENONE	B R AD	G R AB
*RHIZOPOD	ROADSIDE	ROTIFORM	B R AE	G R AD
*RHIZOPUS	ROADSTER	ROTOTILL	B R AG	G R AM
RHODAMIN	*ROADWORK	ROTURIER	B R AN	G R AT
*RHOMBOID	ROBORANT	ROUGHAGE	B R AT	G R AY
*RHONCHUS	ROBOTICS	*ROUGHDRY	B R AW	G R EE
RHYOLITE	ROBOTISM	*ROUGHHEW	B R AY	G R EW
*RHYTHMIC	*ROBOTIZE	*ROUGHISH	B R ED	G R EY
RIBALDLY	*ROCKABYE	ROUGHLEG	B R EE	G R ID
RIBALDRY	*ROCKAWAY	ROULETTE	B R EW	G R IG
RIBBIEST	ROCKETER	ROUNDISH	B R IE	G R IM
RIBGRASS	*ROCKETRY	ROUNDLET	B R IG	G R IN
RIBOSOME	*ROCKFALL	ROUSSEAU	B R IM	G R IP

G R IT	B R AVO	**C R AWL**	D R ESS	**F R YER**
G R OG	**B R AWL**	*C R AZE	D R EST	G R AAL
G R OT	**B R AWN**	*C R AZY	D R IED	G R ACE
G R OW	*B R AXY	**C R EAK**	D R IER	G R ADE
G R UB	*B R AZA	C R EAM	D R IES	G R AFT
G R UM	*B R AZE	C R EDO	D R IFT	G R AIL
K R IS	B R EAD	C R EED	D R ILL	G R AIN
P R AM	**B R EAK**	**C R EEK**	D R ILY	G R AMA
P R AO	B R EAM	C R EEL	**D R INK**	**G R AMP**
P R AT	B R EDE	C R EEP	D R IPT	G R ANA
P R AU	B R EED	C R EME	D R IVE	G R AND
P R AY	B R ENT	C R EPE	D R OIT	G R ANT
P R EE	B R EVE	C R EPT	D R OLL	G R APE
P R EP	B R IAR	**C R EPY**	D R ONE	**G R APH**
P R EX	B R IBE	C R ESS	D R OOL	**G R APY**
P R EY	B R ICK	C R EST	D R OOP	G R ASP
P R IG	B R IDE	**C R ICK**	D R OPT	G R ASS
P R IM	B R IEF	C R IED	D R OSS	G R ATE
P R OA	B R IER	C R IER	**D R OUK**	**G R AVY**
P R OD	B R ILL	C R IES	D R OVE	*G R AZE
P R OF	B R INE	C R IME	D R OWN	G R EAT
P R OG	B R ING	**C R IMP**	D R UID	G R EBE
P R OM	**B R INK**	C R ISP	D R UNK	G R EED
P R OP	**B R INY**	**C R OAK**	D R UPE	**G R EEK**
P R OW	**B R ISK**	C R OCI	D R USE	G R EEN
T R AD	B R ITT	**C R OCK**	**D R YAD**	G R EET
T R AM	B R OAD	**C R OFT**	D R YER	G R EGO
T R AP	B R OAD	C R ONE	**D R YLY**	G R IDE
T R AY	**B R OCK**	**C R ONY**	F R AIL	G R IEF
T R EE	B R OIL	**C R OOK**	**F R AME**	**G R IFF**
T R EF	**B R OKE**	C R OON	**F R ANC**	G R IFT
T R EK	B R OME	C R ORE	**F R ANK**	G R ILL
T R ET	B R OMO	C R OSS	F R AUD	G R IME
T R EY	B R ONC	C R OUP	**F R EAK**	**G R IMY**
T R IG	B R OOD	**C R OWD**	F R EED	G R IND
T R IM	**B R OOK**	**C R OWN**	F R EER	G R IPE
T R IO	B R OOM	*C R OZE	F R EMD	G R IPT
T R IP	B R OSE	C R UDE	**F R ENA**	**G R IPY**
T R OD	**B R OSY**	C R UEL	F R ERE	G R IST
T R OP	**B R OTH**	C R UET	**F R ESH**	G R ITH
T R OT	**B R OWN**	**C R UMB**	F R IAR	G R OAN
T R OW	**B R OWN**	**C R UMP**	F R IED	G R OIN
T R OY	**B R UGH**	C R UOR	F R IER	G R OOM
T R UE	B R UIN	C R USE	F R IES	G R OPE
V R OW	B R UIT	**C R USH**	F R ILL	G R OSS
W R AP	B R UME	C R UST	F R ISE	*G R OSZ
W R EN	B R UNT	**C R WTH**	**F R ISK**	G R OUP
W R IT	B R USH	**C R YPT**	**F R ITH**	G R OUT
B R ACE	B R USK	D R AFF	F R ITT	G R OVE
B R ACH	B R UTE	D R AFT	*F R IZZ	G R OWL
B R ACT	C R AAL	D R AIL	**F R OCK**	G R OWN
B R AID	**C R ACK**	**D R AIN**	F R OND	G R UEL
B R AIL	**C R AFT**	**D R AKE**	F R ONS	**G R UFF**
B R AIN	**C R AKE**	**D R ANK**	F R ONT	G R UME
B R AKE	**C R AMP**	D R APE	F R ORE	**G R UMP**
B R AKY	C R ANE	D R AVE	**F R OSH**	G R UNT
B R AND	**C R ANK**	D R AWL	F R OST	K R AAL
B R ANK	C R APE	D R AWN	**F R OTH**	**K R AFT**
B R ANT	C R APE	D R EAD	**F R OWN**	K R AIT
B R ASH	**C R ASH**	D R EAM	*F R OZE	K R AUT
B R ASS	C R ASS	D R EAR	F R UIT	K R ILL
B R AVA	C R ATE		**F R UMP**	K R ONA

K R ONE	T R AIN	**W R ECK**	**BO R ROW**	**CA R PUS**
K R OON	T R AIT	W R EST	**BO R SCH**	CA R REL
K R UBI	T R AMP	W R IED	**BO R SHT**	**CA R ROM**
P R AAM	T R ANS	W R IER	***BO R ZOI**	CA R ROT
P R AHU	T R APT	W R IES	**BU R BLE**	CA R TEL
P R ANG	T R ASH	W R ING	**BU R BLY**	CA R TER
P R ANK	T R ASS	W R IST	**BU R BOT**	CA R TON
P R ASE	T R AWL	W R ITE	BU R DEN	**CA R TOP**
P R ATE	T R EAD	W R ONG	BU R DIE	**CA R VEL**
P R AWN	T R EAT	W R OTE	BU R EAU	**CA R VEN**
P R EEN	T R END	**W R OTH**	BU R GEE	**CA R VER**
P R ESA	T R ESS	W R UNG	BU R GER	CE R ATE
P R ESE	T R EWS	**BA R BAL**	BU R GLE	**CE R CIS**
P R ESS	T R IAD	**BA R BEL**	BU R GOO	CE R CUS
P R EST	T R IAL	**BA R BER**	BU R IAL	CE R EAL
*P R EXY	T R IBE	**BA R BET**	BU R IED	CE R EUS
P R ICE	T R ICE	**BA R BUT**	BU R IER	CE R ING
P R ICK	**T R ICK**	**BA R DIC**	BU R IES	**CE R IPH**
P R ICY	T R IED	BA R EGE	**BU R ING**	CE R ISE
P R IDE	T R IER	**BA R ELY**	**BU R KER**	CE R ITE
P R IED	T R IES	BA R EST	**BU R LAP**	CE R IUM
P R IER	T R IGO	**BA R FLY**	BU R LER	**CE R MET**
P R IES	T R ILL	**BA R HOP**	**BU R LEY**	CE R OUS
P R ILL	T R INE	BA R ING	BU R NER	CE R TES
P R IMA	T R IOL	BA R ITE	BU R NET	CE R USE
P R IME	T R IPE	**BA R IUM**	BU R NIE	***CE R VIX**
P R IMI	T R ITE	**BA R KER**	BU R RED	**CH R ISM**
P R IMO	T R OAK	**BA R LEY**	BU R RER	**CH R OMA**
P R IMP	**T R OCK**	**BA R LOW**	**BU R ROW**	**CH R OME**
P R INK	T R ODE	**BA R MAN**	BU R SAR	**CH R OMO**
P R INT	T R OIS	**BA R MIE**	BU R TON	**CI R CLE**
P R IOR	T R OKE	BA R ONG	**BY R NIE**	**CI R CUS**
P R ISE	T R OLL	BA R ONY	**BY R OAD**	***CI R QUE**
P R ISM	T R OMP	***BA R QUE**	**CA R ACK**	CI R RUS
P R ISS	T R ONA	BA R RED	***CA R ACK**	**CO R BAN**
P R IVY	T R ONE	BA R REL	**CA R AFE**	**CO R BEL**
*P R IZE	T R OOP	BA R REN	CA R ATE	**CO R BIE**
P R OBE	**T R OOZ**	BA R RET	**CA R BON**	CO R DER
P R OEM	T R OPE	BA R RIO	**CA R BOY**	CO R DON
P R OLE	T R OTH	**BA R ROW**	**CA R CEL**	CO R ING
P R ONE	T R OUT	BA R TER	CA R DER	**CO R IUM**
P R ONG	T R OVE	**BA R YON**	CA R DIA	**CO R KER**
P R OOF	T R UCE	**BA R YTA**	CA R EEN	**CO R MEL**
P R OSE	**T R UCK**	**BA R YTE**	CA R EER	CO R NEA
P R OSO	T R UED	BE R AKE	CA R ESS	CO R NEL
P R OST	T R UER	BE R ATE	**CA R FUL**	CO R NER
P R OSY	T R ULL	**BE R IME**	**CA R HOP**	CO R NET
P R OUD	T R ULY	BE R LIN	**CA R IBE**	CO R NUS
P R OVE	T R UMP	**BE R THA**	CA R IES	CO R ONA
P R OWL	T R UNK	BI R DER	CA R INA	**CO R PSE**
*P R OXY	T R USS	BI R DIE	CA R ING	**CO R PUS**
P R UDE	T R UST	**BI R EME**	CA R LIN	CO R RAL
P R UNE	T R UTH	**BI R KIE**	**CA R MAN**	CO R RIE
P R UTA	**T R YMA**	BI R LER	CA R NAL	**CO R SAC**
P R YER	T R YST	BO R AGE	**CA R NEY**	CO R SET
T R ACE	**V R OOM**	BO R ANE	CA R NIE	***CO R TEX**
T R ACK	**V R OUW**	BO R ATE	**CA R OCH**	CO R TIN
T R ACT	**W R ACK**	BO R DEL	CA R OLI	**CO R VEE**
T R ADE	W R ANG	BO R DER	**CA R PAL**	**CO R VES**
T R AGI	**W R APT**	BO R IDE	**CA R PEL**	**CO R VET**
T R AIK	W R ATH	BO R ING	**CA R PER**	***CO R YMB**
T R AIL	**W R EAK**		**CA R PET**	***CO R YZA**

CU R AGH	**FA R FAL**	GA R LIC	HI R SLE	**MA R LIN**
CU R ARA	**FA R FEL**	GA R NER	**HO R ARY**	**MA R OON**
CU R ARE	FA R INA	GA R NET	HO R NET	*MA R QUE
CU R ARI	**FA R ING**	GA R OTE	**HO R RID**	**MA R RED**
CU R ATE	**FA R MER**	GA R RED	HO R ROR	MA R RER
CU R BER	**FA R ROW**	GA R RET	**HO R SEY**	MA R RON
CU R DLE	FE R BAM	GA R RON	HO R STE	MA R TEN
CU R FEW	FE R INE	GA R TER	**HU R DLE**	MA R TIN
CU R ING	**FE R ITY**	**GA R VEY**	HU R LER	ME R GER
CU R ITE	FE R LIE	GE R BIL	**HU R LEY**	ME R INO
CU R IUM	FE R REL	GE R ENT	**HU R RAH**	ME R LIN
CU R LER	FE R RET	GE R MAN	**HU R RAY**	ME R LON
CU R LEW	**FE R RIC**	GE R MEN	HU R TER	MI R AGE
CU R RAN	FE R RUM	GE R UND	HU R TLE	MI R IER
CU R RIE	FE R ULE	GI R DER	*JA R FUL	MI R ING
CU R SED	**FE R VID**	GI R DLE	**JA R GON**	MI R ROR
CU R SER	FE R VOR	GI R LIE	JA R INA	MO R ALE
CU R TAL	**FI R ING**	GO R GER	*JA R RAH	MO R ALS
CU R TLY	FI R KIN	GO R GET	**JA R RED**	MO R ASS
CU R TSY	FI R MAN	GO R GON	*JA R VEY	MO R EEN
CU R ULE	FI R MER	**GO R HEN**	JE R BOA	MO R GEN
CU R VEY	FI R MLY	**GO R ILY**	*JE R KER	MO R GUE
DA R KEN	FO R AGE	GO R ING	*JE R KIN	MO R ION
DA R KEY	FO R BAD	GU R GLE	**JE R RID**	MO R OSE
DA R KIE	FO R BID	GU R NET	*JE R SEY	MO R RIS
DA R KLE	FO R BYE	**GU R NEY**	**JO R DAN**	MO R SEL
DA R KLY	**FO R CER**	**GY R ATE**	JU R ANT	MO R TAL
DA R NED	FO R EBY	**GY R ENE**	JU R IES	MO R TAR
DA R NEL	FO R EDO	**GY R ING**	JU R IST	MO R ULA
DA R NER	FO R EGO	**GY R OSE**	**KA R ATE**	MU R DER
DA R TER	FO R EST	HA R ASS	KA R OSS	MU R EIN
DA R TLE	**FO R GAT**	HA R BOR	KA R ROO	MU R ING
DE R IDE	**FO R GER**	HA R DEN	KE R MES	*MU R PHY
DE R IVE	**FO R GET**	**HA R DLY**	**KE R MIS**	NA R ROW
DE R MIS	FO R GOT	HA R EEM	KE R NEL	NA R WAL
DE R RIS	FO R INT	HA R LOT	**KE R RIA**	NE R EIS
DI R DUM	**FO R KER**	HA R MER	**KE R SEY**	NE R OLI
DI R ECT	FO R MAL	HA R MIN	*KI R SCH	NO R ITE
DI R ELY	FO R MAT	HA R PER	KI R TLE	NO R MAL
DI R EST	**FO R MEE**	HA R PIN	KO R UNA	NO R MED
DI R HAM	FO R MER	**HA R ROW**	KU R GAN	NU R SER
DI R NDL	FO R MIC	HA R TAL	LA R DER	PA R ADE
DO R ADO	FO R MOL	HE R ALD	LA R DON	**PA R AMO**
DO R BUG	FO R MYL	**HE R BAL**	LA R IAT	PA R ANG
DO R IES	*FO R NIX	**HE R DER**	LA R INE	**PA R APH**
DO R MER	FO R RIT	**HE R DIC**	**LA R KER**	**PA R CEL**
DO R MIE	*FO R WHY	HE R EAT	LA R RUP	**PA R DAH**
DO R MIN	FU R ANE	HE R EIN	*LA R YNX	PA R DEE
DO R PER	FU R IES	HE R EOF	**LO R DLY**	PA R DIE
DO R SAD	FU R LER	HE R EON	LO R EAL	PA R DON
DO R SAL	FU R ORE	**HE R ESY**	LO R ICA	PA R ENT
DO R SER	**FU R RED**	HE R ETO	LU R DAN	**PA R EVE**
DO R SUM	**FU R ROW**	HE R IOT	LU R ING	PA R GET
DU R BAR	GA R AGE	**HE R MIT**	**LU R KER**	**PA R IAH**
DU R ESS	GA R BLE	HE R NIA	LY R ATE	PA R IAN
DU R IAN	GA R CON	**HE R OIC**	**LY R ISM**	PA R IES
DU R ING	**GA R DEN**	HE R OIN	LY R IST	PA R ING
DU R ION	GA R GET	**HE R PES**	MA R AUD	**PA R ISH**
DU R NED	**GA R GLE**	HI R ING	MA R GIN	**PA R ITY**
FA R CER	**GA R ISH**	HI R PLE	MA R INA	**PA R KER**
FA R CIE			MA R INE	
FA R DEL		HI R SEL	*MA R KKA	

PA R LAY	*QU R USH	SH R UNK	ST R OUD	TH R UST
PA R LEY	**RA R EFY**	SI R DAR	ST R OVE	TI R ADE
PA R LOR	RA R ELY	SI R ING	**ST R UCK**	TI R ING
PA R ODY	RA R EST	SI R RAH	ST R UMA	TO R ERO
PA R OLE	**RA R IFY**	SI R REE	ST R UNG	TO R IES
PA R OUS	RA R ING	SO R BET	ST R UNT	TO R OID
PA R RAL	RA R ITY	**SO R BIC**	SU R EST	TO R OSE
PA R RED	RE R EAD	SO R DID	SU R ETY	TO R OUS
PA R REL	RE R ISE	SO R ELY	SU R FER	TO R PID
PA R ROT	RE R OLL	SO R EST	SU R GER	TO R POR
PA R SEC	RU R BAN	**SO R GHO**	SU R REY	*TO R QUE
PA R SER	SA R APE	SO R NER	**SU R TAX**	TO R RID
PA R SON	SA R DAR	SO R REL	**SU R VEY**	TO R ULA
PA R TAN	SA R ODE	SO R ROW	*SY R INX	TU R ACO
PA R TLY	SA R ONG	SO R TER	TA R GET	TU R BAN
PA R TON	SA R SAR	SO R TIE	**TA R IFF**	TU R BID
PA R URA	SA R SEN	SP R AIN	TA R ING	TU R BIT
PA R URE	SA R TOR	SP R ANG	**TA R MAC**	TU R BOT
PA R VIS	**SC R APE**	**SP R AWL**	TA R NAL	TU R EEN
PE R DIE	**SC R AWL**	SP R EAD	TA R PAN	TU R GID
PE R DUE	**SC R EAK**	SP R ENT	TA R PON	TU R GOR
PE R IOD	**SC R EAM**	SP R IER	TA R RED	**TU R KEY**
PE R ISH	SC R EED	SP R ING	TA R SAL	TU R NER
PE R MIT	SC R EEN	SP R INT	TA R SIA	TU R NIP
PE R RON	**SC R EWY**	SP R ITE	TA R SUS	TU R NUP
PE R SON	**SC R IBE**	SP R OUT	TA R TAN	TU R RET
PE R UKE	**SC R IMP**	**SP R UCE**	TA R TAR	TU R TLE
PE R USE	**SC R IPT**	**SP R UCY**	TA R TLY	TU R VES
PH R ASE	**SC R IVE**	SP R UNG	*TA R ZAN	TY R ANT
PI R ACY	SC R OLL	ST R AFE	**TE R APH**	**VA R IED**
PI R ANA	**SC R OOP**	ST R AIN	TE R BIA	VA R IER
PI R ATE	**SC R UFF**	ST R AIT	TE R CEL	VA R IES
PI R AYA	SE R AIL	**ST R AKE**	TE R CET	VA R LET
PO R ISM	SE R APE	ST R AND	TE R EDO	**VE R BAL**
PO R KER	**SE R APH**	ST R ANG	TE R ETE	**VE R BID**
PO R OSE	SE R ATE	ST R ASS	TE R GAL	**VE R DIN**
PO R OUS	SE R DAB	ST R ATA	TE R GUM	**VE R GER**
PO R TAL	SE R EIN	ST R ATH	TE R MER	*VE R IFY
PO R TER	SE R ENE	ST R ATI	**TE R MLY**	**VE R ILY**
PO R TLY	SE R EST	**ST R AWY**	TE R MOR	**VE R ISM**
PU R DAH	SE R IAL	ST R EAK	TE R RAS	VE R IST
PU R ELY	SE R IES	ST R EAM	TE R RET	**VE R ITY**
PU R EST	SE R INE	**ST R EEK**	TE R RIT	**VE R MES**
PU R FLE	SE R ING	ST R EET	TE R ROR	**VE R MIN**
PU R GER	SE R MON	ST R ESS	TH R ALL	**VE R MIS**
PU R IFY	SE R OSA	**ST R ICK**	**TH R ASH**	VE R NAL
PU R INE	SE R OUS	ST R ICT	**TH R AVE**	*VE R NIX
PU R ISM	SE R VAL	ST R IDE	**TH R AWN**	VE R SAL
PU R IST	SE R VER	ST R IFE	**TH R EAD**	VE R SER
PU R ITY	**SH R ANK**	**ST R IKE**	**TH R EAP**	VE R SET
PU R LIN	**SH R EWD**	ST R ING	**TH R EEP**	VE R STE
PU R PLE	**SH R IEK**	ST R IPE	**TH R ESH**	VE R SUS
PU R PLY	**SH R IFT**	ST R IPT	**TH R ICE**	*VE R TEX
PU R RED	**SH R IKE**	**ST R IPY**	**TH R IFT**	**VE R UCA**
PU R SER	SH R ILL	ST R IVE	**TH R ILL**	**VE R VET**
PU R SUE	**SH R IMP**	ST R OBE	**TH R IVE**	**VI R AGO**
PU R VEY	SH R INE	ST R ODE	TH R OAT	**VI R GIN**
PY R ENE	**SH R INK**	**ST R OKE**	TH R ONE	VI R ILE
PY R OLA	**SH R IVE**	ST R OLL	**TH R ONG**	VI R ION
PY R ONE	*SH R OFF	ST R OMA	**TH R OVE**	VI R TUE
PY R OPE	**SH R OUD**	ST R ONG	**TH R USH**	*VO R TEX
PY R ROL	**SH R OVE**	ST R OOK		**WA R BLE**

WA R DEN	*BO R AZON	CA R NAGE	CO R NILY	DE R NIER
WA R DER	BO R DURE	CA R NIES	CO R NUTE	DE R RICK
WA R IER	BO R EDOM	*CA R NIFY	CO R NUTO	DE R VISH
WA R ILY	BO R NEOL	CA R OACH	CO R OLLA	DI R EFUL
WA R ING	BO R NITE	CA R OCHE	CO R ONAL	*DO R HAWK
WA R MER	BO R OUGH	CA R OLER	CO R ONEL	DO R MANT
WA R MLY	BO R SCHT	CA R OLUS	CO R ONER	DO R MICE
WA R MTH	BO R STAL	CA R OTID	CO R ONET	DO R NECK
WA R MUP	BU R BLER	CA R OTIN	CO R PORA	DO R NICK
WA R NER	*BU R DOCK	CA R OUSE	CO R RADE	DU R ABLE
WA R PER	BU R ETTE	CA R PALE	CO R RECT	DU R AMEN
WA R RED	BU R GAGE	CA R PING	CO R RIDA	DU R ANCE
WA R REN	BU R GEON	CA R PORT	CO R RODE	DU R MAST
WA R SAW	BU R GESS	CA R RELL	CO R RODY	FA R ADAY
WA R SLE	BU R GHER	CA R RIED	CO R RUPT	FA R ADIC
WO R KER	BU R GLAR	CA R RIER	CO R SAGE	*FA R AWAY
*WO R KUP	BU R GOUT	CA R RIES	CO R SAIR	FA R CEUR
WO R MER	BU R KITE	CA R RION	CO R SLET	FA R CING
WO R MIL	BU R LESK	CA R ROCH	CO R TEGE	FA R INHA
WO R RIT	BU R NING	CA R ROTY	CO R VINA	FA R MING
WO R SEN	BU R NISH	CA R RYON	CO R VINE	FA R NESS
WO R SER	BU R NOUS	*CA R SICK	CU R ABLE	FA R RAGO
WO R SET	BU R NOUT	CA R TAGE	CU R ACAO	FA R RIER
*WO R THY	BU R SARY	CA R TOON	CU R ACOA	FA R THER
*WU R ZEL	BU R SATE	CA R VING	CU R ATOR	FE R MATA
YA R ROW	BU R SEED	CE R AMAL	CU R BING	FE R MENT
*ZA R EBA	BU R STER	CE R AMIC	CU R CUMA	FE R MION
*ZA R IBA	BU R THEN	CE R ATED	CU R DIER	FE R MIUM
*ZI R CON	BU R WEED	CE R ATIN	CU R DLER	FE R NERY
BA R BATE	CA R ABAO	CE R OTIC	CU R ETTE	FE R RATE
BA R BELL	CA R ABID	CE R TAIN	CU R IOSA	FE R RETY
BA R BULE	CA R ABIN	CE R UMEN	CU R IOUS	FE R RIED
BA R EFIT	CA R ACAL	CE R VINE	CU R LING	FE R RIES
BA R GAIN	CA R ACOL	CH R ISOM	CU R RACH	FE R RITE
BA R GING	CA R ACUL	*CH R ISTY	CU R RACY	FE R ROUS
BA R ILLA	CA R AMEL	*CH R OMIC	CU R RAGH	FE R RULA
*BA R KEEP	*CA R APAX	*CH R OMYL	CU R RANT	FE R RULE
BA R LESS	CA R AVAN	CH R ONIC	CU R RENT	FE R TILE
BA R MAID	CA R AVEL	CH R ONON	CU R RIED	FE R VENT
BA R ONET	*CA R AWAY	CI R CLER	CU R RIER	FE R VOUR
BA R ONNE	CA R BARN	CI R CLET	CU R RISH	FI R EARM
*BA R OQUE	CA R BIDE	CI R CUIT	CU R SING	*FI R EBOX
*BA R RACK	CA R BINE	CI R ROSE	CU R SIVE	FI R EBUG
BA R RAGE	CA R BORA	CI R ROUS	CU R SORY	FI R EDOG
BA R RIER	CA R CASE	CI R SOID	CU R TAIL	*FI R EFLY
BA R RING	CA R CASS	CO R ACLE	CU R TAIN	FI R EMAN
BA R ROOM	CA R DIAC	CO R ANTO	CU R TATE	FI R EPAN
BA R TEND	CA R DING	CO R BEIL	CU R TESY	FI R STLY
BA R WARE	CA R DOON	CO R BINA	CU R TSEY	FO R AGER
BE R EAVE	CA R EFUL	CO R DAGE	CU R TVING	FO R AMEN
BE R ETTA	CA R FARE	CO R DATE	DA R BIES	FO R AYER
*BE R HYME	CA R IBOU	CO R DIAL	DA R EFUL	FO R BADE
BE R LINE	CA R ICES	CO R DOBA	DA R ESAY	FO R BEAR
BE R OBED	CA R IOCA	CO R EIGN	DA R IOLE	FO R BODE
BE R SEEM	CA R IOLE	CO R KAGE	DA R KIES	FO R BORE
BE R SERK	CA R IOUS	CO R KIER	*DA R KISH	FO R CEPS
BI R CHEN	CA R LESS	CO R NCOB	DA R NING	FO R CING
BI R DMAN	CA R LINE	CO R NFED	DA R RING	FO R EARM
BI R ETTA	CA R LING	CO R NICE	DE R AIGN	*FO R EBAY
BI R LING	CA R LISH	CO R NIER	DE R IDER	*FO R EBYE
BO R ACES	CA R LOAD		DE R IVER	FO R EGUT
BO R ACIC	CA R MINE		DE R MOID	FO R EIGN

FO R ELEG	GE R MINA	HO R NITO	MA R TIAN	PA R ONYM
FO R EMAN	GI R AFFE	HO R RENT	MA R TINE	PA R OTIC
*FO R EPAW	GI R ASOL	*HO R RIFY	MA R TINI	PA R OTID
FO R ERUN	GI R DLER	HO R SIER	MA R TLET	*PA R QUET
FO R ESEE	GI R LISH	HO R SILY	*MA R TYRY	PA R RIED
FO R ETOP	GI R OSOL	HO R SING	ME R ISIS	PA R RIES
FO R EVER	*GO R COCK	HU R DIES	MI R IEST	PA R RING
FO R FEIT	GO R GING	HU R DLER	MI R INES	PA R ROTY
FO R FEND	GO R IEST	HU R LING	MO R AINE	PA R SING
FO R GAVE	GO R ILLA	HU R RIER	MO R ELLE	PA R SLEY
FO R GERY	GO R MAND	HU R TFUL	MO R ELLO	PA R SNIP
FO R GING	GU R GLET	*JA R GOON	*MO R PHIC	PA R TAKE
FO R GIVE	GU R NARD	*JA R LDOM	MO R RION	PA R TIAL
FO R GOER	GY R ATOR	*JA R RING	*MO R TIFY	PA R TIED
*FO R KFUL	HA R BOUR	*JA R SFUL	MO R TISE	PA R TIES
FO R KIER	HA R DHAT	*JE R KIES	MU R IATE	PA R TING
FO R LORN	HA R DIER	*JE R REED	MU R RAIN	PA R TITA
FO R MANT	HA R DIES	*JU R IDIC	MU R RINE	PA R TITE
FO R MATE	HA R DILY	*JU R YMAN	NA R CEIN	PA R TLET
*FO R MFUL	HA R DPAN	*KA R AKUL	NA R CISM	PA R TNER
FO R MULA	HA R DSET	KA R TING	NA R CIST	PA R TOOK
FO R SAKE	HA R DTOP	*KE R AMIC	NA R COSE	*PA R TWAY
FO R TIES	HA R ELIP	KE R ATIN	NA R GILE	PA R VENU
*FO R TIFY	HA R IANA	*KE R CHOO	NA R RATE	PA R VISE
FO R TUNE	HA R ICOT	KE R MESS	*NA R THEX	PE R ACID
FO R WARD	*HA R IJAN	KE R NITE	NE R ITIC	PE R CALE
FO R WENT	*HA R MFUL	KE R OGEN	NE R VATE	PE R CENT
FO R WORN	HA R MINE	*KE R YGMA	NE R VILY	PE R CEPT
*FU R BISH	*HA R MONY	*KI R KMAN	NE R VINE	PE R CHER
FU R CATE	HA R NESS	KI R MESS	NE R VING	PE R COID
FU R CULA	HA R PIES	*KU R BASH	NE R VOUS	PE R CUSS
FU R IOSO	HA R PING	LA R CENY	NE R VULE	PE R FECT
FU R IOUS	HA R PIST	LA R DIER	NE R VURE	*PE R FIDY
FU R LESS	HA R POON	LA R DOON	NI R VANA	PE R FORM
FU R LONG	HA R RIED	LA R GESS	NO R LAND	PE R FUME
*FU R METY	HA R RIER	LA R GISH	NO R THER	PE R FUSE
*FU R MITY	HA R RIES	LA R KIER	NU R SERY	PE R GOLA
FU R NACE	HA R RING	LO R DING	NU R SING	PE R HAPS
FU R NISH	HA R SHEN	LO R DOMA	NU R TURE	PE R IAPT
FU R RIER	*HA R SHLY	LO R GNON	PA R ABLE	PE R IDOT
FU R RILY	HA R SLET	LO R IMER	PA R ADER	PE R IGEE
FU R RING	HA R VEST	LO R INER	PA R ADOS	PE R IGON
*FU R ROWY	HE R BAGE	LU R CHER	*PA R ADOX	PE R ILLA
FU R THER	HE R BIER	LY R ATED	PA R AGON	*PE R IQUE
FU R TIVE	HE R DMAN	LY R ICAL	PA R APET	PE R IWIG
GA R BAGE	HE R EDES	MA R ABOU	PA R ASOL	*PE R JURE
GA R BLER	HE R ETIC	MA R ANTA	PA R BOIL	*PE R JURY
GA R BOIL	HE R ITOR	MA R INER	PA R DINE	*PE R KISH
GA R DANT	HE R OINE	MA R ITAL	PA R DNER	PE R LITE
GA R FISH	HE R OISM	*MA R KHOR	PA R EIRA	PE R MUTE
GA R GLER	*HE R OIZE	MA R LIER	PA R ESIS	PE R ORAL
GA R LAND	HE R ONRY	MA R LINE	PA R ETIC	*PE R OXID
GA R MENT	HE R RING	MA R LITE	PA R FAIT	PE R PEND
GA R NISH	HE R SELF	*MA R QUEE	PA R KING	PE R PENT
GA R OTTE	HI R ABLE	*MA R QUIS	*PA R KWAY	*PE R PLEX
GA R PIKE	HI R CINE	MA R RIER	PA R LING	PE R SALT
GA R RING	HI R SUTE	MA R RIES	PA R LOUR	PE R SIST
GA R ROTE	HI R UDIN	*MA R ROWY	PA R LOUS	PE R SONA
GE R BERA	HO R DEIN	MA R SHAL	PA R ODIC	PE R TAIN
GE R ENUK	*HO R IZON	MA R SUPI	PA R ODOS	PE R TURB
GE R MANE	HO R NIER	MA R TAGO	PA R OLEE	PE R USAL
GE R MIER	HO R NILY	MA R TIAL		PE R USER

PE R VADE	SC R AIGH	SP R IGGY	TA R TUFE	TU R NING
PE R VERT	SC R APER	SP R IGHT	TA R WEED	TU R NKEY
PH R ASAL	SC R APIE	SP R INGE	TE R AOHM	TU R NOFF
*PH R ATRY	*SC R APPY	SP R INGY	TE R BIUM	TU R NOUT
PH R ENIC	SC R ATCH	ST R AFER	TE R EBIC	TU R PETH
*PH R ENSY	*SC R AWLY	ST R ANGE	TE R EFAH	TU R TLER
PI R AGUA	*SC R AWNY	ST R ATAL	TE R GITE	TY R ANNY
PI R ANHA	*SC R EAKY	ST R ATUM	TE R MITE	VA R IANT
PI R ATIC	SC R EECH	ST R ATUS	TE R NARY	VA R IATE
PI R OGUE	SC R EWER	ST R AYER	TE R NATE	VA R ICES
*PI R OQUE	SC R IBAL	ST R EAKY	TE R NION	VA R IETY
PO R CINE	SC R IBER	ST R EAMY	TE R PENE	VA R IOLA
PO R KIER	SC R IEVE	ST R ETCH	TE R RACE	VA R IOLE
PO R KIES	*SC R IMPY	ST R ETTA	TE R RAIN	VA R IOUS
PO R RECT	SC R OGGY	ST R ETTO	TE R RANE	VA R MENT
PO R TAGE	SC R OOGE	ST R EWER	TE R REEN	VA R MINT
PO R TEND	SC R OTUM	ST R IATE	TE R RENE	VA R NISH
PO R TENT	SC R OUGE	ST R IDER	TE R RIER	VA R SITY
PO R TICO	*SC R UBBY	ST R IDOR	TE R RIES	VE R ANDA
PO R TION	*SC R UFFY	ST R IGIL	TE R RIFY	VE R BENA
PO R TRAY	SC R UNCH	ST R IKER	TE R RINE	*VE R BIFY
PU R GING	SC R UPLE	ST R INGY	TE R TIAL	VE R BILE
PU R ITAN	SE R FAGE	ST R IPER	TE R TIAN	VE R DANT
PU R LIEU	SE R FDOM	ST R IVER	TH R EADY	VE R DICT
PU R LINE	SE R FISH	ST R OBIC	*TH R IFTY	VE R DURE
PU R LOIN	SE R GING	ST R OBIL	TH R IVER	VE R GING
PU R PORT	SE R IATE	ST R OKER	TH R OATY	VE R GLAS
PU R POSE	SE R ICIN	ST R OPHE	TH R OUGH	VE R IDIC
PU R PURA	SE R IEMA	ST R OYER	TH R OWER	VE R IEST
PU R PURE	SE R INGA	ST R UDEL	TH R REAT	VE R ISMO
PU R RANA	SE R IOUS	SU R BASE	*TH R UMMY	VE R ITAS
PU R RING	SE R PENT	SU R COAT	TH R UPUT	VE R MEIL
PU R SIER	SE R PIGO	SU R FACE	*TH R UWAY	VE R MIAN
PU R SILY	SE R VANT	SU R FEIT	TO R CHON	*VE R MUTH
PU R SING	SE R VICE	SU R FIER	TO R MENT	VE R NIER
PU R SUER	SE R VILE	SU R FING	TO R NADO	VE R RIER
PU R SUIT	SE R VING	SU R GEON	TO R PEDO	VE R SANT
*PU R VIEW	*SH R IEKY	SU R GERY	*TO R QUER	*VE R SIFY
PY R ALID	*SH R IMPY	SU R GING	*TO R QUES	VE R SINE
*PY R AMID	SH R IVEL	SU R MISE	TO R REFY	VE R SING
PY R ETIC	SH R IVER	SU R NAME	TO R RENT	VE R SION
*PY R EXIA	*SH R UBBY	SU R PASS	TO R RIFY	VE R TIGO
PY R OGEN	SI R LOIN	SU R PLUS	TO R SADE	VE R VAIN
PY R OSIS	SI R OCCO	SU R REAL	TO R SION	VI R ELAI
*PY R RHIC	*SK R EEGH	SU R TOUT	TO R TILE	VI R ELAY
PY R RITE	*SK R EIGH	SU R VEIL	TO R TONI	VI R EMIA
PY R ROLE	SO R BATE	SU R VIVE	TO R TRIX	VI R GATE
RA R EBIT	SO R BENT	SY R INGA	TO R TURE	VI R GULE
RE R EDOS	SO R BOSE	SY R INGE	TU R ACOU	VI R OSIS
RE R OUTE	SO R CERY	*SY R PHID	TU R BARY	VI R TUAL
*RO R QUAL	SO R DINE	TA R BUSH	TU R BETH	VO R LAGE
RU R ALLY	SO R DINO	TA R DIER	TU R BINE	WA R BLER
SA R CASM	SO R GHUM	TA R DIES	TU R BITH	WA R FARE
SA R COID	SO R ITES	TA R NISH	TU R DINE	WA R HEAD
SA R COMA	SO R OCHE	TA R RIED	TU R FIER	WA R IEST
SA R COUS	SO R ORAL	TA R RIER	TU R FMAN	WA R ISON
SA R DINE	SO R OSIS	TA R RIES	TU R FSKI	WA R LESS
SA R DIUS	SO R RIER	TA R RING	TU R GENT	WA R LIKE
SA R MENT	SO R RILY	TA R SIER	TU R GITE	*WA R LOCK
SC R AGGY	*SP R AWLY	TA R TANA	TU R KOIS	WA R LORD
SC R AICH	SP R AYER	TA R TISH	TU R MOIL	*WA R MISH
	SP R IEST	TA R TLET	TU R NERY	WA R NING

WA R PAGE	BED R IVEL	*CLE R KISH	FEA R SOME	*HYD R ATOR
*WA R PATH	BEF R IEND	COC R EATE	*FEB R IFIC	*HYD R OGEL
WA R RANT	BEF R INGE	COE R CION	FER R EOUS	*HYD R OGEN
WA R RING	BEG R UDGE	*COE R CIVE	FER R ETER	*HYD R OMEL
WA R RIOR	BER R ETTA	COP R EMIA	FER R IAGE	*HYD R ONIC
*WA R SHIP	BET R AYAL	COR R IDOR	FER R ITIN	*HYD R OPIC
WA R SLER	BET R AYER	COR R IVAL	*FER R YMAN	*HYD R OPSY
WA R STLE	*BEW R AYER	COU R ANTE	FIB R ILLA	*HYD R OSOL
WA R THOG	BIR R ETTA	COU R ANTO	FIB R OSIS	*HYD R OXYL
WA R TIER	BOA R DING	COU R SING	FOR R ADER	*JER R ICAN
WA R TIME	BOA R DMAN	COU R TESY	*FOU R CHEE	*JER R YCAN
*WA R WORK	*BOA R FISH	COU R TIER	*FOU R FOLD	*JOY R IDER
WA R WORN	BOR R OWER	CUP R EOUS	FOU R SOME	LAC R IMAL
WE R GELD	BOT R YOID	*CUR R ENCY	FOU R TEEN	LAC R OSSE
WE R GELT	BOT R YOSE	CUR R ICLE	*FOU R THLY	LAR R IGAN
WE R GILD	BOU R GEON	CUR R IERY	FUR R IERY	LAR R IKIN
*WE R WOLF	BOU R TREE	CUR R YING	FUR R IEST	LAR R UPER
WI R EMAN	BUR R IEST	*CYP R INID	FUR R INER	LAU R EATE
WI R ETAP	BUR R OWER	*CZA R EVNA	FUR R OWER	LEA R IEST
*WI R EWAY	CAB R ESTA	*CZA R ITZA	GAR R ISON	LEA R NING
WI R IEST	CAB R ESTO	DEA R NESS	GAR R OTER	LEP R OTIC
WI R RIER	CAB R ETTA	DEB R UISE	GAR R OTTE	LIB R ETTO
WI R RILY	CAB R ILLA	DEC R EASE	GEA R CASE	LIG R OINE
WI R RING	CAB R IOLE	DEC R EPIT	GEA R LESS	MA R ASMUS
WO R DAGE	*CAP R ICCI	DEC R ETAL	GLO R IOLE	MA R ATHON
WO R DIER	*CAP R IFIG	DEE R SKIN	GLO R IOUS	MA R AUDER
WO R DILY	CAP R IOLE	DEE R WEED	GNA R RING	MA R AVEDE
WO R DING	CAR R IAGE	DEE R YARD	GOU R MAND	MA R BLING
*WO R KBAG	CAR R IOLE	*DEF R AYAL	GUA R ANTY	MA R GARIN
*WO R KBOX	*CAR R ITCH	*DEF R AYER	GUA R DANT	MA R GARIO
*WO R KDAY	CAR R OTIN	DEG R ADER	GUA R DIAN	MA R GINAL
*WO R KING	CAR R YALL	DEG R EASE	GUE R ILLA	MA R GRAVE
*WO R KMAN	CAR R YOUT	DEP R AVER	GUE R NSEY	MA R IGOLD
WO R KOUT	*CHA R ACID	DEP R IVAL	HAI R BALL	MA R INADE
WO R LDLY	*CHA R ACIN	DEP R IVER	HAI R BAND	MA R INARA
WO R MIER	*CHA R COAL	DER R IERE	HAI R IEST	MA R INATE
*WO R MISH	CHA R IEST	DET R ITUS	HAI R LESS	MA R IPOSA
WO R RIED	*CHA R ISMA	DIA R RHEA	*HAI R LIKE	MA R ITIME
WO R RIER	*CHA R LADY	DIC R OTAL	HAI R LINE	MA R KETER
*WO R SHIP	*CHA R LOCK	DIC R OTIC	*HAI R LOCK	MA R LIEST
WO R STED	*CHA R MING	DIE R ESIS	*HAI R WORK	MA R MOSET
*XE R ARCH	CHA R RIER	DIS R OBER	*HAI R WORM	MA R RIAGE
XE R OSIS	CHA R RING	DIU R ESIS	HAR R IDAN	ME R CAPTO
YA R DAGE	CHA R TIST	DIU R ETIC	HAR R OWER	ME R ENGUE
YA R DARM	CHO R AGUS	DOO R BELL	*HAR R UMPH	ME R GENCE
YA R DMAN	*CHO R ALLY	*DOO R JAMB	*HEB R AIZE	ME R IDIAN
*ZA R EEBA	CHO R DATE	*DOO R KNOB	HEI R LESS	ME R INGUE
*ZO R ILLA	CHO R EGUS	DOO R LESS	HEI R LOOM	ME R ISTEM
*ZO R ILLE	*CHO R EMAN	DOO R NAIL	*HEI R SHIP	ME R ISTIC
*ZO R ILLO	CHO R EOID	DOO R POST	HID R OSIS	*MIC R OLUX
BAR R ABLE	CHO R IAMB	DOO R SILL	*HIE R ARCH	*MIC R OMHO
BAR R ANCA	CHO R IOID	DOO R STEP	HIE R ATIC	*MIC R URGY
BAR R ANCO	CHO R TLER	DOO R STOP	HOA R DING	*MOO R FOWL
BAR R ATER	*CHU R CHLY	DOO R YARD	HOA R IEST	MO R ALISM
BAR R ATOR	CHU R NING	DOU R NESS	HOR R IBLE	MO R ALIST
BAR R ATRY	CIR R IPED	*DWA R FISH	*HOR R IBLY	MO R ALITY
BAR R ETOR	CIT R EOUS	*DWA R FISM	*HOR R IFIC	MO R ATORY
BAR R ETRY	CLA R ENCE	FAI R LEAD	*HUA R ACHE	MO R BILLI
BAR R ETTE	CLA R INET	FAI R NESS	*HUA R ACHO	MO R EOVER
BEA R LIKE	CLE R ICAL	*FAI R YISM	*HYD R ACID	MO R IBUND
BEA R SKIN	*CLE R IHEW	FAR R IERY	*HYD R AGOG	MO R ONISM
*BED R ENCH	*CLE R KDOM	FEA R LESS	*HYD R ANTH	MO R ONITY

MO R OSITY	*QUA R TILE	SHI R TING	STU R GEON	WHO R ESON
MO R TALLY	*QUE R CINE	SHO R TAGE	SUR R OUND	*YEA R BOOK
MO R TGAGE	REA R MICE	SHO R TCUT	SUR R OYAL	YEA R LIES
MO R TISER	REA R MOST	SHO R TIES	SWO R DMAN	YEA R LING
MO R TMAIN	REA R OUSE	SHO R TISH	TAR R AGON	YEA R LONG
MO R TUARY	REA R REST	*SIE R OZEM	TAR R IEST	YEA R NING
MU R AENID	REA R WARD	*SKI R MISH	TEA R DOWN	YOU R SELF
MU R ALIST	*REB R ANCH	SKI R TING	TEA R DROP	
MU R DEREE	REC R EANT	SLU R RING	TEA R IEST	
MU R DERER	REC R EATE	SMA R AGDE	TEA R LESS	BEA R
MU R IATED	RED R AWER	SOB R IETY	TER R APIN	BEE R
MU R ICATE	*REF R EEZE	SOR R IEST	TER R ARIA	BIE R
MU R MURER	REG R OOVE	SOR R OWER	*TER R AZZO	BIR R
MU R RELET	*REG R OWTH	SOU R BALL	TER R ELLA	BLU R
NAR R ATER	REO R DAIN	SOU R DINE	TER R IBLE	BOA R
NAR R ATOR	REO R IENT	SOU R NESS	TER R IFIC	BOO R
NA R WHALE	REP R IEVE	SOU R PUSS	TET R ACID	BUH R
NEA R NESS	REP R ISAL	SOU R WOOD	TET R AGON	BUR R
*NEC R OPSY	*REP R OACH	SOV R ANLY	TET R AMER	CHA R
NEC R OSIS	REP R OVAL	SOV R ANTY	TET R APOD	COI R
*NEU R AXON	REP R OVER	SPA R ABLE	TET R ARCH	CUR R
NEU R ITIC	RET R ENCH	SPA R ERIB	*TET R OXID	*CZA R
NEU R ITIS	RET R IEVE	SPA R KIER	THE R EFOR	DEA R
NEU R OSIS	RET R OACT	*SPA R KILY	THE R EMIN	DEE R
NEU R OTIC	RET R OFIT	*SPA R KISH	THE R IACA	DOE R
NIG R OSIN	RET R ORSE	SPA R KLER	THE R MION	DOO R
NIT R ATOR	REW R ITER	SPA R LIKE	THE R MITE	DOR R
NIT R OGEN	*ROO R BACK	SPA R LING	THE R OPOD	DOU R
NIT R OLIC	RUN R OUND	SPA R RIER	THI R LAGE	DUR R
NIT R OSYL	SAC R ARIA	SPA R RING	THI R STER	DYE R
NON R ATED	SAC R ISTY	SPA R SITY	THI R TEEN	FAI R
NON R IGID	SAF R ANIN	*SPE R MARY	*THO R OUGH	FEA R
NON R IVAL	SAP R EMIA	SPE R MINE	THU R IBLE	FIA R
NON R OYAL	SAP R OPEL	SPE R MOUS	THU R IFER	FOU R
NON R URAL	SAU R OPOD	SPI R ACLE	*THY R EOID	GAU R
NUT R IENT	*SCA R CELY	SPI R ALLY	*THY R OXIN	GEA R
PAR R IDGE	*SCA R CITY	SPI R ILLA	TIR R IVEE	GNA R
*PAR R ITCH	*SCA R FPIN	SPO R ADIC	TIT R ABLE	GOE R
PAR R OKET	SCA R IEST	SPO R TFUL	TIT R ATOR	GUA R
PAR R OTER	SCA R IOSE	SPO R TIVE	TSA R EVNA	HAA R
PEA R LASH	SCA R IOUS	SPU R GALL	TUR R ICAL	HAI R
PEA R LITE	SCA R LESS	SPU R IOUS	*TZA R EVNA	HEA R
PEA R MAIN	SCA R RING	SPU R RIER	*TZA R ITZA	HEI R
PEE R LESS	*SCH R IEVE	SPU R RING	*VAG R ANCY	HOA R
PET R OLIC	SCI R OCCO	STA R DUST	*VIB R ANCE	HOE R
PET R ONEL	SCI R RHUS	STA R FISH	*VIB R ANCY	HOU R
PET R OSAL	*SCO R CHER	*STA R GAZE	VIB R ATOR	JEE R
PHA R ISEE	SCO R EPAD	STA R LESS	VIB R ISSA	KEI R
*PHA R MACY	SCO R NFUL	STA R LIKE	VIT R EOUS	KIE R
PLU R ALLY	SCO R PION	STA R LING	WAR R AGAL	KNA R
POO R NESS	SCU R RIED	STA R NOSE	WAR R ANTY	KNU R
POO R TITH	SCU R RIES	STA R RING	WAR R ENER	KYA R
POR R IDGE	SCU R RILE	STA R TLER	WAR R IGAL	LAI R
PRE R ENAL	SEA R CHER	STA R WORT	WEA R ABLE	LEA R
PRO R OGUE	SEC R ETIN	STE R ICAL	WEA R IEST	LEE R
PRU R IENT	SEC R ETLY	STE R IGMA	WEA R IFUL	LEH R
PRU R ITUS	SEC R ETOR	STE R LING	WEI R DIES	LIA R
PSO R ALEA	SER R ANID	STE R NITE	*WHA R FAGE	LIE R
PTE R OPOD	*SFO R ZATO	STE R NSON	*WHE R EVER	LOU R
*PYO R RHEA	SHE R BERT	STE R NWAY	*WHI R RING	MAA R
*QUA R RIER	*SHE R LOCK	STI R RING	*WHO R EDOM	MAI R
*QUA R TERN	SHI R RING	STO R ABLE		MOO R

MUR R	BRIA R	**FAKI R**	**JURO R**	MUTE R
NEA R	BRIE R	***FAQI R**	***KABA R**	NADI R
NOI R	**BUYE R**	FARE R	**KAFI R**	NAME R
PAI R	CABE R	**FAVO R**	**KEBA R**	NAVA R
PAR R	CANE R	**FEMU R**	**KEFI R**	NEVE R
PEA R	CAPE R	FETO R	KITE R	NITE R
PEE R	CARE R	FEUA R	LABO R	NOTE R
PIE R	CATE R	**FEVE R**	LACE R	NUDE R
POO R	**CAVE R**	**FIBE R**	LADE R	PACE R
POU R	CEDA R	**FIFE R**	LAGE R	PALE R
PUR R	CEDE R	FILA R	LAKE R	PAPE R
REA R	**CHAI R**	FILE R	LAME R	PARE R
ROA R	**CHEE R**	FINE R	LASE R	PATE R
RUE R	**CHIR R**	FIRE R	LATE R	**PAVE R**
SCA R	**CHOI R**	**FIVE R**	LAVE R	**PAWE R**
SEA R	**CHUR R**	***FIXE R**	LAYE R	**PAYE R**
SEE R	CIDE R	FLAI R	**LAZA R**	**PAYO R**
SLU R	CIGA R	FLEE R	LEGE R	PETE R
SOA R	CITE R	FLIE R	LEMU R	**PIKE R**
SOU R	CLEA R	FLOU R	LEPE R	PILA R
SPA R	CLOU R	FLUO R	LEVE R	PIPE R
SPU R	CODE R	**FLYE R**	LIBE R	PLIE R
STA R	COLO R	**FOYE R**	LIDA R	**PLYE R**
STI R	COME R	FREE R	LIFE R	**POKE R**
SUE R	COOE R	FRIA R	LIKE R	POLA R
TAH R	COPE R	FRIE R	LINE R	POLE R
TEA R	CORE R	**FRYE R**	LITE R	POSE R
THI R	**COVE R**	**FUME R**	LIVE R	**POWE R**
TIE R	**COWE R**	FURO R	LOBA R	PRIE R
TOR R	CRIE R	GAGE R	LONE R	PRIO R
TOU R	CRUO R	GAME R	LOPE R	**PRYE R**
TSA R	CUBE R	GAPE R	LOSE R	PULE R
TZA R	CURE R	***GAZE R**	LOVE R	PURE R
VAI R	**CYDE R**	GIBE R	LOWE R	**QUEE R**
VEE R	**CYMA R**	GIVE R	LUNA R	RACE R
VIE R	DAMA R	GLAI R	LURE R	RADA R
WAI R	DARE R	GLUE R	MACE R	RAKE R
WAU R	DATE R	GNAR R	**MAJO R**	RAPE R
WEA R	DEAI R	GONE R	**MAKA R**	RARE R
WEE R	DEBA R	GULA R	**MAKE R**	RASE R
WEI R	DEFE R	HALE R	MALA R	RATE R
WHI R	DEMU R	HATE R	MANO R	RAVE R
YEA R	DETE R	**HAYE R**	MASE R	**RAZE R**
YIR R	DICE R	HEDE R	MATE R	**RAZO R**
YOU R	**DIKE R**	**HEWE R**	**MAYO R**	RECU R
BAKE R	DIME R	***HEXE R**	***MAZE R**	REFE R
BALE R	DINA R	HIDE R	METE R	RICE R
BARE R	DINE R	**HIKE R**	MILE R	RIDE R
BASE R	DIRE R	HILA R	MIME R	RIGO R
*BAZA R	DONO R	HIRE R	MINE R	RIME R
BEVO R	DOPE R	**HOME R**	MINO R	RIPE R
BIDE R	DOSE R	HONE R	MISE R	RISE R
BIKE R	DOTE R	HONO R	MITE R	RIVE R
BITE R	DOWE R	**HOPE R**	**MIXE R**	ROGE R
BLEA R	***DOZE R**	**HOVE R**	**MOHU R**	ROPE R
BLUE R	DREA R	HUGE R	MOLA R	ROTO R
BOLA R	DRIE R	**HUMO R**	MOPE R	ROVE R
BONE R	**DRYE R**	**JAGE R**	MOTO R	ROWE R
BORE R	DUPE R	**JAPE R**	**MOVE R**	RULE R
BOWE R	**FACE R**	JIBE R	**MOWE R**	RUMO R
BOXE R	FADE R	***JOKE R**	MUCO R	SABE R
BOYA R	FAKE R		MUSE R	SABI R

SAFE R	TALA R	**BADGE R**	**BOTHE R**	CAUSE R
SAGE R	TALE R	BAILE R	**BOWLE R**	**CAVIA R**
SAKE R	TAME R	BAILO R	**BOWYE R**	CEILE R
SANE R	TAPE R	BAITE R	***BOXCA R**	CELLA R
SAPO R	TAPI R	**BALKE R**	***BOXIE R**	CENSE R
SATY R	TATE R	BALLE R	**BRACE R**	CENSO R
SAVE R	TAWE R	BANDE R	**BRAVE R**	CENTE R
SAVO R	**TAXE R**	BANGE R	**BRAYE R**	**CHAFE R**
SAWE R	TENO R	**BANKE R**	***BRAZE R**	**CHASE R**
SAYE R	THEI R	BANNE R	**BREWE R**	**CHAWE R**
SCAU R	TIGE R	BANTE R	**BRIBE R**	**CHEDE R**
SCOU R	TILE R	**BARBE R**	BRINE R	**CHEWE R**
SEDE R	TIME R	**BARKE R**	**BROKE R**	**CHIDE R**
SENO R	TITE R	BARTE R	**BUCKE R**	**CHIMA R**
SERE R	TONE R	**BASHE R**	**BUDDE R**	**CHIME R**
SEVE R	TOPE R	BASTE R	**BUDGE R**	***CHOKE R**
SEWA R	TOTE R	**BATHE R**	**BUFFE R**	**CHOLE R**
SEWE R	TOWE R	BATTE R	**BUGGE R**	***CHUKA R**
SHEA R	TOYE R	**BAWLE R**	BUGLE R	CINDE R
SHEE R	TRIE R	***BAZAA R**	BULGE R	**CIPHE R**
SHIE R	TRUE R	**BEAKE R**	BULGU R	**CITHE R**
SHIR R	TUBE R	BEARE R	**BUMME R**	**CLAMO R**
SHOE R	TUMO R	BEATE R	**BUMPE R**	**CLAVE R**
SHYE R	TUNE R	**BEAVE R**	**BUNKE R**	**CLAWE R**
SIEU R	TUTO R	**BEDDE R**	BUNTE R	**CLEVE R**
SIKE R	TUYE R	**BEEPE R**	BURGE R	CLOSE R
SIMA R	TWIE R	**BEGGA R**	BURIE R	**CLOVE R**
SITA R	**TWYE R**	BELIE R	**BURKE R**	COALE R
SIVE R	VALO R	BENDE R	BURLE R	COATE R
SIZA R	**VAPO R**	BESTI R	BURNE R	***COAXE R**
SIZE R	VELA R	BETTE R	BURRE R	**COBBE R**
SKIE R	***VEXE R**	BETTO R	BURSA R	**COCKE R**
SKIR R	**VICA R**	***BEZOA R**	**BUSHE R**	**CODDE R**
SLIE R	VIGO R	**BIBBE R**	BUSIE R	**CODGE R**
SMEA R	**VIPE R**	**BICKE R**	**BUSKE R**	**COFFE R**
SNEE R	VISO R	**BIDDE R**	BUSTE R	**COHEI R**
SOBE R	***VIZI R**	**BIGGE R**	BUTLE R	COILE R
SOFA R	***VIZO R**	**BILKE R**	BUTTE R	COINE R
SOLA R	VOLA R	BILLE R	***BUZZE R**	COLLA R
SONA R	**VOME R**	BINDE R	**CADGE R**	COLOU R
SOPO R	VOTE R	BIRDE R	CAGIE R	COLTE R
SORE R	**VOWE R**	BIRLE R	**CAHIE R**	**COMBE R**
SOWA R	WADE R	BISTE R	**CALCA R**	CONCU R
SOWE R	**WAFE R**	BITTE R	**CALKE R**	CONDO R
SPEA R	WAGE R	**BLAME R**	CALLE R	**CONFE R**
SPEE R	**WAKE R**	***BLAZE R**	**CAMBE R**	CONGE R
SPEI R	WALE R	**BLOWE R**	**CAMPE R**	**CONKE R**
SPIE R	WATE R	BOATE R	**CANCE R**	CONNE R
SPOO R	**WAVE R**	**BOBBE R**	CANDO R	**COOKE R**
STAI R	***WAXE R**	BOILE R	**CANKE R**	COOLE R
STEE R	**WEBE R**	BOLTE R	CANNE R	**COOPE R**
STOU R	**WHIR R**	**BOMBE R**	CANTE R	**COPIE R**
SUBE R	WIDE R	BONDE R	CANTO R	**COPPE R**
SUDO R	**WIPE R**	BONIE R	**CAPPE R**	**COPTE R**
SUGA R	WIRE R	***BONZE R**	**CAPTO R**	CORDE R
SUPE R	WISE R	BOOGE R	CARDE R	**CORKE R**
SURE R	**WIVE R**	**BOOKE R**	CAREE R	CORNE R
SWEA R	WOOE R	**BOOME R**	**CARPE R**	**COSHE R**
SWEE R	WRIE R	***BOOZE R**	CARTE R	COSIE R
TABE R	YAGE R	**BOPPE R**	**CARVE R**	COSTA R
TABO R	**ZONE R**	BORDE R	CASTE R	COSTE R
TAKE R	**BACKE R**	**BOSKE R**	CASTO R	COTTA R

COTTE R	DISBA R	**FINDE R**	GETTE R	**HEAVE R**
COUGA R	DITHE R	**FINGE R**	**GEYSE R**	**HECTO R**
COUTE R	DOBBE R	FIRME R	GIAOU R	HEDGE R
COWIE R	**DOCKE R**	FISHE R	**GIBBE R**	**HEEDE R**
*COZIE R	DOCTO R	FITTE R	GILDE R	HEELE R
CRATE R	DODDE R	*FIZZE R	GILLE R	HEFTE R
CRAVE R	DODGE R	FLAKE R	GINGE R	HEIFE R
CROWE R	**DOFFE R**	FLAME R	GINNE R	HELLE R
CULLE R	DOGGE R	FLAVO R	**GIPPE R**	**HELPE R**
CULVE R	DOLLA R	FLAYE R	GIRDE R	HEMME R
CUMBE R	DOLOU R	*FLEXO R	GLAMO R	HERDE R
CUMME R	DOPIE R	FLOWE R	GLIDE R	HILLE R
CUNNE R	DORME R	FLUTE R	**GLOVE R**	**HINDE R**
CUPPE R	DORPE R	**FOAME R**	**GLOWE R**	**HINGE R**
CURBE R	DORSE R	**FODDE R**	**GNAWE R**	**HIPPE R**
CURLE R	DOSSE R	FOETO R	**GOFFE R**	HISSE R
CURSE R	DOTIE R	**FOGGE R**	GOITE R	HITHE R
CUSSE R	DOTTE R	**FOLDE R**	**GOLFE R**	*HOAXE R
CUTLE R	DOUSE R	FOLIA R	GOOBE R	*HOCKE R
CUTTE R	FOOTE R	GOOIE R	**HOGGE R**
CYCLE R	**DOWNE R**	**FORCE R**	**GOPHE R**	HOLDE R
*CYPHE R	**DOWSE R**	**FORGE R**	GORGE R	HOLIE R
DABBE R	DRAPE R	**FORKE R**	GORIE R	HOLLE R
DACKE R	**DRAWE R**	**FORME R**	GOUGE R	HOMIE R
DAGGE R	DRIVE R	FOSTE R	GRADE R	**HONKE R**
DAIKE R	DRONE R	FOWLE R	GRATE R	HONOU R
DAMMA R	**DROVE R**	FRAME R	**GRAVE R**	HOOFE R
DAMME R	**DUBBE R**	FRATE R	*GRAZE R	HOOPE R
DAMNE R	**DUCKE R**	FRILE R	GRIPE R	HOOPE R
DAMPE R	DUELE R	*FRIZE R	GROCE R	HOOTE R
DANCE R	**DUFFE R**	FUELE R	GROPE R	HORRO R
DANDE R	**DUIKE R**	FUHRE R	**GROWE R**	HOSIE R
DANGE R	**DUMPE R**	FULLE R	GUIDE R	HOTTE R
DAPPE R	DUNNE R	FULMA R	GUITA R	HOUSE R
DARNE R	DURBA R	**FUMIE R**	GULPE R	**HOWLE R**
DARTE R	DUSTE R	FUNKE R	**GUMME R**	**HUGGE R**
DASHE R	**DYVOU R**	FURFU R	GUNNE R	**HUMME R**
DAUBE R	**FABLE R**	FURLE R	**GUSHE R**	HUMOU R
DEBTO R	**FACTO R**	FUSSE R	GUTTE R	**HUNGE R**
DECKE R	**FAKEE R**	**GABBE R**	**GYPPE R**	**HUNKE R**
DEFIE R	FALLE R	GADDE R	*HACKE R	HUNTE R
DELVE R	FALTE R	**GAFFE R**	**HAFTE R**	HURLE R
DENIE R	FANNE R	GAGGE R	HAILE R	HURTE R
DEODA R	*FAQUI R	GAINE R	HALTE R	**HUSKE R**
DETOU R	**FARCE R**	GAITE R	**HAMME R**	HUSSA R
DEVOI R	**FARME R**	**GAMBI R**	**HAMPE R**	*JABBE R
DEVOU R	**FATHE R**	GAMIE R	**HANGA R**	*JACKE R
DEWIE R	FATTE R	**GAMME R**	**HANGE R**	JAEGE R
DEXTE R	**FAVOU R**	GANDE R	**HANKE R**	*JAGGE R
DIALE R	**FAWNE R**	GANGE R	**HARBO R**	JAGUA R
DIAPE R	FEARE R	GAOLE R	**HARME R**	JAILE R
DIAPI R	**FEEDE R**	GARNE R	**HARPE R**	JAILO R
DIBBE R	FEELE R	GARTE R	HATTE R	*JAMME R
DICIE R	FELLE R	GASPE R	HAULE R	*JASPE R
DICKE R	**FENCE R**	GASSE R	HAVIO R	*JAZZE R
DIETE R	**FENDE R**	**GATHE R**	*HAWKE R	JEERE R
DIFFE R	**FERVO R**	GAUGE R	**HAWSE R**	*JERKE R
DIGGE R	FESTE R	**GAWKE R**	*HAZIE R	JESTE R
DIMME R	FETTE R	*GEEZE R	**HEADE R**	*JIBBE R
DINNE R	**FIBBE R**	GELDE R	HEALE R	*JIGGE R
DIPPE R	FILLE R	GENDE R	HEARE R	JILTE R

*JINKE R	LEAPE R	**MAIME R**	MULLE R	**PEPPE R**
JITTE R	LEASE R	**MAMME R**	**MUMME R**	PESTE R
*JOBBE R	LEAVE R	MANGE R	**MUMPE R**	PETTE R
*JOGGE R	**LECHE R**	MANNE R	MURDE R	**PEWTE R**
JOINE R	LECTO R	**MAPPE R**	**MURMU R**	**PHYLA R**
JOLTE R	LEDGE R	**MARKE R**	**MUSHE R**	PICKE R
*JOSHE R	LENDE R	MARRE R	MUSTE R	**PIECE R**
*JUDDE R	LESSE R	**MARTY R**	MUTTE R	**PILFE R**
*JUDGE R	LETTE R	**MASHE R**	NAGGE R	PILLA R
*JUICE R	LEVIE R	**MASKE R**	NAILE R	**PINCE R**
*JUMPE R	**LIBBE R**	MASTE R	**NAPPE R**	PINDE R
JUNIO R	**LICKE R**	MATTE R	NATTE R	PINGE R
*JUNKE R	LICTO R	MAUGE R	NECTA R	PINIE R
JUSTE R	LIFTE R	MAULE R	NEEDE R	PINNE R
*KAFFI R	**LIMBE R**	*MAZIE R	NESTE R	**PIPIE R**
KAISE R	LIMIE R	MEAGE R	NESTO R	PITIE R
KANTA R	**LIMME R**	MEANE R	NETHE R	**PLACE R**
KASHE R	LIMNE R	MEDLA R	NETTE R	PLANA R
KEENE R	**LIMPE R**	MEETE R	NEUTE R	PLANE R
KEEPE R	LINEA R	MELDE R	**NICKE R**	PLATE R
KEGLE R	LINGE R	MELTE R	**NIFFE R**	**PLAYE R**
KELTE R	LINIE R	**MEMBE R**	NIGGE R	*PLEXO R
*KICKE R	**LINKE R**	**MEMOI R**	NIPPE R	**PLOVE R**
KIDDE R	LINTE R	MENDE R	NOBLE R	**PLOWE R**
KILLE R	**LIPPE R**	**MENHI R**	NODDE R	POISE R
KILTE R	*LIQUO R	MENTO R	NONPA R	**POKIE R**
KIPPE R	LISPE R	**MERCE R**	NOOSE R	POLDE R
KISSE R	LISTE R	MERGE R	NOSHE R	POLLE R
KNIFE R	LITTE R	METEO R	NOSIE R	PONDE R
KNOWE R	LIVIE R	METIE R	NUDGE R	**POPLA R**
KOSHE R	**LIVYE R**	**MEWLE R**	**NUMBE R**	**POPPE R**
KRATE R	LOADE R	MIDAI R	NURSE R	**PORKE R**
KRONO R	LOAFE R	**MILKE R**	NUTTE R	PORTE R
KRONU R	LOANE R	MILLE R	**PACKE R**	POSEU R
KULTU R	**LOCKE R**	MILTE R	PALIE R	POSTE R
LAAGE R	**LODGE R**	**MIMBA R**	PALLO R	**POTHE R**
LABOU R	LOFTE R	**MINCE R**	**PALMA R**	POTTE R
LACIE R	LOGGE R	MINDE R	**PALME R**	POURE R
LACKE R	LOGIE R	MINTE R	PALTE R	POUTE R
LADDE R	LOITE R	MIOLE R	**PAMPE R**	**POWDE R**
LADLE R	LOLLE R	MIRIE R	PANDE R	**POWTE R**
LAGGE R	LONGE R	MIRRO R	PANIE R	PRATE R
LAMBE R	**LOOKE R**	MISTE R	*PANZE R	**PRAYE R**
LANCE R	LOOPE R	**MITHE R**	**PARKE R**	**PREFE R**
LANDE R	LOOSE R	MITIE R	PARLO R	PRETO R
LANGU R	LOOTE R	**MOBBE R**	PARSE R	**PREWA R**
LANNE R	**LOPPE R**	**MOCKE R**	PASSE R	**PREYE R**
LAPPE R	LOUVE R	**MOHAI R**	PASTE R	**PRICE R**
LAPSE R	**LUBBE R**	MOLDE R	PASTO R	**PRIME R**
LARDE R	LUGGE R	MOLTE R	PATTE R	*PRIZE R
LARKE R	**LUMBA R**	MONGE R	**PAUPE R**	**PROBE R**
LASCA R	**LUMBE R**	MOOTE R	PAUSE R	**PROPE R**
LASHE R	**LUMPE R**	**MOPPE R**	PAVIO R	PROSE R
LASTE R	LUNGE R	MORTA R	**PAMPE R** ~~	**PROVE R**
LATHE R	LUNIE R	MOSSE R	PAWNE R	**PROWA R**
LATTE R	**LUNKE R**	**MOTHE R**	PAWNO R	PRUNE R
LAUDE R	**LURKE R**	MOUSE R	PECKE R	**PUCKE R**
LAVEE R	LUSTE R	**MUCKE R**	PEDLA R	**PUFFE R**
LAWYE R	**MADDE R**	**MUDDE R**	PEDLE R	PULLE R
*LAZIE R	**MAFTI R**	**MUGGA R**	PEELE R	**PULPE R**
LEADE R	*MAHZO R	**MUGGE R**	**PEEPE R**	PULSA R
LEAKE R	MAILE R	**MUGGU R**	PELTE R	PULSE R
			PENNE R	

PUMPE R	RIGOU R	SCALE R	SLATE R	SURGE R
PUNIE R	RIMIE R	SCARE R	SLAVE R	SUTLE R
PUNNE R	**RIMME R**	SCORE R	SLAYE R	**SWAGE R**
PUNTE R	RINGE R	SCOTE R	SLICE R	**SWAYE R**
PURGE R	RINSE R	SEALE R	SLIDE R	**SYPHE R**
PURSE R	RIOTE R	SEAME R	SLIVE R	TABOU R
PUSHE R	**RIPPE R**	SEARE R	SLOPE R	**TACKE R**
PUTTE R	**RISKE R**	SEATE R	SMILE R	TAGGE R
*QINDA R	RITTE R	**SECPA R**	SMITE R	TAILE R
*QINTA R	ROAME R	SECTO R	**SMOKE R**	TAILO R
*QUAKE R	ROARE R	SEEDE R	SNARE R	**TALKE R**
*QUASA R	**ROBBE R**	**SEEKE R**	SNIPE R	**TAMBU R**
*QUAVE R	**ROCKE R**	SEEME R	SNORE R	**TAMPE R**
*QUEUE R	ROLLE R	SEGGA R	**SOAKE R**	**TANKE R**
*QUIVE R	**ROMPE R**	SEINE R	SOARE R	TANNE R
*QUOTE R	ROOFE R	SEISE R	**SOBBE R**	**TAPPE R**
RACIE R	ROOME R	SEISO R	**SOCCE R**	TARTA R
RACKE R	ROOSE R	***SEIZE R**	SOEVE R	TASTE R
RAFTE R	ROOTE R	***SEIZO R**	SOLDE R	TATTE R
RAIDE R	ROPIE R	SELLE R	SOLVE R	TEARE R
RAILE R	ROSIE R	SENDE R	**SOMBE R**	TEASE R
RAISE R	ROSTE R	SENHO R	SONDE R	TEDDE R
RAMME R	ROTTE R	SENIO R	SOONE R	TEEME R
RANCO R	ROUSE R	SENSO R	SORNE R	TEENE R
RANGE R	ROUTE R	SERVE R	SORTE R	TEETE R
RANKE R	***ROZZE R**	SETTE R	SOUCA R	TELFE R
RANTE R	**RUBBE R**	**SEXIE R**	SOUTE R	TELLE R
RAPIE R	RUBIE R	**SHADE R**	**SOWCA R**	**TEMPE R**
RAPPE R	RUDDE R	**SHAKE R**	**SPACE R**	TENDE R
RAPTO R	RUGGE R	**SHAPE R**	SPADE R	TENNE R
RASHE R	RUINE R	SHARE R	SPARE R	TENOU R
RASPE R	**RUMME R**	**SHAVE R**	**SPEWE R**	TENSO R
RASTE R	RUMOU R	**SHEWE R**	**SPICE R**	TENTE R
RATHE R	RUNNE R	**SHIKA R**	SPIDE R	TERME R
RATTE R	RUSHE R	SHINE R	**SPIKE R**	TERMO R
READE R	**SACKE R**	**SHIVE R**	SPINO R	TERRO R
REAME R	SAGGA R	**SHOFA R**	SPRIE R	TESTE R
REAPE R	SAGGE R	**SHOVE R**	STAGE R	TETHE R
REARE R	SAGIE R	**SHOWE R**	STARE R	TETTE R
REAVE R	SAILE R	SIDDU R	STATE R	THALE R
RECTO R	SAILO R	SIDLE R	STAYE R	**THAWE R**
REDDE R	SALTE R	SIFTE R	STIVE R	THENA R
REDEA R	SALVE R	**SIGHE R**	**STOKE R**	**TICKE R**
REEFE R	SALVO R	SIGNE R	STONE R	TIDIE R
REEKE R	**SAMBA R**	SIGNO R	STOPE R	TILLE R
REELE R	**SAMBU R**	SILLE R	STOVE R	TILTE R
REGEA R	SANDE R	SILVE R	STUPO R	**TIMBE R**
REHEA R	SANGA R	**SIMME R**	STYLA R	TINDE R
REIVE R	SANGE R	**SIMPE R**	STYLE R	TINIE R
RELIE R	SANSA R	SINGE R	**SUBPA R**	**TINKE R**
RENDE R	SANTI R	**SINKE R**	**SUCCO R**	TINNE R
RENTE R	SAPOU R	SINNE R	**SUCKE R**	TINTE R
REPAI R	**SAPPE R**	SINTE R	SUDSE R	**TIPPE R**
REPOU R	SARDA R	**SIPPE R**	**SUFFE R**	TITHE R
RESTE R	SARSA R	SIRDA R	SUITO R	TITTE R
RHETO R	SARTO R	SISTE R	SULFU R	**TOCHE R**
RHYME R	SAUCE R	SITTE R	**SULKE R**	TOILE R
RIBBE R	SAUGE R	***SIZIE R**	**SUMME R**	TOLLE R
RIDDE R	SAVIO R	**SKATE R**	SUNDE R	TONGE R
RIEVE R	SAVOU R	**SKEWE R**	**SUPPE R**	TONIE R
RIFLE R	**SAWYE R**	**SKIVE R**	SURFE R	TONNE R
RIGGE R	SCALA R	**SLAKE R**	SURFE R	TOOLE R

TOOTE R	**WAGGE R**	WRITE R	***BLOCKE R**	**BUNGLE R**
TOPPE R	WAILE R	***XYSTE R**	**BLOOME R**	**BURBLE R**
TORPO R	**WAITE R**	YABBE R	**BLOOPE R**	**BURGHE R**
TOSSE R	WAIVE R	YAMME R	BLOTTE R	**BURGLA R**
TOTHE R	**WALKE R**	YAPPE R	**BLOWIE R**	BURRIE R
TOTTE R	**WANDE R**	YAUPE R	**BLUBBE R**	BURSTE R
TOURE R	WANIE R	YAWNE R	**BLUCHE R**	**BUSHIE R**
TOUTE R	WANNE R	YAWPE R	**BLUNDE R**	**BUTCHE R**
TRACE R	**WANTE R**	YELLE R	**BLUNGE R**	**BYLINE R**
TRADE R	**WARDE R**	YELPE R	BLURTE R	***CACKLE R**
TREMO R	WARIE R	YESTE R	**BLUSHE R**	**CADAVE R**
TRIME R	**WARME R**	YODLE R	BLUSTE R	***CAJOLE R**
TROCA R	WARNE R	YONDE R	**BOARDE R**	CALAMA R
TROVE R	**WARPE R**	YONKE R	BOASTE R	CALIBE R
TUBBE R	WASHE R	YOWLE R	**BOGGIE R**	CALIPE R
TUCKE R	WASTE R	***ZAFFA R**	**BOGGLE R**	CALOYE R
TUFTE R	WATTE R	***ZAFFE R**	BOLIVA R	***CAMPHO R**
TUGGE R	**WAVIE R**	***ZAFFI R**	BOLSTE R	CAMPIE R
TUMOU R	***WAXIE R**	***ZANDE R**	**BOODLE R**	**CANDLE R**
TURGO R	WEANE R	***ZANIE R**	**BOOMIE R**	**CANDOU R**
TURNE R	WEARE R	***ZEPHY R**	BOOSTE R	CANNIE R
TUSKE R	**WEAVE R**	***ZIPPE R**	BOSSIE R	CAPERE R
TUSSA R	**WEDDE R**	***ZITHE R**	BOTCHE R	CAROLE R
TUSSE R	**WEEDE R**	***ZOSTE R**	BOTTLE R	CARRIE R
TUSSO R	**WEEPE R**	BABBLE R	**BOUDOI R**	CASHIE R
TUSSU R	**WEEVE R**	***BAFFLE R**	**BOULDE R**	CATCHE R
TWINE R	WEINE R	BAHADU R	**BOUNCE R**	CATERE R
TWOFE R	**WELDE R**	BARRIE R	**BOUNDE R**	CATTIE R
TYPIE R	**WELDO R**	BASILA R	**BOWLDE R**	**CAULKE R**
*VALKY R	WELTE R	**BATCHE R**	**BRAGGE R**	**CAVILE R**
VALOU R	WESTE R	BATTIE R	**BRAIDE R**	CENTAU R
VALUE R	**WETHE R**	BATTLE R	**BRANDE R**	CENTNE R
VALVA R	WETTE R	BAWDIE R	BRANNE R	***CHAFFE R**
VAMPE R	**WHALE R**	**BEADIE R**	BRASIE R	***CHAMBE R**
VAPOU R	**WHINE R**	**BEAMIE R**	BRAWLE R	***CHAMFE R**
VARIE R	**WHITE R**	BEEFIE R	***BRAZIE R**	**CHAMPE R**
VEALE R	***WICKE R**	***BEHAVE R**	BREAKE R	**CHANGE R**
VECTO R	WIDDE R	BELABO R	**BREEDE R**	**CHANTE R**
VEILE R	WIENE R	BELCHE R	**BREVIE R**	**CHANTO R**
VEINE R	**WILDE R**	BENCHE R	**BRIDLE R**	**CHAPTE R**
VELOU R	WILIE R	BESCOU R	BRIEFE R	**CHARGE R**
VENDE R	WILLE R	BESMEA R	**BRIMME R**	CHARIE R
VENDO R	**WINCE R**	BEVELE R	**BRINGE R**	**CHARME R**
VENEE R	**WINDE R**	BICOLO R	BRINIE R	**CHARTE R**
VENTE R	**WINGE R**	BIFILA R	**BROIDE R**	**CHATTE R**
VERGE R	WINIE R	BIPOLA R	BROILE R	***CHAUFE R**
VERIE R	**WINKE R**	BITTIE R	***BRONZE R**	**CHEATE R**
VERSE R	WINNE R	**BLABBE R**	**BROODE R**	***CHECKE R**
VESPE R	WINTE R	**BLADDE R**	**BROTHE R**	CHEDDA R
VETOE R	WIRIE R	BLASTE R	**BROWSE R**	CHEEPE R
VIATO R	**WISHE R**	**BLATHE R**	BRUISE R	CHEERE R
VICTO R	**WITHE R**	BLATTE R	BRUITE R	***CHEQUE R**
VIEWE R	**WOLFE R**	BLEATE R	**BRUSHE R**	CHIGGE R
VIGOU R	**WOLVE R**	BLEEDE R	**BUBBLE R**	CHILLE R
VINIE R	**WONDE R**	**BLENDE R**	***BUCKLE R**	***CHIPPE R**
*VIZIE R	WONNE R	BLESSE R	***BUFFIE R**	**CHIRPE R**
VOICE R	**WOOFE R**	**BLETHE R**	BUGBEA R	**CHITTE R**
VOIDE R	WOOLE R	**BLINDE R**	**BUILDE R**	**CHOOSE R**
VOYEU R	**WORKE R**	**BLINKE R**	BULLIE R	***CHOPPE R**
VULGA R	**WORME R**	BLISTE R	**BUMBLE R**	**CHOUSE R**
WADDE R	WORSE R	**BLITHE R**	**BUNDLE R**	***CHOWDE R**
WAFTE R	**WOWSE R**	BLOATE R		CHUDDA R

CHUDDE R	COUGHE R	DAUNTE R	DREDGE R	FLUNKE R	
CHUGGE R	COULOI R	DAYSTA R	DRESSE R	FLUSHE R	
*CHUKKA R	COULTE R	*DAZZLE R	DRIFTE R	FLUSTE R	
CHUNTE R	COUNTE R	DEBASE R	DRILLE R	FLUTIE R	
CHURNE R	COUPLE R	DEBATE R	DRINKE R	FLUTTE R	
CIRCLE R	COURIE R	DEBONE R	DRIPPE R	*FLYOVE R	
CLABBE R	COURSE R	DECAYE R	DROPPE R	FLYTIE R	
*CLACKE R	COVERE R	DECIDE R	DROWNE R	FOAMIE R	
CLAIME R	COVETE R	DECODE R	DRUBBE R	FOCUSE R	
CLAMBE R	*COZENE R	DECOLO R	DRUDGE R	FONDLE R	
CLAMOU R	CRABBE R	DECOYE R	DRUMME R	FOOTIE R	
CLAMPE R	*CRACKE R	DECREE R	DUCKIE R	FOOTLE R	
CLAPPE R	CRADLE R	DECRIE R	DUELLE R	*FOOZLE R	
*CLAQUE R	CRAMME R	DEFACE R	DUMPIE R	FORAGE R	
CLASHE R	CRAPPE R	DEFAME R	DUSTIE R	FORAYE R	
CLASPE R	CRASHE R	DEFILE R	DUUMVI R	FORBEA R	
CLASSE R	CRAWLE R	DEFINE R	DWELLE R	FOREVE R	
CLATTE R	CREAME R	DEIFIE R	FABULA R	FORGOE R	
CLAVIE R	CREASE R	DELATO R	FADDIE R	FORKIE R	
CLEANE R	CREATO R	DELAYE R	FAGOTE R	FOUNDE R	
CLEARE R	CREEPE R	DELIVE R	FAINTE R	FRACTU R	
CLEAVE R	CRIBBE R	DELUDE R	FAITOU R	FRAKTU R	
*CLICKE R	CRIMME R	DENUDE R	FANCIE R	FRANKE R	
CLIMBE R	CRIMPE R	DEPOSE R	FARCEU R	*FREEZE R	
CLINGE R	CRINGE R	DERIDE R	FARRIE R	FRISEU R	
CLINKE R	CRISPE R	DERIVE R	FARTHE R	FRISKE R	
CLIPPE R	CRITTE R	DERNIE R	FATTIE R	FRITTE R	
CLOBBE R	CRITTU R	DESIRE R	FAVORE R	*FRIZZE R	
*CLOCKE R	CROAKE R	DESPAI R	FEASTE R	FROWNE R	
CLOUTE R	CROFTE R	DESUGA R	FEATHE R	FRUITE R	
CLUBBE R	CROONE R	DEVISE R	FEIGNE R	FUEHRE R	
CLUMBE R	CROPPE R	DEVISO R	FELSPA R	FUELLE R	
CLUNKE R	CROSIE R	DEWATE R	*FEOFFE R	FUMBLE R	
CLUSTE R	CROSSE R	DIASTE R	*FEOFFO R	FUNCTO R	
CLUTTE R	CROWBA R	DIBBLE R	FERVOU R	FUNFAI R	
CLYSTE R	CROWDE R	DIDDLE R	*FETCHE R	FURRIE R	
COACHE R	CROWNE R	DIESTE R	FIDDLE R	FURTHE R	
COASTE R	*CROZIE R	DILATE R	FIELDE R	GABBLE R	
COBBIE R	CRUISE R	DILATO R	FIGHTE R	GAGSTE R	
COBBLE R	CRULLE R	DILUTE R	FIGURE R	GAMBIE R	
COCHAI R	CRUMBE R	DILUTO R	*FILCHE R	GAMBLE R	
*COCKIE R	CRUPPE R	DIMETE R	FILMIE R	GARBLE R	
CODDLE R	CRUSHE R	DINKIE R	FINNIE R	GARGLE R	
COERCE R	CUDBEA R	DIOPTE R	FISHIE R	GAUFFE R	
COHERE R	CUPELE R	DISHIE R	FLAGGE R	*GAWKIE R	
COINFE R	CUPULA R	DITCHE R	FLAMIE R	GEMMIE R	
COINTE R	CURATO R	DIVIDE R	FLANEU R	GENITO R	
COLLIE R	CURDIE R	DIVINE R	FLANGE R	GERMIE R	
COLORE R	CURDLE R	DIVISO R	FLANKE R	GIGGLE R	
*COMAKE R	CURRIE R	DONATO R	FLAPPE R	GIRDLE R	
COMFIE R	CUSHIE R	DOSSIE R	FLASHE R	GLACIE R	
COMPEE R	CUTOVE R	DOTTIE R	FLATCA R	GLADDE R	
CONIFE R	DABBLE R	DOUBLE R	FLATTE R	GLADIE R	
*CONQUE R	DABSTE R	DOUCEU R	FLAVOU R	GLAMOU R	
CONTOU R	DALLIE R	DOWAGE R	FLEECE R	*GLAZIE R	
CORKIE R	DAMAGE R	DOWNIE R	FLENSE R	GLEANE R	
CORNIE R	DANDIE R	DRAFTE R	FLESHE R	GLIMME R	
CORONE R	DANDLE R	DRAGGE R	*FLICKE R	GLISTE R	
CORSAI R	DANGLE R	DRAINE R	FLINDE R	GLITTE R	
COTTIE R	DANSEU R	DRAWBA R	FLINGE R	GLOATE R	
COUCHE R	DASHIE R	DRAWLE R	FLIPPE R	GLOSSE R	
	DAUNDE R	DREAME R	FLOUTE R	GOBBLE R	

GODLIE R	HAVIOU R	KILOBA R	*LYNCHE R	MOURNE R
GOGGLE R	HEADIE R	KINDLE R	MACABE R	MOUSIE R
GRABBE R	HEATHE R	*KNACKE R	*MACHZO R	MOUTHE R
GRAFTE R	HEAVIE R	*KNAPPE R	MALODO R	*MUCKIE R
GRAINE R	*HECKLE R	KNEADE R	MALTIE R	MUDDIE R
GRAMMA R	HEISTE R	KNEELE R	MANAGE R	MUDDLE R
GRANGE R	HEMPIE R	KNITTE R	MANGIE R	*MUFFLE R
GRANTE R	HERBIE R	*KNOCKE R	MANGLE R	MUGGIE R
GRANTO R	HERITO R	KNOLLE R	MANURE R	MUMBLE R
GRAPIE R	HILLIE R	KOTOWE R	MARBLE R	MUNCHE R
GRASPE R	HIPPIE R	*KREUZE R	MARCHE R	MUNSTE R
*GRAZIE R	HIPSTE R	*KRIMME R	MARINE R	MURTHE R
GREASE R	*HITCHE R	KRULLE R	MARLIE R	MUSKIE R
GREETE R	HOARDE R	LABELE R	MARRIE R	*MUZZIE R
GRIEVE R	HOARIE R	LABORE R	*MASQUE R	*MUZZLE R
GRIFTE R	HOBBLE R	*LACQUE R	MASSEU R	*MYNHEE R
GRILLE R	HOISTE R	LACUNA R	MASSIE R	NEEDIE R
GRIMIE R	HOLSTE R	LAMSTE R	MATADO R	NEEDLE R
GRIMME R	HOMAGE R	LANDLE R	MATCHE R	NEGATO R
GRINDE R	HONORE R	LANGUO R	MAUNDE R	NEITHE R
GRINNE R	HOOKIE R	LARDIE R	MEALIE R	NERVIE R
GRIPIE R	HORNIE R	LARKIE R	MEANDE R	NESTLE R
GRIPPE R	HORSIE R	LASHKA R	MEATIE R	NETTIE R
GROANE R	HOSTLE R	LASSOE R	MEDDLE R	NETTLE R
GROOME R	HOTSPU R	LATHIE R	MEGABA R	NEWSIE R
GROOVE R	HOUNDE R	LAUGHE R	MENACE R	NIBBLE R
GROSSE R	HOVERE R	LAUNDE R	MESSIE R	NIGGLE R
GROUPE R	*HOWEVE R	LAYOVE R	METAME R	NIPPIE R
GROUSE R	HUDDLE R	LEACHE R	MIDDLE R	NOBBIE R
GROUTE R	HUMBLE R	LEADIE R	MIDYEA R	NOBBLE R
GROWLE R	HUMIDO R	LEAFIE R	MILKIE R	NONUSE R
GRUBBE R	HURDLE R	LEAGUE R	MILLIE R	NORTHE R
GRUDGE R	HURRIE R	LEARIE R	MINGIE R	NOTCHE R
GRUELE R	HUSKIE R	LEARNE R	MINGLE R	NUBBIE R
GRUMME R	HUSTLE R	LEATHE R	MINICA R	NUCLEA R
GRUNTE R	*JACAMA R	LEGATO R	MINIVE R	PADDLE R
GUARDE R	*JANGLE R	LEGGIE R	MINSTE R	PAINTE R
GUESSE R	JANITO R	LEISTE R	MIRADO R	PALAVE R
GUILDE R	*JEMADA R	LEVATO R	MISAVE R	PALIKA R
GULFIE R	*JEMIDA R	LEVELE R	MISDOE R	PALLIE R
GUMMIE R	*JEWELE R	LIBELE R	MISHEA R	PALMIE R
GUSTIE R	*JINGLE R	LIGHTE R	MISTIE R	PANDOO R
GUTTIE R	*JOCULA R	LIMBIE R	MISUSE R	PANDOU R
GUTTLE R	*JODHPU R	LIMITE R	MITERE R	PANNIE R
*GUZZLE R	*JOGGLE R	LINGIE R	MOBSTE R	PANTHE R
GYRATO R	*JOINDE R	LINTIE R	MODELE R	PAPERE R
*HACKLE R	JOINTE R	*LIQUEU R	MODULA R	PAPPIE R
HAGGLE R	JOLLIE R	LIVENE R	MOLDIE R	PARADE R
HAIRIE R	JOSTLE R	LOATHE R	MONEYE R	PARDNE R
HAMMIE R	JOUSTE R	LOBBYE R	MONIKE R	PARLOU R
HAMSTE R	*JUGGLE R	LOBSTE R	MONITO R	PARTNE R
HANAPE R	*JUGULA R	LOCATE R	MONOME R	PASTIE R
HANDCA R	*JUMBLE R	LOCATO R	MONSTE R	PATAMA R
HANDIE R	*JUNIPE R	LOCULA R	MOOCHE R	PATCHE R
HANDLE R	*KASHMI R	LORIME R	MOONIE R	PAVIOU R
HARBOU R	*KAYAKE R	LORINE R	MOORIE R	PAVISE R
HARDIE R	KEESTE R	LUCIFE R	MOSSIE R	PEACHE R
HARRIE R	KEGELE R	LUNCHE R	MOTTLE R	PEAKIE R
*HATCHE R	KEISTE R	LUPANA R	MOULDE R	PEDDLE R
HAULIE R	KEYSTE R	LURCHE R	MOULTE R	PENSTE R
HAUNTE R	*KHADDA R	LUSTIE R	MOUNTE R	PEOPLE R
HAUTEU R	KIESTE R			

PERCHE R	PRICIE R	RECOVE R	RUNOVE R	SETTLE R
PERUSE R	*PRICKE R	REDUCE R	RUSHIE R	SETTLO R
PETTIE R	PRIMME R	REEDIE R	RUSTIE R	SHADIE R
PHILTE R	PRINKE R	REENTE R	RUSTLE R	SHAKIE R
PHONIE R	PRINTE R	REFINE R	RUTTIE R	SHALIE R
*PIAFFE R	PRIVIE R	REFUSE R	SADDLE R	SHAMME R
PIASTE R	PROCTO R	REFUTE R	SALLIE R	SHARKE R
PICADO R	PRODDE R	REGULA R	SALTIE R	SHARPE R
*PICKEE R	*PROFFE R	REIFIE R	SALUTE R	SHATTE R
*PICKIE R	PROGGE R	REINCU R	SAMBAR	SHEARE R
PIDDLE R	PROOFE R	REINTE R	SAMBHU R	SHEDDE R
PIERCE R	PROSIE R	RELATE R	SAMOVA R	SHEETE R
PILSNE R	PROSPE R	RELATO R	SAMPLE R	SHELLE R
PINCHE R	PROWLE R	RELAXE R	SANDBA R	SHELTE R
PIONEE R	PSALTE R	REMOVE R	SANDBU R	SHELVE R
PISSOI R	PUDDLE R	RENEGE R	SANDIE R	SHIFTE R
PITCHE R	PUGGIE R	RENEWE R	SANTOU R	SHIMME R
PLAGUE R	PULPIE R	RENTIE R	SASSIE R	SHINIE R
PLAITE R	PUMICE R	REOCCU R	SAUNTE R	SHIPPE R
PLANNE R	PUNCHE R	REOFFE R	SAUTOI R	SHIRKE R
PLANTA R	PUNSTE R	REORDE R	SAVIOU R	*SHOCKE R
PLASHE R	PUPILA R	REPAPE R	SAVORE R	SHOOTE R
PLASTE R	PURSIE R	REPINE R	SCALIE R	*SHOPHA R
PLATIE R	PURSUE R	REPLIE R	SCALPE R	SHOPPE R
PLATTE R	PUSHIE R	REPOSE R	SCAMPE R	SHOUTE R
PLEADE R	PUSSIE R	REPOWE R	SCANNE R	SHOWIE R
PLEASE R	PUTTIE R	RESCUE R	SCARIE R	SHRIVE R
PLEATE R	*PUZZLE R	RESIDE R	SCARPE R	*SHUCKE R
PLEDGE R	*QUAFFE R	RESUME R	SCATTE R	SHUDDE R
PLEDGO R	*QUARTE R	RETAKE R	SCAUPE R	SHUNNE R
PLESSO R	*QUELLE R	RETIRE R	SCEPTE R	SHUNTE R
PLINKE R	*QUERIE R	REUTTE R	SCHEME R	SHUTTE R
PLODDE R	*QUESTE R	REVELE R	SCHMEE R	SHYSTE R
PLOTTE R	*QUESTO R	REVERE R	SCHOLA R	SIDECA R
*PLUCKE R	*QUIETE R	REVILE R	SCISSO R	SIGHTE R
PLUGGE R	*QUILTE R	REVISE R	*SCOFFE R	SIGNIO R
PLUMBE R	*QUINTA R	REVISO R	SCOLDE R	SILKIE R
PLUMIE R	*QUITTE R	REVIVE R	SCOOPE R	SIMILA R
PLUMPE R	*QUITTO R	REVOKE R	SCOOTE R	SIMITA R
PLUNDE R	*QUIZZE R	RIBBIE R	SCORNE R	SIMULA R
PLUNGE R	RABBLE R	RIDDLE R	SCOURE R	*SIZZLE R
PLUNKE R	RAFFLE R	RIDGIE R	SCOUTE R	SKEETE R
POACHE R	RAINIE R	RIFFLE R	SCOWDE R	SKELTE R
POINTE R	RALLIE R	RIGHTE R	SCOWLE R	SKIDDE R
POLYME R	RAMBLE R	RIPENE R	SCRAPE R	*SKIMME R
POPOVE R	RAMMIE R	RIPPLE R	SCREWE R	*SKINKE R
POPULA R	RANCHE R	RIVETE R	SCRIBE R	SKINNE R
PORKIE R	RANCOU R	ROASTE R	SCULKE R	*SKIPPE R
POSTWA R	RATTIE R	ROCKIE R	SCULLE R	SKIRTE R
POTTIE R	RATTLE R	ROISTE R	SCUMME R	SKITTE R
POUNCE R	RAVAGE R	ROOSTE R	SCUNNE R	SKIWEA R
POUNDE R	RAVELE R	ROOTIE R	SCUPPE R	*SKULKE R
PRAETO R	RAVENE R	ROTATO R	SCUTTE R	SLABBE R
PRAISE R	REACHE R	ROTATO R	SEAMIE R	SLACKE R
PRANCE R	REACTO R	ROTIFE R	SECEDE R	SLANDE R
PRAWNE R	READIE R	ROUGHE R	SECULA R	SLAPPE R
PREAVE R	REALGA R	ROUNDE R	SECURE R	SLASHE R
PREENE R	REALTE R	ROUSTE R	SEDUCE R	SLATHE R
PREMIE R	REBATE R	ROYSTE R	SEEDIE R	SLATIE R
PRESSE R	REBUKE R	RUDDIE R	*SELTZE R	SLEDDE R
PRESSO R	RECITE R	RUFFLE R	SEMINA R	SLEEPE R
PRESTE R	RECOLO R	RUMBLE R	SENATO R	SLENDE R

SLICKE R	SPIELE R	**STROKE R**	**TEMBLO R**	TUBULA R
SLIMIE R	SPILLE R	**STROYE R**	**TEMPLA R**	**TUMBLE R**
SLIMME R	SPINIE R	STUDIE R	**TEMPTE R**	TUMULA R
SLINGE R	SPINNE R	**STUFFE R**	TENONE R	**TURFIE R**
SLIPPE R	SPITTE R	**STUIVE R**	TENTIE R	TURTLE R
SLITHE R	**SPLICE R**	**STUMPE R**	TERRIE R	TUTELA R
SLOBBE R	SPOILE R	STUNNE R	TESTIE R	**TUTOYE R**
SLOGGE R	**SPONGE R**	STUTTE R	**THANKE R**	**TWEETE R**
SLUBBE R	SPORTE R	**SUBADA R**	THEATE R	*TWEEZE R
SLUGGE R	SPOTTE R	SUBALA R	**THINKE R**	**TWINIE R**
SLUMBE R	SPOUTE R	**SUBDUE R**	**THINNE R**	**TWIRLE R**
SLUMME R	**SPRAYE R**	**SUCCOU R**	**THITHE R**	**TWISTE R**
*SMACKE R	**SPUDDE R**	**SUCKLE R**	**THRIVE R**	**TWITTE R**
SMASHE R	**SPUMIE R**	**SULPHU R**	**THROWE R**	TYPEBA R
SMATTE R	SPURNE R	**SUMPTE R**	**THUMPE R**	VAPORE R
SMEARE R	SPURRE R	**SURFIE R**	**THUNDE R**	VASTIE R
SMELLE R	SPUTTE R	**SWABBE R**	*THYMIE R	**VAULTE R**
SMELTE R	*SQUALO R	**SWAGGE R**	**TICKLE R**	**VAUNTE R**
SMIRKE R	*SQUARE R	**SWAMPE R**	TINGLE R	VAVASO R
SMOLDE R	**STABBE R**	**SWAPPE R**	TINNIE R	VEINIE R
SMOTHE R	STABLE R	**SWARME R**	**TIPPIE R**	VELIGE R
SNAPPE R	**STACKE R**	**SWASHE R**	**TIPPLE R**	VENOME R
SNARLE R	**STAFFE R**	**SWATHE R**	TIPSIE R	VERNIE R
SNEAKE R	STAGGE R	**SWATTE R**	TIPSTE R	VETIVE R
SNEERE R	STAGIE R	**SWEARE R**	TITULA R	VIEWIE R
*SNEEZE R	STAINE R	**SWEATE R**	TOASTE R	VINEGA R
SNICKE R	**STALKE R**	**SWEEPE R**	TODDLE R	**VINTNE R**
SNIFFE R	**STAMME R**	**SWELTE R**	TOGGLE R	**VISITE R**
SNIFTE R	**STAMPE R**	**SWERVE R**	TOLLBA R	**VISITO R**
SNIGGE R	STANDE R	**SWIFTE R**	TOOTLE R	**VITAME R**
SNIPPE R	STAPLE R	**SWIGGE R**	*TORQUE R	**VOCODE R**
SNOOKE R	STARTE R	**SWILLE R**	**TOUCHE R**	VOMITE R
SNOOPE R	**STARVE R**	**SWIMME R**	**TRACKE R**	*VOUCHE R
*SNOOZE R	STEALE R	**SWINGE R**	TRACTO R	VOYAGE R
SNORTE R	STEAME R	**SWISHE R**	TRAILE R	**WABBLE R**
SNOWIE R	STEEPE R	**SWITHE R**	TRAINE R	**WADDLE R**
SNUBBE R	STEERE R	**SWOBBE R**	TRAITO R	**WAGERE R**
SNUFFE R	STELLA R	**SWOONE R**	TRAMCA R	**WAGONE R**
SOAPIE R	**STEMME R**	**SWOOPE R**	**TRAMPE R**	**WAISTE R**
SOCAGE R	STENTO R	**SWOTTE R**	**TRAPPE R**	**WAKENE R**
SOLACE R	**STEPPE R**	TABORE R	**TRAWLE R**	*WALTZE R
SOLDIE R	STERTO R	TABULA R	TREADE R	**WANGLE R**
SOOTHE R	**STICKE R**	**TACKIE R**	TREATE R	**WARBLE R**
SORRIE R	**STIFLE R**	**TACKLE R**	*TREKKE R	**WARRIO R**
SOUNDE R	STINGE R	TALLIE R	**TRICKE R**	**WARSLE R**
SOUTHE R	**STINKE R**	TAMBOU R	**TRIFLE R**	**WARTIE R**
SPALLE R	STINTE R	TANAGE R	TRIGGE R	**WASHIE R**
SPANKE R	STIRRE R	TANGIE R	TRILLE R	*WATCHE R
SPANNE R	**STOCKE R**	TANGLE R	**TRIMME R**	**WATERE R**
SPARGE R	**STOMPE R**	TAPERE R	**TRIPPE R**	**WAVERE R**
SPARKE R	STONIE R	TAPSTE R	**TROCHA R**	**WEARIE R**
SPATTE R	**STOOKE R**	TARDIE R	**TROFFE R**	**WEATHE R**
SPAWNE R	STOOPE R	TARRIE R	TROLLE R	**WEBSTE R**
SPEAKE R	**STOPPE R**	TARSIE R	TROOPE R	**WEEDIE R**
SPEARE R	**STRAFE R**	TATTIE R	TROTTE R	**WEIGHE R**
SPECTE R	**STRAYE R**	TATTLE R	**TROUPE R**	*WELCHE R
SPEEDE R	**STREWE R**	TAUNTE R	TROUSE R	**WELSHE R**
SPELLE R	**STRIDE R**	**TEACHE R**	**TRUCKE R**	*WENCHE R
SPELTE R	STRIDO R	TEARIE R	**TRUDGE R**	*WHACKE R
SPENCE R	**STRIKE R**	**TEETHE R**	TRUSSE R	*WHAPPE R
SPENDE R	STRIPE R	TEGULA R	**TRUSTE R**	**WHEELE R**
SPICIE R	**STRIVE R**	**TELPHE R**	**TRYSTE R**	*WHEEZE R

*WHETHE R	BASIFIE R	BURROWE R	COEDITO R	CUMBERE R
WHETTE R	BATTENE R	BUSHELE R	COENAMO R	CUPELLE R
*WHICKE R	BAYADEE R	BUTTONE R	*COFACTO R	CUSPIDO R
*WHIFFE R	*BEBOPPE R	CADASTE R	*COGNIZE R	CUSTOME R
*WHIMPE R	*BECKONE R	CALCSPA R	*COIFFEU R	CUTWATE R
WHINIE R	BECLAMO R	CALENDA R	COLANDE R	*CYCLECA R
*WHIPPE R	*BEDCHAI R	CALENDE R	COLESSO R	CYLINDE R
WHIRLE R	*BEDCOVE R	CALLIPE R	COLINEA R	*CYMBALE R
*WHISKE R	BEDIAPE R	*CALYPTE R	COLLATO R	CYTASTE R
*WHISPE R	*BEDMAKE R	CAMELEE R	COLLEGE R	DAMPENE R
*WHITHE R	BEFINGE R	CANALLE R	COLLUDE R	DARKENE R
WHITTE R	BEFOULE R	CANCELE R	COLOURE R	DAUGHTE R
*WHIZZE R	BEGETTE R	CANISTE R	COMBATE R	DEADENE R
*WHOEVE R	BEGINNE R	CANVASE R	COMBINE R	DEADLIE R
*WHOOPE R	BEGUILE R	*CAPMAKE R	*COMETHE R	DEBONAI R
*WHOPPE R	*BEHAVIO R	CAPONIE R	COMMONE R	*DEBUNKE R
WIDENE R	BEHOLDE R	CAPSULA R	COMMUTE R	DECANTE R
WIDOWE R	BELABOU R	CAPTURE R	COMPARE R	DECEIVE R
WIELDE R	BELIEVE R	CAREENE R	COMPILE R	*DECEMVI R
WIGGLE R	*BELIQUO R	CAREERE R	COMPLIE R	DECENTE R
*WINCHE R	BELLOWE R	CARESSE R	COMPOSE R	*DECIPHE R
WINDIE R	BEMURMU R	*CARMAKE R	COMPUTE R	DECLARE R
WINGIE R	BEREAVE R	CAROUSE R	CONCEDE R	DECLINE R
WISPIE R	BESETTE R	CATBRIE R	CONDOLE R	DEEMSTE R
WITHIE R	BESIEGE R	CATHETE R	CONDONE R	DEEPENE R
WITTIE R	BETATTE R	CATNAPE R	CONDUCE R	DEFECTO R
WOBBLE R	BETRAYE R	CAVALIE R	CONFIDE R	DEFENDE R
WOODIE R	BEVELLE R	CAVEATO R	CONFINE R	DEFERRE R
WOOLIE R	BEWAILE R	CAVILLE R	CONFUTE R	DEFLATO R
WORDIE R	BEWILDE R	CAVORTE R	CONGENE R	*DEFLOWE R
WORMIE R	*BEWRAYE R	CELLARE R	*CONJURE R	DEFOAME R
WORRIE R	*BICKERE R	CELLULA R	*CONJURO R	DEFOGGE R
WRAPPE R	BICOLOU R	CEMENTE R	CONNIVE R	DEFORME R
WREAKE R	*BICYCLE R	CENSURE R	CONSIDE R	*DEFRAYE R
*WRECKE R	BILANDE R	*CHANCIE R	CONSOLE R	DEGASSE R
WRESTE R	BILINEA R	CHANDLE R	CONSUME R	DEGRADE R
WRINGE R	BILLETE R	*CHAPITE R	CONVENE R	DEHORNE R
WRITHE R	BIMESTE R	CHARRIE R	*CONVEYE R	*DEJEUNE R
WRONGE R	BIOVULA R	CHASSEU R	*CONVEYO R	DELUSTE R
*YACHTE R	BISECTO R	*CHAUFFE R	*CONVOKE R	DEMANDE R
YEARNE R	*BLANCHE R	CHAUNTE R	COPASTO R	DEMEANO R
YIELDE R	BLASTIE R	CHEERIE R	COPLANA R	DEMPSTE R
YODELE R	*BLAZONE R	CHELATO R	CORRIDO R	DEMURRE R
YOUNGE R	*BLEACHE R	*CHICANE R	COSIGNE R	DEPICTE R
YOUNKE R	*BLENCHE R	CHISELE R	COSTUME R	DEPICTO R
*BACHELO R	BLOODIE R	CHORTLE R	COTTAGE R	DEPLORE R
BACILLA R	BLOTTIE R	CINNABA R	COWINNE R	DEPRAVE R
*BACKDOO R	BORDERE R	CIRCULA R	*COWORKE R	DEPRIVE R
*BAGPIPE R	BORROWE R	CISLUNA R	CRANKIE R	DERINGE R
BALANCE R	BOTTOME R	CLAMORE R	CREDITO R	DESALTE R
BALISAU R	BRABBLE R	CLANGOU R	CREMATO R	DESCRIE R
BALLOTE R	BRAINIE R	CLASSIE R	CRIPPLE R	DESERTE R
BALUSTE R	*BREACHE R	CLEANSE R	CROSSBA R	DESERVE R
BANDAGE R	BREATHE R	*CLINCHE R	CROUPIE R	DESIGNE R
BANISHE R	*BROACHE R	CLOISTE R	*CRUCIFE R	DESILVE R
BANISTE R	BROWNIE R	CLOTHIE R	CRUMBIE R	DESPISE R
BANTERE R	BRUSHIE R	COAPPEA R	*CRUNCHE R	DESTRIE R
*BAPTIZE R	BUDGETE R	COAUTHO R	CRUSADE R	DESULFU R
BARRATE R	*BUFFETE R	*COCKSPU R	*CUCUMBE R	DETACHE R
BARRATO R	BURDENE R	CODEBTO R	CUDGELE R	DETAILE R
BARRETO R		CODIFIE R	CULTIVA R	DETAINE R
BARTERE R				DETECTE R

DETECTO R	FILISTE R	GOSSAME R	*KREUTZE R	*MIJNHEE R
DETERGE R	FILMGOE R	GOSSIPE R	LABELLE R	MILLIBA R
DETERRE R	FILTERE R	GOVERNO-R	LABOURE R	MILLINE R
DETESTE R	FINAGLE R	GRABBIE R	LAMENTE R	*MIMICKE R
*DETICKE R	FINGERE R	GRABBLE R	LAMISTE R	MINISTE R
DEVIATO R	FINISHE R	GRANDEU R	LARCENE R	MISALTE R
DEVOURE R	FLAUNTE R	GRANDSI R	LARKSPU R	MISCOLO R
DIALOGE R	FLAVORE R	GRANULA R	LARRUPE R	MISENTE R
DIALYSE R	FLESHIE R	GRAPPLE R	LATEENE R	MISINFE R
*DIALYZE R	*FLETCHE R	GREENIE R	LATHERE R	MISINTE R
DIAMETE R	*FLICHTE R	GRIMACE R	LAUDATO R	MISLAYE R
DICTATO R	*FLINCHE R	GRIPPIE R	LAUGHTE R	MISLIKE R
DIDAPPE R	FLOWERE R	*GRIZZLE R	LAUNCHE R	MISNOME R
*DIEMAKE R	FLYPAPE R	GROUNDE R	LAVALIE R	MISREFE R
*DIFFUSE R	FOMENTE R	GROVELE R	LAVENDE R	MISSTEE R
*DIFFUSO R	FOOTGEA R	GRUELLE R	LAVISHE R	MISTAKE R
DIGESTE R	FOOTWEA R	*GRUFFIE R	*LAWGIVE R	MISTUTO R
DIGESTO R	FOREBEA R	GRUMBLE R	*LAWMAKE R	MODELLE R
DINOSAU R	FOREGOE R	GUNPAPE R	LECTURE R	MODIFIE R
DIRECTO R	FORESEE R	HALLOWE R	LEFTOVE R	MOLESTE R
DISARME R	FORESTE R	*HAMMERE R	LETTERE R	*MONICKE R
DISASTE R	*FORGIVE R	*HAMPERE R	LEVANTE R	MONSIEU R
DISCOLO R	FORRADE R	*HANGOVE R	LEVELLE R	MOREOVE R
DISCOVE R	FORSAKE R	*HANKERE R	LIBELLE R	MORTISE R
*DISFAVO R	FORSWEA R	HARASSE R	LICENCE R	MOTIONE R
DISHONO R	FOSTERE R	HARBORE R	LICENSE R	MOTORCA R
DISINTE R	*FREAKIE R	HARDENE R	LICENSO R	*MOUCHOI R
DISLIKE R	FRESCOE R	*HARKENE R	LINGERE R	MUENSTE R
DISORDE R	*FRIBBLE R	HARROWE R	LIONISE R	MULETEE R
DISPOSE R	FRIVOLE R	HASTENE R	*LIONIZE R	MURDERE R
DISPUTE R	*FRIZZIE R	*HATMAKE R	LISTENE R	MURMURE R
DISROBE R	*FRIZZLE R	*HAVOCKE R	LITTERE R	MUSCULA R
DIVERTE R	FRONDEU R	*HAYMAKE R	LOADSTA R	MUTINEE R
DIVORCE R	FRONTIE R	HEADGEA R	LODESTA R	MUTTERE R
DIVULGE R	FROTTEU R	*HEMIPTE R	LOITERE R	NARRATE R
DODDERE R	FRUITIE R	HINDERE R	LONGHAI R	NARRATO R
DOGNAPE R	FURRINE R	*HOLDOVE R	LONGSPU R	*NECKWEA R
DOMINEE R	FURROWE R	HONOURE R	LONGUEU R	NEIGHBO R
DOOMSTE R	FUSILEE R	HOOPSTE R	LOOSENE R	*NEWCOME R
DOPESTE R	FUSILIE R	HORSECA R	LORDLIE R	*NEXTDOO R
DOUGHIE R	GALLOPE R	HOSPODA R	LOVELIE R	*NIGHTJA R
*DOUZEPE R	GAMESTE R	HOTELIE R	LUMBERE R	NITRATO R
DOWNPOU R	GAMMONE R	*HOWITZE R	MAGISTE R	*NONJURO R
DRAGGIE R	GANGLIA R	*HUCKSTE R	MALIGNE R	NONOWNE R
DRAGSTE R	GANGLIE R	*HYDRATO R	MALINGE R	NONPOLA R
DRENCHE R	GANGSTE R	*JABBERE R	MALTSTE R	NONSKIE R
DRIBBLE R	GANISTE R	*JAPANNE R	MANDATO R	NONSOLA R
DRIVELE R	GARDENE R	*JETLINE R	MANEUVE R	NONSUGA R
DRUMLIE R	GAROTTE R	*JEWELLE R	*MANPOWE R	NONVOTE R
DULCIME R	GARROTE R	*JOKESTE R	*MAPMAKE R	NOTIFIE R
*DUPLEXE R	GASALIE R	*JONGLEU R	MARAUDE R	NUMBERE R
FALCONE R	GASELIE R	*JOYRIDE R	MARKETE R	NUMMULA R
FALTERE R	GASIFIE R	*JUNKETE R	*MARKHOO R	NURTURE R
FAMILIA R	GASOLIE R	*KEYNOTE R	MASSAGE R	*PACIFIE R
FASTENE R	GATHERE R	*KIBITZE R	MASSETE R	*PACKAGE R
FATTENE R	GEOLOGE R	*KIDNAPE R	MEASURE R	PALPATO R
FAVOURE R	GEOMETE R	KILLDEE R	MEDIATO R	PALTERE R
FELDSPA R	GLASSIE R	*KNITWEA R	MENSWEA R	PAMPERE R
FERRETE R	GLIMPSE R	*KNUCKLE R	*METAPHO R	PANDERE R
FETTERE R	GLOBULA R	*KOMONDO R	*MICAWBE R	*PARACHO R
FIDGETE R	GOSPELE R	*KOWTOWE R	MIGRATO R	PARAMOU R
FIGEATE R				PARCENE R

PARDONE R	PREPARE R	REDEEME R	REVEALE R	*SHADOWE R
PARLEYE R	PRESAGE R	REDRAWE R	REVELLE R	SHEATHE R
PARROTE R	PRESIDE R	REFERRE R	REVENGE R	SHIELDE R
PARTAKE R	PRESUME R	REFILTE R	REVENUE R	SHINGLE R
PASSOVE R	PRETTIE R	REFLOWE R	REVERSE R	SHIVERE R
PASTURE R	PREVISO R	REFORME R	REVERTE R	SHOULDE R
PATENTO R	*PRICKIE R	REFUNDE R	REVIEWE R	SHOVELE R
PATTAMA R	PRISONE R	REGAINE R	REVOLTE R	SHREDDE R
PATTERE R	PROCURE R	REGATHE R	REVOLVE R	*SHRIEKE R
PECULIA R	PRODUCE R	REGISTE R	REWARDE R	*SHRIMPE R
PEDALFE R	PROFANE R	*REHAMME R	REWINDE R	*SHRINKE R
PEDALIE R	PROFILE R	REHEATE R	REWRITE R	*SHUFFLE R
PEIGNOI R	PROFITE R	REINDEE R	RICERCA R	SICKENE R
PENCILE R	PROLABO R	REISSUE R	RIMESTE R	SIFFLEU R
PEPPERE R	PROMISE R	*REJECTE R	ROADSTE R	SIGNALE R
*PEPTIZE R	PROMISO R	*REJECTO R	ROCKETE R	SILENCE R
*PERFUME R	PROMOTE R	*REJIGGE R	ROLLOVE R	SILVERE R
PERIPTE R	PROMPTE R	*REJOICE R	ROMANCE R	SIMPERE R
*PERJURE R	PRONATO R	RELAPSE R	ROTURIE R	SINGULA R
PERLUDE R	PROPOSE R	RELEASE R	RUMMAGE R	SINISTE R
PERVADE R	PROVIDE R	RELETTE R	SABOTEU R	*SKETCHE R
PESTERE R	*PROVOKE R	RELIEVE R	SACCULA R	*SKIJORE R
PETIOLA R	*PUCKERE R	RELOADE R	SALVAGE R	*SKYDIVE R
PEWTERE R	PULLOVE R	REMARKE R	SANDBUR R	SLAVERE R
*PHOSPHO R	PULMOTO R	REMEMBE R	SAVORIE R	SLEEKIE R
PIACULA R	PULSATO R	REMINDE R	SAVOURE R	SLEIGHE R
*PICKETE R	PUNISHE R	REMITTE R	SCANTIE R	SLIPOVE R
PILASTE R	PURIFIE R	REMITTO R	SCAPULA R	SLIVERE R
PILFERE R	*PURVEYO R	RENDERE R	SCHILLE R	SLOUCHE R
PILLAGE R	*PUSHOVE R	RENUMBE R	SCHOONE R	SMOOTHE R
PILSENE R	PUTTERE R	REPAIRE R	SCIMETA R	SMOULDE R
PINASTE R	*QUARRIE R	REPEALE R	SCIMITA R	SMUGGLE R
*PINSCHE R	*QUAVERE R	REPEATE R	SCIMITE R	SNAPPIE R
PISCATO R	*QUENCHE R	REPELLE R	*SCLAFFE R	SNATCHE R
*PITCHIE R	*QUIBBLE R	REPENTE R	*SCORCHE R	SNIFFIE R
PLACATE R	*QUIPSTE R	REPLACE R	SCOURGE R	SNIFFLE R
PLAISTE R	*QUIVERE R	REPORTE R	SCOUTHE R	SNIGGLE R
PLANKTE R	RABBITE R	REPROVE R	SCRAPPE R	SNITCHE R
PLAYGOE R	RADIATO R	REPULSE R	SCRAWLE R	SNIVELE R
*PLAYWEA R	RAINWEA R	*REQUIRE R	SCREAME R	SNOBBIE R
PLEDGEO R	RAMPAGE R	*REQUITE R	SCREENE R	SNUFFIE R
PLIGHTE R	RANSOME R	REROLLE R	SCRUBBE R	SNUFFLE R
PLOTTIE R	RAREFIE R	RESELLE R	*SCUFFLE R	SOFTENE R
PLOUGHE R	RATIFIE R	RESERVE R	SCULPTO R	SOLANDE R
*POCKETE R	RAVELLE R	RESETTE R	*SCUTCHE R	SOLDERE R
POETISE R	RAVISHE R	RESHAPE R	SEAFARE R	SONGSTE R
*POETIZE R	REALISE R	RESIGNE R	SEAFLOO R	SORCERE R
POISONE R	*REALIZE R	RESILVE R	SEAMSTE R	SORROWE R
POLESTA R	REAPPEA R	RESISTE R	SEARCHE R	SOUVENI R
POLISHE R	REASONE R	RESISTO R	SEASONE R	SPARKIE R
POLLSTE R	REBUTTE R	RESOLDE R	SEAWATE R	SPARKLE R
POLLUTE R	RECALLE R	RESOLVE R	SECATEU R	SPARRIE R
POMANDE R	RECANTE R	RESORTE R	SECONDE R	SPEEDIE R
PONDERE R	RECEIVE R	RESTORE R	SECRETO R	SPHERIE R
POSTURE R	RECEPTO R	RETAILE R	SEIGNEU R	SPINDLE R
POTTERE R	RECKONE R	RETAILO R	SEIGNIO R	SPINSTE R
POWDERE R	RECLINE R	RETAINE R	SELECTO R	SPLASHE R
PRATTLE R	RECOILE R	RETARDE R	SEMESTE R	SPLATTE R
*PREACHE R	RECORDE R	RETORTE R	*SEQUITU R	SPLENDO R
PREDATO R	REDACTO R	RETURNE R	SERVICE R	SPLINTE R
*PREFACE R		REUNITE R	SERVITO R	SPLITTE R
PREMOLA R		*REVAMPE R	*SHACKLE R	SPLUTTE R

SPONGIE R	STRUTTE R	**TEMPERE R**	**TROUBLE R**	**WANDERE R**
SPOONIE R	**STUBBIE R**	TENDERE R	**TROUVEU R**	**WANTONE R**
SPRAWLE R	**STUCCOE R**	TESTATO R	**TROWELE R**	*WARMAKE R
SPREADE R	**STUMBLE R**	TETRAME R	**TRUCKLE R**	*WARPOWE R
SPRIGGE R	**STYLISE R**	*THATCHE R	TRUNDLE R	WARRENE R
SPRINGE R	*STYLIZE R	**THEREFO R**	TUNNELE R	WARSTLE R
SPRINTE R	SUBAHDA R	**THIRSTE R**	**TURBOCA R**	WATERIE R
SPURRIE R	**SUBFLOO R**	**THRASHE R**	**TURNOVE R**	WATTHOU R
*SQUALLE R	**SUBLIME R**	**THREADE R**	**TWADDLE R**	*WAYFARE R
*SQUANDE R	**SUBORDE R**	**THREAPE R**	**TWANGIE R**	*WAYLAYE R
*SQUASHE R	**SUBORNE R**	**THRESHE R**	**TWANGLE R**	*WEAKENE R
*SQUATTE R	**SUBPOLA R**	**THRILLE R**	**TWIDDLE R**	*WEIGHTE R
*SQUAWKE R	**SUBSIDE R**	*THROBBE R	*TWINKLE R	*WELCOME R
*SQUEAKE R	**SUBSOLA R**	*THRUMME R	*TWITCHE R	WELLDOE R
*SQUEALE R	*SUBVICA R	**THRUSTE R**	*TYPIFIE R	*WHATEVE R
*SQUEEZE R	**SUCCORE R**	**THRUSTO R**	**VALUATO R**	WHEATEA R
*SQUINTE R	**SUFFERE R**	**THURIFE R**	**VALVULA R**	*WHEEDLE R
*SQUIRME R	*SUFFICE R	*THWACKE R	**VANISHE R**	*WHENEVE R
*SQUIRTE R	**SUMMONE R**	**THWARTE R**	**VAPOURE R**	*WHEREVE R
STANCHE R	SUNDERE R	**TINKERE R**	**VARISTO R**	*WHIFFLE R
STARTLE R	**SUPERIO R**	TITRATO R	**VASCULA R**	*WHIPPIE R
STEADIE R	**SUPPLIE R**	TITTERE R	**VAVASOU R**	WHISTLE R
STICKIE R	**SUPPOSE R**	**TOGETHE R**	**VAVASSO R**	WHITENE R
STICKLE R	**SURFACE R**	**TORCHIE R**	**VENEERE R**	WHITTLE R
STINGIE R	**SURMISE R**	TOREADO R	**VENTURE R**	*WHOMEVE R
STINKIE R	**SURNAME R**	TORTURE R	**VERDERE R**	*WHOSEVE R
STIPPLE R	**SURVEYO R**	TOTTERE R	**VERDERO R**	*WIGMAKE R
STITCHE R	**SURVIVE R**	TOWNWEA R	**VERDITE R**	WILLOWE R
*STOCKCA R	**SURVIVO R**	TRADITO R	**VERIFIE R**	*WINGOVE R
STOCKIE R	**SWINDLE R**	**TRADUCE R**	**VIBRATO R**	WINNOWE R
STOPOVE R	*SWITCHE R	**TRAMPLE R**	**VILIFIE R**	WINTERE R
STRAINE R	*SWIZZLE R	**TRANSFE R**	**VILLAGE R**	WIREHAI R
STRANDE R	**TABOURE R**	**TRAPDOO R**	**VINTAGE R**	WITHERE R
STRANGE R	*TAKEOVE R	**TRAVELE R**	**VIOLATE R**	WONDERE R
STRAPPE R	**TAMPERE R**	**TREADLE R**	**VIOLATO R**	WOOLLIE R
STREAKE R	**TARPAPE R**	**TREMBLE R**	**VITIATO R**	WRANGLE R
STREAME R	TATTOOE R	**TRENCHE R**	*VIVIFIE R	WRESTLE R
STREEKE R	**TAUTOME R**	TRESSIE R	**VOLLEYE R**	WRIGGLE R
STRESSO R	**TAVERNE R**	TRESSOU R	**VOUSSOI R**	*YAMMERE R
STRINGE R	*TAXPAYE R	**TRICKIE R**	*VOYAGEU R	*YAWMETE R
STRIPIE R	**TEAMAKE R**	**TRICOLO R**	WAGGONE R	YODELLE R
STRIPPE R	**TEAMSTE R**	**TRIMETE R**	*WALKOVE R	*ZAMINDA R
STROLLE R	TEASELE R	**TRIMOTO R**	**WALLOPE R**	*ZEMINDA R
STRUMME R	TEENAGE R	**TRIUMVI R**	**WALLOWE R**	*ZOOLATE R

S

SABE	SAKE	SANS	SCAD	SCUT
SACK	SAKI	SARD	SCAG	SEAL
SADE	SALE	SARI	SCAM	SEAM
SADI	SALL	SARK	SCAN	SEAR
SAFE	SALP	SASH	SCAR	SEAT
SAGA	SALT	SASS	SCAT	SECT
SAGE	SAME	SATE	SCOP	SEED
SAGO	SAMP	SATI	SCOT	SEEK
SAGY	SAND	SAUL	SCOW	SEEL
SAID	SANE	SAVE	SCUD	SEEM
SAIL	SANG	SAWN	SCUM	SEEN
SAIN	SANK	SCAB	SCUP	SEEP

SEER	SINK	SOAP	STOA	SAICE
SEGO	SIPE	SOAR	STOB	SAIGA
SELF	SIRE	**SOCK**	STOP	SAINT
SELL	SITE	SODA	STOW	SAITH
SEME	SITH	SOFA	STUB	**SAJOU**
SEMI	SITI	SOFT	STUD	SAKER
SEND	**SIZE**	SOIL	STUM	SALAD
SENT	*SIZY	**SOJA**	STUN	SALEP
SEPT	SKAG	SOKE	STYE	SALIC
SERA	SKAT	SOLA	SUBA	SALLY
SERE	SKEE	SOLD	SUCH	SALMI
SERF	SKEG	SOLE	**SUCK**	SALOL
SETA	**SKEP**	SOLI	SUDD	SALON
SEWN	**SKEW**	SOLO	SUDS	SALPA
SEXT	SKID	SOMA	SUER	SALTY
SEXY	**SKIM**	SOME	SUET	SALVE
SHAD	SKIN	SONE	SUGH	SALVO
SHAG	**SKIP**	SONG	SUIT	SAMBA
SHAH	SKIT	SOON	SULK	SAMBO
SHAM	SKUA	SOOT	SUMO	**SAMEK**
SHAT	SLAB	SOPH	SUMP	SANDY
SHAW	SLAG	SORA	SUNG	SANER
SHAY	SLAM	SORB	SUNK	SANGA
SHEA	SLAP	SORD	SUNN	SANGH
SHED	SLAT	SORE	SUPE	SAPID
SHEW	SLAW	SORI	SURA	SAPOR
SHIM	SLAY	SORN	SURD	**SAPPY**
SHIN	SLED	SORT	SURE	SAREE
SHIP	SLEW	SOTH	SURF	SARGE
SHIT	SLIM	SOUL	SWAB	SARIN
SHIV	SLIP	SOUP	SWAG	SAROD
SHMO	SLIT	SOUR	SWAM	SASIN
SHOD	SLOB	SOWN	SWAN	SASSY
SHOE	SLOE	SOYA	SWAP	SATEM
SHOG	SLOG	SPAE	SWAT	SATIN
SHOO	SLOP	SPAN	**SWAY**	SATYR
SHOP	SLOT	SPAR	SWIG	SAUCE
SHOT	SLOW	SPAT	SWIM	**SAUCH**
SHOW	SLUB	SPAY	SWOB	**SAUCY**
SHRI	SLUE	SPED	SWOP	SAUGH
SHUL	SLUG	SPEW	SWOT	SAULT
SHUN	SLUM	SPIC	SWUM	SAUNA
SHUT	SLUR	SPIN	SYBO	SAURY
SIAL	SLUT	SPIT	SYCE	SAUTE
SIBB	SMEW	SPIV	**SYKE**	SAVER
SICE	SMOG	SPOT	SYNC	SAVIN
SICK	SMUG	SPRY	SYNE	SAVOR
SIDE	SMUT	SPUD	SABER	**SAVOY**
SIFT	SNAG	SPUE	SABIN	**SAVVY**
SIGH	SNAP	SPUN	SABIR	SAWER
SIGN	SNAW	SPUR	SABLE	SAYER
SIKE	SNED	STAB	SABOT	SAYID
SILD	SNIB	STAG	SABRA	SAYST
SILK	SNIP	STAW	SABRE	SCALD
SILL	SNIT	STAY	SACRA	SCALE
SILO	SNOB	STEM	SADHE	SCALL
SILT	SNOT	STEP	SADHU	SCALP
SIMA	SNOW	STET	SADLY	**SCALY**
SIMP	SNUB	STEW	SAFER	**SCAMP**
SINE	SNUG	STEY	SAGER	SCANT
SING	SNYE	STIR	SAGUM	SCAPE
SINH	SOAK		**SAHIB**	SCARE

SCARF	**SEIZE**	SHEEN	SIGHT	SLANT
SCARP	SELAH	**SHEEP**	SIGIL	SLASH
SCART	SELLE	SHEER	SIGMA	SLATE
SCARY	SEMEN	SHEET	SIKER	SLATY
SCATT	SEMIS	**SHEIK**	**SILEX**	SLAVE
SCAUP	SENGI	**SHELF**	**SILKY**	SLEEK
SCAUR	SENNA	SHELL	SILLY	SLEEP
SCENA	SENOR	SHEND	SILTY	SLEET
SCEND	SENSA	SHEOL	SILVA	SLEPT
SCENE	SENSE	SHERD	SIMAR	SLICE
SCENT	SENTI	SHIED	SINCE	**SLICK**
SCHAV	SEPAL	SHIEL	SINEW	SLIDE
SCHMO	SEPIA	SHIER	SINGE	SLIER
SCHUL	**SEPOY**	SHIES	SINUS	SLILY
SCHWA	SEPTA	**SHIFT**	SIREE	SLIME
SCION	SERAC	SHILL	SIREN	**SLIMY**
SCOFF	SERAI	**SHILY**	SIRRA	SLING
SCOLD	SERAL	SHINE	SIRUP	SLINK
SCONE	SERER	**SHINY**	SISAL	SLIPE
SCOOP	SERGE	SHIRE	SISSY	SLIPT
SCOOT	SERIF	**SHIRK**	SITAR	SLOID
SCOPE	SERIN	SHIRR	SITUS	**SLOJD**
SCORE	SEROW	SHIRT	SIVER	SLOOP
SCORN	SERRY	SHIST	**SIXMO**	SLOPE
SCOUR	SERUM	**SHIVA**	**SIXTE**	SLOSH
SCOUT	SERVE	**SHIVE**	*SIXTH	SLOTH
SCOWL	SERVO	SHOAL	*SIXTY	SLOYD
SCRAG	SETON	SHOAT	**SIZAR**	**SLUFF**
SCRAM	SETUP	**SHOCK**	**SIZER**	SLUMP
SCRAP	SEVEN	SHOER	**SKALD**	SLUNG
SCREE	SEVER	*SHOJI	SKATE	SLUNK
SCREW	SEWAN	SHONE	SKEAN	SLURB
SCRIM	SEWAR	**SHOOK**	SKEEN	SLURP
SCRIP	SEWER	SHOOL	SKEET	SLUSH
SCROD	**SEXTO**	SHOON	SKEIN	**SLYPE**
SCRUB	**SHACK**	SHOOT	**SKELP**	**SMACK**
SCRUM	SHADE	SHORE	SKENE	SMALL
SCUBA	**SHADY**	SHORL	**SKIED**	SMALT
SCUDO	**SHAFT**	SHORN	SKIER	SMARM
SCUFF	**SHAKE**	SHORT	SKIES	SMART
SCULK	**SHAKO**	SHOTE	**SKIEY**	**SMASH**
SCULL	*SHAKY	SHOTT	*SKIFF	*SMAZE
SCULP	SHALE	SHOUT	SKILL	SMEAR
SCURF	SHALL	SHOVE	**SKIMO**	**SMEEK**
SCUTA	SHALT	**SHOWN**	**SKIMP**	SMELL
SCUTE	SHALY	**SHOWY**	**SKINK**	SMELT
SEAMY	**SHAME**	SHRED	SKINT	**SMERK**
SEBUM	SHANK	**SHREW**	SKIRL	SMILE
SECCO	**SHAPE**	**SHRUB**	SKIRR	**SMIRK**
SEDAN	SHARD	SHRUG	SKIRT	SMITE
SEDER	SHARE	**SHUCK**	SKITE	**SMITH**
SEDGE	**SHARK**	SHUNT	**SKIVE**	**SMOCK**
SEDGY	SHARN	**SHUSH**	SKOAL	**SMOKE**
SEDUM	**SHARP**	SHUTE	**SKULK**	**SMOKY**
SEEDY	SHAUL	**SHYER**	SKULL	SMOLT
SEELY	**SHAVE**	**SHYLY**	SKUNK	SMOTE
SEEPY	**SHAWL**	SIBYL	*SKYEY	SNACK
SEGNO	**SHAWM**	SIDED	**SLACK**	SNAFU
SEGUE	**SHAWN**	SIDLE	SLAIN	SNAIL
SEINE	**SHEAF**	SIEGE	SLAKE	SNAKE
SEISE	SHEAL	SIEUR	SLANG	**SNAKY**
SEISM	SHEAR	SIEVE	SLANK	SNARE

SNARK	SOUND	SPOIL	STEEL	STRUT
SNARL	**SOUPY**	**SPOKE**	STEEP	**STUCK**
SNASH	SOUSE	**SPOOF**	STEER	STUDY
SNATH	SOUTH	**SPOOK**	STEIN	**STUFF**
SNEAK	SOWAR	SPOOL	STELA	STULL
SNEAP	SOWER	SPOON	STELE	STUMP
SNEER	**SOZIN**	SPOOR	STENO	STUNG
SNELL	SPACE	SPORE	STERE	STUNK
SNICK	SPADE	SPORT	STERN	STUNT
SNIDE	SPADO	SPOUT	**STICH**	STUPA
SNIFF	**SPAHI**	SPRAG	**STICK**	STUPE
SNIPE	SPAIL	SPRAT	STIED	STURT
SNOOD	SPAIT	**SPRAY**	STIES	STYLE
SNOOK	**SPAKE**	SPREE	STILE	STYLI
SNOOL	SPALE	SPRIG	STILL	**STYMY**
SNOOP	SPALL	SPRIT	STILT	**SUBAH**
SNOOT	SPANG	SPRUE	STIME	SUBER
SNORE	**SPANK**	SPRUG	**STIMY**	SUCRE
SNORT	SPARE	SPUME	STING	SUDOR
SNOUT	**SPARK**	**SPUMY**	STINK	SUDSY
SNOWY	SPASM	**SPUNK**	STINT	SUEDE
SNUCK	SPATE	SPURN	STIPE	SUGAR
SNUFF	**SPAWN**	SPURT	STIRK	SUING
SOAPY	**SPEAK**	SPUTA	STIRP	SUINT
SOAVE	SPEAN	***SQUAB**	STOAT	SUITE
SOBER	SPEAR	***SQUAD**	**STOCK**	SULFA
SOCLE	**SPECK**	**SQUAT**	STOGY	SULFO
SODDY	SPECS	***SQUAW**	STOIC	**SULKY**
SOFAR	SPEED	***SQUEG**	STOKE	SULLY
SOFTA	SPEEL	***SQUIB**	STOLE	SUMAC
SOFTY	SPEER	***SQUID**	STOMA	SUMMA
SOGGY	SPEIL	**STACK**	STOMP	SUNNA
SOLAN	SPEIR	STADE	STONE	SUNNY
SOLAR	SPELL	**STAFF**	STONY	SUNUP
SOLDI	SPELT	STAGE	STOOD	SUPER
SOLDO	SPEND	STAGY	STOOK	SUPRA
SOLED	SPENT	STAID	STOOL	SURAH
SOLID	SPERM	STAIG	STOOP	SURAL
SOLON	SPICA	STAIN	STOPE	SURER
SOLUM	SPICE	STAIR	STOPT	**SURFY**
SOLUS	**SPICK**	STAKE	STORE	SURGE
SOLVE	**SPICY**	STALE	STORK	SURGY
SONAR	SPIED	STALK	STORM	SURLY
SONDE	SPIEL	STALL	STORY	SURRA
SONIC	SPIER	STAMP	STOSS	SUTRA
SONLY	SPIES	STAND	STOUP	SUTTA
SONNY	**SPIKE**	STANE	STOUR	SWAGE
SONSY	**SPIKY**	STANG	STOUT	SWAIL
SOOEY	SPILE	STANK	STOVE	SWAIN
SOOTH	SPILL	**STAPH**	**STOWP**	SWALE
SOOTY	SPILT	STARE	STRAP	**SWAMI**
SOPHY	SPINE	STARK	STRAW	**SWAMP**
SOPOR	**SPINY**	START	STRAY	**SWAMY**
SOPPY	SPIRE	STASH	STREP	SWANG
SOREL	SPIRT	STATE	STREW	**SWANK**
SORER	**SPIRY**	STAVE	STRIA	SWARD
SORGO	***SPITZ**	STEAD	STRIP	SWARE
SORRY	SPLAT	STEAK	STROP	**SWARF**
SORUS	**SPLAY**	STEAL	STROW	**SWARM**
SOTOL	SPLIT	STEAM	STROY	SWART
SOUGH	SPODE	STEED	STRUM	**SWASH**
		STEEK		

SWATH	SAITHE	SATANG	SCOTIA	SEISIN
SWEAR	**SAIYID**	SATARA	SCOUSE	SEISOR
SWEAT	SALAAM	SATEEN	**SCOUTH**	*SEIZER
SWEDE	SALAMI	SATING	**SCRAPE**	*SEIZIN
SWEEP	SALARY	SATINY	**SCRAWL**	*SEIZOR
SWEER	**SALIFY**	SATIRE	**SCREAK**	**SEJANT**
SWEET	SALINA	SATORI	**SCREAM**	SELDOM
SWELL	SALINE	SATRAP	SCREED	SELECT
SWEPT	SALIVA	SAUCER	SCREEN	SELLER
SWIFT	SALLET	SAUGER	**SCREWY**	SELSYN
SWILL	SALLOW	SAUREL	**SCRIBE**	SELVES
SWINE	SALMON	**SAVAGE**	**SCRIMP**	**SEMEME**
SWING	SALOON	SAVANT	**SCRIPT**	SEMINA
SWINK	SALOOP	SAVATE	**SCRIVE**	**SEMPLE**
SWIPE	SALPID	SAVINE	SCROLL	**SEMPRE**
SWIRL	SALTER	**SAVING**	**SCROOP**	SENARY
SWISH	SALTIE	SAVIOR	**SCRUFF**	SENATE
SWISS	**SALUKI**	**SAVORY**	**SCULPT**	SENDAL
SWITH	SALUTE	SAVOUR	*SCUMMY	SENDER
SWIVE	SALVER	*SAWFLY	**SCURFY**	SENECA
SWOON	SALVIA	**SAWLOG**	**SCURRY**	SENEGA
SWOOP	SALVOR	**SAWNEY**	**SCURVY**	SENHOR
SWORD	SAMARA	**SAWYER**	**SCUTCH**	SENILE
SWORE	**SAMBAR**	*SAXONY	**SCUTUM**	SENIOR
SWORN	**SAMBUR**	**SAYING**	**SCYTHE**	SENITI
SWOUN	**SAMECH**	SAYYID	SEABAG	SENNET
SWUNG	*SAMEKH	*SCABBY	SEABED	SENNIT
SYCEE	SAMIEL	SCALAR	SEADOG	SENORA
SYLPH	SAMITE	SCALER	SEALER	SENSOR
SYLVA	SAMLET	**SCAMPI**	SEAMAN	SENSUM
SYNCH	**SAMPAN**	**SCANTY**	SEAMER	SENTRY
SYNOD	**SAMPLE**	**SCARAB**	SEANCE	SEPSIS
SYREN	**SAMSHU**	**SCARCE**	**SEARCH**	SEPTAL
SYRUP	SANCTA	SCARER	SEARER	SEPTET
SABBAT	SANDAL	**SCAREY**	SEASON	**SEPTIC**
SABBED	SANDER	**SCARPH**	SEATER	**SEPTUM**
SABINE	**SANDHI**	**SCARRY**	SEAWAN	*SEQUEL
SACBUT	SANEST	**SCATHE**	**SEAWAY**	*SEQUIN
SACHEM	SANGAR	**SCATTY**	SECANT	SERAIL
SACHET	SANGER	**SCENIC**	SECEDE	SERAPE
SACKER	SANIES	**SCHEMA**	SECERN	**SERAPH**
*SACQUE	SANING	**SCHEME**	SECOND	SERDAB
SACRAL	SANITY	**SCHISM**	**SECPAR**	SEREIN
SACRED	*SANJAK	**SCHIST**	SECRET	SERENE
SACRUM	SANNOP	*SCHIZO	SECTOR	SEREST
SADDEN	SANNUP	**SCHLEP**	SECUND	SERIAL
SADDHU	SANSAR	**SCHMOE**	SECURE	SERIES
SADDLE	SANSEI	**SCHOOL**	SEDATE	SERINE
SADISM	SANTIR	**SCHORL**	SEDILE	SERING
SADIST	SANTOL	*SCHRIK	SEDUCE	SERMON
SAFARI	SAPOTA	**SCHUIT**	SEEDER	SEROSA
SAFEST	SAPOUR	**SCHUSS**	SEEING	SEROUS
SAFETY	**SAPPED**	SCILLA	**SEEKER**	SERVAL
SAFROL	**SAPPER**	**SCLAFF**	SEEMER	SERVER
SAGBUT	SARAPE	SCLERA	**SEEMLY**	SESAME
SAGEST	SARDAR	*SCOLEX	SEESAW	SESTET
SAGGAR	SARODE	**SCONCE**	SEETHE	**SETOFF**
SAGGED	SARONG	**SCORCH**	SEGGAR	SETOSE
SAGGER	SARSAR	SCORER	**SEICHE**	SETOUS
SAGIER	SARSEN	SCORIA	SEIDEL	SETOUT
SAILER	SARTOR	**SCOTCH**	SEINER	SETTEE
SAILOR	**SASHAY**	SCOTER	SEISER	SETTER

SETTLE	SHINDY	SIMIAN	SLATER	SNAGGY
SEVERE	SHINER	SIMILE	SLAVER	SNAPPY
SEWAGE	SHINNY	SIMLIN	SLAVEY	SNARER
SEWING	SHIRTY	SIMMER	SLAYER	SNARLY
SEXIER	*SHIVAH	SIMNEL	SLEAVE	SNATCH
*SEXILY	SHIVER	SIMONY	*SLEAZY	SNATHE
*SEXISM	*SHLOCK	SIMOOM	SLEDGE	*SNAZZY
SEXIST	SHNAPS	SIMOON	SLEEKY	SNEAKY
*SEXPOT	SHOALY	SIMPER	SLEEPY	SNEESH
SEXTAN	SHODDY	SIMPLE	SLEETY	*SNEEZE
SEXTET	SHOFAR	SIMPLY	SLEEVE	*SNEEZY
SEXTON	SHOGUN	SINEWY	SLEIGH	SNIFFER
SEXUAL	SHOLOM	SINFUL	SLEUTH	*SNIFFY
*SHABBY	SHOPPE	SINGER	SLICER	SNIPER
*SHACKO	SHORAN	SINGLE	SLIDER	SNIPPY
SHADER	SHORTY	SINGLY	SLIEST	SNITCH
SHADOW	SHOULD	SINKER	SLIGHT	SNIVEL
SHADUF	SHOVEL	SINNED	SLIMLY	SNOBBY
SHAGGY	SHOVER	SINNER	SLIMSY	SNOOPY
SHAIRD	SHOWER	SINTER	SLINKY	SNOOTY
SHAIRN	SHRANK	SIPHON	SLIPPY	*SNOOZE
SHAKER	SHREWD	SIPING	SLIPUP	*SNOOZY
SHALED	SHRIEK	SIPPED	SLIVER	SNORER
SHALOM	SHRIFT	SIPPER	SLOGAN	SNOTTY
SHAMAN	SHRIKE	SIPPET	SLOPER	SNOUTY
SHAMES	SHRILL	SIRDAR	SLOPPY	SNUBBY
*SHAMMY	SHRIMP	SIRING	SLOSHY	*SNUFFY
SHAMOY	SHRINE	SIRRAH	SLOUCH	SNUGLY
SHAMUS	SHRINK	SIRREE	SLOUGH	SOAKER
SHANDY	SHRIVE	SISKIN	SLOVEN	SOARER
SHANTI	*SHROFF	SISTER	SLOWLY	SOBBER
SHANTY	SHROUD	SISTRA	SLUDGE	SOBEIT
SHAPER	SHROVE	SITING	SLUDGY	SOBFUL
SHARER	SHRUNK	SITTEN	SLUICE	SOCAGE
SHARIF	SHTETL	SITTER	SLUICY	SOCCER
SHARPY	*SHTICK	*SIZIER	SLUING	SOCIAL
SHAUGH	SICCAN	*SIZING	SLUMMY	SOCKET
SHAVER	SICKEN	*SIZZLE	SLURRY	SOCMAN
SHAVIE	SICKLE	SKATER	SLUSHY	SODDED
SHEATH	*SICKLY	SKATOL	SMALTI	SODDEN
SHEAVE	SIDDUR	SKEANE	SMALTO	SODIUM
SHEENY	SIDING	SKEIGH	SMARMY	SODOMY
SHEEVE	SIDLER	SKERRY	SMARTY	SOEVER
*SHEIKH	SIENNA	*SKETCH	SMEARY	SOFFIT
SHEKEL	SIERRA	SKEWER	SMEGMA	SOFTEN
SHELLY	SIESTA	SKIBOB	SMELLY	SOFTIE
SHELTY	SIFTER	*SKIDDY	*SMILAX	SOFTLY
SHELVE	SIGHER	*SKIDOO	SMILER	SOGGED
*SHELVY	SIGLOS	SKIING	SMIRCH	SOIGNE
SHERIF	SIGNAL	*SKIMPY	*SMIRKY	SOIREE
SHERRY	SIGNER	SKINNY	SMITER	SOLACE
SHEUCH	SIGNET	SKIVER	SMITHY	SOLAND
SHEUGH	SIGNOR	*SKIVVY	SMOGGY	SOLANO
SHEWER	SILAGE	SKLENT	SMOKER	SOLATE
SHIBAH	SILANE	*SKYCAP	*SMOKEY	SOLDAN
SHIELD	SILENI	*SKYMAN	SMOOCH	SOLDER
SHIEST	SILENT	*SKYWAY	SMOOTH	SOLELY
*SHIFTY	SILICA	SLAGGY	SMUDGE	SOLEMN
SHIKAR	SILKEN	SLAKER	SMUDGY	SOLGEL
SHIKSA	SILLER	SLALOM	SMUGLY	SOLIDI
SHIKSE	SILVAN	SLANGY	SMUTCH	SOLING
*SHIMMY	SILVER	SLATCH	SMUTTY	SOLION
				SOLUTE

SOLVER	*SPHINX	*SQUINT	**STODGY**	**STUMPY**
SOMBER	SPICER	*SQUIRE	STOGEY	STUPID
SOMBRE	SPICEY	*SQUIRM	STOGIE	STUPOR
SOMITE	SPIDER	*SQUIRT	**STOKER**	**STURDY**
SONANT	*SPIFFY	*SQUISH	STOLEN	STYLAR
SONATA	SPIGOT	*SQUUSH	STOLID	STYLER
SONDER	**SPIKER**	**SRADHA**	STOLON	STYLET
SONICS	**SPILTH**	STABLE	STOMAL	STYLUS
SONNET	SPINAL	**STABLY**	STONER	**STYMIE**
SONSIE	SPINEL	**STACTE**	STONEY	*STYRAX
SOONER	SPINET	STADIA	STOOGE	SUABLE
SOOTHE	**SPINNY**	STAGER	STOPER	**SUBBED**
SOPITE	SPINOR	**STAGEY**	**STORAX**	**SUBDEB**
SOPPED	SPIRAL	**STAGGY**	STOREY	SUBDUE
SORBET	SPIREA	STALAG	**STORMY**	*SUBFIX
SORBIC	**SPIREM**	**STALKY**	STOUND	**SUBGUM**
SORDID	SPIRIT	STAMEN	STOURE	SUBITO
SORELY	SPITAL	STANCE	STOURY	SUBLET
SOREST	**SPLAKE**	**STANCH**	STOVER	**SUBMIT**
SORGHO	**SPLASH**	*STANZA	STRAFE	SUBORN
SORNER	SPLEEN	**STARCH**	STRAIN	**SUBPAR**
SORREL	SPLENT	STARER	STRAIT	SUBSET
SORROW	**SPLICE**	STARRY	**STRAKE**	SUBTLE
SORTER	SPLINE	STARVE	STRAND	**SUBURB**
SORTIE	SPLINT	STASES	STRANG	**SUBWAY**
SOUARI	SPLORE	STASIS	STRASS	**SUCCAH**
SOUCAR	**SPLOSH**	STATAL	STRATA	**SUCCOR**
SOUDAN	SPOILT	STATER	STRATH	**SUCKER**
SOUGHT	**SPOKEN**	STATIC	STRATI	**SUCKLE**
SOURCE	SPONGE	STATOR	**STRAWY**	**SUDARY**
SOURLY	**SPONGY**	STATUE	**STREAK**	SUDDEN
SOUTER	*SPOOKY	STATUS	STREAM	SUDSER
SOVIET	**SPOONY**	STAYER	**STREEK**	**SUFFER**
SOVRAN	SPORAL	**STEADY**	STREET	*SUFFIX
SOWANS	**SPORTY**	**STEAMY**	STRESS	**SUGARY**
SOWCAR	**SPOTTY**	STEELY	**STRICK**	SUITOR
SOWENS	SPOUSE	STEEVE	STRICT	*SUKKAH
*SOZINE	SPRAIN	STELLA	STRIDE	SULCUS
SPACER	SPRANG	**STEMMA**	STRIFE	SULDAN
SPADER	**SPRAWL**	**STEMMY**	**STRIKE**	**SULFID**
*SPADIX	SPREAD	**STENCH**	STRING	SULFUR
SPAHEE	SPRENT	**STEPPE**	STRIPE	**SULKER**
SPARER	SPRIER	STEREO	STRIPT	SULLEN
SPARGE	SPRING	STERIC	**STRIPY**	**SULPHA**
SPARID	SPRINT	STERNA	STRIVE	SULTAN
*SPARKY	SPRITE	STEROL	STROBE	SULTRY
SPARRY	SPROUT	*STICKY	STRODE	**SUMACH**
SPARSE	**SPRUCE**	STIFLE	**STROKE**	**SUMMED**
SPATHE	**SPRUCY**	STIGMA	STROLL	**SUMMER**
SPAVIE	SPRUNG	STILLY	STROMA	**SUMMIT**
SPAVIN	*SPUNKY	STINGO	STRONG	**SUMMON**
SPECIE	SPURGE	STINGY	**STROOK**	SUNBOW
SPEECH	**SPURRY**	STINKO	STROUD	SUNDAE
SPEEDY	**SPUTUM**	**STINKY**	STROVE	SUNDER
SPEISE	*SQUALL	STIPEL	**STRUCK**	**SUNDEW**
SPEISS	*SQUAMA	STIPES	STRUMA	SUNDOG
*SPELTZ	*SQUARE	STIRPS	STRUNG	**SUNDRY**
SPENCE	*SQUASH	STITCH	STRUNT	**SUNKEN**
SPEWER	*SQUAWK	STITHY	**STUBBY**	**SUNKET**
SPHENE	*SQUEAK	STIVER	**STUCCO**	SUNLIT
SPHERE	*SQUEAL	*STOCKY	**STUDIO**	SUNNED
SPHERY	*SQUILL	STODGE	*STUFFY	SUNSET

SUNTAN	**SABBATH**	SANDHOG	**SCALADE**	SCOUTER
SUPERB	**SABBING**	SANDIER	**SCALADO**	**SCOWDER**
SUPINE	SACATON	SANDLOT	**SCALAGE**	**SCOWLER**
SUPPED	**SACCADE**	**SANDMAN**	SCALARE	**SCRAGGY**
SUPPER	**SACCATE**	**SANDPIT**	**SCALDIC**	**SCRAICH**
SUPPLE	**SACCULE**	SANGRIA	SCALENE	**SCRAIGH**
SUPPLY	*SACKBUT	SANICLE	SCALIER	**SCRAPER**
SURELY	*SACKFUL	SANTIMS	**SCALING**	**SCRAPIE**
SUREST	**SACKING**	SANTOUR	**SCALLOP**	*SCRAPPY
SURETY	**SACLIKE**	*SAPAJOU	**SCALPEL**	**SCRATCH**
SURFER	SACRIST	**SAPHEAD**	**SCALPER**	*SCRAWLY
SURGER	SADDLER	**SAPHENA**	**SCAMPER**	*SCRAWNY
SURREY	SADIRON	SAPIENS	**SCANDAL**	*SCREAKY
SURTAX	SADNESS	SAPIENT	**SCANDIA**	**SCREECH**
SURVEY	**SAFFRON**	SAPLESS	**SCANNED**	**SCREWER**
SUSLIK	**SAFROLE**	**SAPLING**	**SCANNER**	**SCRIBAL**
SUTLER	**SAGAMAN**	SAPONIN	**SCANTLY**	**SCRIBER**
SUTTEE	**SAGGARD**	*SAPPHIC	**SCAPOSE**	**SCRIEVE**
SUTURE	**SAGGING**	**SAPPING**	**SCAPULA**	*SCRIMPY
*SVARAJ	SAGIEST	**SAPROBE**	SCARIER	**SCROGGY**
SVELTE	SAGUARO	**SAPSAGO**	*SCARIFY	**SCROOGE**
*SWABBY	**SAHIWAL**	**SAPWOOD**	**SCARING**	**SCROTUM**
SWAGER	**SAHUARO**	**SARCASM**	SCARLET	**SCROUGE**
*SWAMPY	SAILING	**SARCOID**	**SCARPER**	*SCRUBBY
*SWANKY	**SAINTLY**	**SARCOMA**	**SCARRED**	*SCRUFFY
*SWARAJ	SALABLE	SARCOUS	**SCARVES**	**SCRUNCH**
SWARTH	SALICIN	SARDINE	**SCATTED**	**SCRUPLE**
SWARTY	SALIENT	SARDIUS	**SCATTER**	*SCUFFLE
SWATCH	SALLIED	SARMENT	**SCAUPER**	**SCULKER**
SWATHE	SALLIER	**SASHIMI**	**SCENERY**	SCULLER
SWAYER	SALLIES	**SASSABY**	**SCEPTER**	**SCULPIN**
SWEATY	**SALLOWY**	**SASSIER**	**SCEPTIC**	**SCUMBLE**
SWEENY	SALPIAN	**SASSILY**	**SCEPTRE**	**SCUMMED**
SWEEPY	*SALPINX	SATANIC	*SCHAPPE	**SCUMMER**
SWERVE	**SALSIFY**	**SATCHEL**	**SCHEMER**	SCUNNER
SWEVEN	SALTANT	SATIATE	*SCHERZO	**SCUPPER**
*SWIMMY	*SALTBOX	**SATIETY**	*SCHLEPP	SCURRIL
SWINGE	SALTERN	SATINET	*SCHLOCK	**SCUTAGE**
SWINGY	SALTIER	**SATISFY**	*SCHMALZ	**SCUTATE**
SWIPLE	SALTILY	**SATRAPY**	**SCHMEER**	SCUTTER
SWIRLY	SALTINE	**SATYRID**	**SCHMOOS**	**SCUTTLE**
*SWISHY	SALTIRE	**SAUCING**	*SCHMUCK	**SEABIRD**
SWITCH	**SALTISH**	SAUNTER	**SCHNAPS**	SEABOOT
SWITHE	SALTPAN	SAURIAN	*SCHNOOK	*SEACOCK
SWIVEL	SALUTER	SAUSAGE	**SCHOLAR**	**SEAFOOD**
SWIVET	**SALVAGE**	SAUTOIR	*SCHTICK	**SEAFOWL**
SWOOSH	**SALVING**	SAVABLE	**SCIATIC**	SEAGIRT
SWOUND	**SAMBHAR**	**SAVANNA**	**SCIENCE**	SEALANT
SYLVAN	**SAMBHUR**	SAVELOY	SCISSOR	**SEALERY**
SYLVIN	**SAMBUCA**	SAVIOUR	*SCOFFER	**SEAMARK**
SYMBOL	*SAMBUKE	**SAVORER**	**SCOLDER**	SEAMIER
SYNCOM	SAMISEN	**SAVOURY**	**SCOLLOP**	SEAPORT
SYNDET	**SAMOVAR**	**SAWBILL**	**SCOOPER**	SEAREST
SYNDIC	**SAMPLER**	*SAWBUCK	SCOOTER	**SEASICK**
*SYNTAX	SAMSARA	SAWDUST	**SCOPULA**	SEASIDE
SYNURA	**SANCTUM**	*SAWFISH	*SCORIFY	**SEATING**
SYPHER	SANDBAG	SAWLIKE	**SCORING**	**SEAWALL**
SYPHON	**SANDBAR**	SAWMILL	SCORNER	SEAWANT
*SYRINX	*SANDBOX	*SAXHORN	**SCOTOMA**	**SEAWARD**
SYSTEM	SANDBUR	*SAXTUBA	SCOTTIE	**SEAWARE**
*SYZYGY	**SANDFLY**	**SCABBLE**	**SCOURER**	**SEAWEED**
SABATON		SCABIES	**SCOURGE**	SEBACIC

SEBASIC	SERGING	SHAPEUP	*SHOPBOY	SIGNORY
SECEDER	SERIATE	SHAPING	*SHOPHAR	SILENCE
SECLUDE	SERICIN	SHARING	SHOPMAN	SILENTS
SECONDE	SERIEMA	SHARKER	*SHOPPED	SILENUS
SECONDO	SERINGA	SHARPEN	SHOPPER	SILESIA
SECRECY	SERIOUS	SHARPER	SHORING	SILICIC
SECRETE	SERPENT	SHARPIE	SHORTEN	SILICLE
SECTARY	*SERPIGO	*SHARPLY	SHORTIA	SILICON
SECTILE	SERRATE	SHASLIK	SHORTIE	*SILIQUA
SECTION	SERVANT	SHATTER	SHORTLY	*SILIQUE
SECULAR	SERVICE	SHAVING	SHOTGUN	SILKIER
SECURER	SERVILE	SHEARER	SHOTTED	SILKILY
SEDARIM	SERVING	SHEATHE	SHOTTEN	SILURID
SEDUCER	SESSILE	SHEBANG	SHOUTER	SILVERN
SEEDBED	SESSION	SHEBEAN	SHOVING	SILVERY
SEEDIER	SESTINA	SHEBEEN	*SHOWERY	SILVICS
SEEDILY	SESTINE	SHEDDER	SHOWIER	SIMILAR
SEEDMAN	*SETBACK	SHEENEY	*SHOWILY	SIMIOID
SEEDPOD	SETLINE	SHEENIE	SHOWING	SIMIOUS
SEEMING	SETTING	SHEETER	*SHOWMAN	SIMITAR
SEEPAGE	SETTLER	*SHEGETZ	*SHOWOFF	*SIMPLEX
SEERESS	SETTLOR	SHEITAN	*SHRIEKY	SIMULAR
SEGETAL	SEVENTH	SHELLAC	*SHRIMPY	SINCERE
SEGMENT	SEVENTY	SHELLER	SHRIVEL	SINGLET
SEISING	SEVERAL	SHELTER	SHRIVER	SINKAGE
SEISURE	SEXIEST	SHELTIE	*SHRUBBY	SINLESS
*SEIZING	SEXLESS	SHELVER	SHTETEL	SINNING
*SEIZURE	SEXTAIN	SHELVES	*SHUCKER	SINOPIA
SEJEANT	SEXTANT	SHERBET	SHUDDER	SINSYNE
SELENIC	SEXTILE	SHEREEF	*SHUFFLE	SINUATE
SELFDOM	SFERICS	SHERRIS	*SHERIFF	SINUOUS
SELFISH	SFUMATO	*SHICKSA	SHUNNER	SIPPING
SELLOUT	*SHACKLE	SHIFTER	SHUNTER	SIRLOIN
*SELTZER	*SHADFLY	SHIKARI	*SHUTOFF	SIROCCO
SELVAGE	SHADIER	SHILPIT	SHUTOUT	SISTRUM
SEMATIC	SHADILY	SHIMMER	SHUTTER	SITHENS
SEMIDRY	SHADING	SHINDIG	SHUTTLE	SITTING
SEMIFIT	SHADOOF	SHINGLE	*SHYLOCK	SITUATE
SEMILOG	*SHADOWY	SHINGLY	SHYNESS	*SIXFOLD
SEMIMAT	*SHAHDOM	SHINIER	SHYSTER	SIXTEEN
SEMINAL	SHAITAN	SHINILY	SIALOID	*SIXTHLY
SEMINAR	*SHAKEUP	SHINING	SIAMANG	*SIZABLE
SEMIPRO	SHAKIER	SHINNED	SIAMESE	*SIZIEST
SEMIRAW	*SHAKILY	SHINNEY	SIBLING	*SIZZLER
SENATOR	*SHAKING	SHIPLAP	*SICKBAY	SKATING
SENDOFF	SHALIER	SHIPMAN	*SICKBED	SKATOLE
SENECIO	SHALLOP	*SHIPPED	*SICKISH	SKEETER
SENHORA	SHALLOT	SHIPPEN	SIDEARM	SKELLUM
SENOPIA	SHALLOW	SHIPPER	SIDECAR	SKELTER
SENSATE	SHALLOW	SHIPPON	SIDEMAN	SKEPSIS
SENSING	SHAMBLE	*SHIPWAY	SIDEWAY	*SKEPTIC
SENSORY	SHAMING	SHIRKER	SIEMENS	*SKETCHY
SENSUAL	SHAMMAS	SHITTAH	SIENITE	SKIABLE
*SEPPUKU	*SHAMMED	SHITTIM	SIGANID	SKIDDER
SEPTATE	SHAMMER	*SHIVERY	SIGHTER	SKIDDOO
SEPTIME	SHAMMES	*SHOCKER	SIGHTLY	*SKIDWAY
*SEQUELA	SHAMMOS	SHODDEN	SIGMOID	*SKIFFLE
*SEQUENT	SHAMOIS	SHOEPAC	SIGNIFY	SKILFUL
*SEQUOIA	SHAMPOO	*SHOOFLY	SIGNIOR	SKILLET
SERFAGE	SHANTEY	SHOOTER	SIGNORA	*SKIMMER
SERFDOM	SHANTIH	*SHOPBOY	SIGNORE	SKINFUL
SERFISH	*SHAPELY			*SKINKER

SKINNED	SLOPPED	SNORTER	SORBATE	SPEEDER
SKINNER	SLOTTED	SNOWCAP	SORBENT	SPEEDUP
*SKIPPED	*SLOUCHY	SNOWIER	SORBOSE	SPELEAN
*SKIPPER	SLOUGHY	SNOWILY	SORCERY	SPELLER
*SKIPPET	SLOWISH	SNOWMAN	SORDINE	SPELTER
SKIRRET	SLUBBER	SNUBBER	SORDINO	SPELUNK
SKIRTER	SLUGGED	SNUFFER	SORGHUM	SPENCER
SKITTER	SLUGGER	SNUFFLE	SORITES	SPENDER
SKITTLE	SLUMBER	*SNUFFLY	SOROCHE	SPHENIC
SKIWEAR	SLUMGUM	SNUGGLE	SORORAL	SPHERAL
*SKOOKUM	SLUMMED	SOAKAGE	SOROSIS	SPHERIC
*SKREEGH	SLUMMER	*SOAPBOX	SORRIER	SPICERY
*SKREIGH	SLURRED	SOAPIER	SORRILY	SPICIER
*SKULKER	SLYNESS	SOAPILY	SOTTISH	SPICILY
*SKYDIVE	*SMACKER	SOARING	SOUBISE	SPICING
*SKYHOOK	SMARAGD	SOBERLY	SOUFFLE	SPICULA
*SKYJACK	SMARTEN	SOCAGER	SOULFUL	SPICULE
*SKYLARK	SMARTIE	SOCCAGE	SOUNDER	SPIDERY
SKYLINE	SMARTLY	SOCIETY	SOUNDLY	SPIEGEL
*SKYPHOS	SMASHER	*SOCKEYE	SOUPCON	SPIELER
SKYSAIL	SMASHUP	*SOCKMAN	SOURISH	SPIKING
*SKYWARD	SMATTER	SODDING	SOURSOP	SPILING
SLABBER	SMEARER	SOFTIES	SOUTANE	SPILLER
SLACKEN	SMECTIC	SOIGNEE	SOUTHER	SPINACH
SLACKER	SMEDDUM	SOILAGE	*SOVKHOZ	SPINAGE
*SLACKLY	SMELLER	SOILURE	SOYBEAN	SPINATE
SLANDER	SMELTER	SOJOURN	SPACIAL	SPINDLE
SLAPPED	SMIDGEN	SOKEMAN	SPACING	SPINDLY
SLAPPER	SMIDGIN	SOLACER	SPADING	SPINIER
SLASHER	SMIRKER	SOLANIN	SPAEING	SPINIES
SLATHER	SMITING	SOLANUM	SPALLER	SPINNER
SLATIER	SMITTEN	SOLARIA	SPANCEL	SPINNEY
SLATING	SMOKING	SOLATIA	SPANGLE	*SPINOFF
SLATTED	SMOLDER	SOLDIER	SPANGLY	SPINOSE
SLAVERY	*SMOOCHY	SOLERET	SPANIEL	SPINOUS
SLAVING	*SMOOTHY	SOLFEGE	SPANKER	SPINOUT
SLAVISH	SMOTHER	SOLICIT	SPANNED	SPINULA
SLEDDER	SMUGGLE	SOLIDLY	SPANNER	SPINULE
SLEEKEN	*SMUTCHY	SOLIDUS	SPAREST	SPIRAEA
SLEEKIT	SMUTTED	SOLOIST	SPARGER	SPIRANT
SLEEKLY	SNAFFLE	SOLUBLE	SPARING	SPIREME
SLEEPER	SNAPPED	SOLUBLY	SPARKER	SPIRING
SLEIGHT	SNAPPER	SOLVATE	SPARKLE	SPIROID
SLENDER	SNARLER	SOLVENT	SPAROID	SPIRULA
SLICKER	*SNATCHY	SOLVING	SPARRED	SPITING
*SLICKLY	SNEAKER	SOMEDAY	SPARROW	SPITTED
SLIDING	SNEERER	*SOMEHOW	SPASTIC	SPITTER
SLIMIER	*SNEEZER	SOMEONE	SPATHIC	SPITTLE
SLIMILY	SNICKER	*SOMEWAY	SPATIAL	*SPLASHY
SLIMING	SNIFFER	SONANCE	SPATTED	SPLEENY
SLIMMED	SNIFFLE	SONGFUL	SPATTER	SPLENIA
SLIMMER	SNIFTER	SONLESS	SPATULA	SPLENIC
SLIMPSY	SNIGGER	SONLIKE	SPAWNER	SPLICER
SLINGER	SNIGGLE	*SONOVOX	SPEAKER	SPLOTCH
SLIPOUT	SNIPPED	SONSHIP	SPEARER	SPLURGE
SLIPPED	SNIPPER	SOOTHER	SPECIAL	SPLURGY
SLIPPER	SNIPPET	SOOTHLY	SPECIAL	SPOILER
*SLIPWAY	SNOOKER	SOPHIES	*SPECIFY	SPONDEE
SLITHER	SNOOPER	SOPHISM	*SPECKLE	SPONGER
SLITTED	*SNOOZER	SOPHIST	SPECTER	SPONGIN
SLOBBER	*SNOOZLE	SOPPING	SPECTRA	SPONSAL
SLOGGER	SNORKEL	SOPRANO	SPECTRE	SPONSON

SPONSOR	STAINER	STETSON	STRETTO	**SUBDUER**
SPOONEY	**STALKER**	**STEWARD**	**STREWER**	**SUBECHO**
SPOROID	STAMINA	**STEWBUM**	STRIATE	**SUBEDIT**
SPORRAN	**STAMMEL**	**STEWPAN**	STRIDER	**SUBERIC**
SPORTER	**STAMMER**	**STHENIA**	STRIDOR	**SUBERIN**
SPORULE	**STAMPER**	STIBIAL	STRIGIL	**SUBFUSC**
SPOTTER	**STANDBY**	STIBINE	**STRINGY**	**SUBHEAD**
SPOUSAL	STANDEE	**STIBIUM**	**STRIKER**	**SUBIDEA**
SPOUTER	STANDER	**STICKER**	STRIPER	**SUBITEM**
*SPRAWLY	STANDUP	STICKIT	**STRIVER**	*SUBJECT
SPRAYER	STANING	**STICKLE**	**STROBIC**	*SUBJOIN
SPRIEST	STANNIC	*STICKUM	STROBIL	SUBLATE
SPRIGGY	STANNUM	*STICKUP	**STROKER**	**SUBLIME**
SPRIGHT	**STARDOM**	**STIFFEN**	**STROPHE**	**SUBMISS**
SPRINGE	STARETS	*STIFFLY	**STROYER**	SUBORAL
SPRINGY	STARING	**STIFLER**	STRUDEL	**SUBOVAL**
SPUDDER	STARLET	STINGER	**STUBBLE**	**SUBPART**
SPUMIER	STARLIT	**STINKER**	**STUBBLY**	**SUBPENA**
SPUMING	STARRED	STINTER	STUDDIE	**SUBPLOT**
SPUMONE	STARTER	**STIPEND**	STUDENT	**SUBRACE**
SPUMONI	STARTLE	**STIPPLE**	STUDIED	**SUBRENT**
SPUMOUS	**STARTSY**	STIPULE	STUDIER	**SUBRING**
SPUNKIE	**STARVER**	STIRRED	STUDIES	**SUBRULE**
SPURNER	STATANT	STIRRER	**STUFFER**	**SUBSALE**
SPURRED	**STATELY**	STIRRUP	STUIVER	**SUBSECT**
SPURRER	STATICE	**STOCKER**	**STUMBLE**	SUBSERE
SPURREY	STATING	**STOKING**	**STUMMED**	**SUBSIDE**
SPURTLE	STATION	**STOMACH**	**STUMPER**	**SUBSIDY**
SPUTNIK	STATISM	STOMATA	STUNNED	SUBSIST
SPUTTER	STATIST	STOMATE	STUNNER	SUBSOIL
*SQUABBY	**STATIVE**	**STOMPER**	*STUPEFY	**SUBSUME**
*SQUALID	STATURE	STONIER	STUTTER	SUBTEEN
*SQUALLY	STATUTE	**STONILY**	**STYGIAN**	**SUBTEND**
*SQUALOR	**STAUNCH**	STONING	**STYLATE**	*SUBTEXT
*SQUARER	STEALER	**STONISH**	**STYLING**	SUBTILE
*SQUASHY	**STEALTH**	**STOOKER**	**STYLISE**	SUBTONE
*SQUATTY	STEAMER	STOOLIE	**STYLISH**	**SUBTYPE**
*SQUEAKY	STEARIN	STOOPER	**STYLIST**	SUBUNIT
*SQUEEZE	STEELIE	**STOPGAP**	**STYLITE**	**SUBVENE**
*SQUELCH	STEEPEN	**STOPING**	*STYLIZE	**SUBVERT**
*SQUIFFY	STEEPER	**STOPPED**	**STYLOID**	*SUBZONE
*SQUILLA	STEEPLE	**STOPPER**	STYPSIS	**SUCCEED**
*SQUINCH	**STEEPLY**	**STOPPLE**	**STYPTIC**	**SUCCESS**
*SQUINNY	STEERER	STORAGE	**STYRENE**	**SUCCORY**
*SQUINTY	STELLAR	STORIED	SUASION	**SUCCOTH**
*SQUIRMY	**STEMMED**	STORIES	**SUAVITY**	**SUCCOUR**
*SQUISHY	**STEMMER**	STORING	**SUBACID**	**SUCCUBA**
*SQUOOSH	STEMSON	STOURIE	**SUBADAR**	*SUCCUMB
SRADDHA	*STENCHY	STOUTEN	SUBALAR	**SUCCUSS**
STABBER	STENCIL	**STOUTLY**	SUBAREA	**SUCKLER**
STABILE	**STENGAH**	**STOWAGE**	**SUBARID**	SUCRASE
STABLER	STENTOR	**STRAFER**	**SUBATOM**	SUCROSE
STACKER	**STEPPED**	STRANGE	**SUBBASE**	SUCTION
STADDLE	**STEPPER**	STRATAL	**SUBBASS**	**SUFFARI**
STADIUM	STEPSON	STRATUM	**SUBBING**	*SUFFICE
STAFFER	STERILE	STRATUS	**SUBCELL**	**SUFFUSE**
STAGGED	STERLET	**STRAYER**	**SUBCLAN**	SUGGEST
STAGGER	STERNAL	**STREAKY**	**SUBCOOL**	SUICIDE
STAGGIE	**STERNLY**	**STREAMY**	**SUBDEAN**	SUITING
STAGIER	STERNUM	**STRETCH**	**SUBDUAL**	SULCATE
STAGILY	STEROID	STRETTA	**SUBDUCE**	**SULFATE**
STAGING	STERTOR		**SUBDUCT**	**SULFIDE**

SULFITE	SUTURAL	SYNCARP	*SALVIFIC	SATIRIST
SULFONE	SWABBER	*SYNCHRO	SAMARIUM	*SATIRIZE
SULFURY	SWABBIE	SYNCOPE	SAMENESS	SATURANT
SULLAGE	SWADDLE	SYNERGY	*SAMPHIRE	SATURATE
SULPHID	SWAGGED	SYNESIS	SAMPLING	*SAUCEBOX
SULPHUR	SWAGGER	*SYNGAMY	SANATIVE	SAUCEPAN
SULTANA	SWAGING	*SYNONYM	*SANCTIFY	SAUROPOD
SUMLESS	SWAGMAN	SYNOVIA	SANCTION	SAUTERNE
SUMMAND	SWALLOW	SYNTONY	SANCTITY	SAUTOIRE
SUMMARY	SWAMIES	SYRINGA	SANDARAC	*SAVAGERY
SUMMATE	SWAMPER	SYRINGE	*SANDBANK	SAVAGEST
SUMMERY	SWANNED	*SYRPHID	SANDBURR	SAVAGING
SUMMING	SWANPAN	SYSTOLE	*SANDFISH	SAVAGISM
SUMMONS	SWAPPER	SABBATIC	SANDIEST	SAVANNAH
SUMPTER	SWARMER	SABOTAGE	SANDLIKE	*SAVINGLY
*SUNBACK	*SWARTHY	SABOTEUR	SANDLING	SAVORIER
SUNBATH	SWASHER	SABULOSE	SANDPEEP	SAVORIES
SUNBEAM	SWATHER	SABULOUS	SANDPILE	SAVOROUS
SUNBIRD	SWATTED	SACCULAR	SANDSOAP	SAVOURER
SUNBURN	SWATTER	SACCULUS	*SANDWICH	SAWBONES
SUNDIAL	*SWAYFUL	*SACKLIKE	SANDWORM	SAWHORSE
SUNDOWN	SWEARER	*SACKSFUL	SANDWORT	SAWTOOTH
SUNFAST	SWEATER	SACRARIA	SANENESS	*SAXATILE
SUNFISH	SWEEPER	SACRISTY	SANGAREE	SAYONARA
SUNGLOW	SWEETEN	SADDLERY	SANGUINE	*SCABBARD
SUNLAMP	SWEETIE	SADDLING	SANITARY	SCABIOSA
SUNLAND	SWEETLY	SAFENESS	SANITATE	SCABIOUS
SUNLESS	SWELTER	SAFRANIN	SANITIES	*SCABLIKE
SUNLIKE	SWELTRY	SAGACITY	SANITISE	SCABROUS
SUNNING	SWERVER	SAGAMORE	*SANITIZE	*SCAFFOLD
SUNRISE	SWIFTER	SAGANASH	SANNYASI	SCALABLE
SUNROOF	*SWIFTLY	SAGENESS	SANSERIF	SCALAWAG
SUNROOM	SWIGGER	SAGITTAL	SANTALIC	SCALENUS
SUNSPOT	SWILLER	SAILBOAT	SANTONIN	SCALEPAN
SUNSUIT	SWIMMER	SAILFISH	SAPIDITY	SCALIEST
SUNWARD	SWINDLE	SAINFOIN	SAPIENCE	SCALLION
SUNWISE	SWINGER	SAINTDOM	*SAPIENCY	*SCAMMONY
SUPPING	SWINGLE	SALACITY	*SAPONIFY	*SCAMPISH
SUPPORT	SWINISH	SALADANG	SAPONINE	SCANDENT
SUPPOSE	SWINNEY	SALARIAT	SAPONITE	SCANDIUM
SUPREME	SWIPPLE	SALEABLE	*SAPPHIRE	SCANNING
SURBASE	SWISHER	SALEROOM	*SAPPHISM	SCANSION
SURCOAT	SWITHER	SALESMAN	*SAPPHIST	SCANTIER
SURFACE	*SWITHLY	SALICINE	SAPREMIA	SCANTIES
SURFEIT	SWIVING	SALIENCE	SAPROPEL	*SCAPHOID
SURFIER	*SWIZZLE	SALIENCY	SARABAND	SCAPULAR
SURFING	SWOBBER	SALINITY	SARCENET	*SCARCELY
SURGEON	SWOLLEN	*SALINIZE	SARDONIC	*SCARCITY
SURGERY	SWOONER	SALIVATE	*SARDONYX	*SCARFPIN
SURGING	SWOOPER	SALMONID	SARGASSO	SCARIEST
SURMISE	SWOTTER	SALSILLA	SARMENTA	SCARIOSE
SURNAME	SYCOSIS	SALTBUSH	SARODIST	SCARIOUS
SURPASS	SYENITE	SALTIEST	SARSENET	SCARLESS
SURPLUS	SYLLABI	SALTLESS	SARTORII	SCARRING
SURREAL	*SYLPHID	SALTLIKE	SASSIEST	*SCATBACK
SURTOUT	SYLVINE	SALTNESS	SASSWOOD	SCATTING
SURVEIL	SYLVITE	*SALTWORK	SASTRUGA	SCAVENGE
SURVIVE	SYMBION	SALTWORT	SATANISM	SCENARIO
SUSPECT	SYMBIOT	SALUTARY	SATANIST	SCENICAL
SUSPEND	*SYMPTOM	SALVABLE	SATIABLE	SCEPTRAL
SUSPIRE	SYNAGOG	SALVAGEE	SATINPOD	SCHEDULE
SUSTAIN	SYNAPSE	SALVAGER	SATIRISE	SCHILLER

*SCHIZOID	SCRIBBLE	SECURING	SEMOLINA	*SHADDOCK
*SCHIZONT	SCRIMPIT	SECURITY	SEMPLICE	SHADIEST
*SCHMALTZ	SCROFULA	SEDATION	SENARIUS	*SHADOWER
*SCHMALZY	SCROUNGE	SEDATIVE	SENILELY	*SHADRACH
*SCHMELZE	SCROUNGY	SEDERUNT	SENILITY	*SHAFTING
*SCHMOOSE	SCRUBBER	SEDILIUM	SENNIGHT	*SHAGBARK
*SCHMOOZE	SCRUTINY	SEDIMENT	SENORITA	SHAGREEN
*SCHNAPPS	*SCUFFLER	SEDITION	SENSEFUL	*SHAKEOUT
*SCHNECKE	SCULLERY	SEDULITY	SENSIBLE	*SHAKIEST
*SCHOLIUM	SCULLION	SEDULOUS	SENSILLA	SHALIEST
SCHOONER	SCULPTOR	*SEECATCH	SENSORIA	SHALLOON
*SCHRIEVE	*SCUMLIKE	*SEEDCAKE	SENSUOUS	*SHAMABLE
SCIAENID	*SCUMMING	SEEDCASE	SENTENCE	*SHAMEFUL
SCIATICA	*SCUPPAUG	SEEDIEST	SENTIENT	*SHAMMASH
SCILICET	SCURRIED	SEEDLESS	SENTINEL	*SHAMMIED
SCIMETAR	SCURRIES	SEEDLIKE	SEPARATE	*SHAMMIES
SCIMITAR	SCURRILE	SEEDLING	SEPTARIA	*SHAMMING
SCIMITER	*SCUTCHER	SEEDSMAN	SEPTETTE	*SHAMOSIM
SCINCOID	SCUTELLA	SEEDTIME	SEPTUPLE	*SHAMROCK
SCIOLISM	*SCYPHATE	SEICENTO	*SEQUENCE	*SHANGHAI
SCIOLIST	*SEABEACH	SEIGNEUR	*SEQUENCY	SHANTIES
SCIROCCO	SEABOARD	SEIGNIOR	*SEQUITUR	SHANTUNG
SCIRRHUS	SEABORNE	SEIGNORY	SERAGLIO	*SHASHLIK
SCISSILE	SEACOAST	SEISMISM	*SERAPHIM	SHEALING
SCISSION	SEACRAFT	SELADANG	SERENADE	SHEATHER
SCISSURE	SEADROME	SELAMLIK	SERENATA	SHEDABLE
SCIURINE	SEAFARER	SELCOUTH	SERENITY	SHEDDING
SCIUROID	SEAFLOOR	SELECTEE	*SERFHOOD	SHEENFUL
*SCLAFFER	SEAFRONT	SELECTLY	*SERFLIKE	*SHEEPDOG
SCLEREID	SEAGOING	SELECTOR	SERGEANT	SHEEPISH
SCLERITE	SEALLIKE	SELENATE	SERIALLY	*SHEEPMAN
SCLEROID	SEALSKIN	SELENIDE	SERIATIM	*SHEETFED
SCLEROMA	SEAMIEST	SELENITE	*SERJEANT	SHEETING
SCLEROSE	SEAMLESS	SELENIUM	SEROLOGY	*SHEIKDOM
SCLEROUS	SEAMLIKE	SELFHEAL	SEROSITY	*SHELDUCK
*SCOFFLAW	SEAMOUNT	*SELFHOOD	SEROTINE	*SHELFFUL
SCOLDING	SEAMSTER	SELFLESS	SEROTYPE	*SHELLACK
SCOLIOMA	SEAPIECE	SELFNESS	SERRANID	*SHELVING
*SCOOPFUL	SEAPLANE	SELFSAME	SERVABLE	*SHEPHERD
*SCORCHER	*SEAQUAKE	*SELFWARD	SERVICER	SHERBERT
SCOREPAD	SEARCHER	SELVEDGE	SERVITOR	*SHERLOCK
SCORNFUL	SEASCAPE	SEMANTIC	SESAMOID	SHETLAND
SCORPION	SEASCOUT	SEMESTER	SESSPOOL	SHIELDER
SCOTOPIA	SEASHELL	SEMIARID	SESTERCE	SHIELING
SCOURGER	SEASHORE	SEMIBALD	SETIFORM	SHIGELLA
SCOURING	SEASONAL	SEMICOMA	SETSCREW	*SHIKAREE
SCOUTHER	SEASONER	SEMIDEAF	SETTLING	SHILINGI
SCOUTING	SEATLESS	SEMIDOME	SETULOSE	SHILLALA
SCRABBLE	SEATMATE	SEMIGALA	SETULOUS	SHILLING
*SCRABBLY	SEATRAIN	SEMIHARD	SEVERITY	*SHIMMERY
*SCRAGGLY	*SEATWORK	*SEMIHIGH	SEWERAGE	*SHIMMING
SCRAMBLE	SEAWATER	*SEMIHOBO	*SEXINESS	SHINBONE
SCRANNEL	SECANTLY	SEMIMATT	SEXOLOGY	SHINGLER
SCRAPING	SECATEUR	SEMIMUTE	*SEXTARII	SHINIEST
*SCRAPPED	SECONDER	SEMINARY	*SEXTETTE	SHINLEAF
SCRAPPER	SECONDLY	SEMINUDE	*SEXTUPLE	SHINNERY
SCRAPPLE	SECRETIN	SEMIOSIS	*SEXTUPLY	SHINNING
*SCRATCHY	SECRETLY	SEMIOTIC	*SFORZATO	SHIPLOAD
SCRAWLER	SECRETOR	SEMISOFT	*SHACKLER	SHIPMATE
SCREAMER	SECTORAL	SEMITIST	*SHADBLOW	*SHIPMENT
*SCREECHY	SECUNDUM	SEMITONE	*SHADBUSH	*SHIPPING
SCREENER	SECUREST	SEMIWILD	*SHADCHAN	SHIPSIDE

*SHIPWORM	SIDEREAL	SIRENIAN	SLIPCASE	SNAGLIKE
*SHIPYARD	SIDERITE	SIRVENTE	*SLIPFORM	*SNAPBACK
SHIRRING	*SIDESHOW	SISSYISH	SLIPKNOT	SNAPLESS
SHIRTING	SIDESLIP	SISTERLY	SLIPLESS	SNAPPIER
SHITTING	SIDESPIN	SISTROID	SLIPOVER	*SNAPPILY
SHIVAREE	SIDESTEP	SITARIST	SLIPPAGE	SNAPPING
SHIVERER	*SIDEWALK	SITHENCE	*SLIPPERY	*SNAPPISH
*SHKOTZIM	SIDEWALL	SITOLOGY	SLIPPING	SNAPSHOT
SHLEMIEL	SIDEWARD	*SITZMARK	SLIPSHOD	SNAPWEED
SHOEBILL	*SIDEWAYS	*SIXPENCE	SLIPSOLE	SNATCHER
SHOEHORN	SIDEWISE	*SIXPENNY	SLIPWARE	SNEERFUL
SHOELACE	*SIEROZEM	*SIXTIETH	SLITHERY	*SNICKERY
*SHOEPACK	SIFFLEUR	*SIZEABLE	SLITLESS	SNIFFIER
SHOETREE	SIGHLESS	*SIZINESS	SLITTING	*SNIFFILY
SHOOTING	*SIGHLIKE	SKELETON	SLIVERER	*SNIFFISH
SHOPGIRL	SIGHTSEE	*SKETCHER	*SLIVOVIC	SNIFFLER
*SHOPLIFT	SIGNALER	*SKEWBACK	*SLOBBERY	SNIGGLER
*SHOPPING	SIGNALLY	*SKEWBALD	*SLOBBISH	*SNIPPETY
*SHOPTALK	SIGNIORY	*SKEWNESS	SLOGGING	SNIPPING
*SHOPWORN	SIGNPOST	*SKIAGRAM	SLOPPING	SNITCHER
SHORTAGE	SILENCER	*SKIJORER	*SLOPWORK	SNIVELER
SHORTCUT	SILICATE	SKILLESS	*SLOTBACK	*SNOBBERY
SHORTIES	SILICIDE	*SKILLFUL	SLOTHFUL	SNOBBIER
SHORTISH	*SILICIFY	SKILLING	SLOTTING	*SNOBBILY
SHOTTING	SILICIUM	*SKIMMING	SLOUCHER	*SNOBBISH
SHOULDER	SILICONE	*SKINHEAD	SLOVENLY	SNOBBISM
SHOULDST	SILKIEST	SKINLESS	*SLOWDOWN	SNOUTISH
SHOVELER	*SILKLIKE	*SKINLIKE	SLOWNESS	SNOWBALL
*SHOWBOAT	*SILKWEED	SKINNING	*SLOWPOKE	*SNOWBANK
*SHOWCASE	*SILKWORM	SKIORING	*SLOWWORM	SNOWBELL
*SHOWDOWN	SILLABUB	*SKIPJACK	SLUBBING	SNOWBIRD
*SHOWGIRL	SILLIBUB	SKIPLANE	SLUGABED	*SNOWBUSH
SHOWIEST	*SILOXANE	*SKIPPING	SLUGFEST	SNOWDROP
*SHOWROOM	SILUROID	*SKIRMISH	SLUGGARD	SNOWFALL
SHRAPNEL	SILVERER	SKIRTING	SLUGGING	SNOWIEST
SHREDDER	SILVERLY	*SKITTERY	SLUGGISH	SNOWLAND
*SHREWISH	SILVICAL	*SKITTISH	*SLUMBERY	SNOWLESS
*SHRIEKER	SIMARUBA	*SKULLCAP	SLUMLORD	*SNOWLIKE
SHRIEVAL	*SIMAZINE	*SKYBORNE	SLUMMING	SNOWMELT
*SHRIMPER	SIMOLEON	*SKYDIVER	SLURRING	*SNOWPACK
*SHRINKER	SIMONIAC	*SKYLIGHT	SLYBOOTS	*SNOWPLOW
*SHRIVING	SIMONIES	*SKYWARDS	SMALLAGE	*SNOWSHED
*SHRUNKEN	SIMONIST	*SKYWRITE	SMALLISH	SNOWSHOE
*SHUCKING	*SIMONIZE	*SLABBERY	*SMALLPOX	SNOWSUIT
*SHUDDERY	SIMPERER	SLABBING	SMALTINE	SNUBNESS
*SHUFFLER	*SIMPLIFY	SLAPDASH	SMALTITE	*SNUFFBOX
*SHUNPIKE	SIMPLISM	*SLAPJACK	SMARAGDE	SNUFFIER
*SHUTDOWN	SIMULANT	SLAPPING	SMELTERY	*SNUFFILY
SHUTTING	SIMULATE	SLASHING	SMIDGEON	SNUFFLER
*SHWANPAN	SINAPISM	SLATIEST	*SMITHERY	SNUGGERY
SIBILANT	SINCIPUT	SLATTERN	*SMOCKING	SNUGGEST
SIBILATE	SINECURE	SLATTING	*SMOKEPOT	SNUGGING
SICKENER	SINFONIA	SLAVERER	*SMOKEPOT	SNUGNESS
*SICKERLY	SINGSONG	SLEDDING	SMOOTHEN	*SOAPBARK
SICKNESS	SINGULAR	SLEEKIER	SMOOTHER	SOAPIEST
*SICKROOM	*SINICIZE	SLEEPING	SMOOTHIE	SOAPLESS
SIDEBAND	SINISTER	SLEIGHER	*SMOOTHLY	SOAPSUDS
SIDEHILL	*SINKHOLE	*SLIDEWAY	*SMOTHERY	SOAPWORT
*SIDEKICK	SINOLOGY	SLIMIEST	SMOULDER	*SOBERIZE
SIDELINE	SINUSOID	SLIMMEST	SMUGGLER	SOBRIETY
SIDELING	SIPHONAL	SLIMMING	SMUGNESS	SOCIABLE
SIDELONG	*SIPHONIC	SLIMNESS	SMUTTING	*SOCIABLY

SOCIALLY	SONGLESS	SPARSITY	SPLENIUS	*SQUIREEN
SODALIST	SONGLIKE	SPATTING	SPLINTER	*SQUIRISH
SODALITE	SONGSTER	*SPEAKING	SPLITTER	*SQUIRMER
SODALITY	SONICATE	SPEARMAN	*SPLOTCHY	*SQUIRREL
SODAMIDE	SONORANT	SPECIATE	SPLUTTER	*SQUIRTER
SODDENLY	SONORITY	*SPECIFIC	SPOILAGE	STABLEST
SODOMITE	SONOROUS	SPECIMEN	SPOLIATE	STABLING
*SOFTBACK	SOOCHONG	SPECIOUS	SPONDAIC	STABLISH
SOFTBALL	SOOTHEST	SPECTATE	SPONGIER	STACCATO
SOFTENER	SOOTHING	SPECTRAL	SPONGILY	STAGGARD
*SOFTHEAD	SOOTHSAY	SPECTRUM	SPONGING	STAGGART
SOFTNESS	SORBITOL	SPECULUM	SPONSION	STAGGERY
SOFTWARE	SORCERER	SPEEDIER	SPONTOON	STAGGING
*SOFTWOOD	SOREHEAD	SPEEDILY	*SPOOKISH	STAGIEST
SOILLESS	SORENESS	SPEEDING	SPOONFUL	STAGNANT
SOLANDER	SORICINE	*SPEEDWAY	SPOONIER	STAGNATE
SOLANINE	SORORATE	SPEERING	SPOONIES	STAIRWAY
SOLARISE	SORORITY	SPELAEAN	SPOONING	STAKEOUT
SOLARISM	SORPTION	SPELLING	SPORADIC	STALLION
SOLARIUM	SORRIEST	*SPERMARY	SPORTFUL	STALWART
*SOLARIZE	SORROWER	SPERMINE	SPORTIVE	STAMPEDE
SOLATION	SOUCHONG	SPERMOUS	SPOTLESS	STANCHER
SOLATIUM	*SOUNDBOX	*SPHAGNUM	SPOTTING	*STANCHLY
SOLDERER	SOUNDING	SPHENOID	SPRADDLE	STANDARD
SOLDIERY	SOURBALL	*SPHERICS	SPRATTLE	STANDING
SOLECISE	SOURDINE	SPHERIER	SPRAWLER	STANDISH
SOLECISM	SOURNESS	SPHERING	SPREADER	*STANDOFF
SOLECIST	SOURPUSS	SPHEROID	SPRIGGER	STANDOUT
*SOLECIZE	SOURWOOD	SPHERULE	SPRINGAL	STANDPAT
SOLELESS	SOUTACHE	SPHINGES	SPRINGER	STANHOPE
SOLENESS	SOUTHERN	*SPHINGID	SPRINKLE	STANNARY
SOLENOID	SOUTHING	*SPHYGMUS	SPRINTER	STANNITE
SOLFEGGI	*SOUTHPAW	SPICCATO	*SPROCKET	STANNOUS
SOLIDAGO	SOUTHRON	SPICIEST	SPRYNESS	STAPEDES
SOLIDARY	SOUVENIR	SPICULUM	SPUMIEST	STAPELIA
*SOLIDIFY	SOVRANLY	*SPIFFING	SPURGALL	STARFISH
SOLIDITY	SOVRANTY	SPIKELET	SPURIOUS	*STARGAZE
*SOLIQUID	*SOWBELLY	SPILIKIN	SPURRIER	STARLESS
SOLITARY	SOWBREAD	SPILLAGE	SPURRING	STARLIKE
SOLITUDE	SPACEMAN	*SPILLWAY	SPYGLASS	STARLING
SOLLERET	SPACIOUS	SPINALLY	*SQUABBLE	STARNOSE
SOLONETS	SPADEFUL	SPINDLER	*SQUADRON	STARRING
*SOLONETZ	SPADICES	SPINELLE	*SQUALENE	STARTLER
SOLSTICE	SPADILLE	*SPINIFEX	*SQUALLER	STARWORT
SOLUTION	*SPAGYRIC	SPINLESS	*SQUANDER	STASIMON
SOLVABLE	SPALPEEN	SPINNERY	*SQUARELY	STATABLE
*SOLVENCY	SPANDREL	SPINNING	*SQUAREST	STATEDLY
SOMBRERO	SPANDRIL	SPINSTER	*SQUARING	STATUARY
SOMBROUS	*SPANKING	SPIRACLE	*SQUARISH	STAUMREL
*SOMEBODY	SPANLESS	SPIRALLY	*SQUASHER	STAYSAIL
SOMEDEAL	SPANNING	SPIRILLA	*SQUATTER	STEADIED
SOMERSET	*SPANWORM	SPITBALL	*SQUAWKER	STEADIER
SOMETIME	SPARABLE	SPITEFUL	*SQUEAKER	STEADIES
*SOMEWAYS	SPARERIB	SPITFIRE	*SQUEALER	STEADING
*SOMEWHAT	SPARKIER	SPITTING	*SQUEEGEE	STEALAGE
*SOMEWHEN	*SPARKILY	SPITTOON	*SQUEEZER	STEALING
SOMEWISE	*SPARKISH	SPLASHER	*SQUELCHY	STEALTHY
SONARMAN	SPARKLER	SPLATTER	*SQUIFFED	STEAPSIN
SONATINA	SPARLIKE	SPLENDID	*SQUIGGLE	STEARATE
SONGBIRD	SPARLING	SPLENDOR	*SQUIGGLY	STEARINE
*SONGBOOK	SPARRIER	SPLENIAL	*SQUILGEE	STEATITE
SONGFEST	SPARRING	SPLENIUM	*SQUINTER	STEDFAST

STEENBOK	*STOMACHY	STRUTTER	SUBOVATE	SULPHATE
STEERAGE	STOMATAL	STUBBIER	*SUBOXIDE	SULPHIDE
STEEVING	STOMATIC	*STUBBILY	*SUBPHYLA	SULPHITE
STEGODON	STOMODEA	STUBBING	SUBPOENA	SULPHONE
STEINBOK	STONEFLY	STUBBORN	SUBPOLAR	*SULPHURY
STELLATE	STONIEST	STUCCOER	*SUBPUBIC	SUMMABLE
STELLIFY	*STOPCOCK	*STUDBOOK	SUBSERVE	*SUMMERLY
STEMLESS	STOPOVER	STUDDING	*SUBSHAFT	*SUMMITRY
STEMLIKE	STOPPAGE	*STUDFISH	*SUBSHRUB	SUMMONER
*STEMMERY	STOPPING	STUDIOUS	SUBSIDER	*SUMPWEED
STEMMING	STORABLE	*STUDWORK	SUBSOLAR	*SUNBAKED
STEMWARE	STOTINKA	*STUFFING	SUBSONIC	SUNBATHE
STENOSED	STOUTISH	STULTIFY	SUBSPACE	SUNBURST
STENOSIS	*STOWAWAY	STUMBLER	SUBSTAGE	SUNDERER
STEPDAME	STRADDLE	STUMMING	SUBTILTY	SUNDRIES
STEPLIKE	STRAGGLE	STUMPAGE	SUBTITLE	SUNDROPS
STEPPING	STRAGGLY	STUNNING	SUBTLETY	SUNGLASS
STEPWISE	STRAIGHT	STUNSAIL	SUBTONIC	SUNLIGHT
STERICAL	STRAINER	STURGEON	SUBTOPIC	SUNSCALD
STERIGMA	STRAITEN	STYLISER	SUBTOTAL	SUNSHADE
STERLING	STRAMASH	*STYLIZER	SUBTRACT	SUNSHINE
STERNITE	STRAMONY	SUBABBOT	SUBTRIBE	SUNSTONE
STERNSON	STRANDER	SUBACRID	SUBTUNIC	SUNWARDS
STERNWAY	STRANGER	SUBACUTE	SUBULATE	SUPERADD
STIBNITE	STRANGLE	SUBADULT	SUBURBAN	SUPEREGO
*STICKFUL	STRAPPER	SUBAGENT	SUBURBIA	*SUPERFIX
STICKIER	STRATEGY	SUBAHDAR	*SUBVICAR	SUPERIOR
*STICKILY	STRATIFY	*SUBAXIAL	SUBVIRAL	*SUPERJET
STICKLER	STRATOUS	SUBBREED	*SUBVOCAL	SUPERLIE
*STICKMAN	STRAVAGE	SUBCAUSE	SUCCINCT	SUPERMAN
STICKOUT	STRAVAIG	*SUBCHIEF	SUCCINIC	SUPERNAL
*STICKPIN	STRAWHAT	SUBCLASS	*SUCCINYL	*SUPERSEX
*STIFFISH	STREAKER	*SUBCLERK	SUCCORER	*SUPERTAX
STILBENE	STREAMER	SUBCUTIS	SUCCUBUS	SUPINATE
STILBITE	STREEKER	SUBDEPOT	*SUCHLIKE	SUPINELY
STILETTO	STRENGTH	SUBENTRY	SUCHNESS	SUPPLANT
STILLMAN	STRESSOR	*SUBEPOCH	*SUCKFISH	SUPPLIER
STIMULUS	*STRETCHY	SUBERECT	SUCKLESS	SUPPOSAL
STINGIER	STREUSEL	SUBERISE	*SUCKLING	SUPPOSER
STINGILY	STRICKEN	*SUBERIZE	SUDARIUM	SUPPRESS
STINGRAY	STRICKLE	SUBEROSE	SUDATION	SURCEASE
STINKARD	STRIDENT	SUBEROUS	SUDATORY	SUREFIRE
*STINKBUG	STRIDING	SUBFIELD	SUDSLESS	SURENESS
STINKIER	STRIGOSE	SUBFLOOR	SUFFERER	SURFACER
STINKPOT	STRINGER	SUBFLUID	*SUFFICER	SURFBIRD
STIPPLER	STRIPIER	SUBGENUS	*SUFFIXAL	SURFBOAT
STIRRING	STRIPING	SUBGRADE	SUFFLATE	*SURFFISH
STITCHER	STRIPPED	SUBGROUP	*SUFFRAGE	SURFIEST
STOCCADO	STRIPPER	*SUBHUMAN	SUICIDAL	*SURFLIKE
STOCCATA	STROBILA	*SUBHUMID	SUITABLE	SURGICAL
*STOCKADE	STROBILE	*SUBINDEX	SUITCASE	SURICATE
STOCKCAR	STROBILI	SUBLEASE	SUITLIKE	SURMISER
STOCKIER	STROLLER	SUBLEVEL	*SUKIYAKI	SURMOUNT
*STOCKILY	STRONGYL	SUBLIMER	SULCATED	SURNAMER
*STOCKING	STRONTIA	SUBLIMER	SULFINYL	SURPLICE
*STOCKISH	STRUCKEN	SUBMERGE	SULFONAL	SURPRINT
STOCKIST	STRUGGLE	SUBMERSE	SULFONIC	SURPRISE
*STOCKMAN	STRUMMER	SUBNASAL	SULFONYL	*SURPRIZE
*STOCKPOT	STRUMOSE	SUBNODAL	SULFURET	SURROUND
STOICISM	STRUMOUS	SUBOPTIC	SULFURIC	SURROYAL
STOKESIA	STRUMPET	SUBORDER	SULFURYL	SURVEYOR
		SUBORNER		

SURVIVAL	*SYNONYME	BU S TER	DI S MAY	*JA S PER
SURVIVER	*SYNONYMY	BU S TIC	DI S OWN	JA S SID
SURVIVOR	SYNOPSIS	BU S TLE	DI S PEL	JE S TER
SUSPENSE	*SYPHILIS	BY S SUS	DI S TAL	JE S UIT
SUSURRUS	*SYRPHIAN	CA S ABA	DI S TIL	*JO S EPH
*SUZERAIN	*SYSTEMIC	CA S AVA	DI S USE	*JO S HER
*SVEDBERG		CA S EFY	DO S AGE	JO S TLE
*SWABBING		CA S EIN	DO S SAL	JU S TER
SWAGGING	P S ST	CA S ERN	DO S SEL	JU S TLE
*SWAMPISH	T S AR	CA S HAW	DO S SER	*JU S TLY
*SWANHERD	P S ALM	CA S HEW	DO S SIL	KA S HER
*SWANLIKE	P S HAW	CA S HOO	DU S TER	*KI S HKA
SWANNERY	P S OAS	CA S ING	DU S TUP	*KI S HKE
SWANNING	*P S YCH	CA S INO	FA S CES	KI S MAT
*SWANSKIN	T S ADE	CA S KET	FA S CIA	KI S MET
SWASTICA	T S ADI	*CA S QUE	FA S TEN	KI S SER
*SWASTIKA	T S UBA	CA S SIA	FE S CUE	KO S HER
SWATTING	BA S ALT	CA S SIS	FE S TAL	LA S CAR
*SWAYBACK	BA S ELY	CA S TER	FE S TER	LA S HER
*SWEATBOX	BA S EST	CA S TLE	FI S CAL	LA S ING
SWEEPING	BA S HAW	CA S TOR	FI S HER	LA S SIE
SWEETING	BA S HER	CA S UAL	*FI S HLY	LA S TER
SWEETISH	BA S IFY	CE S IUM	FI S TIC	LA S TLY
SWEETSOP	BA S ING	CE S SUS	FO S SIL	LE S ION
SWELLING	BA S ION	CE S TOS	FO S TER	LE S SEE
*SWIMMING	BA S KET	CE S URA	FU S AIN	LE S SEN
SWIMSUIT	*BA S QUE	CO S HER	FU S ILE	LE S SER
SWINDLER	BA S SET	CO S IER	FU S ION	LE S SON
*SWINEPOX	BA S SLY	CO S IES	FU S SER	LI S PER
*SWITCHER	BA S TER	CO S ILY	FU S TIC	LI S SOM
*SWIZZLER	BE S EEM	CO S INE	GA S BAG	LI S TEL
SWORDMAN	BE S IDE	CO S MIC	GA S CON	LI S TEN
SYBARITE	BE S MUT	CO S MOS	GA S IFY	LI S TER
*SYCAMINE	BE S NOW	CO S SET	GA S KET	LO S ING
*SYCAMORE	BE S TIR	CO S TAR	GA S KIN	LU S TER
*SYCOMORE	BE S TOW	CO S TER	GA S LIT	LU S TRA
*SYCONIUM	BE S TUD	CO S TLY	GA S MAN	LU S TRE
*SYLLABIC	BI S ECT	CU S HAT	GA S PER	LY S ATE
SYLLABLE	BI S HOP	CU S HAW	GA S SED	LY S INE
*SYLLABUB	*BI S QUE	CU S PID	GA S SER	LY S ING
SYLLABUS	BI S TER	CU S PIS	GA S SES	*MA S JID
*SYLVATIC	BI S TRE	CU S SER	GE S TIC	*MA S QUE
*SYMBIONT	BI S TRO	CU S TOM	GO S PEL	MA S TER
*SYMBIOTE	BO S KER	CU S TOS	GO S SAN	*MA S TIX
*SYMBOLIC	BO S KET	CY S TIC	GO S SIP	ME S IAL
*SYMMETRY	BO S OMY	DA S HER	GU S HER	ME S IAN
*SYMPATHY	*BO S QUE	DA S SIE	GU S SET	ME S SAN
*SYMPATRY	BO S TON	DE S ALT	HA S LET	ME S TEE
*SYMPHONY	BU S BOY	DE S AND	HA S SEL	MI S EAT
*SYMPODIA	BU S HEL	DE S CRY	HA S SLE	MI S LIE
*SYMPOSIA	BU S HER	DE S ERT	HA S TEN	MI S LIT
SYNAPSIS	BU S IED	DE S IRE	HI S PID	MI S SEL
*SYNCARPY	BU S IER	DE S IST	HI S SER	MI S SIS
SYNCLINE	BU S IES	DE S MID	HO S IER	MI S SUS
*SYNCYTIA	BU S ILY	DE S ORB	HO S ING	MI S TER
SYNDESIS	BU S ING	DE S POT	HO S TEL	MI S USE
SYNDETIC	BU S KER	DI S ARM	HO S TLY	*MO S QUE
SYNDROME	BU S KIN	DI S BAR	HU S KER	MO S SER
*SYNECTIC	BU S MAN	DI S BUD	HU S SAR	*MU S JID
SYNERGIA	BU S SED	DI S CUS	HU S TLE	MU S LIN
SYNERGID	BU S SES	DI S MAL	HY S SOP	MU S SEL

MU S TEE	RE S EEN	TU S SAL	**BE S IDES**	CO S TATE
MU S TER	RE S ELL	TU S SAR	**BE S IEGE**	CO S TIVE
NA S ION	RE S END	TU S SEH	**BE S LIME**	CO S TREL
NA S TIC	RE S ENT	TU S SER	**BE S MEAR**	CO S TUME
NE S TER	**RE S HIP**	TU S SIS	**BE S MILE**	CU S HIER
NE S TLE	RE S HOE	TU S SLE	***BE S MOKE**	*CU S HILY
NE S TOR	**RE S HOW**	TU S SOR	***BE S PEAK**	CU S HION
NO S HER	RE S IDE	TU S SUR	**BE S TEAD**	CU S SCUS
NO S IER	RE S IFT	VA S SAL	BE S TIAL	CU S TARD
NO S ILY	RE S IGN	**VA S TLY**	**BE S TREW**	CU S TODY
NO S ING	RE S ILE	**VE S ICA**	**BE S TROW**	CY S TEIN
NO S TOC	RE S INY	**VE S PER**	**BE S WARM**	CY S TINE
PA S SEE	RE S IST	VE S PID	**BI S CUIT**	CY S TOID
PA S SEL	***RE S IZE**	VE S SEL	**BI S MUTH**	DA S HEEN
PA S SER	RE S OLD	VE S TAL	**BI S NAGA**	DA S HIER
PA S SIM	RE S OLE	VE S TEE	**BI S TATE**	*DA S HIKI
PA S SUS	RE S ORB	**VE S TRY**	BI S TORT	DA S HPOT
PA S TEL	RE S ORT	**VI S AGE**	**BO S CAGE**	DA S TARD
PA S TER	RE S TER	**VI S ARD**	**BO S KAGE**	DA S YURE
PA S TIL	RE S ULT	**VI S CID**	***BO S QUET**	DE S CANT
PA S TOR	RE S UME	**VI S CUS**	**BO S SDOM**	DE S CEND
PA S TRY	RI S ING	**VI S ING**	**BO S SIER**	DE S CENT
PE S ADE	**RI S KER**	VI S ION	**BO S SIES**	DE S ERVE
PE S ETA	***RI S QUE**	**VI S IVE**	**BO S SISM**	DE S IRER
PE S EWA	RO S ARY	VI S UAL	**BU S HIDO**	DE S MOID
PE S TER	RO S COE	**WA S HER**	**BU S HIER**	DE S PAIR
PE S TLE	RO S ERY	**WA S TER**	***BU S HILY**	DE S PISE
PI S TIL	RO S IER	**WA S TRY**	**BU S HING**	DE S PITE
PI S TOL	RO S ILY	**WE S KIT**	**BU S HMAN**	DE S POIL
PI S TON	RO S ING	**WE S TER**	**BU S HTIT**	DE S POND
PO S ADA	RO S INY	**WI S DOM**	**BU S IEST**	DE S SERT
PO S EUR	RO S TER	**WI S ELY**	**BU S SING**	DE S TAIN
PO S IES	RO S TRA	**WI S ENT**	**BU S TARD**	DE S TINE
PO S ING	RU S HEE	**WI S EST**	**CA S CADE**	DE S TINY
PO S SET	RU S HER	**WI S HER**	**CA S CARA**	DE S TROY
PO S SUM	RU S INE	***XY S TER**	CA S EASE	DE S UGAR
PO S TAL	RU S SET	***XY S TOS**	CA S EATE	DI S ABLE
PO S TER	RU S TIC	***XY S TUS**	CA S EOSE	DI S AVOW
PO S TIN	RU S TLE	***YA S MAK**	CA S EOUS	DI S BAND
PU S HER	SA S HAY	YE S SED	CA S ERNE	DI S CANT
PU S HUP	SE S AME	YE S SES	CA S ETTE	DI S CARD
PU S LEY	SE S TET	YE S TER	***CA S HBOX**	DI S CASE
PU S SLY	SI S KIN	***ZO S TER**	CA S HIER	DI S CEPT
RA S CAL	SI S TER	**BA S CULE**	CA S SABA	DI S CERN
RA S HER	SI S TRA	**BA S EMAN**	CA S SAVA	DI S COID
RA S HLY	SU S LIK	***BA S ENJI**	CA S SINO	DI S CORD
RA S ING	**SY S TEM**	***BA S HFUL**	***CA S SOCK**	DI S CUSS
RA S PER	TA S SEL	***BA S HLYK**	CA S TING	DI S DAIN
RA S SLE	TA S SET	**BA S ILAR**	***CA S TOFF**	DI S EASE
RA S TER	TA S SIE	**BA S ILIC**	CA S UIST	DI S EUSE
RA S URE	TA S TER	BA S INET	CE S SION	DI S GUST
RE S AID	TE S TEE	BA S SIST	CE S SPIT	DI S HELM
RE S AIL	TE S TER	BA S SOON	CE S TODE	DI S HFUL
RE S ALE	TE S TES	**BA S TARD**	CE S TOID	DI S HIER
RE S CUE	TE S TIS	BA S TILE	CI S SOID	DI S HPAN
RE S EAL	TE S TON	**BA S TING**	CI S TERN	DI S HRAG
RE S EAT	TI S ANE	BA S TION	CI S TRON	***DI S JECT**
RE S EAU	TI S SUE		CO S IEST	***DI S JOIN**
RE S ECT	TO S SER		CO S MISM	DI S LIKE
RE S EDA	TO S SUP		CO S MIST	DI S LIMN
RE S EED	**TU S KER**		***CO S SACK**	DI S MAST
RE S EEK	TU S SAH		CO S TARD	DI S MISS

DI S OBEY	FU S TIAN	LA S HINS	NO S IEST	RE S OJET
DI S OMIC	GA S EOUS	LA S HKAR	NO S TRIL	RE S OLVE
DI S PART	GA S KING	LA S SOER	NO S TRUM	RE S OUND
DI S PEND	GA S LESS	LA S TING	**PA S CHAL**	**RE S PECT**
DI S PLAY	GA S SING	LE S BIAN	*PA S QUIL	RE S PELL
DI S PORT	GA S TRAL	LI S SOME	**PA S SADE**	RE S PIRE
DI S POSE	GA S TREA	LI S TING	**PA S SADO**	RE S PITE
DI S PUTE	**GA S TRIC**	LU S TFUL	**PA S SAGE**	**RE S POND**
DI S RATE	GA S TRIN	LU S TIER	PA S SANT	**RE S TACK**
DI S ROBE	GE S TALT	**LU S TILY**	**PA S SING**	**RE S TAFF**
DI S ROOT	**GE S TAPO**	LU S TRAL	PA S SION	RE S TAGE
DI S RUPT	GE S TATE	LU S TRUM	**PA S SIVE**	**RE S TAMP**
DI S SAVE	GE S TURE	**LY S OGEN**	*PA S SKEY	RE S TART
DI S SEAT	GI S ARME	*MA S QUER	PA S TERN	RE S TATE
DI S SECT	GO S HAWK	**MA S SAGE**	PA S TIES	**RE S TFUL**
DI S SENT	GO S LING	MA S SEUR	**PA S TIME**	**RE S TIVE**
DI S SERT	**GO S PORT**	MA S SIER	**PA S TINA**	RE S TOCK
DI S TAFF	**GO S SIPY**	*MA S TIFF	**PA S TING**	**RE S TORE**
DI S TAIN	GO S SOON	ME S SIER	PA S TURE	**RE S TUDY**
DI S TANT	GU S TIER	ME S TESO	**PE S SARY**	**RE S TUFF**
DI S TEND	**GU S TILY**	ME S TINO	PI S CARY	**RE S TYLE**
DI S TENT	*HA S HISH	*ME S TIZA	PI S CINA	RE S UMEN
DI S TICH	*HA S SOCK	*ME S TIZO	PI S CINE	RE S URGE
DI S TILL	HA S TATE	*MI S COOK	PI S MIRE	RI S IBLE
DI S TOME	HE S SIAN	*MI S COPY	PI S SANT	RI S OTTO
DI S TORT	HE S SITE	MI S EASE	PI S SOIR	RI S SOLE
DI S TURB	HI S SELF	*MI S JOIN	PI S TOLE	RO S ARIA
*DI S YOKE	HI S SING	*MI S KEEP	PO S SESS	RO S EATE
DO S SIER	HI S TOID	*MI S KNOW	**PO S TAGE**	**RO S EBAY**
*DU S KISH	HI S TONE	MI S LAIN	**PO S TBAG**	**RO S EBUD**
DU S TBIN	HI S TORY	**MI S LIKE**	*PO S TBOX	RO S ELLE
DU S TIER	HO S ANNA	*MI S MARK	**PO S TBOY**	RO S EOLA
DU S TILY	HO S IERY	MI S RATE	PO S TEEN	RO S ETTE
DU S TMAN	HO S PICE	MI S RULE	PO S TERN	RO S IEST
DU S TPAN	HO S TAGE	MI S SEAT	**PO S TMAN**	RO S OLIO
DY S PNEA	HO S TESS	MI S SIES	PO S TURE	RO S TRAL
DY S URIA	HO S TILE	MI S SILE	PO S TWAR	RO S TRUM
FA S CINE	HO S TLER	MI S SION	*PU S HFUL	**RU S HIER**
FA S CISM	HU S BAND	MI S SORT	PU S HIER	**RU S HING**
FA S CIST	*HU S HABY	MI S SOUT	*PU S HILY	**RU S SIFY**
FA S HION	*HU S HFUL	MI S SSAL	PU S HPIN	RU S TIER
FA S TING	HU S KIER	MI S SUIT	PU S SIER	RU S TILY
FE S TIVE	HU S KIES	MI S TAKE	PU S SIES	SA S HIMI
FE S TOON	*HU S KILY	MI S TIER	PU S SLEY	SA S SABY
*FI S HERY	*HU S KING	MI S TRAL	PU S TULE	SA S SIER
*FI S HEYE	HU S TLER	MI S TUNE	RA S BORA	SA S SILY
*FI S HGIG	*HU S WIFE	MI S USER	RA S PISH	SE S SILE
FI S HIER	*JA S MINE	*MI S YOKE	RE S CALE	SE S SION
FI S HING	JE S SANT	MO S SIER	**RE S CIND**	SE S TINA
FI S HNET	*JE S TFUL	MU S ETTE	RE S CORE	SE S TINE
*FI S HWAY	*JE S TING	MU S ICAL	RE S CUER	SI S TRUM
FI S SATE	JO S TLER	*MU S KILY	*RE S EIZE	**SU S PECT**
FI S SILE	*JU S SIVE	*MU S PIKE	RE S ERVE	**SU S PEND**
FI S SION	*JU S TICE	MU S SING	RE S HAPE	SU S PIRE
FI S SURE	*JU S TIFY	*MY S TERY	RE S HOOT	SU S TAIN
FI S TFUL	*KA S HMIR	*MY S TIFY	RE S IDER	SY S TOLE
FI S TULA	KA S HRUT	NA S ALLY	RE S IDUA	TA S TING
*FO S SICK	KE S TREL	NA S CENT	RE S IDUE	TE S SERA
FU S COUS	KI S TFUL	NE S TLER	RE S MELT	**TE S TACY**
FU S IBLE	LA S AGNA	**NO S EBAG**		TE S TATE
FU S SING	LA S AGNE	NO S EGAY		TE S TIER
FU S SPOT	LA S HING			

TE S TIFY	BED S TRAW	COA S TING	FIS S IPED	*JOY S TICK
TE S TILY	BEE S WING	COI S TREL	*FLA S HGUN	KAI S ERIN
TE S TING	BIA S NESS	COI S TRIL	*FLA S HING	*KEE S HOND
TE S TOON	BIO S COPE	CON S ERVE	FLE S HIER	*KEY S TONE
TE S TUDO	*BIO S COPY	CON S IDER	*FLE S HING	*KIN S FOLK
TI S SUAL	*BIT S TOCK	CON S OLER	*FLE S HPOT	*KLY S TRON
TI S SUEY	BLA S TIER	CON S OMME	*FLY S PECK	LIN S TOCK
TO S SPOT	BLA S TEMA	CON S PIRE	FOR S AKER	*LIP S TICK
TU S SCHE	BLA S TING	CON S TANT	FOR S PENT	*LOB S TICK
TU S SOCK	*BLA S TOFF	CON S TRUE	FOR S WEAR	LOO S ENER
TU S SORE	BLA S TOMA	CON S UMER	FOS S ETTE	LOP S IDED
TU S SUCK	BLA S TULA	COR S ELET	FRE S COER	*LOP S TICK
VA S TIER	*BLE S BUCK	COU S COUS	*FRE S HMAN	MA S SACRE
VA S TITY	BLE S SING	COU S INRY	FRI S ETTE	MA S SEDLY
VE S ICLE	BLI S TERY	*COX S WAIN	FRO S TBIT	MA S SETER
VE S PINE	*BLO S SOMY	CRE S CENT	FRO S TING	MA S SEUSE
VE S TIGE	*BLU S HFUL	*CRE S CIVE	FRU S TULE	MA S SICOT
VE S TING	BLU S TERY	CRE S TING	GEL S EMIA	MA S SIEST
VE S TURE	BOA S TFUL	*CRE S YLIC	*GEM S BUCK	MA S SLESS
VI S CERA	BON S PELL	CRI S PATE	GEM S TONE	MA S TERLY
VI S COID	BON S PIEL	CRI S TATE	*GHA S TFUL	MA S THEAD
VI S COSE	BOU S OUKI	CRO S SARM	GLA S SFUL	MA S TITIS
VI S COUS	BRA S ILIN	CRO S SBAR	GLA S SIER	MA S TLESS
VI S IBLE	BRA S SAGE	*CRO S SBOW	GLA S SILY	MA S TLIKE
VI S ITER	BRA S SARD	CRO S SCUT	GLA S SINE	MA S TODON
VI S ITOR	BRA S SART	CRO S SING	GLA S SMAN	MA S URIUM
*WA S HDAY	BRA S SICA	CRO S SLET	GLI S SADE	*MEM S AHIB
WA S HIER	BRA S SISH	CRO S STIE	GLO S SARY	ME S DAMES
WA S HING	BRI S ANCE	*CRO S SWAY	GLO S SEME	ME S MERIC
WA S HOUT	BRI S LING	CRU S ADER	GLO S SIES	ME S NALTY
WA S HRAG	BRU S HIER	CRU S TOSE	GLO S SINA	ME S OCARP
*WA S HTUB	*BRU S HOFF	CUS S EDLY	GOS S AMER	ME S ODERM
WA S SAIL	BUR S ITIS	CUS S WORD	GOS S IPER	ME S OGLEA
WA S TAGE	BUR S TONE	*DAI S HIKI	GOS S IPRY	ME S OMERE
WA S TERY	CAB S TAND	DAN S EUSE	GOS S YPOL	ME S OSOME
WA S TING	*CAM S HAFT	DIA S PORA	GRI S EOUS	ME S OTRON
WA S TREL	CAP S ICIN	DIA S PORE	GRI S ETTE	*ME S QUITE
WA S TRIE	*CAP S ICUM	DIA S TASE	*GRO S BEAK	ME S SIEST
WE S SAND	CAP S TONE	*DIE S TOCK	GRO S CHEN	ME S SMATE
WE S TERN	CAP S ULAR	DIE S TRUM	GUN S MITH	ME S SUAGE
WE S TING	CAS S ETTE	DIE S TRUS	*GUN S TOCK	*MID S HIPS
*WI S HFUL	CAU S ABLE	*DIP S TICK	GYP S EIAN	*MID S PACE
WI S PIER	CAU S ALLY	DIS S EISE	GYP S EOUS	MI S ADAPT
*WI S PILY	CAU S ERIE	*DIS S EIZE	*GYP S YDOM	MI S AGENT
*WI S PISH	*CAU S EWAY	DIS S ERVE	*GYP S YISH	MI S ALTER
WI S SING	CEN S URER	DIS S UADE	*GYP S YISM	MI S ASSAY
WI S TFUL	CES S POOL	*DOG S BODY	HAU S FRAU	MI S ATONE
*YA S HMAC	CHA S SEUR	DOR S ALLY	*HAY S TACK	MI S AWARE
*YA S HMAK	CHA S TISE	DOS S ERET	*HOG S HEAD	MI S BEGIN
*YE S HIVA	*CHA S TITY	DOW S ABEL	HOL S TEIN	MI S BEGOT
YE S SING	*CHA S UBLE	DRE S SAGE	*HOO S EGOW	MI S BRAND
YE S TERN	*CHE S SMAN	DRE S SING	HOR S ECAR	MI S BUILD
*ZE S TFUL	*CHE S TFUL	*DYE S TUFF	*HOR S EFLY	MI S CIBLE
*BAK S HISH	CHE S TNUT	FAL S ETTO	HOR S EMAN	MI S CLAIM
BAL S AMIC	CHI S ELER	*FAT S TOCK	HOR S IEST	MI S CLASS
BAR S TOOL	CLA S SIER	FEA S ANCE	*HOU S EBOY	MI S COLOR
BAS S INET	*CLA S SIFY	FEA S IBLE	*HOU S EFLY	MI S COUNT
BAS S NESS	CLO S EOUT	FEA S TFUL	HOU S EFUL	MI S DOING
BAS S WOOD	CLU S TERY	FEL S TONE	HOU S EMAN	MI S DOUBT
BED S ONIA	COA S SIST	FES S WISE	HOU S ETOP	MI S DRIVE
BED S TAND	COA S SUME		*HYO S CINE	MI S ENROL
BED S TEAD				MI S ENTER

MI S ENTRY	*MYO S COPE	PRE S CORE	SEA S CAPE	TWI S TING	
MI S ERERE	NAU S EANT	PRE S ENCE	SEA S COUT	VER S EMAN	
MI S EVENT	NAU S EATE	PRE S ERVE	SEA S HELL	VER S ICLE	
MI S FIELD	NAU S EOUS	*PRE S HAPE	SEA S HORE	VOU S SOIR	
MI S GAUGE	NEW S CAST	PRE S IDER	SEA S ONAL	*WAE S UCKS	
MI S GRAFT	NEW S IEST	PRE S IDIA	SEA S ONER	WAI S TING	
MI S GUESS	NEW S LESS	PRE S IDIO	SEI S MISM	WAR S TLER	
MI S GUIDE	*NEW S PEAK	PRE S SMAN	SEN S EFUL	*WHI S PERY	
MI S INFER	NEW S REEL	PRE S SRUN	SEN S IBLE	WHI S TLER	
MI S INTER	NEW S ROOM	PRE S SURE	SEN S IBLE	*WHO S EVER	
MI S LABEL	NON S ENSE	PRE S TAMP	SEN S ILLA	WRE S TLER	
MI S LAYER	NON S KIER	PRE S TIGE	SEN S ORIA	WRI S TLET	
MI S LEARN	NON S OLAR	PRE S UMER	SEN S UOUS	*ZOO S PERM	
MI S LIGHT	NON S OLID	PRI S MOID	SES S POOL	*ZOO S PORE	
MI S LODGE	NON S TICK	PRI S ONER	SET S CREW		
MI S LYING	NON S UGAR	PRI S TANE	*SHA S HLIK		
MI S NOMER	NUI S ANCE	PRI S TINE	SIS S YISH	BAS S	
MI S OLOGY	NUM S KULL	PRO S AISM	SLA S HING	BIA S	
MI S PAINT	NUR S LING	PRO S AIST	SOL S TICE	BOS S	
MI S PARSE	NUT S EDGE	PRO S IEST	STA S IMON	BUS S	
MI S PLACE	NUT S HELL	PRO S PECT	SUB S ERVE	CES S	
MI S PLANT	*PAN S OPHY	PRO S TATE	*SUB S HAFT	CRI S	
MI S PLEAD	PAS S ABLE	PRO S TYLE	*SUB S HRUB	CRU S	
MI S POINT	PAS S BAND	PUI S SANT	SUB S IDER	CUS S	
MI S POISE	*PAS S BOOK	PUL S ATOR	SUB S OLAR	DAI S	
MI S PRINT	*PAS S ERBY	*PUL S EJET	SUB S ONIC	DIE S	
MI S RAISE	PAS S IBLE	*PUL S OJET	SUB S PACE	DOE S	
MI S REFER	PAS S LESS	PUR S IEST	SUB S TAGE	DOS S	
MI S SENSE	PAS S OVER	PUR S LANE	SUD S LESS	FES S	
*MIS S HAPE	PAS S PORT	PUR S UANT	SUN S CALD	FOS S	
MI S SILRY	PAS S WORD	PUS S IEST	SUN S HADE	FUS S	
MI S SOUND	PEA S ECOD	PUS S LIKE	SUN S HINE	GEN S	
MI S SPACE	*PEE S WEEP	*PUS S YCAT	SUN S TONE	HER S	
*MIS S PEAK	PEN S IONE	*QUE S TION	SWA S TICA	HIS S	
MI S SPELL	*PEN S TOCK	*QUI S LING	*SWA S TIKA	JES S	
MI S SPEND	PER S ONAL	RAI S ONNE	TEA S ELER	JOS S	
*MIS S POKE	PER S PIRE	RAM S HORN	TEA S POON	KAA S	
MI S START	PER S UADE	RAN S OMER	TEN S IBLE	KIS S	
MI S STATE	PHA S EOUT	RAT S BANE	TEO S INTE	KOS S	
MI S STEER	PHO S GENE	REA S CEND	THE S AURI	KRI S	
MI S STYLE	*PHO S PHID	REA S CENT	THE S PIAN	KVA S	
MI S TITLE	*PHO S PHIN	REA S ONER	TIN S ELLY	LAS S	
MI S TRACE	*PHO S PHOR	REA S SAIL	TIN S MITH	LES S	
MI S TREAT	*PHY S ICAL	REA S SERT	TIN S TONE	LOS S	
MI S TRESS	*PHY S IQUE	REA S SESS	TIP S IEST	LUE S	
MI S TRIAL	PIA S SABA	REA S SORT	*TIP S TAFF	MAS S	
MI S TRUST	PIA S SAVA	REA S SUME	*TIP S TOCK	MES S	
MI S TRYST	*PIG S TICK	REA S SURE	TOP S TONE	MIS S	
MI S TUTOR	PIL S ENER	*RED S HANK	TRA S HMAN	MON S	
MI S UNION	*PIN S CHER	RED S HIRT	TRE S PASS	MOS S	
MI S USAGE	PLA S MOID	RED S TART	TRE S SIER	MUS S	
MI S VALUE	PLA S TERY	REI S SUER	TRE S SOUR	NAO S	
MI S WRITE	PLA S TRON	REU S ABLE	TRE S SURE	NES S	
*MOS S BACK	PLA S TRUM	ROU S SEAU	TRI S CELE	NEW S	
MO S SIEST	PLU S SAGE	SAL S ILLA	TRI S KELE	NOU S	
MO S SLIKE	POI S ONER	SAN S ERIF	TRI S OMIC	PAS S	
MU S CADEL	POS S IBLE	SAR S ENET	TRI S TATE	PIS S	
MU S CATEL	POT S HARD	SAS S IEST	*TRI S TEZA	PLU S	
MU S CULAR	POT S HERD	SAS S WOOD	TRI S TFUL	PON S	
MU S ICIAN	POT S TONE	SCI S SILE	TRI S TICH	PUS S	
MU S INGLY	PRE S AGER	SCI S SION	TRU S SING	REI S	
MU S KIEST	PRE S CIND	SCI S SURE	TRU S TFUL	RHU S	

SAN S	HERE S	PRIS S	**BEKIS S**	*COZIE S
SAS S	HILU S	PSOA S	**BEVIE S**	*COZZE S
SPON	**HOCU S**	PUBE S	**BICEP S**	CRASE S
SUD S	**HUMU S**	PUBI S	BLINI S	CRASI S
TAS S	HURD S	*PYXI S	**BODIE S**	CRISI S
THI S	*JAKE S	**QUAS S**	BOGIE S	**CROCU S**
THU S	**JUDA S**	RAMU S	**BREEK S**	**CRUCE S**
TOS S	**KUMY S**	REBU S	**BREWI S**	CULLI S
WIS S	**KVAS S**	REGE S	BURIE S	CULTU S
YWI S	LAPI S	RIBE S	BUSIE S	**CUSCU S**
BALA S	LARE S	RISU S	BUSSE S	**CUSPI S**
BANN S	LEGE S	RUBU S	**BYPAS S**	CUSTO S
BASE S	LENE S	SEMI S	**BYSSU S**	CUTLA S
BASI S	LENI S	SHIE S	**CACTU S**	CYESI S
BLES S	LEWI S	SINU S	**CADDI S**	**CYMOU S**
BLIS S	LIME S	SITU S	**CALCE S**	**CYPRE S**
BOGU S	LITA S	SKIE S	CALLU S	**CYPRU S**
BOLA S	LIVE S	SOLU S	**CALVE S**	DALLE S
BOLU S	LOCU S	SORU S	**CAMAS S**	DEBRI S
BONU S	LOES S	SPEC S	**CAMPU S**	DEDAN S
BRAS S	LOGO S	SPIE S	**CANVA S**	**DEFIE S**
BRAW S	LORI S	SPUTA	**CAPIA S**	DEMIE S
CAMA S	LOTO S	STIE S	CARES S	DENIE S
CASU S	LOTU S	STOS S	CARIE S	DERMI S
CHAO S	LOUI S	SWIS S	**CARPU S**	DERRI S
CHES S	LUCE S	TABE S	CASSI S	**DEXIE S**
CLAS S	LUPU S	TALU S	**CAUCU S**	DIDIE S
CONU S	LUSU S	TAMI S	CAULE S	DINGU S
CORP S	LYSI S	TAPI S	CAULI S	DIPSA S
CRAS S	MAGU S	**TAXU S**	**CAVIE S**	DISCU S
CRES S	MANU S	TELO S	CENSU S	DOBIE S
CRIE S	**MAVI S**	**TEXA S**	**CERCI S**	DOGIE S
CROS S	METI S	TONU S	**CERCU S**	DORIE S
CUTE S	MINU S	TOOT S	CEREU S	DURES S
CUTI S	MITI S	TOPO S	CEROU S	**FACIE S**
CYCA S	MODU S	TORU S	CERTE S	**FAECE S**
DEGA S	MOMU S	TRAN S	CESTO S	**FAMOU S**
DEMO S	MONA S	TRAS S	CESTU S	**FASCE S**
DRES S	MUCU S	TRES S	**CHARA S**	**FAUCE S**
DRIE S	NABI S	TREW S	**CHIAU S**	*FIZZE S
DROS S	NARE S	TRIE S	**CHINT S**	FLATU S
FAVU S	NARI S	TROI S	**CHORU S**	FOETU S
FECE S	NATE S	TRUS S	**CIRCU S**	FOLLI S
FETU S	NEGU S	TURP S	CIRRU S	FORTI S
FINI S	NERT S	VAGU S	CITIE S	**FRACA S**
FLIE S	NEVU S	VARU S	CITRU S	**FUCOU S**
FOCU S	**NEXU S**	**VIBE S**	**CIVIC S**	**FUNDU S**
FRIE S	NIDU S	VIRE S	**CLEVI S**	**FUNGU S**
FRON S	NISU S	VIRU S	CLONU S	FURIE S
FUCU S	NODU S	**VOCE S**	**COCCU S**	GABIE S
GAUS S	NOMO S	**WAMU S**	COITU S	GALLU S
GENU S	PARI S	**WIVE S**	COLEU S	GASSE S
GIGA S	**PAVI S**	**WOOP S**	COLIE S	GENIU S
GLAN S	PEDE S	WRIE S	**COMOU S**	GENTE S
GLAS S	PENE S	**XERU S**	CONIE S	GLACI S
GLOS S	PENI S	**YIPE S**	**COPIE S**	GLOMU S
GRAS S	PILU S	YOUR S	CORNU S	GNEIS S
GROS S	PIOU S	*ZOOK S	**CORPU S**	GNOSI S
GUES S	PLIE S	BABIE S	**CORVE S**	GOBIE S
GULE S	POLI S	BAGAS S	COSIE S	GRADU S
GYRU S	PRES S	**BATHO S**	**COSMO S**	GRATI S
HARD S	PRIE S	**BEEVE S**		HAERE S

HAGGI S	PAPPU S	SONIC S	*XYSTU S	CHAMOI S
HALVE S	PARIE S	SOWAN S	YESSE S	CHASSI S
HARAS S	PAROU S	SOWEN S	*YOICK S	*CHEVIE S
HERPE S	PARVI S	SPEIS S	*ZANIE S	*CHLAMY S
HIATU S	PASSU S	STAPE S	*ZOUND S	*CHYMOU S
HOLIE S	PATHO S	STASE S	BADNES S	CIRROU S
HOOVE S	PATOI S	STASI S	*BAFFIE S	CITROU S
HUBRI S	PELVI S	STATU S	BANDIE S	CLARIE S
HYBRI S	PEPLO S	STIPE S	BARLES S	CLASSE S
*JOYOU S	PEPLU S	STIRP S	BAWDIE S	CLASSI S
JURIE S	PHARO S	STRAS S	BEDLES S	CLIVER S
KAROS S	PHASI S	STRES S	BELLIE S	CLYPEU S
KAVAS S	PHYSE S	STYLU S	BENTHO S	COLITI S
KAYLE S	PHYSI S	SULCU S	BESIDE S	COLLIE S
KERME S	PIGNU S	TABBI S	BETIME S	COLLIN S
KERMI S	PILEU S	TARSU S	BIBLES S	COLONU S
KNIVE S	PILOU S	TENNI S	BIGNES S	COMMIE S
KOUMI S	PITIE S	TENUI S	BILIOU S	COMPAS S
*KOUMY S	POGIE S	TERRA S	BILLIE S	CONATU S
KUMIS S	POKIE S	TESTE S	BIOMAS S	CONCUS S
LACHE S	POLEI S	TESTI S	BIONIC S	CONFES S
LADIE S	PONIE S	THEIR S	BIOTIC S	CONGIU S
LAMPA S	POROU S	THESI S	BOBBIE S	COOKIE S
LAPSU S	POSIE S	THOLO S	BOLETU S	COOLIE S
*LAZIE S	*PRAXI S	THYMU S	BONKER S	COPIOU S
LEAVE S	PRECI S	TIDIE S	BOONIE S	COYNES S
LEVIE S	PRIMU S	TIGHT S	BOOTIE S	*CROQUI S
LIMBU S	PTOSI S	TMESI S	BORACE S	CUDDIE S
LITMU S	PYOSI S	TOPHU S	BOSSIE S	CUIRAS S
LOAVE S	RABIE S	TORIE S	BOWLES S	CULLIE S
LUNIE S	RACHI S	TOROU S	BRINIE S	CUMULU S
LUPOU S	RADIU S	TRAGU S	BUBALI S	CUPROU S
MADRA S	RAMOU S	TRAPE S	BUBBIE S	CURIOU S
MANTE S	RAPHI S	TRIEN S	BUDDIE S	CUTLAS S
MANTI S	RECES S	TRIPO S	BUDLES S	*CYCLOP S
*MAQUI S	RECTU S	TSURI S	BUGLOS S	CYPRES S
MATRE S	REGIU S	TURVE S	BULBOU S	*CZARDA S
MEATU S	RELIE S	TUSSI S	BULLIE S	DANDIE S
MEGAS S	REMIS S	TYPHU S	BULLOU S	DARBIE S
MIOSI S	REPAS S	*TZURI S	BURGES S	DARKIE S
MISSI S	REVER S	VALGU S	BURNOU S	DEARIE S
MISSU S	RHESU S	VARIE S	BUTTAL S	DECLAS S
MOLIE S	RICHE S	VENOU S	BUTTIE S	DEGAUS S
MONIE S	RICTU S	VERME S	CAESTU S	DEPRES S
MONTE S	RIMOU S	VERMI S	CALAMU S	DEVIOU S
MORAL S	RUBIE S	VERSU S	CALEND S	DEWLES S
MORAS S	RUCKU S	VILLU S	CALICE S	DIARIE S
MORRI S	RUFOU S	VINOU S	CALLOU S	DICKEN S
MUCOU S	RUGOU S	VISCU S	CALYCE S	DIGRES S
MYASI S	RUMPU S	VITAL S	CANDIE S	DIMNES S
MYOSI S	SANIE S	VIVER S	CANTHU S	DINKIE S
MYTHO S	SCHUS S	VULGU S	CANVAS S	DISCUS S
NAEVU S	SELVE S	WADIE S	CAPLES S	DISMIS S
NAVIE S	SEPSI S	WALIE S	CARCAS S	DOGGIE S
NEREI S	SERIE S	WALRU S	CARICE S	DOLLIE S
NIMBU S	SEROU S	WAMMU S	CARIOU S	DRYNES S
NODOU S	SETOU S	WAMPU S	CARLES S	DUBIOU S
NOESI S	SHAME S	WAVIE S	CARNIE S	DUCHES S
NOWAY S	SHAMU S	WHENA S	CAROLU S	DUCKIE S
NUBLE S	SHNAP S	WHOSI S	CASEOU S	DUENES S
PALAI S	SIGLO S	WOLVE S	CHALLI S	DULNES S
PALPU S		*XYSTO S		

DUNNES S	HAMULU S	LIDLES S	PARESI S	REDRES S
DUTEOU S	HAPLES S	LIMITE S	PARLOU S	REDRIE S
DWARVE S	HARDIE S	LIMULU S	PARODO S	REFLIE S
FAIRIE S	HARNES S	LIONES S	PARRIE S	REFOCU S
FAMULU S	HARPIE S	LIPLES S	PARTIE S	REGLOS S
FANCIE S	HARRIE S	LITOTE S	PASTIE S	REGRES S
FARNES S	HATLES S	LOCULU S	PATNES S	REGULU S
FATLES S	HEAVIE S	LOGGAT S	PATESO S	REPRES S
FATNES S	HEINOU S	LOGGET S	PATASU S	REREDO S
FATTIE S	HEIRES S	LOWNES S	PEERES S	*RHACHI S
FATUOU S	HELICE S	*LYCHNI S	PEGLES S	RHAMNU S
FEELES S	HEREDE S	MADNES S	PELORU S	RHOMBU S
FELLIE S	HIDEOU S	MALLEU S	PENATE S	RIBLES S
FERRIE S	*HIJINK S	MANLES S	PENNIE S	RICINU S
FERROU S	HIPLES S	*MARQUI S	PERCUS S	RICKET S
FEWNES S	HIPNES S	MARRIE S	PERHAP S	RIMLES S
FEYNES S	HITLES S	MATLES S	PETASO S	RIOTOU S
FIBROU S	HOBBIE S	MATRAS S	PETASU S	RODLES S
FILLIE S	HOOKIE S	MEANIE S	PETROU S	RUBIOU S
FINALI S	HOSTES S	MEIOSI S	PHALLU S	RUINOU S
FINLES S	HOTNES S	MERCIE S	PHONIC S	RUNLES S
FITNES S	HUGEOU S	MERISI S	PHONIE S	SADNES S
*FIXING S	HUMERU S	MESEEM S	PHOTIC S	SALLIE S
FOGLES S	HURDIE S	MIDDIE S	PICEOU S	SANTIM S
FOLIOU S	HUSKIE S	MILREI S	PIETIE S	SAPIEN S
FOLLIE S	*HYDROP S	MIMESI S	PIGGIE S	SAPLES S
FORCEP S	HYDROU S	MINIBU S	PILEOU S	SARCOU S
FORTIE S	*JACKAS S	MISBIA S	PITEOU S	SARDIU S
FRONTE S	*JACKIE S	MISSIE S	PLATIE S	SCABIE S
FULNES S	*JACOBU S	MITOSI S	PLUSSE S	SCARVE S
FULVOU S	*JAGLES S	MODULU S	POETES S	SCHMOO S
FUMULU S	JEALOU S	MOLLIE S	POETIC S	SCHNAP S
FUNGOU S	*JEEPER S	MONADE S	POLYPU S	SEERES S
FURIOU S	*JERKIE S	MUDDIE S	POMPOU S	SERIOU S
FURLES S	JETTIE S	MUGGIN S	POPPIE S	SEXLES S
FUSCOU S	*JIMJAM S	MUMMIE S	PORKIE S	SFERIC S
GALLOU S	JOANNE S	MURICE S	POSSES S	SHAMMA S
GALLOW S	*JOBLES S	MYCOSI S	POTTIE S	SHAMME S
GAPOSI S	JOLLIE S	MYIASI S	PRECES S	SHAMMO S
GASEOU S	*JOYLES S	NAPLES S	PREMIS S	SHAMOI S
GASLES S	KALEND S	NEMESI S	PRIAPU S	SHELVE S
*GAWKIE S	KENOSI S	NERVOU S	PRIVIE S	SHERRI S
GAYNES S	KERMES S	NETLES S	PROCES S	SHYNES S
GENESI S	KETOSI S	NEWNES S	PROFES S	SIEMEN S
GIBBOU S	KEYLES S	NEWSIE S	PROTEU S	SILENT S
GLOBOU S	KIDDIE S	NITROU S	PROWES S	SILENU S
GLORIE S	KINESI S	NIVEOU S	*PROXIE S	SILVIC S
GLOTTI S	KIRMES S	NOCUOU S	PULPOU S	SIMIOU S
GLUTEU S	KITTIE S	NODDIE S	PUSSIE S	SINLES S
GODDES S	*KOLKHO S	NOMBLE S	*PYJAMA S	SINUOU S
GODLES S	KOUMIS S	NONPLU S	PYLORU S	SITHEN S
GOODIE S	*KOUMYS S	NONPRO S	PYROSI S	SKEPSI S
GRAMPU S	LAMPER S	NOXIOU S	*PYXIDE S	*SKYPHO S
GRAVIE S	LAPIDE S	NUCLEU S	*QUERIE S	SLYNES S
GRUMOU S	LARGES S	PADDIE S	*QUIETU S	SOFTIE S
GUMLES S	LASHIN S	PANDIE S	RADICE S	SOLIDU S
GUMMOU S	LATICE S	PANTIE S	RANDIE S	SONLES S
GUNLES S	LAWLES S	PAPPIE S	RAUCOU S	SOPHIE S
GUTLES S	LAXNES S	PAPYRU S	RAWNES S	SORITE S
HABITU S	LEGLES S	PARADO S	RAYLES S	SOROSI S
HALITU S	LEMURE S	PARESI S	READIE S	SPINIE S
HALVER S	LEPROU S		RECROS S	SPINOU S
			REDNES S	

SPUMOU S	VERGLA S	BIPAROU S	COENURU S	*DIDYMOU S
STARET S	VERITA S	BIRAMOU S	COLDNES S	DIECIOU S
STORIE S	VICIOU S	BLOODIE S	COLINIE S	DIERESI S
STRATU S	VIROSI S	BLOTLES S	COLOSSU S	DIESTRU S
STUDIE S	VISCOU S	BLUENES S	COLPITI S	DIGGING S
STYPSI S	VOMITU S	BODILES S	*COMBING S	DIMEROU S
SUBBAS S	VOTRES S	BOLDNES S	COMEDIE S	DIOICOU S
SUBMIS S	VOWLES S	BONELES S	COMPLIE S	DIPLOSI S
SUCCES S	WADDIE S	BONINES S	COMPRES S	DIRENES S
SUCCUS S	WAENES S	BOOTLES S	CONGRES S	DISTAVE S
SUMLES S	WALLIE S	BOTANIE S	COOKLES S	DISTRES S
SUMMON S	WANNES S	*BOXINES S	COOLNES S	DIURESI S
SUNLES S	WARLES S	BRIMLES S	COPPERA S	*DIZYGOU S
SURPAS S	WAYLES S	*BRITCHE S	CORDLES S	DOLDRUM S
SURPLU S	WEARIE S	BROWLES S	CORELES S	DOLOROU S
SWAMIE S	WEBLES S	BURSITI S	CORNEOU S	DONENES S
SYCOSI S	WETNES S	BUSHLES S	COSINES S	DOORLES S
SYNESI S	WHEREA S	BUSINES S	COSTLES S	DOPINES S
TABBIE S	WHITIE S	BUSYNES S	COUNTES S	DOURNES S
TALIPE S	*WHIZZE S	BUTTRES S	COUSCOU S	*DOZINES S
TALLIE S	WHOOSI S	BUTYROU S	COVETOU S	DRABNES S
TARDIE S	WIGLES S	CADUCEU S	*COZINES S	DRIPLES S
TARRIE S	WILLIE S	CADUCOU S	CRANKOU S	DRUIDES S
TAXLES S	WITHIE S	CAGINES S	CRANNIE S	DRUTHER S
TEARGA S	WITLES S	CALATHO S	CREMAIN S	DUCTLES S
TEDIOU S	WITNES S	CALATHU S	CREWLES S	DULLNES S
TELESI S	WOENES S	CALCULU S	CRIBROU S	DUMBNES S
TELLIE S	WOOLIE S	CALMNES S	CROPLES S	DURABLE S
TENUOU S	WRYNES S	CALVADO S	CROUPOU S	DUSTLES S
TERRIE S	XEROSI S	CANITIE S	*CRYONIC S	FABULOU S
TETANU S	*ZEALOU S	CANNABI S	*CUFFLES S	FACELES S
THALLU S	*ZEBRAS S	CANONES S	CUMBROU S	FACTIOU S
THERMO S	*ZINCOU S	CANOROU S	CUPREOU S	FADELES S
THIEVE S	*ZYGOSI S	CAPTIOU S	CURELES S	FAIRNES S
THYRSU S	*ZYMOSI S	CARDITI S	CURTNES S	FAMELES S
TIGRES S	*BACCHIU S	CARELES S	CUSTODE S	FASHIOU S
TIMEOU S	BACILLU S	CASHLES S	CUTENES S	FASTNES S
TIPLES S	*BACKLES S	CATERES S	CUTGRAS S	FASTUOU S
TITTIE S	BALDNES S	*CATHEXI S	CYANOSI S	FEARLES S
TOADIE S	BARBLES S	CAUTIOU S	CYSTITI S	*FECKLES S
TODDIE S	BARENES S	CENTESI S	DACTYLU S	FELLNES S
TOELES S	BARKLES S	CERNUOU S	DAFTNES S	FERREOU S
TOPLES S	BARONES S	CERASTE S	DAMPNES S	FETIALI S
*TORQUE S	BASALTE S	CHALLIE S	DANKNES S	FEVEROU S
TOWARD S	BASELES S	CHANTIE S	DARKNES S	FIBROSI S
TOWNIE S	BASENES S	CHAUSSE S	DATELES S	FINENES S
TOYLES S	BASSNES S	*CHIASMU S	DEADNES S	FIRELES S
TRAVOI S	BATHLES S	*CHICNES S	DEAFNES S	FIRMNES S
TRELLI S	BAUDRON S	CHINLES S	DEARNES S	FISHLES S
TRICEP S	BEAMLES S	CHLOROU S	DECOROU S	*FIVEPIN S
TRISMU S	BEATLES S	CHORAGU S	DEEDLES S	FLAGLES S
TROILU S	*BEDWARD S	CHOREGU S	DEEPNES S	FLAMINE S
TSIMME S	BEEFLES S	*CHROMOU S	DEFTNES S	FLAPLES S
TUGLES S	BELTLES S	*CHUCKIE S	DEMONES S	FLATNES S
TUMULU S	*BENDWAY S	CITREOU S	DEMOTIC S	*FLATWAY S
TURKOI S	BIASNES S	CLAWLES S	DENARIU S	FLAWLES S
*TZIMME S	BIBULOU S	CLEMATI S	DESIROU S	*FLEXUOU S
*TZITZI S	BIGAMIE S	CLITORI S	DETRITU S	FLUERIC S
VACUOU S	BIGAMOU S	COALLES S	*DEXTROU S	FLUIDIC S
VARICE S	*BIJUGOU S	COATLES S	DIABETE S	FOAMLES S
VARIOU S	BIMANOU S	CODELES S	DIALYSI S	FONDNES S
VELITE S	BIOLYSI S		DIANTHU S	FOOTLES S

*FORCIPE S	*HAZINES S	*LAZINES S	MELANOU S	*PACKNES S
FORDLES S	HEADLES S	LEADLES S	MELODIE S	PAINLES S
*FORKLES S	HEATLES S	LEAFLES S	*MENFOLK S	PALENES S
FORMLES S	HEDONIC S	LEAKLES S	MENISCU S	*PALEWAY S
FORTRES S	HEEDLES S	LEANNES S	*MEPHITI S	PANCREA S
FOULNES S	HEELLES S	*LECYTHU S	MESDAME S	PANDANU S
*FOXINES S	HEIRLES S	*LEKYTHO S	*METHINK S	PARODIE S
*FOZINES S	HELMLES S	*LEKYTHU S	METRITI S	PASSLES S
FREENES S	HELPLES S	LEUKOSI S	MICROBU S	PASTNES S
FREMITU S	HERBLES S	LEWDNES S	*MIDSHIP S	PATHLES S
FRETLES S	HERCULE S	LIBELOU S	MILDNES S	PATULOU S
FULLNES S	*HIBISCU S	LIFELES S	MINDLES S	PEAKLES S
FUMELES S	HIDELES S	LIGNEOU S	MIRINES S	PEERLES S
FUSELES S	HIDROSI S	LIKENES S	MISCLAS S	PERILOU S
*GADZOOK S	*HIGHNES S	LIMBLES S	MISGUES S	PERTNES S
GAINLES S	HILTLES S	LIMELES S	MISTRES S	PERVIOU S
GALLEAS S	HIVELES S	LIMINES S	MITTIMU S	PETALOU S
GAMASHE S	HOLELES S	LIMPNES S	MODIOLU S	*PHIMOSI S
GAMENES S	HOLINES S	LINELES S	MOLASSE S	*PHTHISI S
GAMINES S	HOMELES S	LINTLES S	MOONLES S	*PHYLAXI S
GARBLES S	HOMINES S	LISTLES S	MOTORBU S	*PHYLESI S
GASTNES S	HOMINIE S	LIVENES S	MOVELES S	PINGRAS S
*GASWORK S	HOODLES S	LOAMLES S	*MUCHNES S	PINKNES S
GATELES S	HOOFLES S	LOFTLES S	MUTENES S	PIPELES S
*GAYWING S	*HOOKLES S	LOGINES S	MUTICOU S	PITHLES S
GEARLES S	HOOPLES S	LONENES S	MUTINIE S	PITILES S
GENEROU S	HOPELES S	LONGNES S	MUTINOU S	*PIXINES S
GENETIC S	HORNFEL S	*LONGWAY S	MYELITI S	PLANLES S
GENITAL S	HORNLES S	LORDLES S	MYOSOTI S	*PLATYPU S
*GEOTAXI S	HOTPRES S	LORDOSI S	NABOBES S	PLAYLES S
GIANTES S	HUGENES S	LORNNES S	NAMELES S	PLOTLES S
GIFTLES S	HUMOROU S	LOSTNES S	NARCOSI S	PLOTTIE S
GLABROU S	*HUMPLES S	LOUDNES S	NATHLES S	PLUGLES S
GLADNES S	HURTLES S	LOVELES S	NAUPLIU S	PLUMBOU S
GLANDER S	HUSTING S	LOVELIE S	NAUSEOU S	PLUVIOU S
GLAUCOU S	*HYMNLES S	LUCKLES S	NAUTILU S	POACEOU S
GLEGNES S	*HYPNOSI S	LUMINOU S	NEARNES S	POETLES S
GLIBNES S	*JOHANNE S	LUSCIOU S	NEATNES S	POKINES S
GLORIOU S	*JUSTNES S	LUSHNES S	NEBULOU S	POLELES S
GLOSSIE S	KEELLES S	LUSTROU S	NECKLES S	POLITIC S
GLUMNES S	KEENNES S	MAILLES S	NECROSI S	*POLYPOU S
GOALLES S	KINDLES S	MALENES S	NEEDLES S	POORNES S
GONENES S	KINDNES S	MAMMATU S	NEURITI S	POPULOU S
GOODNES S	KINESIC S	MAMMITI S	NEUROSI S	PORTLES S
GORGEOU S	KINETIC S	MANDAMU S	NEWSLES S	PORTRES S
GORINES S	*KINFOLK S	MANWARD S	NICENES S	*POXVIRU S
GRACILI S	KINGLES S	MARASMU S	NIGHNES S	PREBLES S
GRACIOU S	*KNICKER S	*MARQUES S	NIGHTIE S	PRECIOU S
GRAYNES S	KNOTLES S	MASSLES S	NORMLES S	*PREFOCU S
GREYNES S	KURTOSI S	MASTITI S	NOSELES S	PRETTIE S
GRIEVOU S	LACELES S	MASTLES S	NOSINES S	PREVIOU S
GRIMNES S	LACINES S	MATELES S	NOTELES S	PRIMNES S
GRISEOU S	LACTEOU S	MATINES S	NOTORNI S	PRINCES S
GUMMOSI S	LAMENES S	*MAZINES S	*NOWADAY S	PRIORES S
GUSTLES S	LAMINOU S	MEALLES S	NUBILOU S	PRIORIE S
GYPSEOU S	LANCIER S	MEANNES S	NUCELLU S	PROGRES S
HAIRLES S	LANDLES S	MEATLES S	NUDENES S	PROPOLI S
HALENES S	LANDMAS S	MEALLES S	NUMBNES S	PROTASI S
HALFNES S	LANKNES S	MEATLES S	NUMEROU S	PROVIRU S
HARDNES S	LAPILLU S	MEATTRES S	NUMINOU S	PRURITU S
HARMLES S	LATENES S	MEEKNES S	NUTGRAS S	PSILOSI S
HAUTBOI S		MEETNES S	*PACIFIE S	PULPLES S

PULVINU S	SANITIE S	SOURPUS S	TENTLES S	VASTNES S
PUMPLES S	SAVORIE S	SPACIOU S	TERMINU S	VEINLES S
PUNINES S	SAVOROU S	SPADICE S	TERMLES S	VENOMOU S
PURENES S	SAWBONE S	SPANLES S	TETANIE S	VENTLES S
PYELITI S	SCABIOU S	SPECIOU S	*TEXTLES S	VERBLES S
*QUADRAN S	SCABROU S	SPERMOU S	THALAMU S	VESTLES S
RACEMOU S	SCALENU S	*SPHERIC S	THANATO S	VICELES S
RACHITI S	SCANTIE S	SPHINGE S	THAWLES S	VICTRES S
RACINES S	SCARIOU S	*SPHYGMU S	THELITI S	VIEWLES S
RAINLES S	SCARLES S	SPINLES S	THEORIE S	VIGOROU S
RAMULOU S	*SCHNAPP S	SPLENIU S	THEWLES S	VILENES S
RANKNES S	SCIRRHU S	SPOONIE S	THINNES S	VIRTUOU S
RAPTNES S	SCLEROU S	SPOTLES S	THOWLES S	VITELLU S
RARENES S	SCURRIE S	SPRYNES S	*THROMBU S	VITREOU S
RASHNES S	SEAMLES S	SPURIOU S	TIDELES S	VOIDNES S
RAVENOU S	SEATLES S	SPYGLAS S	TIDINES S	VOLVULU S
RAYGRAS S	SEDULOU S	STANNOU S	TIDYTIP S	VOMITOU S
REALNES S	SEEDLES S	STAPEDE S	TIMELES S	VOTARES S
REASSES S	SELFLES S	STARLES S	TIMOROU S	VOTELES S
RECKLES S	SELFNES S	STEADIE S	TININES S	VULVITI S
REINLES S	SEMIOSI S	STEMLES S	TINNITU S	*WAESUCK S
REOVIRU S	SENARIU S	STENOSI S	TINTLES S	WAGELES S
RESINOU S	SENSUOU S	STIMULU S	TIRELES S	WAITRES S
RESTLES S	SETULOU S	STRATOU S	TITANES S	WAKELES S
REVERIE S	*SEXINES S	STRUMOU S	TITANOU S	WARDRES S
RHINITI S	*SHAMMIE S	STUDIOU S	TOADLES S	WARINES S
*RHIZOPU S	SHANTIE S	SUBCLAS S	TOMBLES S	WARMNES S
*RHONCHU S	SHORTIE S	SUBCUTI S	TONELES S	WATTLES S
RIBGRAS S	SICKNES S	SUBEROU S	TONETIC S	WAVELES S
RICHNES S	*SIDEWAY S	SUBGENU S	TOOLLES S	WAVINES S
RIFENES S	SIGHLES S	SUCCUBU S	TOPCROS S	*WAXINES S
RIFTLES S	SIMONIE S	SUCHNES S	TORTIOU S	*WEAKNES S
RIGHTIE S	*SIZINES S	SUCKLES S	TORTUOU S	WEEDLES S
RIGOROU S	*SKEWNES S	SUDSLES S	TOUGHIE S	WEIRDIE S
RINGHAL S	SKILLES S	SUNDRIE S	TOWNLES S	WELDLES S
RINGTOS S	SKINLES S	SUNDROP S	TRAMLES S	WELLNES S
RIPENES S	*SKYWARD S	SUNGLAS S	TRAPPOU S	WIDENES S
RISIBLE S	SLIMNES S	SUNWARD S	TREELES S	WIFELES S
ROADLES S	SLIPLES S	SUPPRES S	TRESPAS S	WILDNES S
ROBOTIC S	SLITLES S	SURENES S	TRIGNES S	WILINES S
ROCKLES S	SLOWNES S	SUSURRU S	TRIMNES S	WINDLAS S
ROOFLES S	SLYBOOT S	SYLLABU S	TRINKUM S	WINDLES S
ROOTLES S	SMUGNES S	SYNAPSI S	TROLLIE S	WINELES S
ROPINES S	SNAPLES S	SYNDESI S	TROUSER S	WINGLES S
ROSINES S	SNOWLES S	SYNOPSI S	TROWSER S	WIRELES S
ROSINOU S	SNUBNES S	*SYPHILI S	TRUENES S	WIRINES S
RUCTIOU S	SNUGNES S	TACKLES S	*TRYWORK S	WISENES S
RUDENES S	SOAPLES S	TACTLES S	TUBELES S	WISHLES S
RULELES S	SOAPSUD S	TAILLES S	TUBEROU S	WONDROU S
RUSTLES S	SOFTNES S	TALLNES S	TUBULOU S	WOODLES S
RUTHLES S	SOILLES S	TAMELES S	TUMULOU S	WOOLLIE S
RYEGRAS S	SOLELES S	TAMENES S	TUNELES S	WORDLES S
SABULOU S	SOLENES S	TANTALU S	TURFLES S	*WORKLES S
SACCULU S	SOLONET S	TAPELES S	*TURQUOI S	WORNNES S
SAFENES S	SOMBROU S	TARANTA S	TUSKLES S	*XANTHOU S
SAGENES S	*SOMEWAY S	TARTNES S	TUTORES S	YEARLIE S
SALTLES S	SONGLES S	TAUTNES S	TWIGLES S	*YOKELES S
SALTNES S	SONOROU S	TEARLES S	VAINNES S	*ZANINES S
SAMENES S	SORENES S	TENESMU S	VALOROU S	*ZONELES S
SANENES S	SOURNES S	TENIASI S	VAPOROU S	*ZOONOSI S

T

TABU	THEN	TOOT	TWAE	TARRY
TACE	**THEW**	TOPE	TWAT	TARSI
TACH	**THEY**	TOPH	TWIG	TASSE
TACK	THIN	TOPI	TWIN	TASTE
TACO	THIO	TORA	TWIT	TASTY
TACT	THIR	TORC	TYEE	TATER
TAEL	THIS	TORE	**TYKE**	TATTY
TAHR	THOU	TORI	TYNE	TAUNT
TAIL	THRO	TORN	TYPE	TAUPE
TAIN	THRU	TORO	TYPO	TAWER
TAKE	THUD	TORR	**TYPP**	TAWIE
TALA	THUG	TORT	**TYPY**	TAWSE
TALC	THUS	TORY	TYRE	**TAWNY**
TALE	**TICK**	TOSH	TYRO	**TAXER**
TALI	TIDE	TOSS	**TZAR**	**TAXON**
TALK	TIDY	TOST	**TABBY**	**TAXUS**
TALL	TIED	TOTE	TABER	*TAZZA
TAME	TIER	TOUR	TABES	**TEACH**
TAMP	**TIFF**	TOUT	TABID	TEARY
TANG	TIKE	TOWN	TABLA	TEASE
TANK	TIKI	**TOWY**	TABLE	**TECHY**
TAPA	TILE	TOYO	TABOO	TECTA
TAPE	TILL	TRAD	TABOR	**TEDDY**
TARE	TILT	TRAM	TACET	TEENY
TARN	TIME	TRAP	TACIT	TEETH
TARO	TINE	TRAY	**TACHE**	TEGUA
TARP	TING	TREE	**TACKY**	TEIID
TART	TINT	TREF	**TAFFY**	TEIND
TASK	TINY	TREK	TAFIA	**TELEX**
TASS	TIPI	TRET	TAIGA	TELIA
TATE	TIRE	TREY	TAINT	TELIC
TAUT	TIRL	TRIG	TAKER	TELLY
TAXA	TIRO	TRIM	TAKIN	TELOS
TAXI	TITI	TRIO	TALAR	TEMPI
TEAK	**TIVY**	TRIP	TALER	TEMPO
TEAL	TOAD	TROD	**TALKY**	TEMPT
TEAM	TOBY	TROP	TALLY	**TENCH**
TEAR	TODY	TROT	TALON	TENET
TEAT	**TOFF**	TROW	TALUK	TENIA
TEEM	TOFT	TROY	TALUS	TENON
TEEN	TOFU	TRUE	TAMAL	TENOR
TEFF	TOGA	TSAR	TAMER	TENSE
TELA	TOIL	TUBA	TAMIS	TENTH
TELE	TOIT	TUBE	**TAMMY**	TENTY
TELL	TOKE	**TUCK**	TANGO	TEPAL
TEND	TOLA	TUFA	TANGY	TEPEE
TENT	TOLD	TUFF	TANKA	TEPID
TEPA	TOLE	TUFT	TANSY	TERAI
TERM	TOLL	TULE	TANTO	TERCE
TERN	TOLU	TUMP	TAPER	TERGA
TEST	TOMB	TUNA	TAPIR	TERNE
TETH	TOME	TUNE	TAPIS	TERRA
TEXT	TONE	TUNG	TARDO	TERRY
THAE	TONG	TURD	TARDY	TERSE
THAN	TONY	TURF	TARGE	TESLA
THAT	TOOK	TURN	TAROC	TESTA
THAW	TOOL	TUSH	TAROK	TESTY
THEE	TOOM	TUSK	TAROT	TETRA
THEM	TOON	TUTU	TARRE	**TEUCH**

TEUGH	TINGE	**TOXIC**	TRUSS	**TACTIC**
TEXAS	TINNY	**TOXIN**	TRUST	TAENIA
THACK	**TIPPY**	TOYER	TRUTH	**TAFFIA**
THANE	**TIPSY**	TOYON	**TRYMA**	TAGGED
THANK	TIRED	TRACE	TRYST	TAGGER
THARM	TITAN	**TRACK**	TSADE	TAGRAG
THECA	TITER	TRACT	TSADI	TAHSIL
THEFT	TITHE	TRADE	TSUBA	TAILER
THEGN	TITLE	TRAGI	TUBAL	TAILLE
THEIN	TITRE	TRAIK	**TUBBY**	TAILOR
THEIR	TITTY	TRAIL	TUBER	TAIPAN
THEME	*TIZZY	TRAIN	**TUFTY**	**TAKAHE**
THERE	TOADY	TRAIT	TULIP	**TAKING**
THERM	TOAST	TRAMP	TULLE	**TALCUM**
THESE	TODAY	TRANS	TUMID	TALENT
THETA	**TODDY**	TRAPT	**TUMMY**	TALION
THICK	**TOFFY**	TRASH	TUMOR	**TALKER**
THIEF	TOGUE	TRASS	TUNER	**TALKIE**
THIGH	TOILE	TRAVE	TUNIC	TALLOL
THILL	**TOKAY**	TRAWL	TUNNY	TALLOW
THINE	TOKEN	TREAD	**TUPIK**	**TALUKA**
THING	TOLAN	TREAT	**TUQUE**	TAMALE
THINK	TOLYL	TREND	TURBO	**TAMBAC**
THIOL	TOMAN	TRESS	**TURFY**	**TAMBUR**
THIRD	**TOMMY**	TREWS	TURPS	TAMEIN
THIRL	TONAL	TRIAD	TUTEE	**TAMELY**
THOLE	TONDO	TRIAL	TUTOR	TAMEST
THONG	TONER	TRIBE	TUTTI	**TAMING**
THORN	TONGA	TRICE	TUTTY	**TAMMIE**
THORO	TONIC	**TRICK**	TUYER	**TAMPAN**
THORP	TONNE	TRIED	TWAIN	**TAMPER**
THOSE	TONUS	TRIER	TWANG	**TAMPON**
THRAW	TOOTH	TRIES	**TWEAK**	TANDEM
THREE	TOOTS	TRIGO	TWEED	TANGLE
THREW	*TOPAZ	TRILL	TWEEN	**TANGLY**
THRIP	TOPEE	TRINE	TWEET	TANIST
THROB	TOPER	TRIOL	**TWERP**	**TANKER**
THROE	**TOPHE**	TRIPE	**TWICE**	TANNED
THROW	TOPIC	TRITE	TWIER	TANNER
THRUM	TOPOI	TROAK	TWILL	TANNIC
*THUJA	TOPOS	**TROCK**	TWINE	TANNIN
THUMB	**TOQUE**	TRODE	**TWINY**	TANREC
THUMP	TORAH	TROIS	TWIRL	TANTRA
THURL	**TORCH**	TROKE	**TWIRP**	TAPALO
THUYA	TORIC	TROLL	TWIST	TAPING
THYME	TORII	TROMP	*TWIXT	**TAPPED**
THYMI	TORSE	TRONA	**TWYER**	**TAPPER**
*THYMY	TORSI	TRONE	TYING	**TAPPET**
TIARA	TORSK	TROOP	**TYPAL**	TARGET
TIBIA	TORSO	**TROOZ**	**TYPED**	**TARIFF**
TICAL	TORTE	TROPE	**TYPEY**	TARING
TIDAL	TORUS	TROTH	**TYPIC**	**TARMAC**
TIGER	TOTAL	TROUT	**TYTHE**	TARNAL
TIGHT	TOTEM	TROVE	TABARD	TARPAN
TIGON	TOTER	TRUCE	**TABBED**	TARPON
TILDE	**TOUCH**	**TRUCK**	**TABBIS**	TARRED
TILER	TOUGH	TRUED	TABLET	TARSAL
TILTH	TOUSE	TRUER	TABOUR	TARSIA
TIMER	TOWEL	TRULL	**TACKER**	TARSUS
TIMID	TOWER	TRULY	**TACKET**	TARTAN
TINCT	TOWIE	TRUMP	*TACKEY	TARTAR
TINEA	**TOWNY**	TRUNK	**TACKLE**	TARTLY

*TARZAN	TENREC	THORON	TINIER	TONIER
TASSEL	TENSOR	**THORPE**	TINILY	TONING
TASSET	TENTER	**THOUGH**	TINING	TONISH
TASSIE	TENTIE	THRALL	**TINKER**	TONLET
TASTER	TENUIS	**THRASH**	**TINKLE**	TONNER
TATAMI	TENURE	**THRAVE**	**TINKLY**	TONSIL
TATTED	TENUTO	**THRAWN**	TINMAN	TOOLER
TATTER	TEOPAN	**THREAD**	TINNED	TOOTER
TATTLE	**TEPEFY**	**THREAP**	TINNER	**TOOTHY**
TATTOO	**TEPHRA**	THREAT	TINSEL	TOOTLE
TAUGHT	**TERAPH**	**THREEP**	TINTER	TOOTSY
TAUTEN	TERBIA	**THRESH**	**TIPCAT**	**TOPFUL**
TAUTLY	TERCEL	**THRICE**	**TIPOFF**	**TOPHUS**
TAUTOG	TERCET	**THRIFT**	**TIPPED**	TOPING
TAVERN	TEREDO	THRILL	**TIPPER**	**TOPPED**
TAWDRY	TERETE	**THRIVE**	**TIPPET**	**TOPPER**
TAWNEY	TERGAL	THROAT	**TIPPLE**	**TOPPLE**
TAWPIE	TERGUM	THRONE	TIPTOE	*TOQUET
*TAXEME	TERMER	**THRONG**	**TIPTOP**	TORERO
TAXITE	**TERMLY**	**THROVE**	TIRADE	TORIES
*TAXMAN	TERMOR	**THRUSH**	TIRING	TOROID
*TEABOX	TERRAS	THRUST	TISANE	TOROSE
TEACUP	TERRET	THULIA	TISSUE	TOROUS
TEAPOT	TERRIT	**THUSLY**	TITBIT	TORPID
TEAPOY	TERROR	*THWACK	TITHER	TORPOR
TEARER	TESTEE	**THWART**	TITIAN	*TORQUE
TEASEL	TESTER	*THYMEY	TITMAN	TORRID
TEASER	TESTES	*THYMIC	TITTER	TORULA
*TEAZEL	TESTIS	**THYMOL**	TITTIE	TOSSER
*TEAZLE	TESTON	**THYMUS**	TITTLE	TOSSUP
TECHED	TETANY	**THYRSE**	TITTUP	TOTHER
TECTAL	**TETCHY**	**TICKER**	TMESIS	TOTING
TECTUM	TETHER	**TICKET**	TOASTY	TOTTED
TEDDER	TETRAD	**TICKLE**	TOCHER	TOTTER
TEDIUM	TETRYL	**TICTAC**	TOCSIN	TOUCAN
TEEMER	TETTER	**TICTOC**	TODDLE	**TOUCHE**
TEENER	**THAIRM**	TIDBIT	**TOECAP**	**TOUCHY**
TEENSY	THALER	**TIDDLY**	**TOFFEE**	**TOUGHY**
TEEPEE	**THATCH**	TIDIED	TOGATE	TOUPEE
TEETER	**THAWER**	TIDIER	TOGGED	TOURER
TEETHE	THEINE	TIDIES	TOGGLE	TOUSLE
TEGMEN	THEIRS	**TIDILY**	TOILER	TOUTER
TELEDU	**THEISM**	TIDING	TOILET	*TOUZLE
TELEGA	THEIST	TIEPIN	TOLANE	**TOWAGE**
TELFER	THENAL	TIERCE	TOLEDO	**TOWARD**
TELIAL	THENAR	**TIFFIN**	TOLING	**TOWERY**
TELIUM	**THENCE**	**TIGHTS**	TOLLER	**TOWHEE**
TELLER	**THEORY**	TIGLON	TOLUIC	TOWNEE
TELOME	**THERBY**	TILING	TOLUID	TOWNIE
TELSON	**THERME**	TILLER	TOLUOL	**TOXINE**
TEMPEH	THESIS	TILTER	TOLUYL	**TOXOID**
TEMPER	**THETIC**	TIMBAL	TOMATO	**TOYISH**
TEMPLE	**THIEVE**	**TIMBER**	**TOMBAC**	TRACER
TENACE	**THINLY**	**TIMBRE**	**TOMBAK**	TRADER
TENAIL	**THIRAM**	**TIMELY**	**TOMBAL**	TRAGIC
TENANT	THIRST	TIMING	**TOMBOY**	TRAGUS
TENDER	**THIRTY**	TINCAL	**TOMCAT**	TRAMEL
TENDON	THOLOS	TINDER	**TOMCOD**	TRANCE
TENNER	*THORAX	TINEID	TOMTIT	TRAPAN
TENNIS	THORIA	TINFUL	TONEME	TRAPES
TENOUR	**THORIC**	TINGLE	TONGER	**TRASHY**
TENPIN	**THORNY**	**TINGLY**	TONGUE	TRAUMA

TRAVEL	TRYOUT	*TWANKY	**TALKING**	**TARTUFE**
TREATY	TRYSTE	*TWEAKY	**TALLAGE**	**TARWEED**
TREBLE	TSETSE	**TWEEDY**	**TALLBOY**	TASTING
TREBLY	**TSKTSK**	*TWEEZE	TALLIED	**TATOUAY**
TREFAH	TSURIS	**TWELVE**	TALLIER	TATTIER
TREMOR	TUBATE	**TWENTY**	TALLIES	TATTING
TRENCH	**TUBBED**	TWIBIL	**TALLISH**	TATTLER
TRENDY	**TUBBER**	**TWIGGY**	**TALLITH**	TAUNTER
TREPAN	**TUBFUL**	TWILIT	**TALLOWY**	TAURINE
TREPID	TUBING	TWINER	**TALLYHO**	TAUTAUG
TRESSY	TUBULE	**TWINGE**	**TALOOKA**	*TAXABLE
TREVET	**TUCHUN**	**TWIRLY**	**TAMABLE**	*TAXICAB
TRIAGE	**TUCKER**	**TWITCH**	**TAMANDU**	*TAXIMAN
TRIBAL	**TUCKET**	TWOFER	TAMARAO	*TAXIWAY
*TRICKY	**TUFFET**	**TYCOON**	TAMARAU	**TAXLESS**
TRICOT	TUFTER	**TYMBAL**	TAMARIN	*TAXPAID
TRIENE	TUGGER	**TYMPAN**	**TAMASHA**	*TAXWISE
TRIENS	**TUGRIK**	**TYPHON**	**TAMBALA**	*TAXYING
TRIFID	TUILLE	**TYPHUS**	**TAMBOUR**	**TEABOWL**
TRIFLE	TULADI	**TYPIER**	**TAMBURA**	**TEACAKE**
TRIGLY	**TUMBLE**	*TYPIFY	**TAMPALA**	TEACART
TRIGON	**TUMEFY**	**TYPING**	**TAMPION**	**TEACHER**
TRIJET	TUMOUR	**TYPIST**	TANAGER	**TEARFUL**
TRILBY	TUMULI	TYRANT	**TANBARK**	TEARGAS
TRIMER	TUMULT	*TZETZE	TANGELO	TEARIER
TRIMLY	TUNDRA	*TZURIS	TANGENT	**TEARILY**
TRINAL	TUNICA	**TABANID**	TANGIER	TEAROOM
TRIODE	TUNING	TABARET	TANGLER	**TEASHOP**
TRIOSE	TUNNED	**TABBIED**	**TANGRAM**	TEASING
TRIPLE	TUNNEL	**TABBIES**	**TANKAGE**	TEATIME
TRIPLY	TUPELO	**TABBING**	**TANKARD**	**TEAWARE**
TRIPOD	**TUPPED**	**TABETIC**	**TANKFUL**	**TECHNIC**
TRIPOS	TURACO	TABLEAU	TANNAGE	*TECTRIX
TRISTE	TURBAN	**TABLING**	TANNATE	TEDIOUS
TRITON	TURBID	**TABLOID**	**TANNERY**	TEENAGE
TRIUNE	TURBIT	TABORER	TANNEST	**TEENFUL**
TRIVET	TURBOT	TABORET	TANNING	**TEENTSY**
TRIVIA	TUREEN	TABORIN	**TANNISH**	**TEETHER**
TROCAR	TURGID	TABULAR	TANTARA	TEGULAR
TROCHE	TURGOR	**TACHISM**	**TANTIVY**	**TEGUMEN**
TROGON	**TURKEY**	**TACHIST**	TANTRUM	**TEKTITE**
TROIKA	TURNER	**TACKIER**	**TANYARD**	TELAMON
TROLLY	TURNIP	*TACKIFY	TAPERER	TELEMAN
TROMPE	TURNUP	*TACKILY	**TAPETUM**	TELEOST
TROPHY	TURRET	**TACKLER**	**TAPHOLE**	TELERAN
TROPIC	TURTLE	TACNODE	**TAPIOCA**	TELESIS
TROPIN	TURVES	**TACTFUL**	**TAPPING**	**TELFORD**
TROTYL	**TUSCHE**	TACTILE	**TAPROOM**	TELLIES
TROUGH	**TUSKER**	TACTION	TAPROOT	**TELPHER**
TROUPE	TUSSAH	TACTUAL	TAPSTER	**TEMBLOR**
TROUTY	TUSSAL	**TADPOLE**	**TARBUSH**	**TEMPERA**
TROVER	TUSSAR	**TAFFETA**	TARDIER	**TEMPEST**
TROWEL	TUSSEH	**TAGGING**	TARDIES	**TEMPLAR**
TROWTH	TUSSER	**TAGLIKE**	**TARNISH**	**TEMPLET**
TRUANT	TUSSIS	**TAGMEME**	TARRIED	**TEMPTER**
TRUDGE	TUSSLE	TAILING	TARRIER	**TEMPURA**
TRUEST	TUSSOR	*TAKEOFF	TARRIES	TENABLE
TRUFFE	TUSSUR	**TAKEOUT**	TARRING	**TENANCY**
TRUING	TUTTED	TALARIA	TARSIER	TENDRIL
TRUISM	**TUXEDO**	**TALIPED**	TARTANA	**TENFOLD**
TRUSTY	TUYERE	**TALIPES**	**TARTISH**	TENNIST
TRUSTY	**TWANGY**	TALIPOT	TARTLET	TENONER

TENSILE	*THERAPY	*TIFFANY	TOGGLER	TOUCHER
TENSING	THEREAT	TIGHTEN	TOILFUL	TOUCHUP
TENSION	THEREIN	TIGRESS	TOLIDIN	TOUGHEN
TENSITY	THEREOF	TIGRISH	TOLLAGE	TOUGHIE
TENSIVE	THEREON	TILAPIA	TOLLBAR	TOUGHLY
TENTAGE	THERETO	TILBURY	TOLLMAN	TOURACO
TENTHLY	THERIAC	TILLAGE	TOLLWAY	TOURING
TENTIER	THERMAE	TIMARAU	TOLUATE	TOURISM
TENUITY	THERMAL	TIMBALE	TOLUENE	TOURIST
TENUOUS	THERMEL	TIMBREL	TOLUIDE	TOURNEY
*TEQUILA	THERMIC	TIMEOUS	TOLUOLE	TOWARDS
TERAOHM	THERMIT	TIMEOUT	*TOMBACK	*TOWAWAY
TERBIUM	THERMOS	*TIMOTHY	TOMBOLO	TOWBOAT
TEREBIC	THEROID	TIMPANO	TOMFOOL	TOWHEAD
TEREFAH	THEURGY	TINAMOU	TOMPION	TOWLINE
TERGITE	THIAMIN	TINFOIL	TONETTE	TOWMOND
TERMITE	*THIAZIN	TINGLER	TONGMAN	TOWMONT
TERNARY	*THIAZOL	TINHORN	TONIEST	TOWNIES
TERNATE	*THICKEN	TINIEST	TONIGHT	TOWNISH
TERNION	*THICKET	TINLIKE	TONNAGE	TOWNLET
TERPENE	*THICKLY	TINNIER	TONNEAU	*TOWPATH
TERRACE	THIEVES	TINNILY	TONNISH	TOWROPE
TERRAIN	THIMBLE	TINNING	TONSURE	*TOXEMIA
TERRANE	THINKER	TINTING	TONTINE	*TOXICAL
TERREEN	THINNED	TINTYPE	*TOOLBOX	TOYLESS
TERRENE	THINNER	TINWARE	TOOLING	TOYLIKE
TERRIER	THIONIC	TINWORK	TOOTLER	TRACERY
TERRIES	THIONIN	TIPCART	TOOTSIE	TRACHEA
TERRIFY	THIONYL	TIPLESS	TOPCOAT	TRACHLE
TERRINE	THIRDLY	TIPPIER	TOPFULL	TRACING
TERTIAL	THIRSTY	TIPPING	TOPIARY	TRACKER
TERTIAN	THISTLE	TIPPLER	*TOPKICK	TRACTOR
TESSERA	THITHER	TIPSIER	TOPKNOT	TRADUCE
TESTACY	THORITE	TIPSILY	TOPLESS	*TRAFFIC
TESTATE	THORIUM	TIPSTER	TOPMAST	TRAGEDY
TESTIER	THOUGHT	TISSUAL	TOPMOST	TRAILER
TESTIFY	THREADY	TISSUEY	TOPONYM	TRAINEE
TESTILY	THRIVER	TITANIA	TOPPING	TRAINER
TESTING	THROATY	TITANIC	TOPSAIL	TRAIPSE
TESTOON	THROUGH	TITHING	TOPSIDE	TRAITOR
TESTUDO	THROWER	TITLARK	TOPSOIL	*TRAJECT
TETANAL	*THRUMMY	TITLIST	*TOPWORK	TRAMCAR
TETANIC	THRUPUT	TITRANT	TORCHON	TRAMELL
TETANUS	*THRUWAY	TITRATE	TORMENT	TRAMMED
TETCHED	THUGGEE	TITTIES	TORNADO	TRAMMEL
TETOTUM	THULIUM	TITULAR	TORPEDO	TRAMPER
TETRODE	THUMPER	TOADIED	*TORQUER	TRAMPLE
TEXTILE	THUNDER	TOADIES	*TORQUES	*TRAMWAY
TEXTUAL	*THYMIER	TOADISH	TORREFY	TRANGAM
TEXTURE	*THYMINE	TOASTER	TORRENT	TRANSIT
THALLUS	THYROID	TOBACCO	TORRIFY	TRANSOM
THANAGE	THYRSUS	TOCCATA	TORSADE	*TRAPEZE
THANKER	*THYSELF	TODDIES	TORSION	TRAPPED
*THATCHY	TICKING	TODDLER	TORTILE	TRAPPER
THEATER	TICKLER	TOEHOLD	TORTONI	TRAVAIL
THEATRE	TIDERIP	TOELESS	TORTRIX	TRAVOIS
THEELIN	TIDEWAY	TOELIKE	TORTURE	TRAWLER
THEELOL	TIDIEST	TOENAIL	TOSSPOT	TRAWLEY
THENAGE	*TIEBACK	TOESHOE	TOTABLE	TRAYFUL
THEOLOG	TIERCED	TOGATED	TOTALLY	TREACLE
THEORBO	TIERCEL	TOGGERY	TOTTERY	TREADER
THEOREM		TOGGING	TOTTING	TREADLE

TREASON	TRITIUM	**TUMBRIL**	**TYPEBAR**	**TAMBOURA**
TREATER	TRITOMA	TUMULAR	**TYPESET**	**TAMEABLE**
TREDDLE	TRITONE	TUMULUS	*TYPHOID	**TAMELESS**
TREETOP	**TRIUMPH**	TUNABLE	*TYPHOON	**TAMENESS**
TREFOIL	**TRIVIAL**	**TUNDISH**	*TYPHOSE	**TAMPERER**
TREHALA	**TRIVIUM**	**TUNEFUL**	**TYPICAL**	**TANGENCE**
*TREKKER	**TROCHAL**	TUNICLE	TYPIEST	**TANGENCY**
TRELLIS	**TROCHAR**	TUNNAGE	**TYRANNY**	**TANGIBLE**
TREMBLE	**TROCHEE**	TUNNING	*TZADDIK	**TANGIBLY**
TREMBLY	**TROCHIL**	**TUPPING**	*TZARDOM	TANGIEST
TREMOLO	TRODDEN	TURACOU	*TZARINA	**TANISTRY**
TRENAIL	**TROFFER**	**TURBARY**	*TZARISM	*TANKSHIP
TREPANG	TROILUS	**TURBETH**	*TZARIST	**TANNABLE**
TRESSEL	TROLAND	**TURBINE**	*TZIGANE	**TANTALUM**
TRESTLE	TROLLER	**TURBITH**	*TZIMMES	TANTALUS
TRIABLE	**TROLLEY**	TURBINE	*TZITZIS	**TAPADERA**
TRIACID	TROLLOP	TURDINE	**TABLEFUL**	**TAPADERO**
TRIADIC	**TROMMEL**	**TURFIER**	**TABLETOP**	**TAPELESS**
*TRIAZIN	**TROOPER**	**TURFMAN**	**TABORINE**	**TAPELIKE**
TRIBADE	**TROPHIC**	**TURFSKI**	**TABOURER**	**TAPELINE**
TRIBUNE	TROPINE	**TURGENT**	**TABOURET**	**TAPESTRY**
TRIBUTE	**TROPISM**	TURGITE	**TABULATE**	*TAPEWORM
TRICEPS	TROTTED	TURKOIS	**TACHINID**	**TAPHOUSE**
TRICING	**TROTTER**	**TURMOIL**	**TACHISTE**	TARANTAS
TRICKER	**TROUBLE**	**TURNERY**	**TACITURN**	**TARBOOSH**
TRICKIE	**TROUNCE**	**TURNING**	**TACKIEST**	**TARLATAN**
TRICKLE	**TROUPER**	**TURNKEY**	**TACKLESS**	TARLETAN
*TRICKLY	**TROUSER**	**TURNOFF**	*TACKLING	**TARPAPER**
*TRICKSY	**TRUANCY**	TURNOUT	**TACONITE**	**TARRAGON**
TRICLAD	**TRUCKER**	**TURPETH**	**TACTLESS**	TARRIEST
TRICORN	**TRUCKLE**	TURTLER	**TAFFAREL**	**TARTNESS**
TRIDENT	TRUDGEN	**TUSSOCK**	**TAFFEREL**	**TARTRATE**
TRIDUUM	TRUDGER	TUSSORE	**TAFFRAIL**	**TARTUFFE**
TRIFLER	**TRUFFLE**	TUSSUCK	**TAGALONG**	*TASKWORK
TRIFOLD	TRUMEAU	TUTELAR	**TAGBOARD**	**TASTEFUL**
TRIFORM	**TRUMPET**	**TUTOYER**	TAIGLACH	TATTIEST
TRIGGER	TRUNDLE	TUTTING	*TAILBACK	**TATTOOER**
TRILLER	TRUNNEL	**TWADDLE**	**TAILBONE**	**TAUTNESS**
TRILOGY	TRUSSER	**TWANGLE**	**TAILCOAT**	**TAUTOMER**
TRIMMED	TRUSTEE	**TWASOME**	TAILGATE	**TAUTONYM**
TRIMMER	TRUSTER	**TWATTLE**	TAILLESS	**TAVERNER**
TRINARY	**TRYPSIN**	**TWEEDLE**	**TAILLIKE**	*TAXATION
TRINDLE	**TRYSAIL**	**TWEETER**	**TAILPIPE**	*TAXINGLY
TRINITY	**TRYSTER**	*TWEEZER	**TAILRACE**	*TAXONOMY
TRINKET	**TSARDOM**	*TWELFTH	**TAILSKID**	*TAXPAYER
TRIOLET	TSARINA	**TWIBILL**	**TAILSPIN**	**TEABERRY**
*TRIOXID	TSARISM	**TWIDDLE**	**TAILWIND**	**TEABOARD**
*TRIPACK	TSARIST	**TWIGGEN**	*TAKEDOWN	**TEACHING**
TRIPART	**TSIMMES**	**TWINIER**	*TAKEOVER	**TEAHOUSE**
TRIPLET	TSUNAMI	**TWINING**	*TAKINGLY	*TEAKWOOD
*TRIPLEX	TUATARA	**TWINKLE**	**TALAPOIN**	**TEAMAKER**
TRIPODY	TUATERA	*TWINKLY	**TALESMAN**	**TEAMMATE**
TRIPOLI	**TUBBING**	**TWINNED**	**TALEYSIM**	**TEAMSTER**
TRIPPED	*TUBIFEX	**TWIRLER**	**TALISMAN**	*TEAMWORK
TRIPPER	**TUBLIKE**	**TWISTER**	**TALKABLE**	**TEARDOWN**
TRIPPET	TUBULAR	*TWITCHY	TALLNESS	**TEARDROP**
TRIREME	**TUGBOAT**	**TWITTED**	**TALLYMAN**	TEARIEST
TRISECT	**TUGGING**	**TWITTER**	**TALMUDIC**	**TEARLESS**
TRISEME	TUGLESS	**TWOFOLD**	**TAMANDUA**	**TEASELER**
TRISMUS	TUITION	**TWOSOME**	*TAMARACK	**TEASPOON**
TRISOME	**TUMBLER**	TYMPANA	**TAMARIND**	**TECTONIC**
TRISOMY	**TUMBREL**	*TYMPANY	**TAMARISK**	**TEENAGED**

TEENAGER	*TERRAZZO	*THINKING	TILEFISH	TOLBOOTH
TEETHING	TERRELLA	THINNESS	TILELIKE	TOLERANT
TEETOTAL	TERRIBLE	THINNEST	TILTYARD	TOLERATE
TEETOTUM	TERRIFIC	THINNING	TIMECARD	TOLIDINE
TEGMENTA	TERTIARY	THINNISH	TIMELESS	TOLLGATE
TEGMINAL	TESTATOR	THIONATE	*TIMEWORK	TOLUIDIN
TEGUMENT	TESTICLE	THIONINE	TIMEWORN	*TOMAHAWK
TEIGLACH	TESTIEST	*THIOPHEN	TIMIDITY	TOMALLEY
TELECAST	TETANIES	THIOTEPA	TIMOROUS	TOMBLESS
TELEFILM	TETANISE	THIOUREA	TIMPANUM	*TOMBLIKE
TELEGONY	*TETANIZE	THIRLAGE	TINCTURE	TOMENTUM
TELEGRAM	TETRACID	THIRSTER	TININESS	*TOMMYROT
TELEMARK	TETRAGON	THIRTEEN	TINKERER	TOMOGRAM
TELEPLAY	TETRAMER	THOLEPIN	TINKLING	TOMORROW
TELEPORT	TETRAPOD	*THOROUGH	TINNIEST	TONALITY
TELETHON	TETRARCH	THOUSAND	TINNITUS	TONELESS
TELEVIEW	*TETROXID	THOWLESS	TINPLATE	TONETICS
TELEVISE	*TEXTBOOK	THRALDOM	TINSELLY	TONGUING
TELLTALE	*TEXTLESS	THRASHER	TINSMITH	TONICITY
TELLURIC	*TEXTUARY	THRAWART	TINSTONE	TOOLHEAD
TEMERITY	*TEXTURAL	THREADER	TINTLESS	TOOLLESS
TEMPERER	THALAMUS	THREAPER	TIPPABLE	TOOLROOM
TEMPLATE	THALLIUM	THREATEN	TIPPIEST	TOOLSHED
TEMPORAL	THANATOS	THRENODE	TIPSIEST	TOPCROSS
TENACITY	*THANKFUL	*THRENODY	*TIPSTAFF	*TOPLOFTY
TENACULA	*THATAWAY	THRESHER	*TIPSTOCK	*TOPNOTCH
TENAILLE	*THATCHER	THRILLER	TIRELESS	TOPOLOGY
TENANTRY	THAWLESS	*THROBBER	TIRESOME	*TOPONYMY
TENDANCE	*THEARCHY	*THROMBIN	TIRRIVEE	*TOPOTYPE
TENDENCE	THEBAINE	*THROMBUS	TITANATE	TOPSTONE
TENDENCY	THELITIS	THROSTLE	TITANESS	TORCHERE
TENDERER	*THEMATIC	THROTTLE	TITANISM	TORCHIER
TENDERLY	THEOCRAT	*THRUMMER	TITANITE	TOREADOR
TENEBRAE	*THEODICY	THRUSTER	TITANIUM	TOREUTIC
TENEMENT	*THEOGONY	THRUSTOR	TITANOUS	TORNILLO
TENESMUS	*THEOLOGY	*THUGGERY	TITHABLE	TOROSITY
TENIASIS	*THEONOMY	*THUGGISH	TITHONIA	TORPIDLY
TENORITE	THEORIES	*THUMBKIN	TITIVATE	*TORQUATE
TENOTOMY	THEORISE	*THUMBNUT	TITMOUSE	*TORQUING
TENPENCE	THEORIST	*THUNDERY	TITRABLE	TORTILLA
TENPENNY	*THEORIZE	THURIBLE	TITRATOR	TORTIOUS
TENSIBLE	THEREFOR	THURIFER	TITTERER	TORTOISE
TENTACLE	THEREMIN	*THWACKER	*TITTUPPY	TORTUOUS
TENTIEST	THERIACA	THWARTER	TITULARY	TORTURER
TENTLESS	THERMION	*THWARTLY	*TOADFISH	TOTALISE
TENTLIKE	THERMITE	*THYMIEST	*TOADFLAX	TOTALISM
TEOCALLI	THEROPOD	*THYREOID	TOADLESS	TOTALITY
TEOSINTE	THESAURI	*THYROXIN	TOADLIKE	*TOTALIZE
TEPHRITE	THESPIAN	*TICKLISH	*TOADYISH	TOTALLED
TEPIDITY	THETICAL	*TICKSEED	TOADYISM	TOTEMISM
TERATISM	THEWLESS	*TICKTACK	TOBOGGAN	TOTEMIST
TERATOMA	THIAMINE	*TICKTOCK	TOCOLOGY	TOTEMITE
TERCELET	*THIAZIDE	TIDELAND	TOEPIECE	TOTTERER
TEREBENE	*THIAZINE	TIDELESS	TOEPLATE	TOUGHIES
*TERIYAKI	*THIAZOLE	TIDELIKE	TOGETHER	*TOUGHISH
TERMINAL	*THICKISH	*TIDEMARK	TOILETRY	*TOVARICH
TERMINUS	*THICKSET	TIDINESS	TOILETTE	TOVARISH
TERMLESS	*THIEVERY	TIDYTIPS	TOILSOME	*TOWARDLY
TERMTIME	*THIEVING	TIECLASP	TOILWORN	TOWELING
TERPINOL	*THIEVISH	TIGEREYE	TOKENISM	*TOWNFOLK
TERRAPIN	THINCLAD	TIGERISH	*TOKOLOGY	TOWNLESS
TERRARIA	*THINDOWN	*TIGHTWAD	TOKONOMA	*TOWNSHIP

TOWNSMAN	TREELIKE	TRIPPING	TUBEROID	TWINNING
TOWNWEAR	TREENAIL	TRIPTANE	TUBEROSE	*TWINSHIP
*TOXAEMIA	TREMBLER	*TRIPTYCA	TUBEROUS	TWISTING
*TOXICANT	TRENCHER	*TRIPTYCH	*TUBEWORK	*TWITCHER
*TOXICITY	TREPHINE	TRISCELE	*TUBIFORM	TWITTERY
TRABEATE	TRESPASS	TRISKELE	TUBULATE	TWITTING
TRACHEID	TRESSIER	TRISOMIC	TUBULOSE	*TWOPENCE
*TRACHOMA	TRESSOUR	TRISTATE	TUBULOUS	*TWOPENNY
*TRACHYTE	TRESSURE	*TRISTEZA	TUBULURE	*TYMPANAL
*TRACKAGE	TRIADISM	TRISTFUL	*TUCKAHOE	*TYMPANIC
*TRACKING	TRIANGLE	TRISTICH	TULLIBEE	*TYMPANUM
*TRACKMAN	*TRIARCHY	TRITHING	TUMBLING	*TYPECASE
TRACTATE	*TRIAXIAL	TRITICUM	TUMIDITY	*TYPECAST
TRACTILE	*TRIAZINE	TRIUMVIR	TUMPLINE	*TYPEFACE
TRACTION	*TRIAZOLE	TRIUNITY	TUMULOSE	*TYPIFIER
TRADITOR	TRIBASIC	TRIVALVE	TUMULOUS	*TYPOLOGY
TRADUCER	*TRIBRACH	*TROCHAIC	TUNEABLE	TYRAMINE
TRAGICAL	TRIBUNAL	TROCHILI	TUNELESS	TYRANNIC
TRAGOPAN	TRICHINA	TROCHLEA	TUNGSTEN	TYROSINE
TRAINFUL	TRICHITE	TROCHOID	TUNICATE	*TZAREVNA
TRAINING	TRICHOID	TROILITE	TUNNELER	*TZARITZA
TRAINMAN	*TRICHOME	TROLLIED	TUPPENCE	*TZITZITH
TRAINWAY	*TRICKERY	TROLLIES	*TUPPENNY	
TRAMLESS	TRICKIER	TROLLING	TURBINAL	
TRAMLINE	*TRICKILY	TROMBONE	TURBOCAR	S T AB
TRAMMING	*TRICKISH	TROOPIAL	TURBOFAN	S T AG
*TRAMPISH	TRICOLOR	TROTLINE	*TURBOJET	S T AR
TRAMPLER	TRICORNE	TROTTING	TURFIEST	S T AW
TRAMROAD	TRICTRAC	TROUBLER	TURFLESS	S T AY
*TRANQUIL	*TRICYCLE	TROUPIAL	*TURFLIKE	S T EM
TRANSACT	TRIENNIA	TROUPING	TURGENCY	S T EP
TRANSECT	TRIETHYL	TROUSERS	TURMERIC	S T ET
TRANSEPT	TRIFLING	TROUVERE	TURNCOAT	S T EW
TRANSFER	TRIFOCAL	TROUVEUR	TURNDOWN	S T EY
*TRANSFIX	TRIFORIA	TROWELER	TURNHALL	S T IR
TRANSHIP	TRIGGEST	TROWSERS	TURNOVER	S T OA
TRANSMIT	TRIGGING	TRUANTRY	TURNPIKE	S T OB
TRANSUDE	*TRIGLYPH	*TRUCKAGE	TURNSOLE	S T OP
TRAPBALL	TRIGNESS	*TRUCKING	TURNSPIT	S T OW
TRAPDOOR	TRIGONAL	TRUCKLER	*TURQUOIS	S T UB
*TRAPEZIA	TRIGRAPH	*TRUCKMAN	TURRICAL	S T UD
TRAPLIKE	TRIHEDRA	TRUDGEON	TURTLING	S T UM
TRAPNEST	TRILLION	TRUDGING	TUSKLESS	S T UN
TRAPPEAN	TRILLIUM	TRUEBLUE	*TUSKLIKE	S T YE
TRAPPING	TRILOBAL	TRUEBORN	TUTELAGE	BI T ER
TRAPPOSE	TRILOBED	TRUELOVE	TUTELARY	**S T ACK**
TRAPPOUS	TRIMARAN	TRUENESS	TUTORAGE	S T ADE
*TRAPROCK	TRIMETER	*TRUMPERY	TUTORESS	**S T AFF**
TRAPUNTO	TRIMMEST	TRUNCATE	TUTORIAL	S T AGE
TRASHMAN	TRIMMING	TRUNDLER	TWADDLER	S T AGY
TRAUCHLE	TRIMNESS	TRUNNION	TWANGIER	S T AID
TRAVELER	*TRIMORPH	TRUSSING	TWANGLER	S T AIG
TRAVELOG	TRIMOTOR	TRUSTFUL	*TWELVEMO	S T AIN
TRAVERSE	TRINKUMS	TRUTHFUL	TWIDDLER	S T AIR
TRAVESTY	TRINODAL	*TRYINGLY	TWIGLESS	S T AKE
TRAVOISE	*TRIOXIDE	*TRYWORKS	*TWIGLIKE	S T ALE
TREADLER	TRIPEDAL	TSAREVNA	*TWILIGHT	S T ALK
TREASURE	TRIPHASE	*TSARITZA	TWILLING	S T ALL
TREASURY	TRIPLANE	TUBBABLE	TWINBORN	S T AMP
TREATISE	TRIPLING	TUBELESS	TWINIEST	S T AND
TRECENTO	TRIPLITE	TUBELIKE	*TWINIGHT	S T ANE
TREELESS	TRIPLOID	TUBERCLE	*TWINKLER	S T ANG

S T ANK	S T OVE	BU T ENE	DO T IER	**KI T IES**
S T APH	**S T OWP**	BU T LER	DO T ING	**KI T ING**
S T ARE	S T RAP	BU T TER	DO T TED	***KI T SCH**
S T ARK	S T RAW	BU T TON	DO T TEL	**KI T TED**
S T ART	S T RAY	***BY T ALK**	DO T TER	**KI T TEL**
S T ASH	S T REP	***CA T CHY**	DO T TLE	**KI T TEN**
S T ATE	S T REW	CA T ENA	FA T HER	**KI T TLE**
S T AVE	S T RIA	CA T GUT	FA T HOM	**KI T TLE**
S T EAD	S T RIP	CA T ION	FA T ING	LA T EEN
S T EAK	S T ROP	**CA T ISH**	FA T TED	LA T ELY
S T EAL	S T ROW	**CA T KIN**	FA T TEN	LA T ENT
S T EAM	S T ROY	CA T LIN	FA T TER	LA T EST
S T EED	S T RUM	**CA T NAP**	FE T IAL	LA T HER
S T EEK	S T RUT	**CA T NIP**	FE T ICH	LA T IGO
S T EEL	**S T UCK**	**CA T SUP**	FE T ING	LA T ISH
S T EEP	S T UDY	CA T TED	FE T ISH	LA T RIA
S T EER	**S T UFF**	CA T TIE	FE T TED	LA T TEN
S T EIN	S T ULL	CA T TLE	FE T TER	LA T TER
S T ELA	S T UMP	CE T ANE	FE T TLE	LA T TIN
S T ELE	S T UNG	**CI T HER**	***FI T CHY**	LE T HAL
S T ENO	S T UNK	CI T IED	**FI T FUL**	LE T TED
S T ERE	S T UNT	CI T IES	**FI T TED**	LE T TER
S T ERN	S T UPA	**CI T IFY**	FI T TER	**LI T ANY**
S T ICH	S T UPE	CI T ING	**LI T CHI**
S T ICK	S T URT	CI T OLA	**LI T ERY**
S T IED	S T YLE	CI T OLE	LI T HIA
S T IES	S T YLI	CI T RAL	**LI T HIC**
S T IFF	**S T YMY**	CI T RIC	LI T MUS
S T ILE	**BA T BOY**	CI T RIN	GI T ANO	LI T TEN
S T ILL	**BA T EAU**	CI T RON	GO T TEN	LI T TER
S T ILT	**BA T HER**	CI T RUS	GU T TED	LI T TLE
S T IME	**BA T HOS**	CO T EAU	GU T TER	LI T TLE
S T IMY	BA T ING	CO T ING	GU T TLE	LO T ION
S T ING	**BA T MAN**	CO T TAR	***HA T BOX**	LO T TED
S T INK	BA T TED	CO T TER	**HA T FUL**	LU T EAL
S T IPE	BA T TEN	CO T TON	**HA T ING**	LU T EIN
S T IRK	BA T TER	**CO T YPE**	**HA T ING**	LU T EUM
S T IRP	**BA T TIK**	**CU T EST**	**HA T PIN**	LU T ING
S T OAT	BA T TLE	**CU T ESY**	**HA T RED**	LU T IST
S T OCK	BA T TUE	CU T LAS	**HA T TED**	MA T RES
S T OGY	**BE T AKE**	CU T LER	HA T TER	***MA T RIX**
S T OIC	**BE T HEL**	CU T LET	HE T ERO	MA T RON
S T OKE	BE T IDE	**CU T OFF**	**HI T HER**	MA T TED
S T OLE	**BE T IME**	CU T OUT	HO T BED	MA T TER
S T OMA	BE T ISE	CU T TER	***HO T BOX**	MA T TIN
S T OMP	**BE T ONY**	CU T TLE	HO T DOG	MA T URE
S T ONE	**BE T OOK**	**DA T ARY**	HO T ROD	***MA T ZAH**
S T ONY	**BE T RAY**	**DA T CHA**	HO T TED	***MA T ZOH**
S T OOD	BE T TED	DA T ING	HO T TER	***MA T ZOT**
S T OOK	BE T TER	**DA T IVE**	HU T TED	ME T AGE
S T OOL	BE T TOR	DA T URA	***HU T ZPA**	ME T ATE
S T OOP	***BI T CHY**	**DE T ACH**	***JE T SAM**	ME T EOR
S T OPE	BI T TED	DE T AIL	***JE T SOM**	ME T IER
S T OPT	BI T TEN	DE T AIN	**JE T TED**	ME T ING
S T ORE	BI T TER	DE T ECT	**JE T TON**	ME T TLE
S T ORK	**BO T ANY**	DE T ENT	***JI T NEY**	MI T IER
S T ORM	***BO T CHY**	DE T EST	JI T TER	MI T RAL
S T ORY	**BO T FLY**	**DE T ICK**	KA T ION	MI T TEN
S T OSS	**BO T HER**	DE T OUR	KE T ENE	MO T ILE
S T OUP	BO T TLE	**DI T HER**	KE T ONE	MO T ION
S T OUR	**BO T TOM**	DO T AGE	KE T OSE	MO T TLE
S T OUT	BU T ANE	DO T ARD	**KE T TLE**	MU T ANT

MU T ASE	PI T IED	RE T RIM	TO T ING	**BI T TING**
MU T ATE	PI T IER	RE T TED	TO T TED	*BI T TOCK
MU T EST	PI T IES	RE T UNE	TO T TER	BI T UMEN
MU T INE	**PI T MAN**	RE T URN	TU T TED	BO T ANIC
MU T ING	**PI T SAW**	RE T USE	VA T FUL	BO T CHER
MU T TER	PI T TED	**RE T YPE**	VA T TED	BO T ONEE
MU T TON	PO T AGE	RI T ARD	VE T OER	BO T TLER
MU T UAL	**PO T AGE**	RI T TER	**VE T TED**	BO T ULIN
MU T UEL	**PO T ASH**	RI T UAL	VI T ALS	BU T ANOL
MU T ULE	PO T ATO	RO T ARY	**VI T RIC**	**BU T CHER**
*MY T HIC	**PO T BOY**	**RO T CHE**	VI T TLE	**BU T LERY**
NA T ANT	PO T EEN	RO T GUT	**VO T ARY**	BU T TALS
NA T ION	**PO T FUL**	RO T TED	**VO T ING**	**BU T TERY**
NA T IVE	**PO T HER**	RO T TEN	VO T IVE	BU T TIES
NA T RON	PO T ION	RO T TER	WA T APE	*BU T TOCK
NA T TER	**PO T MAN**	RO T UND	**WA T ERY**	**BU T TONY**
NA T URE	**PO T PIE**	RU T ILE	WA T TER	**BU T YRAL**
NE T HER	PO T SIE	RU T TED	WA T TLE	**BU T YRIC**
NE T TED	PO T TED	SA T ANG	**WE T HER**	**BU T YRIN**
NE T TER	PO T TER	SA T ARA	**WE T TED**	*BU T YRYL
NE T TLE	PO T TLE	SA T EEN	WE T TER	**CA T ALOG**
NE T TLY	PU T LOG	SA T ING	*WI T CHY	**CA T ALPA**
NI T RIC	**PU T OFF**	SA T INY	**WI T HAL**	**CA T ARRH**
NI T RID	PU T OUT	SA T IRE	**WI T HER**	**CA T BIRD**
NI T RIL	PU T RID	SA T ORI	WI T HIN	**CA T BOAT**
NI T WIT	**PU T SCH**	SA T RAP	**WI T ING**	**CA T CALL**
NO T ARY	PU T TEE	**SE T OFF**	**WI T NEY**	**CA T CHER**
NO T ATE	PU T TER	SE T OSE	WI T TED	*CA T CHUP
NO T ICE	**PY T HON**	SE T OUS	WI T TOL	**CA T ECHU**
NO T IFY	RA T ANY	SE T OUT	YT T RIA	CA T ERAN
NO T ING	RA T HER	SE T TEE	*ZI T HER	**CA T ERER**
NO T ION	**RA T IFY**	SE T TER	**BA T CHER**	**CA T FACE**
NU T ANT	RA T INE	SE T TLE	*BA T FISH	**CA T FALL**
NU T ATE	RA T ING	SH T ETL	*BA T FOWL	*CA T FISH
NU T ING	RA T ION	*SH T ICK	*BA T HING	**CA T HEAD**
NU T LET	RA T ITE	SI T ING	**BA T HTUB**	**CA T HECT**
NU T MEG	RA T LIN	SI T TEN	*BA T HYAL	**CA T HODE**
NU T RIA	RA T OON	SI T TER	BA T ISTE	CA T LIKE
NU T TED	RA T TAN	SU T LER	**BA T LIKE**	**CA T LING**
NU T TER	RA T TED	SU T TEE	**BA T SMAN**	**CA T MINT**
PA T ACA	RA T TEN	SU T URE	BA T TEAU	**CA T SPAW**
*PA T CHY	RA T TER	TA T AMI	**BA T TERY**	CA T TAIL
PA T ENT	RA T TER	TA T TED	BA T TIER	CA T TALO
PA T HOS	RA T TLY	TA T TER	**BA T TING**	CA T TALO
PA T INA	RA T TON	TA T TLE	BA T TLER	CA T TIER
PA T INE	RE T AIL	TA T TOO	**BA T WING**	**CA T TILY**
PA T OIS	RE T AIN	TE T ANY	BE T AINE	**CA T TING**
PA T ROL	**RE T AKE**	**TE T CHY**	*BE T AXED	*CA T WALK
PA T RON	RE T ARD	TE T HER	*BE T HANK	CI T ABLE
PA T TED	RE T ELL	TE T RAD	*BE T HINK	CI T ADEL
PA T TEE	RE T ENE	TE T RYL	BE T HORN	CI T HARA
PA T TEN	RE T EST	TE T TER	*BE T HUMP	CI T HERN
PA T TER	RE T IAL	TI T BIT	**BE T IMES**	CI T HREN
PA T TIE	RE T IME	TI T HER	**BE T OKEN**	*CI T IZEN
PE T ARD	RE T INA	TI T IAN	**BE T ROTH**	CI T RATE
PE T ITE	RE T INT	TI T MAN	**BE T TING**	CI T RINE
PE T REL	RE T IRE	TI T TER	**BE T WEEN**	CI T ROUS
PE T ROL	RE T OLD	TI T TIE	*BE T WIXT	CI T TERN
PE T TED	**RE T OOK**	TI T TLE	**BI T ABLE**	CO T ERIE
PE T TER	RE T OOL	TI T TUP	BI T TERN	**CO T HURN**
PE T TLE	RE T ORT	TO T HER	BI T TIER	**CO T IDAL**
*PI T CHY	RE T RAL		BI T TING	**CO T TAGE**

CO T TIER	*FU T HARC	KO T OWER	NI T RITE	PO T TING
CO T TONY	*FU T HARK	LA T AKIA	NI T ROSO	PU T AMEN
*CU T AWAY	*FU T HORC	LA T CHET	NI T ROUS	*PU T REFY
*CU T BACK	*FU T HORK	LA T ENCY	NO T ABLE	PU T TIED
CU T DOWN	*FU T TOCK	LA T ERAD	NO T ABLY	PU T TIER
CU T ICLE	GA T EMAN	LA T ERAL	NO T CHER	PU T TING
CU T LASS	GA T EWAY	LA T HERY	NO T EDLY	RA T ABLE
CU T LERY	GE T AWAY	LA T HIER	NO T HING	RA T AFEE
CU T LINE	GE T TING	LA T HING	NU T GALL	RA T AFIA
CU T OVER	GI T TERN	LA T ICES	NU T LIKE	RA T ATAT
CU T TAGE	GO T HITE	LA T OSOL	NU T MEAT	RA T CHET
CU T TING	GO T THIC	LA T RINE	*NU T PICK	RA T FINK
*CU T WORK	GU T LESS	LA T TICE	NU T WOOD	RA T FISH
CU T WORM	GU T LIKE	LE T DOWN	PA T AMAR	RA T HOLE
DA T ABLE	GU T TATE	LE T TING	PA T CHER	RA T LIKE
DA T EDLY	GU T TERY	LE T TUCE	PA T ELLA	RA T LINE
DE T ENTE	GU T TIER	LI T ERAL	PA T ENCY	RA T TAIL
DE T ERGE	GU T TING	LI T HIUM	*PA T HWAY	RA T TEEN
DE T INUE	GU T TLER	LI T HOID	PA T IENT	RA T TIER
DE T RACT	HAS T ING	LI T ORAL	PA T NESS	RA T TING
DE T RAIN	HA T ABLE	LI T OTES	PA T RIOT	RA T TISH
DE T RUDE	HA T BAND	LI T URGY	PA T ROON	RA T TLER
DI T CHER	*HA T CHEL	LO T TERY	PA T TERN	RA T TOON
DI T HERY	*HA T CHER	LO T TING	PA T TING	RA T TRAP
DI T HIOL	*HA T CHET	LU T EOUS	PE T ASOS	RE T ABLE
DI T TANY	HA T EFUL	LU T HERN	PE T ASUS	RE T AKER
DO T IEST	HA T LESS	MA T INAL	*PE T COCK	RE T ASTE
DO T TIER	HA T LIKE	MA T INEE	PE T IOLE	RE T EACH
DO T TILY	*HA T RACK	MA T LESS	*PE T RIFY	RE T HINK
DO T TING	HA T SFUL	MA T RASS	PE T ROUS	RE T IARY
DO T TREL	HE T AERA	MA T TING	PE T TIER	RE T ICLE
DU T EOUS	HE T AIRA	*MA T TOCK	PE T TILY	RE T INAL
DU T IFUL	*HI T CHER	*MA T ZOON	PE T TING	RE T INOL
FA T ALLY	HI T LESS	*MA T ZOTH	PE T TISH	RE T INUE
*FA T BACK	*HO T CAKE	ME T AMER	PE T UNIA	RE T IREE
FA T BIRD	HO T FOOT	*ME T HOXY	PI T APAT	RE T IRER
FA T EFUL	HO T HEAD	ME T ISSE	PI T CHER	RE T ITLE
FA T HEAD	HO T NESS	*ME T RIFY	PI T EOUS	RE T OUCH
FA T IDIC	HO T SHOT	ME T RIST	PI T FALL	RE T RACE
FA T IGUE	HO T SPUR	MI T ERER	PI T HEAD	RE T RACK
FA T LESS	HO T TEST	MI T ICID	PI T IFUL	RE T RACT
FA T LING	HO T TING	MI T IEST	PI T TING	RE T RAIN
FA T NESS	HO T TISH	MI T OSIS	PO T ABLE	RE T READ
FA T TEST	HU T LIKE	*MI T SVAH	PO T AMIC	RE T REAT
FA T TIER	HU T MENT	*MI T ZVAH	PO T BOIL	RE T RIAL
FA T TIES	HU T TING	*MO T HERY	PO T ENCE	RE T SINA
FA T TILY	*HU T ZPAH	MO T TLER	PO T ENCY	RE T TING
FA T TING	*JE T BEAD	NA T RIUM	PO T HEAD	RE T WIST
FA T TISH	*JE T PORT	NA T URAL	PO T HEEN	RE T YING
FA T UITY	*JE T TIED	NE T LESS	PO T HERB	RO T ATOR
FA T UOUS	JE T TIES	NE T LIKE	PO T HOLE	RO T ATOR
*FE T CHER	*JE T TING	NE T SUKE	*PO T HOOK	RO T IFER
*FE T LOCK	*JI T TERY	NE T TIER	PO T ICHE	RO T TING
FE T TING	*JO T TING	NE T TING	PO T LACH	RO T UNDA
*FI T CHEE	*KA T HODE	NE T TLER	PO T LIKE	RU T HFUL
*FI T CHET	*KA T YDID	NE T WORK	*PO T LUCK	RU T TIER
*FI T CHEW	*KE T CHUP	NI T CHIE	PO T SHOT	RU T TILY
FI T MENT	KE T OSIS	*NI T PICK	PO T TEEN	RU T TING
FI T NESS	*KI T CHEN	NI T RATE	PO T TENT	RU T TISH
FI T TEST	KI T HARA	NI T RIDE	PO T TERY	SA T ANIC
FI T TING	KI T LING	NI T RIFY	PO T TIER	SA T CHEL
	KI T TING	NI T RILE	PO T TIES	SA T IATE

SA T IETY	WA T TEST	BOL T ROPE	CON T INUE	DIS T RAIT
SA T INET	*WE T BACK	*BON T EBOK	CON T INUO	DIS T RESS
SA T ISFY	WE T LAND	*BOO T JACK	CON T RACT	DIS T RICT
SA T RAPY	WE T NESS	BOO T LACE	CON T RAIL	DIS T RUST
SA T YRID	WE T TEST	BOO T LESS	CON T RARY	DOC T ORAL
*SE T BACK	WE T TING	*BOO T LICK	CON T RAST	DOC T RINE
SE T LINE	WE T TISH	BOT T OMER	CON T RITE	DOG T OOTH
SE T TING	WI T HIER	*BOT T OMRY	CON T RIVE	DOT T EREL
SE T TLER	WI T HIES	*BOU T IQUE	COR T ISOL	DOT T IEST
SE T TLOR	WI T HING	*BOX T HORN	COS T LESS	DRU T HERS
SH T ETEL	WI T HOUT	BRA T TICE	*COS T MARY	DUC T LESS
SI T HENS	WI T LESS	BRE T HREN	COS T UMER	DUE T TIST
SI T TING	WI T LING	*BRI T CHES	*COS T UMEY	DUS T HEAP
SI T UATE	WI T LOOF	*BRI T ZSKA	COT T AGER	DUS T IEST
SO T TISH	WI T NESS	BUN T LINE	CRE T ONNE	DUS T LESS
SU T URAL	WI T TIER	BUT T ONER	CRI T ERIA	DUS T LIKE
TA T OUAY	WI T TILY	BUT T RESS	*CRI T IQUE	*DYS T AXIA
TA T TIER	WI T TING	BYS T REET	*CRO T CHET	DYS T OCIA
TA T TING	WO T TETH	*CAL T HROP	CUL T IGEN	DYS T ONIA
TA T TLER	YA T AGAN	CAN T ICLE	CUL T IVAR	DYS T OPIA
TE T ANAL	YT T RIUM	CAN T ONAL	CUL T RATE	FAC T IOUS
TE T ANIC	*ZI T HERN	CAN T RAIP	CUL T URAL	*FAC T OTUM
TE T ANUS	BAC T ERIA	CAP T IOUS	*CUR T ALAX	*FAI T HFUL
TE T CHED	BAC T ERIN	CAP T URER	CUR T NESS	FAL T BOAT
TE T OTUM	BAN T ERER	CAR T LOAD	CUS T ODES	FAL T ERER
TE T RODE	BAN T LING	*CAR T OUCH	CUS T OMER	FAN T ASIA
TI T ANIA	BAP T ISIA	CAS T ANET	CUS T UMAL	FAN T ASIE
TI T ANIC	*BAP T IZER	*CAS T AWAY	CUT T ABLE	FAR T HEST
TI T HING	BAR T ERER	CAS T EISM	CYS T EINE	*FAR T HING
TI T LARK	BAR T ISAN	CAS T RATE	CYS T ITIS	*FAS T BACK
TI T LIST	*BAR T IZAN	CAS T RATO	*DAC T YLIC	FAS T BALL
TI T RANT	BAS T ARDY	CAT T IEST	DAC T YLUS	FAS T ENER
TI T RATE	BAS T ILLE	CAT T LEYA	DAF T NESS	FAS T NESS
TI T TIES	BAT T ALIA	CAU T IOUS	DAL T ONIC	FAS T UOUS
TI T ULAR	BAT T ENER	CEN T AURY	*DEA T HBED	FAT T ENER
TO T ABLE	BAT T ERIE	CEN T ESIS	*DEA T HCUP	FAT T IEST
TO T ALLY	BAT T IEST	CEN T IARE	*DEA T HFUL	*FEA T HERY
TO T TERY	*BEA T IFIC	CEN T RING	DEF T NESS	FES T IVAL
TO T TING	BEA T LESS	CEN T RISM	DEN T ALIA	FET T ERER
TROCHAR	BEE T ROOT	CEN T RIST	DEN T ATED	FET T LING
TU T ELAR	BEL T LESS	CEN T ROID	DEN T ICLE	FIL T ERER
TU T OYER	BEL T LINE	CEN T UPLE	DES T RIER	FIL T RATE
TU T TING	BEN T WOOD	CHA T TING	DES T RUCT	FIS T NOTE
VA T ICAL	BES T IARY	*CHI T CHAT	DEU T ERIC	FIT T ABLE
VA T TING	BES T OWAL	CHI T LING	DEU T ERON	FLA T BOAT
VE T ERAN	BES T RIDE	*CHU T ZPAH	*DEX T RINE	*FLA T FISH
VE T IVER	BIA T HLON	CIS T ERNA	*DEX T ROSE	FLA T FOOT
VE T TING	BIO T ICAL	CLA T TERY	*DEX T ROUS	FLA T FOOT
VI T ALLY	*BIR T HDAY	CLI T ELLA	DIA T OMIC	*FLA T HEAD
VI T AMER	BIS T OURY	CLI T ORIS	DIA T ONIC	FLA T IRON
VI T AMIN	BIT T IEST	CLO T HIER	DIA T RIBE	FLA T LAND
VI T ESSE	*BLA T ANCY	CLO T HING	DIC T ATOR	FLA T LING
VI T IATE	BLA T TING	CLO T TING	DIE T ETIC	FLA T NESS
*VI T RIFY	BLO T LESS	COA T LESS	DIP T ERAL	FLA T TERY
VI T RINE	BLO T TIER	*COA T RACK	DIP T ERAN	FLA T TEST
VI T RIOL	BLO T TING	COA T ROOM	DIP T ERON	FLA T TING
VO T ABLE	BOA T BILL	COA T TAIL	DIS T ANCE	FLA T TISH
VO T RESS	BOA T LOAD	COA T TEND	DIS T ASTE	FLA T WARE
*WA T CHER	BOA T SMAN	COA T TEST	DIS T AVES	*FLA T WASH
WA T ERER	BOA T YARD	CON T AGIA	DIS T INCT	*FLA T WAYS
WA T TAGE	BOL T HEAD	CON T EMPT	DIS T RACT	FLA T WISE
WA T TAPE	BOL T ONIA	CON T INUA	DIS T RAIN	*FLA T WORK

*FLA T WORM	GOA T HERD	LOA T HFUL	*MYS T AGOG	PET T IFOG
*FLE T CHER	GOA T LIKE	LOA T HING	*MYS T ICAL	PEW T ERER
FLU T IEST	GOA T SKIN	LOF T LESS	*MYS T ICLY	*PHO T OMAP
FLU T TERY	GOE T HITE	LOI T ERER	*MYS T IQUE	*PHO T OPIA
FON T ANEL	GRA T EFUL	LOS T NESS	NAE T HING	PHO T OSET
FOO T BALL	GRA T UITY	LUS T IEST	NAU T ICAL	*PIN T SIZE
*FOO T BATH	GUS T ABLE	LUS T IER	NAU T ILUS	*PIS T ACHE
FOO T FALL	GUS T IEST	LUS T RING	NEA T HERD	PIT T ANCE
FOO T GEAR	GUS T LESS	LUS T ROUS	NEA T NESS	PLA T EFUL
FOO T HILL	GUT T ATED	*MAR T YRLY	NEO T ERIC	PLA T ELET
*FOO T HOLD	GUT T IEST	*MAS T ABAH	NES T LIKE	*PLA T FORM
FOO T IEST	GUT T URAL	*MAS T ICHE	NES T LING	PLA T IEST
FOO T LESS	*HAF T ARAH	MA T ELESS	NET T ABLE	PLA T INIC
*FOO T LIKE	*HAF T ORAH	*MA T ELOTE	NET T IEST	PLA T INUM
FOO T LING	*HAP T ICAL	MA T ERIAL	NEU T RINO	PLA T ONIC
*FOO T MARK	HAS T EFUL	MA T ERIEL	*NEX T DOOR	PLA T TING
FOO T NOTE	HAS T ENER	MA T ERNAL	NOC T URNE	*PLA T YPUS
*FOO T PACE	HAT T ERIA	MA T INESS	NON T IDAL	PLE T HORA
*FOO T PATH	HAU T BOIS	MA T TEDLY	NON T ITLE	PLO T LESS
FOO T RACE	*HAW T HORN	MA T TRASS	*NON T OXIC	PLO T TAGE
FOO T REST	*HEA T EDLY	MA T TRESS	NON T RUMP	PLO T TIER
FOO T ROPE	HEA T LESS	MA T URATE	NON T RUTH	PLO T TIES
FOO T SLOG	*HEC T ICAL	MA T URITY	NOR T HERN	PLO T TING
FOO T SORE	HEP T AGON	ME T ALISE	NOR T HING	POE T ICAL
FOO T STEP	*HEP T ARCH	ME T ALIST	NOT T URNO	POE T ISER
FOO T WALL	HIL T LESS	ME T ALLED	NUR T URER	*POE T IZER
FOO T WEAR	HIS T AMIN	ME T ALLIC	PAL T ERER	POE T LESS
*FOO T WORK	HIS T IDIN	ME T ERAGE	PAN T HEON	POE T LIKE
FOO T WORN	HIS T OGEN	ME T HADON	PAN T OFLE	POL T ROON
FOR T IETH	HIS T ORIC	ME T HANOL	PAN T SUIT	*PON T IFEX
FOR T RESS	HUR T LESS	ME T RICAL	PAR T AKER	*PON T IFIC
FOR T UITY	HUS T INGS	ME T RITIS	PAR T ERRE	POR T ABLE
FOS T ERER	HYS T ERIA	*MIS T EACH	PAR T IBLE	*POR T ABLY
FRE T LESS	*HYS T ERIC	*MIS T HINK	PAR T ICLE	POR T ANCE
FRE T SOME	*JET T ISON	*MIS T HROW	PAR T ISAN	POR T HOLE
FRE T TING	*JUS T NESS	*MIS T OUCH	*PAR T IZAN	POR T IERE
*FRE T WORK	KNI T TING	MI T IGATE	PAS T ICCI	POR T LESS
FRI T TING	*KNI T WEAR	MI T TIMUS	*PAS T ICHE	POR T RAIT
FRO T TAGE	*KNO T HOLE	MO T ILITY	PAS T IEST	POR T RESS
FRO T TEUR	KNO T LESS	MO T IONAL	PAS T ILLE	POS T ALLY
FUR T HEST	*KNO T LIKE	MO T IONER	PAS T NESS	POS T ANAL
GAN T LINE	*KNO T WEED	MO T IVATE	PAS T ORAL	POS T CARD
GAN T LOPE	*KOW T OWER	MO T ORBUS	PAS T RAMI	*POS T CAVA
GAS T IGHT	KUR T OSIS	MO T ORCAR	PAS T ROMI	*POS T DATE
GAS T NESS	LAC T EOUS	MO T ORING	PAS T URAL	*POS T FACE
GAS T RAEA	LAI T ANCE	MO T ORISE	PAS T URER	*POS T FORM
GAS T RULA	LAN T HORN	MO T ORIST	PAT T AMAR	POS T HOLE
GEN T RICE	LAT T ERLY	MO T ORMAN	PAT T ERER	*POS T ICHE
*GEO T AXIS	LEA T HERN	*MOU T HFUL	*PAT T YPAN	*POS T IQUE
GES T ICAL	LEA T HERY	*MUL T IJET	PEC T ORAL	POS T LUDE
GES T URAL	LEC T URER	*MUL T IPLY	PEE T WEET	*POS T MARK
*GIF T EDLY	LEF T OVER	*MUS T ACHE	PEN T ACLE	POS T ORAL
GIF T LESS	*LEF T WARD	MU T ATION	PEN T AGON	POS T PAID
GIL T HEAD	*LEF T WING	MU T ENESS	*PEN T ARCH	POS T PONE
GLI T TERY	LET T ERER	MU T ICOUS	PEN T OMIC	POS T URAL
GLU T ELIN	LIN T IEST	MU T ILATE	PEN T OSAN	POS T URER
GLU T TING	LIN T LESS	MU T INEER	*PEP T IZER	POT T ERER
GLU T TONY	LIS T ENER	MU T INIED	PER T NESS	POT T IEST
GNA T HION	LIS T LESS	MU T INIES	PES T ERER	PRA T FALL
GNA T HITE	LIT T ERER	MU T INING	PES T HOLE	*PRA T IQUE
GNA T LIKE	LIT T LISH	MU T INOUS	PET T EDLY	PRA T TLER
*GOA T FISH	LIT T ORAL	MU T TERER	PET T IEST	PRE T ASTE

PRE T ENCE	SAL T IEST	SOF T ENER	TEE T OTAL	WAN T ONLY	
PRE T ENSE	SAL T LESS	*SOF T HEAD	TEE T OTUM	WAR T IEST	
PRE T ERIT	SAL T LIKE	SOF T NESS	TEN T ACLE	*WAR T LIKE	
PRE T REAT	SAL T NESS	SOF T WARE	TEN T IEST	WAS T ABLE	
PRE T TIED	*SAL T WORK	*SOF T WOOD	TEN T LESS	WAS T EFUL	
PRE T TIER	SAL T WORT	SOO T HEST	TEN T LIKE	WAS T ELOT	
PRE T TIES	SAN T ALIC	SOO T HING	TER T IARY	WAS T ERIE	
*PRE T TIFY	SAN T ONIN	SOO T HSAY	TES T ATOR	*WAS T EWAY	
PRO T AMIN	SAR T ORII	SOU T ACHE	TES T ICLE	WAT T HOUR	
PRO T ASIS	SAS T RUGA	SOU T HERN	TES T IEST	WAT T LESS	
PRO T EASE	SAU T ERNE	SOU T HING	*TEX T BOOK	*WEF T WISE	
PRO T EGEE	SAU T OIRE	*SOU T HPAW	*TEX T LESS	WES T ERLY	
PRO T EIDE	SAW T OOTH	SOU T HRON	*TEX T UARY	WES T MOST	
PRO T EOSE	*SCA T BACK	SPA T TING	*TEX T URAL	*WES T WARD	
PRO T OCOL	SCA T TING	SPI T BALL	*THA T AWAY	WET T ABLE	
PRO T OPOD	SCO T OPIA	SPI T EFUL	*THA T CHER	*WHA T EVER	
*PRO T OXID	*SCU T CHER	SPI T FIRE	THE T ICAL	*WHE T TING	
*PRO T OZOA	SCU T ELLA	SPI T TING	TIL T YARD	*WHI T ECAP	
PRO T RACT	SEA T LESS	SPI T TOON	TIN T LESS	*WHI T EFLY	
PRO T RUDE	SEA T MATE	SPO T LESS	TIT T ERER	WHI T ENER	
PUT T ERER	SEA T RAIN	SPO T TING	*TIT T UPPY	WHI T EOUT	
*QUA T ORZE	*SEA T WORK	STA T ABLE	TOR T ILLA	*WHI T RACK	
*QUA T RAIN	SEC T ORAL	STA T EDLY	TOR T IOUS	WHI T TLER	
*QUI T RENT	SEN T ENCE	STA T UARY	TOR T OISE	WHI T TRET	
*QUI T TING	SEN T IENT	STI T CHER	TOR T UOUS	*WID T HWAY	
*QUO T IENT	SEN T INEL	STO T INKA	TOR T URER	WIN T ERER	
RAF T SMAN	SEP T ARIA	SUB T ILTY	TOT T ERER	WIN T ERLY	
RAP T NESS	SEP T ETTE	SUB T ITLE	TRI T HING	WIS T ARIA	
RAT T ENER	SEP T UPLE	SUB T LETY	TRI T ICUM	WIS T ERIA	
RAT T IEST	SES T ERCE	SUB T ONIC	TRO T LINE	WIT T IEST	
RAT T LING	SET T LING	SUB T OPIC	TRO T TING	*WON T EDLY	
REA T TACH	*SEX T ARII	SUB T OTAL	TRU T HFUL	*WOR T HFUL	
REA T TACK	*SEX T ETTE	SUB T RACT	TUR T LING	WOS T TETH	
REA T TAIN	*SEX T UPLE	SUB T RIBE	*TWI T CHER	*WRA T HFUL	
RES T LESS	*SEX T UPLY	SUB T UNIC	TWI T TERY	*WRE T CHED	
RES T ORAL	SHE T LAND	SUI T ABLE	TWI T TING	*WRI T HING	
RES T ORER	SHI T TING	SUI T CASE	*TZI T ZITH	*WRO T HFUL	
RES T RAIN	SHO T TING	SUI T LIKE	VAS T IEST	*XAN T HATE	
RES T RICT	*SHU T DOWN	SWA T TING	VAS T NESS	*XAN T HEIN	
RES T RIKE	SHU T TING	*SWI T CHER	VEN T LESS	*XAN T HENE	
RES T RING	SIS T ERLY	*SYS T EMIC	VEN T URER	*XAN T HINE	
RES T RIVE	SIS T ROID	TAC T LESS	VER T EBRA	*XAN T HOMA	
RES T RUCK	*SIX T IETH	TANGENCE	VER T ICAL	*XAN T HONE	
RES T RUNG	*SKE T CHER	TANGENCY	VER T ICIL	*XAN T HOUS	
RHE T ORIC	*SKI T TERY	TANGIBLE	VES T ALLY	YES T REEN	
*RHY T HMIC	*SKI T TISH	TANGIBLY	VES T IARY	*YOU T HFUL	
RIF T LESS	SLA T IEST	TANGIEST	VES T IGIA	*ZAS T RUGA	
ROO T HOLD	SLA T TERN	*TANKSHIP	VES T LESS		
ROO T IEST	SLA T TING	TANTALUM	VES T MENT		
ROO T LESS	SLI T HERY	TANTALUS	VES T URAL	BAH T	
ROO T LIKE	SLI T LESS	TARLATAN	VIA T ICAL	BAI T	
ROS T ELLA	SLI T TING	TAR T NESS	*VIA T ICUM	BAS T	
ROS T RATE	*SLO T BACK	TAR T RATE	VIC T ORIA	BAT T	
ROU T EMAN	SLO T HFUL	TAS T EFUL	VIC T RESS	BEA T	
ROU T EWAY	SLO T TING	TAT T IEST	VIN T AGER	BEE T	
RUC T IOUS	*SMI T HERY	TAT T OOER	VIR T UOSA	BEL T	
RUS T ICLY	*SMO T HERY	TAU T NESS	VIR T UOSO	BEN T	
RUS T IEST	SMU T TING	TAU T OMER	VIR T UOUS	BES T	
RUS T LESS	SNA T CHER	TAU T ONYM	VOL T AISM	BHU T	
RUS T LING	SNI T CHER	TEC T ONIC	WAI T RESS	BIN T	
RUT T IEST	*SOF T BACK	TEE T HING	WAN T ONER	BIT T	
SAL T BUSH	SOF T BALL				BLA T

BLE T	FOO T	LIS T	RES T	TUF T
BLO T	FOR T	LOF T	RIF T	TWA T
BOA T	FRA T	LOO T	RIO T	TWI T
BOL T	FRE T	LOS T	ROO T	VAS T
BOO T	FRI T	LOU T	ROU T	VEN T
BOR T	GAI T	LUN T	RUN T	VER T
BOT T	GAS T	LUS T	RUS T	VES T
BOU T	GEL T	MAL T	RYO T	**VEX T**
BRA T	GEN T	MAR T	SAL T	VOL T
BRI T	GES T	MAS T	SCA T	**WAF T**
BRU T	GHA T	MAT T	SCO T	WAI T
BUN T	GIF T	MAU T	SCU T	WAN T
BUS T	GIL T	MEA T	SEA T	WAR T
BUT T	GIR T	MEE T	SEC T	WAS T
CAN T	GIS T	MEL T	SEN T	WAT T
CAR T	GLU T	MIL T	SEP T	WEE T
CAS T	GNA T	MIN T	**SEX T**	**WEF T**
CEL T	GOA T	MIS T	SHA T	WEL T
CEN T	GOU T	MIT T	SHI T	WEN T
CHA T	GRA T	**MIX T**	SHO T	WEP T
CHI T	GRI T	MOA T	SHU T	WER T
CIS T	GRO T	MOL T	SIF T	WES T
CLO T	GUS T	MOO T	SIL T	**WHA T**
COA T	HAE T	MOR T	SKA T	**WHE T**
COF T	**HAF T**	MOS T	SKI T	**WHI T**
COL T	HAL T	MOT T	SLA T	WIL T
COO T	HAN T	MUS T	SLI T	WIS T
CUL T	HAR T	MUT T	SLO T	WON T
CUN T	HAS T	NEA T	SLU T	WOR T
CUR T	HEA T	NES T	SMU T	WOS T
CYS T	**HEF T**	NET T	SNI T	WRI T
DAF T	HEN T	NEW T	SNO T	**XYS T**
DAR T	HES T	**NEX T**	SOF T	YET T
DAU T	HIL T	NOW T	SOO T	YUR T
DAW T	HIS T	PAC T	SOR T	**ZES T**
DEB T	HOL T	PAN T	SPA T	BEAS T
DEF T	HOO T	PAR T	SPI T	BEAU T
DEN T	HOS T	PAS T	SPO T	**BEFI T**
DIE T	HUN T	PEA T	STE T	BEGE T
DIN T	HUR T	PEL T	SUE T	BEGO T
DIP T	**JES T**	PEN T	SUI T	BERE T
DIR T	**JIL T**	PER T	SWA T	BESE T
DOA T	**JOL T**	PES T	SWO T	BESO T
DOI T	**JUS T**	PHA T	TAC T	**BHOO T**
DOL T	KAR T	PHO T	TAR T	BIDE T
DOS T	KEE T	PIN T	TAR T	**BIGH T**
DRA T	KEN T	PLA T	TAU T	BIGO T
DUC T	**KEP T**	PLO T	TEA T	BINI T
DUE T	**KHA T**	POE T	TEN T	BION T
DUI T	KIL T	POR T	TES T	BLAS T
DUN T	KIS T	POS T	**TEX T**	BLEA T
FAC T	KNI T	POU T	THA T	BLEN T
FAR T	KNO T	PRA T	TIL T	BLES T
FAS T	**KYA T**	PSS T	TIN T	BLOA T
FEA T	LAS T	PUN T	TOF T	BLUE T
FEE T	LEE T	PUT T	TOI T	BLUN T
FEL T	LEF T	**QUI T**	TOO T	BLUR T
FIA T	LEN T	RAF T	TOR T	BOAR T
FIS T	LES T	RAN T	TOS T	BOAS T
FIX T	LIF T	RAP T	TOU T	BOOS T
FLA T	LIL T	REF T	TRE T	BRAC T
FON T	LIN T	REN T	TRO T	BRAN T

BREN T	DIGI T	GUYO T	PLEA T	SLEE T
BRIT T	DIVO T	**HABI T**	POIN T	SLEP T
BRUI T	**DIXI T**	HADS T	POSI T	SLIP T
BRUN T	DOES T	HAUN T	POUL T	SMAL T
BUIL T	DONU T	HEAR T	PRES T	SMAR T
BURE T	DRAF T	HEIS T	PRIN T	SMEL T
BURN T	DRES T	HELO T	PROS T	SMOL T
BURS T	DRIF T	**HIGH T**	**QUAN T**	SNOO T
BUTU T	DRIP T	HOIS T	**QUAR T**	SNOR T
CADE T	DROI T	HORS T	**QUES T**	SNOU T
CANS T	DROP T	**JABO T**	**QUIE T**	SPAI T
CAPU T	DURS T	**JAUN T**	**QUIL T**	SPEL T
CARA T	DWEL T	**JOIN T**	**QUIN T**	SPEN T
CARE T	**FACE T**	**JOIS T**	**QUIR T**	SPIL T
CHAN T	FAGO T	**JOUS T**	**QUOI T**	SPIR T
CHAP T	FAIN T	**JURA T**	RAME T	SPLA T
CHEA T	FAUL T	**KAPU T**	REAC T	SPLI T
CHER T	FEAS T	KARA T	REBU T	SPOR T
CHES T	FEIN T	KARS T	RECU T	SPOU T
CHOT T	FEIS T	**KEMP T**	REES T	SPRA T
CIVE T	**FIGH T**	KNEL T	REFI T	SPRI T
CLAS T	FILE T	KNOU T	RELE T	SPUR T
CLEA T	FIRS T	**KRAF T**	RELI T	**SQUA T**
CLEF T	FLEE T	KRAI T	REME T	STAR T
CLIF T	FLIN T	KRAU T	REMI T	STIL T
CLIP T	FLOU T	LEAN T	RESE T	STIN T
CLOO T	**FLUY T**	LEAP T	REVE T	STOA T
CLOU T	FOIS T	LEAS T	RIAN T	STOP T
COAC T	FOUN T	LEGI T	RIGH T	STOU T
COAP T	FRIT T	**LICH T**	RIVE T	STRU T
COAS T	FRON T	LICI T	ROAS T	STUN T
COME T	FROS T	LIGH T	ROBO T	STUR T
COMP T	FRUI T	LIMI T	ROOS T	SUIN T
COOP T	**FUME T**	LUNE T	ROSE T	SWAR T
COSE T	GAMU T	LYAR T	ROUS T	SWEA T
COUN T	GAUL T	MAGO T	SABO T	SWEE T
COUR T	GAUN T	MAIS T	SAIN T	**SWEP T**
COVE T	GAVO T	**MAYS T**	SAUL T	**SWIF T**
CRAF T	GEES T	MEAN T	SAYS T	TACE T
CREP T	GEMO T	MERI T	SCAN T	TACI T
CRES T	GENE T	MIDS T	SCAR T	TAIN T
CROF T	GHAS T	**MIGH T**	SCAT T	TARO T
CRUE T	GHAU T	MOIS T	SCEN T	TAUN T
CRUS T	GHOS T	MOTE T	SCOO T	TEMP T
CRYP T	GIAN T	MOUL T	SCOU T	TENE T
CUBI T	GIGO T	MOUN T	**SHAF T**	**THEF T**
CULE T	GLEE T	MULC T	SHAL T	TIGH T
CURE T	GLIN T	NEIS T	SHEE T	TINC T
CURS T	GLOA T	NIGH T	**SHIF T**	TOAS T
DAUN T	GLOS T	PAIN T	SHIR T	TRAC T
DAVI T	GLOU T	PALE T	SHIS T	TRAI T
DEAL T	GRAF T	PEAR T	SHOA T	TRAP T
DEBI T	GRAN T	PETI T	SHOO T	TREA T
DEBU T	GREA T	**PEWI T**	SHOR T	TROU T
DEFA T	GREE T	***PHPH T**	SHOT T	TRUS T
DEIS T	GRIF T	PICO T	SHOU T	TRYS T
DEMI T	GRIP T	PILO T	SHUN T	TWEE T
DEPO T	GRIS T	PIPE T	SIGH T	TWIS T
DERA T	GROU T	PIPI T	SKEE T	***TWIX T**
DICO T	**GRUN T**	**PIVO T**	SKIN T	VALE T
DIDS T	GUES T	PLAI T	SKIR T	VAUL T
DIGH T	GUIL T	PLAN T	SLAN T	VAUN T

VELD T	*BYZAN T	DELIC T	GAINS T	LAMEN T
VERS T	CABLE T	DELIS T	GALIO T	LAMES T
VISI T	CACHE T	DEMAS T	GALOO T	LANCE T
VOMI T	CADEN T	DEMEN T	GAMBI T	LAPPE T
WAIS T	CAHOO T	DEPAR T	GAMES T	LARIA T
WECH T	CALLE T	DEPOR T	GANNE T	LATEN T
WEES T	CAMLE T	DESAL T	GARGE T	LATES T
WHEA T	CANNO T	DESER T	GARNE T	LEARN T
WHIP T	CARPE T	DESIS T	GARRE T	LEGIS T
WHIS T	CARRO T	DESPO T	GASKE T	LEVAN T
WHOR T	CASKE T	DETEC T	GASLI T	LIKES T
WIGH T	CATGU T	DETEN T	GELAN T	LIMPE T
WORS T	CAUGH T	DETES T	GEREN T	LINNE T
WRAP T	CAVEA T	DEVES T	GIBBE T	LIVES T
WRES T	CAVOR T	DEVOU T	GIBLE T	LOCKE T
WRIS T	CEMEN T	DICAS T	GIGLE T	LOCUS T
WURS T	CERME T	DIDAC T	GIGLO T	LOMEN T
YACH T	CHALE T	DIGES T	GIMLE T	*LOQUA T
YEAS T	CHALO T	DIGLO T	GOBBE T	LUCEN T
*ZIBE T	CHAUN T	DIKTA T	GOBLE T	LUTIS T
BAGUE T	CLARE T	DIMOU T	GODWI T	LYRIS T
BALLE T	CLIEN T	DIMWI T	GOGLE T	MAGGO T
BALLO T	CLOSE T	*DIQUA T	GORGE T	MAGNE T
BANDI T	COBAL T	DIREC T	GRIVE T	MAHOU T
BANNE T	COBNU T	DIRES T	GUGLE T	MALLE T
BARBE T	COEMP T	DIVER T	GULLE T	MAMME T
BARBU T	COGEN T	DIVES T	GURNE T	MARKE T
BARES T	COHOR T	DOCEN T	GUSSE T	MARMO T
BARRE T	COLLE T	DOCKE T	HAGBU T	MASCO T
BASAL T	COMBA T	DOPAN T	HALES T	*MATZO T
BASES T	COMFI T	DOUGH T	HALLO T	MAUME T
BASKE T	COMMI T	DREAM T	HAMLE T	MAYES T
BASSE T	COPLO T	DRIES T	HARLO T	MIDGE T
BECKE T	*COQUE T	DRYLO T	HASLE T	MIDGU T
BEFRE T	CORNE T	DULCE T	HEIGH T	MILLE T
BEHES T	CORSE T	DYNAS T	HELME T	MINUE T
BEKNO T	CORVE T	FAGGO T	HENBI T	MISAC T
BEMIS T	COSSE T	*FANJE T	HEPCA T	MISCU T
BENNE T	COVER T	FAUCE T	HEREA T	MISEA T
BESMU T	COWPA T	FERRE T	HERIO T	MISFI T
*BEZAN T	CRAVA T	FIDGE T	HERMI T	MISHI T
BILLE T	CREDI T	FILLE T	HOGNU T	MISLI T
BISEC T	CRUSE T	FINES T	HOLIS T	MODES T
BLUES T	CUBIS T	FLAUN T	HONES T	MODIS T
BOBCA T	CULLE T	FLIES T	HORNE T	MOLES T
BONNE T	CUSHA T	FLIGH T	HOWLE T	MOMEN T
BORSH T	CUTES T	FLUEN T	HUGES T	MONGS T
BOSKE T	CUTLE T	FOMEN T	*JACKE T	MONIS T
BOUGH T	CUTOU T	FORES T	JENNE T	MOPPE T
BOWPO T	CYGNE T	FORGA T	JESUI T	MOTMO T
BREAS T	DACOI T	FORGE T	*JUNKE T	MULLE T
BREVE T	DAKOI T	FORGO T	JURAN T	MUSCA T
BRIGH T	DECAN T	FORIN T	JURIS T	MUSKE T
BRULO T	DECEI T	FORMA T	KAINI T	MUSKI T
BRUNE T	DECEN T	FORRI T	KAPUT T	MUTAN T
BUCKE T	DECOC T	FOUGH T	KEYSE T	MUTES T
BUDGE T	DEDUC T	FREES T	KISMA T	MYSOS T
BUFFE T	DEFEA T	FRIGH T	KISME T	NATAN T
BULLE T	DEFEC T	FUNES T	*KLEPH T	NAUGH T
BURBO T	DEGUS T	*FYLFO T	KNIGH T	NIDGE T
BURNE T	DEHOR T	GADGE T	KRUBU T	NITWI T
BYPAS T	*DEJEC T		LABRE T	NOCEN T

NONFA T	*RAMJE T	SACBU T	SUBMI T	VIBIS T
NOUGA T	RAPIS T	**SACHE T**	SUBSE T	VIOLE T
NOUGH T	RARES T	SADIS T	**SUMMI T**	VOLAN T
NUDES T	REBAI T	SAFES T	**SUNKE T**	VOLOS T
NUDIS T	RECAN T	SAGBU T	SUNLI T	**WADSE T**
NUGGE T	RECAS T	SAGES T	SUNSE T	WALLE T
NUTAN T	RECEN T	SALLE T	SURES T	WALNU T
NUTLE T	**RECEP T**	SAMLE T	**SWIVE T**	WAUCH T
PACKE T	REDAC T	SANES T	**SYNDE T**	WAUGH T
PALES T	REDOU T	SAVAN T	TABLE T	WEIGH T
PALLE T	REEDI T	SCHIS T	**TACKE T**	WESKI T
PANDI T	REEMI T	**SCHIS T**	TALEN T	**WHILS T**
PAPIS T	**REFEC T**	**SCHUI T**	TAMES T	*WHISH T
PAREN T	REFLE T	**SCRIP T**	TANIS T	*WICKE T
PARGE T	REGEN T	**SCULP T**	**TAPPE T**	**WIDES T**
PARRO T	REGLE T	SECAN T	TARGE T	**WIDGE T**
PATEN T	REGRE T	SECRE T	TASSE T	**WIGLE T**
PEANU T	REHEA T	**SEJAN T**	**TAUGH T**	WILLE T
PEDAN T	*REJEC T	SELEC T	TEAPO T	WISEN T
PEEWI T	**REKNI T**	SENNE T	TENAN T	WISES T
PELLE T	RELEN T	SENNI T	TERCE T	**WOMBA T**
PENUL T	RELIC T	SEPTE T	TERRE T	WORRI T
PERMI T	RELIS T	SERES T	TERRI T	WORSE T
PICKE T	RELUC T	SESTE T	THEIS T	WRIES T
PIGLE T	REMEE T	SETOU T	THIRS T	**WRIGH T**
PIGNU T	REMEL T	**SEXIS T**	THREA T	YCLEP T
PIOLE T	REMIN T	**SEXTE T**	THROA T	YOGUR T
*PIQUE T	RENNE T	*SEXPO T	**THRIF T**	*ZEALO T
PLACE T	REPAS T	SHIES T	THRUS T	BABBIT T
PLAIN T	REPEA T	**SHRIF T**	**THWAR T**	*BACKLI T
PLANE T	REPEN T	SIGNE T	**TICKE T**	*BACKOU T
PLIAN T	REPOR T	SILEN T	TIDBI T	*BACKSE T
PLIGH T	RESEA T	**SIPPE T**	**TIPCA T**	BAILOU T
POCKE T	RESEC T	SLIES T	**TIPPE T**	BALLAS T
PONEN T	RESEN T	**SLIGH T**	TITBI T	*BANQUE T
POPPE T	RESIF T	SOBEI T	TOILE T	BAPTIS T
POSSE T	RESIS T	**SOCKE T**	**TOMCA T**	BAREFI T
POTEN T	RESOR T	**SOFFI T**	TOMTI T	BARONE T
PREAC T	RESUL T	SONAN T	TONLE T	BASINE T
PRESE T	RETES T	SONNE T	*TOQUE T	BASSIS T
PRIES T	RETIN T	SORBE T	TREVE T	BAWSUN T
PRIVE T	RETOR T	SORES T	**TRIJE T**	BAYONE T
PROBI T	REVER T	**SOUGH T**	TRIVE T	BEARCA T
PROFI T	REVES T	SOVIE T	TRUAN T	BECRUS T
*PROJE T	REVOL T	SPIGO T	TRUES T	BEDFAS T
PROMP T	RIBLE T	SPINE T	TRYOU T	BEDIGH T
PROSI T	RIDEN T	SPIRI T	**TUCKE T**	BEDPOS T
PULLE T	RILLE T	SPLEN T	**TUFFE T**	BENEFI T
PULPI T	RIPES T	SPLIN T	TUMUL T	BENEMP T
PUNDI T	RIPOS T	SPOIL T	TURBI T	BEPAIN T
PUPPE T	ROBUS T	SPREN T	TURBO T	*BEQUES T
PURES T	**ROCHE T**	SPRIN T	TURRE T	BESHOU T
PURIS T	**ROCKE T**	SPROU T	TWILI T	*BETWIX T
PUTOU T	RODEN T	*SQUIN T	**TYPIS T**	BEVOMI T
*QIVIU T	*ROQUE T	*SQUIR T	TYRAN T	*BEZZAN T
*QUAIN T	ROTGU T	STRAI T	VACAN T	BIBELO T
RABBE T	ROUPE T	STREE T	VARLE T	BIGGES T
RABBI T	RUDES T	STRIC T	**VELVE T**	BISCUI T
RACHE T	RUNLE T	STRIP T	VERIS T	BISTOR T
RACIS T	RUNOU T	STRUN T	VERSE T	BLANKE T
RACKE T	RUSSE T	STYLE T	**VERVE T**	BLATAN T
RAGOU T	**SABBA T**	SUBLE T		BLOWOU T

BOMBAS T	COAGEN T	CROCHE T	DOPIES T	GABBAR T
BONESE T	COALPI T	*CROCKE T	DORMAN T	GABFES T
BONIES T	COCOMA T	*CROQUE T	DOTIES T	GALIPO T
BOOKLE T	COCONU T	CROWNE T	DOUBLE T	GALLAN T
BOOMLE T	COENAC T	CRUMPE T	DOVECO T	GALLNU T
BORSCH T	COEREC T	CULPRI T	DRABBE T	GALLOO T
*BOSQUE T	*COEXER T	CULTIS T	DRAGNE T	GAMIES T
*BOUQUE T	*COEXIS T	CULVER T	DRAUGH T	GANTLE T
*BOWKNO T	*COFFRE T	*CUMQUA T	DRIBLE T	GARDAN T
*BOWSHO T	COHABI T	CURRAN T	DROPLE T	GARMEN T
*BOXIES T	COLLEC T	CURREN T	DROPOU T	GELLAN T
BOYCOT T	COMBUS T	CYCLIS T	DROUGH T	GESTAL T
BRACHE T	COMFOR T	*CZARIS T	DRUGGE T	GIGABI T
*BRIQUE T	COMMEN T	DADAIS T	DUALIS T	GILBER T
BRISKE T	*COMPAC T	DASHPO T	DUELIS T	GILLNE T
*BROCKE T	COMPAR T	*DECRYP T	DUNNES T	*GJETOS T
BROUGH T	COMPLO T	DEFAUL T	DURMAS T	GLAIKE T
BULLBA T	COMPOR T	DEFIAN T	FADDIS T	GLAIKI T
BUMBOA T	COMPOS T	DEFICI T	FALLOU T	GNOMIS T
BUNDIS T	CONCEI T	DEFLEC T	FANTAS T	GOOIES T
BUOYAN T	CONCEN T	DEFROS T	FANWOR T	GORIES T
BURGOU T	CONCEP T	DELIGH T	FASCIS T	GOSPOR T
BURNOU T	CONCER T	DELIMI T	FATTES T	GOURME T
BUSHTI T	CONCOC T	DEMERI T	FAUVIS T	GRAVES T
BUSIES T	CONDUC T	DEMOUN T	FEEDLO T	GRAYOU T
CABARE T	CONDUI T	DENTIS T	FELWOR T	GROMME T
CABINE T	CONFEC T	DEPAIN T	FERMEN T	GRUMME T
CAGIES T	CONGES T	DEPOSI T	FERVEN T	GUNBOA T
*CAJAPU T	CONNEC T	DESCAN T	FEUDIS T	GUNSHO T
*CAJUPU T	CONSEN T	DESCEN T	FIDEIS T	GURGLE T
CALLAN T	CONSIS T	DESSER T	FIGMEN T	GYMNAS T
CALUME T	CONSOR T	DETRAC T	FIGWOR T	HABITA T
CAMBIS T	CONSUL T	DEVIAN T	FILBER T	*HACKBU T
CANDEN T	CONTAC T	DEWIES T	FILEMO T	HADDES T
CAPELE T	CONTEN T	DIALEC T	FILMSE T	HAIRCU T
CARPOR T	CONTES T	DIALIS T	FINFOO T	HALBER T
CASUIS T	*CONTEX T	DIARIS T	FISHNE T	HALIBU T
CATBOA T	CONTOR T	DICIES T	*FITCHE T	HANDOU T
CATHEC T	CONVEC T	DILUEN T	FITMEN T	HANDSE T
CATMIN T	CONVEN T	DIMMES T	FITTES T	HANGOU T
CELLIS T	CONVER T	DINGBA T	FLASKE T	HAPLON T
CESSPI T	CONVIC T	DISCAN T	FLATLE T	HARDHA T
CHALLO T	COOKOU T	DISCEP T	FLUTIS T	HARDSE T
CHAPLE T	COOLAN T	DISGUS T	*FLYBEL T	HARICO T
CHARIO T	COPILO T	*DISJEC T	*FLYBOA T	HARPIS T
CHEMIS T	*COPYCA T	DISMAS T	*FLYPAS T	HARSLE T
CHEROO T	COPYIS T	DISPAR T	FOLDOU T	HARVES T
*CHEVIO T	CORONE T	DISPOR T	*FOLKMO T	*HATCHE T
CHUTIS T	CORREC T	DISROO T	FONDAN T	*HAYLOF T
*CHYMIS T	CORRUP T	DISRUP T	FOREGU T	*HAZIES T
CIGARE T	CORSLE T	DISSEA T	FORFEI T	HEADSE T
CINEAS T	COSIES T	DISSEC T	FORMAN T	HELIAS T
CIRCLE T	COSMIS T	DISSEN T	FORWEN T	HELLCA T
CIRCUI T	COULDS T	DISSER T	FRAUGH T	HIDEOU T
CLAMAN T	COUPLE T	DISTAN T	FREIGH T	HINDGU T
CLAUCH T	COURAN T	DISTEN T	FRESHE T	HIPPES T
CLAUGH T	COWIES T	DISTOR T	FRISKE T	*HIPSHO T
CLEMEN T	CRAMPI T	DOGCAR T	FUGUIS T	HOLDOU T
CLOSES T	CREDEN T	DOGTRO T	FULGEN T	HOLIBU T
COADMI T	CRESSE T	DONNER T	FUMIES T	HOLIES T
	*CRICKE T	DOORMA T	FUSSPO T	HOMIES T
				HOOKLE T

HORREN T	MIDMOS T	PIERRO T	*RACQUE T	REVUIS T
HOTFOO T	MIGRAN T	PIETIS T	RADIAN T	RIBWOR T
HOTSHO T	MINARE T	PIGBOA T	RAGWOR T	RIMIES T
HOTTES T	MIRIES T	PIGMEN T	RAIMEN T	RINGEN T
*HOWBEI T	MISCAS T	PINIES T	RAINOU T	RINGLE T
HUTMEN T	MISEDI T	PIPIES T	RAMPAN T	RIPPLE T
HYDRAN T	MISMEE T	*PIQUAN T	RAMPAR T	RIVULE T
HYGEIS T	MISPAR T	PISSAN T	RAPPOR T	ROLLOU T
*HYMNIS T	MISSEA T	PITAPA T	RAREBI T	ROMAUN T
*JACKPO T	MISSOR T	*PLACKE T	RATATA T	ROOTLE T
*JACONE T	MISSOU T	PLAUDI T	RATCHE T	ROPIES T
JESSAN T	MISSUI T	PLAYAC T	READAP T	ROSIES T
*JETPOR T	MITIES T	PLAYLE T	READMI T	ROWBOA T
*JUDOIS T	MONOCO T	PLEDGE T	READOP T	RUBIES T
*JUJUIS T	MOONLE T	PLENIS T	READOU T	RUMMES T
*KAJEPU T	MOONLI T	PLUMME T	REAGEN T	RUNDLE T
KASHRU T	MOONSE T	POKIES T	REALIS T	*SACKBU T
KILOBI T	MORDAN T	POLECA T	REALLO T	SACRIS T
KINGLE T	MORDEN T	POLLIS T	REBOAN T	SAGIES T
*KUMQUA T	MUGWOR T	POLOIS T	RECEIP T	SALIEN T
LACIES T	MUSKRA T	POLYCO T	RECHAR T	SALTAN T
LAMBAS T	NAILSE T	PORREC T	RECHEA T	SANDLO T
LAMBEN T	NARCIS T	PORTEN T	RECOUN T	SANDPI T
LAMBER T	NASCEN T	POTSHO T	RECRUI T	SAPIEN T
LANGUE T	NEGLEC T	PRECAS T	REDBAI T	SARMEN T
LATCHE T	NOBLES T	PRECEN T	REDCOA T	SATINE T
LAWSUI T	NONSUI T	PRECEP T	REDDES T	SAWDUS T
*LAZARE T	NOSIES T	PREDIC T	REDOUB T	SCARLE T
*LAZIES T	NUTMEA T	PREEMP T	REDRAF T	SEABOO T
LEAFLE T	*NYMPHE T	PREFEC T	REDROO T	SEAGIR T
LEFTIS T	PAGEAN T	PREHEA T	*REEJEC T	SEALAN T
LENIEN T	PALETO T	PRELEC T	REELEC T	SEAPOR T
LEVERE T	PALIES T	PRESEN T	REENAC T	SEARES T
LIMIES T	PALMIS T	PRESIF T	REEREC T	SEAWAN T
LINECU T	PANDEC T	PRETES T	REFIGH T	SEGMEN T
LINIES T	PARAPE T	*PRETEX T	REFLEC T	SEJEAN T
LINOCU T	PARFAI T	PREVEN T	REFLOA T	SELLOU T
LOCKNU T	*PARQUE T	*PRICKE T	REFRAC T	SEMIFI T
LOCKOU T	PARTLE T	PRODUC T	REFRON T	SEMIMA T
LOGIES T	PASSAN T	*PROJEC T	REGNAN T	*SEQUEN T
LOOKOU T	PATIEN T	PROPHE T	REGRAF T	SERPEN T
LOOSES T	PATRIO T	*PROPJE T	REGRAN T	SERVAN T
LUNIES T	PAYMEN T	PROSEC T	REGREE T	SEXIES T
MADDES T	PEACOA T	PROTEC T	RELIAN T	SEXTAN T
MADWOR T	PEASAN T	PROTES T	RELIGH T	SHALLO T
MAILLO T	PECCAN T	PROTIS T	REMNAN T	SHERBE T
MANCHE T	PELTAS T	PROVOS T	REMOUN T	SHEROO T
MANHUN T	PENDAN T	PRUDEN T	REPAIN T	SHILPI T
MANIHO T	PENDEN T	PSCHEN T	REPLAN T	SHUTOU T
MANTLE T	PENNAN T	PULLOU T	REPOSI T	SINGLE T
MANUMI T	PERCEN T	PULSAN T	REPRIN T	*SIZIES T
MARGEN T	PERCEP T	PUNGEN T	REPTAN T	SKILLE T
MARPLO T	PERFEC T	PUNIES T	*REQUES T	*SKIPPE T
MARTLE T	PERIAP T	PURPOR T	RESHOO T	SKIRRE T
*MAZIES T	PERIDO T	PURSUI T	RESMEL T	SLEEKI T
MEANES T	PERPEN T	*QUADRA T	RESOJE T	SLEIGH T
MEDIAN T	PERSAL T	*QUARTE T	RESPEC T	SLIPOU T
MEGABI T	PERSIS T	*QUERIS T	RESTAR T	SNIPPE T
MELILO T	PERVER T	*QUILLE T	RETRAC T	SOLERE T
*MESQUI T	PIANIS T	*QUINNA T	RETREA T	SOLICI T
METRIS T	*PICQUE T	*QUINTE T	RETWIS T	SOLOIS T
*MEZQUI T	PIEFOR T	RACIES T	REVISI T	SOLVEN T

SOPHIS T	TONIGH T	WHITES T	*BOUGHPO T	COASSIS T
SORBEN T	TOPCOA T	WILDCA T	*BOWFRON T	COATTES T
SPARES T	TOPKNO T	WILIES T	*BOWSPRI T	COBBIES T
SPINOU T	TOPMAS T	WINGLE T	BRACELE T	*COCKBOA T
SPIRAN T	TOPMOS T	WINIES T	BRACTLE T	*COCKIES T
SPRIES T	TORMEN T	WIPEOU T	BRAGGAR T	*COCKLOF T
SPRIGH T	TORREN T	WIRIES T	BRAGGES T	*COCKSHU T
STARLE T	TOSSPO T	WITHOU T	BRASSAR T	*COEFFEC T
STARLI T	TOURIS T	WOODCU T	BREADNU T	COGNOVI T
STATAN T	TOWBOA T	WOODLO T	BREAKOU T	COHEREN T
STATIS T	TOWMON T	WORKOU T	*BRICKBA T	COLEWOR T
STERLE T	TOWNLE T	WOULDS T	BRINIES T	COLLARE T
STICKI T	*TRAJEC T	WROUGH T	BROOKLE T	COLONIS T
STUDEN T	TRANSI T	YOGHUR T	*BROWBEA T	COLORAN T
STYLIS T	TRIDEN T	*ZIKURA T	BROWNOU T	COLORIS T
SUBDUC T	TRINKE T	BACCARA T	*BUCKSHO T	*COMFIES T
SUBEDI T	TRIOLE T	*BACCHAN T	*BUFFIES T	COMPLEA T
*SUBJEC T	TRIPAR T	*BACKLIS T	BULLIES T	*COMPLEC T
SUBPAR T	TRIPLE T	*BACKMOS T	BULLPOU T	CONFLIC T
SUBPLO T	TRIPPE T	*BACKRES T	BULLSHI T	CONFRON T
SUBREN T	TRISEC T	*BACKSEA T	BURGONE T	*CONJUNC T
SUBSEC T	TRUMPE T	BAILMEN T	BURRIES T	CONODON T
SUBSIS T	TSARIS T	*BAKEMEA T	BUSHGOA T	*CONQUES T
*SUBTEX T	TUGBOA T	BALLONE T	BUSHIES T	CONSTAN T
SUBUNI T	TURGEN T	*BANJOIS T	BYSTREE T	CONTEMP T
SUBVER T	TURNOU T	*BANKRUP T	CABALIS T	CONTRAC T
SUGGES T	TYPESE T	BANNERE T	*CACHALO T	CONTRAS T
SUNFAS T	TYPIES T	BAREFOO T	*CACHEPO T	COPAREN T
SUNSPO T	*TZARIS T	BARGHES T	CALAMIN T	CORKIES T
SUNSUI T	VAGRAN T	BARGUES T	CAMPIES T	CORNIES T
SUPPOR T	VALIAN T	BASEMEN T	*CAMSHAF T	CORSELE T
SURCOA T	VARMEN T	BASSINE T	CANNIES T	COSECAN T
SURFEI T	VARIAN T	BATTIES T	CANOEIS T	COTENAN T
SURTOU T	VARMIN T	BAWDIES T	CANONIS T	*COUCHAN T
SUSPEC T	VEINLE T	BEADIES T	*CANZONE T	COULDES T
SYMBIO T	VERDAN T	BEAMIES T	CARBURE T	COVALEN T
TABARE T	VERDIC T	BECARPE T	CARCANE T	COVENAN T
TABORE T	VERIES T	*BEDQUIL T	CARRYOU T	COVERLE T
TACHIS T	VERSAN T	*BEECHNU T	CASEMEN T	*CRACKPO T
TAKEOU T	VIADUC T	BEEFIES T	CASTANE T	CREODON T
TALIPO T	VIBRAN T	BEETROO T	CATALYS T	CRESCEN T
TANGEN T	VILAYE T	*BEKNIGH T	CATAPUL T	CROSSCU T
TANNES T	VINIES T	BELLWOR T	CATARAC T	CROSSLE T
TAPROO T	VIOLEN T	BENEDIC T	CATTIES T	*CROTCHE T
TARTLE T	VIOLIS T	BERGAMO T	CELLARE T	*CROWFOO T
TEACAR T	WALKOU T	BESOUGH T	CENTRIS T	CRYOSTA T
TELEOS T	WANIES T	BESPREN T	CERAMIS T	CUCURBI T
TEMPES T	WANNES T	BETELNU T	CEREMEN T	CURDIES T
TEMPLE T	WARIES T	BIGAMIS T	CERVELA T	CUSHIES T
TENNIS T	WARRAN T	BITTIES T	CHARIES T	DAMEWOR T
THEREA T	WASHOU T	BIVALEN T	CHARTIS T	DAMNDES T
THERMI T	WATTES T	*BLACKOU T	*CHECKOU T	DANEWOR T
*THICKE T	WAVELE T	BLOWIES T	CHESTNU T	DARNDES T
THOUGH T	WAVIES T	BLUECOA T	*CHEVALE T	DASHIES T
THRUPU T	*WAXIES T	BOBBINE T	CHILIAS T	*DAYLIGH T
TIDIES T	*WEBFOO T	BODEMEN T	*CHITCHA T	DEADBEA T
TIMEOU T	WERGEL T	BOGGIES T	CLAIMAN T	DEBUTAN T
TINIES T	WETTES T	BONGOIS T	CLARINE T	DECADEN T
TIPCAR T	WHATNO T	BOOKRES T	CLOSEOU T	DECEDEN T
TITLIS T	WHEREA T	BOOMIES T	CLOUDLE T	DECREPI T
TITRAN T	*WHIFFE T	BOTANIS T	*CLUBFOO T	DEFEREN T
TONIES T	*WHIPPE T	*BOUFFAN T	CLUBROO T	DEFORES T

DEMIVOL T	FABULIS T	GALAVAN T	*HOBBYIS T	LUMINIS T
DEMOCRA T	FADDIES T	GALIVAN T	*HOLDFAS T	LUNGWOR T
DEMONIS T	FAINEAN T	GASLIGH T	HOMILIS T	LUSTIES T
DEMOTIS T	FALCONE T	GASTIGH T	HONEWOR T	LUTANIS T
DEPONEN T	FALTBOA T	GATEPOS T	*HOOFBEA T	LUTENIS T
DERELIC T	*FANLIGH T	GAUNTLE T	*HOOKIES T	LYRICIS T
DESELEC T	FARTHES T	GEMMIES T	HORNIES T	MAINMAS T
DESINEN T	FATALIS T	GERMIES T	HORNPOU T	*MAKEFAS T
DESTRUC T	FATTIES T	GIGAWAT T	HORNWOR T	MALAPER T
DIALLIS T	FECULEN T	GLADDES T	HORSIES T	MALEDIC T
*DIFFRAC T	FEMINIS T	GLADIES T	*HOTCHPO T	MALEMIU T
DIGAMIS T	FIGURAN T	GOALPOS T	*HUMBLES T	MALTIES T
DILATAN T	FILAMEN T	GODLIES T	HUMORIS T	MALTREA T
DILIGEN T	FILMIES T	GRADIEN T	*HUSKIES T	MANGIES T
DINKIES T	FINALIS T	GRAPIES T	*HYGIEIS T	MANIFES T
DIPLOMA T	FINNIES T	GREENLE T	*JACKBOO T	MANTELE T
DIRIMEN T	FIREBOA T	GRIEVAN T	*JAILBAI T	MARABOU T
DISCOUN T	FIREBRA T	GRIMIES T	*JINGOIS T	MARLIES T
DISCREE T	*FISHBOL T	GRIMMES T	*JOHNBOA T	MARMOSE T
DISHERI T	FISHIES T	GRIPIES T	*JOLLIES T	MARTINE T
DISHIES T	FLAGRAN T	GRUMMES T	*JUBILAN T	MASSICO T
*DISJOIN T	FLAMEOU T	GUARDAN T	*JUDGMEN T	MASSIES T
*DISJUNC T	FLAMIES T	GULFIES T	KEELBOA T	*MAXICOA T
DISMOUN T	FLATBOA T	GUMMIES T	*KILOVOL T	MEALIES T
DISPIRI T	FLATFOO T	*GUNFIGH T	*KILOWAT T	MEATIES T
DISPLAN T	FLATTES T	GUNFLIN T	*KINGBOL T	MEDALIS T
*DISQUIE T	FLEAWOR T	GUNPOIN T	*KINGPOS T	MEGAVOL T
DISTINC T	*FLESHPO T	GUSTIES T	*KNOCKOU T	MEGAWAT T
DISTRAC T	*FLIPPAN T	GUTTIES T	LAKEPOR T	MELANIS T
DISTRAI T	FLOWERE T	GYROSTA T	LAMPPOS T	MELODIS T
DISTRIC T	FLUTIES T	HABITAN T	LANCELE T	*MERCHAN T
DISTRUS T	FOAMIES T	HAGADIS T	LANNERE T	MESSIES T
DITHEIS T	*FOGFRUI T	HAIRIES T	LAPIDIS T	METALIS T
DIVALEN T	FOLDBOA T	*HALAKIS T	LARDIES T	*MIDNIGH T
DOCUMEN T	*FOLKMOO T	*HAMMIES T	LARKIES T	MIDPOIN T
*DOGFIGH T	FOOTIES T	HANDCAR T	LATHIES T	MILEPOS T
DOGGIES T	FOOTRES T	*HANDFAS T	LAYABOU T	MILITAN T
DOMINAN T	FORECAS T	HANDIES T	LEADIES T	MILKIES T
DOORPOS T	FOREFOO T	HANDLIS T	LEADWOR T	*MILKWOR T
DORMIEN T	FOREMAS T	*HANDWRI T	LEAFIES T	MINGIES T
DOSSERE T	FOREMOS T	HANGNES T	LEARIES T	*MIQUELE T
DOTTIES T	FOREPAR T	HARDBOO T	LEGALIS T	MISADAP T
DOUGHNU T	FOREPAS T	HARDIES T	LEGGIES T	MISAGEN T
DOWNBEA T	FOREWEN T	*HAZELNU T	LIBELAN T	MISBEGO T
DOWNCAS T	*FORKIES T	*HEADHUN T	LIBELIS T	MISCOUN T
DOWNIES T	*FORKLIF T	HEADIES T	*LICKSPI T	MISDOUB T
DRAGONE T	FORSPEN T	HEADMOS T	LIFEBOA T	MISEVEN T
DRIBBLE T	FOVEOLE T	HEADRES T	LIGAMEN T	MISGRAF T
DROPSHO T	FRAGMEN T	*HEAVYSE T	LILLIPU T	MISLIGH T
DROPWOR T	FRAGRAN T	HEDONIS T	LIMBIES T	MISPAIN T
DRUGGIS T	*FRANKES T	*HELICOP T	LINGIES T	MISPLAN T
DRUMBEA T	*FREAKOU T	HELIPOR T	LINGUIS T	MISPOIN T
DRUPELE T	FREEBOO T	HELLBEN T	LINIMEN T	MISPRIN T
DRYPOIN T	*FREQUEN T	*HELPMEE T	LINTIES T	MISSTAR T
DUBONNE T	FRONTLE T	HEMOSTA T	LITIGAN T	MISTIES T
*DUCKIES T	FROSTBI T	*HEMPIES T	*LOBBYIS T	MISTREA T
DUELLIS T	FRUITLE T	HERBIES T	LOCALIS T	MISTRUS T
DUETTIS T	FUMIGAN T	HESITAN T	LODGMEN T	MISTRYS T
*DUMPCAR T	FURRIES T	HILLIES T	LONGBOA T	MOBOCRA T
DUMPIES T	FURTHES T	HINDMOS T	LORIKEE T	MOLDIES T
DUSTIES T	FUTURIS T	*HIPPIES T	LOYALIS T	MONOCRA T
DYNAMIS T	GADABOU T	HOARIES T	LUCULEN T	MONODIS T

MONOTIN T	*PAVEMEN T	*PROHIBI T	REINDUC T	SATURAN T
MONUMEN T	PEAKIES T	PROSAIS T	REINFEC T	SAVAGES T
MOONIES T	PEDERAS T	PROSIES T	REINSER T	SCALIES T
MOONSHO T	PEDIMEN T	PROSPEC T	REINVEN T	SCANDEN T
MOONWOR T	PEETWEE T	PROTRAC T	REINVES T	SCARIES T
MOORIES T	*PENCHAN T	PRURIEN T	*RELAXAN T	*SCHIZON T
MOORWOR T	PENITEN T	PSALMIS T	RELEVAN T	SCILICE T
MORALIS T	PENLIGH T	PUGGIES T	RELUCEN T	SCIOLIS T
MOSSIES T	PENPOIN T	PUGILIS T	REMANEN T	SCRIMPI T
MOTORIS T	PETTIES T	PUISSAN T	RENITEN T	SEACOAS T
MOUSIES T	PETULAN T	PULPIES T	REORIEN T	SEACRAF T
*MOVEMEN T	PHALLIS T	*PULSEJE T	RESCRIP T	SEAFRON T
*MUCKIES T	PHANTAS T	*PULSOJE T	RESIDEN T	SEAMIES T
MUDDIES T	PHASEOU T	PURSIES T	RESONAN T	SEAMOUN T
MUGGIES T	PHEASAN T	PURSUAN T	RESOUGH T	SEASCOU T
*MULTIJE T	PHONIES T	PURULEN T	RESTRIC T	SECURES T
MUNIMEN T	PHOTOSE T	*PUSHCAR T	RESUBMI T	SEDERUN T
MURALIS T	*PICKIES T	PUSHIES T	RETICEN T	SEDIMEN T
MURRELE T	PIECRUS T	PUSSIES T	RETIRAN T	SEEDIES T
MUSKIES T	PIEDFOR T	*PUSSYCA T	RETROAC T	SEMIMAT T
*MUZZIES T	PIEDMON T	PYROSTA T	RETROFI T	SEMISOF T
*MYOBLAS T	PIEPLAN T	*QUADRAN T	REVEHEN T	SEMITIS T
NANOWAT T	PILEWOR T	*QUICKSE T	REVENAN T	SENNIGH T
NATIVIS T	PINKROO T	*QUIETIS T	REVEREN T	SENTIEN T
NAUSEAN T	PINPOIN T	*QUITREN T	RHEOSTA T	SERGEAN T
NAVICER T	*PITCHOU T	*QUOTIEN T	RIBBIES T	*SERJEAN T
NEEDIES T	*PLANCHE T	RAINCOA T	RICCHIES T	SHADIES T
NEPOTIS T	PLANGEN T	RAINIES T	*RICOCHE T	*SHAKEOU T
NERVIES T	PLATELE T	RALLYIS T	RIDGIES T	*SHAKIES T
NESCIEN T	PLATIES T	RAMMIES T	RIGHTIS T	SHALIES T
NETTIES T	PLAYSUI T	RATTIES T	RIGORIS T	SHERBER T
NEWSCAS T	PLEASAN T	REACCEN T	RINGBOL T	SHINIES T
NEWSIES T	PLUMELE T	REACCEP T	ROBORAN T	*SHIPMEN T
NIELLIS T	PLUMIES T	REACTAN T	ROCKIES T	*SHOPLIF T
NIHILIS T	POIGNAN T	READDIC T	RONDELE T	SHORTCU T
NIPPIES T	POKEROO T	READIES T	ROOTIES T	SHOULDS T
NOBBIES T	POLEMIS T	*READJUS T	ROSEROO T	*SHOWBOA T
NONADUL T	POLYGLO T	REANOIN T	ROUNDLE T	SHOWIES T
NONELEC T	POPULIS T	REARMOS T	ROYALIS T	SIBILAN T
NONEVEN T	PORKIES T	REARRES T	RUBAIYA T	SIGNPOS T
NONGUIL T	PORTRAI T	REASCEN T	RUDDIES T	SILKIES T
NOVELIS T	POTTIES T	REASSER T	RUDIMEN T	SIMONIS T
NUBBIES T	*PRAEFEC T	REASSOR T	RUMINAN T	SIMULAN T
NUTRIEN T	PRAELEC T	RECOMMI T	RUNABOU T	SINCIPU T
*PACIFIS T	PREADAP T	RECREAN T	RURALIS T	SITARIS T
PAGANIS T	PREADMI T	RECUSAN T	RUSHIES T	*SKYLIGH T
PALLIES T	PREADOP T	REDEFEA T	RUSTIES T	SLATIES T
PALMIES T	PREADUL T	REDIGES T	RUTILAN T	SLIMIES T
*PAMPHLE T	PREALLO T	REDIREC T	RUTTIES T	SLIMMES T
PANELIS T	PRECINC T	REDOLEN T	SAILBOA T	SLIPKNO T
PANTSUI T	PREELEC T	REDSHIR T	SALARIA T	SLUGFES T
PAPPIES T	PREENAC T	REDSTAR T	SALTIES T	*SMOKEPO T
PARAKEE T	*PREEXIS T	REEDIES T	SALTWOR T	SNAPSHO T
PARAMEN T	PREGNAN T	REENLIS T	SANDIES T	SNOWIES T
*PARAQUA T	PRELIMI T	*REEXPOR T	SANDWOR T	SNOWMEL T
*PARAQUE T	PREPLAN T	REFEREN T	*SAPPHIS T	SNOWSUI T
PARODIS T	PREPRIN T	REFLUEN T	SARCENE T	SNUGGES T
*PAROQUE T	PRETERI T	REFORES T	SARODIS T	SOAPIES T
PARROKE T	PRETREA T	REFORMA T	SARSENE T	SOAPWOR T
PASSPOR T	PRICIES T	*REFOUGH T	SASSIES T	SODALIS T
PASTIES T	PRIMMES T	REGIMEN T	SATANIS T	SOLECIS T
PATULEN T	PRINTOU T	REIMPOR T	SATIRIS T	SOLLERE T

SOMERSE T	STRUMPE T	TENEMEN T	TWINIES T	WEARIES T
*SOMEWHA T	SUBABBO T	TENTIES T	*TWINIGH T	WEEDIES T
SONGFES T	SUBADUL T	TERCELE T	*TYPECAS T	WELDMEN T
SONORAN T	SUBAGEN T	TESTIES T	VALVELE T	WESTMOS T
SOOTHES T	SUBDEPO T	THEOCRA T	VASTIES T	*WHINCHA T
SORRIES T	SUBEREC T	THEORIS T	VEGETAN T	WHINIES T
SPICIES T	*SUBSHAF T	*THICKSE T	VEGETIS T	WHITEOU T
SPIKELE T	SUBTRAC T	THINNES T	*VEHEMEN T	WHITTRE T
*SPROCKE T	SUCCINC T	THRAWAR T	VEINIES T	*WHODUNI T
SPUMIES T	SULFURE T	*THUMBNU T	VEINULE T	WILLYAR T
*SQUARES T	SUNBURS T	*THYMIES T	VELVERE T	WINDIES T
STABLES T	SUNLIGH T	TINNIES T	VESICAN T	WINGIES T
STAGGAR T	*SUPERJE T	TIPPIES T	VESTMEN T	WISPIES T
STAGIES T	SUPPLAN T	TIPSIES T	VIEWIES T	WITHIES T
STAGNAN T	SURFBOA T	TOLERAN T	VIGILAN T	WITTIES T
STAKEOU T	SURFIES T	*TOMMYRO T	VIRULEN T	*WOODCHA T
STALWAR T	SURMOUN T	TOTEMIS T	VISCOUN T	WOODIES T
STANDOU T	SURPRIN T	*TOXICAN T	VISITAN T	WOOLIES T
STANDPA T	SWIMSUI T	TRANSAC T	VITALIS T	WORDIES T
STARDUS T	*SYMBION T	TRANSEC T	*VIVISEC T	*WORKBOA T
STARWOR T	TABOURE T	TRANSEP T	VOCALIS T	WORMIES T
STEDFAS T	TACKIES T	TRANSMI T	VOLITAN T	WORMROO T
STICKOU T	TAILCOA T	TRAPNES T	VOTARIS T	WOULDES T
STINKPO T	TANGIES T	TRIGGES T	WAINSCO T	WRISTLE T
STOCKIS T	TARRIES T	TRIMMES T	*WARCRAF T	*YOGHOUR T
*STOCKPO T	TATTIES T	*TURBOJE T	WARTIES T	*ZIGGURA T
STONIES T	TEARIES T	TURFIES T	WASHIES T	*ZIKKURA T
STRAIGH T	TEGUMEN T	TURNCOA T	WASTELO T	
STRAWHA T	TELECAS T	TURNSPI T	*WATCHOU T	
STRIDEN T	TELEPOR T	*TWILIGH T	*WAXPLAN T	

V

VAGI	VEST	VUGG	VEENA	VIDEO
VAIL	VETO	VUGH	VEERY	VIEWY
VAIN	VEXT	VACUA	VEGAN	VIGIL
VAIR	VIAL	VAGAL	VELAR	VIGOR
VALE	VICE	VAGUE	VELDT	VILLA
VAMP	VIDE	VAGUS	VELUM	VIMEN
VANE	VIER	VAKIL	VENAL	VINAL
VANG	VIEW	VALET	VENGE	VINCA
VARA	VILE	VALID	VENIN	VINIC
VARY	VILL	VALOR	VENOM	VINYL
VASE	VINA	VALSE	VENUE	VIOLA
VAST	VINE	VALUE	VERGE	VIPER
VEAL	VINO	VALVE	VERSE	VIRAL
VEEP	VINY	VANDA	VERSO	VIREO
VEER	VIOL	VAPID	VERST	VIRES
VEIL	VIRL	VAPOR	VERTU	VIRGA
VEIN	VISA	VARIA	*VARIX	VIRID
VELA	VISE	VARNA	VERVE	VIRTU
VELD	VITA	VARUS	VESTA	VIRUS
VENA	VIVA	VARVE	VETCH	VISIT
VEND	VIVE	VARY	*VEXER	VISOR
VENT	VOID	VASTY	*VEXIL	VISTA
VERA	VOLE	VATIC	VIAND	VITAL
VERB	VOLT	VAULT	VIBES	VITTA
VERT	VOTE	VAUNT	VICAR	VIVID
VERY	VROW	VEALY	*VICHY	*VIXEN

*VIZIR	VAULTY	VIATOR	*VACANCY	VENATIC
*VIZOR	VAUNTY	VIBIST	VACCINA	VENDACE
VOCAL	VAWARD	VIBRIO	VACCINE	VENISON
VOCES	VEALER	VICING	*VACUITY	VENOMER
VODKA	VECTOR	VICTIM	VACUOLE	VENTAGE
VODUN	VEEPEE	VICTOR	VACUOUS	VENTAIL
VOGIE	VEGETE	VICUNA	VAGRANT	VENTRAL
VOGUE	VEILER	VIEWER	VALANCE	VENTURE
VOICE	VEINAL	VIGOUR	VALENCE	VENTURI
VOILE	VEINER	VIKING	*VALENCY	VERANDA
VOLAR	VELATE	VILLUS	*VILIFY	VERBENA
VOLTA	VELLUM	VINEAL	VALIDLY	*VERBIFY
VOLTE	VELOCE	VINERY	VALLATE	VERBILE
VOLTI	VELOUR	VINIER	VALONIA	VERDANT
VOLVA	VELURE	VINING	VALUATE	VERDICT
VOMER	VELVET	VINOUS	VALVATE	VERDURE
VOMIT	VENDEE	VIOLET	VALVULA	VERGING
VOTER	VENDER	VIOLIN	VALVULE	VERGLAS
VOUCH	VENDOR	VIRAGO	VAMOOSE	VERIDIC
VOWEL	VENDUE	VIRGIN	VAMPIRE	VERIEST
VOWER	VENEER	VIRILE	*VAMPISH	VERISMO
VROOM	VENERY	VIRION	*VANDYKE	VERITAS
VROUW	VENIAL	VIRTUE	VANILLA	VERMEIL
VULGO	VENINE	VISAGE	VANTAGE	VERMIAN
VULVA	VENIRE	VISARD	VANWARD	*VERMUTH
VYING	VENOSE	VISCID	*VAPOURY	VERNIER
VACANT	VENOUS	VISCUS	*VAQUERO	VERRUCA
VACATE	VENTER	VISING	VARIANT	VERSANT
VACUUM	VENULE	VISION	VARIATE	*VERSIFY
VADOSE	VERBAL	VISIVE	VARICES	VERSINE
VAGARY	VERBID	VISUAL	VARIETY	VERSING
VAGILE	VERDIN	VITALS	VARIOLA	VERSION
VAGINA	VERGER	VITRIC	VARIOLE	VERTIGO
VAGROM	VERIER	VITTLE	VARIOUS	VERVAIN
VAHINE	*VERIFY	VIVACE	VARMENT	VESICLE
VAKEEL	VERILY	*VIVARY	VARMINT	VESPINE
VALGUS	VERISM	VIVERS	VARNISH	VESTIGE
VALINE	VERIST	*VIVIFY	VARSITY	VESTING
VALISE	VERITY	VIXARD	VASTIER	VESTURE
*VALKYR	VERMES	*VIZIER	VASTITY	VETERAN
VALLEY	VERMIN	*VIZSLA	VATICAL	VETIVER
VALOUR	VERMIS	VOICER	VATTING	VETTING
VALUER	VERNAL	VOIDER	VAULTER	*VEXEDLY
VALUTA	*VERNIX	VOLANT	VAUNTER	VIADUCT
VALVAL	VERSAL	VOLERY	VAUNTIE	VIBRANT
VALVAR	VERSER	VOLLEY	VAVASOR	VIBRATE
VAMOSE	VERSET	VOLOST	VAWNTIE	VIBRATO
VAMPER	VERSTE	VOLUME	VEBROSE	VIBRION
VANDAL	VERSUS	VOLUTE	VEDALIA	*VICARLY
VANISH	*VERTEX	*VOLVOX	VEDETTE	*VICEROY
VANITY	VERVET	VOMICA	VEGETAL	VICINAL
VANMAN	VESICA	VOMITO	*VEHICLE	VICIOUS
VAPORY	VESPER	VOODOO	VEILING	VICOMTE
VAPOUR	VESPID	*VORTEX	VEINIER	*VICTORY
VARIED	VESSEL	VOTARY	VEINING	VICTUAL
VARIER	VESTAL	VOTING	VEINLET	VICUGNA
VARIES	VESTEE	VOTIVE	VEINULE	VIDETTE
VARLET	VESTRY	VOYAGE	VELAMEN	VIDICON
VASSAL	VETOER	VOYEUR	VELIGER	VIDUITY
VASTLY	VETTED	VULGAR	VELITES	VIEWIER
VATFUL	VIABLE	VULGUS	VELOUTE	VIEWING
VATTED	VIATIC			VILAYET

VILLAGE	*VAGILITY	*VEILLIKE	VESTLESS	VISCERAL
VILLAIN	VAGINATE	VEINIEST	*VESTLIKE	VISCOUNT
VILLEIN	*VAGOTOMY	VEINLESS	VESTMENT	*VISELIKE
VINASSE	*VAGRANCY	*VEINLIKE	VESTURAL	VISIONAL
VINEGAR	VAINNESS	VEINULET	VESUVIAN	VISITANT
VINIEST	VALENCIA	VELARIUM	*VEXATION	VITALISE
VINTAGE	VALERATE	VELARIZE	*VEXILLUM	VITALISM
VINTNER	VALERIAN	VELLEITY	*VEXINGLY	VITALIST
VIOLATE	VALIANCE	*VELOCITY	VIATICAL	VITALITY
VIOLENT	*VALIANCY	VELVERET	*VIATICUM	*VITALIZE
VIOLIST	VALIDATE	VENALITY	*VIBRANCE	VITAMINE
VIOLONE	*VALIDITY	VENATION	*VIBRANCY	VITELLIN
VIRELAI	*VALKYRIE	VENDETTA	VIBRATOR	VITELLUS
VIRELAY	VALORISE	VENDIBLE	VIBRISSA	VITIATOR
VIREMIA	*VALORIZE	*VENDIBLY	*VIBURNUM	VITILIGO
VIRGATE	VALOROUS	VENEERER	VICARAGE	VITREOUS
VIRGULE	VALUABLE	VENENATE	VICARATE	VITULINE
VIROSIS	*VALUABLY	VENENOSE	VICARIAL	*VIVACITY
VIRTUAL	VALUATOR	VENERATE	VICELESS	*VIVARIUM
VISCERA	VALVELET	VENEREAL	*VICENARY	*VIVERRID
VISCOID	VALVULAR	VENETIAN	VICINAGE	*VIVIFIER
VISCOSE	*VAMBRACE	*VENGEFUL	*VICINITY	*VIVIPARA
VISCOUS	VANADATE	VENOMOUS	VICTORIA	*VIVISECT
VISIBLE	VANADIUM	VENOSITY	VICTRESS	*VIZCACHA
VISITER	VANGUARD	VENTLESS	VIEWIEST	*VIZIRATE
VISITOR	VANILLIN	VENTURER	VIEWLESS	VOCALISE
VITALLY	VANISHER	*VERACITY	VIGILANT	*VOCALISM
VITAMER	*VANQUISH	*VERANDAH	VIGNETTE	VOCALIST
VITAMIN	*VAPIDITY	VERATRIA	*VIGORISH	*VOCALITY
VITESSE	VAPORING	VERATRIN	VIGOROSO	*VOCALIZE
VITIATE	VAPORISE	VERATRUM	VIGOROUS	VOCATION
*VITRIFY	*VAPORISH	*VERBALLY	VILENESS	*VOCATIVE
VITRINE	*VAPORIZE	*VERBATIM	VILIFIER	*VOICEFUL
VITRIOL	VAPOROUS	VERBIAGE	VILIPEND	VOIDANCE
*VIVIFIC	VAPOURER	VERBLESS	VILLADOM	VOIDNESS
VOCABLE	VARIABLE	VERBOTEN	VILLAGER	VOLATILE
*VOCABLY	*VARIABLY	*VERDANCY	VILLAINY	*VOLCANIC
VOCALIC	VARIANCE	VERDERER	VILLATIC	VOLITANT
*VOCALLY	VARICOSE	VERDEROR	*VINCIBLE	VOLITION
VOCODER	*VARIEDLY	VERDITER	*VINCULUM	VOLITIVE
VOICING	*VARIFORM	VERECUND	*VINEYARD	VOLLEYER
VOLANTE	VARIORUM	VERGENCE	VINIFERA	VOLPLANE
VOLCANO	VARISTOR	VERIFIER	VINOSITY	VOLTAISM
VOLTAGE	VARLETRY	*VERJUICE	VINTAGER	VOLUTION
VOLUBLE	*VARNISHY	VERMOULU	VIOLABLE	VOLVULUS
VOLUTIN	VASCULAR	*VERMOUTH	VIOLATER	*VOMITIVE
VOMITER	*VASCULUM	VERNACLE	VIOLATOR	*VOMITORY
VOMITUS	*VASIFORM	VERNICLE	VIOLENCE	VOMITOUS
VORLAGE	VASTIEST	VERONICA	*VIOMYCIN	*VORACITY
VOTABLE	VASTNESS	VERSEMAN	VIRGINAL	VOTARESS
VOTRESS	VATICIDE	VERSICLE	VIRICIDE	VOTARIST
*VOUCHEE	VAULTING	VERTEBRA	VIRIDIAN	VOTEABLE
*VOUCHER	VAUNTFUL	VERTICAL	*VIRIDITY	VOTELESS
VOWLESS	VAVASOUR	VERTICIL	VIRILISM	VOUSSOIR
VOYAGER	VAVASSOR	VESICANT	VIRILITY	*VOWELIZE
VULGATE	VEGANISM	VESICATE	*VIROLOGY	*VOYAGEUR
VULPINE	VEGETANT	VESICULA	VIRTUOSA	*VULCANIC
VULTURE	VEGETATE	VESPERAL	VIRTUOSO	VULVITIS
*VYINGLY	VEGETIST	*VESPIARY	VIRTUOUS	
VACATION	*VEGETIVE	VESTALLY	VIRUCIDE	
*VACCINIA	*VEHEMENT	VESTIARY	VIRULENT	K V AS
*VAGABOND	*VEILEDLY	VESTIGIA	*VISCACHA	K V ASS

SCHA V	PA V ANE	*CI V ILLY	RA V ENER	CON V ENER
BE V IES	PA V ING	CO V ERER	RA V IOLI	CON V ERGE
BO V INE	PA V IOR	CO V ETER	RE V ALUE	CON V ERSE
CA V EAT	PA V ISE	CU V ETTE	RE V ELER	CON V EXLY
CA V ERN	*QI V IUT	DE V ALUE	RE V ELRY	*CON V EYER
CA V IAR	RA V AGE	DE V ELOP	RE V ENGE	*CON V EYOR
CA V IES	RA V INE	DE V IANT	RE V ENUE	*CON V INCE
CA V ING	RA V ING	DE V IATE	RE V ERER	*CON V OKER
CA V ITY	RA V ISH	DE V ILRY	RE V ERIE	*CON V OLVE
CA V ORT	RE V AMP	DE V IOUS	RE V ERSE	CON V ULSE
CI V ICS	RE V EAL	DE V ISAL	RE V ERSO	COR V ETTE
CI V ISM	RE V ERB	DE V ISEE	RE V ILER	*CRA V ENLY
CO V ERT	RE V ERE	DE V ISER	RE V ISAL	CRE V ALLE
CO V ING	RE V ERS	DE V ISOR	RE V ISER	CRE V ASSE
DE V EIN	RE V ERT	DE V OICE	RE V ISIT	CUL V ERIN
DE V EST	RE V ERY	DE V OLVE	RE V ISOR	DIS V ALUE
DE V ICE	RE V EST	DE V OTEE	RE V IVAL	DRI V ELER
DE V ISE	RE V IEW	DI V ERSE	RE V IVER	*DRI V EWAY
DE V OID	RE V ILE	DI V IDER	RE V OICE	*FER V ENCY
DE V OIR	RE V ISE	DI V INER	RE V OKER	FLA V ONOL
DE V OTE	RE V IVE	DI V ISOR	RE V OLVE	FLA V ORER
DE V OUR	RE V OKE	DI V ORCE	RE V UIST	*FLA V OURY
DE V OUT	RE V OLT	DI V ULGE	RE V VING	FRI V OLER
DI V ERT	RE V VED	DO V ECOT	RI V ALRY	GAL V ANIC
DI V EST	RI V AGE	*DO V EKEY	RI V ETER	GRA V AMEN
DI V IDE	RI V ING	*DO V EKIE	RI V IERA	*GRA V ELLY
DI V INE	SA V AGE	DU V ETYN	RI V IERE	GRA V ITON
DI V ING	SA V ANT	FA V ORER	RI V ULET	GRO V ELER
DO V ISH	SA V ATE	FO V EOLA	RO V VING	*HEA V ENLY
DY V OUR	SA V INE	FO V EOLE	SA V ABLE	*HEA V YSET
FA V ELA	SA V ING	GA V OTTE	SA V ANNA	NER V IEST
FA V OUR	SA V IOR	HA V EREL	SA V ELOY	NON V IRAL
GA V AGE	SA V ORY	HA V IOUR	SA V IOUR	NON V OCAL
GA V IAL	SA V OUR	HO V ERER	SA V ORER	NON V OTER
GI V ING	SO V IET	*JA V ELIN	SA V OURY	PAR V ENUE
GO V ERN	SO V RAN	*JU V ENAL	SE V ENTH	PAR V OLIN
HA V IOR	TA V ERN	*LA V ROCK	SE V ENTY	PER V ADER
*JO V IAL	VI V ACE	LE V ATOR	SE V ERAL	PER V ERSE
KA V ASS	*VI V ARY	LE V ELER	SE V VERE	PER V IOUS
LA V ABO	VI V ERS	LE V ELLY	*SO V KHOZ	PLU V IOSE
LA V AGE	*VI V IFY	LE V ERET	VA V ASOR	PLU V IOUS
LA V EER	*WA V ERY	LE V ULIN	*VI V IFIC	*POX V IRUS
LA V ING	WA V IER	LI V ABLE	WA V ELET	PRE V IOUS
LA V ISH	WA V IES	LI V ENER	*WA V EOFF	PRE V ISOR
LE V ANT	*WA V ILY	LO V ABLE	WA V ERER	*PRO V ENLY
LE V IED	WA V ING	*MO V ABLY	WA V IEST	PRO V IDER
LE V IER	WI V ERN	MO V ELES	BIO V ULAR	*PRO V INCE
LE V IES	WI V ING	NA V ETTE	*BRE V ETCY	PRO V IRUS
LE V ITY	*WY V ERN	NA V VIES	*BRE V IARY	*PRO V OKER
LI V ELY	BE V ELER	NI V EOUS	CAL V ADOS	PUL V ILLI
LI V ERY	BE V OMIT	NO V ATIN	CAL V ARIA	PUL V INUS
LI V EST	*BI V ALVE	NO V ELLA	CAN V ASER	*PUR V EYOR
LI V IER	*BI V INYL	NO V ELLY	CER V ELAT	*QUA V ERER
LI V ING	BI V OUAC	NO V ELTY	*CER V ICAL	*QUI V ERER
LI V YER	CA V ALLA	PA V IOUR	*CHE V ALET	REO V IRUS
LO V AGE	*CA V ALLY	PA V ISER	*CHE V ERON	SAL V ABLE
LO V ELY	*CA V ALRY	PI V OTAL	*CHI V ALRY	SAL V AGER
LO V ELY	CA V EMAN	*PO V ERTY	*CHI V AREE	SAL V AGER
LO V ING	CA V ETTO	RA V AGER	*CLA V ICLE	*SAL V IFIC
NA V AID	CA V IARE	RA V ELER	CLE V EITE	SCA V ENGE
NO V ICE	CA V ILER	RA V ELIN	*COE V ALLY	SEL V EDGE
		RA V ELLY		SER V ABLE

SER V ICER	SLA V ERER	SUB V IRAL	TRA V ERSE	* * *
SER V ITOR	SLI V ERER	*SUB V OCAL	TRA V ESTY	
SHI V AREE	*SLI V OVIC	SUR V EYOR	TRA V OISE	SHI V
SHI V ERER	SLO V ENLY	SUR V IVAL	TRI V ALVE	SPI V
SHO V ELER	SNI V ELER	SUR V IVER	VAL V ELET	GANE V
SIL V ERER	SOL V ABLE	SUR V IVOR	VAL V ULAR	MOSHA V
SIL V ERLY	*SOL V ENCY	*SYL V ATIC	VEL V ERET	
SIL V ICAL	SOU V ENIR	TRA V ELER	VOL V ULUS	
SIR V ENTE	*SUB V ICAR	TRA V ELOG	VUL V ITIS	

W

WACK	WEEN	WINY	WAKEN	WHEEL
WADE	WEEP	WIPE	WAKER	WHEEN
WADI	WEER	WIRE	WALER	WHEEP
WADY	WEET	WIRY	WALLA	*WHELK
WAFF	WEFT	WISE	WALLY	WHELM
WAFT	WEIR	WISH	*WALTZ	WHELP
WAGE	WEKA	WISP	WAMUS	WHERE
WAIF	WELD	WISS	WANEY	*WHICH
WAIL	WELL	WIST	WANLY	*WHIFF
WAIN	WELT	WITE	WARTY	WHILE
WAIR	WEND	WITH	WASHY	WHINE
WAIT	WENT	WIVE	WASPY	WHINY
WAKE	WEPT	WOAD	WASTE	WHIPT
WALE	WERE	WOKE	WATAP	WHIRL
WALK	WERT	WOLD	WATCH	WHIRR
WALL	WEST	WOLF	WATER	WHISH
WALY	WHAM	WOMB	WAUGH	*WHISK
WAME	WHAP	WONT	WAVER	WHIST
WAND	WHAT	WOOD	WAVEY	WHITE
WANE	WHEE	WOOF	*WAXEN	WHITY
WANT	WHEN	WOOL	*WAXER	*WHIZZ
WANY	WHET	WORD	WEALD	WHOLE
WARD	WHEW	WORE	WEARY	*WHOMP
WARE	WHEY	WORK	WEAVE	WHOOP
WARK	WHID	WORM	*WEBBY	WHORE
WARM	WHIM	WORN	WEBER	WHORL
WARN	WHIN	WORT	WECHT	WHORT
WARP	WHIP	WOST	WEDEL	WHOSE
WART	WHIR	WOVE	WEDGE	WHOSO
WARY	WHIT	WRAP	WEDGY	*WHUMP
WASH	*WHIZ	WREN	WEEDY	WIDDY
WASP	WHOA	WRIT	WEENY	WIDEN
WAST	WHOM	*WYCH	WEEPY	WIDER
WATT	WHOP	WYLE	WEEST	WIDOW
WAUK	WICH	WYND	WEIGH	WIDTH
WAUL	WICK	WYNN	WEIRD	WIELD
WAUR	WIDE	WYTE	WELCH	WIGAN
WAVE	WIFE	WACKE	WELSH	WIGHT
WAVY	WILD	*WACKY	WENCH	WILCO
WAWL	WILE	WADDY	WENNY	WILLY
*WAXY	WILL	WADER	WETLY	WINCE
WEAK	WILT	WAFER	*WHACK	WINCH
WEAL	WILY	WAGER	WHALE	WINDY
WEAN	WIND	WAGON	WHANG	WINEY
WEAR	WINE	WAHOO	WHARF	WINGY
WEED	WING	WAIST	WHAUP	*WINZE
WEEK	WINK	WAIVE	WHEAL	WIPER
WEEL	WINO		WHEAT	WIRER

WIRRA	WADING	WARPER	*WHEEZY	WINDER
WISED	WADMAL	WARRED	*WHELKY	WINDLE
WISER	WADMEL	WARREN	WHENAS	WINDOW
WISHA	WADMOL	WARSAW	WHENCE	WINDUP
WISPY	WADSET	WARSLE	*WHERRY	WINERY
WITAN	WAEFUL	WASHER	*WHERVE	WINGER
WITCH	*WAFERY	WASTER	*WHIDAH	WINIER
WITEN	*WAFFIE	WASTRY	WHILOM	WINING
WITHE	*WAFFLE	WATAPE	WHILST	WINISH
WITHY	WAFTER	WATERY	*WHIMSY	WINKER
WITTY	WAGGED	WATTER	WHINER	WINKLE
WIVER	WAGGER	WATTLE	*WHINEY	WINNED
WIVES	WAGGLE	WAUCHT	*WHINNY	WINNER
*WIZEN	WAGGLY	WAUGHT	*WHIPPY	WINNOW
WOALD	WAGGON	*WAVERY	*WHIRLY	WINTER
WOFUL	WAGING	WAVIER	*WHIRRY	WINTLE
WOKEN	WAHINE	WAVIES	*WHISHT	WINTRY
WOMAN	WAILER	*WAVILY	*WHISKY	WIPING
*WOMBY	WAITER	WAVING	WHITEN	WIRIER
WOMEN	WAIVER	*WAXIER	WHITER	WIRILY
*WONKY	*WAKIKI	*WAXILY	*WHITEY	WIRING
WOODY	WAKING	*WAXING	*WHOLLY	WISDOM
WOOER	WALIES	*WAYLAY	WHOMSO	WISELY
WOOLY	WALING	WEAKEN	*WHOOSH	WISENT
WOOPS	WALKER	*WEAKLY	WHOSIS	WISEST
WOOSH	*WALKUP	WEALTH	*WHYDAH	WISHER
*WOOZY	WALLAH	WEANER	*WICKED	WISING
WORDY	WALLET	WEAPON	*WICKER	*WITCHY
WORLD	WALLIE	WEARER	*WICKET	WITHAL
WORMY	WALLOP	WEASEL	*WICOPY	WITHER
WORRY	WALLOW	WEASON	WIDDER	WITHIN
WORSE	WALNUT	WEAVER	WIDDIE	WITING
WORST	WALRUS	*WEBFED	WIDDLE	WITNEY
WORTH	WAMBLE	WEDDER	WIDEST	WITTED
WOULD	*WAMBLY	WEDELN	WIDGET	WITTOL
WOUND	WAMMUS	WEDGIE	WIDISH	WIVERN
WOVEN	*WAMPUM	WEEDER	WIELDY	WIVING
WRACK	WAMPUS	*WEEKLY	WIENER	*WIZARD
WRANG	WANDER	WEENIE	WIENIE	*WIZZEN
WRAPT	WANDLE	WEENSY	*WIFELY	WOBBLE
WRATH	WANGAN	WEEPER	WIFING	*WOBBLY
WREAK	WANGLE	WEEVER	WIGEON	WOEFUL
WRECK	WANGUN	WEEVIL	WIGGED	WOLFER
WREST	WANIER	WEEWEE	WIGGLE	WOLVER
WRIED	WANING	WEIGHT	WIGGLY	WOLVES
WRIER	WANION	WEINER	WIGLET	WOMBAT
WRIES	WANNED	WEIRDO	WIGWAG	WOMERA
WRING	WANNER	WEIRDY	*WIGWAM	WONDER
WRIST	WANTER	WELDER	*WIKIUP	WONNED
WRITE	WANTON	WELDOR	WILDER	WONNER
WRONG	WAPITI	WELKIN	WILDLY	WONTON
WROTE	WARBLE	WELTER	WILFUL	WOODEN
WROTH	WARDEN	WESKIT	WILIER	WOODSY
WRUNG	WARDER	WESTER	WILILY	WOOFER
WURST	WARIER	WETHER	WILING	WOOLEN
WABBLE	WARILY	WETTED	WILLER	WOOLER
*WABBLY	WARING	WETTER	WILLET	WOOLIE
WADDER	WARMER	*WHACKY	WILLOW	WOOLLY
WADDIE	WARMLY	WHALER	WIMBLE	WORKER
WADDLE	WARMTH	*WHAMMY	WIMPLE	*WORKUP
WADDLY	WARMUP	*WHARVE	WINCER	WORMER
WADIES	WARNER	*WHEEZE	WINCEY	WORMIL

WORRIT	WARFARE	WEASAND	*WHIFFER	*WILLOWY
WORSEN	WARHEAD	WEATHER	*WHIFFET	*WINCHER
WORSER	WARIEST	*WEAZAND	*WHIFFLE	WINCING
WORSET	WARISON	*WEBBING	*WHIMPER	WINDAGE
*WORTHY	WARLESS	*WEBFOOT	*WHIMSEY	WINDBAG
WOWSER	WARLIKE	WEBLESS	WHINIER	WINDIER
WRAITH	*WARLOCK	*WEBLIKE	WHINING	WINDIGO
WRASSE	WARLORD	WEBSTER	*WHIPPED	WINDILY
*WRATHY	*WARMISH	*WEBWORM	*WHIPPER	WINDING
WREATH	WARNING	WEDDING	*WHIPPET	WINDROW
WRENCH	WARPAGE	*WEDLOCK	*WHIPRAY	*WINDWAY
WRETCH	*WARPATH	WEEDIER	*WHIPSAW	WINESOP
WRIEST	WARRANT	WEEDILY	WHIRLER	*WINGBOW
WRIGHT	WARRING	*WEEKDAY	WHIRRED	WINGIER
WRISTY	WARRIOR	*WEEKEND	*WHISKER	WINGLET
WRITER	*WARSHIP	WEIGELA	*WHISKEY	WINGMAN
WRITHE	WARSLER	WEIGHER	*WHISPER	WINIEST
*WURZEL	WARSTLE	*WEIGHTY	WHISTLE	WINNING
*WYVERN	WARTHOG	WEIRDIE	*WHITELY	*WINNOCK
WABBLER	WARTIER	WEIRDLY	WHITEST	WINSOME
WADABLE	WARTIME	*WELCHER	*WHITHER	WINTERY
WADDIED	*WARWORK	WELCOME	WHITIES	WIPEOUT
WADDIES	WARWORN	WELFARE	WHITING	WIREMAN
WADDING	WASHIER	WELSHER	*WHITISH	WIRETAP
WADDLER	WASHING	WELTING	*WHITLOW	*WIREWAY
WADMAAL	WASHOUT	*WENCHER	WHITTER	WIRIEST
WADMOLL	WASHRAG	WENDIGO	WHITTLE	*WISHFUL
WAENESS	*WASHTUB	WENNISH	*WHIZZED	WISPIER
*WAESUCK	WASSAIL	WERGELD	*WHIZZER	*WISPILY
WAFTAGE	WASTAGE	WERGELT	*WHIZZES	*WISPISH
WAFTURE	WASTERY	WERGILD	*WHOEVER	WISTFUL
WAGERER	WASTING	*WERWOLF	*WHOLISM	WITHIER
*WAGGERY	WASTREL	WESSAND	*WHOOPEE	WITHIES
WAGGING	WASTRIE	WESTERN	*WHOOPER	WITHING
*WAGGISH	*WATCHER	WESTING	*WHOOPLA	WITHOUT
WAGONER	WATERER	*WETBACK	WHOOSIS	WITLESS
WAGSOME	WATTAGE	WETLAND	*WHOPPER	WITLING
WAGTAIL	WATTAPE	WETNESS	WHORING	WITLOOF
WAILFUL	WATTEST	WETTEST	*WHORISH	WITNESS
WAISTER	WAVELET	WETTING	WHORTLE	WITTIER
WAITING	*WAVEOFF	WETTISH	*WICKAPE	WITTILY
*WAKANDA	*WAVEOFF	*WHACKER	*WICKING	WITTING
*WAKEFUL	WAVERER	WHALING	*WICKIUP	*WOADWAX
WAKENER	WAVIEST	WHANGEE	*WICKYUP	WOBBLER
*WALKING	*WAXBILL	*WHAPPER	WIDENER	WOENESS
WALKOUT	*WAXIEST	WHATNOT	WIDGEON	WOESOME
*WALKWAY	*WAXLIKE	WHEATEN	WIDOWER	*WOLFISH
*WALLABY	*WAXWEED	WHEEDLE	WIELDER	*WOLFRAM
WALLEYE	*WAXWING	WHEELER	*WIFEDOM	*WOMANLY
WALLIES	*WAXWORK	WHEELIE	*WIGGERY	WOMMERA
*WALTZER	*WAXWORM	*WHEEPLE	WIGGING	WONNING
*WAMEFOU	*WAYBILL	*WHEEZER	WIGGLER	WOODBIN
*WAMEFUL	WAYLESS	WHEREAS	WIGLESS	*WOODBOX
*WAMPISH	WAYSIDE	WHEREAT	*WIGLIKE	WOODCUT
WANGLER	*WAYWARD	*WHEREBY	WILDCAT	WOODHEN
WANIEST	*WAYWORN	WHEREIN	WILDING	WOODIER
WANIGAN	*WEAKISH	*WHEREOF	WILDISH	WOODLOT
WANNESS	*WEALTHY	*WHEREON	WILIEST	WOODMAN
WANNEST	WEARIED	WHERETO	WILLFUL	WOODSIA
WANNING	WEARIER	*WHETHER	WILLIED	*WOODWAX
WANTAGE	WEARIES	WHETTER	WILLIES	WOOLIER
WARBLER	WEARISH	*WHICKER	WILLING	WOOLIES

WOOLLEN	WALLAROO	WAVINESS	*WHIPPIER	WINGSPAN
WOOLMAN	WALLOPER	*WAXBERRY	*WHIPPING	WINNABLE
WOOMERA	WALLOWER	*WAXINESS	*WHIPTAIL	WINNOWER
WOORALI	WANDERER	*WAXPLANT	*WHIPWORM	WINTERER
WOORARI	WANDEROO	*WAYFARER	*WHIRRING	WINTERLY
WORDAGE	WANNIGAN	*WAYGOING	*WHISPERY	*WIREDRAW
WORDIER	WANTONER	*WAYLAYER	WHISTLER	WIREHAIR
WORDILY	WANTONLY	*WEAKENER	*WHITECAP	WIRELESS
WORDING	*WARCRAFT	*WEAKFISH	*WHITEFLY	*WIRELIKE
*WORKBAG	*WARDENRY	*WEAKLING	WHITENER	*WIREWORK
*WORKBOX	WARDRESS	*WEAKNESS	WHITEOUT	*WIREWORM
*WORKDAY	WARDROBE	WEANLING	*WHITRACK	WIRINESS
*WORKING	WARDROOM	*WEAPONRY	WHITTLER	WISEACRE
*WORKMAN	*WARDSHIP	WEARABLE	WHITTRET	WISENESS
WORKOUT	WAREROOM	WEARIEST	*WHIZBANG	*WISHBONE
WORLDLY	WARFARIN	WEARIFUL	*WHIZZING	WISHLESS
WORMIER	WARINESS	WEEDIEST	*WHODUNIT	WISPIEST
*WORMISH	*WARMAKER	WEEDLESS	*WHOMEVER	*WISPLIKE
WORRIED	WARMNESS	*WEEDLIKE	*WHOREDOM	WISTARIA
WORRIER	*WARMOUTH	*WEEKLONG	WHORESON	WISTERIA
*WORSHIP	WARPLANE	*WEFTWISE	.*WHOSEVER	*WITCHERY
WORSTED	*WARPOWER	WEIGELIA	WIDENESS	*WITCHING
WOTTETH	*WARPWISE	*WEIGHMAN	*WIDTHWAY	*WITHDRAW
WOULDST	WARRAGAL	*WEIGHTER	*WIFEHOOD	WITHERER
WRANGLE	WARRANTY	WEIRDIES	WIFELESS	*WITHHOLD
WRAPPER	WARRENER	*WELCOMER	*WIFELIKE	WITHIEST
WRASTLE	WARRIGAL	WELDLESS	*WIGMAKER	WITTIEST
WREAKER	WARSTLER	WELDMENT	WILDFIRE	*WIZARDRY
WREATHE	WARTIEST	*WELLADAY	*WILDFOWL	WOBEGONE
*WRECKER	*WARTLIKE	*WELLAWAY	*WILDLIFE	*WOLFFISH
WRESTER	*WASHABLE	WELLBORN	WILDLING	*WOLFLIKE
WRESTLE	*WASHBOWL	*WELLCURB	WILDNESS	WOMANISE
WRIGGLE	WASHIEST	WELLDOER	*WILDWOOD	*WOMANISH
*WRIGGLY	*WASHROOM	*WELLHEAD	WILINESS	*WOMANIZE
WRINGER	WASTABLE	WELLHOLE	WILLIWAU	WONDERER
WRINKLE	WASTEFUL	WELLNESS	*WILLIWAW	WONDROUS
*WRINKLY	WASTELOT	WELLSITE	WILLOWER	*WONTEDLY
WRITHEN	WASTERIE	WEREGILD	*WILLYARD	WOODBIND
WRITHER	*WASTEWAY	*WEREWOLF	WILLYART	WOODBINE
WRITING	*WATCHCRY	WESTERLY	*WILLYWAW	*WOODCHAT
WRITTEN	*WATCHDOG	WESTMOST	WINDBURN	*WOODCOCK
WRONGER	*WATCHEYE	*WESTWARD	*WINDFALL	WOODIEST
WRONGLY	*WATCHFUL	*WETPROOF	*WINDFLAW	WOODLAND
WROUGHT	*WATCHMAN	WETTABLE	WINDGALL	*WOODLARK
*WRYNECK	*WATCHOUT	*WHALEMAN	WINDIEST	WOODLESS
WRYNESS	WATERAGE	*WHARFAGE	WINDLASS	WOODLORE
WADEABLE	WATERBED	*WHATEVER	WINDLESS	WOODNOTE
*WAESUCKS	WATERDOG	WHEATEAR	WINDLING	WOODPILE
WAGELESS	WATERIER	*WHEEDLER	WINDMILL	*WOODRUFF
WAGGONER	WATERILY	*WHEELING	*WINDPIPE	*WOODSHED
WAGONAGE	WATERING	*WHEELMAN	*WINDSOCK	WOODSMAN
*WAHCONDA	WATERISH	*WHENEVER	*WINDWARD	*WOODWIND
WAILSOME	WATERLOG	*WHEREVER	WINELESS	*WOODWORK
WAINSCOT	WATERLOO	*WHETTING	*WINESHOP	*WOODWORM
WAISTING	WATERMAN	*WHEYFACE	WINESKIN	*WOOINGLY
WAITRESS	*WATERWAY	*WHIFFLER	*WINGBACK	WOOLFELL
*WAKELESS	WATTHOUR	*WHIMBREL	WINGDING	WOOLIEST
*WAKENING	WATTLESS	*WHINCHAT	*WINGEDLY	WOOLLIER
*WAKERIFE	*WAVEBAND	WHINIEST	WINGIEST	WOOLLIES
*WALKAWAY	*WAVEFORM	*WHIPCORD	WINGLESS	*WOOLLIKE
*WALKOVER	WAVELESS	*WHIPLASH	*WINGLIKE	*WOOLPACK
*WALKYRIE	*WAVELIKE	*WHIPLIKE	*WINGOVER	*WOOLSACK

*WOOLSHED	B W ANA	*T W IXT	NE W ISH	*BO W KNOT
*WOOLSKIN	D W ARF	T W YER	NE W TON	BO W LDER
*WORDBOOK	D W ELL	BA W BEE	NO W AYS	BO W LESS
WORDIEST	D W ELT	*BA W DRY	NO W ISE	*BO W LFUL
WORDLESS	D W INE	BA W LER	PA W NEE	*BO W LIKE
*WORDPLAY	S W AGE	BA W TIE	PA W NER	BO W LINE
*WORKABLE	S W AIL	BE W AIL	PA W NOR	BO W LING
*WORKADAY	S W AIN	BE W ARE	*PA W PAW	*BO W SHOT
*WORKBOAT	S W ALE	BE W EEP	PE W TER	CO W BANE
*WORKBOOK	S W AMI	BE W ORM	PO W DER	CO W BELL
*WORKFOLK	S W AMP	BE W RAP	PO W TER	*CO W BIND
*WORKLESS	S W AMY	BE W RAY	*PO W WOW	*CO W BIRD
*WORKLOAD	S W ANG	BO W ERY	RA W ISH	*CO W EDLY
*WORKROOM	S W ANK	BO W FIN	RE W AKE	*CO W FISH
*WORKSHOP	S W ARD	BO W ING	RE W ARD	CO W GIRL
*WORKWEEK	S W ARE	BO W LEG	RE W ARM	*CO W HAGE
*WORMHOLE	S W ARF	BO W LER	RE W ASH	*CO W HAND
WORMIEST	S W ARM	BO W MAN	RE W ELD	*CO W HERB
*WORMLIKE	S W ART	BO W POT	RE W IND	*CO W HERD
WORMROOT	S W ASH	*BO W WOW	RE W IRE	*CO W HIDE
WORMSEED	S W ATH	BO W YER	RE W OKE	CO W IEST
*WORMWOOD	S W EAR	*BY W ORD	RE W ORD	*CO W LICK
WORNNESS	S W EAT	*BY W ORK	RE W ORK	CO W LING
*WORTHFUL	S W EDE	CO W AGE	RE W OVE	*CO W POKE
WOSTTETH	S W EEP	CO W ARD	RE W RAP	*CO W SHED
WOULDEST	S W EER	*CO W BOY	RO W ING	*CO W SKIN
*WRACKFUL	S W EET	CO W IER	*SA W FLY	CO W SLIP
WRANGLER	S W ELL	CO W MAN	SA W LOG	DE W ATER
*WRAPPING	S W EPT	CO W PAT	SA W NEY	*DE W CLAW
*WRATHFUL	S W IFT	CO W PEA	SA W YER	DE W DROP
*WRECKAGE	S W ILL	*CO W POX	SE W AGE	DE W FALL
*WRECKFUL	S W INE	CO W RIE	SE W ING	DE W IEST
*WRECKING	S W ING	DA W TIE	SO W ANS	DE W LESS
WRESTLER	S W INK	DE W IER	SO W CAR	DO W ABLE
*WRETCHED	S W IPE	DE W ILY	SO W ENS	DO W AGER
WRIGGLER	S W IRL	DE W LAP	TA W DRY	DO W NIER
WRISTLET	S W ISH	DE W OOL	TA W DRY	FE W NESS
*WRITHING	S W ISS	DE W ORM	TA W NEY	FO W LING
WRONGFUL	S W ITH	DO W ERY	TA W PIE	*FO W LPOX
*WROTHFUL	S W IVE	DO W NER	*TH W ACK	*GA W KIER
	S W OON	DO W SER	TH W ART	*GA W KIES
	S W OOP	FA W NER	TO W AGE	*GA W KISH
H W AN	S W ORD	FO W LER	TO W ARD	*HA W KING
S W AB	S W ORE	GA W KER	TO W ERY	*HA W KISH
S W AG	S W ORN	GA W SIE	TO W HEE	*HO W BEIT
S W AM	S W OUN	GE W GAW	TO W NEE	*HO W EVER
S W AN	S W UNG	*HA W KER	TO W NIE	*HO W WDAH
S W AP	T W AIN	*HA W KEY	VA W ARD	*JA W BONE
S W AT	T W ANG	*HA W KIE	WO W SER	*JA W LIKE
S W AY	T W EAK	HA W SER	YA W NER	*JA W LINE
S W IG	T W EED	HO W LER	YA W PER	*JE W ELER
S W IM	T W EEN	HO W LET	YO W LER	*JE W ELRY
S W OB	T W EET	*KO W TOW	*BA W COCK	*JE W FISH
S W OP	T W ERP	LA W FUL	BA W DIER	LA W LESS
S W OT	T W ICE	LA W INE	BA W DIES	LA W LIKE
S W UM	T W IER	LA W ING	*BA W DILY	LA W SUIT
T W AE	T W ILL	LA W MAN	*BA W DRIC	LO W BORN
T W AT	T W INE	LA W YER	BA W SUNT	LO W BRED
T W IG	T W INY	LO W BOY	*BE W EARY	*LO W BROW
T W IN	T W IRL	LO W ERY	*BE W ITCH	LO W DOWN
T W IT	T W IRP	LO W ING	*BE W ORRY	LO W LAND
Y W IS	T W IST	LO W ISH	*BO W HEAD	LO W LIFE

LO W NESS	*CLO W NERY	SNO W MELT	STO W	HARRO W
*MA W KISH	*CLO W NISH	*SNO W PACK	THA W	*HAYMO W
NE W BORN	*COB W EBBY	*SNO W PLOW	THE W	*HEEHA W
*NE W MOWN	*COG W HEEL	*SNO W SHED	TRO W	HOLLO W
NE W NESS	*CRA W FISH	SNO W SHOE	VIE W	*JIGSA W
*NE W SBOY	*CRA W LWAY	SNO W SUIT	VRO W	*KOWTO W
NE W SIER	CRE W LESS	*STO W AWAY	WHE W	MALLO W
NE W SIES	*CRO W FOOT	SUN W ARDS	BEDE W	MARRO W
NE W SMAN	*CRO W STEP	THA W LESS	BELO W	MEADO W
NO W HERE	CUT W ATER	THE W LESS	BYLA W	MELLO W
PA W NAGE	*DOG W ATCH	THO W LESS	CAHO W	MILDE W
*PO W DERY	*DRA W BACK	TRO W ELER	KOTO W	MINNO W
RA W HIDE	DRA W BORE	TRO W SERS	MACA W	MORRO W
RA W NESS	*DRA W DOWN	*TRY W ORKS	MIAO W	NARRO W
RE W AKEN	DRA W TUBE	VIE W IEST	NOHO W	NEPHE W
RE W EAVE	FLA W LESS	VIE W LESS	PAPA W	*PAWPA W
RE W EIGH	FLO W ERER		PILA W	PILLO W
RE W IDEN	FLO W ERET		PSHA W	PITSA W
RE W OKEN	*FLY W HEEL	BLA W	RENE W	*POWWO W
RE W OUND	*GAS W ORKS	BLO W	RESA W	REAVO W
RE W OVEN	*GAY W INGS	BRA W	RESE W	REDRA W
RE W RITE	*GLO W WORM	BRE W	RESO W	REFLE W
RO W BOAT	GRE W SOME	BRO W	SCRE W	REFLO W
*RO W LOCK	*LAY W OMAN	CHA W	SERO W	REGLO W
SA W BILL	*MAD W OMAN	CHE W	SHRE W	REGRE W
*SA W BUCK	*MID W ATCH	CHO W	SINE W	REGRO W
SA W DUST	NAR W HALE	CLA W	*SQUA W	RESHO W
*SA W FISH	NON W HITE	CLE W	STRA W	REVIE W
SA W LIKE	NON W OODY	CRA W	STRE W	RIPSA W
SA W MILL	NON W OVEN	CRE W	STRO W	SALLO W
TO W ARDS	*PIN W HEEL	CRO W	THRA W	SALLO W
*TO W AWAY	*PLO W BACK	DHO W	THRE W	SEESA W
TO W BOAT	*PLO W HEAD	DRA W	THRO W	SHADO W
TO W HEAD	PLO W LAND	DRE W	VROU W	SORRO W
TO W LINE	*REA W AKEN	FLA W	WIDO W	SUNBO W
TO W MOND	SEA W ATER	FLE W	BARLO W	SUNDE W
TO W MONT	*SHO W BOAT	FLO W	BARRO W	TALLO W
TO W NIES	*SHO W CASE	FRO W	BASHA W	WALLO W
TO W NISH	*SHO W DOWN	GLO W	BELLO W	WARSA W
*TO W PATH	*SHO W GIRL	GNA W	BESNO W	WILLO W
TO W ROPE	SHO W IEST	GRE W	BESTO W	WINDO W
VA W NTIE	*SHO W ROOM	GRO W	BILLO W	WINNO W
VO W LESS	*SKE W BACK	KNE W	BORRO W	YARRO W
*YA W PING	*SKE W BALD	KNO W	*BOWWO W	YELLO W
*BED W ARDS	*SKE W NESS	MEO W	BURRO W	*BACKSA W
*BLO W BACK	*SKY W ARDS	PHE W	BYELA W	*BESHRE W
*BLO W FISH	*SKY W RITE	PLO W	CALLO W	BESTRE W
*BLO W HARD	*SLO W DOWN	PRO W	CASHA W	BESTRO W
*BLO W HOLE	SLO W NESS	SCO W	CASHE W	*BUCKSA W
BLO W IEST	*SLO W POKE	SHA W	CURFE W	CATSPA W
*BLO W PIPE	*SLO W WORM	SHE W	CURLE W	*CUMSHA W
*BLO W TUBE	*SNO W BALL	SHO W	CUSHA W	*DAYGLO W
ʿBOB W HITE	*SNO W BANK	SKE W	FALLO W	*DEWCLA W
*BRO W BEAT	SNO W BELL	SLA W	FARRO W	DISAVO W
BRO W LESS	SNO W BIRD	SLE W	FELLO W	*FITCHE W
BRO W NIER	*SNO W BUSH	SLO W	*FOGBO W	*FLYBLO W
*BRO W NISH	SNO W DROP	SME W	FOLLO W	*FOREPA W
BRO W NOUT	SNO W FALL	SNA W	FURRO W	FRETSA W
*CHO W CHOW	*SNO W IEST	SNO W	GEEGA W	*HACKSA W
*CHO W TIME	SNO W LAND	SPE W	GEWGA W	HANDSA W
CLA W LESS	SNO W LESS	STA W	*GUFFA W	HOOSGO W
	*SNO W LIKE	STE W	HALLO W	*JACKDA W

*LOCKJA W	RINGTA W	CARASSO W	*FURBELO W	*ROUGHHE W
LONGBO W	SEMIRA W	*CHECKRO W	*GANGPLO W	*SCOFFLA W
*LOWBRO W	SHALLO W	*CHOWCHO W	*HAWKSHA W	SETSCRE W
MISDRA W	*SOMEHO W	*CLERIHE W	*HEDGERO W	*SHADBLO W
MISGRO W	SPARRO W	*COCKCRO W	*HIGHBRO W	*SIDESHO W
*MISKNO W	SUNGLO W	COLESLA W	*HONEYDE W	*SNOWPLO W
MISTBO W	SWALLO W	*CROSSBO W	*HOOSEGO W	*SOUTHPA W
MOONBO W	*WHIPSA W	CURASSO W	*KICKSHA W	TELEVIE W
*PRESHO W	*WHITLO W	DISALLO W	*LOBBYGO W	TOMORRO W
*PREVIE W	WINDRO W	DISENDO W	*MACCABA W	*WILLIWA W
*PURVIE W	*WINGBO W	*FEVERFE W	*MACKINA W	*WILLYWA W
RAINBO W	BEDSTRA W	*FOOFARA W	*MISTHRO W	*WINDFLA W
REENDO W	*BESHADO W	*FOREKNO W	*PEEPSHO W	*WIREDRA W
*RIKSHA W	.BUNGALO W	*FORESHO W	*RICKSHA W	*WITHDRA W

X

XYST	*BO X ING	*BO X HAUL	*SI X FOLD	FLE X
*XEBEC	DE X IES	*BO X IEST	SI X TEEN	FLU X
XENIA	DE X TER	*BO X LIKE	*SI X THLY	HOA X
XENIC	DE X TRO	*BO X WOOD	*TA X ABLE	*JIN X
XENON	*FI X ATE	*CO X ALGY	*TA X ABLE	LYN X
XERIC	*FI X ITY	*CO X COMB	*TA X ICAB	MIN X
XERUS	*FI X URE	*DE X TRAL	*TA X IMAN	PRE X
*XYLAN	*FO X IER	*DE X TRAN	*TA X IWAY	ROU X
*XYLEM	*FO X ILY	*DE X TRIN	TA X LESS	BEAU X
*XYLOL	*FO X ING	*FI X ATIF	*TA X PAID	*BEMI X
*XYLYL	*HE X ADE	*FI X EDLY	*TA X WISE	BORA X
*XYLENE	*HE X ANE	*FI X INGS	*TA X YING	CALI X
*XYLOID	*HE X ONE	*FI X TUTE	TE X TILE	*CALY X
*XYLOSE	*HE X OSE	*FO X FIRE	TE X TUAL	CARE X
*XYSTER	*LA X ITY	*FO X FISH	TE X TURE	*CIME X
*XYSTOS	LU X ATE	*FO X HOLE	*TO X EMIA	*CODE X
*XYSTUS	*LU X URY	*FO X IEST	*TO X ICAL	CULE X
*XANTHIC	*MA X IMA	*FO X LIKE	*VE X EDLY	*CYLI X
*XANTHIN	*MA X IXE	*FO X SKIN	*WA X BILL	DESE X
*XERARCH	*MY X OID	*FO X TAIL	*WA X IEST	*DEWA X
XEROSIS	*MY X OMA	*HE X AGON	*WA X LIKE	GALA X
*XIPHOID	*PA X WAX	*HE X APLA	*WA X WEED	*HAPA X
*XYLIDIN	*SA X ONY	*HE X APOD	*WA X WING	HELI X
*XANTHATE	SE X IER	*HE X EREI	*WA X WORK	*HYRA X
*XANTHEIN	*SE X ILY	*HE X OSAN	*WA X WORM	*KYLI X
*XANTHENE	*SE X ISM	LA X NESS	*COE X TEND	LATE X
*XANTHINE	SE X IST	*LE X ICAL	*FLA X SEED	MIRE X
*XANTHOMA	*SE X POT	*LE X ICON	*FLE X IBLE	MURE X
*XANTHONE	SE X TAN	*MA X ILLA	*FLE X UOSE	*PHLO X
*XANTHOUS	SE X TET	*MA X IMAL	*FLE X UOUS	RADI X
*XENOGAMY	SE X TON	*MA X IMUM	*GLO X INIA	REDO X
*XENOGENY	SE X UAL	*MA X WELL	*PRO X EMIC	*REFI X
*XENOLITH	*TA X EME	*MI X TURE	*PRO X IMAL	RELA X
*XEROSERE	TA X ITE	NO X IOUS	*QUI X OTIC	REME X
*XYLIDINE	*TA X MAN	*PY X IDES	*QUI X OTRY	REMI X
*XYLOCARP	TO X INE	*SA X HORN	*REE X PORT	*REWA X
*XYLOTOMY	TO X OID	*SA X TUBA		SILE X
	TU X EDO	SE X IEST		TELE X
	*WA X IER	SE X LESS	CAL X	*VARI X
*BO X CAR	*WA X ILY	SE X TAIN	COA X	*BIFLE X
*BO X FUL	*WA X ING	SE X TANT	CRU X	*BOLLI X
*BO X IER	*BO X FISH	SE X TILE	FLA X	*BOLLO X

*BOMBY X	*POLLE X	*BROADA X	*PILLBO X	*CURTALA X
*CAUDE X	*PREFI X	*CARAPA X	*POSTBO X	*HARUSPE X
*CERVI X	*PREMI X	*CASHBO X	*POSTFI X	*HERETRI X
*CLIMA X	*PRETA X	*COALBO X	*PRINCO X	*HERITRI X
*COCCY X	*PROLI X	*COANNE X	*REAFFI X	*MATCHBO X
*COMMI X	*REFLE X	*COMPLE X	REANNE X	*MICROLU X
*CONVE X	*REFLU X	*CONFLU X	*RECTRI X	*MILLILU X
*CORTE X	*SCOLE X	*FEEDBO X	*REINDE X	*PARALLA X
*COWPO X	*SMILA X	*FIREBO X	*SALPIN X	*PONTIFE X
*DIPLE X	*SPADI X	*FLUMMO X	*SALTBO X	*PRECIEU X
*DUPLE X	*SPHIN X	*FOWLPO X	*SANDBO X	*QUINCUN X
*FORNI X	STORA X	*GEARBO X	*SIMPLE X	*SARDONY X
*HALLU X	*STYRA X	*HELLBO X	*SOAPBO X	*SAUCEBO X
*HATBO X	*SUBFI X	*JUKEBO X	*SONOVO X	*SMALLPO X
*HOTBO X	*SUFFI X	*LOCKBO X	*TECTRI X	*SNUFFBO X
*LARYN X	SURTA X	*MAILBO X	*TOOLBO X	*SOUNDBO X
*LUMMO X	*SYNTA X	*MINIMA X	TORTRI X	*SPINIFE X
*MASTI X	*SYRIN X	*NARTHE X	*TRIPLE X	*SUBINDE X
*MATRI X	*TEABO X	*PACKWA X	*TUBIFE X	*SUPERFI X
*MENIN X	*THORA X	*PANCHA X	*WOADWA X	*SUPERSE X
NONTA X	*VERNI X	*PARADO X	*WOODBO X	*SUPERTA X
*PAXWA X	*VERTE X	*PEMPHI X	*WOODWA X	*SWEATBO X
*PEGBO X	*VOLVO X	*PERPLE X	*WORKBO X	*SWINEPO X
*PHENI X	*VORTE X	*PHALAN X	*BICONVE X	*TOADFLA X
*PICKA X	*BANDBO X	*PHARYN X	*CICATRI X	*TRANSFI X
*POLEA X	*BEESWA X	*PHOENI X	*CRUCIFI X	

Y

YACK	YODH	*YEUKY	YAUPER	YARDAGE
YAFF	YOGA	YIELD	YAUPON	YARDARM
YAGI	YOGH	YINCE	YAWNER	YARDMAN
YALD	YOGI	YIPES	YAWPER	*YASHMAC
YANG	YOKE	YIRTH	YCLEPT	*YASHMAK
YANK	YOLK	YODEL	YEARLY	YATAGAN
YARD·	YOND	YODLE	YEASTY	*YAWPING
YARE	YONI	YOGEE	YEELIN	*YCLEPED
YARN	YORE	YOGIC	YELLER	YEALING
YAUD	YOUR	YOGIN	YELLOW	YEARNER
YAUP	YOWE	YOKEL	YELPER	YEGGMAN
YAWL	YOWL	*YOLKY	YEOMAN	*YELLOWY
YAWN	YUAN	YOUNG	YESSED	*YESHIVA
YAWP	YUGA	YOURN	YESSES	YESSING
YEAH	YULE	YOURS	YESTER	YESTERN
YEAN	YURT	YOUSE	YIPPED	YIELDER
YEAR	YWIS	YOUTH	YIPPEE	*YIPPING
YEGG	YACHT	YOWIE	YIPPIE	YODELER
YELD	YAGER	YUCCA	YODLER	YOGHURT
YELK	YAHOO	YULAN	YOGINI	YOUNGER
YELL	YAIRD	*YUMMY	YOGURT	YOUNKER
YELP	YAMEN	YUPON	*YOICKS	*YOYTHEN
YERK	YAMUN	YABBER	YOKING	YPERITE
YETI	YAPOK	YAMMER	YONDER	YTTRIUM
YETT	YAPON	*YANQUI	YONKER	*YACHTING
YEUK	YAULD	*YAPOCK	YOUPON	*YACHTMAN
YILL	YEARN	YAPPED	YOWLER	*YAHOOISM
YIPE	YEAST	YAPPER	YTTRIA	*YAMMERER
YIRD	YENTA	YARROW	*YACHTER	*YARDBIRD
YIRR	YERBA	*YASMAK	*YAPPING	*YARDWAND

*YARMELKE	S Y KE	L Y SSA	HA Y ING	ST Y LAR
*YARMULKE	S Y NC	L Y TIC	*HA Y MOW	ST Y LER
*YATAGHAN	S Y NE	L Y TTA	HE Y DAY	ST Y LET
*YAWMETER	T Y EE	*M Y OPY	*HE Y DEY	ST Y LUS
YEANLING	T Y KE	N Y ALA	HO Y DEN	ST Y MIE
*YEARBOOK	T Y NE	N Y LON	*JA Y GEE	*ST Y RAX
YEARLIES	T Y PE	*N Y MPH	*JA Y VEE	*TH Y MEY
YEARLING	T Y PO	*P Y GMY	*JO Y FUL	*TH Y MIC
YEARLONG	T Y PP	P Y LON	*JO Y OUS	TH Y MOL
YEARNING	T Y PY	P Y OID	*JO Y POP	TH Y MUS
*YEOMANRY	T Y RE	P Y RAN	KA Y LES	TH Y RSE
*YESHIVAH	T Y RO	P Y RIC	KE Y SET	TO Y ISH
YESTREEN	*W Y CH	*P Y XIE	*KE Y WAY	TR Y OUT
YODELLER	W Y LE	*P Y XIS	LA Y MAN	TR Y STE
*YOGHOURT	W Y ND	S Y CEE	*LA Y OFF	TU Y ERE
*YOKELESS	W Y NN	S Y LPH	*MA Y DAY	VO Y AGE
*YOKELISH	W Y TE	S Y LVA	*MA Y FLY	VO Y EUR
*YOKEMATE	X Y ST	S Y NCH	*MA Y HAP	*WA Y LAY
*YOUNGISH	*Z Y ME	S Y NOD	*MA Y HEM	*WH Y DAH
YOURSELF	*B Y LAW	S Y REN	*MA Y POP	*ZO Y SIA
*YOUTHFUL	*B Y WAY	S Y RUP	M Y ASIS	BA Y ONET
YTTERBIA	C Y ANO	T Y ING	M Y CELE	*BA Y WOOD
YULETIDE	C Y CAD	T Y PAL	M Y ELIR	BO Y COTT
	C Y CAS	T Y PED	M Y OPIA	*BO Y HOOD
	C Y CLE	T Y PEY	M Y OSIN	CA Y ENNE
	C Y CLO	T Y PIC	M Y OSIS	*CH Y MIST
B Y RE	C Y DER	T Y THE	M Y OTIC	*CH Y MOUS
B Y RL	*C Y LIX	V Y ING	M Y RIAD	CL Y PEUS
B Y TE	C Y MAR	*X Y LAN	M Y RICA	CL Y STER
C Y AN	C Y MOL	*X Y LEM	M Y RTLE	CO Y NESS
C Y MA	C Y NIC	*X Y LOL	M Y SELF	*CR Y BABY
C Y ME	C Y TON	*X Y LYL	M Y SOST	CR Y OGEN
C Y ST	D Y ING	BA Y AMO	M Y STIC	*CR Y PTIC
D Y AD	F Y TTE	BA Y ARD	M Y THOS	CR Y STAL
D Y ER	G Y PSY	BE Y LIC	NO Y ADE	*DA Y BOOK
D Y KE	G Y RAL	*BE Y LIK	*PA Y DAY	*DA Y GLOW
D Y NE	G Y RON	BE Y OND	PA Y NIM	DA Y LILY
F Y CE	G Y RUS	BO Y ARD	*PA Y OFF	DA Y LONG
F Y KE	H Y DRA	BO Y ISH	PA Y OLA	DA Y MARE
G Y BE	H Y DRO	BR Y ONY	PE Y OTE	DA Y ROOM
G Y RE	H Y ENA	CA Y MAN	PE Y OTL	DA Y SIDE
G Y RI	H Y ING	CA Y USE	PH Y LAE	DA Y SMAN
G Y RO	H Y MEN	*CH Y MIC	PH Y LAR	DA Y STAR
G Y VE	H Y OID	CO Y ISH	PH Y LON	DA Y TIME
H Y LA	*H Y PHA	CO Y OTE	*PH Y LUM	DO Y ENNE
H Y MN	*H Y RAX	CO Y POU	PH Y SES	DR Y NESS
H Y PO	H Y SON	CR Y PTO	*PH Y SIC	FE Y NESS
H Y TE	*K Y ACK	DA Y BED	PH Y SIS	*FL Y ABLE
K Y AR	*K Y AT	*DA Y FLY	PH Y TIN	*FL Y AWAY
K Y AT	K Y RIE	DO Y LEY	PH Y TON	*FL Y BELT
K Y TE	*K Y THE	DR Y LOT	*PS Y CHE	*FL Y BLOW
L Y NX	L Y ARD	FL Y ING	*PS Y CHO	*FL Y BOAT
L Y RE	L Y ART	FL Y MAN	PS Y LLA	*FL Y LEAF
L Y SE	L Y ASE	*FL Y SCH	RH Y MER	*FL Y OVER
M Y NA	L Y CEA	*FL Y WAY	*RH Y THM	*FL Y PAST
P Y IC	L Y CEE	FR Y PAN	RH Y TON	FL Y TIER
P Y IN	L Y ING	GA Y ETY	SA Y ING	FL Y TING
P Y RE	*L Y MPH	GE Y SER	SA Y YID	*FL Y TRAP
R Y KE	L Y NCH	GL Y CAN	SC Y THE	GA Y NESS
R Y ND	L Y RIC	GL Y CIN	*SK Y CAP	GL Y CINE
R Y OT	L Y SIN	GL Y COL	*SK Y MAN	*GL Y PTIC
S Y BO	L Y SIS	*GL Y CYL	*SK Y WAY	*GR Y PHON
S Y CE				

*HA Y COCK	*SK Y LARK	*CIT Y FIED	*POL Y MATH	FLA Y
*HA Y FORK	SK Y LINE	*CIT Y WARD	*POL Y PARY	FLE Y
HA Y LAGE	*SK Y PHOS	*CLA Y BANK	*POL Y PIDE	FOG Y
*HA Y LOFT	SK Y SAIL	*CLA Y LIKE	*POL Y PNEA	*FOX Y
*HA Y RACK	*SK Y WARD	*CLA Y MORE	*POL Y PODY	*FOZ Y
*HA Y RICK	SL Y NESS	*CLA Y WARE	*POL Y POID	FRA Y
HA Y RIDE	SO Y BEAN	*COP Y BOOK	*POL Y PORE	FUM Y
HA Y SEED	ST Y GIAN	*COP Y DESK	*POL Y POUS	FUR Y
*HA Y WARD	ST Y LATE	*COP Y HOLD	*POL Y SEMY	GAB Y
*HA Y WIRE	ST Y LING	*COR Y PHEE	*POL Y SOME	GAM Y
*JA Y BIRD	ST Y LISE	COT Y LOID	POL Y TENE	GAP Y
*JA Y WALK	ST Y LISH	*CRA Y FISH	*POL Y TENY	GLE Y
*JO Y ANCE	ST Y LIST	*DIC Y CLIC	*POL Y TYPE	GOB Y
*JO Y LESS	ST Y LITE	*DID Y MIUM	POL Y URIA	GOR Y
*JO Y RIDE	*ST Y LIZE	*DID Y MOUS	*POL Y ZOAN	GRA Y
*KA Y AKER	ST Y LOID	*DID Y NAMY	*POL Y ZOIC	GRE Y
*KE Y HOLE	ST Y PSIS	*DIH Y BRID	PON Y TAIL	*HAZ Y
KE Y LESS	ST Y PTIC	*DIH Y DRIC	*QUA Y SIDE	HOL Y
KE Y NOTE	ST Y RENE	*DIZ Y GOUS	*RUB Y LIKE	HOM Y
KE Y STER	*TH Y MIER	*GAN Y MEDE	*SPH Y GMUS	JOE Y
*KE Y WORD	*TH Y MINE	*GRA Y BACK	SPR Y NESS	JUR Y
*KR Y PTON	TH Y ROID	*GRA Y FISH	STA Y SAIL	LAC Y
*LA Y AWAY	TH Y RSUS	GRA Y LING	*SWA Y BACK	LAD Y
LA Y ETTE	*TH Y SELF	GRA Y NESS	TID Y TIPS	LAK Y
LA Y OVER	TO Y LESS	GRE Y NESS	*WHE Y FACE	*LAZ Y
LO Y ALLY	TO Y LIKE	*HOK Y POKY		LEV Y
LO Y ALTY	TR Y PSIN	*HOL Y TIDE		LIL Y
*MA Y BUSH	TR Y SAIL	*KAL Y PTRA	BAB Y	LIM Y
MA Y ORES	TR Y STER	*KAR Y OTIN	BEV Y	LIN Y
*MA Y WEED	VO Y AGER	*LAD Y BIRD	BOD Y	LOG Y
M Y ALGIA	*WA Y BILL	*LAD Y FISH	BOG Y	LOR Y
M Y COSIS	WA Y LESS	*LAD Y HOOD	BON Y	LUN Y
M Y ELINE	WA Y SIDE	*LAD Y LIKE	*BOX Y	MAN Y
M Y ELOID	*WA Y WARD	*LAD Y LOVE	BRA Y	*MAZ Y
M Y ELOMA	*WA Y WORN	*LAD Y PALM	BUO Y	MIR Y
M Y IASIS	*WR Y NECK	*LAD Y SHIP	BUR Y	MIT Y
M Y OSOTE	WR Y NESS	*LEC Y THUS	BUS Y	MOL Y
M Y OTOME	*YO Y THEN	*LEK Y THOS	CAG Y	MON Y
PA Y ABLE	*BAB Y HOOD	*LEK Y THUS	CAV Y	NAR Y
PA Y LOAD	BAR Y TONE	*MAN Y FOLD	CIT Y	NAV Y
PA Y MENT	*BIC Y CLER	*MOL Y BDIC	CLA Y	NIX Y
PA Y ROLL	*BIC Y CLIC	*PLA Y BACK	CLO Y	NOS Y
PE Y TRAL	*BOD Y SURF	*PLA Y BILL	COL Y	PAL Y
PE Y TREL	*BOD Y WORK	*PLA Y BOOK	CON Y	PAT Y
*PH Y TANE	*BUO Y ANCE	*PLA Y DOWN	COP Y	PIL Y
*PH Y TOID	*BUO Y ANCY	PLA Y GIRL	COW Y	PIN Y
*PL Y WOOD	*BUS Y BODY	PLA Y GOER	*COZ Y	PIP Y
*PR Y THEE	BUS Y NESS	PLA Y LAND	DAV Y	PIT Y
*PS Y CHIC	*BUS Y WORK	PLA Y LESS	DEF Y	*PIX Y
PS Y LLID	BUT Y LATE	*PLA Y LIKE	DEM Y	PLA Y
PT Y ALIN	BUT Y LENE	*PLA Y MATE	DEN Y	PLO Y
RA Y LESS	BUT Y RATE	*PLA Y ROOM	DEW Y	POG Y
RE Y NARD	BUT Y ROUS	PLA Y SUIT	DID Y	POK Y
RO Y ALLY	*CAL Y CATE	*PLA Y TIME	DOG Y	POL Y
RO Y ALTY	*CAL Y CEAL	*PLA Y WEAR	DOP Y	PON Y
RO Y STER	*CAL Y CINE	*POL Y BIRD	DOR Y	POS Y
*SH Y LOCK	*CAL Y CULI	POL Y GALA	DOT Y	PRA Y
SH Y NESS	*CAL Y PTER	*POL Y GAMY	*DOX Y	PRE Y
SH Y STER	*CAL Y PTRA	POL Y GENE	*DOZ Y	PUN Y
*SK Y DIVE	*CAP Y BARA	POL Y GLOT	DRA Y	*QUA Y
*SK Y HOOK	CAR Y ATID	*POL Y GONY	DUL Y	*QUE Y
*SK Y JACK	CAR Y OTIN	*POL Y GYNY	DUT Y	RAC Y

REL Y	BEIG Y	CATT Y	DICE Y	*FLAK Y
RIM Y	BELA Y	*CHEV Y	*DICK Y	FLAM Y
ROP Y	BELL Y	*CHEW Y	DILL Y	FLAW Y
ROS Y	BEND Y	*CHIV Y	DIML Y	*FLAX Y
RUB Y	BENN Y	*CHOK Y	DING Y	*FLUK Y
SAG Y	BERR Y	*CIVV Y	DINK Y	FLUT Y
SEX Y	BIAL Y	CLAR Y	DIPP Y	*FLYB Y
SHA Y	BIDD Y	COBB Y	DIRT Y	FOAM Y
*SIZ Y	*BIFF Y	*COCK Y	DISH Y	FOGE Y
SLA Y	BIGL Y	COLL Y	DITT Y	FOGG Y
SPA Y	BILG Y	*COMF Y	*DIVV Y	FOLL Y
SPR Y	BILL Y	COMM Y	*DIZZ Y	FOOT Y
STA Y	BITS Y	CONE Y	DOBB Y	FORA Y
STE Y	BITT Y	CONK Y	DODG Y	FORB Y
SWA Y	BLIM Y	COOE Y	DOGE Y	*FORK Y
THE Y	BLOW Y	COOK Y	DOGG Y	FORT Y
TID Y	BLUE Y	COOL Y	DOIL Y	FUBS Y
TIN Y	BOBB Y	CORB Y	DOLL Y	FUGG Y
TIV Y	BOGE Y	CORK Y	DONS Y	FULL Y
TOB Y	BOGG Y	CORN Y	DOOL Y	*FUNK Y
TOD Y	BONE Y	COSE Y	*DOOZ Y	FUNN Y
TON Y	BONN Y	COVE Y	DOPE Y	FURR Y
TOR Y	BOOB Y	COWR Y	DORM Y	*FURZ Y
TOW Y	BOOM Y	COYL Y	DORT Y	FUSS Y
TRA Y	BOOT Y	*COZE Y	DOTT Y	FUST Y
TRE Y	*BOOZ Y	*CRAZ Y	DOWD Y	*FUZZ Y
TRO Y	BOSK Y	CREP Y	DOWN Y	GABB Y
TYP Y	BOSS Y	CRON Y	DOWR Y	GAIL Y
VAR Y	BOUS Y	CUBB Y	DOYL Y	GALL Y
VER Y	BRAK Y	CUDD Y	DRIL Y	GAME Y
VIN Y	*BRAX Y	CULL Y	DRYL Y	GAPP Y
WAD Y	BRIN Y	CUPP Y	DUCH Y	GASS Y
WAL Y	BRIN Y	CURD Y	*DUCK Y	GAUD Y
WAN Y	BROS Y	CURL Y	DUDD Y	*GAUZ Y
WAR Y	BUBB Y	CURR Y	DULL Y	*GAWK Y
WAV Y	BUDD Y	CURV Y	DUMM Y	GAWS Y
*WAX Y	*BUFF Y	CUSH Y	DUMP Y	GAYL Y
WHE Y	BUGG Y	CUTE Y	DUNG Y	GEMM Y
WIL Y	BULG Y	CUTT Y	DUST Y	GERM Y
WIN Y	BULK Y	DADD Y	FADD Y	GIDD Y
WIR Y	BULL Y	*DAFF Y	FAER Y	GILL Y
*ZAN Y	BULL Y	DAIL Y	FAIR Y	GIMP Y
BADD Y	BUMP Y	DAIR Y	FANC Y	GINN Y
BADL Y	BUNN Y	DAIS Y	FANN Y	GIPS Y
*BAFF Y	BURL Y	DALL Y	FARC Y	GIRL Y
BAGG Y	BURR Y	DAND Y	FATL Y	GLAD Y
BALK Y	BUSB Y	DARK Y	FATT Y	GLAR Y
BALL Y	BUSH Y	DASH Y	FAWN Y	*GLAZ Y
BALM Y	BUST Y	DAUB Y	FELL Y	GLOR Y
BAND Y	BUTT Y	DEAR Y	FENN Y	GLUE Y
BARK Y	*BYWA Y	DECA Y	FERL Y	GODL Y
BARM Y	CABB Y	DECO Y	FERN Y	GOLL Y
BARN Y	CADD Y	DECR Y	FERR Y	GOOD Y
BASS Y	CADG Y	DEED Y	FIER Y	GOOE Y
BATT Y	CAGE Y	DEIF Y	FIFT Y	GOOF Y
BAWD Y	CAMP Y	DEIT Y	FILL Y	GOON Y
BAWT Y	CAND Y	DELA Y	FILM Y	GOOS Y
BEAD Y	CANN Y	DELL Y	FINN Y	GORS Y
BEAK Y	CANT Y	DERA Y	FIRR Y	GOUT Y
BEAM Y	CARN Y	DERB Y	FISH Y	GRAP Y
BEEF Y	CARR Y	DERR Y	FITL Y	GRAV Y
BEER Y	CASK Y	DIAR Y	*FIZZ Y	GRIM Y

GRIP Y	*JENN Y	LUCK Y	NAPP Y	*POCK Y
GULF Y	*JERK Y	LUMP Y	NAST Y	PODG Y
GULL Y	*JERR Y	LUST Y	NATT Y	POES Y
GULP Y	*JETT Y	MADL Y	NAVV Y	POGE Y
GUMM Y	*JIFF Y	MALM Y	NEED Y	POKE Y
GUNN Y	*JIMM Y	MALT Y	NERB Y	POPP Y
GUPP Y	*JIMP Y	MAME Y	NETT Y	PORG Y
GURR Y	*JOLL Y	MAMM Y	NEWL Y	PORK Y
GUSH Y	*JOLT Y	MANG Y	NEWS Y	POTS Y
GUST Y	*JOTT Y	MANL Y	NIFT Y	POTT Y
GUTS Y	*JOWL Y	MARL Y	NINN Y	POUT Y
GUTT Y	*JUIC Y	MARR Y	NIPP Y	*PREX Y
GYPS Y	*JUMP Y	MASH Y	NITT Y	PRIC Y
HAIR Y	*JUNK Y	MASS Y	NOBB Y	PRIV Y
*HAMM Y	*JUTT Y	MATE Y	NOBL Y	PROS Y
HAND Y	KAUR Y	MEAL Y	NODD Y	*PROX Y
*HANK Y	KELP Y	MEAN Y	NOIS Y	PUDG Y
HAPL Y	KERR Y	MEAT Y	NOOK Y	*PUFF Y
*HAPP Y	KIDD Y	MEIN Y	NOSE Y	PUGG Y
HARD Y	KILT Y	MERC Y	NOWA Y	PULP Y
HARP Y	*KINK Y	MERR Y	NUBB Y	PUNK Y
HARR Y	KITT Y	MESH Y	NUTT Y	PUNN Y
HEAD Y	*KOOK Y	MESS Y	PADD Y	PUNT Y
HEAV Y	LACE Y	MIDD Y	PALL Y	PUPP Y
HEDG Y	LAIT Y	*MIFF Y	PALM Y	PURS Y
HEFT Y	LANK Y	MILK Y	PALS Y	PUSH Y
*HEMP Y	LARD Y	MILT Y	PAND Y	PUSS Y
HENR Y	LARK Y	MINC Y	PANS Y	PUTT Y
HERB Y	LATH Y	MING Y	PANT Y	*PYGM Y
HERR Y	*LAXL Y	MINN Y	PAPP Y	*QUAK Y
HILL Y	LEAD Y	MINT Y	PARD Y	*QUER Y
HINN Y	LEAF Y	MIRK Y	PARR Y	RAGG Y
*HIPP Y	LEAK Y	MISS Y	PART Y	RAIN Y
HOAG Y	LEAR Y	MIST Y	PAST Y	RALL Y
HOAR Y	LEAV Y	MOLD Y	PATL Y	RAMM Y
*HOBB Y	LEDG Y	MOLL Y	PATS Y	RAND Y
*HOKE Y	LEER Y	MOMM Y	PATT Y	RANG Y
HOLE Y	LEFT Y	MONE Y	*PAWK Y	RASP Y
HOME Y	LEGG Y	MOOD Y	PEAK Y	RATT Y
HONE Y	LIMB Y	MOON Y	PEAT Y	RAWL Y
*HONK Y	LIME Y	MOOR Y	PEAV Y	READ Y
HOOE Y	LIND Y	MORA Y	*PECK Y	REDL Y
*HOOK Y	LINE Y	MOSE Y	PEER Y	REDR Y
HOOL Y	LING Y	MOSS Y	PENN Y	REED Y
HORN Y	LINK Y	MOTE Y	PEON Y	REEF Y
HORS Y	LINT Y	MOTH Y	PEPP Y	REEK Y
HOTL Y	LIPP Y	MOUS Y	PERD Y	REFL Y
*HUBB Y	LOAM Y	*MUCK Y	PERK Y	REFR Y
*HUFF Y	LOBB Y	MUDD Y	PERR Y	REIF Y
*HULK Y	LOFT Y	MUGG Y	PESK Y	REKE Y
*HUMP Y	LOGG Y	MUHL Y	PETT Y	RELA Y
*HUNK Y	LOLL Y	MULE Y	PHON Y	REPA Y
HURL Y	LOOB Y	MUMM Y	*PICK Y	REPL Y
HURR Y	LOOE Y	MURK Y	PIET Y	RESA Y
*HUSK Y	LOON Y	MURR Y	PIGG Y	RETR Y
HUSS Y	LOOP Y	MUSH Y	PIGM Y	RIBB Y
*JACK Y	LOPP Y	MUSK Y	PINE Y	RIDG Y
*JAGG Y	LORR Y	MUSS Y	PINK Y	RILE Y
*JANT Y	LOSS Y	MUST Y	PITH Y	RISK Y
*JAZZ Y	LOUR Y	*MUZZ Y	PLAT Y	*RITZ Y
*JELL Y	LOUS Y	*MYOP Y	PLAT Y	ROCK Y
*JEMM Y	LOWL Y	NANN Y	PLUM Y	ROIL Y

ROOK Y	SOPP Y	TUBB Y	BARLE Y	BROWN Y
ROOM Y	SORR Y	TUFT Y	BARON Y	*BRUMB Y
ROOT Y	SOUP Y	TUMM Y	BASEL Y	BRUSH Y
ROUP Y	SPIC Y	TUNN Y	BASIF Y	BRYON Y
ROWD Y	SPIK Y	TURF Y	BASSL Y	*BUBBL Y
RUDD Y	SPIN Y	TUTT Y	BATBO Y	*BUNCH Y
RUGB Y	SPIR Y	TWIN Y	*BAULK Y	BURBL Y
RUMM Y	SPLÁ Y	TYPE Y	*BAWDR Y	BURLE Y
RUNN Y	SPRA Y	VAST Y	*BEACH Y	BUSBO Y
RUNT Y	SPUM Y	VEAL Y	BEAUT Y	BUSIL Y
RUSH Y	STAG Y	VEER Y	*BEECH Y	*BYPLA Y
RUST Y	STIM Y	VEIN Y	BELAD Y	CAGIL Y
RUTT Y	STOG Y	*VICH Y	BELFR Y	CALOR Y
SADL Y	STON Y	VIEW Y	BENDA Y	CANAR Y
SALL Y	STOR Y	*WACK Y	BETON Y	CANOP Y
SALT Y	STRA Y	WADD Y	BETRA Y	CARBO Y
SAND Y	STRO Y	WALL Y	BEWRA Y	CARNE Y
SAPP Y	STUD Y	WANE Y	BIGAM Y	CASEF Y
SASS Y	STYM Y	WANL Y	BINAR Y	*CATCH Y
SAUC Y	SUDS Y	WART Y	BIOPS Y	CAUSE Y
SAUR Y	SULK Y	WASH Y	*BITCH Y	CAVIT Y
SAVO Y	SULL Y	WASP Y	*BLABB Y	CELER Y
SAVV Y	SUNN Y	WAVE Y	BLAST Y	*CHAFF Y
SCAL Y	SURF Y	WEAR Y	BLEAR Y	*CHALK Y
SCAR Y	SURG Y	*WEBB Y	BLENN Y	CHALL Y
SEAM Y	SURL Y	WEDG Y	BLIME Y	*CHAMM Y
SEDG Y	SWAM Y	WEED Y	*BLOCK Y	*CHAMP Y
SEED Y	TABB Y	WEEN Y	BLOOD Y	*CHANC Y
SEEL Y	TACK Y	WEEP Y	BLOOM Y	CHANT Y
SEEP Y	TAFF Y	WENN Y	BLOTT Y	CHARR Y
SEPO Y	TALK Y	WETL Y	BLOUS Y	CHATT Y
SERR Y	TALL Y	WHIN Y	*BLOWB Y	*CHEEK Y
SHAD Y	TAMM Y	WHIT Y	BLOWS Y	CHEER Y
*SHAK Y	TANG Y	WIDD Y	*BLOWZ Y	CHEES Y
SHAL Y	TANS Y	WILL Y	BLUEL Y	CHERR Y
SHIL Y	TARD Y	WIND Y	BLUES Y	CHERT Y
SHIN Y	TARR Y	WINE Y	BLURR Y	CHEST Y
SHOW Y	TAST Y	WING Y	BODIL Y	*CHICL Y
SHYL Y	TATT Y	WISP Y	BOSOM Y	CHILL Y
SILK Y	TAWN Y	WITH Y	BOTAN Y	*CHINK Y
SILL Y	TEAR Y	WITT Y	*BOTCH Y	*CHIPP Y
SILT Y	TECH Y	*WOMB Y	BOTFL Y	*CHIRP Y
SISS Y	TEDD Y	*WONK Y	BOUNC Y	CHITT Y
*SIXT Y	TEEN Y	WOOD Y	BOUNT Y	*CHIVV Y
SKIE Y	TELL Y	WOOL Y	BOWER Y	*CHOKE Y
*SKYE Y	TENT Y	WOOL Y	BRAGG Y	CHOOS Y
SLAT Y	TERR Y	*WOOZ Y	BRAIN Y	*CHOPP Y
SLIL Y	TEST Y	WORD Y	BRAND Y	*CHUBB Y
SLIM Y	*THYM Y	WORM Y	BRANN Y	*CHUCK Y
SMOK Y	TINN Y	WORR Y	BRASH Y	*CHUFF Y
SNAK Y	TIPP Y	*YEUK Y	BRASS Y	*CHUMM Y
SNOW Y	TIPS Y	*YOLK Y	BRATT Y	*CHUNK Y
SOAP Y	TITT Y	*ZINC Y	BRAWL Y	CICEL Y
SODD Y	*TIZZ Y	*ZING Y	BRAWN Y	CITIF Y
SOFT Y	TOAD Y	*ZINK Y	*BREEZ Y	*CLAMM Y
SOGG Y	TODA Y	*ZIPP Y	*BRICK Y	CLASS Y
SONL Y	TODD Y	*ZLOT Y	BRION Y	CLAYE Y
SONN Y	TOFF Y	BAILE Y	BROLL Y	CLERG Y
SONS Y	TOKA Y	*BAKER Y	*BRONZ Y	*CLIFF Y
SOOE Y	TOMM Y	BALDL Y	BROOD Y	CLING Y
SOOT Y	TOWN Y	BAREL Y	BROOM Y	*CLIQU Y
SOPH Y	TRUL Y	BARFL Y	BROTH Y	CLODD Y

CLOGG Y	DEARL Y	FIRML Y	GLAIR Y	HORSE Y
CLOTT Y	DEATH Y	*FISHL Y	GLASS Y	HOSTL Y
CLOUD Y	DECUR Y	*FITCH Y	GLEAM Y	HOURL Y
*CLUBB Y	*DEEJA Y	*FIXIT Y	GLEET Y	*HUMBL Y
*CLUMP Y	DEEPL Y	*FLABB Y	GLOOM Y	HUNGR Y
CLUMS Y	DEFRA Y	FLAGG Y	GLOSS Y	HURLE Y
*CODIF Y	DENAR Y	*FLAPP Y	GLUMP Y	HURRA Y
*COGWA Y	DEPLO Y	*FLASH Y	GNARL Y	*JALOP Y
COLDL Y	DEPUT Y	FLATL Y	GNATT Y	*JAPER Y
COLON Y	DESCR Y	*FLECK Y	GOBON Y	*JARVE Y
COMED Y	DHOOL Y	FLEDG Y	GOGGL Y	*JAUNT Y
COMEL Y	DIGAM Y	FLEEC Y	GOODB Y	*JERSE Y
COMIT Y	DIMIT Y	*FLESH Y	GOODL Y	*JIGGL Y
*COMPL Y	DIMPL Y	FLEUR Y	GOOGL Y	*JIMIN Y
*CONCH Y	DINGE Y	FLIMS Y	GOONE Y	*JINGL Y
CONVE Y	DINGH Y	FLINT Y	GOOSE Y	*JITNE Y
CONVO Y	DINKE Y	FLOUR Y	GORIL Y	*JOCKE Y
*COOKE Y	DINKL Y	*FLUFF Y	GRABB Y	*JOHNN Y
COOLL Y	DIPOD Y	*FLUKE Y	GRAIN Y	*JOUNC Y
COROD Y	DIREL Y	*FLUNK Y	GRANN Y	*JUNGL Y
COSIL Y	DISMA Y	FLURR Y	GRASS Y	*JUSTL Y
COSTL Y	*DJINN Y	*FLYWA Y	GRAYL Y	KEENL Y
COUNT Y	DONKE Y	*FOLKS Y	GREAS Y	KERSE Y
*COWBO Y	DOUBL Y	FONDL Y	GREED Y	*KEYWA Y
*CRABB Y	DOUGH Y	FOREB Y	GREEN Y	KIDNE Y
*CRACK Y	DOURL Y	*FORWH Y	GREMM Y	KINDL Y
CRAFT Y	DOWER Y	FOULL Y	GREYL Y	KINGL Y
CRAGG Y	DOYLE Y	*FOXIL Y	GRIPE Y	*KLUTZ Y
*CRANK Y	*DOZIL Y	FREAK Y	GRIPP Y	*KNOBB Y
CRANN Y	DRABL Y	FREEL Y	GRISL Y	KNOLL Y
*CRAPP Y	*DRAFF Y	*FRENZ Y	GRITT Y	KNOTT Y
CRAWL Y	DRAFT Y	FRETT Y	GROGG Y	KNURL Y
*CREAK Y	DRAGG Y	FRIAR Y	GROOV Y	LACIL Y
CREAM Y	DRAWL Y	FRILL Y	GROUT Y	*LACKE Y
CREAS Y	DREAM Y	FRING Y	GROWL Y	LAMEL Y
CREEP Y	DREAR Y	*FRISK Y	GRUBB Y	LANEL Y
CREPE Y	DREGG Y	*FRIZZ Y	*GRUFF Y	LASTL Y
*CRIMP Y	DRESS Y	FROGG Y	GRUMP Y	LATEL Y
CRISP Y	DRIFT Y	FROST Y	GUILT Y	*LAXIT Y
*CROAK Y	DRIPP Y	*FROTH Y	GULLE Y	*LAZIL Y
CROUP Y	DROLL Y	*FROUZ Y	GURNE Y	LEACH Y
*CROWD Y	DROOP Y	*FROWS Y	*HACKL Y	LEALT Y
CRUDD Y	DROPS Y	*FROWZ Y	HARDL Y	LEEWA Y
*CRUMB Y	DROSK Y	FRUIT Y	HAULM Y	LEGAC Y
*CRUMM Y	DROSS Y	*FRUMP Y	*HAWKE Y	LENIT Y
CRUST Y	DROWS Y	GADFL Y	*HAZIL Y	LEVIT Y
CUDDL Y	DRUML Y	GAIET Y	HEART Y	LIKEL Y
CULLA Y	DUALL Y	GAINL Y	*HEATH Y	LIMPL Y
CURAC Y	DUPER Y	*GALAX Y	HERES Y	LIMPS Y
CURTL Y	FAIRL Y	GALLE Y	*HEYDA Y	LINSE Y
CURTS Y	*FAKER Y	GAMEL Y	*HEYDE Y	LITAN Y
CURVE Y	FAMIL Y	GAMIL Y	*HICKE Y	LIVEL Y
CUTES Y	FAULT Y	GANGL Y	*HIGHL Y	LIVER Y
DAINT Y	FEALT Y	GANTR Y	*HOCKE Y	LOGIL Y
DAMPL Y	*FECKL Y	GARVE Y	HOLIL Y	LOGWA Y
DARKE Y	FEIST Y	GASIF Y	HOMEL Y	LONEL Y
DARKL Y	FELON Y	GAYET Y	HOMIL Y	LONGL Y
DATAR Y	FERIT Y	GENTR Y	HOMIN Y	LOONE Y
DAUBR Y	*FILTH Y	GHARR Y	*HONKE Y	LORDL Y
*DAYFL Y	FINEL Y	GHOST Y	*HOOKE Y	LOUDL Y
DEADL Y	FINER Y	GIGGL Y	HOORA Y	LOUNG Y
DEAFL Y		GLADL Y	HORAR Y	LOVEL Y

LOWBO Y	NOTIF Y	PUGGR Y	SANIT Y	SLINK Y
LOWER Y	NUBBL Y	PULLE Y	SASHA Y	SLIPP Y
LUNAC Y	NUDIT Y	*PUNCH Y	SATIN Y	SLOPP Y
*LUXUR Y	NUMBL Y	PUNIL Y	SAVOR Y	SLOSH Y
MAGUE Y	*PACIF Y	*PUNKE Y	*SAWFL Y	SLOWL Y
MAINL Y	*PACKL Y	PUREL Y	SAWNE Y	SLUDG Y
MALAD Y	PAINT Y	PURIF Y	*SAXON Y	SLUIC Y
*MAMME Y	PALEL Y	PURIT Y	*SCABB Y	SLUMM Y
MANGE Y	PALTR Y	PURPL Y	SCANT Y	SLURR Y
MARBL Y	PANTR Y	PURVE Y	SCARE Y	SLUSH Y
MARGA Y	*PAPAC Y	PUSLE Y	SCARR Y	SMARM Y
MARSH Y	PAPER Y	PUSSL Y	SCATT Y	SMART Y
MAUND Y	PARIT Y	*QUAGG Y	SCREW Y	SMEAR Y
*MAYDA Y	PARLA Y	*QUALM Y	*SCUMM Y	SMELL Y
*MAYFL Y	PARLE Y	*QUARR Y	SCURF Y	*SMIRK Y
*MAZIL Y	PAROD Y	*QUEAS Y	SCURR Y	SMITH Y
MEANL Y	PARTL Y	*QUEAZ Y	SCURV Y	SMOGG Y
MEASL Y	PASTR Y	*QUINS Y	SEAWA Y	*SMOKE Y
MEDLE Y	*PATCH Y	*QUIRK Y	SEEML Y	SMUDG Y
MEETL Y	*PAYDA Y	RACIL Y	SENAR Y	SMUGL Y
MELOD Y	*PEACH Y	RAMIF Y	SENTR Y	SMUTT Y
MEMOR Y	PEARL Y	RANKL Y	*SEXIL Y	SNAGG Y
*MICKE Y	PEAVE Y	RAREF Y	*SHABB Y	SNAPP Y
MIDDA Y	*PEBBL Y	RAREL Y	SHAGG Y	SNARL Y
*MIDWA Y	PELTR Y	RARIF Y	*SHAMM Y	*SNAZZ Y
*MIGHT Y	PENUR Y	RARIT Y	SHAMO Y	SNEAK Y
MILAD Y	PHONE Y	RASHL Y	SHAND Y	*SNEEZ Y
MINIF Y	PHOOE Y	RATAN Y	SHANT Y	*SNIFF Y
MISER Y	PIGST Y	RATIF Y	SHARP Y	SNIPP Y
MISLA Y	*PIMPL Y	RATTL Y	SHEEN Y	SNOBB Y
MISSA Y	PINER Y	REALL Y	SHELL Y	SNOOP Y
*MIZZL Y	*PINKL Y	REALT Y	SHELT Y	SNOOT Y
*MODIF Y	PIRAC Y	REBUR Y	*SHELV Y	*SNOOZ Y
MOIET Y	*PITCH Y	RECOP Y	SHERR Y	SNOTT Y
*MONKE Y	PLAGU Y	REDBA Y	*SHIFT Y	SNOUT Y
MONOD Y	PLASH Y	REDEF Y	*SHIMM Y	SNUBB Y
MOOLE Y	PLENT Y	REDEN Y	SHIND Y	*SNUFF Y
MOSTL Y	*PLISK Y	REMED Y	SHINN Y	SNUGL Y
MOTLE Y	PLOID Y	REPLA Y	SHIRT Y	SODOM Y
MOULD Y	PLOTT Y	RESIN Y	SHOAL Y	SOFTL Y
MOUSE Y	*PLUCK Y	REVER Y	SHODD Y	SOLEL Y
MOUTH Y	*PLUMM Y	RHEUM Y	SHORT Y	SOREL Y
MULLE Y	PLUSH Y	RICHL Y	*SICKL Y	SOURL Y
*MURPH Y	*POACH Y	*RICKE Y	SIMON Y	*SPARK Y
MURRE Y	POETR Y	RIDLE Y	SIMPL Y	SPARR Y
MUSCL Y	POINT Y	RIGHT Y	SINEW Y	SPEED Y
MUTIN Y	*POKIL Y	RIPPL Y	SINGL Y	SPHER Y
NAMEL Y	POLIC Y	ROPER Y	SKERR Y	SPICE Y
NAPER Y	POLIT Y	ROPIL Y	*SKIDD Y	*SPIFF Y
*NAZIF Y	POORL Y	ROSAR Y	*SKIMP Y	SPINN Y
NEARB Y	POPER Y	ROSER Y	SKINN Y	SPONG Y
NEARL Y	PORTL Y	ROSIL Y	*SKIVV Y	*SPOOK Y
NEATL Y	POTBO Y	ROSIN Y	*SKYWA Y	SPOON Y
NEBUL Y	*POUCH Y	ROTAR Y	SLAGG Y	SPORT Y
NETTL Y	PREPA Y	RUBBL Y	SLANG Y	SPOTT Y
NICET Y	PRETT Y	*RUFFL Y	SLAVE Y	SPRUC Y
NIDIF Y	PRICE Y	RUMBL Y	*SLEAZ Y	*SPUNK Y
NIGHT Y	*PRICK Y	RUMPL Y	SLEEK Y	SPURR Y
NINET Y	PRIML Y	RUNWA Y	SLEEP Y	STABL Y
NOBOD Y	PRIOR Y	SAFET Y	SLEET Y	STAGE Y
NOSIL Y	PRISS Y	SALAR Y	SLIML Y	STAGG Y
NOTAR Y	PUDDL Y	SALIF Y	SLIMS Y	STALK Y

STARR Y	THORN Y	WAGGL Y	*BEEFIL Y	*CARAWA Y
STEAD Y	THUSL Y	*WAMBL Y	BEGGAR Y	*CARNIF Y
STEAM Y	*THYME Y	WARIL Y	BELLBO Y	CARROT Y
STEEL Y	TIDDL Y	WARML Y	*BELTWA Y	CATTIL Y
STEMM Y	TIDIL Y	WASTR Y	*BEWEAR Y	CAUTER Y
*STICK Y	TIMEL Y	WATER Y	*BEWORR Y	*CAVALL Y
STILL Y	TINGL Y	*WAVER Y	*BHEEST Y	*CAVALR Y
STING Y	TINIL Y	*WAVIL Y	*BIBBER Y	CENTUR Y
STINK Y	TINKL Y	*WAXIL Y	BIGGET Y	*CERTIF Y
STITH Y	TOAST Y	*WAYLA Y	BIGGIT Y	*CHANTE Y
*STOCK Y	TOMBO Y	*WEAKL Y	BIGOTR Y	*CHANTR Y
STODG Y	TOOTH Y	*WEEKL Y	*BIKEWA Y	*CHARIL Y
STOGE Y	TOOTS Y	WEENS Y	BILIAR Y	*CHARIT Y
STONE Y	TOUCH Y	WEIRD Y	*BILLOW Y	*CHARPO Y
STORE Y	TOUGH Y	*WHACK Y	BINDER Y	*CHEAPL Y
STORM Y	TOWER Y	*WHAMM Y	BIOGEN Y	*CHICOR Y
STOUR Y	TRASH Y	*WHEEZ Y	BIOLOG Y	*CHIEFL Y
STRAW Y	TREAT Y	*WHELK Y	BIONOM Y	*CHILDL Y
STRIP Y	TREBL Y	*WHERR Y	BIPART Y	*CHIMBL Y
STUBB Y	TREND Y	*WHIMS Y	*BLACKL Y	*CHIMLE Y
*STUFF Y	TRESS Y	*WHINE Y	*BLANKL Y	*CHIMNE Y
STUMP Y	*TRICK Y	*WHINN Y	BLARNE Y	*CHINCH Y
STURD Y	TRIGL Y	*WHIPP Y	*BLEAKL Y	*CHINTZ Y
SUBWA Y	TRILB Y	*WHIRL Y	*BLIGHT Y	*CHOOSE Y
SUDAR Y	TRIML Y	*WHIRR Y	BLINDL Y	*CHRIST Y
SUGAR Y	TRIPL Y	*WHISK Y	*BLOTCH Y	*CHURCH Y
SULTR Y	TROLL Y	*WHITE Y	*BLOWFL Y	*CHUTNE Y
SUNDR Y	TROPH Y	*WHOLL Y	*BLUEJA Y	CILIAR Y
SUPPL Y	TROUT Y	*WICOP Y	*BOBBER Y	CINDER Y
SUREL Y	TRUST Y	WIELD Y	BOBSTA Y	*CIPHON Y
SURET Y	TUMEF Y	*WIFEL Y	BOLONE Y	*CIVILL Y
SURRE Y	TURKE Y	WIGGL Y	BOOTER Y	*CLARIF Y
SURVE Y	TWANG Y	WILDL Y	*BRAMBL Y	CLARIT Y
*SWABB Y	*TWANK Y	WILIL Y	*BRANCH Y	CLEANL Y
*SWAMP Y	*TWEAK Y	WINCE Y	*BRAVER Y	CLEARL Y
*SWANK Y	TWEED Y	WINER Y	*BREATH Y	CLERIS Y
SWART Y	TWENT Y	WINTR Y	*BREVIT Y	*CLERKL Y
SWEAT Y	TWIGG Y	WIRIL Y	*BREWER Y	*CLIQUE Y
SWEEN Y	TWIRL Y	WISEL Y	BRIBER Y	*CLUTCH Y
SWEEP Y	*TYPIF Y	*WITCH Y	*BRIEFL Y	*COALIF Y
*SWIMM Y	VAGAR Y	WITNE Y	*BRISKL Y	*COCKIL Y
SWING Y	VALLE Y	*WOBBL Y	BRISTL Y	*COCKNE Y
SWIRL Y	VANIT Y	WOODS Y	BROADL Y	*COCKSH Y
*SWISH Y	VAPOR Y	WOOLL Y	BRUTEL Y	*COGENC Y
*SYZYG Y	VASTL Y	*WORTH Y	BRUTIF Y	*COLICK Y
*TACKE Y	VAULT Y	*WRATH Y	BUGGER Y	*COMFRE Y
TAMEL Y	VAUNT Y	WRIST Y	BUIRDL Y	*COMPAN Y
TANGL Y	VENER Y	YEARL Y	BURSAR Y	*COMPON Y
TARTL Y	*VERIF Y	YEAST Y	*BUSHIL Y	*COOKER Y
TAUTL Y	VERIL Y	*ZINCK Y	BUTLER Y	COOPER Y
TAWDR Y	VERIT Y	*ZONAR Y	BUTTER Y	*COPYBO Y
TAWNE Y	VESTR Y	BAIRNL Y	BUTTON Y	CORNIL Y
TEAPO Y	*VILIF Y	BALCON Y	*CACHEX Y	CORROD Y
TEENS Y	VINER Y	BALONE Y	*CADENC Y	COTTON Y
TEPEF Y	*VIVAR Y	BATTER Y	*CALCIF Y	COUNTR Y
TERML Y	*VIVIF Y	*BAWDIL Y	CALLBO Y	COURTL Y
TETAN Y	VOLER Y	BEADIL Y	CALUMN Y	*COWEDL Y
TETCH Y	VOLLE Y	BEAMIL Y	*CALVAR Y	*COXALG Y
THEOR Y	VOTAR Y	BEANER Y	*CAMPIL Y	*CRACKL Y
THERB Y	*WABBL Y	BEASTL Y	CANNER Y	*CRANKL Y
THINL Y	WADDL Y	*BEATIF Y	CANNIL Y	*CRINKL Y
THIRT Y	*WAFER Y	BEDIRT Y	CANONR Y	CRISPL Y

*CRUCIF Y	DYNAST Y	GALLER Y	*HODADD Y	LOYALL Y
CRUDIT Y	*FACTOR Y	GALLFL Y	HOLIDA Y	LOYALT Y
CRUELT Y	*FACULT Y	*GANGWA Y	*HOLYDA Y	LUCENC Y
*CRUMBL Y	FAINTL Y	GATEWA Y	HONEST Y	LULLAB Y
*CRUMPL Y	*FAIRWA Y	GAUDER Y	HORNIL Y	LUSTIL Y
*CRUNCH Y	*FALLAC Y	GAUNTR Y	*HORRIF Y	LYINGL Y
CRUSIL Y	*FALSIF Y	*GEMMIL Y	HORSIL Y	*MAGNIF Y
*CRYBAB Y	FALSIT Y	GEODES Y	HOSIER Y	*MAJEST Y
*CUBICL Y	FANTAS Y	GEOLOG Y	*HUMANL Y	*MALARK Y
CURSOR Y	FARADA Y	GETAWA Y	*HUMIDL Y	MALMSE Y
CURTES Y	*FARAWA Y	GHASTL Y	*HUSHAB Y	*MAMMAR Y
CURTSE Y	FATALL Y	GHOSTL Y	HUSKIL Y	*MANGAB Y
*CUSHIL Y	FATTIL Y	GINGEL Y	*HYDROX Y	MANGIL Y
CUSTOD Y	FATUIT Y	GINGER Y	HYMNAR Y	MANUAR Y
*CUTAWA Y	FELONR Y	GLORIF Y	*HYMNOD Y	*MARROW Y
CUTLER Y	FEODAR Y	*GLOWFL Y	*JAGGAR Y	*MARTYR Y
DACOIT Y	FERNER Y	GOSSIP Y	*JAGGER Y	MASONR Y
*DAKOIT Y	FERRET Y	GRAMAR Y	*JALOPP Y	MASTER Y
*DAMNIF Y	FEUDAR Y	GRANAR Y	*JELLIF Y	MATTER Y
DANDIL Y	*FIDGET Y	GRANDL Y	*JEWELR Y	MEATIL Y
DARESA Y	*FIFTHL Y	GRAPER Y	*JIMMIN Y	*MEDIAC Y
DATEDL Y	*FILMIL Y	GRATIF Y	*JITTER Y	MERCER Y
DAUBER Y	FINALL Y	GRAVEL Y	*JOBBER Y	MERCUR Y
DAYLIL Y	*FINICK Y	GRAVIT Y	*JOINER Y	MESALL Y
DEANER Y	*FIREFL Y	GREATL Y	*JOINTL Y	MESSIL Y
DEATHL Y	FIRSTL Y	GREENL Y	*JOLLIF Y	*METHOX Y
*DECENC Y	*FISHER Y	GRIML Y Y	*JOLLIT Y	*METRIF Y
DEERFL Y	*FISHWA Y	*GRIZZL Y	*JOURNE Y	*MICRIF Y
DENSIF Y	*FIXEDL Y	GROCER Y	*JUSTIF Y	*MILDEW Y
DENSIT Y	FLAUNT Y	GROSSL Y	*KILLJO Y	MILIAR Y
DESTIN Y	*FLAVOR Y	*GROUCH Y	*KNAVER Y	*MILKIL Y
DESTRO Y	*FLESHL Y	*GRUFFL Y	*KNUCKL Y	*MIMICR Y
DEVILR Y	*FLIGHT Y	*GRUMPH Y	*KOLACK Y	MISALL Y
*DIARCH Y	*FLOWER Y	GUNNER Y	*LACQUE Y	*MISCOP Y
DICLIN Y	*FLUENC Y	GUNPLA Y	LACTAR Y	MISERL Y
*DICYCL Y	FLUIDL Y	GUSTIL Y	LAMPRE Y	MISPLA Y
DIETAR Y	*FLUNKE Y	GUTTER Y	LANIAR Y	MISREL Y
*DIGNIF Y	*FLYAWA Y	*HACKNE Y	LARCEN Y	MISTIL Y
DIGNIT Y	*FOAMIL Y	*HALFWA Y	LATENC Y	*MOCKER Y
DINGIL Y	*FOCALL Y	*HALLWA Y	LATHER Y	MODEST Y
DISOBE Y	*FOLKWA Y	HAMMIL Y	LAUNDR Y	MOISTL Y
DISPLA Y	FOOLER Y	HANDIL Y	*LAYAWA Y	MOLLIF Y
DITHER Y	*FOOTBO Y	HARDIL Y	*LECHER Y	MONKER Y
DITTAN Y	*FOOTWA Y	*HARMON Y	LEGALL Y	MONOEC Y
DODDER Y	*FOPPER Y	*HARSHL Y	LENGTH Y	*MONTHL Y
DODGER Y	*FOREBA Y	*HAUGHT Y	LEPROS Y	MOONIL Y
DOGGER Y	FORGER Y	*HAUTBO Y	LEVELL Y	MORTAR Y
DOORWA Y	*FORTIF Y	*HAZELL Y	LIBERT Y	*MORTIF Y
DOTTIL Y	FOUNDR Y	HEADIL Y	LIBRAR Y	*MOTHER Y
*DOUGHT Y	FRAILT Y	*HEADWA Y	*LICHTL Y	MOUSIL Y
*DOVEKE Y	*FRANKL Y	*HEALTH Y	LIFEWA Y	*MOVABL Y
DRAPER Y	*FRECKL Y	*HEALTH Y	LIGHTL Y	*MUCKIL Y
*DRIZZL Y	*FREEWA Y	HEARSA Y	LIGNIF Y	MUDDIL Y
*DROSHK Y	FRESHL Y	HELLER Y	*LINKBO Y	MUGGIL Y
DROUTH Y	*FRIZZL Y	HELOTR Y	*LIQUEF Y	*MUMMER Y
DUALIT Y	*FROWST Y	HENNER Y	*LIQUIF Y	*MUMMIF Y
DUBIET Y	FULLER Y	HERONR Y	LITTER Y	*MUSKIL Y
*DULCIF Y	*FURMET Y	*HICKOR Y	LITURG Y	*MUZZIL Y
*DUMPIL Y	*FURMIT Y	*HIGHBO Y	LOATHL Y	*MYOLOG Y
DUOPOL Y	FURRIL Y	*HIGHWA Y	LOCALL Y	*MYSTER Y
DUSTIL Y	*FURROW Y	HISTOR Y	LOFTIL Y	*MYSTIF Y
*DYARCH Y	GAINSA Y	HOARIL Y	LOTTER Y	NAIVET Y

NASALL Y	PLAGUE Y	RECTOR Y	SCROGG Y	SOMEDA Y
NAUGHT Y	*PLAYBO Y	REEDIF Y	*SCRUBB Y	*SOMEWA Y
NECTAR Y	*PLAYDA Y	*REENJO Y	*SCRUFF Y	SOOTHL Y
NEEDIL Y	PLENAR Y	REENTR Y	SEALER Y	SORCER Y
NEOLOG Y	PLIANC Y	REGALL Y	SECREC Y	SORRIL Y
NEOTEN Y	*PLOWBO Y	REGENC Y	SECTAR Y	SOUNDL Y
NERVIL Y	*PLUMPL Y	REMARR Y	SEEDIL Y	SPANGL Y
*NEWSBO Y	PORTRA Y	*REPLEV Y	SEMIDR Y	*SPECIF Y
NIGHTL Y	POSTBO Y	RESTUD Y	SENSOR Y	SPICER Y
NIGRIF Y	POTENC Y	RETIAR Y	SEVENT Y	SPICIL Y
NIMIET Y	POTTER Y	REUNIF Y	*SHADFL Y	SPIDER Y
NINTHL Y	POULTR Y	REVELR Y	SHADIL Y	SPINDL Y
NIPPIL Y	*POVERT Y	RHATAN Y	*SHADOW Y	SPINNE Y
NITRIF Y	*POWDER Y	RIBBON Y	*SHAKIL Y	*SPLASH Y
NOBBIL Y	*PREACH Y	*RICKET Y	SHANTE Y	SPLEEN Y
NOONDA Y	PRELAC Y	RIFLER Y	*SHAPEL Y	SPLURG Y
NOSEGA Y	*PRICKL Y	RIGHTL Y	*SHARPL Y	SPOONE Y
NOTABL Y	*PRIMAC Y	RIGIDL Y	SHEENE Y	*SPRAWL Y
NOTEDL Y	PRIMAR Y	RIVALR Y	SHINGL Y	SPRIGG Y
NOVELL Y	PRIMEL Y	ROADWA Y	SHINIL Y	SPRING Y
NOVELT Y	PRIORL Y	ROBBER Y	SHINNE Y	SPURRE Y
NULLIF Y	*PRIVAC Y	ROBOTR Y	*SHIPWA Y	*SQUABB Y
NULLIT Y	*PRIVIT Y	*ROCKAB Y	*SHIVER Y	*SQUALL Y
NUMMAR Y	PROBIT Y	*ROCKER Y	*SHOOFL Y	*SQUASH Y
NUNNER Y	PRODIG Y	ROGUER Y	*SHOPBO Y	*SQUATT Y
NURSER Y	PROGEN Y	ROLLWA Y	SHORTL Y	*SQUEAK Y
*PAGEBO Y	PROSIL Y	ROOKER Y	*SHOWER Y	*SQUIFF Y
PAISLE Y	PROSOD Y	*ROPEWA Y	*SHOWIL Y	*SQUINN Y
*PALFRE Y	PRUDER Y	ROSEBA Y	*SHRIEK Y	*SQUINT Y
PALMAR Y	PSALTR Y	ROUGHL Y	*SHRIMP Y	*SQUIRM Y
*PANICK Y	PUBERT Y	ROUNDL Y	*SHRUBB Y	*SQUISH Y
PANOPL Y	*PUCKER Y	ROYALL Y	*SICKBA Y	STAGIL Y
*PARKWA Y	*PUDENC Y	ROYALT Y	SIDEWA Y	STANDB Y
PARROT Y	*PUFFER Y	RUDDIL Y	SIGHTL Y	*STARCH Y
PARSLE Y	PULPIL Y	RUDESB Y	SIGNIF Y	STARTS Y
*PARTWA Y	PURSIL Y	RUNAWA Y	SIGNOR Y	STATEL Y
*PASSKE Y	*PUSHIL Y	RURALL Y	SILKIL Y	STEEPL Y
PATENC Y	PUSSLE Y	RUSSIF Y	SILVER Y	*STENCH Y
*PATHWA Y	*PUTREF Y	RUSTIL Y	*SIXTHL Y	STERNL Y
PAUCIT Y	*QUALIF Y	RUTTIL Y	*SKETCH Y	*STIFFL Y
*PAUGHT Y	*QUALIT Y	SAINTL Y	*SKIDWA Y	STONIL Y
*PAUNCH Y	*QUAVER Y	SALLOW Y	*SLACKL Y	STOUTL Y
*PECCAR Y	*QUEENL Y	SALSIF Y	SLAVER Y	STREAK Y
PEDLAR Y	*QUEERL Y	SALTIL Y	SLEEKL Y	STREAM Y
PENALL Y	*QUICKL Y	SANDFL Y	*SLICKL Y	STRING Y
PENALT Y	*QUIETL Y	SASSAB Y	SLIMIL Y	STUBBL Y
*PEPPER Y	*QUINAR Y	SASSIL Y	SLIMPS Y	*STUPEF Y
*PERFID Y	*QUIVER Y	SATIET Y	*SLIPWA Y	SUAVIT Y
*PERJUR Y	*RACEWA Y	SATISF Y	*SLOUCH Y	SUBSID Y
PESSAR Y	*RACKET Y	SATRAP Y	SLOUGH Y	SUCCOR Y
*PETRIF Y	RAGGED Y	SAVELO Y	SMARTL Y	SULFUR Y
PETTIL Y	RAILWA Y	SAVOUR Y	*SMOOCH Y	SUMMAR Y
*PHLEGM Y	RAINIL Y	SCANTL Y	*SMOOTH Y	SUMMER Y
*PHONIL Y	RAUCIT Y	*SCARIF Y	*SMUTCH Y	SURGER Y
*PHRATR Y	*RAUNCH Y	SCENER Y	*SNATCH Y	*SWARTH Y
*PHRENS Y	RAVELL Y	*SCORIF Y	SNOWIL Y	SWEETL Y
PIGGER Y	READIL Y	SCRAGG Y	*SNUFFL Y	SWELTR Y
PIGSNE Y	REALIT Y	*SCRAPP Y	SOAPIL Y	*SWIFTL Y
PILLOR Y	REAPPL Y	*SCRAWL Y	SOBERL Y	SWINNE Y
*PILLOW Y	RECARR Y	*SCRAWN Y	SOCIET Y	*SWITHL Y
PIOSIT Y	RECENC Y	*SCREAK Y	SOLIDL Y	SYNERG Y
PISCAR Y	*RECTIF Y	*SCRIMP Y	SOLUBL Y	*SYNGAM Y

SYNTON Y	TURBAR Y	*ZOOLOG Y	*BURGUND Y	COOINGL Y
*TACKIF Y	TURNER Y	*ZOOTOM Y	*BUSYBOD Y	*COQUETR Y
*TACKIL Y	TURNKE Y	*ZYMURG Y	*BUTCHER Y	CORDURO Y
TALLBO Y	*TWINKL Y	*BACKSTA Y	*CABLEWA Y	*CORNETC Y
TALLOW Y	*TWITCH Y	*BADGERL Y	*CADUCIT Y	CORONAR Y
TANNER Y	*TYMPAN Y	BANALIT Y	*CAJOLER Y	*COSTMAR Y
TANTIV Y	TYRANN Y	BANDITR Y	*CALAMAR Y	*COSTUME Y
TATOUA Y	*VACANC Y	*BARBERR Y	*CALAMIT Y	COURTES Y
*TAXIWA Y	*VACUIT Y	BARRATR Y	*CANDIDL Y	COUSINR Y
TEARIL Y	*VALENC Y	BARRETR Y	CANINIT Y	*COVERTL Y
TEENTS Y	VALIDL Y	*BASICIT Y	CANNONR Y	*COWARDL Y
TENANC Y	*VAPOUR Y	BASILAR Y	*CAPACIT Y	*COWBERR Y
TENSIT Y	VARIET Y	*BASKETR Y	*CASTAWA Y	*CRAMOIS Y
TENTHL Y	VARSIT Y	BASTARD Y	CASUALL Y	*CRANKIL Y
TENUIT Y	VASTIT Y	*BAYBERR Y	CASUALT Y	*CRAVENL Y
TERNAR Y	*VERBIF Y	*BEACHBO Y	*CATCHFL Y	*CRAWLWA Y
TERRIF Y	*VERSIF Y	*BEAUTIF Y	CATEGOR Y	*CREAMER Y
TESTAC Y	*VEXEDL Y	*BEGGARL Y	CATENAR Y	*CROCKER Y
TESTIF Y	*VICARL Y	BESTIAR Y	CAUSALL Y	*CROSSWA Y
TESTIL Y	*VICERO Y	*BIFIDIT Y	*CAUSEWA Y	*CRYOGEN Y
*THATCH Y	*VICTOR Y	*BIGEMIN Y	*CAVITAR Y	*CUBICIT Y
*THERAP Y	VIDUIT Y	*BIHOURL Y	CELERIT Y	CULINAR Y
THEURG Y	VIRELA Y	*BILBERR Y	*CELIBAC Y	*CUPIDIT Y
*THICKL Y	VITALL Y	BIOASSA Y	*CEMETER Y	*CURRENC Y
THIRDL Y	VITRIF Y	*BIOMETR Y	CENTAUR Y	CURRIER Y
THIRST Y	*VOCABL Y	*BIOSCOP Y	*CEREMON Y	*CUSHION Y
THREAD Y	*VOCALL Y	*BIRTHDA Y	CETOLOG Y	CUSSEDL Y
*THRIFT Y	VYINGL Y	BISTOUR Y	*CHAMBRA Y	*CUTCHER Y
*THRUMM Y	*WAGGER Y	*BITCHER Y	*CHANCER Y	*CYTOGEN Y
*THRUWA Y	*WALKWA Y	BITINGL Y	*CHANCIL Y	*CYTOLOG Y
TIDEWA Y	*WALLAB Y	*BIWEEKL Y	*CHARLAD Y	DARINGL Y
*TIFFAN Y	*WASHDA Y	*BIYEARL Y	*CHASTIT Y	DEACONR Y
TILBUR Y	WASTER Y	*BLACKBO Y	*CHEERIL Y	DEBILIT Y
*TIMOTH Y	*WEALTH Y	*BLACKFL Y	*CHEMURG Y	DECENAR Y
TINNIL Y	WEEDIL Y	*BLATANC Y	*CHICCOR Y	*DELEGAC Y
TIPSIL Y	*WEEKDA Y	*BLAZONR Y	*CHIMBLE Y	*DELICAC Y
TISSUE Y	*WEIGHT Y	BLISTER Y	*CHIVALR Y	*DELIVER Y
TOGGER Y	WEIRDL Y	BLOODIL Y	*CHOIRBO Y	DELUSOR Y
TOLLWA Y	*WHEREB Y	*BLOOMER Y	*CHORALL Y	*DEMAGOG Y
TOPIAR Y	*WHIMSE Y	*BLOSSOM Y	*CHRONAX Y	*DENAZIF Y
TORREF Y	*WHIPRA Y	*BLUBBER Y	*CHURCHL Y	DERISOR Y
TORRIF Y	*WHISKE Y	BLUSTER Y	CINERAR Y	*DETOXIF Y
TOTALL Y	*WHITEL Y	*BODINGL Y	*CIRCUIT Y	*DEVIANC Y
TOTTER Y	*WIGGER Y	BORINGL Y	*CIVILIT Y	*DEVILTR Y
TOUGHL Y	*WILLOW Y	*BOTCHER Y	*CLASSIF Y	*DEWBERR Y
TOURNE Y	WINDIL Y	*BOTTOMR Y	CLATTER Y	DIABLER Y
*TOWAWA Y	*WINDWA Y	BOUNDAR Y	*CLEMENC Y	*DIAPHON Y
TRACER Y	WINTER Y	*BOVINEL Y	CLINALL Y	*DIDYNAM Y
TRAGED Y	*WIREWA Y	*BOVINIT Y	*CLOWNER Y	DILATOR Y
*TRAMWA Y	*WISPIL Y	*BOWINGL Y	CLUSTER Y	*DIPLOID Y
TRAWLE Y	WITTIL Y	*BOXBERR Y	*COAGENC Y	DISARRA Y
TREMBL Y	*WOMANL Y	BRAINIL Y	*COBWEBB Y	DISUNIT Y
*TRICKL Y	WORDIL Y	*BRAZENL Y	*COEMBOD Y	*DIVINIT Y
*TRICKS Y	*WORKDA Y	*BREVETC Y	*COEMPLO Y	DOCILIT Y
TRILOG Y	WORLDL Y	*BREVIAR Y	COEVALL Y	*DOGBERR Y
TRINAR Y	*WRIGGL Y	BRIDALL Y	COLLIER Y	*DOGGEDL Y
TRINIT Y	*WRINKL Y	BROGUER Y	*COLLOQU Y	*DOGSBOD Y
TRIPOD Y	WRONGL Y	BROIDER Y	*COLOTOM Y	*DOMESDA Y
TRISOM Y	*YELLOW Y	*BRYOLOG Y	*COMMONL Y	*DOOMSDA Y
TROLLE Y	*ZEDOAR Y	*BULLYBO Y	*CONICIT Y	*DORMANC Y
TRUANC Y	*ZINCIF Y	*BUOYANC Y	CONTRAR Y	DORSALL Y
	*ZINKIF Y	BURGLAR Y	*CONVEXL Y	DOTINGL Y

*DOUGHBO Y	*FUGACIT Y	*HEXARCH Y	*LIQUIDL Y	MONETAR Y
*DOWNPLA Y	*FUMATOR Y	*HIDEAWA Y	LITERAC Y	MONITOR Y
*DOXOLOG Y	*FUMITOR Y	HILARIT Y	LITERAR Y	*MONOGAM Y
*DRAUGHT Y	FUNERAR Y	*HOGMANA Y	*LIVIDIT Y	MONOGEN Y
*DRIVEWA Y	*FURMENT Y	*HOGMENA Y	*LIVINGL Y	*MONOGYN Y
DROLLER Y	FURRIER Y	*HOKYPOK Y	LOBLOLL Y	MONOLOG Y
*DROUGHT Y	FUTILIT Y	*HOLOGYN Y	*LOBOTOM Y	*MONOPOD Y
DRUDGER Y	FUTURIT Y	*HOMEBOD Y	LOCALIT Y	*MONOPOL Y
*DUDISHL Y	GADGETR Y	*HOMOGON Y	LOCUTOR Y	MONOTON Y
DULCETL Y	*GAPINGL Y	*HOMOLOG Y	LOGOTYP Y	*MOPINGL Y
DUOPSON Y	GARGANE Y	*HOMONYM Y	LOSINGL Y	MORALIT Y
*DYSPEPS Y	GELIDIT Y	HONORAR Y	LOVELIL Y	MORATOR Y
*FACIALL Y	GEOGNOS Y	*HOROLOG Y	*LOVINGL Y	*MORDANC Y
*FACILIT Y	*GEOMANC Y	*HORRIBL Y	LUCIDIT Y	MORONIT Y
*FADEAWA Y	GEOMETR Y	*HORSEFL Y	LUMINAR Y	MOROSIT Y
*FALCONR Y	*GEOPHAG Y	*HOUSEBO Y	*LYSOGEN Y	MORTALL Y
FARRIER Y	*GIFTEDL Y	*HOUSEFL Y	*MACCABO Y	MORTUAR Y
FATALIT Y	*GIMMICK Y	*HUMIDIF Y	*MACCOBO Y	*MOTHERL Y
*FATHERL Y	GINGELE Y	*HUMIDIT Y	*MAHOGAN Y	MOTILIT Y
*FEATHER Y	GINGELL Y	*HUMILIT Y	MAINSTA Y	*MOTIVIT Y
*FEDERAC Y	GINGERL Y	*HYDROPS Y	*MAJORIT Y	*MOTORWA Y
*FELICIT Y	*GIVEAWA Y	*HYPOGYN Y	*MALARKE Y	*MOVEABL Y
FELINEL Y	GLASSIL Y	*JACKSTA Y	MALIGNL Y	*MOVINGL Y
FELINIT Y	*GLAZIER Y	*JAGGHER Y	MANNERL Y	*MUCIDIT Y
*FELLOWL Y	GLITTER Y	*JANISAR Y	MANUALL Y	*MUCOSIT Y
*FEMINAC Y	GLOSSAR Y	*JANIZAR Y	*MARKEDL Y	*MUDPUPP Y
*FEMINIT Y	GLUTTON Y	*JAPINGL Y	*MARTYRL Y	*MULBERR Y
*FERACIT Y	GORBELL Y	*JEALOUS Y	MASSEDL Y	*MULTIPL Y
FERETOR Y	*GORBLIM Y	*JEJUNIT Y	MASTERL Y	MUSINGL Y
*FEROCIT Y	GOSSIPR Y	*JEOPARD Y	MATTEDL Y	*MUSKETR Y
*FERVENC Y	*GRAMERC Y	*JESUITR Y	MATURIT Y	*MYCOLOG Y
*FETOLOG Y	GRATUIT Y	*JOCOSIT Y	*MAUMETR Y	*MYOPATH Y
*FIDELIT Y	*GRAVELL Y	*JOKINGL Y	MEDIALL Y	*MYSTICL Y
FINALIT Y	GREENER Y	*JOVIALT Y	MENIALL Y	*NABOBER Y
FINITEL Y	*GREENFL Y	*JUGGLER Y	MENOLOG Y	NASALIT Y
*FINNICK Y	GRINDER Y	*JURATOR Y	MESNALT Y	*NASCENC Y
*FIRECLA Y	GROGGER Y	*KNACKER Y	*METONYM Y	NATALIT Y
*FISCALL Y	*GRUFFIL Y	*KNIGHTL Y	*MICRURG Y	NATATOR Y
FLATTER Y	GUARANT Y	*KOLINSK Y	MIDSTOR Y	NATIVEL Y
*FLAVOUR Y	GUERNSE Y	LABIALL Y	MILITAR Y	NATIVIT Y
*FLICKER Y	GULOSIT Y	LABILIT Y	MILLIAR Y	*NAUMACH Y
*FLUIDIT Y	*GYNANDR Y	*LACKADA Y	*MINACIT Y	*NECROPS Y
*FLUMMER Y	*GYNARCH Y	LAMASER Y	MINATOR Y	NIHILIT Y
FLUTTER Y	*GYNIATR Y	*LAMBENC Y	MINISTR Y	NOBILIT Y
*FOLDAWA Y	*GYRATOR Y	LANDLAD Y	MINORIT Y	NODALIT Y
*FOREBOD Y	*HAGBERR Y	LANOSIT Y	*MISAPPL Y	NODOSIT Y
*FORELAD Y	HARLOTR Y	LAPIDAR Y	MISASSA Y	*NOMARCH Y
*FOREPLA Y	*HATCHER Y	*LAPIDIF Y	*MISCARR Y	NOMOLOG Y
FORESTA Y	*HATCHWA Y	*LATCHKE Y	MISENTR Y	NONDAIR Y
FORESTR Y	*HEADACH Y	LATENTL Y	*MISOGAM Y	*NONEMPT Y
*FORMALL Y	*HEADSTA Y	LATINIT Y	*MISOGYN Y	NONENTR Y
*FORMERL Y	*HEATEDL Y	LATTERL Y	MISOLOG Y	*NONHARD Y
FORTUIT Y	*HEAVENL Y	LAVATOR Y	MISSILR Y	NONMONE Y
*FOURTHL Y	*HEGEMON Y	LEATHER Y	*MIXOLOG Y	NONPART Y
*FREAKIL Y	*HEGUMEN Y	LEGALIT Y	*MOBILIT Y	*NONWOOD Y
*FRENZIL Y	*HELICIT Y	LEGENDR Y	MODALIT Y	*NORMALC Y
*FRIENDL Y	*HERALDR Y	LEGERIT Y	MOLALIT Y	NORMALL Y
*FRIPPER Y	*HEREDIT Y	LENIENC Y	MOLARIT Y	NOSOLOG Y
*FRIZZIL Y	*HERMITR Y	LETHALL Y	*MOMENTL Y	NUBILIT Y
*FROMENT Y	*HEXAPOD Y	*LETHARG Y	MONANDR Y	NUGATOR Y
*FRUCTIF Y		LIENTER Y	*MONARCH Y	NUMERAR Y
*FRUMENT Y		LIMITAR Y		PADUASO Y

*PANDOWD Y	*PROVENL Y	*ROCKETR Y	*SILICIF Y	STANNAR Y	
*PANSOPH Y	*PSALMOD Y	ROGATOR Y	SILVERL Y	STATEDL Y	
*PAPERBO Y	PSALTER Y	ROLLAWA Y	*SIMPLIF Y	STATUAR Y	
*PAPISTR Y	*PUBLICL Y	*ROLLICK Y	SINOLOG Y	STEALTH Y	
*PASSERB Y	PULINGL Y	ROSEMAR Y	SISTERL Y	STELLIF Y	
PATENTL Y	*PUNDITR Y	ROTATOR Y	SITOLOG Y	*STEMMER Y	
*PEACOCK Y	*PUNGENC Y	*ROUGHDR Y	*SIXPENN Y	STERNWA Y	
*PECCANC Y	*PUNITOR Y	ROUTEWA Y	*SKITTER Y	*STICKIL Y	
*PEDAGOG Y	*PUPILAR Y	*ROVINGL Y	*SLABBER Y	STINGIL Y	
PEDANTR Y	*PUPPETR Y	RUGOSIT Y	*SLIDEWA Y	STINGRA Y	
*PEDDLER Y	*PYROLOG Y	RURALIT Y	*SLIPPER Y	*STOCKIL Y	
*PEDOLOG Y	*QUACKER Y	RUSTICL Y	SLITHER Y	*STOMACH Y	
PENALIT Y	*QUAGMIR Y	SACRIST Y	*SLOBBER Y	STONEFL Y	
*PENDENC Y	*QUANDAR Y	SADDLER Y	SLOVENL Y	*STOWAWA Y	
PENOLOG Y	*QUANTIF Y	SAGACIT Y	*SLUMBER Y	STRAGGL Y	
*PERIGYN Y	*QUANTIT Y	SALACIT Y	SMELTER Y	STRAMON Y	
*PERIPET Y	*QUIDDIT Y	SALIENC Y	*SMITHER Y	STRATEG Y	
PETALOD Y	*QUIXOTR Y	SALINIT Y	*SMOOTHL Y	STRATIF Y	
PETTEDL Y	*RABBITR Y	SALUTAR Y	*SMOTHER Y	*STRETCH Y	
*PHANTAS Y	RABIDIT Y	*SANCTIF Y	*SNAPPIL Y	*STUBBIL Y	
*PHARMAC Y	RADIALL Y	SANCTIT Y	*SNICKER Y	STULTIF Y	
*PHYLLAR Y	RADIANC Y	SANITAR Y	*SNIFFIL Y	SUBENTR Y	
*PICNICK Y	RAGINGL Y	SAPIDIT Y	*SNIPPET Y	SUBTILT Y	
PILOSIT Y	RAILLER Y	*SAPIENC Y	*SNOBBER Y	SUBTLET Y	
*PIPINGL Y	RAMOSIT Y	*SAPONIF Y	*SNOBBIL Y	SUDATOR Y	
*PIQUANC Y	*RAMPANC Y	*SAVAGER Y	*SNUFFIL Y	*SULPHUR Y	
*PITCHIL Y	RANDOML Y	*SAVINGL Y	SNUGGER Y	*SUMMERL Y	
PLAGIAR Y	*RAPACIT Y	*SCAMMON Y	SOBRIET Y	*SUMMITR Y	
PLASTER Y	RAPIDIT Y	*SCARCEL Y	*SOCIABL Y	SUPINEL Y	
PLEURIS Y	RASCALL Y	*SCARCIT Y	SOCIALL Y	SWANNER Y	
*PLUGUGL Y	*RAVINGL Y	*SCHMALZ Y	SODALIT Y	*SYMMETR Y	
*PLUMBER Y	*RECODIF Y	*SCRABBL Y	SODDENL Y	*SYMPATH Y	
PLURALL Y	*RECONVE Y	*SCRAGGL Y	SOLDIER Y	*SYMPATR Y	
PODIATR Y	*RECOVER Y	*SCRATCH Y	SOLIDAR Y	*SYMPHON Y	
POLARIT Y	REDEPLO Y	*SCREECH Y	*SOLIDIF Y	*SYNCARP Y	
*POLYGAM Y	*REEMBOD Y	SCROUNG Y	SOLIDIT Y	*SYNONYM Y	
*POLYGON Y	*REEMPLO Y	SCRUTIN Y	SOLITAR Y	*TAKINGL Y	
*POLYGYN Y	REFINER Y	SCULLER Y	*SOLVENC Y	TANGENC Y	
*POLYPAR Y	REGALIT Y	SECANTL Y	*SOMEBOD Y	TANGIBL Y	
*POLYPOD Y	REGISTR Y	SECONDL Y	SONORIT Y	TANISTR Y	
*POLYSEM Y	REGNANC Y	SECRETL Y	SOOTHSA Y	TAPESTR Y	
*POLYTEN Y	*REMODIF Y	SECURIT Y	SORORIT Y	*TAXINGL Y	
*POMOLOG Y	RENOTIF Y	SEDULIT Y	SOVRANL Y	*TAXONOM Y	
*POPINJA Y	*REOCCUP Y	SEIGNOR Y	SOVRANT Y	TEABERR Y	
POROSIT Y	*REPACIF Y	SELECTL Y	*SOWBELL Y	TELEGON Y	
*PORPHYR Y	*REPURIF Y	SEMINAR Y	*SPARKIL Y	TELEPLA Y	
*PORTABL Y	RESINIF Y	SENILEL Y	SPARSIT Y	TEMERIT Y	
POSINGL Y	*RESUPPL Y	SENILIT Y	SPEEDIL Y	TENACIT Y	
POSOLOG Y	RESURVE Y	*SEQUENC Y	*SPEEDWA Y	TENANTR Y	
POSTALL Y	*REVERIF Y	SERENIT Y	*SPERMAR Y	TENDENC Y	
POTATOR Y	REVISOR Y	SERIALL Y	*SPILLWA Y	TENDERL Y	
*POTBELL Y	*REVIVIF Y	SEROLOG Y	SPINALL Y	TENOTOM Y	
*PRETTIF Y	*RHAPSOD Y	SEROSIT Y	SPINNER Y	TENPENN Y	
PRIESTL Y	*RHEOLOG Y	SEVERIT Y	SPIRALL Y	TEPIDIT Y	
*PRIGGER Y	RIBALDL Y	*SEXOLOG Y	*SPLOTCH Y	TERTIAR Y	
*PRINCEL Y	RIBALDR Y	*SEXTUPL Y	SPONGIL Y	*TEXTUAR Y	
PRINTER Y	*RIGIDIF Y	*SHIMMER Y	*SQUAREL Y	*THATAWA Y	
PRIORIT Y	RIGIDIT Y	SHINNER Y	*SQUELCH Y	*THEARCH Y	
*PROMPTL Y	RIMOSIT Y	*SHUDDER Y	*SQUIGGL Y	*THEODIC Y	
*PROPERT Y	RITUALL Y	*SICKERL Y	STAGGER Y	*THEOGON Y	
*PROPHEC Y	*ROCKAWA Y	SIGNALL Y	STAIRWA Y	*THEOLOG Y	
*PROPHES Y		SIGNIOR Y	*STANCHL Y	*THEONOM Y	

*THIEVER Y	TRAINWA Y	*VAPIDIT Y	*VIRIDIT Y	*WIDTHWA Y
*THRENOD Y	TRAVEST Y	*VARIABL Y	VIRILIT Y	*WINGEDL Y
*THUGGER Y	*TREASUR Y	*VARIEDL Y	*VIROLOG Y	WINTERL Y
*THUNDER Y	*TRIARCH Y	VARLETR Y	VITALIT Y	*WITCHER Y
*THWARTL Y	*TRICKER Y	*VARNISH Y	*VIVACIT Y	*WIZARDR Y
TIMIDIT Y	*TRICKIL Y	*VEILEDL Y	*VOCALIT Y	*WONTEDL Y
TINSELL Y	TRIUNIT Y	VELLEIT Y	*VOMITOR Y	*WOOINGL Y
*TITTUPP Y	TRUANTR Y	*VELOCIT Y	*VORACIT Y	*WORDPLA Y
TITULAR Y	*TRUMPER Y	VENALIT Y	*VULGARI Y	*WORKADA Y
TOCOLOG Y	*TRYINGL Y	*VENDIBL Y	WALKAWA Y	*XENOGAM Y
TOILETR Y	TUMIDIT Y	VENOSIT Y	WANTONL Y	*XENOGEN Y
*TOKOLOG Y	*TUPPENN Y	*VERACIT Y	*WARDENR Y	*XYLOTOM Y
TOMALLE Y	TURGENC Y	*VERBALL Y	WARRANT Y	*YEOMANR Y
TONALIT Y	TUTELAR Y	*VERDANC Y	*WASTEWA Y	*ZEALOTR Y
TONICIT Y	TWITTER Y	*VESPIAR Y	*WATCHCR Y	*ZOOLATR Y
*TOPLOFT Y	*TWOPENN Y	VESTALL Y	WATERIL Y	*ZOOMETR Y
TOPOLOG Y	*TYPOLOG Y	VESTIAR Y	*WATERWA Y	*ZYGOSIT Y
*TOPONYM Y	VAGILIT Y	*VEXINGL Y	*WAXBERR Y	*YUMM Y
*TOROSIT Y	*VAGOTOM Y	*VIBRANC Y	*WEAPONR Y	*ZEST Y
TORPIDL Y	*VAGRANC Y	*VICENAR Y	*WELLADA Y	*ZYMOLOG Y
TOTALIT Y	*VALIANC Y	*VICINIT Y	*WELLAWA Y	
*TOWARDL Y	*VALIDIT Y	VILLAIN Y	WESTERL Y	
*TOXICIT Y	*VALUABL Y	VINOSIT Y	*WHISPER Y	
			*WHITEFL Y	

Z

*ZANY	*ZOMBI	*ZIPPER	*ZECCHIN	*ZABAIONE
*ZARF	ZONAL	*ZIRCON	*ZEDOARY	*ZABAJONE
ZEAL	ZONER	*ZITHER	*ZELKOVA	*ZAIBATSU
*ZEBU	*ZOOID	*ZIZITH	*ZEMSTVO	*ZAMINDAR
ZEIN	*ZOOKS	*ZIZZLE	*ZEOLITE	*ZANINESS
ZERO	ZORIL	*ZODIAC	*ZESTFUL	*ZARATITE
ZEST	*ZOWIE	*ZOFTIG	*ZIKURAT	*ZARZUELA
ZETA	*ZADDIK	*ZOMBIE	*ZILLION	*ZASTRUGA
*ZINC	*ZAFFAR	*ZONARY	*ZINCATE	*ZEALOTRY
ZING	*ZAFFER	*ZONATE	*ZINCIFY	*ZECCHINO
ZITI	*ZAFFIR	*ZONING	*ZINCITE	*ZEMINDAR
ZOEA	*ZAFFRE	*ZONKED	*ZINCKED	*ZEPPELIN
*ZOIC	*ZAFTIG	*ZONULA	*ZINCOID	*ZIBELINE
ZONE	*ZANANA	*ZONULE	*ZINCOUS	*ZIGGURAT
*ZOOM	*ZANDER	*ZOSTER	*ZINGANO	*ZIKKURAT
ZOON	*ZANIER	*ZOUAVE	*ZINGARA	*ZINCKING
ZORI	*ZANIES	*ZOUNDS	*ZINGARO	*ZIRCONIA
*ZYME	*ZAREBA	*ZOYSIA	*ZINKIFY	*ZIRCONIC
ZAIRE	*ZARIBA	*ZYGOMA	*ZITHERN	*ZOMBIISM
*ZAMIA	*ZEALOT	*ZYGOTE	*ZOARIUM	*ZONATION
*ZANZA	*ZEATIN	*ZYMASE	*ZOISITE	*ZONELESS
*ZAYIN	*ZEBECK	*ZACATON	*ZONATED	*ZONETIME
*ZEBEC	*ZECHIN	*ZAMARRA	*ZOOGLEA	*ZOOCHORE
*ZEBRA	*ZENANA	*ZAMARRO	*ZOOLOGY	*ZOOGENIC
*ZESTY	*ZENITH	*ZANYISH	*ZOOTOMY	*ZOOGLOEA
*ZIBET	*ZEPHYR	*ZAPATEO	*ZORILLA	*ZOOLATER
*ZILCH	*ZEUGMA	*ZAPTIAH	*ZORILLE	*ZOOLATRY
*ZINCY	*ZIBETH	*ZAPTIEH	*ZORILLO	*ZOOMANIA
*ZINGY	*ZIGZAG	*ZAREEBA	*ZYGOSIS	*ZOOMETRY
*ZINKY	*ZILLAH	*ZEALOUS	*ZYMOGEN	*ZOOMORPH
*ZIPPY	*ZINCIC	*ZEBRASS	*ZYMOSIS	*ZOONOSIS
*ZIRAM	*ZINCKY	*ZEBRINE	*ZYMURGY	*ZOOPHILE
*ZLOTY	*ZINNIA	*ZEBROID	*ZYZZYVA	*ZOOPHYTE

*ZOOSPERM	*JE Z AIL	*BA Z OOKA	*BEN Z IDIN	*FRI Z
*ZOOSPORE	*LA Z IED	*BE Z IQUE	*BEN Z OATE	*FRI Z
*ZUCCHINI	*LA Z IER	*BE Z ZANT	*BLA Z ONER	*FUZ Z
*ZWIEBACK	*LA Z IES	*BI Z ARRE	*BLA Z ONRY	*JAZ Z
*ZYGOSITY	*LA Z ILY	*BI Z NAGA	*BLI Z ZARD	*JEE Z
*ZYGOTENE	*LA Z ING	*BU Z ZARD	*BOU Z OUKI	*PHI Z
*ZYMOGENE	*LA Z ULI	*BU Z ZWIG	*BRA Z ENLY	*QUI Z
*ZYMOLOGY	*LI Z ARD	*CA Z IQUE	*BRA Z ILIN	*RAZ Z
	*MA Z ARD	*CO Z ENER	*BUZ Z WORD	RIT Z
	*MA Z IER	*DA Z ZLER	*CAN Z ONET	*BLIT Z
*C Z AR	*MA Z ING	*DO Z ENTH	*CRU Z EIRO	*BORT Z
T Z AR	*MA Z UMA	*FA Z ENDA	*DIA Z EPAM	*FRIZ Z
*BA Z AAR	*ME Z CAL	*FU Z ZING	*DOU Z EPER	*GROS Z
*BE Z ANT	*ME Z UZA	*GA Z ELLE	*FOR Z ANDO	*HAFI Z
*BE Z OAR	*MI Z ZEN	*GA Z ETTE	*FRI Z ETTE	*HERT Z
*BI Z ONE	*MI Z ZLE	*GI Z ZARD	*FRI Z ZIER	*KLUT Z
*BU Z ZER	*MI Z ZLY	*GU Z ZLER	*FRI Z ZILY	NERT Z
*BY Z ANT	*MU Z HIK	*HA Z ELLY	*FRI Z ZLER	*SPIT Z
*CO Z IER	*MU Z JIK	*HA Z IEST	*GAD Z OOKS	*TOPA Z
*CO Z IES	*MU Z ZLE	*JA Z ZMAN	*GLA Z IERY	TROO Z
*CO Z ZES	*NA Z IFY	*JE Z EBEL	*GRA Z IOSO	*WALT Z
*DA Z ZLE	*NO Z ZLE	*LA Z ARET	*GRI Z ZLER	*WHIZ Z
*DE Z INC	*PI Z AZZ	*LA Z IEST	*MAR Z IPAN	*BLINT Z
*DO Z ILY	*PI Z ZLE	*LA Z YISH	*MOZ Z ETTA	*CHINT Z
*DO Z ING	*PU Z LER	*LO Z ENGE	*MUZ Z IEST	*HALUT Z
*FI Z GIG	*PU Z ZLE	*MA Z IEST	*PIZ Z ERIA	*KIBIT Z
*FI Z ZER	*RE Z ONE	*MA Z URKA	*POZ Z OLAN	*KOLHO Z
*FI Z ZES	*RO Z ZER	*MA Z ZARD	*RHI Z OBIA	*KOLKO Z
*FI Z ZLE	*SI Z IER	*MA Z ZILY	*RHI Z OPOD	*PIZAZ Z
*GA Z ABO	*SI Z ING	*ME Z QUIT	*RHI Z OPUS	*QUART Z
*GA Z EBO	*SI Z ZLE	*ME Z UZAH	*SIT Z MARK	*SPELT Z
*GA Z ING	*SO Z INE	*MO Z ETTA	*SWI Z ZLER	*CHALUT Z
*GU Z ZLE	*SY Z YGY	*MU Z ZIER	*WHI Z BANG	*KIBBUT Z
*HA Z ARD	*VI Z ARD	*MU Z ZILY	*WHI Z ZING	*KOLKHO Z
*HA Z IER	*VI Z IER	*MU Z ZLER	*ZAR Z UELA	*SCHMAL Z
*HA Z ILY	*VI Z SLA	*RA Z ZING		*SHEGET Z
*HA Z ING	*WI Z ARD	*SI Z ABLE		*SOVKHO Z
*HA Z ZAN	*WI Z ZEN	*SI Z IEST	*BUZ Z	*SOLONET Z
*HU Z ZAH	*ZI Z ITH	*SI Z ZLER	*CHE Z	
*JA Z ZER	*ZI Z ZLE	*ZY Z ZYVA	*FIZ Z	

CHAPTER 2

□□□

Two-Letter Words

If there's one list in this book that you should memorize, this is it.

AA	BE	ET	LA	OM	SO
AD	BI	FA	LI	ON	TA
AE	BO	GO	LO	OP	TI
AH	BY	HA	MA	OR	TO
AI	DA	HE	ME	OS	UN
AM	DE	HI	MI	OW	UP
AN	DO	HO	MY	OX	US
AR	EF	ID	NA	OY	UT
AS	EH	IF	NO	PA	WE
AT	EL	IN	NU	PE	XI
AW	EM	IS	OD	PI	YA
AX	EN	IT	OE	RE	YE
AY	ER	JO	OF	SH	
BA	ES	KA	OH	SI	

CHAPTER 3

□□□

Three-Letter Words Formed from Two-Letter Words

B AA	P AN	M AT	F AY	G EL	P ET
C AD	R AN	O AT	G AY	M EL	R ET
D AD	T AN	P AT	H AY	S EL	S ET
F AD	W AN	S AT	J AY	G EM	V ET
H AD	B AR	T AT	L AY	H EM	W ET
L AD	E AR	V AT	M AY	R EM	Y ET
M AD	F AR	W AT	N AY	B EN	
P AD	G AR	D AW	P AY	F EN	A GO
R AD	J AR	H AW	R AY	H EN	E GO
S AD	L AR	J AW	S AY	M EN	
T AD	M AR	M AW	W AY	P EN	
W AD	O AR	P AW	Y AY	S EN	A HA
H AE	P AR	R AW		T EN	S HE
K AE	T AR	S AW	A BA	W EN	T HE
M AE	W AR	T AW	O BE	Y EN	C HI
N AE	Y AR	W AW	O BI	F ER	G HI
S AE	G AS	Y AW	O BO	H ER	K HI
W AE	H AS	F AX	A BY	P ER	P HI
A AH	P AS	L AX		S ER	M HO
H AH	V AS	P AX		P ES	O HO
P AH	W AS	R AX	O DE	R ES	R HO
R AH	B AT	S AX	A DO	Y ES	T HO
Y AH	C AT	T AX		F ET	
B AN	E AT	W AX	A EF	G ET	D ID
C AN	F AT	Z AX	R EF	J ET	F ID
F AN	G AT	B AY	Y EH	L ET	G ID
G AN	H AT	C AY	B EL	M ET	L ID
M AN	L AT	D AY	D EL	N ET	M ID

R ID	P OD	O OW	S UP	AN A	BO W
K IF	R OD	S OW	T UP	AN D	BO X
D IN	S OD	T OW	Y UP	AN E	BO Y
F IN	T OD	V OW	B US	AN I	
G IN	Y OD	W OW	J US	AN T	
J IN	H OE	Y OW	P US	AN Y	DA B
K IN	J OE	B OX	B UT	AR C	DA D
L IN	R OE	C OX	C UT	AS H	DA G
P IN	W OE	F OX	G UT	AS K	DA K
R IN	N OH	G OX	H UT	AS P	DA M
S IN	O OH	L OX	J UT	AS S	DA W
T IN	P OH	O OX	M UT	AT E	DA Y
V IN	D OM	S OX	N UT	AW A	DE I
W IN	C ON	B OY	O UT	AW E	DE L
Y IN	D ON	F OY	P UT	AW L	DE N
B IS	E ON	G OY	R UT	AW N	DE S
S IS	F ON	H OY	T UT	AX E	DE V
V IS	I ON	S OY		AY E	DE W
W IS	M ON	T OY	A WE		DE X
A IT	S ON		E WE		DE Y
B IT	T ON	A PE	O WE	BA A	DO C
F IT	V ON	O PE		BA D	DO E
G IT	W ON		P YA	BA G	DO G
K IT	Y ON	A RE	R YA	BA H	DO L
L IT	B OP	I RE	A YE	BA L	DO M
N IT	C OP		D YE	BA N	DO N
P IT	F OP	A SH	E YE	BA R	DO R
S IT	L OP	P SI	L YE	BA T	DO T
T IT	M OP		P YE	BA Y	DO R
U IT	O OP	E TA	R YE	BE D	DO W
W IT	S OP	U TA	T YE	BE E	
	T OP		W YE	BE G	EF F
	W OP	B UN		BE L	EF T
O KA	D OR	D UN		BE N	EL D
	G OR	F UN	AA H	BE T	EL F
A LA	M OR	G UN	AA L	BI B	EL K
	N OR	H UN	AD D	BI D	EL L
A MA	T OR	J UN	AD O	BI G	EL M
E ME	C OS	M UN	AD Z	BI N	EM E
A MI	K OS	N UN	AH A	BI O	EN D
	B OW	P UN	AI L	BI S	EN G
A NA	C OW	S UN	AI M	BI T	EN S
	D OW	T UN	AI R	BO A	ER A
B OD	H OW	C UP	AI T	BO B	ER E
C OD	L OW	D UP	AM A	BO D	ER G
G OD	M OW	H UP	AM I	BO G	ER N
H OD	N OW	P UP	AM P	BO P	ER R
N OD			AM U	BO T	ER S

ES S	HI S	LO P	NU N	* * *	TA U
ET A	HI T	LO T	NU T	RE B	TA V
ET H	HO B	LO W		RE D	TA W
	HO D	LO X	OD D	RE E	TA V
FA D	HO E		OD E	RE F	TA X
FA G	HO G	MA C	OF F	RE I	
FA N	HO P	MA D	OF T	RE M	TI C
FA R	HO T	MA E	OH M	RE P	TI E
FA T	HO W	MA G	OH O	RE S	TI L
FA X	HO Y	MA N	ON E	RE T	TI N
FA Y		MA P	OP T	RE V	TI P
	IN K	MA R	OR A	RE X	TI T
GO A	IN N	MA T	OR B		TO D
GO B	IS M	MA W	OR C		TO G
GO D	IT S	MA Y	OR E	SH H	TO M
GO O			OR T	SH Y	TO N
GO R		ME L	OS E	SI B	TO P
GO X	JO B	ME N	OW E	SI M	TO R
GO Y	JO E	ME T	OW L	SI N	TO T
	JO G	ME W		SI P	TO W
		MI B		SI S	TO Y
HA D	KA B	MI D	PA D	SI T	
HA E	KA E	MI G	PA H	SI X	UP O
HA G	KA X	MI L	PA L	SO L	US E
HA H	KA Y	MI M	PA M	SO N	UT A
HA J		MI R	PA N	SO P	
HA M	LA B	MI X	PA P	SO T	WE B
HA P	LA C		PA R	SO U	WE D
HA S	LA D	NA B	PA S	SO W	WE E
HA T	LA G	NA E	PA T	SO X	WE N
HA W	LA M	NA G	PA W	SO Y	WE T
HA Y	LA P	NA P	PA X		
HE M	LA R	NA Y	PA Y	TA B	YA Y
HE N	LA T	NO B	PE A	TA D	YE A
HE P	LI B	NO D	PE D	TA E	YE H
HE R	LI D	NO G	OE E	TA G	YE N
HE X	LI E	NO H	PE G	TA J	YE P
HE Y	LI N	NO M	PE N	TA M	YE S
HI C	LI P	NO O	PE P	TA N	YE T
HI E	LI T	NO R	PE R	TA O	
HI M	LO B	NO T	PE S	TA P	
HI N	LO G	NO W	PE T	TA R	
HI P	LO O	NU B	PE W	TA T	

CHAPTER 4

□□□

Prefixes, Suffixes, and Plurals

PREFIXES

The criteria for an acceptable Scrabble® prefix is:

1. The word cannot contain a hyphen.
2. The root or base word must be able to stand alone.

The following are acceptable prefixes:

A	BI	DIS	IN	PAR	SUPER
AB	CO	EM	INTER	PARA	TRANS
ABS	COL	EN	MAL	POST	TRI
AD	COM	EX	MICRO	PRE	ULTRA
ANTE	CON	FORE	MIS	PRO	UN
ANTI	DE	HAY	NON	RE	UNI
AUTO	DI	IL	ORTHO	SEMI	UP
BE	DIA	IM	OVER	SUB	

A-		BOUGHT	NORMAL	AD-		RIFT
BASE		BOUND	OUT	APT		SCRIPT
BASH		BOUT	REACT	AXIAL		VENT
BEAM		BREAST	SENT	DRESS		VERB
BED		BRIDGE	SOLVE	DUCT		VERSE
BET		BUT	USE	HERE		VICE
BETTER		BUTTED	USER	JOIN		VISOR
BETTING		BUTTER	VOLT	JOINT		
BIDE		BUZZ	YE	JUDGE		ANTE-
BLOOM				JUROR		DATE
BOARD		AB-	ABS-	MAN		LOPE
BODE		BE	TRACT	MIRE		TYPE
BOIL		BEY		MIX		
BOON		DUCE	* * *	OPTION		* * *

269

ANTI-
- BODY
- DOTE
- FAT
- HERO
- KING
- LOG
- MASK
- NODE
- POLE
- POPE
- RUST
- SKID
- SMOG

AUTO-
- BUS
- CADE
- GIRO
- GYRO
- MATE
- SOME
- TYPE

BE-
- BLOOD
- BOP
- BOPPER
- CALM
- CAME
- CAP
- CARPET
- CAUSE
- CHALK
- CHANCE
- CHARM
- CLAMOR
- CLASP
- CLOAK
- CLOG
- CLOTHE
- CLOUD
- CLOWN
- COME
- COMING
- COWARD
- CRAWL
- CRIME
- CROWD
- CRUST
- CUDGEL
- CURSE
- DABBLE
- DAZZLE
- DECK
- DELL
- DEVIL
- DEW
- DIAPER
- DIM
- DOTTED
- DRAPE

DRENCH
DROLL
DUMB
DUNCE
FALL
FINGER
FLAG
FLEA
FLECK
FLOWER
FOG
FOOL
FORE
FOUL
FOULER
FRET
FRIEND
FRINGE
GALL
GAZE
GET
GIRDLE
GLAD
GLOOM
GONE
GOT
GOTTEN
GRIM
GRIME
GROAN
GRUDGE
GUILE
GULF
GUM
GUN
HALF
HAVE
HEAD
HIND
HOLD
HOLDER
HOOF
HOWL
JEWEL
JUMBLE
KISS
KNIGHT
KNOT
LABOR
LACED
LADY
LAY
LEAP
LIKE
LIQUOR
LITTLE
LIVE
LONG
LOW
LYING
MADAM
MEAN

MINGLE
MIRE
MIST
MIX
MOAN
MOCK
MUDDLE
MURMUR
MUSE
MUZZLE
NAME
PAINT
PIMPLE
QUEST
RASCAL
RAKE
RATE
RINGED
ROBED
ROUGED
SCORCH
SCREEN
SEEM
SET
SETTER
SHADOW
SHAME
SHIVER
SHOUT
SHREW
SHROUD
SIEGE
SLIME
SMEAR
SMIRCH
SMOKE
SMOOTH
SMUDGE
SMUT
SNOW
SOOTHE
SOUGHT
SPEAK
SPOUSE
SPREAD
STOW
STREW
STRIDE
STUD
SWARM
TAKE
TAXED
THANK
THINK
THORN
THUMP
TIDE
TIME
TIMES
TOKEN
TOOK
TRAY

TROTH
VOMIT
WAIL
WARE
WEARY
WEEP
WIG
WINGED
WORM
WORRY
WRAP

BI-
- ANNUAL
- AXAL
- AXIAL
- CHROME
- COLOR
- CONVEX
- CORN
- CUSPID
- DENTAL
- FACIAL
- FOCAL
- FOLD
- FORKED
- GOT
- LINEAR
- MANUAL
- METAL

CO-
- ACT
- ACTION
- ACTIVE
- ADMIRE
- ADMIT
- AGENCY
- AGENT
- ANNEX
- APPEAR
- ASSIST
- ASSUME
- ATTEND
- ATTEST
- AUTHOR
- AXAL
- CAIN
- CHAIR
- CHIN
- COON
- CREATE
- DEBTOR
- DERIVE
- EDITOR
- EFFECT
- EMBODY
- EMPLOY
- ENACT
- ENURE
- ENZYME
- EQUAL

EQUATE
ERECT
EXERT
EXIST
EXTEND
FACTOR
HABIT
HOG
LESSEE
LESSOR
LOCATE
LOG
MAKER
MATE
MEDIAN
MEDIC
MET
NATION
PALM
PARENT
PASTOR
PATRON
PECK
PIED
PIER
PIES
PILOT
PIOUS
PLOT
REDEEM
REIGN
RING
ROTATE
SET
STAR
TENANT
TIDAL
TING
TYPE
UPON
WAGE
WARD
WINNER
WORKER

COL-
- DISH
- LAPSE
- LARD
- LATE
- LET
- LIES
- LOP
- ON

COM-
- ATIC
- BAT
- BUST
- FIT
- FORT
- MIX

MOVE
MUTE
PACT
PADRE
PARE
PART
PEER
PLAIN
PLIER
PLIES
PLOT
POSE
POST
POUND
PRESS
PRIZE

CON-
CAVE
DENSE
DOLE
DONE
DUCE
DUCT
FINE
FIRM
FLUX
FOCAL
FOUND
FRONT
FUSE
GLOBE
JOIN
JUROR
QUEST
SENT
SERVE
SIGN
SOLE
SORT
TACT
TEMPT
TEND
TENT
TEST
TEXT
TORT
TOUR
TRACT
TRAIL
TRITE
VENT
VERGE
VERSE
VEX

DE-
AIR
ASH
BARK
BASE
BIT

BONE
BRIEF
BRUISE
BUG
BUNK
BUT
BYE
CAMP
CANE
CANTER
CARE
CAY
CEASE
CENT
CIDER
CLAIM
CLASS
CODE
COLOR
COY
LAY
LEAD
LEGACY
LIGHT
LIME
LIST
LOUSE
MARK
MAST
MEAN
MERIT
MOB
MODE
MOUNT
NATURE
NOTE
PAINT
PART
PEND
PLOY
PLUME
POLISH
PORT
POSE
POT
PRESS
RAIL
RANGE
RAT
RAY
RIDE
SALT
SAND
SELECT
SERVE
SEX
SIGN
SILVER
SIRE
SPITE
SPOIL
SUGAR

SULFUR
TAIL
TENT
TEST
TESTER
TICK
TOUR
TRACT
TRAIN
VALUE
VEIN
VEST
VICE
VISE
VISOR
VOICE
VOID
VOTE
WAN
WATER
WAX
WOOL
WORM

DI-
ACID
ARIES
ATOM
BASIC
CAST
COT
DAPPER
OXIDE
PHASE
POLE
REST
VAN
VERSE
VEST
VINE
VISOR

DIA-
GRAM
LIST
LOGIC
METER
MINE
PAUSE
PHONE
SPORE

DIS-
ABLE
ABUSE
AGREE
ALLOW
ARM
ARRAY
AVOW
BAND
BAR

BOUND
BOWEL
BUD
CASE
CLAIM
CLOSE
COLOR
CORD
COUNT
COVER
CROWN
CUSS
EASE
ENDOW
FAVOR
FROCK
GORGE
GRACE
GUST
HELM
JOIN
LIKE
LODGE
LOYAL
MAST
MAY
MISS
MOUNT
OBEY
ORDER
OWN
PATCH
PLACE
PLAY
PLUME
PORT
POSE
PRIZE
PROOF
PROVE
QUIET
ROBE
ROOT
SAVE
SEIZE
SERVE
SOLVE
TASTE
TILL
TORT
TRACT
TRAIN
TRAIT
TRUST
UNION
UNITE
UNITY
USE
VALUE
YOKE

* * *

EM-
BANK
BARK
BARRED
BATTLE
BED
BITTER
BLAZE
BODY
BORDER
BOSOM
BOSS
BOW
BOWEL
BRACE
IRATE
MET
PALE
PANEL
PLACE
PLANE
PLOY
POISON
POWER
PRESS
PRIZE

EN-
ABLE
ABLER
ACT
ACTIVE
ACTOR
AMOUR
ATE
CAGE
CAMP
CASE
CASH
CHAIN
CHANT
CHASER
CIPHER
CIRCLE
CLASP
CLOSE
CLOSER
CODE
CORE
CRUST
CRYPT
CYST
DAMAGE
DANGER
DIVE
DOWER
DUE
FETTER
FEVER
FIN
FLAME
FOLD

EN-
FOLDER
FORCE
FRAME
GENDER
GIRDLE
GLUT
GORGE
GRAFT
GRAIL
GRAIN
GRAM
GRAVE
GRAVER
GROSS
GULF
HALO
ISLE
JAMBED
JOIN
JOY
KINDLE
LACE
LARGE
LARGER
LIST
LIVEN
MESH
NOBLE
NOBLER
OUNCE
PLANE
RAGE
RAPT
RAVISH
RICH
RICHER
ROBE
ROLL
ROLLER
ROLLING
ROOT
SAMPLE
SCONCE
SCROLL
SERF
SHEATH
SHRINE
SHROUD
SIGN
SKY
SLAVE
SLAVER
SNARE
SNARL
SOUL
SPHERE
SUE
SURE
SURER
SWATHE
TAIL

THRONE
TIRE
TITLE
TOIL
TOMB
TOPIC
TRAILS
TRANCE
TRAP
TREAT
TREATY
TREE
TRENCH
TRIES
TRUST
TRY
TWINE
TWIST
VENOM
VIABLE
VISION
WHEEL
WIND
WOMB
WRAP

EX-
ACT
ACTION
ACTOR
ALTER
AMEN
AMPLE
ARCH
CHANGE
CITE
CLAIM
HALE
PLAIN
PLANT
PORT
POSE
POUND
PRESS
PULSE
SECT
TEND
TENT
TOLL
TOLLING
TORT
TRACT

FORE-
ARM
BAY
BEAR
BODE
BODY
BOOM
BY
BYE

CAST
DATE
DECK
DO
DOOM
FACE
FEEL
FEND
FOOT
GO
GUT
HAND
HEAD
HOOF
KNOW
LADY
LEG
LIMB
LOCK
MAN
MAST
MILK
MOST
NAME
NOON
PART
PAST
PAW
PEAK
PLAY
RANK
RUN
SAID
SAIL
SEE
SEER
SHOW
SIDE
SKIN
STAY
TELL
TIME
TOP
WARN
WENT
WORD
WORN
YARD

HAY-
COCK
FORK
LOFT
MAKER
MOW
RACK
RIDE
SEED
STACK
WARD
WIRE
* * *

IL-
LEGAL
LIQUID
LOGIC

IM-
AGE
AGING
BALM
BARK
BED
BITTER
BLAZE
BODY
BOSOM
BROWN
BRUTE
MANE
MATURE
MERGE
MESH
MIX
MOBILE
MODEST
MORAL
PACT
PAINT
PAIR
PALE
PANEL
PARITY
PEACH
PLANT
PLEAD
PLEDGE
PLIED
PLIES
PLY
POLICY
POLITE
PORT
PORTER
POSE
POSTER
POTENT
POUND
POWER
PRESS
PRINT
PRISON
PROPER
PROVE
PULSE
PURE
PURITY

IN-
ACTION
ACTIVE
ARCH
ARM
BEING

BOARD
BORN
BOUND
BOUNDS
BREED
BUILT
BURST
BYE
CAGE
CASE
CITE
CIVIL
CLASP
CLIP
CLOSE
CLOSER
COG
COME
COMING
CORPSE
CREASE
CREATE
CROSS
CRUST
CULT
CUR
CURVE
CUS
DEED
DENT
DEVOUT
DIRECT
DOCILE
DOLE
DOOR
DOORS
DOW
DRAFT
DRAWN
DUCE
DUCT
DUE
EARTH
EDIBLE
EDITED
EQUITY
EXACT
EXPERT
FAMOUS
FANCY
FARE
FIELD
FIRM
FIRMLY
FLAME
FLEXED
FLIGHT
FLOW
FLUENT
FLUX
FOLD
FOLDER

FORM	STANCE	MICRO-	GIVE	SPOKE
FORMAL	STAR	BAR	GRAFT	SPOKEN
FORMER	STATE	BUS	GROW	START
FRINGE	STEAD		GUESS	STATE
FRUGAL	STEP	MIS-	GUIDE	STEER
FUSE	STILL	ADD	HEAR	STEP
FUSION	STROKE	AGENT	HIT	STOP
GATE	SURE	AIM	INFER	STYLE
GATHER	SWATHE	ALLY	JOIN	SUIT
GOING	TACT	ALTER	JUDGE	TAKE
GOT	TAKE	APPLY	KEEP	TAKER
GRAFT	TEND	ASSAY	KNOW	TEACH
GRAIN	TENDED	ATE	LABEL	TEND
GROUP	TENDER	ATONE	LABOR	TERM
GROWN	TENSE	AVER	LAIN	THINK
GROWTH	TENT	AWARD	LAY	THROW
GULF	THRONE	BEGIN	LAYER	TIER
HABIT	TIME	BEGOT	LEAD	TIME
HALE	TITLE	BIAS	LEARN	TITLE
HAUL	TOMB	BILL	LIE	TOOK
HUMAN	TONE	BIND	LIGHT	TOUCH
HUMANE	TONER	BRAND	LIKE	TRACE
JURY	TORT	BUILD	LIT	TREAT
LACE	TOWN	CALL	LIVE	TRIAL
LAID	TREAT	CARRY	LODGE	TRUST
LAND	TRENCH	CAST	LYING	TRYST
LAY	TRUST	CHIEF	MARK	TUNE
LAYER	TWINE	CLAIM	MATCH	TUTOR
LET	URBANE	CLASS	MATE	TYPE
LIER	VALID	COIN	MEET	UNION
MATE	VENT	COLOR	MOVE	USAGE
MESH	VEST	COOK	NAME	USE
MOST	VIABLE	COPY	PAGE	USER
NERVE	VITAL	COUNT	PAINT	VALUE
POUR	VOICE	CUE	PART	WORD
PUT	WALL	CUT	PATCH	WRITE
QUEST	WARD	DATE	PEN	YOKE
QUIET	WARDS	DEAL	PLACE	
ROAD	WEAVE	DEED	PLEAD	NON-
RUSH	WIND	DEEM	POINT	ACID
SANE	WRAP	DO	POISE	ADULT
SANITY		DOER	PRINT	AGE
SCRIBE	INTER-	DOING	PRIZE	BANK
SCROLL	ACT	DONE	QUOTE	BASIC
SEAM	CUT	DOUBT	RAISE	BEING
SECT	LAP	DRAW	RATE	BOOK
SET	MIX	DRIVE	READ	CASH
SETTER	RING	EASE	REFER	DAIRY
SHEATH	SEX	EAT	RELY	ELECT
SHORE	TIE	EDIT	RULE	EMPTY
SHRINE	WAR	ENROLL	SAY	ENTRY
SIDE		ENTER	SEAT	EQUAL
SIGHT	MAL-	ENTRY	SEND	EVENT
SISTER	LARD	EVENT	SENSE	FARM
SNARE	LOW	FAITH	SHAPE	FAT
SOLE	MY	FIELD	SHOD	FATAL
SOUL	ODOR	FILE	SORT	FLUID
SPAN	POSED	FIRE	SOUND	FOCAL
SPHERE	TIER	FIT	SPACE	FOOD
SPIRIT	TREAT	FORM	SPEAK	GAME
STABLE		FRAME	SPELL	GREEN
STALL	* * *	GAUGE	SPEND	GUILT

NON-	AGE	GOAD	RAN	WARY
HERO	ALL	GROW	RANK	WEAK
HUMAN	APT	HAND	RASH	WEAR
IDEAL	ARCH	HANG	RATE	WEEN
JUROR	ARM	HARD	RICH	WET
LEGAL	ATE	HATE	RIDE	WIDE
LIFE	AWE	HAUL	RIFE	WILY
LOCAL	BAKE	HEAD	RIPE	WIND
MAN	BEAR	HEAP	RODE	WISE
METAL	BET	HEAR	RUDE	WORD
MONEY	BID	HEAT	RULE	WORE
MORAL	BIG	HIGH	RUN	WORK
NAVAL	BITE	HOLD	SAD	WORN
OBESE	BLOW	HOLY	SALE	WOUND
OWNER	BOLD	HOPE	SALT	WROUGHT
PAGAN	BOOK	HOT	SAVE	ZEAL
PAPAL	BORE	HUNG	SAW	
PARTY	BORN	HUNT	SEA	PAR-
PLUS	BORNE	IDLE	SEAS	BOIL
POLAR	BOUGHT	JOY	SEE	DINE
QUOTA	BRED	JUST	SEED	DONER
RATED	BUSY	KEEN	SEER	EVE
RIGID	BUY	KILL	SELL	FLESH
RIVAL	CALL	KIND	SET	FOCAL
ROYAL	CAME	LAID	SEW	GET
RURAL	CAST	LAIN	SHOE	GO
SENSE	COAT	LAND	SHOT	KING
SKID	COLD	LAP	SICK	LANCE
SKIER	COME	LATE	SIDE	LAY
SLIP	COOK	LAX	SIZE	RED
SOLAR	COOL	LAY	SLIP	RIDGE
SOLID	COY	LEAF	SLOW	SING
STICK	CRAM	LEAP	SOAK	SNIP
STOP	CROP	LET	SOFT	SON
SUCH	DARE	LEWD	SOLD	TAKE
SUGAR	DEAR	LIE	SOON	TAKER
SUIT	DECK	LIVE	SOUL	TAN
TAX	DO	LOAD	SPIN	TIED
TIDAL	DOER	LONG	STAY	TIES
TITLE	DOSE	LOOK	STEP	TON
TOXIC	DRAW	LORD	STIR	TOOK
TRUMP	DRY	LOUD	SUP	VENUE
TRUTH	DUE	LOVE	SURE	VISE
UNION	DYE	LYING	TAKE	
URBAN	EASY	MAN	TAME	PARA-
USE	EAT	MANY	TART	DROP
USER	FAR	MEEK	TASK	FORM
USING	FAST	MELT	TAX	PET
VIRAL	FAT	MEN	THIN	SANG
VOCAL	FEAR	MILD	TIME	SHAH
VOTER	FEED	MIX	TIRE	SITE
WHITE	FILL	MUCH	TOIL	SOL
WOODY	FISH	NEAR	TONE	VANE
WOVEN	FLOW	NEAT	TOOK	
ZERO	FLY	NEW	TOP	POST-
	FOND	NICE	TRIM	AGE
	FOUL	PASS	TURN	ALLY
ORTHO-	FREE	PAY	URGE	ANAL
TIC	FULL	PERT	USE	BAG
	GILD	PLAY	VIEW	BOX
OVER-	GIRD	PLUS	VOTE	BOY
ABLE	GLAD	PLY	WARM	CARD
ACT				

DATE	MOLAR	LONG	BURY	FEED
FACE	NAME	MOTE	BUS	FELL
FIX	NATAL	NOUN	BUT	FLEX
FORM	PACK	PANE	BUTTING	FIGHT
HOLE	PAID	PHASE	BUTTON	FILTER
MAN	PARE	PONE	CALL	FIND
MARK	PAY	POSE	CANE	FIRE
PAID	PLACE	PYLON	CAP	FLEW
PONE	PLAN	RATE	CARRY	FLIES
WAR	PLANT	ROGUE	CAST	FLOW
	PRINT	SECT	CHANGE	FLOWER
	PUNCH	SING	CHART	FLY
PRE-	SAGE	STATE	CHOOSE	FORGE
ACT	SCORE	STYLE	CLAD	FOUGHT
ADAPT	SELL	TEASE	CLAIM	FOUND
ADMIT	SENT	TEND	CLASP	FRONT
ADOPT	SERVE	TEST	CLEAN	FUSE
ADULT	SET	TRACT	CLOTHE	GAUGE
AGED	SHAPE	UNION	COAL	GAVE
ALLOT	SHOW	VIRUS	COCK	GEAR
AMBLE	SIDE	WAR	CODIFY	GILD
AMP	SIFT		COIL	GIVE
ANAL	SOAK	**RE-**	COIN	GLAZE
ARM	SOLD	ACTIVE	COLOR	GLOSS
AVER	STAMP	ACTOR	COMMIT	GLOW
AXIAL	TASTE	ABSORB	CONVEY	GRADE
BEND	TAX	ACCEDE	COOK	GRAFT
BILL	TEEN	ACCENT	CORD	GREW
BIND	TEND	ACCEPT	CROWN	GRIND
BLESS	TENSE	ACCUSE	CURVE	GROOVE
BOIL	TEST	ADAPT	DATE	GORGE
BOUND	TEXT	ADD	DEAR	HAMMER
CAST	TREAT	ADDICT	DEEM	HANDLE
CENT	UNION	ADORN	DEFEAT	HANG
CHECK	UNITE	AFFIX	DEFY	HARDEN
CHILL	VENT	AGENT	DEMAND	HEAR
CITED	VIEW	ALLOT	DIRECT	HEARSE
CLEAN	VISE	ALTER	DIVIDE	HEEL
COOK	VISOR	ANNEX	DOCK	HEM
COOL	WAR	ANOINT	DRAW	HINGE
CURE	WARM	ARGUE	DRIED	HOUSE
DATE	WARN	AROUSE	DRIES	HUNG
DAWN	WASH	ASCEND	DRILL	IMAGE
DIAL	WRAP	ASCENT	DRIVE	IMPORT
DUSK		ASSAIL	DRY	IMPOSE
ELECT	**PRO-**	ASSORT	DYE	INCITE
ENACT	BAND	ASSUME	EARN	INDEX
EXIST	CARP	ATTACH	ECHO	INDUCE
FACE	CLAIM	ATTACK	EDIT	INFORM
FIX	CURE	ATTAIN	EJECT	INJURE
FOCUS	DUCE	AWAKE	EMBARK	INSERT
FORM	FILE	AWAKEN	EMBODY	INTER
FRANK	FIT	BAIT	EMERGE	INVENT
GAME	FOUND	BID	EMIT	INVITE
HEAT	FUSE	BIND	ENDOW	INVOKE
HUMAN	GRADE	BIRTH	ENJOY	JUDGE
JUDGE	GRAM	BLOOM	EQUIP	KEY
LEGAL	JET	BOIL	ERECT	KNIT
LIMIT	LABOR	BOP	EVOKE	LABEL
MAN	LAPSE	BRANCH	EXPEL	LACE
MEDIC	LATE	BUFF	EXPORT	LAPSE
MEN	LEG	BURIAL	FALL	LEARN
MIX				

RE-
LEND
LETTER
LINE
LIST
LIT
LOAN
MAIL
MANNED
MAP
MARQUE
MEMBER
MEET
MEND
MERGE
MET
MOLD
MOTION
NATURE
OBJECT
OIL
OPPOSE
PACIFY
PASS
PEOPLE
PERK
PIN
PLAN
PLATE
PLEDGE
PLUNGE
POWER
PRICE
PROBE
PURIFY
PURSUE
QUITE
RISE
ROLL
ROLLER
SAID
SAIL
SALUTE
SAW
SAY
SCREEN
SCRIPT
SEAT
SEE
SEEK
SEEN
SEIZE
SEND
SEW
SHIP
SHOW
SIFT
SILVER
SIZE
SMELT
SMOOTH
SOLD

SOLDER
SOUGHT
SPELL
SPREAD
SPRING
STACK
STRIKE
STRUCK
STRUNG
STUDY
STUFF
SUMMON
SUPPLY
TAILOR
TASTE
TIME
TINT
TITLE
TRIM
TUNE
TWIST
TYING
UTTER
VEST
VOICE
WAKE
WAN
WEIGH
WELD
WIN
WOKE
WOKEN
WON
WROUGHT
ZONE

SEMI-
ARID
BALD
COMA
DEAF
DOME
GALA
HIGH
HOBO
LOG
MUTE
NUDE
RAW
SOFT
TONE
WILD

SUB-
ABBOT
ACID
ACRID
ACUTE
ADULT
AGENT
AREA
ARID

ATOM
AXIAL
BASE
BASS
BED
BREED
CAUSE
CELL
CLAN
CLASS
CLERK
DEAN
DEPOT
DUAL
DUCE
DUCT
DUE
ECHO
EDIT
ENTRY
ERECT
FIELD
FIX
FLOOR
FLUID
GRADE
GROUP
GUM
HEAD
HUMAN
HUMID
IDEA
INDEX
JOIN
LEVEL
LIME
NASAL
OPTIC
ORAL
ORDER
OVAL
OXIDE
PAR
POLAR
RACE
RING
RULE
SECT
SHAFT
SHRUB
SOIL
SOLAR
SONIC
STAGE
TEND
TONIC
TOPIC
TRIBE
TUNIC
URBAN
VOCAL
ZONE

* * *
SUPER-
ADD
JET
LIE
SEX

TRANS-
ACT
SECT
FIX

TRI-
METER
MOTOR
OXIDE
PACK
PART
PHASE
PLANE
POD
SECT
SOME
STATE
UNITY
VALVE

ULTRA-
RED

UN-
ABATED
ABUSED
ACTED
AGED
AGEING
AGILE
AGING
AIMED
AIRED
ALLIED
ANCHOR
ANELED
APT
APTLY
ARGUED
ARTFUL
ATONED
AVOWED
AWARE
AWED
BACKED
BAKED
BAR
BARBED
BASED
BATED
BEAR
BELIEF
BELT
BEND
BID

BIDDEN
BIND
BITTED
BLAMED
BLEST
BLOODY
BODIED
BONED
BONNET
BOSOM
BOWED
BOX
BRACE
BRED
BREECH
BROKE
BUILD
BUNDLE
BURIED
BURNT
CAKE
CANDID
CASE
CAUGHT
CAUSED
CHANCY
CHARGE
CHARY
CHASTE
CHIC
CHOKE
CHURCH
CLENCH
CLINCH
CLOAK
CLOSE
CLOUD
CLOYED
COATED
COCK
COFFIN
COIL
COMELY
COMIC
CREATE
CROWN
CURED
CURSED
DAMPED
DARING
DECKED
DENIED
DEVOUT
DIMMED
DOCK
DOER
DOUBLE
DREAMT
DRIED
DRUNK
DULLED
DYED

				UP-
EARTH	LEAD	PURGED	STICK	
EDIBLE	LEASED	PUZZLE	STOP	BEAR
ENVIED	LED	QUIET	STRESS	BEARER
ERASED	LETHAL	RAISED	STUNG	BIND
EVADED	LET	RANKED	SUBTLE	BOIL
EXOTIC	LETTED	RAZED	SUNK	BORE
EXPERT	LEVEL	READY	SWATHE	BUILD
FADED	LEVIED	REASON	SWEAR	BYE
FADING	LIMBER	REELER	SWAYED	CAST
FAITH	LIVE	REEVE	TAGGED	CHUCK
FALLEN	LIVELY	RENT	TAKEN	CLIMB
FANCY	LOBED	REPAIR	TEACH	CURL
FENCE	MAKER	RESTED	THINK	DATER
FEARED	MAN	RHYMED	TILLED	DIVE
FED	MAPPED	RIFLED	TILTED	DRY
FELT	MARRED	RIG	TRUSTY	FIELD
FILIAL	MASKER	RIMED	TUNE	FLOW
FILMED	MATED	RISEN	TUFTED	FOLD
FIRED	MATTED	ROOF	VARIED	GATHER
FITLY	MEANT	ROUGH	VEINED	GAZE
FIX	MEET	ROUND	VEXED	GOING
FLEXED	MELLOW	ROVE	VIABLE	GROWTH
FOLDER	MENDED	ROVEN	VOCAL	HEAP
FORCED	MET	RUSHED	VOICE	HEAVER
FORGOT	MEW	SALTED	WALLED	HOARD
FORKED	MILLED	SAVED	WARIER	HOLDER
FREE	MIXT	SAY	WARIEST	LAND
FROCK	MODISH	SEAM	WARILY	LANDER
FUNNY	MOLTEN	SEIZED	WARMED	LEAP
FUSED	MORAL	SEW	WARNED	LIGHT
GALLED	MOVING	SEXUAL	WARPED	PILE
GENIAL	MOWN	SHADED	WEANED	PITY
GIFTED	NEEDED	SHARED	WEIGHT	PROP
GLAZED	NOISY	SHARP	WEPT	RAISE
GOT	NOTED	SHED	WETTED	RAISER
GOTTEN	OILED	SHELL	WIFELY	ROOTER
GOWNED	ORNATE	SHIFT	WILLED	ROSE
GRACED	OWNED	SHIP	WINDER	ROUSE
GRADED	PAGED	SHRUNK	WISDOM	RUSH
GREEDY	PAIRED	SHUT	WISH	SEND
HAILED	PARTED	SICKER	WIT	SETTER
HAIR	PAYING	SIGHT	WON	SHIFT
HALLOW	PEG	SILENT	WOODED	SOAR
HALVED	PEOPLE	SINFUL	WOOED	SPRING
HASTY	PILE	SLAKED	WORKED	STAIR
HEALED	PITIED	SLING	WORN	STARE
HELM	PLACED	SOAKED	WRUNG	STATER
HEROIC	PLIANT	SOBER		STEP
HEWN	PLOWED	SOLID	UNI-	STIR
HIP	POETIC	SORTED	AXIAL	STOOD
HIRED	POISED	SOUGHT	COLOR	SWEEP
HOOD	POLLED	SOURED	CORN	TEAR
HOPED	POSED	SOWN	CYCLE	THROW
HOUSE	POSTED	SPEAK	FACE	TILT
HUNG	PRETTY	SHERE	FORM	TIME
HUSK	PRICED	SPOILT	SEX	TOWNER
IDEAL	PRIMED	SPRUNG	SON	TREND
JOYFUL	PRIZED	SPUN	VALVE	WAFT
KENNEL	PROBED	STABLY	VERSE	WELL
KINGLY	PRUNED	STEEL	VOCAL	
KNIT	PUCKER	STEP		∗ ∗ ∗

SUFFIXES

The criteria for an acceptable Scrabble® suffix is:

1. No letter can be dropped when adding the suffix.
2. The suffix, in most cases, does not have a meaning of its own.
3. The use of the suffix changes the meaning of the base or root word or converts it to another part of speech.

The following are acceptable suffixes:

ABLE	ED	FOLD	ISM	LET	SHIP
AGE	EE	FUL	IST	LIKE	SOME
AL	EER	GRAPHER	ITIS	LING	STER
AN	EN	HOOD	ITY	LY	TH
ANCE	ER	IBLE	IVE	MENT	ULE
ATION	ERY	IE/Y	IZE	NESS	WARD
CLE	ESE	IER	KIN	OCK	WAYS
CY	ESS	ING	LER	OUS	WISE
DOM	ETTE	ISH	LESS	RY	Y

-ABLE
 AGREE
 BREAK
 DETECT
 EAT
 EXCHANGE
 IMPRESSION
 PREFER
 READ
 TREASON
 UNDERSTAND

-AGE
 ACRE
 CART
 CELLAR
 HERMIT
 ORPHAN
 PACK
 PEER
 STOP
 VICAR

-AL
 BESTOW
 BETROTH
 COAST
 EDUCATION
 FICTION
 MUSIC

 OCCASION
 PROVISION
 RENEW
 WITHDRAW

-AN
 REPUBLIC

-ANCE
 FORBEAR
 FURTHER
 UTTER

-ATION
 BOTHER
 FLIRT
 SEDIMENT

-CLE
 MONO
 UN

-CY
 BANKRUPT
 CAPTAIN
 CHAPLAIN
 COLONEL
 NORMAL

 * * *

-DOM
 BORE
 DUKE
 EARL
 FILM
 HEATHEN
 MARTYR
 OFFICIAL
 SAVAGE
 VILLA

-ED
 BOOT
 LAND
 MONEY
 TALENT
 ROOT
 UMBRELLA
 WOOD

-EE
 BIOGRAPH
 MURDER
 TEST
 TOWN
 STAND

-EER
 AUCTION
 PAMPHLET

 SLOGAN
 SONNET

-EN
 BLACK
 DARK
 DEEP
 EARTH
 FAST
 FRIGHT
 GOLD
 HARD
 LENGTH
 MOIST
 SHORT
 SILK
 WOOD

-ER
 FOREIGN
 HEAD
 HUNT
 PAINT
 TROT

-ERY
 BREW
 COOK
 DEAN
 FISH

 FOOL
 ROOK

-ESE
 JOURNAL
 TRANSLATION

-ESS
 AUTHOR
 COUNT
 MURDER

-ETTE
 CELLAR
 FLANNEL
 KITCHEN
 LEADER
 SERMON

-FOLD
 TWO
 TEN
 THOUSAND

-FUL
 FORGET
 HAND

-GRAPHER
 PHOTO
 TELE

***	***			
-HOOD	**-IST**	CAB	SHIP	**-STER**
BACHELOR	BALLOON	EYE	TREAT	GAME
FALSE	COLON	FLAT		PUNT
FATHER	COPY	IS	**-NESS**	SPEED
NEIGHBOR	NOVEL	KING	DIVINE	SPIN
PRIEST	ROYAL	LEAF	DRUNKEN	TAP
	SAD	NECK	GOOD	TRICK
-IBLE	VIOLIN	OWE	HARSH	
CONVERT		RING	KIND	**-TH**
DISCERN	**-ITY**		PREPARED	FOUR
	COMICAL	**-LIKE**	SWEET	HUNDRED
-IE/Y	HISTORIC	CHILD	WICKED	SIX
DEAR	SENTIMENTAL	GENTLEMAN		THIRTEEN
HANK		GOD	**-OCK**	THOUSAND
NIGHT	**-IVE**	LADY	BULL	
	ATTRACT	SPORTSMAN	HILL	**-ULE**
-IER	CREAT			NOD
HOTEL	POSSESS	**-LING**	**-OUS**	
	PRODUCT	CAT	DANGER	**-WARD**
-ING	INSTINCT	NURSE	MOUNTAIN	BACK
INN		PRINCE	MURDER	DOWN
OFF	**-IZE**	SAP	THUNDER	EAST
OUT	CIVIL	SEED		FOR
SACK	FAMILIAR	UNDER	**-RY**	HEAVEN
SHIRT	LEGAL		CHEMIST	HOME
SKIRT	MATERIAL	**-LY**	DRUDGE	LAND
	NATIONAL	COWARD	NURSE	ON
-ISH	PATRON	DEAD	PEASANT	UP
AMATEUR	SOBER	EARTH	RIVAL	
BOOK		GENTLEMAN	YEOMAN	**-WAYS**
BOY	**-KIN**	GREAT		LENGTH
CHILD	LAMB	HEAVEN	**-SHIP**	NO
FEVER	MUNCH	KIND	AUTHOR	SIDE
DEVIL		KING	CENSOR	
FOOL	**-LER**	LEISURE	FELLOW	**-WISE**
GIRL	CUT	LIVE	FRIEND	CLOCK
GREEN		LOVE	HARD	LENGTH
HELL	**-LESS**	MAN	LADY	CRAB
POP	CEASE	MASTER	MEMBER	LIKE
SELF	COUNT	MONTH	SCHOLAR	NO
	FEAR	SCHOLAR	TOWN	OTHER
-ISM	LIFE	USUAL		POKER
ALCOHOL	DOUBT		**-SOME**	
BARBAR	NUMBER	**-MENT**	BURDEN	**-Y**
DESPOT	TAME	ACKNOWLEDGE	FEAR	EARTH
HERO	TIRE	ARRANGE	LONE	CHOOSE
IMPERIAL		BEWILDER	QUARREL	CRAFT
PARALLEL	**-LET**	EMPLOY	TIRE	FISH
PATRIOT	ARM	ENDOW	TROUBLE	SLANG
IMPERIAL	BOOK	ENLIGHTEN		WOODS
		REFRESH	***	

PLURALS

Pluralization can create some of the most spirited disagreements in a Scrabble® game. Keep in mind that a plural may sound new and unusual to you and may even be omitted from some dictionaries, but

if the rules are followed you should have little difficulty claiming the rights to use the plural.

1. Most nouns become plural with the addition of "s" or "es".
2. If pluralization requires the removal of a letter or letters or the addition of an apostrophe, under Scrabble® rules, the plural cannot be made.
3. Most exceptions to the rules are listed in the dictionary, here are a few:

OX-	EN
CHILD-	REN
LARVA-	E
TABLEAU-	X
MORCEAU-	X
CHERUB-	IM
ANTENNA-	E
FORMULA-	E
NEBULA-	E
ALGA-	E
ALUMNA-	E
PLATEAU-	X
BUREAU-	X
ADIEU-	X
KIBBUTZ-	IM

CHAPTER 5

□□□

Quick-Check Usage Guide

This section lists all the official Scrabble® words that fall into one of six major categories of special knowledge:

> Animal
> Legal
> Medical
> Military
> Nautical
> Performing Arts

Players using an unusual word in one of these categories need only provide the subject or category (very often a precise definition is not known even by the individual playing the word) and in a very few seconds, using the Quick-Check Usage Guide, the authenticity of the word can be verified. The Quick-Check Usage Guide can also be used to review your knowledge of the specific terms in the specific fields provided.

ANIMAL WORDS

AARDVARK	ACTINIA	AIVR	ALBICORE	ANACONDA
AARDWOLF	ADDAX	ALAN	ALEVIN	ANHINGA
AASVOGEL	ADDER	ALAND	AMADAVAT	ANI
ABALONE	AEDES	ALANT	ANABAS	ANOA
ACCENTOR	AI	ALBACORE	ANABLEPS	ANOLE

ANTLION	BORZOI	CHARR	DAKERHEN	GARPIKE
ANURAN	BOSHBOK	CHEBEC	DASYURE	GARRON
AOUDAD	BOSHVARK	CHEGOE	DECAPOD	GAVIAL
APHID	BOSSY	CHETAH	DESMAN	GAYAL
APHIDIAN	BOVID	CHEWINK	DEVON	GECKO
APTERYX	BOVINE	CHIGETAI	DIKDIK	GELADA
ARACHNID	BOWFIN	CHIGOE	DINGO	GEMSBOK
ARANEID	BRACH	CHILOPOD	DIPLOPOD	GEMSBUCK
ARAPAIMA	BRAHMA	CHIMAERA	DIPNOAN	GENET
ARGALI	BRAIZE	CHINCH	DOBBIN	GENETTE
ARGUS	BRANT	CHIRO	DODO	GEODUCK
ARIEL	BRANTAIL	CHOUGH	DORBUG	GERBIL
ASCARID	BRIARD	CHUB	DORHAWK	GERENUK
ASCARIS	BRIT	CHUKAR	DORMICE	GILTHEAD
ASCIDIAN	BROCKET	CHUKKAR	DORMOUSE	GLED
ASP	BRUIN	CLERID	DOVEKEY	GLEDE
ASPIC	BRULOT	CLOWDER	DOVEKIE	GNU
ASPIS	BRUMBY	CLUMBER	DRONGO	GOA
ASPISH	BUBAL	CLUPEOID	DRUMFISH	GOBY
AUDAD	BULLBAT	COALA	DUIKER	GODWIT
AUK	BULLHEAD	COALFISH	DUROC	GOLDBUG
AUKLET	BULLOCK	COATI		GOLDEYE
AVIAN	BURBOT	COBIA		GORAL
AVOCET	BUSHBECK	COCCID	EAGLET	GORCOCK
AVOSET	BUSHGOAT	COCHIN	EELPOUT	GOSHAWK
AXIS	BUSHTIT	COCKEREL	EGRET	GOURAMI
AXOLOTL	BUT	COHO	EIDER	GRAMPUS
	BUTEO	COHOG	ELAND	GRAYBACK
		COLIN	ELAPHINE	GRAYFISH
BABIRUSA		COMATULA	ELAPID	GRAYLAG
BANGTAIL	CABRILLA	CONY	ELAPINE	GRAYLING
BASENJI	CACHALOT	COOT	ELATER	GREBE
BATFISH	CACIQUE	COQUINA	ELATERID	GREYHEN
BAUDRONS	CACOMIXL	CORBIE	ELVER	GRILSE
BAWTIE	CADWELL	CORBINA	EMYD	GRISON
BAYARD	CAHOW	CORBY	EOHIPPUS	GRIVET
BEARCAT	CAIMAN	CORGI	ERGATE	GROSBEAK
BELLBIRD	CAPUCHIN	CORVINE	ESCOLAR	GRUNION
BILLBUG	CAPYBARA	COYPOU	EULACHON	GUAN
BILLFISH	CARABAO	COYPU	EURO	GUENON
BITTERN	CARABID	CRAPPIE	EYAS	GUNNEL
BIVALVE	CARACAL	CRAWDAD	EYRA	GURNARD
BIVALVED	CARACARA	CREODONT		GURNET
BLACKCAP	CARANGID	CREVALLE	FATBACK	GURNARD
BLACKFIN	CARIBE	CRICETID	FATBIRD	GWEDUC
BLAUTOK	CARIBOU	CRINOID	FATLING	GWEDUCK
BLEAK	CATTALO	CROOK	FATSTOCK	
BLENNY	CAVALLA	CUDDY	FENNEC	
BLESBOK	CAVEFISH	CULEX	FIGETER	HABU
BLOODFIN	CAVY	CULICID	FILEFISH	HAGDON
BLOWFLY	CAYMAN	CULICINE	FINFOOT	HAGFISH
BLUEBILL	CAYUSE	CULVER	FIREBRAT	HAGGARD
BLUEGILL	CAZIQUE	CUNNER	FITCH	HALFBEAK
BLUEHEAD	CEBID	CURASSOW	FOOLFISH	HANGBIRD
BOARFISH	CEBOID	CUSCUS	FOXFISH	HANUMAN
BOATBILL	CERASTES	CUSHAT		HARRIER
BOBOLINK	CERO	CUSK		HART
BOCACCIO	CETE	CYCLOPS	GALAGO	HATTERIA
BOMBYCID	CHACMA	CYGNET	GALAH	HAWKEY
BOMBYX	CHAFER	CYPRINID	GAMBUSIA	HAWKIE
BONACI	CHALCID		GANNET	HELLERI
BONITO	CHARACID	DABCHICK	GANOID	HIND
BONTEBOK	CHARACIN	DACE	GARFISH	HOATZIN
			GARGANEY	HOGNOSE

HOODIE	LAVEROCK	MURAENID	PEKE	REREMICE
HOOPOE	LEMUROID	MURINE	PERCOID	RHEA
HOOPOO	LEPORID	MURRE	PETREL	RHEBOK
HOWLET	LEPRINE	MURRELET	PEWEE	RICEBIRD
HYLA	LEPROSE	MURRY	PHASMID	RIDLEY
	LEVERET	MUSCA	PHILMEL	RINGDOVE
INCONNU	LIMPKIN	MUSPIKE	PHOCINE	RINGHALS
INDRI	LINGCOD	MUSQUASH	PHOEBE	ROBALO
IXODID	LINNET		PIDDOCK	ROCKLING
	LINSANG	NENE	PIEBALD	ROEBUCK
JABIRU	LOACH	NEWT	PIGFISH	ROSEFISH
JACAMAR	LOBEFIN	NILGAI	PILCHARD	ROTCH
JACANA	LONGSPUR	NILGAU	PINFISH	ROTCHE
JACKAROO	LOOKDOWN	NILGHAI	PINTADO	ROUEN
JACKDAW	LORIKEET	NILGHAU	PINTANO	ROUGHLEG
JACKFISH	LORIS	NOCTULE	PIPEFISH	RUDD
JACOBIN	LORY	NOTORNIS	PIPIT	RUDDOCK
JAVELINA	LUCE	NUMBFISH	PIRARUCU	RUFFE
JENNET	LUNKER	NUTRIA	PLACOID	
JENNY		NYALA	PLAICE	SAHIWAL
JERBOA	MACACO	NYLGHAI	PLANARIA	SAIGA
JOCKO	MACAQUE	NYLGHAU	PLATY	SAITHE
JOEY	MAGOT		PLATYPUS	SAKER
JUMBUCK	MAGPIE	OARFISH	PLOVER	SALADANG
JUNCO	MAMBA	OCTOPI	POCHARD	SALMONID
JUREL	MANAKIN	OCTOPOD	POGY	SALUKI
	MANGABEY	OKAPI	POLLACK	SAMBAR
KABELJOU	MANGABY	OLDWIFE	POTTO	SAMBHAR
KAE	MARGAY	OMNIVORA	POULT	SAMBHUR
KAGU	MARKHOR	OMNIVORE	POYOU	SAMBUR
KAKA	MARMOSET	OPAH	PUFFIN	SAMLET
KAKAPO	MARMOT	OQUASSA	PUPFISH	SANDFISH
KALONG	MARTLET	ORANG	PYRALID	SANDPEEP
KEA	MAVIS	ORC		SASIN
KEESHOND	MEDAKA	ORIBI	QUAHAUG	SASSABY
KERRY	MEGAPODE	ORMER	QUETZAL	SAUGER
KESTREL	MELOID	ORTOLAN	QUEY	SAUREL
KIANG	MENDIGO	ORYX		SAIRY
KILLDEE	MERLE	OSCINE	RAINBIRD	SAWBILL
KILLDEER	MERLIN	OSPREY	RAMSHORN	SCALARE
KINGBIRD	MESSAN	OUISTITI	RANID	SCAUP
KIWI	MIDGE	OURANG	RASBORA	SCIAENID
KOALA	MISSEL	OUZEL	RATEL	SCINCOID
KOEL	MOJARRA	OVENBIRD	RATFISH	SCIURINE
KOKANEE	MOKE	OVIBOS	RATITE	SCOTER
KOLINSKI	MOLA	OVIPARA	RATTAIL	SCULPIN
KOLINSKY	MOLDWARP	OXPECKER	REDBONE	SCUP
KOMONDOR	MOLLIE		REDBUG	SCUPPAUG
KOODOO	MOLLUSC	PACA	REDFIN	SERIEMA
KRAIT	MOLLUSK	PADNAG	REDFISH	SERIN
KUDU	MOLOCH	PAGURIAN	REDHORSE	SEROTINE
	MONEYEYE	PALFREY	REDLEG	SERRANID
LABROID	MOONFISH	PANGOLIN	REDPOLL	SERVAL
LACERTID	MOPOKE	PAPILLON	REDSHANK	SHOEBILL
LACEWING	MOSSBACK	PARD	REDSTART	SHRIKE
LAMPYRID	MOUFFLON	PARDINE	REDUVIID	SILD
LANGSHAN	MOUFLON	PARGO	REDWING	SILURID
LANGUR	MUDPUPPY	PAROQUET	REE	SKUA
LANNER	MULEY	PARR	REEDBIRD	SLOWWORM
LANNERET	MUNGOOSE	PARTAN	REEDBUCK	SMEW
LAPIN	MUNTJAC	PECCARY	REITBOK	SMOLT
LAPWING	MUNTJAK	PEKAN	REQUIN	SORA

SORD	TAUTOG	TOMTIT	VERVET	WISENT
SPARID	TEG	TOURACO	VESPINE	WOODCHAT
SPARLING	TEIID	TRAGOPAN	VIREO	WRASSE
SPLAKE	TEKEDYE	TREPANG	VISCACHA	WRYNECK
SPRUG	TELEOST	TROILUS	VIVERRID	
STARNOSE	TENCH	TROUPIAL	VIVIPARA	XERUS
STEGODON	TENREC	TUATARA	VIZSLA	
STIRK	TERCEL	TUATERA		YAPOCK
STUDFISH	TETRA	TULADI	WALLAROO	YAPOK
SURICATE	THEROPOD	TULLIBEE	WANDEROO	YAUD
SUSLIK	THROSTLE	TUNICATE	WAPITI	YEANLING
	TIGLON	TYEE	WARMOUTH	YOWE
TAKAHE	TIGON		WARRAGAL	YOWIE
TAKIN	TINAMOU	UMBRETTE	WARRIGAL	
TALAPOIN	TIT	UNGULATE	WARSAW	ZANDER
TAMANDUY	TITLARK	UTA	WEEVER	ZEBU
TAMANDUA	TITMAN		WEKA	ZIBET
TAMARAO	TITMOUSE	VEDALIA	WHIMBREL	ZIBETH
TAMARIN	TODY	VEFRY	WHIPRAY	ZORIL
TATOQUAY	TOGUE	VENDACE	WHYDAH	ZORILLA
TAUTAUG	TOMCOD	VERDIN	WILLET	ZORILLE

LEGAL WORDS

ABJURE	COLESSEE	IMPLEAD	LIBELANT	PROVISO
ABJURER	COLESSOR	INFRACT	LIBELEE	PURVIEW
ADJUDGE		INFRINGE	LIBELER	
AFFIANT	DELICT		LIBELIST	RECUSANT
ARRAIGN	DEMESNE	JURA	LIBELLED	RECUSE
ARRESTER	DEVISEE	JURAL	LIBELLEE	REPLEVY
ARRESTOR	DEVISOR	JURANT	LIBELLER	
ARROGATE	DRAWEE	JURAT	LIBELLING	SOKE
ASSIGNEE	DROIT	JURATORY	LIBELOUS	SOLON
ASSIGNOR		JURIDIC	LIBER	SUBORN
ASSIZE	EMPOWER	JURYMAN		SUBORNER
	ENACTIVE	JUS	MITTIMUS	
	ENACTOR		MORTMAIN	TALESMAN
CANON	ENACTORY	LACHES		TERMOR
CANONESS	ENFEOFF	LEGALESE	NOLO	TESTACY
CANONISE	ENTAIL	LEGALISM		TESTATE
CANONIST	ESTOPPEL	LEGALIST	OYER	TESTATOR
CANONIZE	ESTOVERS	LEGATE	OYEZ	
CASUS	ESTREAT	LEGATEE		VERECUND
CAVEAT		LEGATINE	PANDECT	
CAVEATOR	HYPOTHEC	LEGATING	POIND	
COGNOVIT		LEGATOR	PRAECIPE	
COHEIR	• • •	LIBEL	PRAEDIAL	

MEDICAL WORDS

ABALATION	ADDUCTOR	ADRENAL	ALIENIST	AMNESIC
ABORNING	ADENITIS	AFFERENT	AMENT	AMNESTIC
ABSCESS	ADENOID	AGRAPHIA	AMENTIA	AMNIOTE
ACIDOSIS	ADENOMA	AILMENT	AMNESIA	ANDROGEN
ACROTISM	ADIPOSIS	ALEXIA	AMNESIAC	ANEMIA

ANGINA	COLPITIS	HEMATOID	LUMBAR	NARCOSE
ANGIOMA	COMATOSE	HEMATOMA	LUPUS	NARCOSIS
ANODYNE	CONTAGIA	HEMOLYZE	LYMPH	NECROSIS
ANOXEMIA	CORPSMAN	HEMOSTAT	LYMPHOMA	NECROPSY
ANTHELIX	CUPPING	HERNIA	LYSIN	NEOPLASM
ANURESIS	CYSTITIS	HERNIATE	LYSINE	NEPHRISM
ANURIA		HERPES	LYSIS	NEURON
APHTHA	DENGUE	HILUM	LYSOGEN	NEUROSIS
APLASIA	DERMA	HYDATID	LYSSA	NEUROTIC
APOMIXIS	DESMOID	HYPHEMIA		NODE
APOPLEXY	DIAGNOSE	HYPO	MAINLINE	NOMA
APRAXIA	DIALYTIC	HYPOGYNY	MALADY	NONA
ASCITES	DIALYZER	HYPONOIA	MALAISE	
ASCORBIC	DIARRHEA	HYPOPNEA	MALARIA	OMENTUM
ASPHYXIA	DIURESIS	HYPOPYON	MALINGER	ONCIDIUM
ASPHYXY	DIZYGOUS	HYPOXIA	MALLEOLI	ONCOLOGY
ASPIRANT	DOC	HYTE	MANUS	ORCHITIS
ASTASIA	DURAL		MASTITIS	ORTHOTIC
ATARAXIC	DYSLEXIA	ID	MASTOID	OSTEITIS
ATAXIA	DYSPNEA	ILEITIS	MEDIAD	OSTEOID
ATAXIC	DYSPNOEA	ILEUM	MEDICO	OSTEOMA
ATHEROMA	DYSTAXIA	ILEUS	MELANISM	OSTIUM
ATONY	DYSTONIA	ILIA	MELANOMA	OSTOMY
ATOPY	DYSURIA	IMPETIGO	MENARCHE	OTALGIA
ATRESIA		IRITIS	MEROPIA	OTITIS
ATROPHIA	ECTHYMA	ISCHEMIA	METRITIS	OVIDUCT
ATROPHY	EMBOLISM		MILIARIA	
AURIST	EMBOLUS	JIMJAMS	MIOSIS	PANDEMIC
AUTOPSIC	ENDEMIC	JUGULATE	MIOTIC	PATHOGEN
AUTOTOMY	ENDOCARP		MITRAL	PEDOLOGY
	ENDODERM	KAHUNA	MOLLUSK	PELLAGRA
BACTERIN	EPILEPSY	KELOID	MONECIAN	PEPSIN
BEDSONIA	EREPSIN	KIBE	MONGOL	PEPTIC
BENNY	ERETHISM	KURU	MONO	PERONEAL
BERBERIN	ERYTHRON		MOTILE	PETECHIA
BERIBERI	ESTRIN	LACUNOSE	MOTORIC	PHLEGM
BIGHEAD	ESTRIOL	LAKING	MUCIN	PHOBIA
BIOSCOPY	ESTROGEN	LAZAR	MUCOSA	PHTHISIS
BISTOURY	ESTRONE	LAZARET	MUSCLY	PHYSIC
BITEWING	ETIOLOGY	LEMNISCI	MUSCULAR	PIAN
BLEB		LENITIVE	MYALGIA	PINTA
BRONCHI	FIBROMA	LEPROSY	MYCOSIS	PITH
BULIMIA	FIBROSIS	LESION	MYELIN	PLACEBO
BULLA	FLEXOR	LETHAL	MYELOID	PLEURA
BUNION	FROSTBITE	LEUCEMIA	MYELOMA	PLEURISY
BURSITOS	FURUNCLE	LEUKEMIA	MYIASIS	POLYPUS
		LEUKEMIC	MYOBLAST	POLYURIA
CALVARIA	GANGRENE	LEUKOMA	MYOGENIC	POSOLOGY
CANCROID	GENITURE	LEUKON	MYOGRAPH	POX
CARDITIS	GLAUCOMA	LEUKOSIS	MYOID	PREMUNE
CAROTID	GLEET	LIBIDO	MYOLOGY	PRESSOR
CATARRH	GLENOID	LIENAL	MYOMA	PROCAINE
CATHETER	GLIAL	LIGAMENT	MYOPATHY	PRODROME
CATLING	GRIPPE	LIMBIC	MYOPE	PROPHAGE
CAUL	GUMMA	LIPOMA	MYOPIA	PROPHASE
CAUTERY	GYNIATRY	LIVERISH	MYOPY	PROVIRUS
CENTESIS		LIVID	MYOSCOPE	PRURIGO
CICATRIX	HAKIM	LOBOTOMY	MYXEDEMA	PRURITUS
CLONUS	HAPLOPIA	LOCHIA	MYXOCYTE	PSILOSIS
COLIC	HEMAGOG	LORDOSIS	MYXOID	PTOSIS
COLITIS	HEMAL	LUES	MYXOMA	PURBLIND
COLOTOMY	HEMATIC	LUETIC	* * *	PUS

PYELITIS	* * *	SOPOR	THELITIS	* * *
PYEMIA	SCHIZO	SPASM	THROE	VARICOSE
PYGIDIUM	SCHIZOID	SPASTIC	THROMBUS	VARIOLA
PYLORUS	SCIATICA	SPECULUM	THYMUS	VERNIX
PYODERMA	SCOLEX	SPRUE	TIC	VIROLOGY
PYOGENIC	SCOLIOMA	STENOSED	TINEA	VIROSIS
PYOID	SCOTOMA	STENOSIS	TIZZY	VULVA
PYORRHEA	SCOTOPIA	STOUND	TONUS	VULVITIS
PYOSIS	SCROFULA	STUPE	TOXAEMIA	
PYREXIA	SCROGGY	STYE	TOXEMIA	WEN
PYROGEN	SCURVY	SUBVIRAL	TRACHOMA	WHITLOW
PYURIA	SEMICOMA	SYCOSIS	TREPHINE	WINDBURN
	SEMIDEAF	SYNAPSIS	TUMOUR	
RALE	SENILELY		TUSSIS	XANTHOMA
REGORGE	SENOPIA	TAKING	TYPHUS	XEROSIS
REOVIRUS	SENSORIA	TENACULA		XYSTER
RESECT	SEQUELA	TENOTOMY	ULCEROUS	
RHEUM	SEROLOGY	TERATOMA	URIC	ZOOGLEA
RHINITIS	SEROSA	TESTIS	UROSCOPY	ZOSTER
ROENTGEN	SETON	TETANUS	UVEA	
RUBELLA	SEXOLOGY	TETANY	UVULA	
RUBEOLA	SHAMAN	TETTER	UVULITIS	

MILITARY WORDS

AGGER	BORDURE	CULET	FAULD	HAYWARD
AIRBURST	BOWMAN	CULVERIN	FEDAYEE	HIPPARCH
AIRHEAD	BOWYER	CUTLAS	FENCIBLE	HOPLITE
ALCAIDE	BRISANCE	CUTLASS	FIRELOCK	HOWITZER
ALCAZAR	BURGONET		FLANCARD	HUSSAR
AMTRAC	BYRNIE	DEBOUCH	FOEMAN	
ANABASIS		DEBOUCHE	FOILSMAN	IMPI
ANGARY	CAMAIL	DEBRIEF	FOIN	IRONCLAD
ANTITANK	CAMION	DECURION	FOXHOLE	
ANTIWAR	CAMISADO	DECURY	FRAG	JAMBEAU
ARM	CANNON	DEFILADE	FRAGGING	JANIZARY
ARMADA	CANNONRY	DEMOB	FUSIL	JAWAN
ARMAMENT	CARABIN	DESTRIER	FUSILEER	JEMADAR
ARMATURE	CARABINE	DISHELM	FUSILIER	JERRY
ARMET	CASCABEL	DOGFACE		JINGAL
ARMIES	CASEMATE	DOGFIGHT	GANTLOPE	JINGALL
ARMIGER	CASERN	DOUGHBOY	GARRISON	
ARMIGERO	CASERNE	DRUMFIRE	GHAZI	KAMIKAZE
ARMORER	CASQUE	DUD	GISARME	KLEPHT
ARQUEBUS	CAUDILLO		GLAIVE	KNIGHTLY
	CHAMFRON	ENCAMP	GORGET	KRIS
BALLISTA	CHAPE	ENFILADE	GREAVE	
BARBICAN	CHASSEUR	ENLISTEE	GRENADE	LAAGER
BARBUT	CHAUSSES	ENLISTER	GUERILLA	LANGRAGE
BARD	CLAYMORE	ENSIFORM	GUNROOM	LEAGUER
BARESARK	CONELRAD	ENSIGNCY	GUNSHIP	LONGBOW
BARRAGE	CORSELET	EQUERRY	GYRENE	LOOIE
BASINET	COSSACK	EQUITES		
BASTION	COUTER	EVZONE	HACKBUT	MAILLESS
BATTALIA	CROSSBOW		HALBERD	MANCIPLE
BILLET	CUIRASS	FALCHION	HALBERT	MANGONEL
BILLETER	CUISH	FALLBACK	HAUBERK	MANTELET
BINNACLE	CUISSE	FASCINE	HAWKISH	MANTLET

MARCHER	PAVISER	RECRUIT	SKIRMISH	VAMBRACE
MARTELLO	PELE	REDAN	SOLDIER	VANQUISH
MESSMAN	PELTAST	REDCOAT	SOLDIERY	VELITES
MESSMATE	PELTATE	REDEPLOY	SPAHI	VENTAIL
MIQUELET	PENTOMIC	REDOUBT	SPEARER	
MORION	PERDU	REGIMENT	SPEARMAN	WARCRAFT
MUNIMENT	PERDUE	RITTER	SPONTOON	WARHEAD
MUNITION	PETARD		STALAG	WARISON
	PETRONEL	SABATON	STINKPOT	WARLESS
NAUMACHY	PEYTRAL	SABER	STRAFE	WARLIKE
NAPALM	PEYTREL	SAGUM	STRAFER	WARLORD
NONCOM	PHALANX	SALIENT	SUBDEPOT	WARMAKER
NUKE	PICKEER	SALLET	SUTLER	WARPLANE
	PIKE	SALVO	SWORDMAN	WARPOWER
OUTWAR	PIKEMAN	SANGAR		WARRED
	PLEBE	SAPPER		WARRING
PALIKAR	POILU	SARGE	TAMPION	WARWORK
PALLETTE	POMPOM	SCIMETAR	TARGE	WARWORN
PANDOUR	PROLONGE	SCIMITAR	TASSET	
PANOPLY		SCIMITER	TESTUDO	
PANZER	RAVELIN	SERGEANT	THANE	YATAGHAN
PAULDRON	REARWARD	SERJEANT	TOPKICK	
PAVIS	REB	SHAKO		
PAVISE	REBELDOM	SHOGUN	UHLAN	
				* * *

NAUTICAL WORDS

ABAFT	BELAY	BULKHEAD	COMPASS	DOWNHAUL
ABEAM	BENTHAL	BUMBOAT	CONN	DOWNWIND
ABOARD	BENTHIC	BUMKIN	CORVET	DRAGNET
AFT	BENTHOS	BUNTLINE	CORVETTE	DRAIL
AFTMOST	BERTH	BUOY	COXSWAIN	DRIFT
AHOY	BEVOR	BUOYAGE	CREWLESS	DRIFTAGE
AHULL	BIBB	BUOYANCE	CREWMAN	DROGUE
AIRBOAT	BIBBED	BUOYANCY	CROJIK	DROMOND
ALEE	BIDARKA	BURGEE	CUTWATER	DUGOUT
AMIDSHIP	BIDARKEE	BURTON		
APORT	BILANDER		DAHABEAH	DUNNAGE
ARGOSY	BILGE	CAIQUE	DAHABIEH	EARING
ARK	BIREME	CARAVEL	DAHABIYA	EASTER
ARMADA	BOATEL	CARINATE	DAVIT	EASTING
ASEA	BOATMAN	CARLING	DEADWOOD	EASTWARD
ASTERN	BOATSMAN	CARRACK	DEBARK	EUPHROE
AWASH	BOBSTAY	CARVEL	DECKING	EURIPOS
AWEATHER	BOGAN	CATBOAT	DHOW	EXEC
AWEIGH	BOLLARD	CATFALL	DINGEY	
	BOLTROPE	CATHEAD	DINGHY	FAIRLEAD
BACKOUT	BOSUN	CATSPAW	DISMAST	FALTBOAT
BACKSTAY	BOTEL	CATTED	DOCKAGE	FELUCCA
BARQUE	BOTTOMRY	CHANDLER	DOCKER	FERRYMAN
BARRATER	BOUSE	CHANTEY	DOCKHAND	FID
BARRATOR	BOWSPRIT	CHANTY	DOCKLAND	FIREROOM
BARRATRY	BOXHAUL	CHINE	DOCKSIDE	FIRTH
BATEAU	BRAIL	CLUBHAUL	DOCKYARD	FLEMISH
BATTEAU	BREAM	COASTING	DOGGER	FLOTA
BEACH	BRIG	COBLE	DORIES	FLOTILLA
BEAM	BROACH	COCKBILL	DOGWATCH	FLOTSAM
BECKET	BUGEYE	COCKBOAT	DORY	FLUYT

FLYBOAT	JETSOM	MOOR	SANDBAR	* * *
FOLDBOAT	JETTISON	MOORAGE	SCEND	
FOOTROPE	JIBB	MOORING	SCHUIT	TAFFAREL
FOREBODY	JIBBOOM		SCOW	TAFFEREL
FOREBOOM	JIBE	NAUMACAY	SCUBA	TAFFRAIL
FOREDECK	JIBER	NAVICERT	SCULL	TANKSHIP
FOREMAST	JOHNBOAT	NAVIES	SCULLER	TARTANA
FOREPEAK		NERITIC	SEABAG	TELEMAN
FORESAIL	KEDGE	NORTHING	SEABEACH	TEXAS
FORESTAY	KEEL		SEABED	THOLEPIN
FOREYARD	KEELAGE	OARSMAN	SEABOOT	TIDELAND
FRIGATE	KEELBOAT	ONSHORE	SEABORNE	TIDELESS
FUTTOCK	KEELHAUL	ORLOP	SEACOCK	TIDEMARK
	KEELLESS	OUTBOARD	SEACRAFT	TIDERIP
GALLEASS	KEELSON	OUTHAUL	SEADROME	TIDEWAY
GALLEON	KELSON	OUTSAIL	SEAFARER	TOPMAST
GALLEY	KETCH		SEAFLOOR	TOPSAIL
GALLIES	KEVEL	PARRAL	SEAFRONT	TOPSIDE
GALLIOT	KEVIL	PARREL	SEAGOING	TORPID
GANGWAY	KILLICK	PATAMAR	SEAMARK	TOWBOAT
GANTLINE		PATTAMAR	SEAMOUNT	TRIMARAN
GARBOARD	LAGAN	PELAGIC	SEAWARD	TRYSAIL
GARVEY	LAGEND	PELORUS	SEAWAY	TSUBA
GENOA	LANCE	PHAROS	SEXTANT	TSUNAMI
GONDOLA	LANCER	PILOTAGE	SHIPLOAD	TYE
GRAPLIN	LANYARD	PINNACE	SHIPMAN	
GRAPLINE	LARBOARD	PIRAGUA	SHIPMATE	UMIAK
GRAPNEL	LASCAR	PIRATIC	SHIPSIDE	UNANCHOR
GUNROOM	LATEEN	PIROGUE	SHIPWAY	UNDERSEA
GUNWALE	LATEENER	PIROQUE	SHORAN	UNDERSET
GUYOT	LAVEER	POLYNYA	SICKBAY	UNDERTOW
GYBE	LEADSMAN	PORTLESS	SKEG	UNMOOR
GYROSTAT	LEE	PRAM	SKIFF	UNSHIP
	LEEBOARD	PRATIQUE	SKYSAIL	UPWIND
	LEEWARD	PRAU	SLATCH	
HAAF	LEEWAY	PROW	SLIPWAY	VANG
HADAL	LIMEY	PURSER	SLOOP	VEDETTE
HALLIARD	LINER		SOFAR	VESSEL
HALYARD	LOCKAGE	RANDAN	SONAR	
HANK	LOGBOOK	RANKER	SONARMAN	WAISTER
HARPING	LONGBOAT	RATLIN	SONDER	WARDROOM
HATCHWAY	LONGSHIP	RATLINE	SPAR	WATERMAN
HAULYARD	LUFF	RATTLING	SPARLIKE	WATERWAY
HAWSE	LUGGER	RAZEE	SPARRED	WHARFAGE
HAWSER	LUGSAIL	RECHART	SPARRING	WHEELMAN
HEADRACE	LUMPER	REDOCK	SPENCER	WHERRY
HEADSAIL		RESAIL	SPONSON	WHERVE
HEADSTAY	MAINMAST	RESHIP	SPRIT	WORKBOAT
HELM	MAINSAIL	REEF	STAYSAIL	
HELMLESS	MAINSTAY	REEFER	STEAMER	XEBEC
HELMSMAN	MAINTOP	REGATTA	STEEVE	
HOY	MAKEFAST	RHUMB	STEEVING	YACHTER
HUSSAR	MARLINE	RIGGING	STEMSON	YACHTING
	MARLING	ROBAND	STERN	YACHTMAN
INBOARD	MASTHEAD	ROBBIN	STERNSON	YARDARM
INHAUL	MASTLESS	ROGER	STERNWAY	YAW
INHAULER	MAYDAY	ROWLOCK	STRAKE	YAWL
IRONCLAD	MIDSHIP	RUDDER	STUNSAIL	
	MISHIPS		SURFBOAT	ZONETIME
JACKSTAY	MIZEN	SAILER	SURFY	
JACKY	MIZZEN	SALTIE	SWABBIE	
JAYGEE	MOONSAIL	SAMPAN	SWIFTER	
JETSAM				

PERFORMING ARTS WORDS

ALLEGRO	CITOLE	JONGLEUR	* * *	SEGNO
ALMAH	CITTERN	JOTA	PANPIPE	SEGUE
ALT	CLAQUE	JUBA	PAS	SEMPLICE
ALTHORN	CLAQUER		PAVAN	SEMPRE
ARIETTA	CLAQUEUR	KOLO	PAVANE	SITARIST
ARIETTE	CLAVIER		PAVIN	SONATINA
ARIOSE	CLEF	LANCIERS	PIANISM	SORDINE
ARIOSO	CORYPHEE	LANDLER	PIBROCH	SUBITO
ARMONICA	COULISSE	LARGO	PIU	SUBTONIC
	CZARDAS	LEGATO	PLAGAL	
BALLONNE		LENTO	PLECTRUM	TAMBOURA
BARRE	DANSEUR	LIED	PLIE	TAMBUR
BATTERIE	DANSEUSE		POINTE	TAMBURA
BATTU	DISEUSE	MAXIXE	PRESA	TANTARA
BAYADEER	DIVA	MAZURKA	PRESTO	TANTO
BAYADERE	DULCIMER	MBIRA		THEORBO
BEGUINE		MEDIANT	RAGA	THEREMIN
BOWING	FADING	MELODISE	REDOWA	THRENODE
BOWINGLY	FADO	MELODIST	REVERB	THRENODY
BRAVURA	FIGURANT	MELODIZE	REVUIST	THRUM
BUFFO	FLAUTIST	MODERATO		THRUMMER
	FRUG	MORRIS	SACKBUT	TRITONE
CELESTA	FUGATO	MOSSO	SAGBUT	TUCKET
CELESTE	FURIOSO	MOTET	SAMBUCA	TUTTI
CEMBALO		MOTIVIC	SAMBUKE	
CHAINE	GALLIARD	MUDRA	SAMISEN	UT
CHANSON	GALOP		SAROD	
CHANT	GAVOT	NAUTCH	SARODE	VIGOROSO
CHASSE	GAVOTTE	NOH	SARODIST	
CITHARA			SAXTUBA	ZANZA
CITHER	HABANERA	OBLIGATO	SCENA	ZAPATEO
CITHERN	HAUTBOY	ORATORIO	SCHERZO	
CITOLA	* * *	OUD	SECONDO	